Cisco CallManager Fundamentals

John Alexander
Chris Pearce
Anne Smith
Delon Whetten

Cisco Press

Cisco Press
201 W 103rd Street
Indianapolis, IN 46290 USA

Cisco CallManager Fundamentals

John Alexander

Chris Pearce

Anne Smith

Delon Whetten

Copyright© 2002 Cisco Press

Published by:
Cisco Press
201 West 103rd Street
Indianapolis, IN 46290 USA

Printed in the United States of America 2 3 4 5 6 7 8 9 0

Library of Congress Cataloging-in-Publication Number: 00-105375

ISBN: 1-58705-008-0

2nd Printing October 2001

Warning and Disclaimer

This book is designed to provide information about Cisco CallManager. Every effort has been made to make this book as complete and as accurate as possible, but no warranty or fitness is implied.

The information is provided on an "as is" basis. The authors, Cisco Press, and Cisco Systems, Inc., shall have neither liability nor responsibility to any person or entity with respect to any loss or damages arising from the information contained in this book.

The opinions expressed in this book belong to the authors and are not necessarily those of Cisco Systems, Inc.

Trademark Acknowledgments

All terms mentioned in this book that are known to be trademarks or service marks have been appropriately capitalized. Cisco Press or Cisco Systems, Inc., cannot attest to the accuracy of this information. Use of a term in this book should not be regarded as affecting the validity of any trademark or service mark.

Feedback Information

At Cisco Press, our goal is to create in-depth technical books of the highest quality and value. Each book is crafted with care and precision, undergoing rigorous development that involves the unique expertise of members from the professional technical community.

Readers' feedback is a natural continuation of this process. If you have any comments regarding how we could improve the quality of this book or otherwise alter it to better suit your needs, you can contact us through e-mail at feedback@ciscopress.com. Please make sure to include the book title and ISBN in your message.

We greatly appreciate your assistance.

Publisher	John Wait
Editor-In-Chief	John Kane
Cisco Systems Management	Michael Hakkert
	Tom Geitner
	William Warren
Acquisitions Editor	Amy Lewis
Managing Editor	Patrick Kanouse
Development Editor	Andrew Cupp
Project Editor	Marc Fowler
	Beatriz Valdés
Copy Editor	Ginny Kaczmarek

Technical Editors

Faraz Aladin	Bob Bell	Adrian Brookes
Mick Buchanan	Thomas Chan	Dave Corley
Abid Fazal	Graham Gudgin	Addis Hallmark
Lee Ji	Ketil Johansen	Bill W. King
Doys Kurian	Jackie Lee	Rowan McFarland
Scott A. Morrison	Mark Nelson	Thang Nguyen
Richard B. Platt	Bernie Rodríguez	Vishwanath Shenoy
Chris Spain	Rohit Srivastava	Aaron Tong
Todd Truitt	Manoshi Vasudevan	Scott Veibell
Triston Whetten	Wilf Wong	Liang Wu

Team Coordinator	Tammi Ross
Cover Designer	Louisa Klucsnik
Production Team	Argosy
Indexer	Tim Wright

CISCO SYSTEMS

Corporate Headquarters
Cisco Systems, Inc.
170 West Tasman Drive
San Jose, CA 95134-1706
USA
http://www.cisco.com
Tel: 408 526-4000
  800 553-NETS (6387)
Fax: 408 526-4100

European Headquarters
Cisco Systems Europe
11 Rue Camille Desmoulins
92782 Issy-les-Moulineaux
Cedex 9
France
http://www-europe.cisco.com
Tel: 33 1 58 04 60 00
Fax: 33 1 58 04 61 00

Americas Headquarters
Cisco Systems, Inc.
170 West Tasman Drive
San Jose, CA 95134-1706
USA
http://www.cisco.com
Tel: 408 526-7660
Fax: 408 527-0883

Asia Pacific Headquarters
Cisco Systems Australia, Pty.,
Ltd
Level 17, 99 Walker Street
North Sydney
NSW 2059 Australia
http://www.cisco.com
Tel: +61 2 8448 7100
Fax: +61 2 9957 4350

Cisco Systems has more than 200 offices in the following countries. Addresses, phone numbers, and fax numbers are listed on the Cisco Web site at www.cisco.com/go/offices

Argentina • Australia • Austria • Belgium • Brazil • Bulgaria • Canada • Chile • China • Colombia • Costa Rica • Croatia • Czech Republic • Denmark • Dubai, UAE • Finland • France • Germany • Greece • Hong Kong • Hungary • India • Indonesia • Ireland • Israel • Italy • Japan • Korea • Luxembourg • Malaysia • Mexico • The Netherlands • New Zealand • Norway • Peru • Philippines • Poland • Portugal • Puerto Rico • Romania • Russia • Saudi Arabia • Scotland • Singapore • Slovakia • Slovenia • South Africa • Spain • Sweden • Switzerland • Taiwan • Thailand • Turkey • Ukraine • United Kingdom • United States • Venezuela • Vietnam • Zimbabwe

About the Authors

John Alexander is the director of the CallManager software development at Cisco Systems, Inc. He has more than 30 years of experience in software development, including more than 20 years of management experience. His experience is primarily in the field of voice communications, including call processing, voice messaging, call center, and switching systems. John was a member of the team that developed and implemented the CallManager software.

Chris Pearce is a technical leader in the CallManager software group at Cisco Systems, Inc. He has 10 years of experience in telecommunications. His primary areas of expertise include call routing, call control, and telephone features. Chris was a member of the team that developed and implemented the CallManager software from its early stages, and he was directly involved in developing the system architecture and design.

Anne Smith is a technical writer in the CallManager software group at Cisco Systems, Inc. She has eight years of documentation experience, including six years of writing and developing technical documentation. She was a member of the team that developed the CallManager documentation from its early stages.

Delon Whetten is the manager of the Core Call Processing team in the CallManager software group at Cisco Systems, Inc. He has more than 25 years of software development experience. His experience has been centered on communication systems and includes the design and development of message switching, voice messaging, video teleconferencing, and VoIP call processing systems. Delon was a member of the team that developed and implemented the CallManager software from its early stages, and he was directly involved in developing the system architecture and design.

About the Technical Reviewers

Faraz Aladin, CCIE #3134, has been in the voice and data networking industry for about 13 years, with the last five at Cisco Systems, Inc. He has been intimately involved with the Cisco AVVID Architecture and Solutions team from inception. Faraz was part of the team that wrote the *IP Telephony Design Guide* and the *QoS Design Guide*, and he has written other architecture papers and a design guide for Catalyst 6500 switches. Faraz holds a degree in engineering.

Bob Bell started with Cisco Systems, Inc. with the Selsius Systems acquisition in 1998 and has been a telecommunications engineer specializing in protocols since 1980. He is involved in IEEE 802, IETF, and is currently the chair of EIA/TIA TR41.4 IP Telephony Infrastructures and Gateways.

Adrian Brookes is a development manager with Cisco Systems, Inc. working on the Cisco AVVID product range. He gained his extensive telecommunications knowledge from previous posts with major manufacturers and service providers and continues to be at the forefront of technology. Adrian is based in the European theatre (Europe/Middle East/Asia).

Mick Buchanan, CCNA, CIPT, MCP, CNE, began working with CallManager in 1998 as one of the original Selsius Systems customer support engineers. He is currently responsible for maintaining Cisco's Dallas Technical Briefing Center for product demonstrations on the entire line of Cisco AVVID IP Telephony products.

Thomas Chan is a manager in the software development group at Cisco Systems, Inc. He holds a master's degree in computer science from the University of California and has worked for Cisco Systems since 1999.

Dave Corley, a senior product line manager for Cisco Systems, Inc. in the Enterprise Voice/Video Business Unit, is responsible for definition and marketing of Cisco CallManager. He previously served in technical and marketing positions with Selsius Systems, Incite, and Voice Control Systems. Dave holds a bachelor's degree in aerospace engineering and a master of science degree in mechanical engineering. He and his wife attempt to raise two unruly but lovable kids from their home in Plano, Texas.

Abid Fazal is an integration engineer with Cisco Systems, Inc. He has worked as a system and network engineer and manager for more than seven years. For the last 12 months he has been focusing on system integration of IP telephony technologies.

Graham Gudgin, CCIE #2370, is a member of the Cisco AVVID Solutions Engineering Team at Cisco Systems, Inc. Graham is responsible for IP telephony network design.

Addis Hallmark, CCNA, CIPT, MCSE, MCP+I, is a technical marketing engineer with Cisco Systems, Inc. Addis has been involved with the testing, installing, administering, and deployment of Cisco CallManager since its 2.x release.

Lee Ji is a software engineer in the CallManager software group at Cisco Systems, Inc. in Dallas, Texas. He has worked in the telecommunications industry since 1993. For the last year, he has been focusing on IP telephony technologies.

Ketil Johansen, CCIE #1145, is a systems engineer with Cisco Systems, Inc. in Denmark. Ketil has worked with networking technologies since 1984. The last two years he has been focusing on IP telephony technologies.

Bill W. King, CIPT, is a technical marketing manager in the Enterprise Voice/Video Business Unit within Cisco Systems, Inc. Bill joined Cisco Systems in 1999 and is responsible for competitive analysis and for developing customer and consultant outbound marketing information for the Cisco AVVID IP Telephony solution sets.

Doys Kurian, formerly with Cisco Systems, Inc., was a software test technician specializing in Call Detail Records.

Jackie Lee is a manager in the Software Development group at Cisco Systems, Inc.

Rowan McFarland is a software engineer with Cisco Systems, Inc. His responsibilities include software conference bridge, media termination point, and music on hold server development. This includes kernel mode device drivers that are used for real-time RTP streaming. Rowan has been working in the telecommunications industry for the last 12 years and has worked on a variety of projects, mainly focusing on embedded development.

Scott A. Morrison is a systems engineer with Cisco Systems, Inc. providing DoD with solutions, specializing in IP telephony. Prior to coming to Cisco, Scott was a test engineer at JCIET (Joint Combat Identification and Evaluation Team) where he installed, tested, evaluated, and provided technical feedback on Cisco's IP Telephony products, including Cisco CallManager.

Mark Nelson is a programmer for Cisco Systems, Inc. He is the author of *The Data Compression Book* and the *Serial Communications Developers Guide*.

Thang Nguyen is a software engineer in the CallManager software group at Cisco Systems, Inc. Thang has more than 10 years of experience, with background in ATM, SS7, wireless data, and VoIP.

Richard B. Platt is a senior director of development within the Enterprise Voice/Video Business Unit at Cisco Systems, Inc.

Bernie Rodríguez is a network engineer with Texas Instruments, Inc.

Vishwanath Shenoy is a senior systems analyst with InfoSys Technologies Ltd. in Bangalore, India. He has worked on Java Applications since 1996. In the last 18 months, he has been involved in the development of the Administrative Reporting Tool (ART) for Cisco CallManager.

Chris Spain is a technical marketing manager at Cisco Systems, Inc. Chris is a 20-year veteran of the telecommunications industry, with tenure in PBX development, TDM wide area networking, Frame Relay, ATM, and IP. Most recently, Chris has been focusing on IP telephony design.

Rohit Srivastava is a consultant for Cisco Systems, Inc.

Aaron Tong is a software engineer with Cisco Systems, Inc. in the EVVBU Voice Applications.

Todd Truitt is a technical marketing engineer for the Cisco Systems AVVID Design Team.

Manoshi Vasudevan has provided software development in the CTI area on several standard protocol/APIs, such as TSAPI, CSTA, JTAPI, and TAPI, for the last 12 years. She has a master of science and a bachelor's degree in electrical engineering. Currently, she manages a group that is responsible for implementation of TAPI and JTAPI providers for the Cisco CallManager.

Scott Veibell is currently the manager of five key teams for Cisco CallManager Development: QA, Integration, Critical Accounts, Solutions Test, and Engineering Field Trials for Cisco Systems, Inc. Before that, Scott was in technical marketing. Before joining Cisco, Scott was part of the original team (Incite, a division of Intecom, and later Selsius Systems, a wholly owned subsidiary of Intecom) that developed CallManager to switch H.320 video over isoEthernet. He was a member, and later the manager, of the technical support department for Selsius Systems. Scott has also held positions as a manufacturing engineer for Texas

Instruments and was an Army (Combat Engineer) officer. Scott holds a bachelor's degree in mining engineering from the University of Idaho.

Triston Whetten is a test engineer in the CallManager Integration group at Cisco Systems, Inc. He has worked with CallManager since release 2.2 in 1999. Triston is currently working toward his bachelor's degree in computer science.

Wilf Wong is a development manager with Cisco Systems, Inc. He has a master's degree in computer science from the University of Michigan, Ann Arbor, and has been working in voice and data technologies since 1981. He has been working in the IP telephony technologies at Cisco Systems since 1998.

Liang Wu is a software engineer in the CallManager software group at Cisco Systems, Inc. For the last five years, he has been focusing on PBX/Enterprise communication systems.

Dedication

John Alexander:

This book is dedicated to my wife, Lee. Without her patience and support, I could not have contributed to the book.

Chris Pearce:

To all of my teachers;
to Mom and Dad;
and, especially, to Clay.

Anne Smith:

To my parents: Mom for teaching me strength, focus, and endurance; Dad for teaching me to be smart and always try harder. Dad, it's not Michener but at least it's 600 pages.

To Ruby and Bill for their constant support.

To Herb, best friend, partner, lover, and husband, for his support, patience, and love.

Delon Whetten:

To my wife, Loraine, for her endless encouragement and support, and for allowing me to spend the many weekends and long nights that were spent working on this project at her expense. Without her support, my involvement in this project would not have happened. I also appreciate the support and encouragement from my sons Jonathan and Mark.

Acknowledgments

Chris Pearce would like to thank the following people in particular: Gene Arantowicz, Chris Spain, Faraz Aladin, and the EVVBU technical marketing group for information relating to Cisco CallManager deployment models; Luc Bouchard, for information relating to Enhanced 911; Craig Cotton for his MCS server matrices and information relating to Cisco-certified servers; Richard Platt for information relating to TDM versus packet-switched architectures; Jan Willem Ruys, for information relating to and his effort in encoding the Netherlands dial plan; Triston Whetten for help testing change notification logic; Mike Sandman, for his telecom history Web page (www.sandman.com/telhist.html) with great pictures; and Todd Truitt, for his great information relating to gateways and quality of service.

Anne Smith would like to thank the following people in particular: Addis Hallmark and Triston Whetten for being so knowledgeable and easy to work with; Brian Sedgley for knowing everything and always finding a few minutes for me; Mick Buchanan for being such a great reviewer; Scott Veibell for his constant encouragement, counsel, and support; and Richard Platt for his vision and guidance. I also thank Delon, Chris, and John for making this book possible and making the experience an enjoyable one with teamwork, high standards of excellence, and dedication.

The authors would like to acknowledge the contribution of the following people for their assistance on this book: Faraz Aladin, Gene Arantowicz, Darren Baker, Ho Bao, Rick Baugh, Bob Bell, Adrian Brookes, Mick Buchanan, Ray Cetrone, Thomas Chan, Gerardo Chaves, Cliff Chew, Rita Chow, Tony Collins, Dave Corley, Darrick Deel, Richard Dunlap, Clay Eddings, Denny Farmer, Abid Fazal, Bill Forsythe, Andy Francke, Graham Gudgin, Duane Guthrie, Paul Hahn, Sofian Halim, Addis Hallmark, Joel Hamilton, Stuart Hamilton, Marquis Harper, Ron Higgins, John Houston, Lee Ji, Ketil Johansen for having such high standards and expecting us to live up to them, Terry McKeon, Bill W. King, Mike Knappe, Monica Shen Knotts, Ed Kostenbauder, Doys Kurian, Jackie Lee, Victor Lee, Rowan McFarland, Susie Minatrea, Priya Mollyn, Scott Morrison, Charlie Munro, Karl Nakamura, Mark Nelson, Thang Nguyen, Donald Pitschel, Jared Page, Dave Patton, Richard Platt, Ken Pruski, Akanksha Puri, Bernie Rodriguez, Jeff Sanders, Susan Sauter, Herb Sayre, Brian Sedgley, Chris Spain, Rohit Srivastava, Ty Thorsen, James Tighe, Todd Truitt, David Tucker, Manoshi Vasudevan, Scott Veibell, Andy Vu, Hau Vu, Triston Whetten, Wilf Wong, Liang Wu, Tony Zhu, Conrad Zgliczynski.

To the folks at Cisco Press, Alicia Buckley, John Kane, Kathy Trace, and everyone else who contributed to the book, we thank you. We especially thank Drew Cupp and Amy Lewis for their hard work on this title and hand-holding throughout the writing process.

The authors would like to acknowledge the following authors of engineering documents that were important to the quality of this book during the research phase: Pranab Bajpai, Dee Booth, Santhosh Cheeniyil, Cliff Chew, Dave Corley, Mustapha El-Habbal, Clint D. Entrop, Andy Francke, Heather Gray, Duane Guthrie, Sofian Halim, John Houston, InfoSys, Akash Jain, Venkatesh Jayaraman, Lee Ji, Joanna Jiang, Senthil Kumar, Jackie Lee, Sam Lee, Rowan McFarland, Ravi Mulam, Charlie Munro, Ping Ni, Dinh Nguyen, Thang Nguyen, Andy

Pepperell, Ashok Ranganath, Vishwanath Shenoy, Sanjay Sheth, Eddie Soliman, Rohit Srivastava, Nageswara Rao Vankayala, Winnie Wong, Liang Wu, Tony Zhu, and Jamie Zhuang.

We also owe our thanks to everyone in the following groups for their contribution to the Cisco AVVID technology: EVVBU Engineering, Quality Assurance, Integration, Test, Project Management, Technical Marketing, Product Management, Documentation, Cisco TAC, and Marketing.

Contents at a Glance

Contents

Foreword

In July of 1997, the engineering group from Selsius Systems, a small startup in Dallas, Texas, co-founded by David Tucker and me, connected two normal-appearing phones into a 10 Mbps Ethernet LAN. On one of the phones in the lab, I dialed a four-digit extension in a very ordinary way, which in turn caused the second phone to ring in a very ordinary way on David's desk. He answered the phone with the customary "Hello," and I replied with an uncustomary response, "Can you hear me?!" Thus began the third technology evolution in the long history of the telephone. Although the "phone call" appeared ordinary on the outside, everything inside was vastly different from the first generation of analog telephony and substantially different from the second generation of TDM digital telephony. This was the first time that a telephone call had been made entirely with Internet technology consisting of a true IP phone (connected over Ethernet), over an IP network, managed by an IP-connected server appropriately named the CallManager.

Since that fateful day in 1997, the IP telephony industry in general and the original Selsius Systems in particular have developed and evolved at Internet speed. Selsius Systems was acquired by Cisco Systems in November of 1998. At Cisco, the number of customers has grown from dozens to many thousands worldwide. Revenues have increased 50 percent to 100 percent sequentially quarter to quarter. Third-generation IP phones with built-in Web browsers and servers have been introduced. The CallManager code base has grown from several hundred thousand lines of C++ code to more than 2 million. And the engineering staff has grown from the original 30 engineers to more than 1000 engineers.

There are many components that comprise the Cisco AVVID (Architecture for Voice, Video, and Integrated Data) IP Telephony solution; nevertheless, Cisco CallManager is the heart of the solution. The content of this book is the first public glimpse into the core of the CallManager. The authors carefully discuss the fundamental design, its evolution, and the motives behind the current architecture. Over the course of its seven-year life, CallManager has undergone several major transitions. This is perhaps its key to success: the ability to adapt and change at Internet speed. The fundamental philosophy has remained intact; however, much of the underlying architecture has either evolved or been redesigned resulting in a system that supports tens of thousands of devices and is deployed in thousands of companies all over the world.

Three of the authors of this book, John Alexander, Chris Pearce, and Delon Whetten, are three of the original designers of the CallManager. Anne Smith was one of the original writers of the CallManager documentation. Today, John's role is director for Cisco CallManager development. Chris continues as the lead architect. Delon manages the core group of call processing. And Anne leads much of the supporting documentation effort. My association with the authors and the Cisco CallManager product spans a decade, but in Internet time, the equivalent is closer to 50 years. Nevertheless, this book represents the first book, written by the first designers, of the first IP telephony solution ever!

Richard B. Platt
Senior Director of Development
Enterprise Voice/Video Business Unit
Cisco Systems, Inc.

Introduction

In June 2000, Cisco Systems, Inc., released Cisco CallManager 3.0. CallManager is the heart of the Cisco Architecture for Voice, Video, and Integrated Data (AVVID) IP Telephony solution. CallManager provides administrators a platform by which they can manage their enterprise's voice communications over the same network on which they manage their enterprise's data communications. It enables devices that speak dozens of different protocols to communicate together with seeming effortlessness and supports both enterprise and endpoint applications. As of the time of this writing, Cisco Systems has released Cisco CallManager 3.1(1).

We, the writers of this book, have been intimately involved with CallManager since its inception in 1997. And as the years have gone by, we've watched as both the capability and the complexity of the product have increased. Features that seemed obvious to us during CallManager development have sometimes proved less than obvious to those who have actually deployed CallManager. Furthermore, although the *Cisco CallManager Administration System Guide* is very good at telling you how to accomplish specific tasks, it isn't always as good at telling you why you need to accomplish a specific task, or in providing you with a framework for understanding how different CallManager concepts work together.

Therefore, we have tried to distill our knowledge of CallManager into these few hundred pages in the hopes that you will find here what you might not have found elsewhere: a blueprint that will reveal order amid the dozens of devices and the hundreds of features that CallManager supports.

Objectives

This book provides a view of the Cisco AVVID IP Telephony solution that centers around CallManager. This information helps you put together in your mind the various pieces of CallManager so that you can better understand how to design and implement your own CallManager system. By learning how CallManager processes information, you can configure and troubleshoot your system more effectively.

This book is most relevant to CallManager system administrators who are responsible for configuring CallManager, integrating it into their networks, and maintaining it. This book is also appropriate for network architects looking to integrate Cisco AVVID IP Telephony with third-party applications and for people interested in the nuts and bolts of a VoIP solution.

Organization

This book is meant to complement the information already available on Cisco Connection Online (www.cisco.com) and in the Cisco CallManager end-user documentation. This book does not provide detailed configuration information or step-by-step instructions. Information is provided in the following chapters:

- Chapter 1, "Cisco CallManager Architecture," provides an overview of VoIP telephony. It describes the hardware and software components that make up Cisco AVVID IP Telephony and outlines several methods for deploying a Cisco AVVID IP Telephony solution.

- Chapter 2, "Call Routing," discusses the fundamental building blocks of CallManager's call routing infrastructure and describes how you can apply these building blocks to solve complex routing problems that most enterprises face.

- Chapter 3, "Station Devices," describes the station devices supported by CallManager. It categorizes them by protocol and then subdivides them by device capabilities. It describes how you can write your own Cisco IP Phone services.

- Chapter 4, "Trunk Devices," details the gateway protocols supported by CallManager, including H.323 and Media Gateway Control Protocol (MGCP). It describes how the H.323 protocol signals to gateways, to other CallManager clusters, and to H.323 gatekeepers.

- Chapter 5, "Media Processing," discusses allocation and control of media processing resources, such as conference bridges, transcoders, and music on hold (MOH) servers. It explains media connection processing and call preservation.

- Chapter 6, "Manageability and Monitoring Tools," describes tools that you can use to make CallManager easier to manage. It explains in some detail the plug-ins and applications that work with CallManager to assist with system monitoring.

- Chapter 7, "Call Detail Records," describes the facilities provided for controlling the generation and storage of Call Detail Records (CDRs) and Call Management Records (CMRs), and it provides information on how to access, interpret, and use the stored data.

- Appendix A, "Feature List," provides a list of CallManager and Cisco IP Phone features. Features that are new to CallManager release 3.1 are indicated.

- Appendix B, "Cisco Integrated Solutions," details Cisco solutions that can be used in conjunction with CallManager or other components in the Cisco AVVID IP Telephony system.

- Appendix C, "Glossary of Terms and Acronyms," provides definitions for important terms.

Book Features and Text Conventions

Each chapter provides basic information about the subject matter, followed by more detailed information. In the body of Chapter 1 is a block diagram of Cisco CallManager's internal components. This diagram is subsequently presented in the introduction of each chapter of the book. The CallManager components that are covered in a particular chapter are highlighted in this diagram. Every chapter ends with a summary section that highlights the critical information that the chapter presents.

If you are new to CallManager, you can often read just the first few sections of each chapter to get a feel for the information. Then you can return to read the more detailed sections as your knowledge of the product increases and you find yourself looking for more answers. For the "old-timers" out there who have been working with CallManager since 1998, the deeper you go into the sections, the more rewarded with information you will be.

This book uses the following formatting conventions to convey additional meaning:

- Key terms are *italicized* the first time they are used and defined.
- Notes emphasize information of a noteworthy or unusual nature.
- Hints are handy information bits about the subject.
- Commands, IP phone buttons and soft keys, CallManager Administration fields and check boxes, GUI items, menus, menu items, radio buttons, pull-down boxes and items, settings, values, system parameters, and actions are presented in **boldface**.

Target Release—Cisco CallManager 3.1

This book targets Cisco CallManager Release 3.1(1), released during the third quarter of calendar year 2001. Most of the material this book presents should apply for many releases to come. Long printing lead times and subsequent 3.1(x) releases might render some of this information out-of-date, but we have tried to protect against that wherever possible by foreseeing those changes.

Cisco CallManager Architecture

Cisco Architecture for Voice, Video and Integrated Data (Cisco AVVID) is a suite of components that includes Internet Protocol (IP) telephony communications. Cisco CallManager is the call routing and signaling component for *IP telephony* in a Cisco AVVID IP Telephony network. The term IP telephony describes telephone systems that place calls over the same type of data network that makes up the Internet.

Telephone systems have been around for more than 100 years. Small, medium, and large businesses use them to provide voice communications between employees within the business and to customers outside the business. The public telephone system itself is a very large network of interconnected telephone systems.

What makes IP telephony systems in general, and Cisco CallManager in particular, different is that they place calls over a computer network. The phones that CallManager controls plug directly into the same IP network as your PC, rather than into a phone jack connected to a telephones-only network.

Phone calls placed over an IP network differ fundamentally from those placed over a traditional telephone network. To understand how IP calls are different, you must first understand how a traditional telephone network works.

In many ways, traditional telephone networks have advanced enormously since Alexander Graham Bell invented the first telephone in 1876. Fundamentally, the traditional telephone network is about connecting a long, dedicated circuit between two telephones.

Traditional telephone networks fall into the following four categories:

- Key systems
- Private Branch eXchanges (PBXs)
- Class 5 switches
- Class 1 to 4 switches

A *key system* is a very small-scale telephone system designed to handle telephone communications for a small office of 1 to 25 users. Key systems can be either analog, which means they use the same 100-year-old technology of your home phone, or digital, which means they use the 30-year-old technology of a standard office phone.

A *PBX* is a corporate telephone office system. These systems scale from the small office of 20 people to large campuses (and distributed sites) of 30,000 people. However, because of the nature of the typical circuit-switched architecture, no PBX vendor manufactures a single system that scales throughout the entire range. Customers must replace major portions of their infrastructure if they grow past their PBX's limits.

A *Class 5 switch* is a national telephone system operated by a local telephone company (called a *local exchange carrier* [LEC]). These systems scale from about 2000 to 100,000 users and serve the public at large.

Long distance companies (called *interexchange carriers* [IECs or IXCs]) use *Class 1 to 4 switches*. They process truly mammoth levels of calls and connect calls from one Class 5 switch to another.

Despite the large disparity in the number of users supported by these types of traditional networks, the core technology is circuit-based. Consider an old-time telephone operator. He or she sits in front of a large plugboard with hundreds of metal sockets and plugs. (Figure 1-1 shows a picture of an early PBX.) When a subscriber goes off-hook, a light illuminates on the plugboard. The operator plugs in the headset and requests the number of the party from the caller. After getting the number of the called party and finding the called party's socket, the operator checks to see if the called party is busy. If not, the operator then connects the sockets of the calling and called parties with a call cable, thus completing a circuit between them. The circuit provides a conduit for the conversation between the caller and the called party.

Today's central switching office—specifically, its call processing software—is simply a computerized replacement for the old-time telephone operator. Obeying a complex script of rules, the call processing software directs the collection of the number of the called party, looks for the circuit dedicated to the called party, checks to see if the line is busy, and then completes the circuit between the calling and called parties.

In the past, this circuit was an analog circuit from end to end. The voice energy of the speaker was converted into an electrical wave that traveled to the listener, where it was converted back again into a sound wave. Even today, the vast majority of residential telephone users still have an analog circuit that runs from their phone to the phone company's central switching office, while digital circuits run between central switching offices.

This reliance on circuits characterizes traditional telephone systems and gives rise to the term *circuit switching*. A characteristic of circuit switching is that once the telephone system collects the number of the called party, and establishes the circuit from the calling party to the called party, this circuit is dedicated to the conversation between calling and called parties. The resources allocated to the conversation cannot be reused for other purposes, even if the calling and called parties are silent on the call. Furthermore, if something happens to disrupt the circuit between the calling and called parties, they can no longer communicate.

Figure 1-1 *An Early PBX*

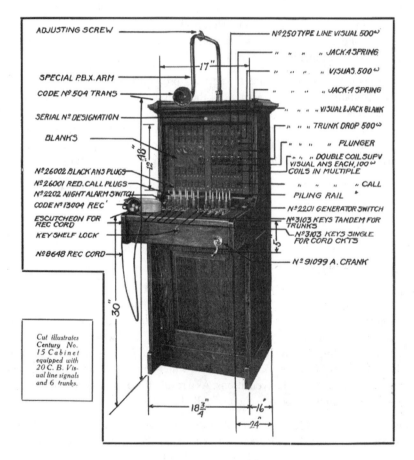

Do You Want a Real Good
P. B. X. Switchboard?

LOOK THIS OVER CAREFULLY
AND
WRITE TODAY FOR PRICES

CENTURY TELEPHONE CONSTRUCTION CO.

BUFFALO, N. Y.   BRIDGEBURG, ONT.

Like the central switching office, CallManager is a computerized replacement for a human operator. However, CallManager relies on packet switching to transmit conversations. *Packet switching* is the mechanism by which data is transmitted through the Internet. Web pages, e-mail, and instant messaging are all conveyed through the fabric of the Internet by packet switching.

In packet switching, information to be conveyed is digitally encoded and broken down into small units called *packets*. Each packet consists of a header section and the encoded information. Among the pieces of header information is the network address of the recipient of the information. Packets are then placed on a router-connected network. Each router looks at the address information in each packet and decides where to send the packet. The recipient of the information can then reassemble the packets and convert the encoded data back into the original information.

Packet switching is more resilient to network problems than circuit switching, because each packet contains the network address of the recipient. If something happens to the connection between two routers, a router with a backup connection can forward the information to the backup router, which in turn will look at the address of the recipient and determine how to reach it. Furthermore, if the sender and recipient are not communicating, the resources of the network are available to other users of the network.

In circuit-switched voice communications, an entire circuit is consumed when a conversation is established between two people. The system encodes the voice in a variety of manners, but the standard for voice encoding in the circuit-switched world is *pulse code modulation (PCM)*. Because PCM is the de facto standard for voice communications in the circuit-switched world, it comes as no surprise that a PCM-encoded voice stream fills the capacity of a single voice circuit.

An interesting wrinkle about voice encoding is introduced by packet-switched communications. Even if circuit-switched systems encoded the voice stream according to a more efficient scheme, there is little incentive to do so, because a circuit is fully reserved no matter how much data you place on it. In the packet-switched world, however, a more efficient encoding scheme means that for the same amount of voice traffic, you can place a smaller number of packets on the network, which in turn means that the same network can carry a larger number of conversations. As a result, the packet-switched world has given rise to several different encoding schemes called *codecs*.

Different types of voice encoding offer different benefits, but generally the more high fidelity the voice quality, the more bandwidth that the resulting media stream requires. This statement does not hold so true for those codecs that attempt to minimize bandwidth. As the amount of bandwidth that you are willing to permit the voice stream to consume decreases, the more clever and complex the codec must become to maintain voice quality. The codecs that attempt to minimize the bandwidth required for a voice stream require complex mathematical calculations that attempt to predict in advance information about the volume and frequency level of an utterance. Such codecs are highly optimized for the spoken voice. Furthermore, these calculations are often so computationally intensive that software cannot perform them quickly enough; only specialized hardware with digital signal processors (DSPs) can handle the computations efficiently. As a result, codec support often differs substantially from device to device in the Voice over IP (VoIP) network.

Because not all network devices understand all codecs, an important part of establishing a packet voice call is the negotiation of a voice codec to be used for the conversation. This codec negotiation is a part of a packet-switched call that does not assume nearly the same importance on a circuit-switched call. Chapter 5, "Media Processing," discusses codecs in more detail.

The rest of this chapter discusses the following topics:

- Circuit-switched systems
- Cisco AVVID IP Telephony networks
- Enterprise deployment of Cisco CallManager clusters

Circuit-Switched Systems

A *circuit-switched system* is typically a vertically integrated, monolithic computer system. A mainframe cabinet houses a proprietary processor, often along with a redundant processor, which in turn is connected with a bus to cabinets containing switch cards, line cards, and trunk cards.

Line cards control station devices (usually phones) and trunk cards control trunk devices (connections to other telephone systems). A wire runs from a station into a line card and carries both the call signaling and the encoded voice of the station device. Similarly, wires called *trunks* connect circuit-switched systems together with trunk cards. Line and trunk cards forward received call signaling to the call processing software, while the encoded media is available to the switch cards. Figure 1-2 demonstrates this architecture.

Call Establishment in a Circuit-Switched Telephone System

Call establishment with a circuit-switched system consists of two phases: a session establishment phase and a media exchange phase.

The session establishment phase is the phase in which the telephone system attempts to establish a conversation. During this phase, the telephone system finds out that the caller wants to talk to someone, locates and alerts the called party, and waits for the called party to accept the call. As soon as the telephone system determines that the called party wants to take the call, it connects an end-to-end circuit between the caller and called user, which permits them to begin the media exchange phase.

The media exchange phase is the phase in which the endpoints actually converse over the connection that the session establishment phase forges.

Figure 1-2 *Traditional Circuit-Switched Architecture*

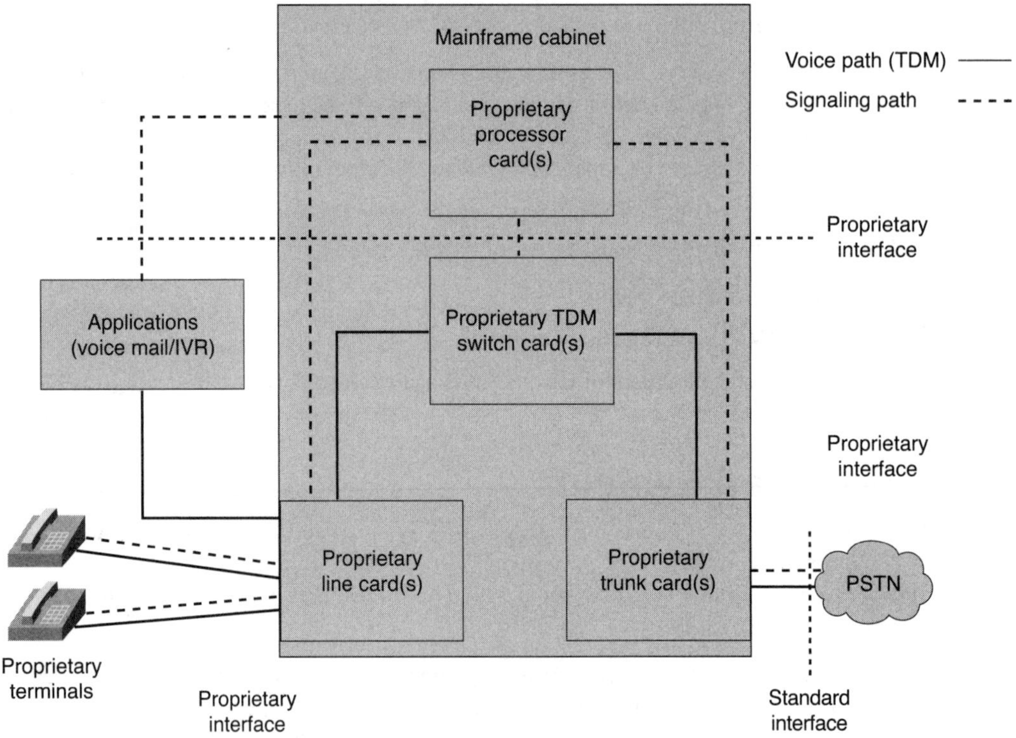

Session establishment is the purview of *call signaling protocols*. Call signaling protocol is just a fancy term for the methods that coordinate the events required for a caller to tell the network to place a call, provide the telephone number of the destination, ring the destination, and connect the circuits when the destination answers. There are dozens of call signaling protocols, of which the following are just a sample:

- Rudimentary indications that can be provided over analog interfaces

- Proprietary digital methods

- Various versions of ISDN Basic Rate Interface (BRI), which are implementations of ITU-T Q.931

- Various versions of ISDN Primary Rate Interface (PRI), which are also implementations of ITU-T Q.931

- Integrated Services User Part (ISUP), which is part of Signaling System 7 (SS7)

All of these protocols serve the purpose of coordinating the establishment of a communications session between calling and called users.

As part of the session establishment phase, the telephone network reserves and connects circuits from the caller to the called user. Circuit-switched systems establish circuits with commands to their switch cards. Switch cards are responsible for bridging the media from one line or trunk card to another card in response to directives from the call processing software.

Once a circuit-switched system forges an end-to-end connection, the end devices (also called *endpoints*) can begin the media exchange phase. In the media exchange phase, the endpoints encode the spoken word into a data stream. By virtue of the circuit connection, a data stream encoded by one endpoint travels to the other endpoint, which decodes it.

One feature to note is that in a circuit-switched system, the telephone network's switches are directly involved in both the call signaling and the media exchange. The telephone system must process the events from the caller and called user as part of the session establishment, and then it issues commands to its switch cards to bridge the media. Both the call signaling and the media follow the same path.

Call signaling protocols sometimes embed information about the voice-encoding method to be used to ensure that the endpoints communicate using a common encoding scheme. For voice communications, however, this media negotiation does not assume the importance it does in a packet-based system, where endpoints generally have more voice-encoding schemes to choose from.

In summary, a circuit-switched system goes through the following steps (abstracted for clarity) to establish a call:

Step 1 **Call signaling**—Using events received from the line and trunk cards, the telephone system detects an off-hook event and dialed digits from the caller, uses the dialed digits to locate a destination, offers the call to the called user, and waits for the called user to answer. When the called user answers, the telephone system fully connects a circuit between the caller and called user.

Step 2 **Media exchange**—By virtue of their connected circuit, the calling and called users can converse. The calling user's phone encodes the caller's speech into a data stream. The switch cards in the telephone system forward the data stream along the circuit until the called user's phone receives and decodes it. Both the call signaling and the media follow a nearly identical path.

Cisco AVVID IP Telephony Networks

A Cisco AVVID IP Telephony network is a packet-based system. Cisco CallManager is a member of a class of systems called *softswitches*. In a softswitch-based system, the call signaling components and device controllers are not separated by a hardware bus running a proprietary protocol, but instead are separate boxes connected over an IP network and talking through open and standards-based protocols.

CallManager provides the overall framework for communication within the corporate enterprise environment. CallManager handles the signaling for calls within the network and calls that originate or terminate outside the enterprise network. In addition to call signaling, CallManager provides call feature capabilities, the capability for voice mail interaction, and an application programming interface (API) for applications. Among such applications are Cisco IP Auto Attendant (Cisco IP AA), Cisco IP SoftPhone, Cisco IP Interactive Voice Response (IVR), Cisco IP Contact Center (IPCC), and Cisco WebAttendant.

A Cisco AVVID IP Telephony network is by nature more open and distributed than a traditional telephone system. It consists of a set number of servers that maintain static provisioned information, provide initialization, and process calls on behalf of a larger number of client devices. Servers cooperate with each other in a manner termed *clustering*, which presents administrators with a single point of provisioning, offers users the illusion that their calls are all being served by the same CallManager node, and enables the system to scale and provide reliability.

The remainder of this section discusses the following topics:

- "Cisco CallManager History" presents a short history of CallManager.
- "Cisco-Certified Servers for Running Cisco AVVID IP Telephony" describes the Windows 2000 servers that CallManager runs on.
- "Windows 2000 Services on Cisco AVVID IP Telephony Servers" presents the services that run on the server devices in a Cisco AVVID IP Telephony network.
- "Client Devices that Cisco CallManager Supports" presents the station, trunking, and media devices that CallManager supports.
- "Call Establishment in a Cisco AVVID IP Telephony Network" describes how a Cisco AVVID IP Telephony system places telephone calls.
- "Cisco AVVID IP Telephony Clustering" describes Cisco AVVID IP Telephony clustering.

Cisco CallManager History

There have been several releases of the software that would become Cisco CallManager release 3.1. It started in 1994 as a point-to-point video product, but it was recast as an IP-based telephony system in 1997. By 2001, it is able to support as many as 100,000 users.

1994—Multimedia Manager

Cisco CallManager release 3.1 began in 1994 as Multimedia Manager 1.0. Multimedia Manager was the signaling controller for a point-to-point video product. Multimedia Manager was developed under HP-UX in the language SDL-88.

Specification and Description Language (SDL), is an International Telecommunication Union (ITU)-standard (Z.100) graphical and textual language that many telecommunications specifications use to describe their protocols. An SDL system consists of many independent state machines, which communicate with other state machines solely through message passing and are thus object-oriented. Furthermore, because SDL is specifically designed for the modeling of real-time behavior, it is extremely suitable for call processing software.

Although Multimedia Manager 1.0 was developed in HP-UX, it was produced to run on Microsoft Windows NT 3.51. Each Multimedia Manager server was a signaling source and sink only. Multimedia Manager 1.0 managed connections by sending commands to network hubs, which contained the matrix for the video connections. Each hub contained 12 hybrid Ethernet/time-division multiplexing (TDM) ports. Each port could serve either a PC running videoconferencing software or a subhub that managed four PRI interfaces for calls across the public network. In addition, hubs could be chained together using hybrid Ethernet/TDM trunks. At that point in time, the software was somewhat of a hybrid system; Multimedia Manager, running on a Microsoft Windows NT 3.51 Server, handled the call signaling and media control over IP like a softswitch, but the media connections were still essentially circuit-based in the network hubs.

Figure 1-3 depicts CallManager as it existed in 1994.

1997—Selsius-CallManager

Although Multimedia Manager 1.0 worked wonderfully, by 1997 it was clear that Multimedia Manager was not succeeding in the marketplace. Customers were reluctant to replace their Ethernet-only network infrastructure with the hybrid Ethernet/TDM hubs required to switch the bandwidth-hungry video applications. At that point, Multimedia Manager 1.0 changed from a videoconferencing solution to a system designed to route voice calls over an IP network. Unlike the hybrid solution, which required intervening hubs to connect a virtual circuit between endpoints, media signaling traveled over the IP infrastructure directly from station to station. In other words, the system became a packet-switched telephone system.

The change required the development of IP phones and IP gateways. The database, which had been a software application running under Windows NT, became a set of Web pages connected to a Microsoft Access database. The new interface permitted administrators to modify the network configuration from any remote machine's Web browser.

Figure 1-3   *Cisco CallManager in 1994*

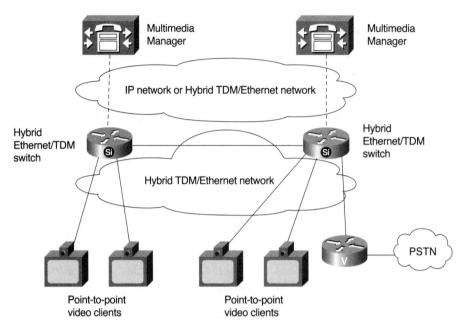

The call processing software, too, changed. It incorporated new code to control the IP phones and gateways. For this purpose, the Skinny Client Control Protocol (SCCP) and Skinny Gateway Control Protocol (SGCP) were invented. In addition, the software supported Microsoft NetMeeting, an application that uses the H.323 protocol to support PC-to-PC packet voice calls.

At the same time, the call processing software had finally outgrown the SDL development tools. To ensure that the code base could continue to grow, the pure SDL code was converted into a C++ based SDL application engine that duplicated all of the benefits that the previous pure SDL environment had provided.

Selsius-CallManager 1.0 was born. It permitted Skinny Protocol station-to-station and station-to-trunk calls. Each Selsius-CallManager supported 200 feature phones with features such as transfer and call forward.

Figure 1-4 depicts CallManager as it existed in 1997.

Figure 1-4   *Cisco CallManager in 1997*

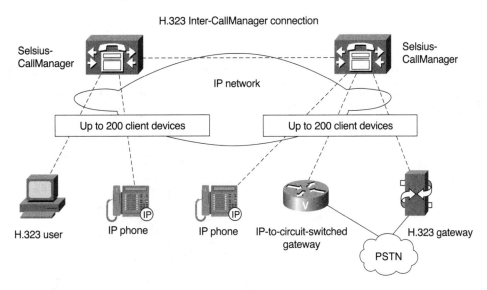

2000—Cisco CallManager Release 3.0

CallManager received a great deal of attention from the marketplace. By 1998, CallManager 2.0 had been released, and Cisco Systems, Inc., had become interested in the potential of the product.

After acquiring the CallManager product as a result of Cisco Systems' acquisition of Selsius Systems in 1998, Cisco concentrated on enhancing the product. Cisco was also simultaneously undertaking a huge design and re-engineering effort to provide both scalability and redundancy to the system. Clustering was introduced, and the Specification and Description Language (SDL) engine became the Signal Distribution Layer (SDL) engine, which permits the sending of signals directly from one CallManager to another. A redundancy scheme allowed stations to connect to any CallManager in a cluster and operate as if they were connected to their primary CallManager. Support for Media Gateway Control Protocol (MGCP) was added, as was the Cisco IP Phone 7960, which provided a large display, soft keys, and access to network directories and services.

By mid-2000, Cisco CallManager release 3.0 was complete. It permitted feature-rich calls between H.323 stations and gateways, MGCP gateways, and Skinny Protocol stations and gateways. Each cluster supported up to 10,000 endpoints, and multiple cluster configurations permitted the configuration of up to 100,000 endpoints.

Figure 1-5 depicts Cisco CallManager release 3.0.

Figure 1-5 *Cisco CallManager in 2000*

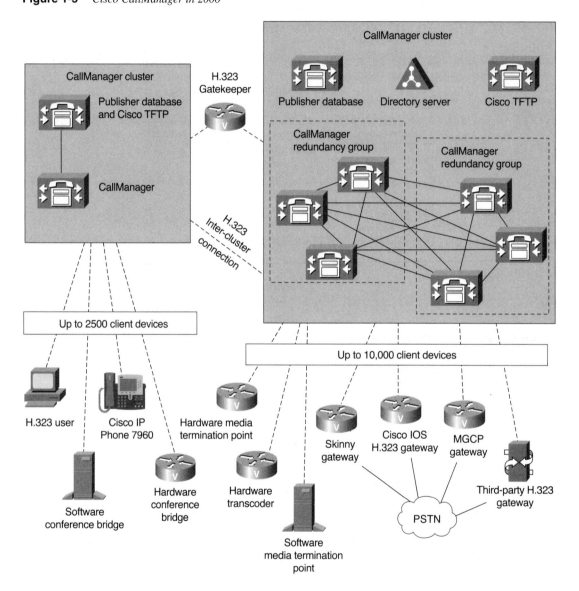

2001—Cisco CallManager Release 3.1

Cisco CallManager release 3.1 builds on the foundation of Cisco CallManager 3.0. The platform supports more gateway devices and station devices, adds enhancements to serviceability, and adds more features. Among the specific enhancements are

- Music on hold (MOH) servers
- Media resource devices available to the cluster, rather than individual CallManager nodes
- Support for digital interfaces on MGCP gateways
- Call preservation between IP Phones and MGCP gateways on server failure
- Generic database support for third-party devices
- Hoteling
- Overlap sending
- Support for extensible markup language (XML) and HTML applications in Cisco IP Phones
- Support for telephony applications through Telephony Application Programming Interface (TAPI) and Java TAPI (JTAPI)
- Support for Cisco IP Phones 7910 and 7940

Cisco-Certified Servers for Running Cisco AVVID IP Telephony

CallManager and its associated services run on a Windows 2000 Server. However, because voice applications are so critical to an enterprise's function, Cisco Systems requires that CallManager be installed only on certified server platforms.

Cisco has certified the following servers:

- Cisco MCS-7825-800
- Cisco MCS-7835-1000
- Compaq DL320
- Compaq DL380
- IBM xSeries 330
- IBM xSeries 340

The Cisco MCS-7825-800 and Cisco MCS-7835-1000 ship with an installation disk that contains all of the Windows 2000 services that are required to create a working IP telephony network. The Compaq and IBM servers are hardware-only; you must order a software-only version on CallManager to install on these servers.

Cisco AVVID IP Telephony consists of a suite of applications that you can provision in numerous ways for flexibility. For example, although a server contains applications for managing the database, device initialization, device control, software conferencing, and voice mail, you might decide to reserve an entire server for just one of these functions in a large, differentiated Cisco AVVID IP Telephony deployment.

Cisco offers the following MCS 7800 series servers:

- The *MCS-7825-800 server* is a slim but powerful server, suitable for smaller installations. It ships with either Cisco CallManager or Cisco IP/IVR. Through Cisco CallManager's clustering (see the section "Cisco AVVID IP Telephony Clustering") architecture, you can achieve high levels of availability and scalability.

- The *MCS-7835-1000 server* is a high-availability server platform that delivers the high performance required by enterprise networks. In addition to using CallManager clustering to achieve scalability and availability, it features a redundant hot-plug power supply and redundant hot-plug hard drives using RAID-1 disk mirroring to ensure maximum availability. If a power supply or hard drive fails, you can replace it without powering down the server or affecting service. In the case of the hard drive, as soon as you insert a replacement drive, the integrated RAID controller mirrors the data from the primary drive to the new drive without any user intervention.

Table 1-1 presents specifications for these MCS 7800 series servers.

Table 1-1 *Specifications for MCS 7800 Series Servers*

Feature	MCS-7825-800	MCS-7835-1000
Operating System	Windows 2000	Windows 2000
Intel Pentium III Processor	800 MHz	1 GHz
RAM	512 MB	1 GB
Hard Drives	Single 20 GB Fast ATA (7200 rpm)	Dual 18.2 GB Ultra3 SCSI 10,000 rpm
Hardware RAID Controller	No	Yes
Hot-Plug Redundant Power Supply	No	Yes
Size (1 U = 4.3 cm)	1 U	3 U
Maximum IP Phones	500	2500
Participation in Cisco CallManager Clusters	Yes	Yes
Maximum Users in Cluster	2500	10,000
Maximum IP IVR/Auto Attendant ports	30	48

The Compaq servers that Cisco has certified have the specifications shown in Table 1-2. These servers mirror the Cisco MCS 7800 series servers in function. The Compaq DL320 is suitable for smaller installations, while the Compaq DL380 supports larger clusters.

Table 1-2   *Specifications for Cisco-Certified Compaq Servers*

Feature	DL320	DL380
Operating System	Windows 2000	Windows 2000
Intel Pentium III Processor	800 MHz	1 GHz
RAM	512 MB	1 GB
Hard Drives	Single 20 GB	Dual 18.2 GB
	Fast ATA	Ultra3 SCSI
	(7200 rpm)	10,000 rpm
Hardware RAID Controller	No	Yes
Hot-Plug Redundant Power Supply	No	Yes
Size (1 U = 4.3 cm)	1 U	3 U
Maximum IP Phones	500	2500
Participation in Cisco CallManager Clusters	Yes	Yes
Maximum Users in Cluster	2500	10,000
Maximum IP IVR/Auto Attendant ports	30	48

At the time of this writing, information on the IBM servers was not yet available.

Windows 2000 Services on Cisco AVVID IP Telephony Servers

Cisco AVVID IP Telephony relies on several Windows 2000 services, of which Cisco CallManager is only one. Cisco AVVID IP Telephony uses the Windows 2000 services described in Table 1-3.

Table 1-3   *Windows 2000 Services that Run on a Cisco AVVID IP Telephony Server*

Name	Description
Cisco CallManager	Provides call signaling and media control signaling for up to 2500 devices.
Cisco IP Voice Media Streaming Application	Provides H.323 media termination, music on hold, and G.711 media mixing capabilities.

continues

Table 1-3   *Windows 2000 Services that Run on a Cisco AVVID IP Telephony Server (Continued)*

Name	Description
Cisco Messaging Interface	Permits Simple Message Desk Interface (SMDI) communications to voice-mail systems over an RS-232 connection.
Cisco MOH Audio Translator	Converts G.711 music source files to G.729a music source files for providing music on hold to G.729a-capable devices.
Cisco RIS Data Collector	Collects serviceability information from all cluster members for improved administrability.
Cisco Telephony Call Dispatcher	Allows users such as switchboard attendants to receive and quickly transfer calls to other users in the organization; provides automated routing capabilities.
Cisco TFTP	Provides preregistration information to devices, including a list of CallManager servers with which the devices are permitted to register, firmware loads, and device configuration files.
Database Notification	A change notification server and watchdog process that ensures that all Cisco AVVID IP Telephony applications on a server are working properly.
Publisher Database	Serves as the primary read-write data repository for all Cisco AVVID IP Telephony applications in the cluster. The Publisher database replicates database updates to all Subscriber databases in the cluster.
Subscriber Database	Serves as a backup read-only database for Cisco AVVID IP Telephony applications running on the server, should the applications lose connectivity to the Publisher database.

Client Devices that Cisco CallManager Supports

In a Cisco AVVID IP Telephony network, CallManager is the telephone operator, and it places calls on behalf of many different endpoint devices. These devices can be classified into the following categories:

- **Station devices**—Station devices are generally telephone handsets. CallManager offers four different types of handsets, which it controls with Skinny Protocol. The Cisco IP Phone 7910 is an entry-level station with a single line appearance and a two-line display. The Cisco IP Phone 7935 is a speakerphone console designed for use in conference rooms. The Cisco IP Phone 7940 supports two line appearances and offers a more powerful nine-line display with soft keys and status lines. The Cisco IP Phone 7960 supports up to six line appearances and has the same display as the Cisco IP Phone 7940.

However, station devices need not be physical handsets. CallManager also supports H.323 user clients, such as NetMeeting, which runs as a software application on a user's PC, and Cisco SoftPhone, which connects to CallManager using the TAPI application interface.

Chapter 3, "Station Devices," goes into more detail about station devices.

- **Gateway devices**—Gateway devices provide access from one telephone system to another. This access can be from one network of CallManager servers to another, from a CallManager network to a PBX, or from a CallManager network to a public network such as a Class 4 or Class 5 switch. (But note that intercluster H.323 trunks provide an alternative for connecting CallManager networks together without requiring a gateway device.)

  CallManager supports a wide range of gateway devices. The Cisco 2600, 3600, and 5300 series routers can connect to CallManager using the H.323 protocol. The Cisco VG200 gateway communicates to CallManager using MGCP. The Cisco Catalyst 4000 and 6000 switches offer a set of Voice Interface Cards (VICs) that communicate with CallManager using MGCP also in 3.1.

  Each gateway type manages a set of traditional telephony interfaces. These interfaces can be analog interfaces (the same type of telephone interface that probably runs into your home), digital interfaces such as T1 and E1 Call Associated Signaling (CAS), or any of eight flavors of ISDN Primary Rate Interface (PRI).

  Chapter 4, "Trunk Devices," goes into more detail about trunk devices.

- **Media processing devices**—Media processing devices perform codec conversion, media mixing, and media termination functions. CallManager controls media processing devices using Skinny Protocol. Four types of media processing devices exist.

  — **Transcoding resources**—These exist to perform codec conversions between devices that otherwise could not communicate because they do not encode voice conversations using a common encoding scheme. If CallManager detects that two endpoints cannot interpret each other's voice-encoding schemes, it inserts a transcoder into the conversation. Transcoders serve as interpreters. When CallManager introduces a transcoder into a conversation, it tells the endpoints in the conversation to send their voice streams to the transcoder instead of to each other. The transcoder translates an incoming voice stream from the codec that the sender uses into the codec that the recipient uses, and then forwards the voice stream to the recipient. The Catalyst 4000 and 6000 platforms offer a blade that performs transcoding functions. *Blades* are cards that are the width of the chassis that they are going into, and they contain the digital signal processors (DSPs) that perform codec conversion and media mixing.

— **Unicast conferencing devices**—These exist to permit Ad Hoc and Meet-Me conferencing. When an endpoint wishes to start a multiparty conversation, all of the other parties in the conversation need to receive a copy of its voice stream. If several parties are speaking at once in a conversation, some component in the conversation needs to combine the independent voice streams present at a particular instant into a single burst of sound to be played through the telephone handset.

Unicast conferencing devices perform the functions of both copying a conference participant's voice stream to other participants in the conference and mixing the voice streams into a single stream. When you initiate a conference, CallManager looks for an available Unicast conferencing device and dynamically redirects all participants' voice streams through the device. The Catalyst 4000 and 6000 platforms offer a blade that performs mixing functions. In addition, the Cisco IP Voice Media Streaming Application is a software application that can mix media streams encoded according to the G.711 codec.

— **Media Termination Point (MTP) resources**—These devices exist to allow users to invoke features such as hold and transfer, even when the person they are conversing with is using an H.323 endpoint such as NetMeeting. Older H.323 devices do not tolerate interruptions in their media sessions very well. Attempts to place these devices on hold will cause them to terminate their active call. A media termination device serves as a proxy for these old H.323 devices and allows them to be placed on hold as part of feature operation. The Catalyst 4000 and 6000 platforms offer blades that perform media termination functions, and the Cisco IP Voice Media Streaming Application is a software application that can perform media termination functions for calls that use the G.711 codec.

— **Music on Hold (MOH) resources**—These exist to provide users a music source when you place them on hold. When you place a user on hold, CallManager renegotiates the media session between the party you place on hold and the music on hold device. For as long as you keep the user on hold, the music on hold device transmits its audio stream to the held party. When you remove the user from hold, CallManager renegotiates the media stream between your device and the user.

Table 1-4 provides a comprehensive (at the time of this writing) list of the devices that CallManager supports.

Table 1-4   *Client Devices that Cisco CallManager Supports*

Name	Type	Description
Cisco IP Phone 7910	Station	Single-line appearance phone with 2-line black-and-white alphanumeric display
Cisco IP Phone 7940	Station	Dual-line appearance phone with 9-line grayscale graphical display
Cisco IP Phone 7935	Station	Speakerphone console with alphanumeric display designed for use in conference rooms
Cisco IP Phone 7960	Station	6-line appearance phone with 9-line grayscale graphical display
Microsoft NetMeeting	Station	Windows-based H.323 software client application
Cisco SoftPhone	Application	Windows-based TAPI software client application
Cisco 1750 Gateway	Gateway	H.323 gateway FXS, FXO, and E&M analog interfaces
Cisco 2600 Series Gateways	Gateway	H.323 gateway with FXS, FXO, and E&M analog interfaces, and T1 and E1 CAS, user- and network-side PRI digital interfaces
Cisco 3600 Gateway	Gateway	MGCP and H.323 gateway with FXS, FXO, and E&M analog interfaces, and T1 and E1 CAS, user- and network-side PRI digital interfaces
Cisco 3810 V3 Gateway	Gateway	H.323 gateway with FXS, FXO, and E&M analog interfaces, and T1 and E1 CAS digital interfaces
Cisco 5300 Series Gateways	Gateway	H.323 gateway with T1 and E1 CAS, user- and network-side PRI digital interfaces
Cisco 7200 Gateway	Gateway	H.323 gateway with T1 CAS, user- and network-side PRI digital interfaces
Cisco DT-24+	Gateway	MGCP gateway with user- and network-side PRI digital interfaces
Cisco DE-30+	Gateway	MGCP gateway with user- and network-side PRI digital interfaces
Cisco Catalyst 4000	Gateway	A platform for which blades controlled with MGCP are available that provide FXS, FXO, and E&M analog interfaces, T1 and E1 CAS, and user- and network-side PRI digital interfaces

continues

Table 1-4 *Client Devices that Cisco CallManager Supports (Continued)*

Name	Type	Description
Cisco Catalyst 6000	Gateway	A platform for which blades controlled with MGCP are available that provide FXS analog interfaces and user- and network-side PRI digital interfaces
Cisco VG200 Gateway	Gateway	MGCP gateway with FXS and FXO analog interfaces and T1 CAS, user- and network-side PRI digital interfaces
Cisco Catalyst 4000	Media	A platform for which blades controlled with Skinny Protocol are available that provide conferencing, transcoding, and media termination
Cisco Catalyst 6000	Media	A platform for which blades controlled with Skinny Protocol are available that provide conferencing, transcoding, and media termination
Cisco IP Voice Media Streaming Application	Media	G.711 conferencing and media termination software application

Call Establishment in a Cisco AVVID IP Telephony Network

Although a circuit-based system relies on a switch card to forge a media connection between two devices, a packet-based system uses no switch cards at all. Rather, the calling device streams media over the IP network directly to the called device. This point bears repeating, because it is a fundamental difference between circuit-switched and packet-switched systems in the enterprise: In a traditional circuit-switched system, both the signaling path and the media path run into the central cabinet, with the call processing software controlling the media on behalf of the devices by talking to a switch card. In a softswitch, the call processing software terminates the signaling path and coordinates the media session directly with the calling and called devices, which initiate the media exchange on their own. In processing a call, Cisco AVVID IP Telephony performs the following steps:

Step 1 **Call signaling**—An IP telephony device sends a request to CallManager to originate a call. The request contains the address of the destination to be called. CallManager locates the called party, sends a new call event to the called device, and waits for the called device to respond with an answering event.

Step 2 **Media control**—When the called device answers, CallManager determines the details of the media session to be established. CallManager must ensure that the two devices can communicate with a common voice-encoding scheme, and it must provide each device with the IP address and port on which the other device has chosen to receive media.

Step 3 **Media exchange**—After the media session is negotiated and the addresses exchanged, each device streams media directly through the IP network to the other device. Unlike a circuit-switched system, CallManager does not bridge the media streams. Media termination is a function of the endpoints themselves.

Figure 1-6 illustrates a comparison between the circuit-switched and packet-switched call models.

Using the IP network as a virtual matrix offers some remarkable benefits. The Internet is an IP network that spans the globe. A computer on the Internet can talk to its neighbor as easily as it talks to one that is 1000 miles away. Similarly, without the need to connect circuits one leg at a time across long distances, one CallManager can connect calls between IP phones separated by area codes or even country codes as easily as it can connect two IP phones in the same building.

Furthermore, IP networks are distributed by their nature. A traditional circuit-based solution requires that all of the wires for your voice network run into the same wiring closet. This means that the telephone system can intercept events from the line and trunk cards and gain access to the media information that the devices send to connect them in the matrix. CallManager is able to communicate with devices by establishing virtual wires through the fabric of the IP network, and the devices themselves establish virtual wires with each other when they start exchanging media. This feature makes CallManager more scalable than traditional circuit-switched systems. Figure 1-7 offers a comparison.

Another major benefit of CallManager is that it resides on the same network as your data applications. The Cisco AVVID IP Telephony model is a traditional Internet client-server model. CallManager is simply a software application running on your data network with which clients (telephones and gateways) request services using standard or open interfaces. This coresidency between your voice and data applications allows you to integrate traditional data applications (such as Web servers and directories) into the interface of your voice devices. The use of standard Internet protocols for such applications (HTML and XML) means that the skills for developing such applications are readily available, if you wish to customize the services available to your voice devices.

Finally, CallManager interacts with IP devices on the network using standard or open protocols, which allows you to mix and match equipment from other vendors when building your voice network. For devices, CallManager supports the open Skinny Protocol to phones, gateways, and transcoding devices; MGCP to gateway devices; and H.323 to user and gateway devices. For server applications, CallManager supports TAPI and JTAPI.

Figure 1-6 *Circuit-Switched Call vs. Packet-Switched Call*

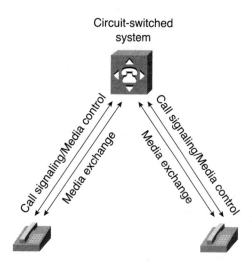

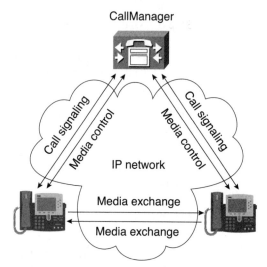

Phones are connected directly into the circuit-switched system.

1 Call signaling: The system detects a call request and extends the call to the destination. Negotiation of the type of connection usually occurs as part of the call signaling itself.

2 Media exchange: When the call is answered, the circuit-switched system must bridge the voice stream. Both call signaling and media exchange are centralized.

Phones connect to CallManager through a network of routers.

1 Call signaling: CallManager detects a call request and extends the call to the destination.

2 Media control (sometimes, but not always, part of call signaling): When the destination answers, the endpoints must negotiate a codec and exchange addresses for purposes of exchanging media.

3 Media exchange: The phones exchange media directly with each other. The media often follows a completely different set of routers from the call signaling. Call signaling and media control are centrally managed, but the high-bandwidth media is distributed.

Figure 1-7   *Cisco AVVID IP Telephony Scalability*

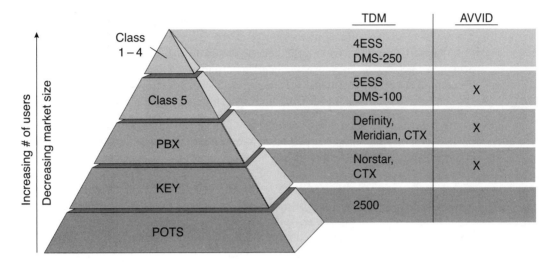

Cisco AVVID IP Telephony Clustering

A traditional telephone system tends to come packaged in a large cabinet with racks of outlying cabinets to house the switch cards, line cards, and trunk cards. A Cisco AVVID IP Telephony network, however, is composed of a larger number of smaller, more specialized components. This allows you to more closely tailor your telephone network to your organization's needs.

This focus on the combined power of small components extends to the call processing component of a Cisco AVVID IP Telephony network: Cisco CallManager. Up to eight servers can cooperatively manage the call processing for the enterprise. Such a set of networked servers is called a CallManager cluster. Clustering helps provide the wide scalability of a Cisco AVVID IP Telephony network, redundancy in the case of network problems, ease of use for administrators, and feature transparency between users.

Clustering allows for flexibility and growth of the network. In release 3.1, clusters can contain up to eight servers, which together can support 10,000 endpoints. If your network serves a smaller number of users, you can buy fewer servers. (Cisco CallManager can support larger networks—up to 100,000 users—through the use of *intercluster trunking*.) As your network grows, you can simply add more servers. Clustering allows you to expand your network seamlessly.

The idea behind a cluster is that of a virtual telephone system. A cluster allows administrators to provision much of their network from a central point. Cluster cooperation works so effectively that users might not realize that more than one CallManager node handles their calls. A guiding philosophy of clustered operation is that if a user's primary CallManager experiences an outage, the user cannot distinguish any change in phone operation when it registers with a secondary or tertiary CallManager. Thus, to the users and the administrators, the individual servers in the cluster appear as one large telephone system, even if your users reside in completely different geographical regions.

Clustering requires a certain amount of bandwidth. Unless a LAN connects two servers in the network, they should not be part of the same cluster. Only if your network includes highly reliable, high-bandwidth—T3 or better—connections between two remote sites should you consider putting cluster members on either side of the connection. Rather, either remote sites should run independent clusters—a model called *distributed call processing*—or devices in remote sites should be managed by a cluster of servers that reside in a central site, a model called *centralized call processing*. Large networks tend to deploy a combination of distributed and centralized call processing systems.

Clustering and Reliability

Clustering provides for high reliability of a Cisco AVVID IP Telephony network. In a traditional telephone network, there is a fixed association between a telephone and the call processing software that serves it. Traditional telephone vendors provide reliability through the use of redundant components installed in the same chassis. Table 1-5 draws a comparison between a traditional telephone system's redundant components and Cisco AVVID IP Telephony redundancy.

Table 1-5   *Comparison Between Traditional Telephone System Redundancy and Cisco AVVID Redundancy*

Function	PBX	Cisco AVVID
Processor unit	Redundant	Up to 8 servers (1 for the Publisher database service, 1 for Cisco TFTP, 6 for Cisco CallManager)
Media switching	Redundant TDM switch	Distributed IP network (multipath)
Intercabinet interfaces	Redundant	Distributed IP interfaces (multipath)
Intracabinet buses	Redundant TDM bus	Redundant Ethernet buses
Power supplies	Redundant	Redundant
Line cards	Single (usually 24)	Not applicable
Power to phones	In-line (phantom)	In-line (phantom), third pair, or external
Phones	Single interface	Can be triple-homed

CallManager redundancy works differently. The redundancy model differs by Cisco AVVID IP Telephony component. Clustering has one meaning in regard to the database, another meaning in regard to CallManager nodes, and a third meaning in regard to the client devices.

Database Clustering

To serve calls for client devices, CallManager needs to retrieve settings for those devices. In addition, the database is the repository for information such as service parameters, features, and the route plan. The database layer is a set of dynamic link libraries (DLLs) that provide a common access point for data insertion, retrieval, and modification of the database. The database itself is Microsoft SQL Server 7.0 standard edition.

If the database resided on a single machine, the phone network would be vulnerable to a machine or network outage. Therefore, the database uses a replication strategy to ensure that every server can access important provisioning information even if the network fails.

Each CallManager cluster consists of a set of networked databases. One database, the Publisher, provides read and write access for database administrators and for CallManager nodes themselves. For large installations, it is recommended that the Publisher reside on a separate server to prevent database updates from impacting the real-time processing that CallManager does as part of processing calls.

In normal operations, all CallManager nodes in a cluster retrieve information from the Publisher. However, the Publisher maintains a TCP connection to each server in the cluster that runs a CallManager. When database changes occur, the Publisher database replicates the changed information to Subscriber databases on each of these connected servers. The Publisher replicates all information other than Publisher Call Detail Records (CDRs). In addition, the Publisher serves as a repository for CDRs written by all CallManager nodes in the cluster.

In a large campus deployment, a server is often dedicated to handling the Publisher database. This server is often a high availability system with hardware redundancy, such as dual power supply and Redundant Array of Independent Disks (RAID) disk arrays.

Subscriber databases are read-only. CallManager nodes access the Subscriber databases only in cases when the Publisher is not available. Even so, CallManager nodes continue operating with almost no degradation. If the Publisher is not available, CallManager nodes write CDRs locally and replicate them to the Publisher when it becomes available again. Figure 1-8 shows database clustering.

Figure 1-8   *Database Clustering*

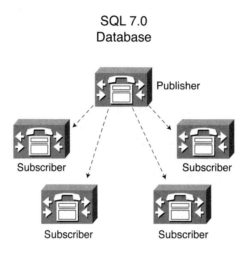

SQL 7.0
Database

Publisher

Subscriber

Subscriber

Subscriber

Subscriber

Cisco CallManager Clustering

Although the database replicates nearly all information in a star topology (one Publisher, many Subscribers), CallManager nodes replicate a limited amount of information in a fully meshed topology (every server publishes information to every other server).

CallManager uses a fully meshed topology rather than a star topology because it needs to be able to respond dynamically and robustly to changes in the network. Database information changes relatively rarely, and the information in the database is static in nature. For example, the database allows you to specify which CallManager nodes can serve a particular device, but the information does not specifically indicate to which server a device is currently registered. Therefore, a star topology that prevents database updates but permits continued operation if the Publisher database is unreachable serves nicely.

CallManager, on the other hand, must respond to the dynamic information of where devices are currently registered. Furthermore, because processing speed is paramount to CallManager, it must store this dynamic information locally to minimize network activity. Should a server fail or the network have problems, a fully meshed topology allows devices to locate and register with backup CallManager nodes. It also permits the surviving reachable CallManager nodes to update their routing information to extend calls to the devices at their new locations.

Figure 1-9 shows the connections between CallManager nodes in a cluster.

Figure 1-9 *Cisco CallManager Clustering*

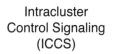

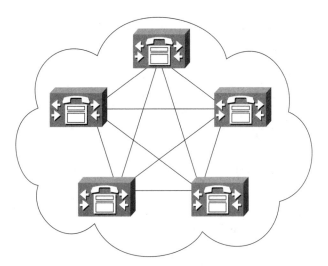

When devices initialize, they register with a particular CallManager node. The CallManager node to which a device registers must get involved in calls to and from that device. Each device has an address, either a directory number or a route pattern (see Chapter 2, "Call Routing," for more information about call routing). The essence of the inter-CallManager replication is the advertisement of the addresses of newly registering devices from one CallManager to another. This advertisement of address information minimizes the amount of database administration required for a Cisco AVVID IP Telephony network. Instead of having to provision specific ranges of directory numbers for trunks between particular CallManager nodes in the cluster, the cluster as a whole can automatically detect the addition of a new device and route calls accordingly.

The other type of communication between CallManager nodes in a cluster is not related to locating registered devices. Rather, it occurs when a device controlled by one CallManager node calls a device controlled by a different CallManager node. One CallManager node must signal the other to ring the destination device. The second type of communication is hard to peg. For lack of a better term, it is called Intracluster Control Signaling (ICCS).

Understanding this messaging requires knowing more about CallManager architecture. CallManager is roughly divided into six layers:

- Link
- Protocol
- Aggregator
- Media Control
- Call Control
- Supplementary Service

Figure 1-10 depicts this architecture. At the beginning of each subsequent chapter of this book, there is a copy of this figure with shading to indicate the components of CallManager that are covered in that particular chapter.

The Link Layer is the most basic. Its function is to ensure that if a device sends a packet of information to CallManager, or CallManager sends a packet of information to a device, the sent packet is received. CallManager uses two methods of communication. The TCP protocol is by far the most commonly used. TCP underlies much communication on the Internet. It provides for reliable communication between peers using the IP protocol. CallManager uses TCP for call signaling and media control with IP Phones, H.323 gateways, media devices, and other CallManager nodes. The UDP protocol is a protocol in which a sent packet is not guaranteed to be received. CallManager uses UDP for communication with MGCP gateways. Although UDP itself is not reliable, the MGCP protocol is designed to handle instances where the IP network loses the message; in such a case, the MGCP protocol retransmits its last message.

The Protocol Layer includes the logic that CallManager uses to manage the different types of devices that it supports. These devices include the media devices, trunk devices, and station devices. The Protocol Layer also supports third-party integration with CallManager through the TAPI and JTAPI protocols.

The Aggregator Layer allows CallManager to properly handle the interactions between groups of related devices. The media resource manager, for example, permits one CallManager node to locate available media devices, even if they are registered to other CallManager nodes. The route list performs a similar function for gateways. Line control permits CallManager to handle IP Phones that share a line appearance, even if the IP Phones are registered with different CallManager nodes.

The Media Control Layer handles the actual media connections between devices. It handles the media control portion of setting up a call, but it also handles more complicated tasks. For instance, sometimes CallManager must introduce a transcoding device to serve as an interpreter for two devices that don't talk the same codec. In this case, one call between two devices consists of multiple media hops through the network. The Media Control Layer coordinates all of the media connections.

Figure 1-10 *Layers Within Cisco CallManager*

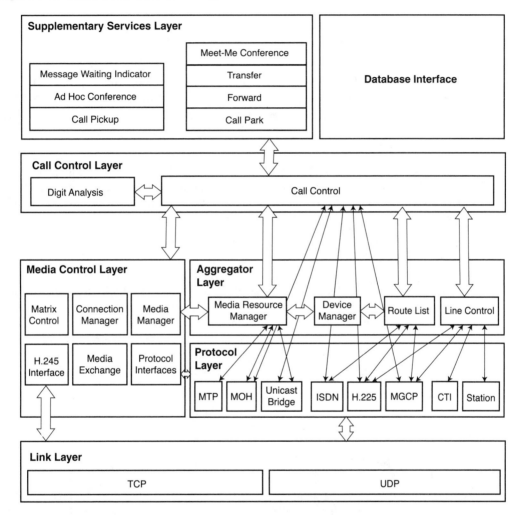

The Call Control layer handles the basic call processing of the system. It locates the destination that a caller dials and coordinates the Media Control, Aggregator, and Protocol Layers. Furthermore, it provides the primitives that the Supplementary Service Layer uses to relate independent calls.

The Supplementary Service Layer relates independent calls together as part of user-requested features such as call transfer, conference, and call forwarding.

Within each layer, the SDL application engine manages state machines. These state machines each handle a small bit of the responsibility of placing calls in a CallManager network. For example, one kind of state machine is responsible for handling station devices, while another type is responsible for handling individual calls on station devices. These state machines are essentially small event-driven processes, but they do not show up on Microsoft Windows 2000's Task Manager. Rather, the SDL application engine manages these tasks.

These state machines perform work through the exchange of proprietary messages. Before Cisco CallManager release 3.0 was created, these messages were strictly internal to CallManager. With the release of Cisco CallManager 3.0, these messages could travel from a state machine in one CallManager node directly to another state machine managed by a different CallManager node.

This mechanism is, in fact, what allows a CallManager cluster to operate with perfect feature transparency. The same signaling that occurs when a call is placed between two devices managed by the same CallManager node occurs when a call is placed between two devices managed by different CallManager nodes.

Architecturally, intracluster communication tends to occur at the architectural boundaries listed in Figure 1-10. Take, for example, the situation that occurs when two devices that share a line appearance register with different CallManager nodes. When someone dials the directory number of the line appearance, both devices ring. Even though the state machine responsible for managing each station is on its own CallManager node, both of these state machines are associated with a single state machine that is responsible for managing line appearances. (These can reside on one of the two CallManager nodes in question, or possibly on a third CallManager node). The ICCS, however, guarantees that the feature operates the same, no matter how many CallManager nodes are handling a call.

The architectural layers are rather loosely coupled. In theory, a call between two devices registered to different CallManager nodes in the cluster could involve up to seven CallManager nodes, though in practice, only two are required.

Device Redundancy

In a traditional telephone system, the phone is a slave to the call processing logic in the cabinet; it is unaware of the operating condition of its master. Consequently, the secondary master must maintain the state of the endpoint. For this reason, traditional telephone system architectures are redundant architectures rather than distributed architectures: maintaining state across more than a single backup processor is excessively complex and difficult. In the Cisco AVVID IP Telephony architecture, the endpoint is aware of the operational status of the server, as well as its own connectivity states. As a result, the endpoints determine which CallManager nodes serve them. You can provision each endpoint with a list of candidate servers. If the server to which an endpoint is registered has a software problem, or a network connectivity glitch prevents the endpoint from contacting the server, the endpoints move their registration to a secondary or even tertiary CallManager. Phones in active conversations, assuming that the media path is not interrupted, maintain their audio connection to the party to which they are streaming. However, because CallManager is not available to the phone during this interim, users cannot access features on the preserved call. Once the call terminates and the phone reregisters, the phone regains access to CallManager features.

Figure 1-11 shows an example of this behavior in action. On the left, three phones are homed to CallManager SanJoseC in a cluster, and each has multiple CallManager nodes configured for redundancy. CallManager SanJoseC fails. As a result, all phones that were registered with CallManager SanJoseC switch over to their secondary CallManagers. One phone moves to CallManager SanJoseB, and the other phones move to CallManager SanJoseA.

Figure 1-11 *Device Redundancy*

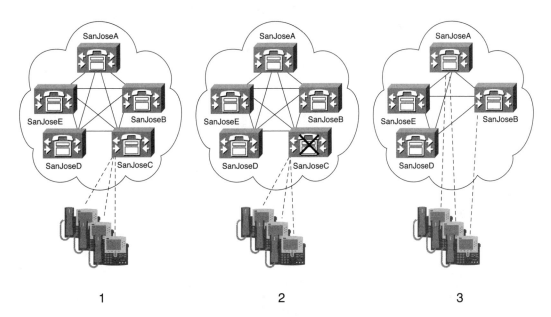

Deployment of Servers Within a Cisco CallManager Cluster

Each CallManager node in a cluster can support up to 2500 phones. A CallManager cluster can support up to 10,000 phones. Adding multiple clusters permits as many phones as you need.

Within a cluster, several strategies exist for deployment of servers. Different strategies exist for clusters up to 2500 users, sites between 2500 and 5000 users, sites between 5000 and 10,000 users, and sites above 10,000 users.

Up to 2500 Users

Two deployment models exist for sites up to 2500 users.

The first model requires two servers. In this model, one server houses the Publisher and Cisco TFTP, and it serves as a backup CallManager. The other server houses a primary CallManager. Under normal operating conditions, all devices in the cluster register to the second server, but if the second server is unavailable, the first server takes over CallManager responsibilities. Figure 1-12 shows this deployment model.

Figure 1-12   *Deployment Model 1 for up to 2500 Users*

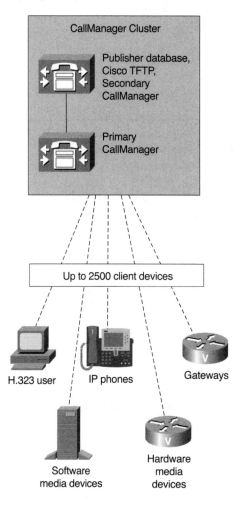

The second deployment model requires a third server. In this model, the first server houses the Publisher database and Cisco TFTP. The second server houses a primary CallManager. The third server houses a backup CallManager. Under normal operating conditions, call devices in the cluster register to the second server, but if the second server is unavailable, the third server takes over CallManager responsibilities. Figure 1-13 shows this deployment model.

Figure 1-13 *Deployment Model 2 for up to 2500 Users*

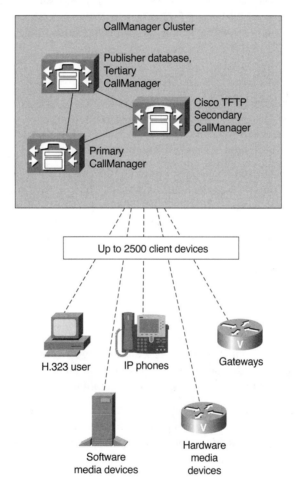

The second deployment model has the advantage of eliminating the risk that database activity on the Publisher database degrades performance of CallManager if the primary CallManager is unavailable. Furthermore, both deployment models permit the use of the locations feature of CallManager as an admissions control mechanism. (Admissions control is a means by which you can prevent your IP network from carrying so much voice traffic that the quality of individual calls degrades because of dropped packets.)

2500 to 5000 Users

Cluster sizes of between 2500 and 5000 users require four servers. One server houses the Publisher database and Cisco TFTP. The second server houses a CallManager that serves as primary CallManager for the first 2500 users. The third server houses a CallManager that serves as primary CallManager for the second 2500 users. The fourth server runs a CallManager that serves as a backup if either of the other CallManager servers becomes unavailable. Figure 1-14 shows this deployment model.

5000 to 10,000 Users

Cluster sizes of between 5000 and 10,000 users require eight servers. One server houses the Publisher database. Another server houses Cisco TFTP so that devices can get their settings and firmware loads from Cisco TFTP without competing with CallManager for processor resources.

CallManager runs on the remaining six servers. These servers consist of two replication groups of three servers each. The three CallManager nodes within a replication group together control 5000 users. In each replication group, the first server handles 2500 users, the second server handles 2500 users, and the third server provides a backup in case either of the other servers in the group becomes unavailable. Figure 1-15 shows this deployment model.

More than 10,000 Users

When the number of users climbs above 10,000, a single cluster cannot manage all devices. However, you can connect CallManager clusters together through either gateways or direct CallManager-to-CallManager connections called *intercluster trunks*. These trunks run the H.323 protocol. Figure 1-16 shows this configuration.

Between clusters, you can achieve dial-plan management either by configuring your route plan to route calls across the appropriate intercluster trunks or through the use of an H.323 gatekeeper. If you need admissions control, you achieve it through the use of an H.323 gatekeeper.

Figure 1-14 *Deployment Model for 2500 to 5000 Users*

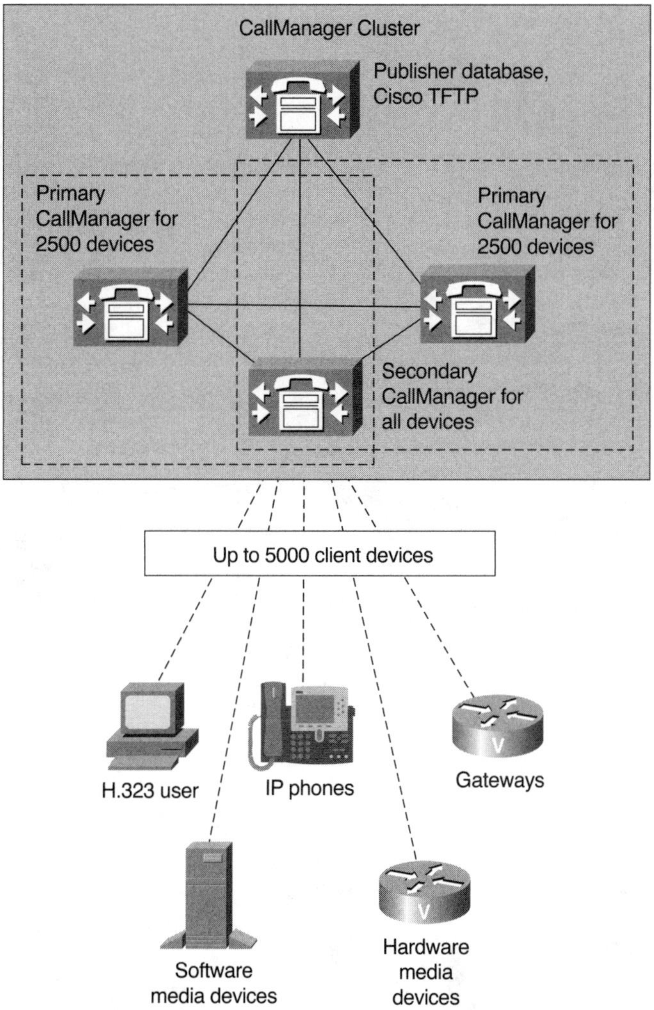

CallManager Cluster

Publisher database,
Cisco TFTP

Primary
CallManager for
2500 devices

Primary
CallManager for
2500 devices

Secondary
CallManager for
all devices

Up to 5000 client devices

H.323 user

IP phones

Gateways

Software
media devices

Hardware
media
devices

Figure 1-15 *Deployment Model for 5000 to 10,000 Users*

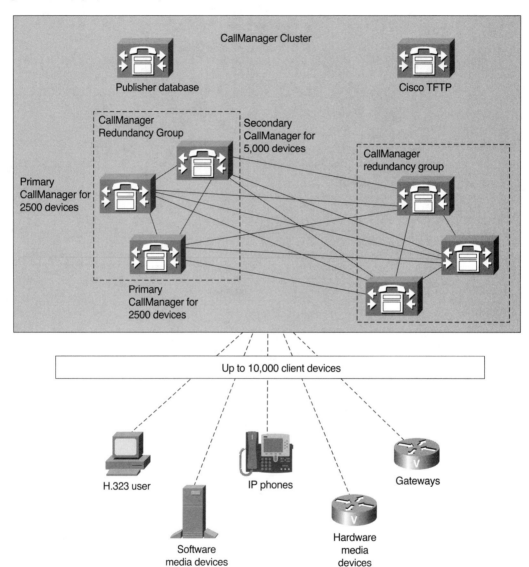

Figure 1-16 *Deployment Model for More than 10,000 Users*

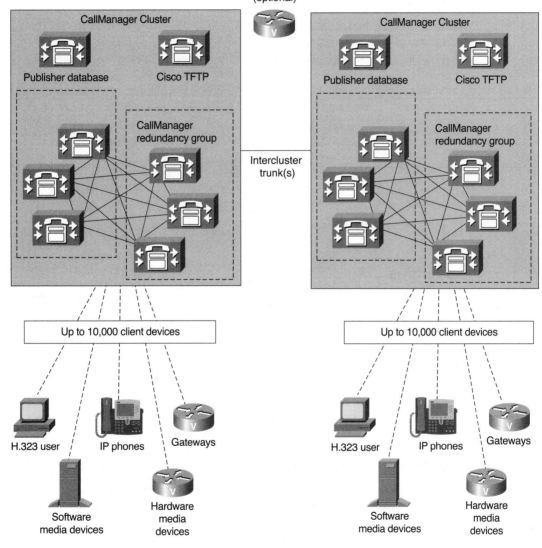

Enterprise Deployment of Cisco CallManager Clusters

This section provides an overview of the ways in which you can deploy Cisco CallManager throughout your enterprise. It addresses network infrastructure, admissions control, and supported CallManager topologies.

The excellent Cisco document DOC-7811103, *Cisco IP Telephony Network Design Guide,* which is also publicly available at www.cisco.com/univercd/cc/td/doc/product/voice/ ip_tele/, addresses all of the content in this section in far greater detail. The contents of this section have been stolen shamelessly from it. If you are already thoroughly acquainted with the aforementioned Cisco document, you might wish to skip the rest of this chapter. In any case, we strongly recommend you read the document to supplement the information contained here.

This section covers two main topics:

- "Network Topologies" describes the supported deployment strategies for a CallManager network.
- "Quality of Service" describes the methods by which you can ensure that voice traffic does not experience degradation when the network becomes congested.

Network Topologies

CallManager can be deployed in several different topologies. This section provides an overview of the following topologies:

- Single-site model
- Multiple-site model with independent call processing
- Multiple-site IP WAN model with distributed call processing
- Multiple-site model with centralized call processing
- Combined multiple-site model

Single-Site Model

The single-site model consists of a single site or campus served by a LAN. A cluster of up to eight servers (one dedicated to the Publisher database, one dedicated to the TFTP service, and six running CallManager) provides telephony service to up to 10,000 IP-enabled voice devices within the campus. Calls outside of the campus environment are served by IP-to-Public Switched Telephony Network (PSTN) gateways. Because bandwidth is often overprovisioned and undersubscribed on the LAN, there is usually no need to worry about admissions control.

Figure 1-17 presents a picture of the single-site model.

Figure 1-17 *Single-Site Model*

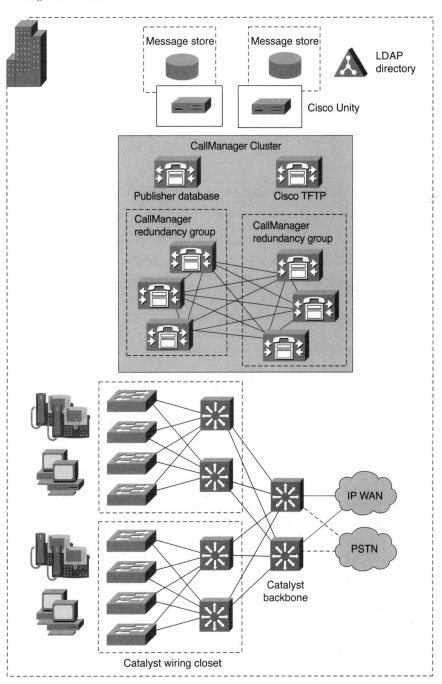

Multiple-Site Model with Independent Call Processing

The multiple-site model consists of multiple sites or campuses, each of which runs an independent cluster of up to eight servers. Each cluster provides telephony service for up to 10,000 IP-enabled voice devices within a site. Because bandwidth is often over-provisioned and undersubscribed on the LAN, there's usually no need to worry about admissions control.

IP-to-PSTN gateways handle calls outside or between each site. The multiple-site model with independent call processing allows you to use the same infrastructure for both your voice and data. However, because of the absence of an IP WAN, you cannot take advantage of the economies of placing voice calls on your existing WAN, because these calls must pass through the PSTN.

Figure 1-18 presents a picture of the multiple-site model with independent call processing.

Multiple-Site IP WAN Model with Distributed Call Processing

From CallManager's point of view, the multiple-site IP WAN model with distributed call processing is identical to the multiple site model with independent call processing. From a practical point of view, they differ markedly.

Whereas the multiple-site model with independent call processing uses only the PSTN for carrying voice calls, the multiple-site IP WAN model with distributed call processing uses the IP WAN for carrying voice calls when sufficient bandwidth is available. This allows you to take advantage of the economies of routing calls over the IP WAN instead of the PSTN.

In such a case, you can set up each site with its own CallManager cluster and interconnect the sites with PSTN-enabled H.323 gateways, such as Cisco 2600, 3600, and 5300 series routers, under H.323 gatekeeper control. Each cluster provides telephony service for up to 10,000 IP-enabled voice devices. You can add other clusters, which allows your network to support vast numbers of users.

This type of deployment allows you to bypass the public toll network when possible and also guarantees that remote sites retain survivability should the IP WAN fail. Using an H.323 gatekeeper allows you to implement a quality of service (QoS) policy that guarantees the quality of voice calls between sites. The same voice codec must apply to all intersite calls.

Two chief drawbacks of this approach are increased complexity of administration, because each remote site requires its own database, and less feature transparency between sites.

Because each site is an independent cluster, for all users to have access to conference bridges, music on hold (MOH) servers, and transcoders, you must deploy these resources in each site. Figure 1-19 presents a picture of the multiple-site IP WAN model with distributed call processing.

Figure 1-18 *Multiple-Site Model with Independent Call Processing*

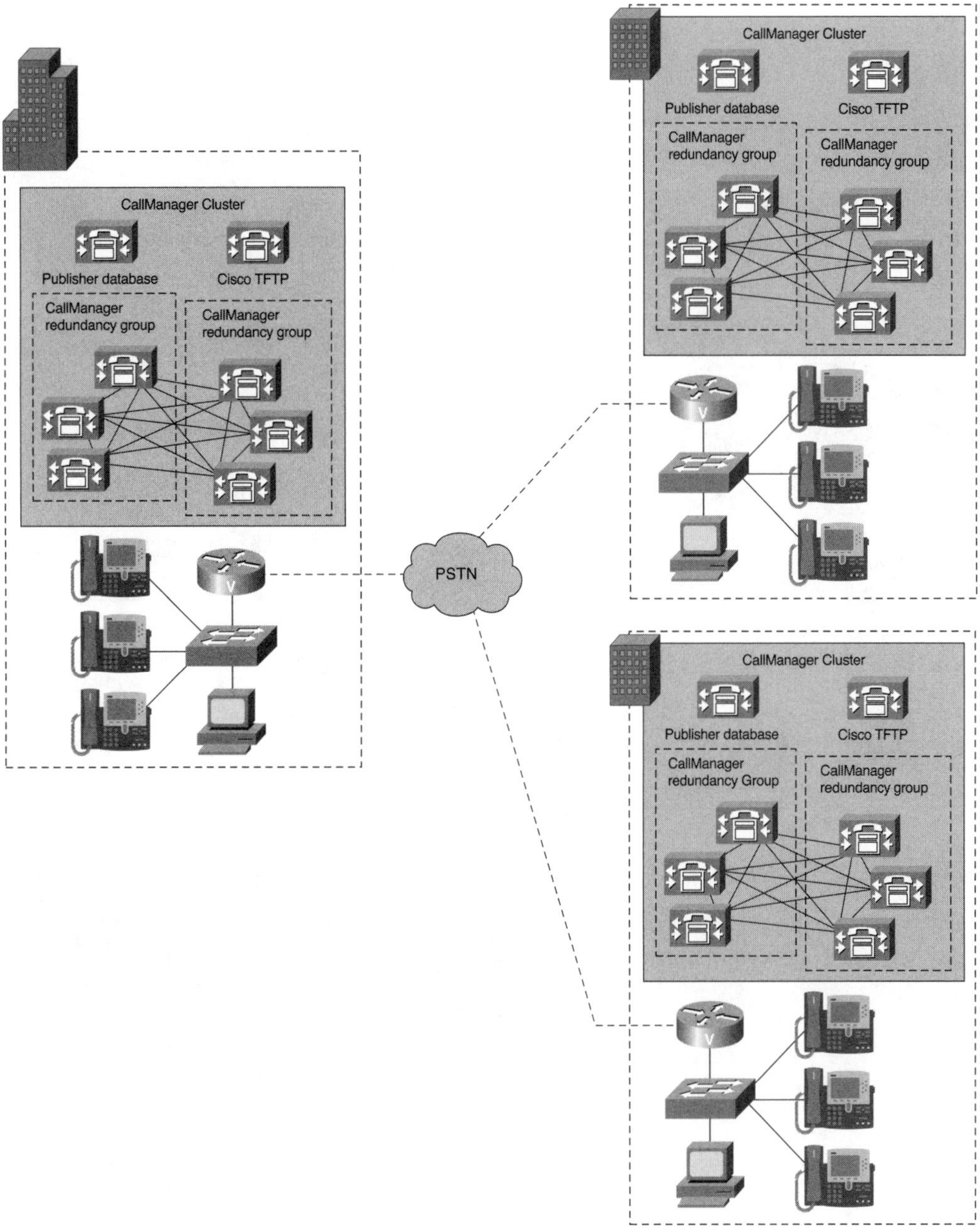

Figure 1-19 *Multiple-Site IP WAN Model with Distributed Call Processing*

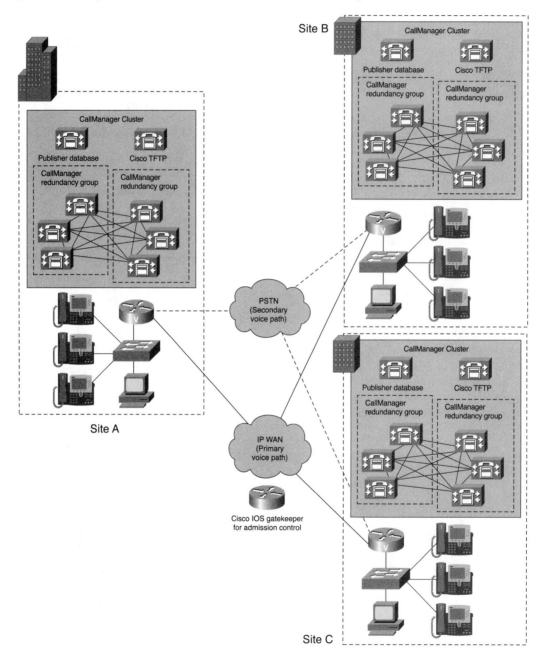

Multiple-Site Model with Centralized Call Processing

In a multiple-site model with centralized call processing, a CallManager cluster in a centralized campus processes calls placed by IP telephony devices both in the centralized campus and also in remote sites connected by an IP WAN. This type of topology is called a *hub-and-spoke topology*: the centralized campus is the hub, while the branch offices sit at the end of IP WAN spokes radiating from the campus.

To CallManager, the multiple-site model with centralized call processing is nearly identical to the single-site model. However, guaranteeing voice quality between branch sites and the centralized site requires the use of a QoS policy that integrates the locations feature of CallManager. Locations requires that all phones must register with a single CallManager. As a result, when using the multiple-site model with centralized call processing, the maximum supported cluster size consists of three CallManagers, and the secondary and tertiary CallManagers must operate purely as redundant servers. At any one time, the same CallManager node must serve all devices in the cluster.

Deploying a multiple-site model with centralized call processing offers easier administration and true feature transparency between the centralized and remote sites. However, because you cannot deploy a fully meshed cluster, maximum cluster size drops from 10,000 users to 2,500 users. Furthermore, should the IP WAN fail, devices in remote sites will be unable to place or receive calls, unless you configure dial backup.

Because all sites are served by one cluster, you only need to deploy voice mail, conference bridges, and transcoders in the central site, and all remote sites can access these features. Figure 1-20 presents a picture of the multiple-site model with centralized call processing.

Combined Multiple-Site Model

You can deploy the centralized and distributed models in tandem. If, for example, you have several large sites with a few smaller branch offices all connected by the IP WAN, you can connect the large sites using a distributed model, while serving the smaller branch offices from one of your main campuses using the centralized model. This hybrid model relies on complementary use of the locations feature of CallManager and gatekeepers for call-admission control. Figure 1-21 presents a picture of the combined multiple-site model.

Quality of Service (QoS)

Your network's available bandwidth ultimately determines the number of VoIP calls that your network can handle. As the amount of traffic on an IP network increases, individual data streams suffer packet loss and packet latency. In the case of voice traffic, this can mean clipped, choppy, and garbled messages. QoS mechanisms safeguard your network from such conditions.

Figure 1-20 *Multiple-Site Model with Centralized Call Processing*

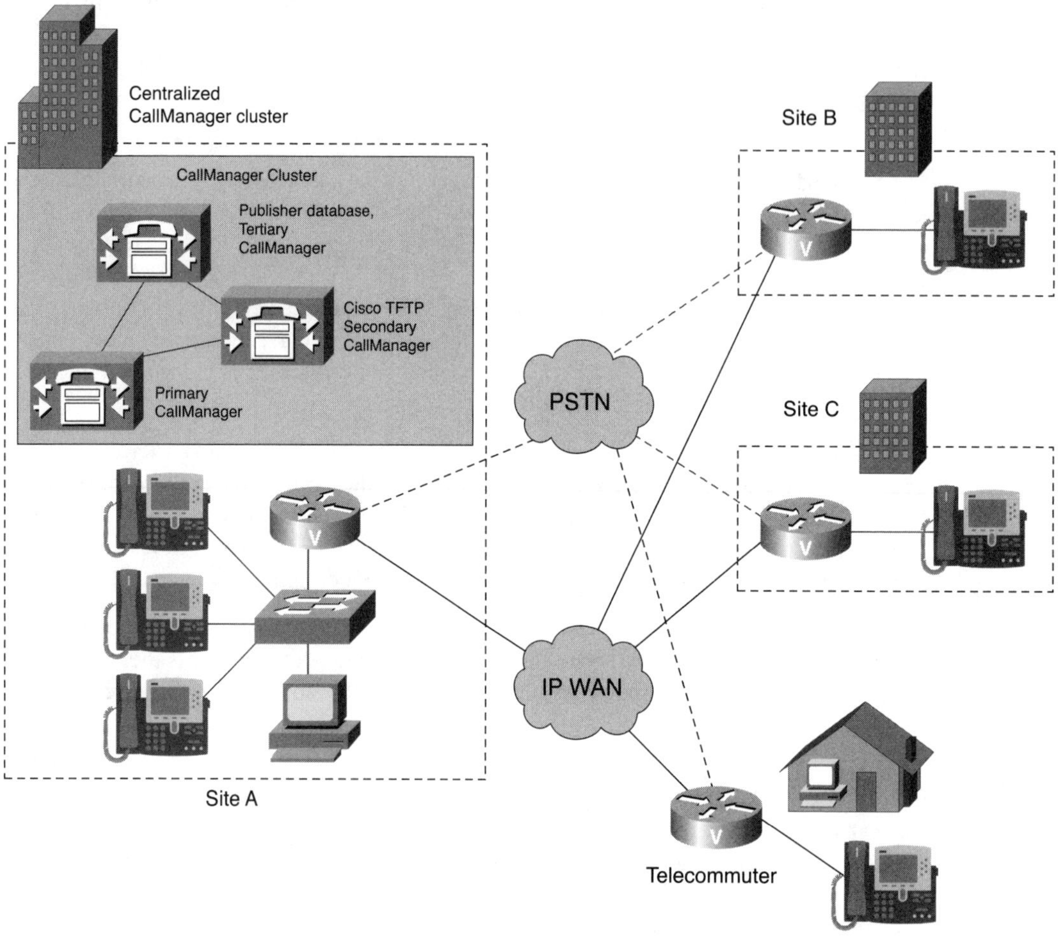

Unlike data traffic, voice traffic can survive some loss of information. Humans are good at extracting information from an incomplete data stream, while computers are not. Data traffic, on the other hand, can deal with delayed transmission, whereas delayed transmission can destroy the intelligibility of a conversation. *Traffic classification* permits you to categorize your traffic into different types. Traffic classification is a prerequisite to *traffic prioritization,* the process of applying preferential treatment to certain types of traffic. Traffic prioritization allows you to minimize the latency that a voice connection experiences at the expense of the latency that a data connection experiences.

Figure 1-21 *Combined Multiple-Site Model*

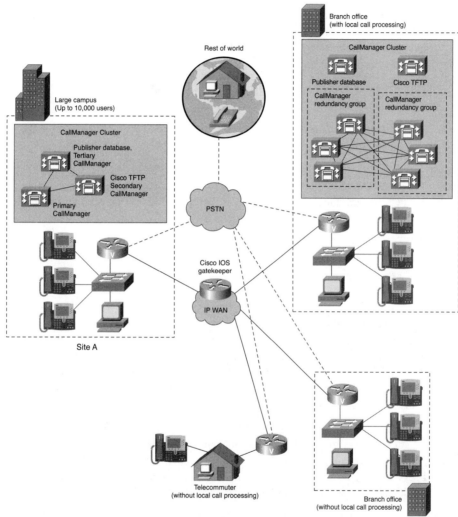

The *Cisco AVVID QoS Design Guide* for CallManager 3.0(5), order number DOC-7811549, which is publicly available at www.cisco.com/univercd/cc/td/doc/product/voice/ip_tele/, covers QoS in a Cisco AVVID IP Telephony network in much greater detail than this section, which just provides an overview.

Admissions control mechanisms prevent an IP network from becoming clogged with traffic to the point of unusability. When a network's capacity is consumed, admissions control mechanisms prevent new traffic from being added to the network.

When calls traverse the WAN, admissions control assumes paramount importance. Within the LAN, on a switched network, life is good; if you classified your information properly, then either you have enough bandwidth or you do not. Links to remote sites across the IP WAN, however, can be a scarce resource. A 10-Mbps or 100-Mbps Ethernet connection can support hundreds of voice calls, but a 64-kbps ISDN link can route only a few calls before becoming overwhelmed.

This section describes the mechanisms that CallManager uses to enhance voice traffic on the network. It covers the following topics:

- "IP Precedence" discusses traffic classification and traffic prioritization, features by which you can give voice communications preferential treatment on your network.

- "Regions" discusses how you can conserve network bandwidth over bandwidth-starved IP WAN connections.

- "Cisco CallManager Locations" describes a method of admissions control that functions within CallManager clusters.

- "H.323 Gatekeeper" describes a method of admissions control that functions between CallManager clusters.

IP Precedence

IP precedence provides a means of traffic classification and is important in configuring your traffic prioritization. By assigning voice traffic a routing priority higher than data traffic, you can ensure that the latency-intolerant voice packets are passed through your IP fabric more readily than latency-tolerant data packets. By assigning voice-related signaling a higher routing priority than data traffic, you guarantee that CallManager quickly provides a dial tone to users who go off-hook.

The Cisco 7900 series phones, as well as the Cisco 12SP+ and 30VIP phones, all send out 802.1Q packets with **class of service** and **type of service** fields set to 5 for the voice stream and 3 for the signaling streams. CallManager permits you to set its **class of service** and **type of service** fields to 3. In contrast, most data devices encode either no 802.1Q information or a default value of 0 for the **class of service** and **type of service** fields.

When present, the **class of service** and **type of service** fields permit the routers in your IP network to place incoming packets into processing queues according to the priority values encoded in the packet. By more quickly servicing queues into which higher priority packets are placed, a router can guarantee that higher priority packets experience less delay. Because all Cisco IP Phones encode their packets with **type of service** and **class of service** values of 5 and data devices do not, in effect, the **type of service** and **class of service** fields permit you to classify the type of data passing through your network. This allows you to ensure that voice transmissions experience less latency. Figure 1-22 presents an example.

Figure 1-22 *IP Precedence Example*

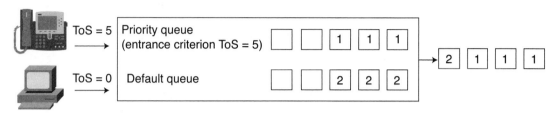

Figure 1-22 depicts two devices that send information through a network router. The Cisco IP Phone 7960 categorizes its traffic with **type of service** 5, while the PC categorizes its traffic with **type of service** 0. The router reads packets from both devices from the network and places them in queues based on the **type of service** field. Packets classified with **type of service** 5 go on a priority queue, while other packets go on the default queue.

When the router decides to forward the packet out to the network again, it sends packets from the priority queue in preference to those on the default queue. Therefore, even if the Cisco IP Phone 7960 and PC send their packets to the router at the same time, the router will forward all of the packets sent by the IP Phone before forwarding any of the packets from the PC. This minimizes the latency (or end-to-end trip time) required for packets from the IP Phone but increases the latency experienced by the PC. Thus the router properly handles the latency-intolerant voice packets.

Regions

Like IP precedence, regions play an important role in ensuring the quality of voice calls within your network.

Regions allow you to constrain the codecs selected when one device calls another. Most often, you use regions to limit the bandwidth used when calls are placed between devices connected by an IP WAN. However, you can also use regions as a way of providing higher voice quality at the expense of network bandwidth for a preferred class of users.

When you define a new region, Cisco CallManager Administration asks you to define the compression type used for calls between devices within the region. You also define, on a region-by-region basis, compression types used for calls between the region you are creating and all other regions.

You associate regions with device pools. All devices contained in a given device pool belong to the region associated with that device pool. When an endpoint in one device pool calls an endpoint in another, the codec used is constrained to what is defined in the region. If, for some reason, one of the endpoints in the call cannot encode the voice stream according to the specified codec, CallManager attempts to introduce a transcoder (see Chapter 5) to allow the endpoints to communicate.

Figure 1-23 depicts a configuration that uses three regions to constrain bandwidth between end devices. Phones 1000 and 2000 are in the main campus, while phone 3000 is in a branch office. Calls within the main campus use the G.711 codec, as do calls from phone 1000 to phone 3000. Calls between phone 2000 and phone 3000 use the G.729 codec.

Figure 1-23 *Regions Overview*

	Region 1	Region 2	Region 3
Region 1	G.711		
Region 2	G.711	G.711	
Region 3	G.711	G.729	G.711

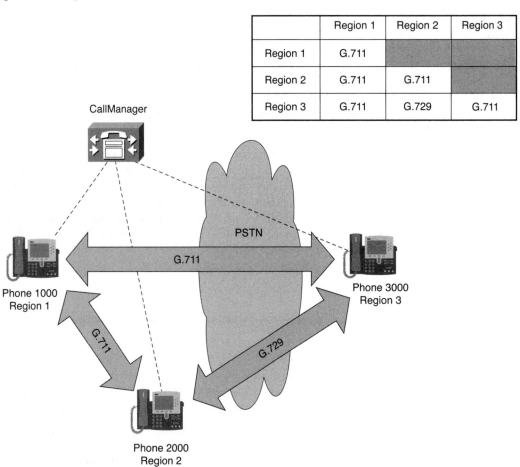

Cisco CallManager Locations

Locations is a form of admissions control. A location defines a topological area connected to other areas by links of limited bandwidth. With each location, you specify the amount of bandwidth available between users in that location and other locations in your network.

CallManager allows users to place an unlimited number of calls between devices within the same location, but when a user places a call to another location, CallManager temporarily deducts the bandwidth associated with the selected codec from the interlocation bandwidth remaining. When a user's call terminates, CallManager returns the allocated bandwidth to the pool of available bandwidth. Users who attempt to place a call when there is no more bandwidth available receive a fast busy tone. Several design caveats must be considered when using locations.

- Locations requires that all devices in a cluster register with the same CallManager node, with other CallManager nodes used solely for backup purposes. The locations feature is essentially a bandwidth counter that CallManager maintains. If CallManager notes that a call is being placed from one location to another, it decrements the call bandwidth from the bandwidth permitted for each location. The problem is that these counts are maintained on a basis that is strictly per CallManager node. Multiple CallManager nodes in a cluster means multiple independent bandwidth counters, and because any CallManager node in a cluster might serve a particular endpoint's call, there is no way that the counters can remain synchronized.

- Locations requires that you deploy your voice network in a Hub-and-spoke topology. Although locations allow you to configure admissions control, the locations mechanism is topologically ignorant. Having only one bandwidth counter for all interlocation calls means that all calls from one location to any other location must traverse only one logical network link, which limits deployment strictly to Hub-and-spoke topologies. Figure 1-24 elaborates.

Locations has two other features:

- CallManager permits calls that use media termination devices to complete, even if the bandwidth counter reports that no bandwidth is available.

- Bandwidth is deducted from the bandwidth count only after a call reaches the connected state. As a result, if multiple calls are established across a network link at the same time, locations can allow more calls to be established than the network link supports.

Figure 1-24 *Hub-and-Spoke Topology Restriction*

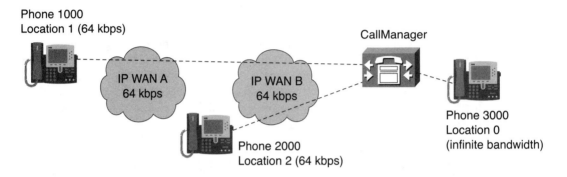

Not supported: Locations in a hierarchical topology

Phone 1000
Location 1 (64 kbps)

CallManager

IP WAN A
64 kbps

IP WAN B
64 kbps

Phone 3000
Location 0
(infinite bandwidth)

Phone 2000
Location 2 (64 kbps)

Wrong: Calls from Phone 1000 to Phone 3000 decrement Location 1's bandwidth counter but not Location 2's. CallManager allows 64 kbps of calls from Location 1 to Location 0 and, at the same time, 64 kbps of calls from Location 2 to Location 0. IP WAN B is overwhelmed.

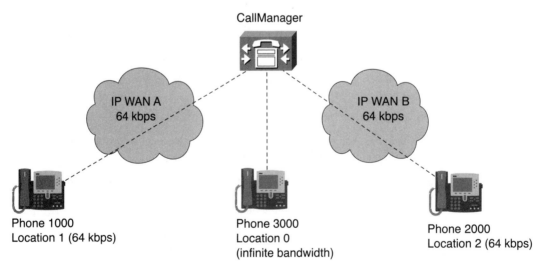

Supported: Locations in a hub-and-spoke topology

CallManager

IP WAN A
64 kbps

IP WAN B
64 kbps

Phone 1000
Location 1 (64 kbps)

Phone 3000
Location 0
(infinite bandwidth)

Phone 2000
Location 2 (64 kbps)

Right: Calls from Phone 1000 to Phone 2000 decrement both Location 1 and Location 2's bandwidth counts. Calls from Phone 1000 to Phone 3000 decrement Location 1's bandwidth count, allowing Phone 2000 to call Location 0 if necessary. The IP WAN is never overwhelmed.

H.323 Gatekeeper

CallManager can be configured to use an H.323 gatekeeper for admissions control between CallManager clusters. Before placing an H.323 call, a gatekeeper-enabled CallManager makes a Registration, Admissions, and Status (RAS) protocol admissions request (ARQ) to the H.323 gatekeeper.

The H.323 gatekeeper associates the requesting CallManager with a zone and can track calls that come into and go out of the zone. If the bandwidth allocated for a particular zone is exceeded, the H.323 gatekeeper denies the call attempt, and the caller hears a fast busy tone. Essentially, an H.323 gatekeeper provides a locations-like functionality for the H.323 domain. However, unlike locations, a chief advantage of an H.323 gatekeeper configuration is that if not enough bandwidth is available to place the call across the IP WAN, you can configure the call to route out a PSTN gateway instead. Figure 1-25 presents a picture of a gatekeeper-enabled configuration.

Figure 1-25 *H.323 Gatekeeper-Based Call Admissions Control*

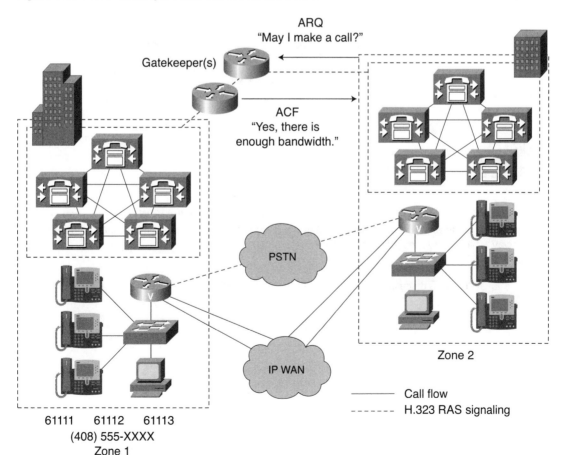

To configure fallback through the PSTN, you must configure the route plan to choose an alternate route if the gatekeeper rejects the call attempt. To configure PSTN fallback, you must configure a route list that contains two route groups. The first route group contains the intercluster trunk that routes outgoing calls over the IP WAN. If insufficient bandwidth is available, however, the H.323 gatekeeper rejects this outgoing call attempt. This call rejection triggers the alternate route associated with the route list. When CallManager selects this alternate route, it transforms the dialed digits to the destination's address as seen from the PSTN's point of view and offers the call to the PSTN gateway. Figure 1-26 demonstrates fallback routing through the PSTN.

Figure 1-26 *Fallback Routing Through the PSTN*

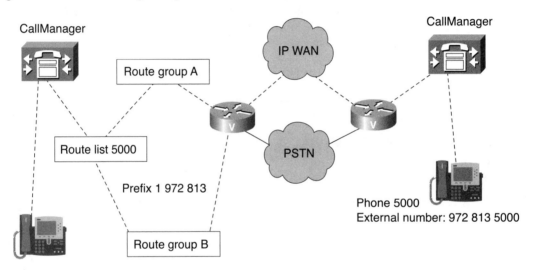

A call from Phone 1000 to Phone 5000 first attempts to route across the IP WAN. If the gatekeeper denies the call attempt, the route list modifies the dialed number and again offers the call to the gateway, which routes the call across the PSTN.

Chapter 2 discusses call routing in much more detail.

Summary

This chapter has provided an overview of Cisco AVVID IP Telephony.

It covered VoIP and how Cisco AVVID IP Telephony differs from traditional telephone systems. It described how you can use VoIP to achieve savings by routing your telephone calls over the IP WAN.

The chapter discussed Cisco CallManager, the heart of Cisco AVVID IP Telephony. The chapter recounted a short history of how CallManager has evolved and discussed the following components of a Cisco AVVID IP Telephony network:

- The Cisco-certified servers on which CallManager runs
- The Windows 2000 services that provide IP telephony in a Cisco AVVID IP Telephony network
- The client devices that CallManager supports

The chapter covered the phases that CallManager goes through to set up a call and described CallManager's clustering strategy for providing high availability and scalability. It described several different deployment models for CallManagers within a cluster.

Finally, the chapter described several methods of deploying clusters to serve both campuses and campuses with remote offices. In addition, it summarized the methods of traffic classification, traffic prioritization, and admissions control (both locations-based and gatekeeper-based) by which you can guarantee good voice quality in your network.

Call Routing

This chapter covers call routing in Cisco CallManager. CallManager provides an extremely flexible set of tools with which you can control call routing in your enterprise, but this flexibility comes with a price: complexity. This chapter covers routing from the very beginning. It discusses the route pattern, which is CallManager's central routing concept, and it discusses wildcards, which are the basic building blocks of the route pattern. It discusses how CallManager uses route patterns to select destinations based on the digits that users dial.

From this foundation, the chapter delves further into ever more complex topics. This chapter consists of the following sections:

- "The Three Responsibilities of Call Routing" briefly discusses the tasks that CallManager's routing logic must accomplish.

- "The Seven Fundamentals of Call Routing" elaborates on the seven basic features— route patterns, route filters, dialing transformations, translation patterns, route lists, calling search spaces, and partitions—that CallManager uses to solve call routing problems.

- "Route Patterns and Route Filters" talks about the route pattern, CallManager's fundamental call routing concept, by which you can assign addresses to devices in your network.

- "Dialing Transformations" discusses the mechanisms by which you can alter the calling and called numbers as CallManager routes them during calls.

- "Translation Patterns" defines a method by which you can assign aliases to other route patterns. This method is often called on to resolve thorny call routing problems.

- "Route Lists and Route Groups" defines a method by which you can organize your gateways into ordered lists so that you can ensure both that your gateways are fully utilized and that you use them in the most cost-efficient manner.

- "Calling Search Spaces and Partitions" defines a method by which you can customize routing on a user-by-user basis to accomplish complex tasks, such as routing calls by the type or the geographic location of the calling user.

- "Case Studies" provides some extensive examples by which you can see how all of the call routing concepts work together to solve complex problems.

- "Miscellaneous Solutions" provides specific solutions for call routing problems that administrators are commonly called on to solve. The solutions in this section often did not fit nicely in other sections of this chapter.

- "The North American Numbering Plan" talks about how CallManager knows how to route calls to the North American network. It also shows you how to replace CallManager's North American knowledge with call routing knowledge for non-North American networks.

- "Troubleshooting" discusses some common problems that administrators encounter when configuring their enterprise dial plans.

Figure 2-1 shows the block structure of CallManager. The shaded parts of Figure 2-1 are covered in this chapter.

This chapter is sprinkled with numerous examples throughout. These examples might be difficult to wade through, but they provide solutions to many common problems. By fully understanding how the examples work, you will be able both to improve on them and to discover solutions to problems that this chapter does not fully address.

The Three Responsibilities of Call Routing

The call routing component of Cisco CallManager has three main responsibilities:

- To determine which endpoint CallManager should ring based on the digits you dial

- To perform address translation

- To support individualized routing

The first responsibility is to determine which endpoint CallManager should ring based on the digits you dial. These endpoints are often other IP Phones, but they could just as easily be numbers controlled by other systems, such as the Public Switched Telephone Network (PSTN), other Private Branch eXchanges (PBXs), or other CallManager clusters. Furthermore, the digits you dial can sometimes not even correspond to a physical destination at all. Numbers such as call park codes, Meet-Me conference codes, and translation patterns (the section "Translation Patterns" describes the way to provide aliases for numbers) do not cause any specific device to ring. Rather, they allow CallManager to treat your call in special ways, depending on the type of number. For example, dialing a call park code allows you to retrieve a party who has been held from another station; dialing a Meet-Me conference code allows you to join a multiparty conversation; dialing a translation pattern can redirect your call to a different destination; and dialing a Computer Telephony Interface (CTI) Route Point can pass control of your call to an application such as an automated attendant. Call routing concepts, such as route patterns, underlie CallManager's treatment of all of these virtual endpoints.

Figure 2-1 *CallManager Block Structure Diagram*

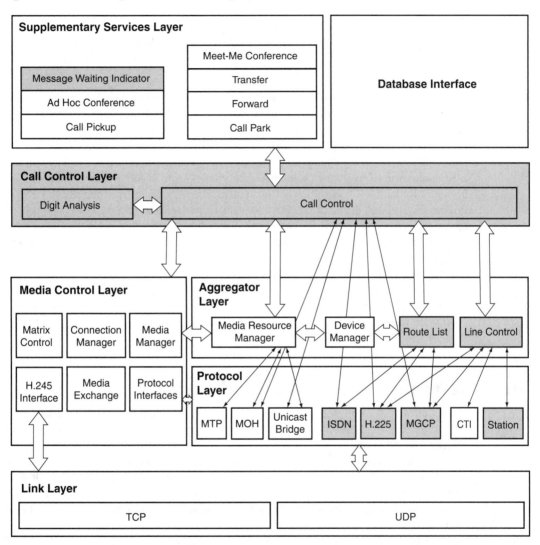

The call routing component's second responsibility is to perform address translation. Address translation allows you to modify the dialed digits and the calling number as the call propagates through a network. Such address translation is important when a network must pass a call from a private network with its private numbering plan to the PSTN with a standardized numbering plan. For example, most PBXs require users to dial an access code to place calls to the PSTN. If CallManager does not first remove the access code before offering the call to the PSTN, the PSTN rejects the call attempt. Imagine what happens if you dial an access code of 9 for calls you make from your home phone; most likely, the PSTN plays an announcement that you have composed your number incorrectly, or worse, it routes your call to a completely different destination. CallManager's address translation capabilities allow you to enforce a private numbering plan while simultaneously reconciling it against the PSTN's numbering plan. The section "Dialing Transformations" discusses address translation in more detail.

CallManager's third responsibility is to support individualized routing, which means that the destination you reach when you dial a number might differ completely from the destination your neighbor reaches when your neighbor dials the same number. This capability is useful to support routing by class of calling user, by organization, or by geographic location. For example, routing by class of calling user permits you to restrict calls made from lobby phones while allowing your executives full access to international numbers. Routing by organization permits you to route calls made by different departments in your enterprise to different locations, so calls from engineers to a technical support organization route to a different place than calls made by marketing executives. Taken to an extreme, routing by organization allows you to control entirely different enterprises using a single CallManager. Routing by geographic location allows you to deploy a single CallManager in one geographic location that controls phones in different geographic locations. Customizing the call routing for users in different geographic locations allows you to ensure that emergency calls from a particular location route to the appropriate emergency response center. You can also control costs by routing calls across your IP network instead of the PSTN, a process called *toll bypass* or *toll restriction*.

The Seven Fundamentals of Call Routing

Cisco CallManager Administration presents several items in the **Route Plan** menu related to routing. However, this chapter describes routing concepts, not particular administration screens. By understanding the underlying concepts, you can better develop your enterprise's call routing infrastructure. For example, the Route Pattern Configuration screen (shown in Figure 2-2) incorporates several routing concepts: route patterns, route filters, transformations, route lists, and partitions. This chapter does not directly deal with the Route Pattern Configuration screen, but when you understand the components that make up the Route Pattern Configuration screen, building an individual route pattern is straightforward. Figure 2-2 demonstrates how an excerpt from a single screen—the Route Pattern Configuration screen in this case—incorporates several (but not all) routing concepts.

Figure 2-2 *Route Pattern Configuration Screen*

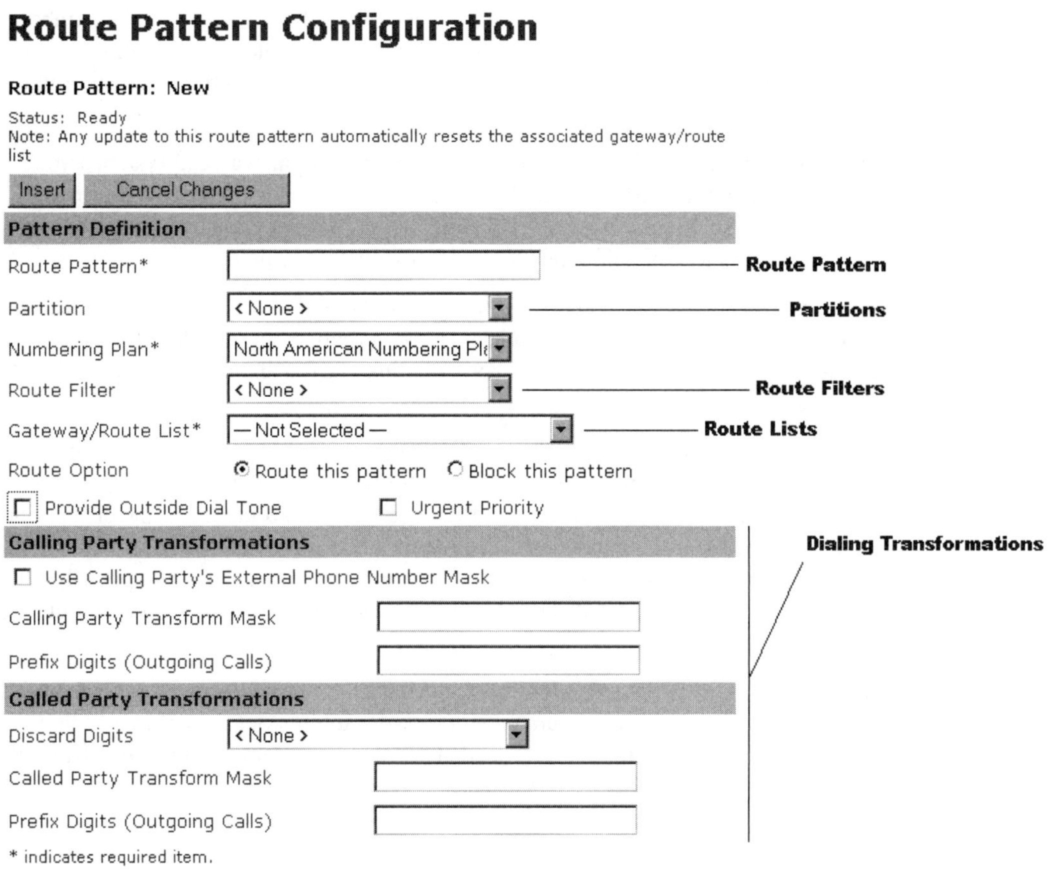

Route Pattern Configuration

Route Pattern: New

Status: Ready
Note: Any update to this route pattern automatically resets the associated gateway/route list

[Insert] [Cancel Changes]

Pattern Definition

Route Pattern*	[ ]	——————— **Route Pattern**
Partition	< None > ▼	——————— **Partitions**
Numbering Plan*	North American Numbering Pl▼	
Route Filter	< None > ▼	——————— **Route Filters**
Gateway/Route List*	— Not Selected — ▼	——— **Route Lists**
Route Option	⦿ Route this pattern ○ Block this pattern	
☐ Provide Outside Dial Tone	☐ Urgent Priority	

Calling Party Transformations   **Dialing Transformations**

☐ Use Calling Party's External Phone Number Mask

Calling Party Transform Mask   [   ]

Prefix Digits (Outgoing Calls)   [   ]

Called Party Transformations

Discard Digits   < None > ▼

Called Party Transform Mask   [   ]

Prefix Digits (Outgoing Calls)   [   ]

* indicates required item.

CallManager uses seven major concepts to fulfill its responsibilities:

- Route patterns
- Route filters
- Dialing transformations
- Translation patterns
- Route lists
- Calling search spaces
- Partitions

Route patterns and *route filters* permit CallManager to fulfill its primary responsibility of locating a destination. Route patterns are the addresses you assign to devices. For instance, associating the route pattern 8*XXX* with a gateway means that when you dial a number between 8000 and 8999, your call routes out that gateway. Route filters are more esoteric. Used in conjunction with the special route pattern wildcard @, route filters restrict the scope of the @ wildcard.

Dialing transformations, along with several miscellaneous gateway and system settings, permit CallManager to modify dialed digits and calling numbers before the destination receives a call. Also, by modifying dialed digits before passing a call to another network, you can affect which destination the other network ultimately dials.

Translation patterns provide a level of routing indirection that can resolve complicated scenarios. They are another feature that helps the call routing component fulfill its primary responsibility of selecting a destination. You can think of a translation pattern as an alias for another route pattern.

Route lists are a mechanism that allows CallManager to choose from available gateways when placing a call to another network. Route lists are composed of route groups, which in turn are composed of gateways. When CallManager selects a route list as the destination for a call, it begins searching in a linear fashion for an available gateway from among the gateways that the route list's route groups contain. If a gateway is busy, temporarily unreachable, or nonexistent, CallManager chooses another gateway to which to route the call.

Calling search spaces and *partitions* allow CallManager to provide individualized routing. These features allow you to configure networks to use toll restriction, enforce calling restrictions by user, or configure networks that serve independent organizations with fully or partially segregated routing plans for multiple tenant environments.

Route Patterns and Route Filters

This section introduces the basic building blocks of call routing: route patterns and route filters.

A route pattern is an address, much like your mailing address. When a user dials a number, Cisco CallManager tries to figure out to which destination to deliver the call. It performs this function by looking at all of the route patterns you have configured and then figuring out which route pattern is the best fit for the number the user has dialed. CallManager then attempts to offer the call to the endpoint that you have associated with the route pattern.

Do not confuse the concept of route pattern that this section discusses with the Route Pattern Configuration screen in Cisco CallManager Administration. The Route Pattern Configuration screen allows you to associate an address with a destination and contains other settings that let you modify the calling and called numbers. One of the fields on the

Route Pattern Configuration screen takes a route pattern as input; so does one of the fields on the Translation Pattern Configuration screen. Figure 2-3 shows the field on the Translation Pattern Configuration screen that takes a route pattern as input.

Figure 2-3 *Route Pattern Field in the Translation Pattern Configuration Screen*

Translation Pattern Configuration

Translation Pattern: New

Status: Ready

Insert	Cancel Changes

Pattern Definition

Translation Pattern	9.@	—————— **A route pattern**

Partition   < None >

Numbering Plan*   North American Numbering Pl∢

Route Filter   < None >

Calling Search Space < None >

Route Option   ● Route this pattern   ○ Block this pattern

☑ Provide Outside Dial Tone   ☑ Urgent Priority

Calling Party Transformations

☐ Use Calling Party's External Phone Number Mask

Calling Party Transform Mask

Prefix Digits (Outgoing Calls)

Called Party Transformations

Discard Digits   < None >

Called Party Transform Mask

Prefix Digits (Outgoing Calls)

* indicates required item.

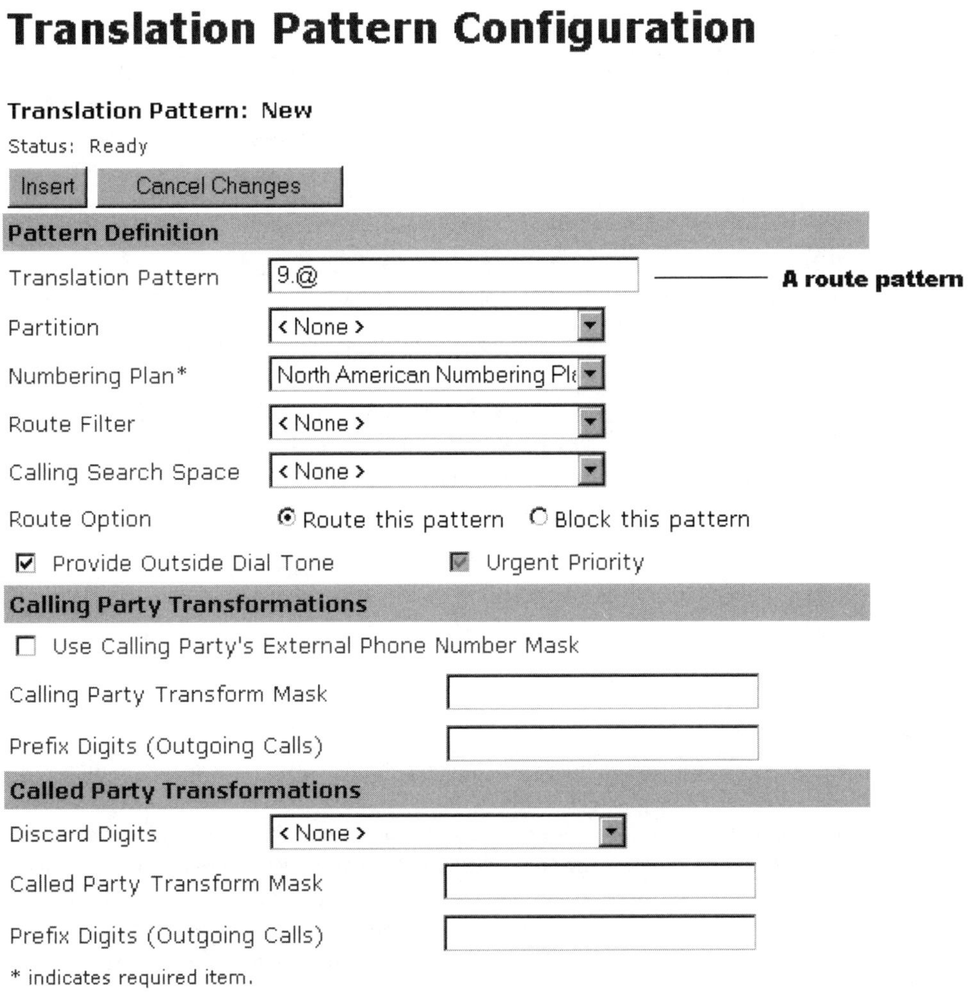

Many different Cisco CallManager Administration screens allow you to enter route patterns. For example, the directory numbers you assign to phones are actually route patterns, as are Meet-Me conference numbers, message waiting on/off numbers, call park numbers, call pickup group numbers, and translation patterns.

A route pattern is a sequence of digits and other alphanumeric characters. When the digits are all numeric, as is usually the case with directory numbers, CallManager rings the device with which you have associated the route pattern only when a user dials the exact numerical sequence. By including non-numeric characters called *wildcards* in a route pattern, you tell CallManager to ring the associated device for a range of dialed numbers. For instance, if you assign the route pattern 8XXX to a device, CallManager rings the device when users dial numbers in the range from 8000 to 8999.

Route filters are a special range-refining mechanism. You use route filters with route patterns that contain the special @ wildcard. The @ wildcard allows you to represent the PSTN with a single route pattern. When you must limit the types of PSTN calls (such as emergency, local, long distance, and international) that users can place, route filters limit the scope of the @ wildcard.

This section discusses the following topics:

- "Wildcards" describes the building blocks out of which you build route patterns.
- "Dialing Behavior" describes how CallManager processes digits from a calling user and selects a destination.
- "Dialing Behavior Refinements" elaborates on the basic procedure discussed in the section "Dialing Behavior" by introducing the **Urgent Priority** check box and explaining the logic that underlies outside dial tone.
- "Other Wildcards (@ and .)" revisits some complex wildcards that the section "Wildcards" introduces but only glosses over.
- "Route Filters" introduces a mechanism by which you can narrow the scope of the @ wildcard.

Wildcards

A house address is a specific sequence of digits and alphabetic characters that allows the postal service to identify a package's destination. A route pattern is like a house address for a callable endpoint, but unlike a house address, the addresses that a telephone system uses must provide a means by which the administrator can specify a range of addresses. You can enter individual addresses for every phone your network manages, but if users need to dial out of a gateway to the PSTN, the number of individual addresses becomes too vast to configure. Clearly, requiring the configuration of every single telephone number in the PSTN is not reasonable.

Route patterns use wildcards, which are digit placeholders that permit you to specify quickly a range of matching digits. For example, instead of configuring every individual number from 7000 to 7999 to route a call across a gateway to another network, by configuring 7XXX, you can tell CallManager to send all calls that begin with the digit 7 and are followed by three digits (in the range 0 to 9) to the gateway.

There is more to it, but first look at the basic wildcards, which Table 2-1 summarizes.

Table 2-1   *Wildcard Summary*

Wildcard	Description
0, 1, 2, 3, 4, 5, 6, 7, 8, 9, *, #	These look like digits, but they are actually simple wildcards. Each matches exactly one occurrence of the corresponding digit in a dialed digit string.
[xyz...]	This notation allows you to specify a set of matching digits. For example, [357] matches one occurrence of either the digit 3, 5, or 7.
[...x-y...]	Placing a hyphen between any two digits within square brackets causes one occurrence of any digits within the range to match, including the digits themselves. You can use range notation along with set notation. For example, [3-69] matches one occurrence of a digit 3, 4, 5, 6, or 9.
[^x-y]	If the first character after the open angle bracket is a carat, the expression matches one occurrence of any digit (including * and #) *except* those specified. For example, [^1-8] matches one occurrence of a digit 9, 0, *, or #.
wildcard?	A question mark following any wildcard or bracket expression matches zero or more occurrences of any digit that matches the previous wildcard. For example, 9[12]? matches the empty string, 9, 91, 92, 912, 9122, 92121, and many others.
wildcard+	A plus sign following any wildcard or bracket expression matches one or more occurrences of any digit that matches the previous wildcard. For example, 3[1-4]+ matches 31, 3141, 3333, and many others.
X	The X wildcard is a convenience wildcard that matches one occurrence of any digit in the range 0 to 9. This wildcard is functionally equivalent to the range expression [0-9].
!	The ! wildcard is a convenience wildcard that matches one or more occurrences of any digit in the range 0 to 9. This wildcard is functionally equivalent to the range expression [0-9]+.
. and @	The section "Other Wildcards (@ and .)" discusses these wildcards.

Route Patterns and grep(1)

UNIX users may have noticed a strong similarity between route patterns and regular expressions. UNIX has a robust command line interface that offers many elegant text-processing tools. One tool, grep(1), uses regular expressions to fulfill a common need for those who regularly work with command line interfaces, searching through a text stream for the occurrence of a specified word.

For example, if you had a directory containing text files of letters and memos and you needed to find all files that related to your taxes, you might tell grep(1) to look for the word "tax." However, because "tax" might start a sentence, a simple search for "tax" would fail to find occurrences of the capitalized "Tax." Although you could do two different searches, combining the two searches and weeding out duplicate hits would be onerous, and furthermore, more complicated search criteria might vastly increase the number of individual searches that you would have to do. Using the regular expression "[Tt]ax" is one way you can find all instances of the word "tax," both capitalized and lowercase.

To do the search, grep(1) looks through every individual line of every file looking for *specific* substrings that match the *general* pattern that the regular expression represents. Grep(1) prints *all* matching lines.

On the other hand, the call routing component does the opposite. It takes the *specific* sequence of digits dialed by the user and examines every *general* route pattern looking for the best *single* match.

Furthermore, although grep(1) concerns itself about what text strings currently match a regular expression, because users enter digits one by one, the call routing component must concern itself not only with which route patterns match the current sequence of dialed digits, but also with which route patterns might match if the user dials more digits. For example, the digit string 100 does not match the route pattern 1000, but if the user dials another 0, the route pattern matches perfectly. If CallManager were to take into account only the collected digits at a given moment in time, it would provide reorder tone to the user, because 100 does not match the route pattern 1000. Instead, CallManager realizes that if the user continues dialing, at some point in the future the collected digits might match a configured route pattern. Therefore, CallManager applies reorder tone only when the digits it has collected can never match a configured route pattern.

Dialing Behavior

The call routing component's behavior is sometimes counterintuitive, so a better understanding of the process it uses to select a destination can allow you to better troubleshoot problems.

In collecting a user's digits, the call routing component goes through the following steps:

Step 1   Compare the current sequence of dialed digits against the list of all route patterns and determine which route patterns currently match. Call the set of current matches *currentMatches*.

— If *currentMatches* is empty, the user's dialed digit string does not currently correspond with a destination.

— If *currentMatches* contains one or more members, the call routing component determines the *closest match*. The closest match is the route pattern in *currentMatches* that matches the fewest number of route patterns. For example, the dialed digit string 2000 matches both route pattern 2XXX and 20XX. Although there are 1000 different dialed digit strings that match 2XXX, only 100 dialed digit strings match 20XX, and 20XX is therefore the closest match.

Step 2 Simultaneously, determine whether different route patterns might match if the user were to dial more digits. Call the condition of having potential matches for a dialed digit string *potentialMatches*.

— If *potentialMatches* holds true, the call routing component waits for the user to dial another digit. If the user dials another digit, the sequence of events restarts at step 1 using the new digit string.

— If *potentialMatches* no longer holds true or a dialing timeout has elapsed, then the call routing component selects a destination.

— To select a destination, the call routing component looks at the closest match. The section "Example 2: Closest Match Routing" elaborates on closest match routing. If there is no closest match, the user's dialed digit string does not correspond with a destination. Furthermore, no more digits are forthcoming. CallManager rejects the call attempt.

— Otherwise, the CallManager extends the call to the device associated with the closest match.

Examples can best explain this process. The following sections present three examples:

• "Example 1: Simple Call Routing" presents an example in which exactly one route pattern ultimately matches.

• "Example 2: Closest Match Routing" presents an example in which multiple route patterns match and CallManager uses the closest match routing algorithm to select a route pattern.

• "Example 3: Wildcards That Match Multiple Digits" presents an example that demonstrates the effect of wildcards that match multiple digits.

For purposes of the examples, assume that CallManager has been configured with the route patterns in Table 2-2.

Table 2-2 *Basic Dialing Behavior Example Route Patterns*

Route Pattern	Description
1100	Matches exactly the dialed digit string 1100
1200	Matches exactly the dialed digit string 1200

continues

Table 2-2   *Basic Dialing Behavior Example Route Patterns (Continued)*

Route Pattern	Description
120X	Matches dialed digit strings in the range 1200-1209
130	Matches exactly the dialed digit string 130
1300	Matches exactly the dialed digit string 1300
13!	Matches all dialed digit strings of any length that begin with digit sequence 13

Example 1: Simple Call Routing

In this example, a calling user goes off-hook and dials 1100. On collecting the final digit of the dialed digit string, CallManager selects exactly one route pattern and offers the call to the associated destination.

When the user goes off-hook, CallManager begins its routing process. The current set of dialed digits is empty. The set of current matches, *currentMatches*, is empty. Every route pattern in the table is a potential match at this point, so the condition of having potential matches, *potentialMatches*, is true. Table 2-3 shows the current set of potential matches. As long as *potentialMatches* holds true, CallManager must wait for more digits.

Table 2-3   *Patterns That Can Match, Example 1, No Dialed Digits*

Currently Dialed Digits: <None>
Current Matches
<None>
Patterns That Can Still Match
1100
1200
120X
130
1300
13!
Patterns That Can No Longer Match
<None>

When the user dials 1, the state of affairs does not change. No current match exists, and every route pattern in the table is a potential match.

Dialing another 1 eliminates many route patterns as possible matches. The patterns 1200, 120X, 130, 1300, and 13! are no longer potential matches for the dialed digit string. The only route pattern that remains in contention is 1100. However, *currentMatches* is still empty and *potentialMatches* still holds true. Even though 1100 is the only route pattern that the user could dial that might result in a match, CallManager must wait until the user does, in fact, dial the full string. Table 2-4 shows the current set of potential matches.

Table 2-4 *Patterns That Can Match, Example 1, Dialed Digits 11*

Currently Dialed Digits: 11

Current Matches
<None>
Patterns That Can Still Match
1100
Patterns That Can No Longer Match
~~1200~~
~~120X~~
~~130~~
~~1300~~
~~13!~~

The next 0 does not change the situation.

When the user dials the final 0, *currentMatches* contains route pattern 1100. Furthermore, as further digits would not result in a different route pattern matching, *potentialMatches* does not hold true. CallManager extends the call to the device associated with route pattern 1100. Table 2-5 shows the final set of potential matches.

Table 2-5 *Patterns That Can Match, Example 1, Dialed Digits 1100*

Currently Dialed Digits: 1100

Current Matches
1100
Patterns That Can Still Match
<None>
Patterns That Can No Longer Match
~~1200~~
~~120X~~
~~130~~

continues

Table 2-5   *Patterns That Can Match, Example 1, Dialed Digits 1100 (Continued)*

~~1300~~
~~13!~~

Example 2: Closest Match Routing

In this example, a calling user goes off-hook and dials 1200. On collecting the final digit of the dialed digit string, CallManager determines that two route patterns match the dialed digit string and uses the closest matching routing algorithm to select which route pattern is awarded the call.

The closest match for a dialed digit string is simply the route pattern that matches the fewest number of digit strings of equal length to the dialed digit string. For example, whereas the route pattern 1000 matches exactly one dialed digit string, the route pattern 1XXX, which matches any dialed digit string in the range 1000 to 1999, matches 1000 possible dialed digit strings. In any comparison between route patterns 1000 and 1XXX, the closest match routing algorithm gives route pattern 1000 precedence.

The qualification "of equal length to the dialed digit string" in the preceding paragraph handles cases in which one or more of the route patterns being examined contains a wildcard that matches multiple dialed digits. For example, route pattern 1! matches any dialed digit string beginning with 1, and route pattern 13! matches any dialed digit string beginning with 13. The ! wildcard in these route patterns might match one, two, or more digits. As a result, the number of dialed digit strings that match either of these route patterns is infinite.

To decide among them, CallManager restricts the calculation of number of potentially matching dialed digit strings to only those of the same length as the dialed digit string itself. For instance, given the route patterns 1! and 13! and a dialed digit string of 13000, CallManager determines how many 5-digit dialed digit strings could potentially match both route patterns. Thus, 13!, which matches 1000 5-digit strings, takes precedence over 1!, which matches 10,000 possible 5-digit strings.

Returning to the example, when the user goes off-hook, CallManager begins its routing process. The current set of dialed digits is empty. The set of current matches, *currentMatches*, is empty. Every route pattern in the table is a potential match at this point, so the condition of having potential matches, *potentialMatches*, is true. As long as *potentialMatches* holds true, CallManager must wait for more digits. Table 2-6 shows the current set of potential matches.

Table 2-6   *Patterns That Can Match, Example 2, No Dialed Digits*

Currently Dialed Digits: <None>
Current Matches
<None>

Table 2-6 *Patterns That Can Match, Example 2, No Dialed Digits (Continued)*

Patterns That Can Still Match
1100
1200
120X
130
1300
13!
Patterns That Can No Longer Match
<None>

When the user dials 1, the situation does not change. No current match exists, and every route pattern in the table is a potential match.

Dialing 2 eliminates route patterns 1100, 130, 1300, and 13! as possible matches. The patterns 1200 and 120X are the only route patterns that can match. Table 2-7 shows the current set of potential matches.

Table 2-7 *Patterns That Can Match, Example 2, Dialed Digits 12*

Currently Dialed Digits: 12

Current Matches
<None>
Patterns That Can Still Match
1200
120X
Patterns That Can No Longer Match
~~1100~~
~~130~~
~~1300~~
~~13!~~

The next 0 does not change the situation.

When the user dials the final 0, *currentMatches* contains both route pattern 1200 and route pattern 120X. Furthermore, as further digits would not result in a different route pattern matching, *potentialMatches* does not hold true and CallManager must select a destination.

As 1200 is a closer match than 120X, CallManager extends the call to the device that owns route pattern 1200. Table 2-8 shows the final set of potential matches.

Table 2-8 *Patterns That Can Match, Example 2, Dialed Digits 1200*

Currently Dialed Digits: 1200	
Current Matches	
1200	Selected: Matches exactly one number
120X	Not selected: Matches 10 different numbers
Patterns That Can Still Match	
<None>	
Patterns That Can No Longer Match	
~~1100~~	
~~130~~	
~~1300~~	
~~13!~~	

Example 3: Wildcards That Match Multiple Digits

When a route pattern contains a wildcard that matches multiple digits, CallManager often must wait for an interdigit timeout to expire before it can route the call. This situation occurs because even if the route pattern containing the wildcard already matches, the user might intend to dial further digits. The most trivial example of this behavior is the route pattern !, which matches one or more occurrence of any number of digits. If a user dials 123 and matches the route pattern !, CallManager must continue to wait, because it has no assurances that the user is not planning to dial 1234. Routing the call prematurely might cause CallManager to send an incomplete dialed digit string to an adjacent network.

In the following example, a calling user goes off-hook and dials 1300. The route pattern 13! ensures that condition *potentialMatches* always holds true. Even if CallManager finds that route pattern 13! is the best match out of set *currentMatches*, CallManager must continue to wait, because it has no way of knowing if the user is really finished dialing.

In this example, when the user goes off-hook, CallManager begins its routing process. The current set of dialed digits is empty. The set of current matches, *currentMatches*, is empty. Every route pattern in the table is a potential match at this point, so the condition of having potential matches, *potentialMatches*, is true. As long as *potentialMatches* holds true, CallManager must wait for more digits. Table 2-9 shows the current set of potential matches.

Table 2-9 *Patterns That Can Match, Example 3, No Dialed Digits*

Currently Dialed Digits: <None>

Current Matches
<None>

Patterns That Can Still Match
1100
1200
120X
130
1300
13!

Patterns That Can No Longer Match
<None>

When the user dials 1, the situation does not change. No current match exists, and every route pattern in the table is a potential match.

Dialing 3 eliminates route patterns 1100, 1200, and 120X as possible matches, whereas 130, 1300, and 13! are still possible matches. Table 2-10 shows the current set of potential matches.

Table 2-10 *Patterns That Can Match, Example 3, Dialed Digits 13*

Currently Dialed Digits: 13

Current Matches
<None>

Patterns That Can Still Match
130
1300
13!

Patterns That Can No Longer Match
~~1100~~
~~1200~~
~~120X~~

The next 0 causes *currentMatches* to contain route patterns 130 and 13!. However, *potentialMatches* holds true, because the user's next digit might allow the same (13!) or a different (1300) route pattern to match. Table 2-11 shows the current set of potential matches.

Table 2-11 *Patterns That Can Match, Example 3, Dialed Digits 130*

Currently Dialed Digits: 130
Current Matches
130
13!
Patterns That Can Still Match
1300
13!
Patterns That Can No Longer Match
~~1100~~
~~1200~~
~~120X~~

The fact that route pattern 13! shows up in both the list of current matches and the list of potential matches needs explaining. When a route pattern ends with a multiple match wildcard (!, range expressions ending with ? such as [1-5]?, or range expressions ending with + such as [1-5]+), CallManager recognizes that even though the current dialed number matches the route pattern, the user might intend to dial further digits.

The final 0 eliminates route pattern 130 as a possible match. *CurrentMatches* contains route patterns 1300 and 13!. CallManager cannot attempt a closest match routing determination, however, because route pattern 13! not only matches the current digit string (1300), but also matches a longer digit string (13000). The ! wildcard at the end of a route pattern means that condition *potentialMatches* always holds true. Table 2-12 shows the current set of potential matches.

Table 2-12 *Patterns That Can Match, Example 3, Dialed Digits 1300*

Currently Dialed Digits: 1300
Current Matches
1300
13!
Patterns That Can Still Match
13!

Table 2-12 *Patterns That Can Match, Example 3, Dialed Digits 1300 (Continued)*

Patterns That Can No Longer Match
~~1100~~
~~1200~~
~~120X~~
~~130~~

In such a case, the only event that allows CallManager to select a destination is an interdigit timeout. On receiving an interdigit timeout, CallManager knows that no more digits are forthcoming and can make a routing selection. In this example, after the timeout, CallManager selects route pattern 1300 using closest match routing rules. Table 2-13 shows the final list of potential matches.

Table 2-13 *Patterns That Can Match, Example 3, Dialed Digits 1300 with Timeout*

Currently Dialed Digits: 1300	
Current Matches	
1300	Selected: Matches exactly one number
13!	Not selected: Matches 10 different four-digit numbers
Patterns That Can Still Match	
<None>	Interdigit timeout means no further digits are forthcoming
Patterns That Can No Longer Match	
~~1100~~	
~~1200~~	
~~120X~~	
~~130~~	

The system interdigit timeout defaults to 10 seconds. To change it, change the value associated with the CallManager service parameter **TimerT302_msec**. **TimerT302_msec** defines the duration of the interdigit timer in milliseconds. It defaults to 10,000 milliseconds.

Overlapped Sending and Non-North American Numbering Plans

The previous section demonstrates that when you end a route pattern with a wildcard that matches multiple digits (! or range expressions ending in + or ?), CallManager must wait for the system interdigit timeout to expire before it can route the call. So why would you ever end a route pattern with a wildcard that matches multiple digits?

Many countries have variable-length national dialing plans. Unlike North America, in which the length of a public telephone number is fixed at 10 digits, countries with variable-length dial plans require users to dial a varying number of digits to identify a number in the PSTN. For instance, in Finland, a numbering area equivalent to a North American area code is called a Telealue (TLA). Some TLAs are a single digit (2, 3, 5, 6, 9), while other TLAs are two digits (13, 14, 15, 16, 17, 18, 19). Within a TLA, different carriers own different number blocks, which range from three to five digits long. For instance, one carrier controls block 422 in TLA 19, while another carrier controls block 4251 in TLA 19. In other words, one carrier handles calls made from within Finland that begin with the six digits 019422, while the other handles calls from within Finland that begin with the seven digits 0194251. (Users within Finland dial 0 before dialing the TLA.) Finally, subscriber numbers range from three to five digits long. As a result, the number of a Finnish resident is of an indeterminate length (in practice, eight or nine digits, but this value does not reflect mobile numbers or service numbers).

Because the number of digits in countries with variable-length numbering plans is so dependent on the particular digits dialed, such countries rely on *overlapped sending* in the PSTN to figure out how many digits to collect and where to route the call.

Overlapped sending is kind of like a bucket brigade. Figure 2-4 shows the principle under which overlapped sending works. Figure 2-4 depicts a network of four nodes (A, B, C, and D) and three users (1, 2, and 3). User 1 wishes to call User 3, whose number is 0123333, composed of a one-digit region identifier (0), a three-digit node identifier (123), and a three-digit subscriber number (333). User 2's number is 01244444, composed of a one-digit region identifier (0), a three-digit node identifier (124), and a four-digit subscriber number (4444).

In Figure 2-4, no single node in the network understands the complete dialing plan. Node A understands that when a user attached to node A dials 0, it should send the call to node B. When node B receives the call, it recognizes that it needs more digits to determine the final destination and asks node A to pass on any digits that node A receives from User 1.

Node B understands that it must collect three digits before it can route the call further. If the digits are 123, it routes the call to node C. If the digits are 124, it routes the call to node D.

Nodes C and D, in turn, manage their portions of the numbering plan. Node C understands that it must collect three digits to select a subscriber, while node D requires four digits to select a subscriber. When User 1 dials 0123, node B offers the call to node C.

Node C performs the same steps that node B does when it receives a call. Node C recognizes that it requires three digits to make a routing selection and asks node B to pass on any digits that node B receives from node A (which, in turn, receives them from User 1). When node C receives the last three digits, it routes the call to User 3. Thus, in the manner that water buckets pass from hand to hand in a bucket brigade until they reach the fire, digits pass from node to node until they reach the spot that needs them.

Figure 2-4   *Overlapped Sending in a Simple Network*

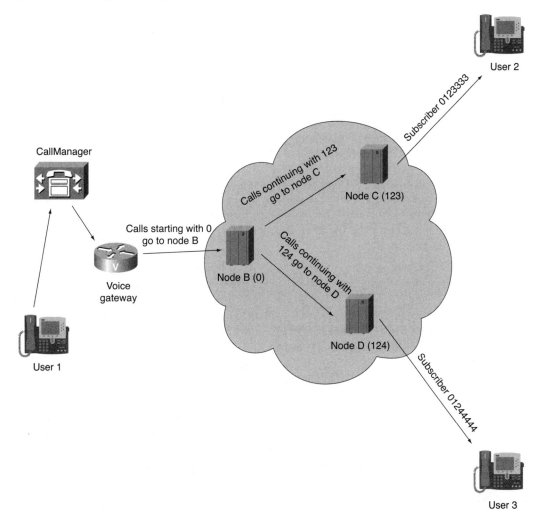

Versions of CallManager before release 3.1 do not support overlapped sending, but rather require that you provision knowledge of your entire network's numbering plan as route patterns. This requirement is acceptable for numbers within your network and for public numbers in a fixed numbering plan (because, for example, you can just configure a pattern like 9.XXXXXXXXXX to handle all patterns in the North American numbering plan). But variable-length numbering plans require the configuration of large numbers of such patterns just to provide network access.

Hence, in CallManager releases 3.0 and earlier, if you were an administrator in a country with variable-length numbering plans, you had three options.

- Configure very specific route patterns on your trunk interfaces, in effect encoding the national network's knowledge of the national numbering plan into the database. This option requires a significant knowledge of your country's numbering plan, the patience to enter all of the route patterns, and constant monitoring of changes to the national numbering plan so that you can update your route patterns.

- Replace CallManager's knowledge of the North American numbering plan with your country's numbering plan. Like the first option, this option requires extensive knowledge of your country's numbering plan, but it is a better solution because it means you can use the @ wildcard to represent your country's numbering plan. (For more information about the @ wildcard, see the section "Other Wildcards [@ and .].") However, the Technical Assistance Center (TAC) will not support any unofficial changes you make to the North American numbering plan. The section "The North American Numbering Plan" describes how you can replace the North American numbering plan.

- Configure gateways with steering codes followed with the ! wildcard (which matches multiple digits). For example, imagine that in the sample network depicted in Figure 2-4, Node A was CallManager, the remaining nodes were the PSTN, and you associated the route pattern 0! with the gateway to node B. When User 1 dials 0, CallManager continues collecting digits from User 1 until the interdigit timeout expires, whereupon CallManager offers the complete number to the PSTN.

At the time of this writing, most administrators choose the third option, but also configure a few specific route patterns to handle numbers that their users often dial, relying on closest match routing to eliminate the interdigit timeout. Users strongly dislike long interdigit timeouts, because while CallManager is waiting for the timeout to expire, users think that something is wrong with the system. One approach to eliminate interdigit timeout is to use # as an interdigit timeout character. For example, assume that your external access code to a variable-length dialing plan is 0. If you configure 0!, when users dial any digit sequence beginning with 0, CallManager waits for interdigit timeout and then ships all dialed digits to the PSTN.

However, if you also configure 0!#, users who have been trained to terminate all external dialed number sequences with # can avoid the interdigit timeout. Because the ! wildcard matches only the digits 0 through 9, dialing # removes the 0! route pattern from contention, leaving only 0!#. Because 0!# is not terminated with a wildcard that matches multiple dialed digits, condition *potentialMatches* ceases holding true and CallManager can route the call immediately. Pressing # is analogous to pressing the **SEND** button on a call made from a cell phone.

The good news is that CallManager release 3.1 supports overlapped dialing, rendering much of the advice in this section obsolescent. If your PSTN supports overlapped sending, simply configure your route patterns with the *steering code* alone (without the trailing !

wildcard); when CallManager offers the call to the associated gateway or route list, the PSTN prompts CallManager to pass any further digits along.

The bad news is that CallManager supports overlapped dialing only for gateways with digital interfaces that use the Media Gateway Control Protocol (MGCP) protocol. If your network uses Cisco H.323 gateways for access to the PSTN, and your country uses a variable-length numbering plan, you must still choose from one of the three options this section presents.

One final comment: Even if you can take advantage of overlapped sending in your network, by replacing the North American numbering plan with a partial or complete one of your own, you can enforce calling restrictions on your users using route filters. For example, you might configure a national numbering plan for your country that includes only region codes, but which does not try to control routing all the way to the exchange level. By making CallManager responsible for collecting all of the digits up to the region code, you can configure route filters to block calls to a particular region or to route them across your private network. Then, once CallManager hands the partially dialed digit string to the PSTN, the PSTN can initiate overlapped sending to collect the remainder of the digits.

Using route filters with variable-length numbering plans requires that you replace the North American numbering plan with one of your own. In a pure overlapped sending environment, once CallManager passes a call off to the PSTN, users can then dial any number the PSTN supports—including those to pay services—because the PSTN, not CallManager, processes those digits. The section "The North American Numbering Plan" describes how you can replace the North American numbering plan.

Dialing Behavior Refinements

The section "Dialing Behavior," for purposes of clarity, describes a simplified version of CallManager's call routing logic. The actual process is more involved. This section discusses two refinements to the basic dialing procedure:

- "Urgent Route Patterns" describes route pattern urgency, which can interrupt interdigit timing when CallManager must route a call immediately.
- "Outside Dial Tone" describes the logic that determines when CallManager applies outside dial tone.

Urgent Route Patterns

As the preceding section mentions, when CallManager receives digits from the user, it waits to route the call until it is sure that it needs no more digits. A case in point is route patterns that end in a wildcard that matches multiple digits. CallManager must wait for the interdigit timeout to expire before it offers the call to the selected destination.

But if you need a call to route the very moment that a user provides sufficient dialed digits, you can use the **Urgent Priority** check box on the Route Pattern Configuration screen to short-circuit the dialing procedure.

An urgent route pattern only has an observable effect if your dial plan contains overlapping route patterns. Your call routing plan contains overlapping route patterns if it is possible to dial a sequence of digits so that the call routing component can select a current match but must continue to wait for more digits because there are also potential matches. For example, if you assign directory number 99110 to a phone and also configure a gateway with route pattern 9.911 (for emergency services in North America), you create a dial plan with overlapping route patterns. When a user in an emergency situation dials 9911, CallManager waits for the interdigit timeout to expire before routing the call, because CallManager does not know whether the user intends to dial 0 to complete a call to the station instead of the emergency response center.

You can use the **Urgent Priority** check box to protect yourself from this sort of configuration. By marking the 9.911 route pattern as urgent, you tell CallManager to route the call to the emergency center the instant that a user dials 9911. (Note, however, that in the example provided, marking the 9.911 route pattern as urgent has the side effect of preventing any user from dialing the phone with directory number 99110.)

Another common usage of the **Urgent Priority** check box comes into play for administrators in countries with variable-length numbering plans. The simplest configuration for countries with variable-length numbering plans is to configure a gateway with an outside access code (for example, 0) followed by the ! wildcard. However, this configuration introduces interdigit timeout into all external numbers that users dial. By configuring specific route patterns for numbers that their users commonly dial, administrators can eliminate the interdigit timeout for the commonly dialed patterns. Table 2-14 provides a sample configuration and explanation of a U.K. dialing plan.

Table 2-14 *Sample U.K. Dialing Plan*

Route Pattern	Priority	Description
9.00!	Normal	International calls
9.0[1-57-9]XXXXXXX 9.0[1-57-9]XXXXXXXX 9.0[1-57-9]XXXXXXXXX	Normal	National calls, which can be 9, 10, or 11 digits (not counting the external access code), depending on the specific digits dialed after the 0[1-57-9] portion of the route pattern.
		This kind of overlapping route pattern configuration means that users who dial a national number requiring a lesser number of digits (9 in this example) must wait for the interdigit timer to expire before CallManager routes the call, because CallManager cannot be certain that the user does not intend to dial further digits.

Table 2-14 *Sample U.K. Dialing Plan (Continued)*

9.037[0485]XXXXXX	Urgent	More specific numbers in the national network. Marking these as urgent means that when CallManager selects these as the best match, it stops the interdigit timer.
9.08[56]0XXXXXXX		
9.0802XXXXXXX		
		For instance, the first of these route patterns, 9.037[0485]XXXXXX, is a 10-digit number (not counting the external access code). The national route pattern 9.0[1-57-9]XXXXXXXX would normally match this route pattern, but the longer route pattern 9.0[1-57-9]XXXXXXXXX causes CallManager to keep the interdigit timer running. Marking 9.037[0485]XXXXXX as urgent causes CallManager to route the more specific route pattern immediately when a user dials it.

Two points about urgent route patterns to note especially:

- First, an urgent route pattern only takes effect if it is the best match at the time. If you define an urgent route pattern XXXX, a normal route pattern 8XXX, and a normal route pattern 80000, when users dial 8000, CallManager continues to wait for more digits, because the normal route pattern 8XXX is the best match.

- Second, defining an urgent route pattern limits the total number of route patterns you can usefully assign. If you define the route pattern 999 as an urgent route pattern, users can never dial longer digit sequences that begin with 999, because the urgent route pattern always takes priority.

Outside Dial Tone

Another subject that the call routing procedure described in section "Dialing Behavior" omits is providing outside dial tone. Outside dial tone is an indication that users expect when CallManager routes their calls off of the local network. To apply outside dial tone, check the **Outside Dial Tone** check box on the Route Pattern or Translation Pattern Configuration screens for each route pattern that you consider to be off-network. For dialed digit strings that can match those patterns, the call routing component then applies outside dial tone at some point during the dial sequence.

You cannot explicitly configure the point in the dialing sequence when CallManager applies outside dial tone. In addition, the decision to apply outside dial tone is completely independent of whether or where the route pattern contains a "." wildcard (described in the section ". Wildcard"). Rather, the call routing component applies outside dial tone at the point when all potential matches for a dialed digit string have had their **Outside Dial Tone** box checked.

For example consider the route patterns 9000 and 91XXXXXXX. 91XXXXXXX belongs to a trunk device and has had its **Outside Dial Tone** box checked. Table 2-15 shows these route patterns.

Table 2-15 *Outside Dial Tone Example 1, Configured Route Patterns*

Configured Route Patterns	Outside Dial Tone Check Box
9000	Do not apply outside dial tone
91XXXXXXX	Apply outside dial tone

When a user goes off-hook, CallManager applies inside dial tone. Table 2-16 depicts the current dialing state.

Table 2-16 *Outside Dial Tone Example 1, Dialed Digits <None>*

Currently Dialed Digits: <None>	
Current Matches	
<None>	
Patterns That Can Still Match	
9000	Do not apply outside dial tone
91XXXXXXX	Apply outside dial tone
Patterns That Can No Longer Match	
<None>	
Actions Taken: Apply inside dial tone	

The user dials 9 and CallManager turns off inside dial tone. At this point, CallManager cannot tell whether the user intends to dial the on-network number 9000 or the off-network number 91XXXXXXX, so it waits for the next digit. Table 2-17 depicts the current dialing state.

Table 2-17 *Outside Dial Tone Example 1, Dialed Digits 9*

Currently Dialed Digits: 9	
Current Matches	
<None>	

Table 2-17   *Outside Dial Tone Example 1, Dialed Digits 9 (Continued)*

Patterns That Can Still Match	
9000	Do not apply outside dial tone
91XXXXXXX	Apply outside dial tone
Patterns That Can No Longer Match	
<None>	
Actions Taken: Turn off inside dial tone	

If the user then dials 1, CallManager eliminates the route pattern 9000 from its list of potential matches. At this point, all remaining candidates have had their **Outside Dial Tone** box checked, and the call routing component chooses this moment to apply outside dial tone (see Table 2-18).

Table 2-18   *Outside Dial Tone Example 1, Dialed Digits 91*

Currently Dialed Digits: 91	
Current Matches	
<None>	
Patterns That Can Still Match	
91XXXXXXX	Apply outside dial tone
Patterns That Can No Longer Match	
~~9000~~	~~Do not apply outside dial tone~~
Actions Taken: All route patterns require outside dial tone. Apply outside dial tone.	

Now assume that an additional route pattern, 9124, has been configured. This route pattern could be a station device, call park, or Meet-Me conference code. Table 2-19 depicts this configuration.

Table 2-19   *Outside Dial Tone Example 2, Configured Route Patterns*

Configured Route Patterns	Outside Dial Tone Check Box
9000	Do not apply outside dial tone
9124	Do not apply outside dial tone
91XXXXXXX	Apply outside dial tone

The steps that CallManager takes when the user goes off-hook and dials 9 are identical to those in Example 1. However, Table 2-20 shows that when the user dials the subsequent 1, CallManager waits, because at least one of the route patterns that can still match does not require outside dial tone.

Table 2-20 *Outside Dial Tone Example 2, Dialed Digits 91*

Currently Dialed Digits: 91	
Current Matches	
<None>	
Patterns That Can Still Match	
9124	Do not apply outside dial tone
91XXXXXXX	Apply outside dial tone
Patterns That Can No Longer Match	
~~9000~~	~~Do not apply outside dial tone~~
Actions Taken: <None>	

As long as what the user dials keeps the route pattern 9124 in contention as a possible match, CallManager defers applying outside dial tone. For example, if the user continues by dialing 2 (yielding currently dialed digits of 912), CallManager continues to defer application of outside dial tone. However, if instead of dialing 2, the user dials 7 (yielding currently dialed digits of 917), the route pattern 9124 can no longer match, and CallManager applies outside dial tone, because all potentially matching route patterns have had their **Outside Dial Tone** box checked.

If your system is experiencing delayed outside dial tone, be sure to look for route patterns that overlap with the route patterns for which you are expecting to hear outside dial tone, but for which you have not checked the **Outside Dial Tone** box. These conflicting route patterns might be Meet-Me conference or call park ranges, in which case you need to change these ranges so that they do not conflict with the off-network route pattern in question.

On the other hand, if you receive outside dial tone sooner than expected (usually because you wish to use access codes that are longer than a single digit), introduce a new route pattern that is identical to your access code, but do not check the **Outside Dial Tone** box. (You can assign this route pattern to the same gateway or route list to which the full route pattern connects.) CallManager suppresses outside dial tone until the user dials the last digit of the access code. Table 2-21 presents an example in which the access code for external numbers is 999.

Table 2-21 *Outside Dial Tone Example 3, Configured Route Patterns*

Configured Route Patterns	Outside Dial Tone Check Box
999	Do not apply outside dial tone
999.1XXXXXXX	Apply outside dial tone

Just as in the previous examples, CallManager applies inside dial tone when the user goes off-hook and turns off inside dial tone after the user dials 9. Table 2-22 depicts the dialing state when the user dials 99.

Table 2-22   *Outside Dial Tone Example 3, Dialed Digits 99*

Currently Dialed Digits: 99	
Current Matches	
<None>	
Patterns That Can Still Match	
999	Do not apply outside dial tone
999.1XXXXXXX	Apply outside dial tone
Patterns That Can No Longer Match	
<None>	
Actions Taken: <None>	

CallManager continues suppressing outside dial tone because route pattern 999 might still match the user's dialed digits. Table 2-23 presents the dialing state when the user dials another 9 (yielding dialed digits of 999).

Table 2-23   *Outside Dial Tone Example 3, Dialed Digits 999*

Currently Dialed Digits: 999	
Current Matches	
999	
Patterns That Can Still Match	
999.1XXXXXXX	Apply outside dial tone
Patterns That Can No Longer Match	
<None>	
Actions Taken: All route patterns require outside dial tone. Apply outside dial tone.	

Adding the route pattern 999 thus suppresses outside dial tone until the moment that you want it applied.

Other Wildcards (@ and .)

The section "Route Patterns and Route Filters" deliberately glosses over some of the most common wildcards you use: the @ and . wildcards.

@ Wildcard

Unlike the convenient wildcards X and ! and the range-matching notations, the @ wildcard does not represent any particular set of matching characters. The @ wildcard causes CallManager to add the set of national route patterns for the numbering plan that you specify in the **Numbering Plan** drop-down list on the Route Pattern or Translation Pattern Configuration screens. One way to think of the @ pattern is that it matches any number that you can dial from your North American home phone. For example, specifying the @ pattern along with the North American numbering plan allows users to dial 911 and 555 1212 and 1 800 555 1212 and 011 33 12 34 56 78 90.

The @ pattern is a macro. When you configure it, CallManager looks up a list of route patterns associated with the dialing plan you have specified and adds them individually. This might cause the CallManager to appear to violate closest match routing rules.

For instance, different individual route patterns in the North American numbering plan match the four dialing strings 911 and 555 1212 and 1 800 555 1212 and 011 33 12 34 56 78 90. Table 2-24 shows some sample route patterns.

Table 2-24 *Sample Route Patterns in the North American Numbering Plan*

Dialing String	Matching Route Pattern	Description
911	[2-9]11	Services (311, 411, 611, 911)
555 1212	[2-9]XX XXXX	7-digit dialing
1 800 555 1212	1 [2-9]XX [2-9]XX XXXX	11-digit dialing
011 33 12 34 56 78 90	011 3[0-469] !	International calls to the valid 2-digit country codes in the range 30–39

Assume that you place the route pattern @ on a gateway that you want to use for all of your outbound calls. You have another gateway that you prefer to use for 7-digit local calls, so you configure the route pattern XXX XXXX on it. But when you dial 555 1212, your calls route out the first gateway. What is happening?

From your point of view, you configured the route patterns in Table 2-25.

Table 2-25 *Closest Matching and the @ Wildcard, User-Configured Patterns*

Route Pattern	Selected Destination
@	Gateway 1
XXX XXXX	Gateway 2

The specific route pattern XXX XXXX definitely appears to match fewer route patterns than the @ pattern. However, CallManager interprets @ as a macro expansion and actually treats your configuration as shown in Table 2-26.

Table 2-26 *Closest Matching and the @ Wildcard, CallManager-Expanded Patterns*

Route Pattern	Selected Destination
[2-9]11	Gateway 1
[2-9]XX XXXX	Gateway 1
1 [2-9]XX [2-9]XX XXXX	Gateway 1
011 3[0-469] !	Gateway 1
XXX XXXX	Gateway 2

When a user dials 555 1212, both [2-9]XX XXXX and XXX XXXX match. [2-9]XX XXXX is the more specific, and thus the call routes to gateway 1.

To avoid this situation, when you configure route patterns that you wish to take precedence over the @ pattern, either be as specific as possible in describing your route patterns, or preferably, use route filters (described in the section "Route Filters").

. Wildcard

The . wildcard is unlike other wildcards in that it does not match digits at all. Rather, the call routing component uses the . wildcard to fulfill its secondary responsibility of address translation.

The . wildcard functions solely as a delimiter. When it appears in a route pattern, it divides the dial string into PreDot and PostDot sections. This has no effect on what digit strings the route pattern matches. Rather, you use the . wildcard in conjunction with *digit discarding instructions*.

Digit discarding instructions are one way to tell the call routing component which dialed digits should be kept before the call is offered to the selected device. Most digit discarding instructions can be used only in conjunction with route patterns that contain the @ wildcard. However, some digit discarding instructions rely on the PreDot section that the . wildcard defines. Further details about digit discarding instructions (and other transformations) are in the section "Digit Discarding Instructions."

Route Filters

As described, the @ wildcard is an all-or-nothing affair. When present, it matches all of the valid numbers for the national numbering plan specified, even those you would prefer your users did not dial.

Route filters are the mechanism by which you can cause CallManager to add only a subset of the route patterns for a given numbering plan. For example, using route filters, you can cause an @ pattern to match only the national emergency numbers. You can also use route filters to distinguish local calls from long distance calls or to limit access to toll services.

Route filters are a test that CallManager applies to individual route patterns in a numbering plan included by the @ wildcard. CallManager examines each valid route pattern in the numbering plan and applies the test. If a particular route pattern passes the test, CallManager adds it into its routing tables, and users are able to dial numbers that match the route pattern. If a particular route pattern fails the test, CallManager skips over it, and users are unable to dial numbers that match the route pattern. Route filters work by allowing CallManager to add only the subset of a numbering plan whose *tags* fulfill the constraints that *operators* impose.

Route Filter Length Limitation

The maximum length of the route filter, written out as a textual expression and not including any tags with values of NOT-SELECTED, must not exceed 1024 characters. If you need a more complicated route filter, you can usually split the route filter across several route patterns. For instance, say you need to define the route pattern 9.@ and apply a route filter that includes emergency calls, calls to information services, international calls, and calls to a variety of specific area codes. The total length of the filter required, however, exceeds the 1024-character limit.

Route filters of this length consist of several clauses connected by the OR operator. To resolve this problem, break the route filter up into several route filters where different clauses of the long route filter are joined by the OR operator. Then associate the smaller route filters with the duplicate copies of the route pattern.

For instance, the example filter describes emergency calls *or* calls to information services *or* international calls *or* calls to a variety of specific area codes. You can break up the lengthy clause by defining one 9.@ with a route filter for emergency calls, another 9.@ with a route filter for information services, another 9.@ with a route filter for international calls, and other 9.@ route patterns with route filters for the specific area codes. Because each route filter selects a different subset of the numbering plan, it is perfectly fine to reuse the same route pattern multiple times.

Tags

Tags are named substrings of individual route patterns for a given national numbering plan.

For instance, the route pattern 1 [2-9]XX [2-9]XX XXXX exists in the North American numbering plan. It is composed of four sections. The first section, 1, denotes the call as a toll call. The second section matches an area code. The office code and the subscriber follow. The numbering plan file for the North American numbering plan encodes this knowledge as the tags LONG-DISTANCE-DIRECT-DIAL, AREA-CODE, OFFICE-CODE, and SUBSCRIBER. In contrast, the route pattern [2-9]XX XXXX contains only the OFFICE-CODE and SUBSCRIBER tags.

Table 2-27 shows the tags that the North American numbering plan contains, and it provides representative digit strings for each tag. Bold type in Table 2-27 indicates the section of the example number that corresponds to the listed tag.

Table 2-27   *Tags in the North American Numbering Plan*

Tag Name	Example Number	Description
AREA-CODE	1 **214** 555 1212	The area code in an 11-digit long distance call
COUNTRY-CODE	01 1 **33** 1234567890 #	The country code in an international call
END-OF-DIALING	01 1 33 1234567890 **#**	The #, which ends interdigit timeout in international calls
INTERNATIONAL-ACCESS	**01** 1 33 1234567890 #	The initial 01 of an international call
INTERNATIONAL-OPERATOR	01 **0**	The digit that denotes the operator component of an international call
LOCAL-AREA-CODE	**214** 555 1212	The area code in a 10-digit local call
LOCAL-DIRECT-DIAL	**1** 555 1212	The initial 1 some 7-digit calls require
LOCAL-OPERATOR	**0** 555 1212	The initial 0 some operator-assisted 7-digit calls require
LONG-DISTANCE-DIRECT-DIAL	**1** 214 555 1212	The initial 1 required for long distance direct-dial calls
LONG-DISTANCE-OPERATOR	**0** 214 555 1212	The initial 0 required for operator-assisted long distance calls
NATIONAL-NUMBER	01 1 33 **1234567890** #	The national number component of an international call
OFFICE-CODE	1 214 **555** 1212	The office or exchange code of a North American call
SATELLITE-SERVICE	01 1 881 **4** 1234 #	A specific value associated with calls to the satellite country code

continues

Table 2-27 *Tags in the North American Numbering Plan (Continued)*

Tag Name	Example Number	Description
SERVICE	1 **411**	Access to local telephony provider services
SUBSCRIBER	1 214 555 **1212**	A particular extension a given exchange serves
TRANSIT-NETWORK-ESCAPE	**101** 0321 1 214 555 1212	Long distance carrier code
TRANSIT-NETWORK	101 **0321** 1 214 555 1212	The escape sequence used for entering a long distance carrier code

Operators

Operators are the functions that determine whether a given route pattern passes the tests you specify.

There are four operators:

- <tag> EXISTS, whose test is passed if the route pattern under inspection contains the specified tag.

- <tag> DOES-NOT-EXIST, whose test is passed if the route pattern under inspection does not contain the specified tag.

- <tag> == <value>, whose test is met if 1) the route pattern under inspection contains the tag and 2) a non-empty intersection exists for the set of route patterns that the pattern expression in <value> matches and the set of route patterns that the pattern expression associated with tag matches.

- <tag> NOT-SELECTED, whose test is passed under all conditions. The NOT-SELECTED operator is a value that exists only in CallManager Administration to represent that you have not selected an operator for a particular tag. It simply means "none of the above."

An example might help clarify the tortured description of the == operator. One route pattern defined in the North American numbering plan is [2-9]XX XXXX (see Figure 2-5). This pattern consists of an office code and a subscriber. The first section of the route pattern, [2-9]XX, corresponds to the tag OFFICE-CODE.

Figure 2-5 *Pattern [2-9]XX XXXX in the North American Numbering Plan*

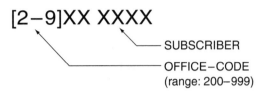

Let us say that you specify OFFICE-CODE == [1-3]XX in a route filter. When determining whether to add the pattern [2-9]XX XXXX into the routing tables, CallManager intersects the route pattern [2-9]XX from the numbering plan with the route pattern [1-3]XX in the route filter. [2-9]XX matches all dialed digit strings in the range 200–999, while route pattern [1-3]XX matches all dialed digit strings in the range 100–399. The intersection of these sets is all dialed digit strings in the range 200–399. As a result, CallManager determines that the route pattern under inspection matches the filter's test. It inserts into the internal routing tables the route pattern that represents the intersection of the value you specified and the entry in the numbering plan, namely, [23]XX XXXX. Figure 2-6 depicts the application of the route filter.

You can string operators together with the Boolean operators AND and OR. When you string operators together with OR, CallManager includes a route pattern under inspection if either of the specified conditions exist. When you string operators together with AND, CallManager includes a route pattern under inspection only if both of the specified conditions exist.

For example, the route filter AREA-CODE EXISTS OR SERVICE EXISTS causes CallManager to include both the route pattern [2-9]11, which matches information and emergency services in the North American numbering plan, and the route pattern 1 [2-9]XX [2-9]XX XXXX, which matches long distance toll calls in the North American numbering plan. [2-9]11 contains the SERVICE tag, and 1 [2-9]XX [2-9]XX XXXX contains the AREA-CODE tag.

However, the route filter AREA-CODE EXISTS AND SERVICE EXISTS causes CallManager to include absolutely no route patterns, because no number in the North American numbering plan has both an area code and a service number.

Figure 2-6 *Intersection of Two Pattern Ranges Because of a Route Filter*

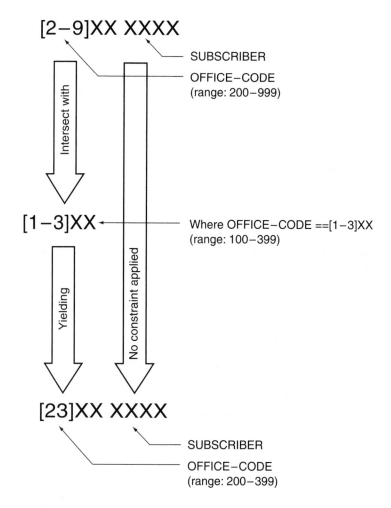

Route Filter Operation

When an @ pattern has an associated filter, the filter affects the macro expansion that takes place. Before adding an individual route pattern from the numbering plan to the system, CallManager checks to see if that particular route pattern passes the tests specified in the route filter. If the route pattern does not qualify, CallManager will not add it, which means that users cannot dial it.

It is important to note that route filters in themselves do not explicitly block calls. They tell CallManager not which patterns to exclude but which patterns to include. A route filter that specifies AREA-CODE == 900 does not eliminate calls to area code 900 (reserved for toll services in the United States); rather, it tells CallManager to include only those route patterns in the North American numbering plan where the area code is 900. In other words, it configures the system so that toll number calls are the only destination users can dial. (You *can* block these numbers. See the section "Routing by Class of Calling User" for details.)

The best way to see how route filters operate is to look at some examples. For instructive purposes, these examples use the North American numbering plan and assume that the @ pattern expands only to the route patterns in Table 2-28.

Table 2-28   *Route Patterns Used for Route Filter Example*

Route Pattern	Description	Tags
[2-9]11	311, 411, 611, 911	SERVICE
[2-9]XX XXXX	7-digit dialing	OFFICE-CODE
		SUBSCRIBER
[2-9]XX [2-9]XX XXXX	10-digit dialing	LOCAL-AREA-CODE
		OFFICE-CODE
		SUBSCRIBER
1 [2-9]XX [2-9]XX XXXX	11-digit dialing	LONG-DISTANCE-DIRECT-DIAL
		AREA-CODE
		OFFICE-CODE
		SUBSCRIBER
01 1 3[0-469] !	International dialing to valid 2-digit country codes in the range 30–39	INTERNATIONAL-ACCESS
		INTERNATIONAL-DIRECT-DIAL
		COUNTRY-CODE
		NATIONAL-NUMBER

If you specify the route pattern 9.@ with no route filter, CallManager indiscriminately adds each route pattern in Table 2-28, preceded by 9. Thus, users can dial 9 911 and 9 555 1212, as well as 9 1 900 555 1212. Table 2-29 lists the route patterns that CallManager adds.

Table 2-29   *Route Patterns Added When No Route Filter Is Specified*

Added Route Patterns	Tags in the Route Pattern
9 [2-9]11	SERVICE
9 [2-9]XX XXXX	OFFICE-CODE, SUBSCRIBER

continues

Table 2-29 *Route Patterns Added When No Route Filter Is Specified (Continued)*

Added Route Patterns	Tags in the Route Pattern
9 [2-9]XX [2-9]XX XXXX	LOCAL-AREA-CODE, OFFICE-CODE, SUBSCRIBER
9 1 [2-9]XX [2-9]XX XXXX	LONG-DISTANCE-DIRECT-DIAL, AREA-CODE, OFFICE-CODE, SUBSCRIBER
9 011 3[0-469] !	INTERNATIONAL-ACCESS, INTERNATIONAL-DIRECT-DIAL, COUNTRY-CODE, NATIONAL-NUMBER

If instead, you add the same route pattern but use a route filter that specifies SERVICE EXISTS, CallManager adds only those route patterns that contain the SERVICE tag. (In North America, the SERVICE tag matches numbers such as 411 for directory information and 911 for emergency services.) Your users can access network services but no other numbers. Table 2-30 lists the added route patterns.

Table 2-30 *Route Patterns Added for the Route Filter SERVICE EXISTS*

Accepted Route Patterns (Contain SERVICE Tag)	Tags in the Route Pattern
9 [2-9]11	SERVICE
Rejected Route Patterns	**Tags in the Route Pattern**
9 [2-9]XX XXXX	OFFICE-CODE, SUBSCRIBER
9 [2-9]XX [2-9]XX XXXX	LOCAL-AREA-CODE, OFFICE-CODE, SUBSCRIBER
9 1 [2-9]XX [2-9]XX XXXX	LONG-DISTANCE-DIRECT-DIAL, AREA-CODE, OFFICE-CODE, SUBSCRIBER
9 011 3[0-469] !	INTERNATIONAL-ACCESS, INTERNATIONAL-DIRECT-DIAL, COUNTRY-CODE, NATIONAL-NUMBER

The route filter COUNTRY-CODE DOES-NOT-EXIST eliminates the international dialing route pattern. Users can access network services and local and long distance numbers. Table 2-31 lists the added route patterns.

Table 2-31 *Route Patterns Added for the Route Filter COUNTRY-CODE DOES-NOT-EXIST*

Accepted Route Patterns (Lack COUNTRY-CODE Tag)	Tags in the Route Pattern
9 [2-9]11	SERVICE
9 [2-9]XX XXXX	OFFICE-CODE, SUBSCRIBER
9 [2-9]XX [2-9]XX XXXX	LOCAL-AREA-CODE, OFFICE-CODE, SUBSCRIBER
9 1 [2-9]XX [2-9]XX XXXX	LONG-DISTANCE-DIRECT-DIAL, AREA-CODE, OFFICE-CODE, SUBSCRIBER

Table 2-31 *Route Patterns Added for the Route Filter COUNTRY-CODE DOES-NOT-EXIST (Continued)*

Rejected Route Patterns	Tags in the Route Pattern
9 011 3[0-469] !	INTERNATIONAL-ACCESS, INTERNATIONAL-DIRECT-DIAL, COUNTRY-CODE, NATIONAL-NUMBER

The route filter AREA-CODE == [89]00 OR AREA-CODE == 888 OR AREA-CODE == 877 demonstrates the way in which the equal operator can constrain a route pattern. This filter allows users to dial 11-digit numbers to the toll-free ranges 800, 877, or 888 and to the toll range 900. Table 2-32 lists the added route patterns.

Table 2-32 *Route Patterns Added for the Route Filter AREA-CODE == [89]00 OR AREA-CODE == 888 OR AREA-CODE == 877*

Added Route Patterns (Contain AREA-CODE Tag, Constrained to Specified Ranges)	Tags in the Route Pattern
9 1 **[89]00** [2-9]XX XXXX	LONG-DISTANCE-DIRECT-DIAL, AREA-CODE, OFFICE-CODE, SUBSCRIBER
9 1 **888** [2-9]XX XXXX	LONG-DISTANCE-DIRECT-DIAL, AREA-CODE, OFFICE-CODE, SUBSCRIBER
9 1 **877** [2-9]XX XXXX	LONG-DISTANCE-DIRECT-DIAL, AREA-CODE, OFFICE-CODE, SUBSCRIBER
Filtered Route Patterns (Lack AREA-CODE Tag)	**Tags in the Route Pattern**
9 [2-9]11	SERVICE
9 [2-9]XX XXXX	OFFICE-CODE, SUBSCRIBER
9 [2-9]XX [2-9]XX XXXX	LOCAL-AREA-CODE, OFFICE-CODE, SUBSCRIBER
9 011 3[0-469] !	INTERNATIONAL-ACCESS, INTERNATIONAL-DIRECT-DIAL, COUNTRY-CODE, NATIONAL-NUMBER

The bold type in the above table shows that the values specified on the equals operator have constrained the area code substring of the North American numbering plan to a particular range. In each case, the generalized substring [2-9]XX, which matches any digit string between 200 and 999, has been modified so that it matches only the intersection between the substring and value specified in the route filter.

Useful Route Filters for the North American Numbering Plan

This section presents some route filter configurations for the North American numbering plan that you might find useful.

It describes how to use route filters to do the following:

- Block calls where the user has selected a long distance carrier
- Block international calls
- Route just local numbers
- Route just toll-free numbers
- Eliminate interdigit timing between 7-digit and 10-digit route patterns
- Block 900 numbers

Block Calls Where the User Has Selected a Long Distance Carrier

In North America, users can select a long distance carrier by dialing at the beginning of their number the digits 101 followed by a 4-digit carrier code. CallManager digit discarding instructions (see the section "Digit Discarding Instructions") call this type of dialing 10-10-Dialing.

On the North American numbering plan Route Filter screen, the tag TRANSIT-NETWORK-ESCAPE filters numbers in which the user has included the 101 carrier selection digits. Configuring a route filter with the value TRANSIT-NETWORK-ESCAPE DOES-NOT-EXIST blocks calls that include the carrier selection code.

The difference between configuring a route filter to block long distance carrier selection and using the digit discarding instructions **10-10-Dialing** is that the route filter blocks a user's call attempt if the user dials the carrier selection code, while the digit discarding instructions permit the call to go through but silently strip out the carrier selection portion of the dialed number.

Block International Calls

You can block international calls with the route filter INTERNATIONAL-ACCESS DOES-NOT-EXIST. In the North American numbering plan file, the tag INTERNATIONAL-ACCESS corresponds to the initial 01 of international dialed calls. By specifying a route filter that prevents CallManager from including route patterns beginning with this tag, you prevent CallManager from matching any numbers beginning with 01. You block international calls by never adding them in the first place.

Route Just Local Numbers

Routing just local numbers typically requires stringing together several route filter clauses joined by OR.

Local calls can vary dramatically by geographical region. Some regions have 7-digit local calls, some metropolitan regions have a mixture of 7- and 10-digit local calls, and other regions have 10-digit local calls.

7-Digit Dialing   If your region has 7-digit dialing and you wish to permit users to dial *only* 7-digit numbers, defining the route filter SERVICE DOES-NOT-EXIST AND LOCAL-AREA-CODE DOES-NOT-EXIST AND AREA-CODE DOES-NOT-EXIST AND INTERNATIONAL-ACCESS DOES-NOT-EXIST should suffice. Filtering against SERVICE DOES-NOT-EXIST blocks calls to information and emergency services, LOCAL-AREA-CODE blocks ten-digit calls, AREA-CODE DOES-NOT-EXIST blocks 11-digit long distance calls, and INTERNATIONAL-ACCESS blocks international calls.

If you wish to, say, permit calls to services, long distance calls, or international calls, you simply exclude the appropriate operator expression from the proposed route filter.

The LOCAL-AREA-CODE section of the defined route filter deserves some more explanation. You might have noticed that in some cases, a proposed route filter uses the tag AREA-CODE and in other cases it uses the tag LOCAL-AREA-CODE. The tag LOCAL-AREA-CODE represents the area code as it appears in 10-digit numbers.

Some metropolitan regions of North America require users to dial ten digits for all of their local calls. This means that CallManager must include both 7-digit patterns and 10-digit patterns in its expansion of the North American numbering plan, because you can deploy CallManager in different geographic regions. Because of CallManager's analysis process, however, unless you explicitly exclude the 10-digit pattern when you are in a 7-digit dialing region, CallManager will wait for the interdigit timer to expire before offering your 7-digit calls to the PSTN.

On the other hand, the AREA-CODE tag represents the area code as it appears in 11-digit numbers (typically direct-dial and calling-card long distance calls) in the North American numbering plan. Using two different tag names for essentially the same subsection of a North American number assists those administrators in 10-digit dialing regions who wish to permit 10-digit local calls while blocking 11-digit toll calls. By specifying the filter AREA-CODE DOES-NOT-EXIST, such administrators can screen out all of the toll calls while leaving the 10-digit calls untouched. The section "Eliminate Interdigit Timing Between 7-Digit and 10-Digit Patterns" expands on this wrinkle of CallManager's North American numbering plan.

Metro Dialing

Some geographical regions have *metro dialing*. In metro dialing, a user in a home area code needs to dial only seven digits, but a few neighboring area codes, also local calls, require the user to dial ten digits. Metro dialing is typically the most problematic, because some 11-digit calls might actually be local calls, while some 10-digit calls might be toll calls. In such cases, you might need to specify criteria down to the office code level to provide full local access. (Another approach is to define an @ pattern to perform general filtering and to define separate specific patterns, such as 972 813 XXXX, to handle the exceptional cases.)

If your region has metro dialing, define a route filter in which one clause specifies 7-digit dialing and subsequent clauses define the nontoll area codes on an area-code-by-area-code basis. For instance, in the Dallas-Fort Worth area in 1995, the following route filter would provide general metro dialing access from the point of view of a user in the 972 area code:

> LOCAL-AREA-CODE DOES-NOT-EXIST AND AREA-CODE DOES-NOT-EXIST AND INTERNATIONAL-ACCESS DOES-NOT-EXIST
>
> OR
>
> LOCAL-AREA-CODE == 214
>
> OR
>
> LOCAL-AREA-CODE == 817

Because the user in the 972 area code dials seven digits to call other numbers in the 972 area code, the first part of this route filter handles any 7-digit calls that the user in the 972 area code dials. The second part of this route filter handles 10-digit calls starting with 214 that the user dials, and the third part of this route filter handles 10-digit calls starting with 817 that the user dials.

You can add exceptional cases as additional clauses or as separate route patterns.

Note especially the use of the tag LOCAL-AREA-CODE. The LOCAL-AREA-CODE tag represents an area code as dialed as part of a 10-digit North American number (for example, 214 555 1212). The same area code in an 11-digit North American number (0 214 555 1212 and 1 214 555 1212) corresponds to the tag AREA-CODE.

10-Digit Dialing   A 10-digit dialing route filter is like a metro dialing routing filter, but you need not include the route filter for 7-digit dialing. For instance, in the Dallas-Fort Worth area in 2000, the following route filter provides general 10-digit dialing access:

> LOCAL-AREA-CODE == 214
>
> OR
>
> LOCAL-AREA-CODE == 817
>
> OR
>
> LOCAL-AREA-CODE == 972
>
> OR
>
> LOCAL-AREA-CODE == 940

Again, you can add exceptional cases (11-digit local calls) as additional clauses or as separate route patterns.

Route Toll-Free Numbers

In the North American numbering plan, area codes 800, 877, and 888 are dedicated to toll-free numbers. The following route filter provides access to only these services:

AREA-CODE == 800

OR

AREA-CODE == 877

OR

AREA-CODE == 888

Eliminate Interdigit Timing Between 7-Digit and 10-Digit Patterns

Because some geographical regions use 7-digit dialing and others use 10-digit dialing, the North American numbering plan shipped with CallManager must accommodate both types of dialing. Furthermore, because the IP network permits stations homed to a particular CallManager to be in different geographical locations, CallManager must be able to support both types of dialing simultaneously.

As a result, the North American numbering plan shipped with CallManager includes both route patterns [2-9]XX XXXX and [2-9]XX [2-9]XX XXXX. The problem that occurs is with the 10-digit route pattern in place, users of the 7-digit pattern must wait for the interdigit timeout to expire before CallManager routes their 7-digit calls.

Eliminating the interdigit timeout means configuring CallManager to eliminate the 10-digit route pattern for users of 7-digit dialing. CallManager includes a preconfigured route filter that you can assign to patterns that the 7-digit dialers use. This route filter is called **7-digit dialing**.

Block 900 Numbers

The previous route filters in this section operate by using inclusion. That is, the clauses provided define a subset of the North American numbering plan that includes only those patterns that you wish to be routed and excludes those patterns you wish to block.

As long as the restrictions placed use the EXISTS or DOES-NOT-EXIST operators, you can use one route filter to define which patterns should be routed. EXISTS specifies that CallManager should route all valid number ranges for a particular tag, while DOES-NOT-EXIST specifies that CallManager should route no valid number ranges for a particular tag.

When you need to specify only *some* of the valid number ranges for a particular tag, use the == operator. However, CallManager does not support a != (not-equals) operator. As a result, although you can specify a route filter such as AREA-CODE == 900, rather than blocking 900 numbers, this filter routes 900 numbers and blocks all other types of calls.

However, you can still block 900 numbers with the use of two route patterns. First, configure an @-pattern with the route filter AREA-CODE == 900. On the route pattern, however, click the radio button **Block This Pattern**. This configuration specifies that CallManager should block all external calls with area code 900.

To make all non-900-numbers route, configure another @-pattern with no route filter at all. Using closest match routing rules (see the section "Example 2: Closest Match Routing"), if a user dials a dialed digit string containing an area code of 900, the route pattern with the route filter AREA-CODE == 900 matches, which causes CallManager to block the call. Because an external call to another area code matches only the unfiltered pattern, CallManager routes the call.

An example can best illustrate the process that occurs. Table 2-33 shows a representative sample of route patterns that CallManager adds when you specify the route pattern 9.@.

Table 2-33 *Sample Route Patterns Added By 9.@*

Route Pattern	Description
9 [2-9]11	Services (311, 411, 611, 911)
9 [2-9]XX XXXX	7-digit dialing
9 1 [2-9]XX [2-9]XX XXXX	11-digit dialing
9 011 3[0-469] !	International calls to the valid 2-digit country codes in the range 30–39

When you specify the route filter, AREA-CODE == 900, CallManager includes only those route patterns that have an area code tag. Furthermore, CallManager constrains the route pattern so that the tag can match the number 900 (see Table 2-34).

Table 2-34 *Route Pattern Added by 9.@ Where AREA-CODE == 900*

Route Pattern	Description
9 1 900 [2-9]XX XXXX	11-digit dialing to the 900 area code

When you add both route patterns and specify that CallManager should route calls to 9.@ but block calls to 9.@ where AREA-CODE == 900, the routing tables appear as displayed in Table 2-35.

Table 2-35   *Combined Routing Tables*

Route Pattern	Treatment
9 [2-9]11	Route this pattern
9 [2-9]XX XXXX	Route this pattern
9 1 [2-9]XX [2-9]XX XXXX	Route this pattern
9 011 3[0-469] !	Route this pattern
9 1 900 [2-9]XX XXXX	Block this pattern

If a user dials 911 or a 7-digit number, it is evident that CallManager routes the call. When a user dials an 11-digit number, however, closest match routing rules ensure that the user's call is handled properly. Table 2-36 shows that when a user dials 9 1 214 555 1212, CallManager finds a unique match for the 9.@ route pattern and routes the call.

Table 2-36   *Routing Treatment for Number 9 1 214 555 1212*

Currently Dialed Digits: 9 1 214 555 1212	
Current Matches	
9 1 [2-9]XX [2-9]XX XXXX	Route this pattern
Patterns That Can Still Match	
<None>	
Patterns That Can No Longer Match	
~~9 [2-9]11~~	
~~9 [2-9]XX XXXX~~	
~~9 011 3[0-469] !~~	
~~9 1 900 [2-9]XX XXXX~~	
Actions Taken: <None>	

When a user dials 9 1 900 555 1212, on the other hand, CallManager finds two matching route patterns in the routing tables, uses closest match routing rules to select between them, and then applies the appropriate treatment. Table 2-37 shows CallManager selecting the blocked route pattern 9.@ where AREA-CODE == 900 over the more generic route pattern 9.@. As a result, CallManager rejects calls to 900 numbers.

Table 2-37 *Routing Treatment for Number 9 1 900 555 1212*

Currently Dialed Digits: 9 1 900 555 1212	
Current Matches	
9 1 900 [2-9]XX XXXX	Block this pattern
	Selected: Matches 8,000,000 numbers
9 1 [2-9]XX [2-9]XX XXXX	Route this pattern
	Not selected: Matches 6,400,000,000 numbers
Patterns That Can Still Match	
<None>	
Patterns That Can No Longer Match	
~~9 [2-9]11~~	
~~9 [2-9]XX XXXX~~	
~~9 011 3[0-469].!~~	
Actions Taken: <None>	

This strategy of configuring a general route pattern to allow most calls through, but then configuring specific route patterns with blocking treatment to screen a very specific small set of calls, recurs often in enterprise deployments.

Dialing Transformations

Dialing transformations allow the call routing component to modify either the calling number or the dialed digits of a call. Transformations that modify the calling number are calling party transformations, while those that modify the dialed digits are called party transformations.

Translation Patterns vs. Dialing Transformations

Cisco CallManager also uses a concept called *translation patterns* (described in section "Translation Patterns"), and indeed, translation patterns rely heavily on dialing transformations to operate. But translation patterns and dialing transformations are separate concepts. Dialing transformations is a generic concept that refers to any setting in CallManager that can change the calling number or dialed digits. Dialing transformations appear not only on the Transformation Pattern Configuration screen, but also on the Route Pattern Configuration screen, numerous gateway configuration screens, and in service parameters.

Calling party transformations affect the calling number but not the calling name of a call. For example, when one Cisco IP Phone 7960 calls another, normally the called phone sees two pieces of information: the directory number of the calling phone and the any display name that you have entered on the Directory Number Configuration screen for the calling phone. Figure 2-7 depicts the display of a Cisco IP Phone 7960 that is receiving a call and the corresponding configuration fields in the Directory Number Configuration screen of the calling phone.

Figure 2-7   *Calling Number and Name During Call Presentation*

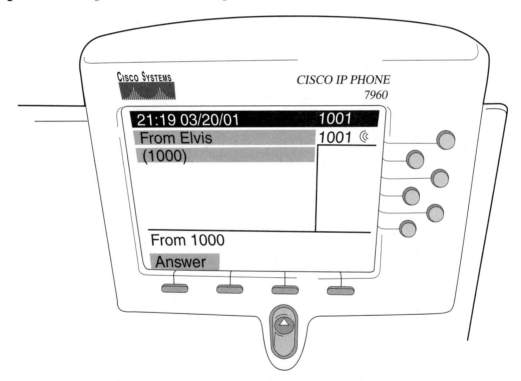

The **Display** field in the Directory Number Configuration screen has limited scope. CallManager presents it for station-to-station calls within the cluster, but when a call leaves the private network, there is often no provision in the network protocol to provide calling party name information to the PSTN. Some protocols, however, do provide for transmission of the calling number, and CallManager transmits the calling number whenever the protocol permits.

You usually need calling party transformations only for display purposes. For instance, enterprises very commonly require that the central switchboard number for an organization be provided as the calling number for all external calls. Even when you wish to actually transmit the calling party's *direct inward dial (DID)* number, however, you still must configure some sort of calling party transformation. The PSTN usually wants to see the number of the calling user's address *from the PSTN's point of view* rather than the internal directory number you have assigned your user. Calling party transformations are not limited to calls to the PSTN, though. If you so choose, you can apply them to calls between your users.

Called party transformations modify the digits the calling user actually dials. Often, they do not affect which destination CallManager selects, because the selection is based on the digits that the calling user dials, not the transformed called number. The transformation just modifies those digits before CallManager sends them to a selected device. However, if the selected device looks at the dialed digits to further route the call, the transformation can indeed affect which device ultimately receives the call. This sort of steering occurs most often when CallManager offers a call with a modified called number to a gateway connected to an adjacent network.

This section discusses the transformations permitted at different stages of the transformation process. It covers the following topics:

- "When Cisco CallManager Can Apply Dialing Transformations" discusses five opportunities during the call routing process that CallManager has to apply dialing transformations.

- "About Device Types That Cisco CallManager Supports" provides an overview of the types of station and trunk devices that CallManager supports, because routing settings are often particular to only certain types of devices.

- "About Masks" discusses masking, an operation that commonly occurs during many stages of the call routing process.

- "Dialing Transformation-Related Service Parameters" discusses some CallManager service parameters that relate to calling and called party transformations. The transformations these settings provide are somewhat inconsistent. Some apply to inbound calls, while others apply to outbound calls. Most settings take effect for only some of the devices that CallManager supports.

- "Transformations on the Originating Device" discusses the first opportunity that CallManager has to transform calling and called numbers, at the point where CallManager first receives a call. These transformations are highly device-dependent.

- "Transformations in Translation Patterns, Route Patterns, and Route Lists" discusses the second, third, and fourth opportunities where CallManager can transform calling and called numbers. These transformations are very regular, and thus, this section can discuss them as a group.

- "Transformations on the Terminating Device" discusses the fifth and final opportunity where CallManager can transform calling and called numbers, just before CallManager offers the call to the destination. Just like the transformation on the originating device, transformations on the terminating device are highly device-dependent.

When Cisco CallManager Can Apply Dialing Transformations

Calling and called party transformations can occur in five stages during CallManager's routing process. These stages occur in order, though not all of them need to occur. For instance, if the number that the user dials does not correspond to a translation pattern or route list, then no translation-pattern-based or route-list-based transformations occur. The five stages, in order, are

1 At the originating device

2 As part of translation pattern

3 As part a route pattern

4 As part of a route list's operation

5 At the terminating device

A Detour to Discuss the Stages of Call Routing

To fully understand the stages of call routing means understanding a little of what goes on in the internal logic of CallManager. CallManager consists of a large number of independent logical components that interact in a complex manner. Each logical component has very limited responsibilities to reduce the complexity of any individual component. For example, to each Cisco IP Phone 7960, CallManager assigns one component whose responsibility is to serve as a control point for actions (going off-hook, pressing buttons, and so on) that a user performs. But when a Cisco IP Phone 7960 places a call, CallManager dynamically creates a component that understands how to perform the functions of a call. Other components handle the high-level concepts of "call transfer" or "two-party call" or "route pattern lookup." To process a simple station-to-station call, CallManager passes messages among at least 40 components.

When this section talks about a transformation occurring at the originating device, it does not mean that the physical device itself or even the software embedded within it is applying a dialing transformation. Rather, it means that the logical component in CallManager that represents the originating device is applying a dialing transformation.

This is not to say that devices themselves never have call routing capabilities of their own. Cisco IOS gateways, in particular, have very robust dialing transformation capabilities, but those capabilities are outside the scope of this book.

First, CallManager settings for the originating device can modify the dialed digits before control of the call passes the digits to the call routing component. This process happens, for instance, when a call from the PSTN comes into CallManager. Depending on what digits the PSTN sends, you might find it necessary to convert the address from a PSTN address to a local directory number.

Second, if the destination selected is a *translation pattern*, CallManager applies the calling and called party transformations associated with the translation pattern to change the calling and called numbers. After CallManager applies the dialing transformation, digit analysis uses the resulting called number to select another destination. Sometimes, the transformed digits cause CallManager to match a new translation pattern. In such a case, CallManager applies the calling and called party transformations of the newly selected translation pattern to select a new destination. CallManager breaks such chains of translation patterns after ten iterations to prevent infinite routing loops. The section "Translation Patterns" contains further information about translation patterns.

The third opportunity that the call routing component has to apply dialing transformations is when the dialed digits match a route pattern or directory number. When the dialed digits select a route pattern, CallManager applies the calling and called party transformations configured on the Route Pattern Configuration screen.

Fourth, after any translation patterns have been analyzed, if the destination is a route list (described in the section "Route Lists and Route Groups"), CallManager applies any calling and called party transformations specified on the route between the route list and individual route groups within the route list. Unlike other transformations in this sequence, transformations on a route list *override* the ones that the route pattern or translation pattern applies. In all other cases, the changes that CallManager applies are cumulative. For instance, if CallManager prepends the digit 9 to a dialed number of 1000 at the originating device, and the terminating device subsequently prepends an 8, the resulting called number is 891000. On the other hand, if a called party transformation on the route pattern prepends the digit 9 to the dialed number 1000, but a called party transformation on the route between the route list and an individual route group prepends an 8, the resulting called number is 81000, not 981000. The settings on the route undo the transformations that the route pattern applies. This behavior allows you to define transformations on a route pattern that are correct for most cases, but that you wish to supersede for calls out particular route groups.

Finally, CallManager can modify the calling and called parties just before handing the call to the associated device.

Figure 2-8 shows a picture of the transformation process. A Cisco IP Phone 7960 places a call. When CallManager passes the call request to call control, CallManager modifies the digits according to any dialing transformations configured for the phone. If the digits provided match a translation pattern, CallManager applies the dialing transformations configured for the translation pattern. At some point, CallManager selects a destination and applies any dialing transformations configured for the route pattern or directory number selected. If a route list is the target of the call, CallManager applies any dialing transformations on specific routes selected. Finally, CallManager applies any dialing transformations configured on the terminating device. All of these opportunities to transform the calling number and called number means that they can differ quite dramatically by the time CallManager has routed a call.

Figure 2-8   *Locations Where Transformations Occur*

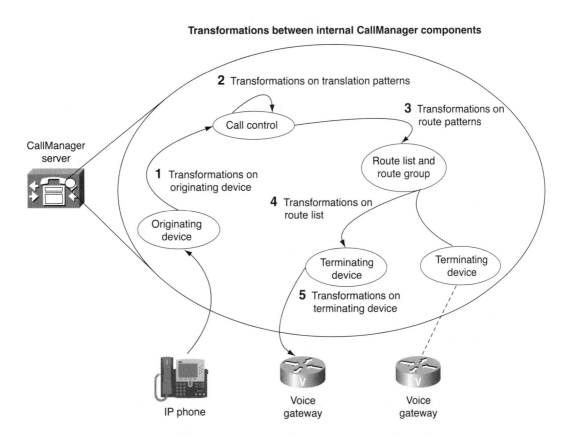

About Device Types That Cisco CallManager Supports

Although CallManager can transform the calling and called numbers at the originating and terminating devices, the dialing transformations available are often quite protocol-dependent. For instance, the dialing transformations that you can configure for an analog phone connected to the Cisco VG200, which uses the MGCP, are not the same as those that you can configure for the Cisco 2600 router, which uses the H.323 protocol.

Chapter 4, "Trunk Devices," and Chapter 3, "Station Devices," go into great detail about the specific gateway and station devices that CallManager supports. However, this chapter groups these devices into categories to help guide you through the many protocol-specific call routing settings. The following section clearly defines these categories.

CallManager devices can be roughly divided into two classes: station devices and trunk devices. Furthermore, each class of devices can be divided by protocol type: Skinny Protocol (Client or Gateway), MGCP, and H.323.

Station Device Categories

Station devices are the devices that users interact with directly—in other words, phones. Each station device has transformations that are particular to it. There are three classes of station devices:

- **Skinny**—Stations that implement the Skinny Protocol, such as the Cisco 7900 series of phones and Cisco 12SP+ and 30VIP. This category also includes plain old telephone service (POTS) stations driven from Skinny Protocol gateways, such as the AS-2, AS-4, and AS-8.

  The Cisco IP Phone 7910 is a single-line IP Phone with a two-line textual display; the Cisco IP Phone 7940 is a two-line IP Phone with a large graphical display; Cisco IP Phone 7935 is a speakerphone console with a two-line textual display designed for conference rooms; and the Cisco IP Phone 7960 is a six-line IP Phone with a large graphical display. If you own an older version of CallManager, you might have the Cisco IP Phones 12SP+ or 30VIP, which more closely resemble a traditional PBX phone. Other than the settings associated with the station's line, no transformation-related fields exist.

  In addition to pure IP Phone devices, CallManager supports POTS stations behind Skinny Protocol gateways such as the AS-2, AS-4, and AS-8. You may have these gateways if you own an older version of CallManager.

- **MGCP**—POTS phones driven from gateways that use the MGCP protocol, such as the VG200.

- **H.323**—Direct clients such as NetMeeting and POTS phones driven from gateways that use the H.323 protocol, like the Cisco 2600, 3600, 5300, and 7200 series of routers.

Trunk Device Categories

Trunk devices provide access to other networks. These networks can be other CallManager clusters, private TDM networks, or PSTNs. Each trunk device has transformations that are particular to it. CallManager supports three classes of trunk devices:

- **Skinny**—Analog gateways that implement the Skinny Gateway Protocol. If you have an older version of CallManager, you might have the AT-2, AT-4, or AT-8 analog gateways.

- **MGCP**—Analog and digital trunks driven from gateways that use the MGCP protocol, such as the VG200, Catalyst 6000 T1 Voice over IP (VoIP) gateway, Catalyst 6000 E1 VoIP gateway, Cisco DT-24+, and Cisco DE-30+ gateways.

- **H.323**—Direct H.323 links to other clusters and Cisco PRI and analog gateways that use the H.323 protocol, such as the Cisco 2600, 3600, 5300, and 7200 series routers.

About Masks

CallManager uses a common operation called *masking* throughout the transformation process, so it is worthwhile to discuss it before continuing.

Mask operations allow you to suppress leading digits, to change existing digits while leaving others unmodified, and to insert leading digits. A mask operation requires two pieces of information, the number to be masked and the mask itself.

In the mask operator, the number is overlaid by the mask, aligned so that the last character of the mask overlays the last digit of the number. Where the mask contains a digit, the mask's digit supersedes the number's digit. Where the mask contains an X, the corresponding digit of the number is used. And if the number is longer than the mask, the mask obscures the extra digits, as if the stencil were opaque at that point.

Figure 2-9 presents some examples.

Figure 2-9   *Transformation Mask Operation*

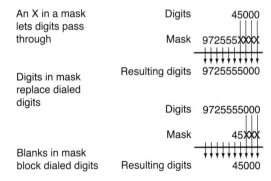

Dialing Transformation-Related Service Parameters

Numerous CallManager settings related to call routing exist as service parameters. CallManager service parameters do not automatically take effect for every CallManager in a cluster. Rather, service parameters take effect only for the specific CallManager you select in Cisco CallManager Administration In most cases, you want these settings to take effect for an entire CallManager cluster, so be sure to set the service parameters for every CallManager in the cluster.

Another important point to note about service parameters is that when these parameters take effect for a particular gateway type, the settings apply to all gateways that your CallManager controls and not individual gateways. For instance, if you configure the StripPoundCalledPartyFlag for a particular CallManager, all gateways connected to that CallManager modify the dialed digits in accordance with the StripPoundCalledPartyFlag. The service parameter does not permit you to use the StripPoundCalledPartyFlag for one particular gateway connected to CallManager while other gateways connected to CallManager ignore the service parameter.

Furthermore, CallManager service parameters related to routing do not always apply to all gateway protocols. The section "About Device Types That Cisco CallManager Supports" describes the device types that CallManager supports.

Service parameters are a vestige of the call routing settings that existed in the *scm.ini* file before release 3.0. Although Cisco CallManager 3.1 provides alternative ways to achieve the functions that most of these settings provide, these settings still are effective.

Table 2-38 shows the list of routing-related service parameters and a checklist of which protocols for which the settings take effect.

Table 2-38 *Supported Service Parameter Dialing Transformations by Device Type*

Service Parameter Dialing Transformation	Skinny Station Devices	MGCP Station Devices	H.323 Station Devices	Skinny Trunk Devices	MGCP Trunk Devices	H.323 Trunk Devices
CgpnScreeningIndicator				$\sqrt{}$		
MatchingCgpnWithAttendantFlag				$\sqrt{}^2$	$\sqrt{}^2$	
SendingCompleteIndicator				$\sqrt{}^1$		
OverlapReceivingForPriFlag				$\sqrt{}^1$		
StripPoundCalledPartyFlag				$\sqrt{}$	$\sqrt{}$	$\sqrt{}$
UnknownCallerID				$\sqrt{}$		
UnknownCallerIDFlag				$\sqrt{}$		
UnknownCallerIDText				$\sqrt{}$		
NumberingPlanInfo				$\sqrt{}^1$		

1   T1-PRI and E1-PRI interfaces only

2   FXO interfaces only

CgpnScreeningIndicator

CgpnScreeningIndicator affects calls that CallManager routes out MGCP digital gateways. The *Cgpn* in **CgpnScreeningIndicator** stands for *calling party number*.

The value associated with the parameter is an integer value. The setting allows you to specify the value of the screening indicator field in the calling party number information element of the Integrated Services Digital Network (ISDN) protocol. This element indicates to the attached ISDN network whether CallManager scrutinized the calling number it provides.

Table 2-39 shows the values the setting takes, along with a description of the meaning that the ISDN protocol assigns to these settings.

Table 2-39   *Values of CgpnScreeningIndicator*

Value	Description
0	User provided, not screened: The user device provides the value in the calling number and CallManager did not scrutinize it.
1	User provided, verified and passed: The user device provides the value in the calling number. CallManager checks it against a list of acceptable numbers and declares it acceptable.
2	User provided, verified and failed: The calling user device provides the value in the calling number. CallManager checks it against a list of acceptable numbers, but it is not valid.
3	Network provided: CallManager provides the calling number.
4	Default: CallManager sets up its default value for the screening indicator—user provided, not screened.

Only change this setting if the attached ISDN network rejects your outbound calls because it finds the value of the screening indicator unacceptable. (Determining this fact requires detailed debugging of the trace file.) However, the value you set has no effect on the tasks CallManager actually performs in relation to the calling number. In other words, CallManager performs no actual screening and verification of the calling number. Rather, it simply changes the value of the ISDN field it provides to the ISDN network to provide flexibility in interworking with different varieties of ISDN.

MatchingCgpnWithAttendantFlag

This setting provides a simple way to emulate the functionality of a small PBX or key system. Small PBXs typically associate inbound analog trunks on a one-for-one basis with user stations. The PBX offers incoming calls over an analog trunk to the corresponding station, and conversely, outbound calls from the station select the corresponding analog trunk. This allows a small business to provide internal users with unique external directory numbers but still to use low-cost analog loop start trunks.

An analog loop start trunk is just like the analog phone line that most people have at home. Analog loop start trunks have limited ability to communicate calling and called party information. When a user places a call from a private network to the PSTN, no way exists for the private network to indicate to the PSTN the public phone number of the calling user. Rather, the PSTN uses the number assigned to the loop start trunk as the calling number. Similarly, when the PSTN offers the call to the private network, the PSTN has no way to provide the actual digits the calling user dialed; rather, it assumes that the inbound call directly terminates on the appropriate phone.

This setting works with analog gateways running the Skinny Gateway Control Protocol and with Cisco MGCP gateways. The gateway setting Attendant DN described in the section "Attendant DN" automatically routes incoming calls from an analog trunk to the specified directory number. This behavior is exactly what is required to handle the trunk-to-station behavior of a small PBX.

The setting **MatchingCgpnWithAttendantFlag** handles the station-to-trunk calls. When this value is set to T, CallManager makes sure that the trunk selected for a station's outbound call is the same as that it uses to handle the station's inbound calls. To perform this function, it routes the outbound call out the trunk whose Attendant DN is the directory number of the calling station.

This setting works best if you have a single gateway for external calls, because you can assign a single route pattern such as 9.@ to the gateway and ensure that CallManager presents all users' external calls to this gateway. If you have several gateways, to ensure that CallManager presents a given user's external call to the associated gateway, you need either to place all of your gateways in a route list (see the section "Route Lists and Route Groups" for more information) or to use calling search spaces and partitions to route the calling user to the appropriate gateway (see the section "Calling Search Spaces and Partitions").

SendingCompleteIndicator and OverlapReceivingForPriFlag

These values work in tandem. They enable *overlapped receiving.*

Many countries implement national numbering plans that use variable-length subscriber numbers. Complicated tables of area codes or city codes determine the actual length of a subscriber. Unless a telephone system intimately understands the country's numbering plan, efficiently giving calls to and receiving calls from such networks requires providing or receiving digits one at a time.

Receiving digits one at a time from the network is called overlapped receiving. By default, overlapped receiving is enabled and the sending complete indicator is disabled.

If your route plan contains route patterns that begin with similar digit strings (for instance, 9XXX and 9XXXX), leaving overlapped receiving enabled can cause routing delays when CallManager receives calls over trunks that use these settings. Disable this capability by changing the **OverlapReceivingForPriFlag** to F.

StripPoundCalledPartyFlag

Administrators who manage call routing for countries with variable-length numbering plans for which CallManager support does not yet exist must configure route patterns such as 0! to get CallManager to provide the proper number of digits to the PSTN. Because route patterns ending in the ! wildcard introduce interdigit timing on all calls, such administrators often also configure equivalent route patterns (in this case, 0!#) so that knowledgeable users who terminate their outbound calls with a # need not wait for the interdigit timeout to expire.

Before such calls enter the PSTN, the dialed # must be stripped. This setting is disabled by default. When set to T, CallManager strips the final # (if it exists) of a dialed digit string before CallManager routes the call out the gateway.

UnknownCallerID, UnknownCallerIDFlag, and UnknownCallerIDText

UnknownCallerId, **UnknownCallerIdFlag**, and **UnknownCallerIdText** affect calls that originate from a gateway. When calls arrive from the PSTN, often caller ID is not available. Setting the **UnknownCallerIdFlag** to T tells CallManager to provide a calling number and name for inbound calls that do not contain such information. The contents of **UnknownCallerIDText** become the calling name, and the contents of **UnknownCallerID** become the calling number.

NumberingPlanInfo

Calls to ISDN and H.323 networks include information that attempts to classify the number dialed. The section "Called Party IE Number Type" discusses this information in more detail.

This information, however, tends to be rather troublesome in practice, because many networks are particular about the manner in which the information is encoded. The **NumberingPlanInfo** service parameter provides a way to tweak this information if your system is having difficulty communicating with a connected system. The **NumberingPlanInfo** service parameter takes the following values:

- 0 disables the setting, which causes CallManager to format the numbering plan information according to the call routing component's best judgment and the settings on the terminating device.

- 1 causes CallManager to encode the numbering plan field of the called party information element to **Unknown**, if the type of number field of the called party information element, as determined by CallManager, is also **Unknown**.

- 2 causes Cisco CallManager to encode the numbering plan field of the called party information element as **Private**, and the type of number field of the called party information element as **Unknown**.

If the system you have connected CallManager to is complaining about the encoding of the called number—a fact you can determine only through detailed analysis of the call rejection messages the connected system returns—changing this setting might resolve the problem.

Transformations on the Originating Device

This section describes the first opportunity CallManager has to transform the calling or called numbers—when the component that controls the caller's device offers the call to the call control component. These dialing transformations vary from device type to device type. The section "About Device Types That Cisco CallManager Supports" describes the device types that CallManager supports.

Table 2-40 provides an overview of the different kinds of originating device dialing transformations, along with a checklist of which protocols support which transformations.

External Phone Number Mask

All station devices use the Directory Number Configuration screen. This screen contains a field that is important in transformations, the **External Phone Number Mask**. Although the external phone number mask does not, in itself, effect any transformations, it allows you to configure a line's number from the PSTN's point of view—the line's external number. When you configure a value in this field, the value also shows up in the top line of the Cisco IP Phone 7940 and 7960 as the phone's external phone number.

For station-to-station calls, the calling line's directory number shows up as the calling number. However, for station-to-trunk calls, you can configure the destination route pattern so that it instead uses the line's external number as the calling number.

The external phone number mask is truly a mask (see the section "About Masks"). If you are fortunate enough to be able to map the final digits of a phone's external number directly to its internal extension, and if you are using autoregistration, you can use a mask value in this field instead of an individual number, and it saves you some data entry. (For information about autoregistration, see Chapter 3.)

Table 2-40   *Supported Originating Device Dialing Transformation by Device Type*

Originating Device Dialing Transformation	Skinny Station Devices	MGCP Station Devices	H.323 Station Devices	Skinny Trunk Devices	MGCP Trunk Devices	H.323 Trunk Devices
External Phone Number Mask	√	√	√			
Prefix Digits	√[1]	√		√	√[3]	√[8]
Num Digits	√[2]	√			√[4]	√
Expected Digits	√[2]	√			√[5]	
Attendant DN				√	√[6]	
CallerID Enable				√		
Sig Digits					√[7]	√

1   On POTS phones controlled by gateways that use the Skinny Gateway Protocol, this setting is called Prefix DN; this setting does not exist for IP Phones

2   Only for POTS phones controlled by gateways that use the Skinny Gateway Protocol

3   On T1-CAS, T1-PRI, and E1-PRI interfaces, where it is called Prefix DN

4   On FXO interfaces, this setting does not exist

5   On FXO, T1-PRI, and E1-PRI interfaces, this setting does not exist

6   On T1-CAS interfaces

7   On T1-PRI and E1-PRI interfaces

8   Called Prefix DN

For example, assume your system uses four-digit directory numbers. Furthermore, your site does not require overlapping dial plans (as might be required for multiple tenants) and it is small enough that it is served by a single area code and office code (say, 214 and 555, respectively). When you specify the mask 214555XXXX in the Cisco CallManager Configuration screen under the **System** menu, when a new device registers, CallManager automatically assigns it the external phone number mask 214555XXXX. When it receives its directory number (say, 1212), this configuration tells CallManager that the newly registered line's external phone number is 2145551212. If you also check the **Use External Phone Number Mask** check box for the route pattern that routes calls to the PSTN, CallManager presents your users' full external numbers to the PSTN when they place calls.

The external phone number mask also provides you with a means by which you can hide the external phone number of your users when they place external phone calls. If you set a phone's external phone number mask to your switchboard number and then check the **Use External Phone Number Mask** check box on the route pattern you use for routing external calls, CallManager presents the switchboard number as the calling phone's calling number.

Prefix Digits

These fields crop up under slightly different names in many of the devices. You can usually find these fields by clicking on specific ports in the gateway configuration screen.

Prefix Digits can contain a sequence of digits (*, #, 0 through 9). CallManager Administration also calls this field *Prefix DN*. **Prefix Digits** can contain a sequence of digits (*, #, 0 through 9). When a gateway configured with prefix digits receives a call from an associated gateway, CallManager modifies the dialed digits by prepending the digits you specify to the dialed number. For example, if a gateway provides the dialed digits 1000 and you specify prefix digits of 3, CallManager modifies the dialed digits to 31000.

Some subtleties exist about how prefix digits operate with different types of gateways. When CallManager connects to a gateway using a digital telephony protocol such as H.323 or ISDN, inbound calls from these gateways usually provide all of the digits the calling user dialed in the call setup attempt. This type of dialing is called *enbloc dialing*.

When CallManager connects to a gateway using an analog protocol or by a digital protocol such as MGCP, particularly when a POTS phone is connected to the gateway, the digits the user dials arrive from the gateway one by one. This type of digit collection is called *overlapped dialing*. When you configure prefix digits in conjunction with a gateway controlling a POTS station, CallManager immediately attempts to route the call based on the configured prefix digits. In the usual case, the prefix digits you specify are not sufficient for CallManager to select a destination, and CallManager waits for further digits from the calling user.

However, you can implement a hotline or Private Line Automatic Ringdown (PLAR) function with POTS phones by relying on CallManager's treatment of Prefix Digits. PLAR is a feature whereby CallManager can ring a specified extension the moment that a user places a call from a particular station. This feature works only with the Cisco AS-2, Cisco AS-4, Cisco AS-8, and Cisco VG200 gateways. POTS phones connected to other gateways such as the Cisco 24XX and Cisco 36XX routers connect to CallManager by a digital telephony protocol, H.323.

PLAR works when the Prefix Digits you specify are sufficient to permit CallManager to immediately select a destination. In this case, CallManager immediately offers the call to the specified destination. For instance, if your enterprise has a security desk with number 61111, by configuring prefix digits of 61111 for an analog gateway with an attached analog phone, you cause CallManager to immediately ring the security desk when a user picks up the POTS phone.

(The section "Hotline Functionality" describes a different way that you can configure PLAR, one that works with all devices but which requires a slightly more complicated configuration.)

Expected Digits and Num Digits

The gateway settings **Expected Digits** and **Num Digits** work in tandem. Expected Digits tells CallManager how many digits you expect the calling user to be dialing. **Num Digits** tells CallManager how many of those digits are significant to selecting a destination.

Num Digits is the easier of these settings to explain. Its heritage is the trunk interfaces, where you can often predict which digits a connected network sends. On a trunk interface, these settings tell CallManager to expect to receive *n* digits, the last *m* of which are significant for routing purposes. For instance, the central office might provide seven digits as the called number, but because the first three digits are always the office code, you just want to use the last four digits to route the call. Configuring **7** for **Expected Digits** and **4** for **Num Digits** causes CallManager to ignore the first three digits sent by the central office. If your dial plan is reasonably simple, as is often the case if your enterprise is smaller than 1000 users, using **Num Digits** provides you a simple way to maintain a 4- or 5-digit dial plan for your internal phones. (If your enterprise needs to support a large number of users whose external numbers are connected to a large number of telephone exchanges, **Num Digits** is often not powerful enough to handle the routing of your inbound calls. The section "Extension Mapping from the Public to the Private Network" describes how you can use translation patterns to route your inbound calls.)

Although the **Num Digits** setting tells CallManager how many digits you wish to keep, the **Expected Digits** setting tells CallManager how many digits the PSTN is going to send. When the gateway to which CallManager is connected uses enbloc dialing, the **Expected Digits** setting is superfluous; because the call setup attempt contains all of the digits the calling user dialed, CallManager can immediately use the **Num Digits** setting to extract the digits that you wish to route with. **Expected Digits** is a setting applicable to gateways connected to CallManager by protocols that use overlapped dialing. In such instances, CallManager needs to know how many digits to collect before using the **Num Digits** setting to extract the digits you wish to route with.

When you configure these settings for a station device, they behave identically to this setting on a trunk device. CallManager ignores the first few digits that the user dials and uses subsequent digits to route the call.

Attendant DN

Analog trunks are just like the analog phone lines that run into most people's houses. On an analog phone line, when a user goes off-hook, the phone places voltage on the line and the central office prepares to place a call. In the case of tone dialing, the central office connects your line to a tone detector, which listens to the stream of tones that emanate as you dial your phone and converts them to dialed digits.

When you configure an analog gateway, CallManager plays the part of the central office. However, Cisco analog gateways do not contain tone detectors. As a result, when CallManager detects that the trunk has been taken off-hook, it must dial a preconfigured number. This number is the **Attendant DN**. **Attendant DN** is a setting that is much like Prefix Digits, which is described in the section "Prefix Digits"; when a call comes in over the gateway, CallManager automatically provides the specified digits to the call routing component.

Caller ID Enable

A calling party transformation specific to the analog gateways is the **Caller ID Enable** check box. You can find this check box by clicking a configured port on the Gateway Configuration screen.

Caller ID is a mechanism by which the central office delivers textual and numeric information about the calling user. The PSTN sends caller ID on a 1200-bps carrier wave between the first and second rings. The analog gateways can process this signal and provide it to CallManager. Checking this check box tells the gateway to provide this information when the PSTN offers a call to CallManager.

Sig Digits Check Box and Num Digits

Digital trunk devices support variants of the ISDN signaling protocol. ISDN differs from analog protocols in that ISDN endpoints interpret the voltage levels on the trunk as either on or off values. This interpretation allows CallManager to assign meanings to particular patterns of on and off values and receive information, such as the calling and called party, directly in the call attempt. Unlike the analog gateways, which must dial a preconfigured number, digital gateways receive called party information directly in the call setup message. CallManager can transform this information by using settings on the Gateway Configuration screen.

Digital gateways have no setting that corresponds to the Expected Digits settings, because the call setup request usually encodes all the digits of the called number.

For digital gateways, the **Num Digits** setting (see the section "Expected Digits and Num Digits") is actually configured using two settings: the **Sig Digits** check box and the **Num Digits** field. If you leave the **Sig Digits** check box unchecked, CallManager will process all digits of the called number. However, if you check the **Sig Digits** check box, the number in the **Num Digits** check box indicates how many of the final digits of the dialed number that CallManager should use to route the call. For example, if the **Sig Digits** check box is checked and Num Digits is four, when CallManager receives a call for 9725551212, CallManager truncates all but the last four digits and routes using the digits 1212.

When used in conjunction with overlapped receiving (see the section "SendingCompleteIndicator and OverlapReceivingForPriFlag"), the **Num Digits** field might not operate as you expect. The **Num Digits** setting operates only on the first batch of digits the calling gateway provides to CallManager. In overlapped receiving, the gateway does not provide all of the digits at once. In fact, the first message that the gateway sends to CallManager often contains no digits at all. As a result, Cisco CallManager probably will not suppress any of the digits coming in from the gateway.

For example, assume you have set **Num Digits** to **4** and the gateway provides the digits 9725551212 one digit at a time. The first digit (9) arrives and CallManager applies the **Num Digits** setting to it. Because the **Num Digits** setting specifies to keep four of the initial digits, CallManager keeps the first digit. Then CallManager passes through all of the subsequent digits without complaint. Had all of the digits arrived in the call setup, CallManager would have truncated 9725551212 to 1212. When using overlapped receiving, unless you know that the initial setup that the gateway sends to CallManager contains more digits than the **Num Digits** setting, do not use the **Num Digits** setting.

Transformations in Translation Patterns, Route Patterns, and Route Lists

This section describes the second through fourth opportunities during which the CallManager can apply transformations as part of the routing process. The second opportunity occurs if the dialed digits match a translation pattern, the third occurs when a route pattern is ultimately selected, and the fourth occurs if the selected destination is a route list.

The section "Translation Patterns" describes translation patterns, and the section "Route Lists and Route Groups" describes route lists. However, it is worth noting here that the transformations associated with a route list *override* those that the route pattern applies. That is, although other dialing transformations you apply have a cumulative effect, the transformations you specify on a route between a route list and a route group undo any transformations that the Route Pattern Configuration screen applies. This capability allows you to define default dialing transformations on the route pattern, which you selectively override if a call goes out a particular set of gateways. For instance, in North America, long distance carriers expect to receive ten digits for calls to the PSTN. However, local carriers expect the digit 1 to precede long distance calls. Typically, to save costs, enterprises prefer their long distance calls to route directly to a long distance carrier. However, if all gateways to the long distance carrier are busy, by using a route list, you can route the call to a gateway connected to a local carrier as an alternate choice. In such a case, you could define dialing transformations on the route pattern to throw away the access code and long distance 1 that the user dials so that calls to the long distance carrier consist only of ten digits. If the route list determines that all gateways to the long distance carrier are busy, however, by setting different dialing transformations on the route group containing gateways to the local carrier, you can cause CallManager to discard only the access code and keep the initial 1 on the long distance call.

To prevent a particular route group from overriding the transformations you associate with a route pattern, leave the transformation mask fields of the route group empty and be sure to select **<None>** rather than **NoDigits** for digit discarding instructions.

Called Party Transformations

Three types of called party transformations can be configured in the call routing component and on route lists. They are as follows:

- Digit discarding instructions, which you use primarily with the @ wildcard and allow you to discard meaningful subsections of numbers in the national network. They are critical for implementing toll bypass solutions, where the long distance number that the calling user has dialed must be converted into a local number from which CallManager passes the digits to the PSTN.

- Called party transformation mask, which allows you to suppress leading digits, change existing digits while leaving others unmodified, and insert leading digits.

- Prefix digits, which allow you to prepend one or more digits to the called number.

CallManager applies the transformations in the order listed.

Digit Discarding Instructions

Digit discarding instructions allow you perform conversions of a dialed number specific to a national numbering plan. For the North American numbering plan, you can strip access codes, suppress long distance carrier selection, convert numbers to achieve toll bypass operations, and strip trailing # from international number sequences. Because digit discarding instructions are dial-plan specific, this section describes only those digit discarding instructions that apply to the North American numbering plan.

In general, digit discarding instructions apply only to route patterns that contain the @ wildcard. However, you can use the digit discarding instruction PreDot with route patterns that use the . wildcard even if they do not contain the @ wildcard.

Digit discarding instructions consist of one or more of the following identifiers grouped into three sections. The access code section lets you remove initial digits from a dialed string. The toll bypass section allows you to turn dial strings that represent long distance calls into dial strings that represent local calls. Finally, the trailing-# instruction lets you strip a dialed end-of-dialing terminator from international calls to prevent it from going to an adjacent network (which might have trouble processing it).

Digit discarding instruction identifiers are additive, so the digit discarding instruction **PreDot 10-10-Dialing** combines the effects of each individual identifier. If you do not wish to discard any digits, select **NoDigits**.

Table 2-41 describes the groups and identifiers and provides sample dialed digit strings. Substrings in bold denote which digits CallManager discards.

Table 2-41 *Digit Discarding Instructions Groups and Identifiers*

Instructions	Discarded Digits (for Route Pattern 9.8@)	Used For
Access Code		
PreDot	**98** 1 214 555 1212	Stripping access codes
PreAt	**98** 1 214 555 1212	Stripping access codes
Toll Bypass		
11/10D->7D	98 **1010321 1 214** 555 1212	Toll bypass to a 7-digit dialing region
11D->10D	98 **1010321 1** 214 555 1212	Toll bypass to a 10-digit dialing region
IntlTollBypass	98 **011 33** 0123456789 #	Toll bypass from country to country
10-10-Dialing	98 **1010321** 1 214 555 1212	Long distance carrier code suppression
Trailing-#		
Trailing-#	98 011 33 0123456789 **#**	Suppression of end-of-dialing character

Called Party Transformation Mask

Values in this field can truncate or expand the dialed digit string and change individual digits before CallManager sends the digits to a connected network or device. The section "About Masks" discusses mask operation.

Prefix Digits

This field can contain *, #, or digits 0 through 9. CallManager prepends this field to the called number before it is sent to the next stage of the routing process.

Calling Party Transformations

Three types of calling party transformations can be configured in the call routing component and on route lists:

- **Use External Phone Number Mask** check box, which instructs the call routing component to use a calling station's external phone number rather than its directory number as the calling number.

- Calling party transformation mask, which allows you to suppress leading digits, change existing digits, leave other digits unmodified, and insert leading digits.
- Prefix digits, which allow you to prepend the specified digits to the calling number.

CallManager applies the transformations in the order listed.

Use External Phone Number Mask Check Box

Setting this flag sets the calling number to the external phone number mask configured on the calling line, rather than the directory number of a calling line. See the section "About Masks" for details about the ways that masks work and the section "External Phone Number Mask" for more details about the external phone number mask.

If no external phone number mask is configured on the calling line, or if the call originates from a device that does not have an external phone number mask setting, the call routing component uses the directory number (in the case of calling user devices) or the provided calling number (in the case of calling trunk devices) instead.

Calling Party Transformation Mask

Values in this field can truncate or expand the calling number and change individual digits before CallManager sends the calling number to a connected switch or device. The section "About Masks" discusses mask operation.

The section "External Phone Number Mask" describes one method by which you can cause PSTN users to see your company switchboard's number as the calling number, rather than the direct number of your users when they place calls to the PSTN. Calling party transformation masks provide another method. By specifying your switchboard's number as a calling party transformation mask in the Route Pattern Configuration screen, you cause CallManager to replace the calling user's calling number with that of the company switchboard.

Prefix Digits

This field can contain *, #, or digits 0 through 9. CallManager prepends this field to the calling number before sending it to the next stage of the routing process.

Transformations on the Terminating Device

Trunk devices have settings that relate to the calling and called numbers. The settings described in this section correspond to the fifth and final place in CallManager where transformations can occur in the call routing process. Table 2-42 describes the dialing transformations and provides a checklist of which settings affect which gateways.

Table 2-42 *Supported Terminating Device Dialing Transformations by Device Type*

Terminating Device Dialing Transformation	Skinny Station Devices	MGCP Station Devices	H.323 Station Devices	Skinny Trunk Devices	MGCP Trunk Devices	H.323 Trunk Devices
Caller ID DN					$\sqrt{}^1$	$\sqrt{}$
Calling Party Selection					$\sqrt{}^2$	$\sqrt{}^3$
Presentation Bit					$\sqrt{}^2$	$\sqrt{}^3$
Called Party IE Number Type					$\sqrt{}^2$	$\sqrt{}^3$
Calling Party IE Number Type					$\sqrt{}^2$	$\sqrt{}^3$
Called Party IE Numbering Plan					$\sqrt{}^2$	$\sqrt{}^3$
Calling Party IE Numbering Plan					$\sqrt{}^2$	$\sqrt{}^3$
Number of Digits to Strip					$\sqrt{}^2$	
Display IE Delivery					$\sqrt{}$	$\sqrt{}$
Redirecting Number IE Delivery					$\sqrt{}$	

1 T1-CAS, T1-PRI and E1-PRI interfaces only

2 T1-PRI and E1-PRI interfaces only

3 Only on H.323 gateways, not intercluster trunks

Caller ID DN

Caller ID DN provides a mechanism to set the calling number of calls that CallManager extends to a gateway. It is a mask value (see the section "About Masks"). Values set in this field operate on the calling number that previous transformation steps generate.

Calling Party Selection

Calling Party Selection has one of three values: **Originator**, **First Redirect Number**, and **Last Redirect Number**.

This setting determines what number is presented as the calling number when call forwarding occurs.

If no forwarding at all has occurred, all three values (**Originator**, **First Redirect Number**, and **Last Redirect Number**) contain the calling number of the originator. If CallManager has forwarded the call once, both the first redirect number and last redirect number are the calling number of the forwarding phone, while the originator is the calling number of the originator. If CallManager has forwarded the call twice, the originator is the calling number of the calling user, the first redirect number is the calling number of the first forwarding phone, and the last redirect number is the calling number of the last forwarding phone. If the call forwards more than once, the last redirect number reflects the calling number of the last device to forward the call.

Why would you set this field? If the system that the gateway is connected to is in charge of maintaining the billing records for calls from CallManager, you might wish to bill not the actual originator of a call, but the party that caused the call to forward out the gateway. If the adjacent system uses the calling number to determine who to bill, this setting effectively allows you to control the billing.

Presentation Bit

The presentation bit has values of **None**, **Allowed**, and **Restricted**. If set to **None** or **Allowed** (either value has the same effect), this setting indicates to the attached network that the called party is allowed to see the calling number. If this field is set to **Restricted**, the called party is prohibited from seeing the calling number.

Called Party IE Number Type

This setting has values of **Cisco CallManager**, **Unknown**, **National**, and **International**. The setting dictates how CallManager represents the called number to the network to which the gateway provides access.

Calls to ISDN networks include not only the dialed digits but also an indication of what the calling system believes the numbers represent. The **Type of number** field indicates to the system that receives the call whether the digits provided represent a national number, an international number, or whether the calling system even knows what the nature of the dialed number is. Although this setting was a nice idea on the part of the architects of ISDN, in practice, it (and its brethren, **Calling Party IE Number Type**, **Called Party Numbering Plan**, and **Calling Party Numbering Plan**) usually just causes problems. For example, one setting that the ISDN messages permit is **Private**, which represents to the called system that the calling system believes the provided digits are a number on a privately owned network. PSTN systems may decide that they do not want to route calls tagged with the type of number **Private**, even if the actual digits contained in the call setup represent an actual PSTN number. Conversely, if the PSTN is providing you with a Centrex service (in which the PSTN operates as a PBX so that you can network remote offices), the PSTN might require the type of number be encoded as **Private** for an interoffice call, even if the provided digits are sufficient to allow the PSTN to route the call to a remote office. In summary, even if the digits you provide are correct, the system to which you offer the call might reject the call if the **Type of number** field is not what it expects. Therefore, CallManager provides settings to permit you to control the **Type of number** and **Numbering plan** fields in case the network to which you connect your gateway is particular about the encoding of these fields.

By default, this value is set to **Cisco CallManager**, which means CallManager fills in this number as best it can. This setting usually works fine. If the pattern the calling user dials matches an @ pattern, CallManager fills in the number as national or international based on the numbering plan (see the section "The North American Numbering Plan"). For non-@ patterns, CallManager punts and encodes the number as **Unknown**.

If an attached network has problems with the number type that CallManager encodes, changing this setting may resolve the problem. Particularly if you live in a country that does not use the North American numbering plan and you have configured specific route patterns to route calls out gateways, you may find that the PSTN balks at CallManager's encoding of the number type as **Unknown**. Changing this setting to **National** can resolve the problem.

Calling Party IE Number Type

This setting has values of **Cisco CallManager**, **Unknown**, **National**, and **International**. The setting dictates how CallManager represents the calling number to the network to which the gateway provides access.

By default, CallManager encodes the number as **Unknown**, and this setting works in most cases. If an attached network has problems with the number type that CallManager encodes, changing this setting may resolve the problem.

Called Numbering Plan

ISDN networks expect telephone systems to provide not only the number type of a called number, but also the numbering plan it believes the number applies. This setting has values of **Cisco CallManager**, **ISDN**, **National Standard**, **Private**, and **Unknown**.

By default, CallManager encodes the number as **ISDN**. If an attached network has problems with the default numbering plan that CallManager encodes, changing this setting can resolve the problem.

Calling Numbering Plan

This setting has values of **Cisco CallManager**, **ISDN**, **National Standard**, **Private**, and **Unknown**.

By default, CallManager encodes the number as **ISDN**. If an attached network has problems with the default numbering plan that CallManager encodes, changing this setting can resolve the problem.

Number of Digits to Strip

Setting this value instructs CallManager to strip the specified number of digits from the beginning of all called numbers before passing the call to an adjacent network. If you administer a network in a country with a variable-length dialing plan, you might find this setting useful, because the discarding mechanisms that digit discarding instructions (see the section "Digit Discarding Instructions") provide are not available, and because called party transform masks enable you only to truncate a number to a fixed number of final digits.

Display IE Delivery

This setting controls the delivery of the display information element (IE). The display information element permits a telephone system to ask another system to display the contained information. Many telephone systems use it to communicate the display name of the calling user. When you enable this option for a particular gateway, CallManager places the contents of the **Display** field (on the Directory Number Configuration screen) into the display information element before CallManager extends a call to the attached gateway.

Redirecting Number IE Delivery

This setting controls the delivery of the redirecting number information element. Suppose that a phone on a telephone system calls another phone on the same telephone system, and the call forwards to different telephone system that manages the voice messaging system for the enterprise. The new telephone system needs to know what directory number the caller originally dialed so that the voice messaging system can deliver the caller's voice message to the correct voice messaging box number. The redirecting number information element permits one telephone system to communicate this information to another. Enabling this flag permits CallManager to communicate the original dialed number to the connected network.

Translation Patterns

Translation patterns are a mechanism that allows you to introduce a level of routing indirection into the call routing process. They allow you to define aliases for the endpoints in your network.

Why do you need to define such aliases? This section discusses a few reasons:

- Security desk and operator functionality
- Hotline functionality
- Extension mapping from the public to your private network

- Insertion of access codes in the **Received Calls** and **Missed Calls** menus of Cisco IP Phones
- Multiple tenant applications

You configure translation patterns almost exactly like route patterns. They have the same calling and called party transformations, and they use the same wildcard notation.

Unlike route patterns, translation patterns do not correspond to a physical or logical destination. Instead, a translation pattern relies on the calling and called party transformations to perform its function. Although route patterns use transformations simply a way to change the presentation of the calling or called parties, translation patterns use the results of called party transformations as a set of digits for a new analysis attempt. Cisco CallManager then uses the results of the second analysis attempt to determine which destination to ring.

The second analysis attempt might itself match a translation pattern. In this case, CallManager applies the calling and called party transformations of the matching translation pattern and uses the results as the input for another analysis attempt. To prevent routing loops, CallManager breaks chains of translation patterns after ten iterations.

An example might help to explain. Imagine that you have the translation patterns and route patterns listed in Table 2-43.

Table 2-43   *Translation Pattern Example*

Configured Translation and Route Patterns
Translation Pattern: 1XXX
Called Party Transformation Mask: 2XXX
Translation Pattern: 2XXX
Prefix Digits: 8
Route pattern: 8.XXXX
Gateway: Gateway A

When a user dials the number 1000, this configuration causes CallManager to offer the user's call to Gateway A with a called number of 82000. This process consists of the following steps:

Step 1   The dialed digits 1000 match the translation pattern 1XXX. CallManager applies the called party transformation mask 2XXX to the dialed digits 1000, yielding 2000.

Step 2   CallManager uses the resulting number, 2000, as the input for another analysis attempt. This attempt matches the translation pattern 2XXX. CallManager applies the prefix digit 8 to the digits 2000, yielding 82000.

Step 3 CallManager uses the resulting number, 82000, as the input for another analysis attempt. This attempt matches the route pattern 8.XXXX. CallManager offers the call to Gateway A, the gateway associated with the route pattern.

One configuration field that appears for translation patterns, but which does not appear for route patterns, is *calling search space*. When the new analysis is attempted, the analysis is attempted using the calling search space configured for the translation pattern, rather than the calling search space of the originating device. This behavior can allow a user to call a number in a partition that the user's calling search space would not normally permit the user to dial. The section "Calling Search Spaces and Partitions" describes calling search spaces and partitions.

Translation patterns, therefore, differ from route patterns; when route patterns match, CallManager always extends the call to the destination associated with the route pattern. The dialing transformations that CallManager applies have a purely cosmetic effect in that they change the calling number and called number, but do not cause CallManager to select a different destination. (However, if the destination to which CallManager offers the call is a gateway or other CallManager cluster, the gateway or CallManager cluster can use the transformed called number to decide where to route the call.)

On the other hand, translation patterns have no associated destination. The called party number transformations that CallManager applies do directly affect which destination CallManager selects, because CallManager uses the results of the transformation to select a new destination. The new analysis attempt might match a route pattern or directory number, or the attempt may match another translation pattern, in which case CallManager attempts another analysis. Figure 2-10 presents a flowchart of this process.

Figure 2-10 *Translation Pattern Flowchart*

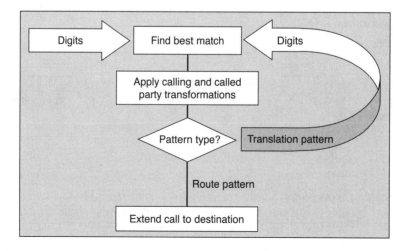

The rest of this section describes different translation pattern configurations:

- "Security Desk and Operator Functionality" discusses a mechanism by which you can associate an easily remembered directory number with an emergency service, while maintaining a fixed-length directory number plan.

- "Hotline Functionality" discusses a mechanism by which you can automatically ring a particular extension when a phone goes off-hook.

- "Extension Mapping from the Public to the Private Network" describes how you can map the discontinuous number ranges that the telephone company might assign you to a contiguous range for internal extensions.

- "Insertion of Access Codes in the **Received Calls** and **Missed Calls** Menus of Cisco IP Phones" describes how you can use translation patterns to insert outside access codes for calls that your users receive. Inserting the access codes allows your users to use the **Dial** soft key on the **Received Calls** and **Missed Calls** menus of their IP Phones. Normally, users must use the **EditDial** soft key to modify the number of a received or missed call in order to return a received or missed call.

- "Multiple Tenant Applications" discusses a few strategies that use translation patterns to deal with the problems that arise when different organizations with independent dial plans share a single CallManager.

Security Desk and Operator Functionality

The operator or security desk is often just a phone in your network with a standard 4- or 5-digit extension. However, for the desk to be useful with the least amount of hassle for your users, it is desirable to be able to assign these special extensions a directory number that is out of the ordinary (such as 0) and thus easier for your users to remember in an emergency.

One way to accomplish this task is, of course, to assign unusual directory numbers directly to these stations. However, having unusual directory numbers in a particular number block makes configuration of inbound routing more complex. Inbound calls often route based on the last four or five digits of an externally published number. If you want these special stations to receive inbound calls for other networks, you have to configure special routing to convert very specific extension numbers to your unusual numbers.

Translation patterns allow you to give numbers that are compatible with the rest of your numbering plan to these special stations, but to assign them aliases in the cluster. This allows your users to have easy-to-remember emergency numbers without the pain of configuring all ingresses to the cluster with special routing instructions.

To configure a dialing alias, specify the alias as a translation pattern and make sure that calling users include the partition that contains the translation pattern in their calling search spaces. In the called party transformation mask, enter the extension that you want to be called. In the translation calling search space, enter a calling search space that contains the partition associated with the destination extension.

Figure 2-11 shows a security desk example.

Figure 2-11 *Security Desk Example*

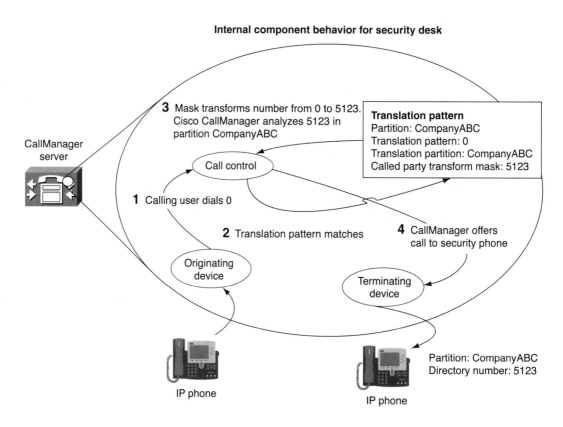

The example relies on the provision of the translation and route patterns in Table 2-44.

Table 2-44 *Security Desk Example Patterns*

Configured Route and Translation Patterns	Comments
Partition: CompanyABC	Translation calling search space CompanyABC contains partition CompanyABC.
Translation pattern: 0	
Translation calling search space: CompanyABC	
Called party transformation mask: 5123	

Table 2-44   *Security Desk Example Patterns (Continued)*

Configured Route and Translation Patterns	Comments
Partition: CompanyABC Route pattern: 5123	5123 is a phone with directory number 5123. CallManager considers directory numbers as route patterns and these can be the destination that a translation pattern selects.

When the calling user dials 0, CallManager performs the following steps:

Step 1   The dialed digit 0 matches the translation pattern 0. CallManager applies the called party transformation mask 5123 to convert the called number to 5123.

Step 2   CallManager uses the resulting number, 5123, as the input for another analysis attempt. This attempt matches the security phone's directory number. CallManager offers the call to the security phone with dialed digits of 5123.

Hotline Functionality

A hotline or private line automatic ringdown (PLAR) configuration causes a specified destination to ring immediately when the hotline extension goes off-hook. It is simply a special case of an operator configuration.

In an operator configuration, translation patterns cause the operator extension to ring when a single digit is dialed. In a hotline configuration, the specified destination rings before a user dials any digits. By specifying a translation pattern containing no digits, you can cause the transformation and reanalysis to occur immediately after the user takes the phone off-hook.

The only wrinkle is that of interdigit timing. Translation patterns always have urgent priority, which means that as soon as the user enters a digit sequence for which a translation pattern is the best match, the call routing component applies the translation immediately, even if subsequent digits would cause a different route pattern to match. This behavior means that if you configure a hotline translation pattern and group it in the same route partition as all of your other route patterns and directory numbers, whenever any device goes off-hook for any reason, the hotline extension rings. Users never have the opportunity to dial any digits.

To prevent this behavior from occurring, you must put the hotline translation pattern in its own partition and configure the hotline extension's calling search space so that it looks in the hotline partition to resolve its analysis requests. The section "Calling Search Spaces and Partitions" discusses calling search spaces and partitions.

Figure 2-12 shows an example of hotline configuration.

Figure 2-12 *Hotline Configuration*

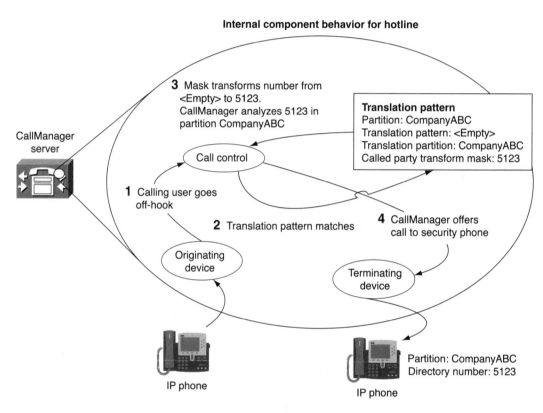

The example relies on the provision of the translation and route patterns in Table 2-45.

Table 2-45 *Hotline Configuration Example Route Patterns*

Configured Route and Translation Patterns	Comments
Partition: Hotline Translation pattern: <Empty> Translation calling search space: CompanyABC Called party transformation mask: 5123	Translation calling search space CompanyABC contains partition CompanyABC.
Partition: CompanyABC Route pattern: 5123	5123 is a phone with directory number 5123. CallManager considers directory numbers as route patterns and these can be the destination that a translation pattern selects.

When the calling user whose calling search space includes the Hotline partition goes off-hook, CallManager performs the following steps:

Step 1   When the user goes off-hook, this provides CallManager with an empty set of dialed digits, which match the translation pattern <Empty> in the Hotline partition. CallManager applies the called party transformation mask 5123 to convert the called number to 5123.

Step 2   CallManager uses the resulting number, 5123, as the input for another analysis attempt. The calling search space that CallManager uses for the analysis attempt is the calling search space of the translation pattern, CompanyABC. This attempt matches the hotline's directory number. CallManager offers the call to the hotline phone with dialed digits of 5123.

Extension Mapping from the Public to the Private Network

If your campus grows past 1000 users, you might need to use translation patterns to preserve your internal extension numbering scheme. Local phone carriers often sell numbers in blocks of 1000. For example, if a single exchange serves your campus, the phone company might lease you the block of 1000 numbers from 813 5000 to 813 5999.

As long as you do not exceed 1000 users, it is possible to use gateway settings to map the block of 1000 users that the phone company assigns you to your internal numbering scheme. For example, if you prefer your users to be in the numbering range 8000 to 8999, when the PSTN provides 813 5XXX as the called number, you can use dialing transformations on the Gateway Configuration screen to strip all but the final three digits and prepend an 8 (see the section "Transformations on the Originating Device").

However, if your network grows past 1000 users, there is no guarantee that the next block of 1000 numbers that the phone company assigns you will be contiguous with your previous range. In fact, even if the same central office serves you, the phone company might assign you a different exchange number. At this point, performing a transformation in the gateway does not work.

For instance, let us say that the phone company has given you two ranges, 813 5XXX and 828 9XXX. You can no longer just keep the last three digits and prepend 8 in the Gateway Configuration screen, because a call to 813 5000 and a call to 828 9000 both get transformed to the directory number 8000.

However, if you choose to keep the final four instead of the final three digits, the discontinuity of the numbering range affects your internal numbering plan. A call to 813 5000 is transformed to 5000, while a call to 828 9000 is transformed to 9000. Setting aside for a moment that your existing users (who were in the range 8000 to 8999) can no longer receive calls until you renumber them to the 5000 range, the split numbering range at the central office is now visible to your internal network. If you have previously set up an initial steering digit of 5 for features such as call park or for intercluster calls, the split numbering range might force you to reorganize your numbering plan, probably to the frustration of your users.

On the other hand, anticipating that your campus might grow to beyond 1000 users, if you keep the 7000 to 7999 range open (or better yet, assign users 5-digit directory numbers), by using translation patterns, you can map inbound calls in the 813 5XXX range to the internal 8XXX range while directing inbound calls in the 828 9XXX range to the internal 7XXX range.

To configure this setup, perform no transformations at the inbound gateway. Instead, set up two translation patterns in a partition visible only to your inbound gateways (see the section "Calling Search Spaces and Partitions"). Set one translation pattern to 813 5XXX with a called party transformation mask of 8XXX, and set the other translation pattern to 828 9XXX with a called party transformation mask of 7XXX.

When an inbound call arrives in the 813 5XXX range, the corresponding translation pattern matches, and CallManager transforms the called number to 8XXX. Then, because translation patterns cause reanalysis to occur, CallManager uses the transformed digits to select the actual destination to ring. Figure 2-13 shows the behavior that occurs when a call comes in for 8135123.

The example relies on the provision of the translation and route patterns in Table 2-46.

Table 2-46 *Patterns for Transforming Inbound Calls to Deal with a Discontinuous Numbering Range*

Configured Route and Translation Patterns	Comments
Partition: InboundTranslations Translation pattern: 8135XXX Translation calling search space: CompanyABC Called party transformation mask: 8XXX	Translation calling search space CompanyABC contains partition CompanyABC.
Partition: CompanyABC Route pattern: 8123	8123 is a phone with directory number 8123. CallManager considers directory numbers as route patterns and these can be the destination that a translation pattern selects.

Figure 2-13 *Transforming Inbound Calls to Deal with a Discontinuous Numbering Range*

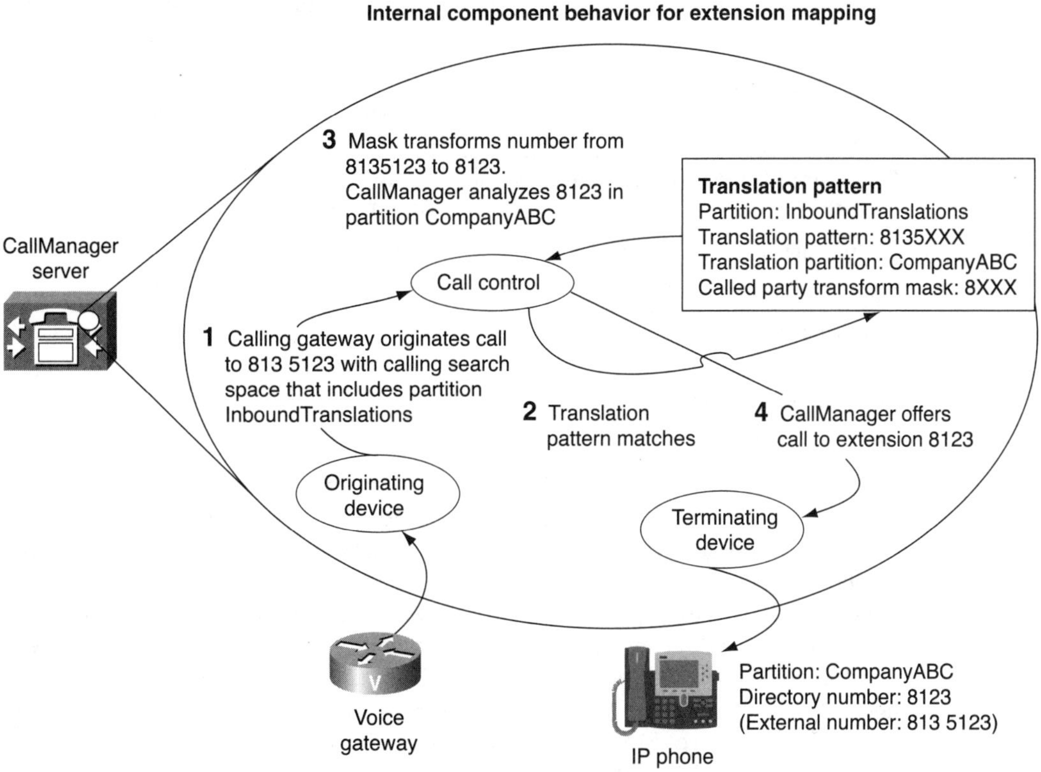

Internal component behavior for extension mapping

When the PSTN sends a call through the gateway to 8138123, CallManager performs the following steps:

Step 1   The gateway provides CallManager with the digits 8138123, which matches the translation pattern 8135XXX in the InboundTranslations partition. CallManager applies the called party transformation mask 8XXX to convert the called number to 8123.

Step 2   CallManager uses the resulting number, 8123, as the input for another analysis attempt. The calling search space that CallManager uses for the analysis attempt is the calling search space of the translation pattern, CompanyABC. This attempt matches the phone with directory number 8123. CallManager offers the call to the phone with dialed digits of 8123.

The above translation patterns suffice for a company of up to 1000 users. If your network grows past 1000 users and the phone company gives you numbers in the 828 9XXX range, by adding the following translation patterns, you can map the 9XXX range (which probably overlaps with your outside access code) to 7XXX. Table 2-47 shows the translation pattern that maps the new range.

Table 2-47 *Translation Pattern for Transforming Inbound Calls to Deal with a Discontinuous Numbering Range*

Configured Route and Translation Patterns	Comments
Partition: InboundTranslations	Translation calling search space CompanyABC contains partition CompanyABC.
Translation pattern: 8289XXX	
Translation calling search space: CompanyABC	
Called party transformation mask: 7XXX	

Directory Number Lengths and Cisco CallManager

CallManager has no particular reliance on 4-digit directory numbers. You can use any number of digits for your internal extensions and adjust the translation tables appropriately. For example, if the example network this section presented used 5-digit extensions in the range 50000–51999, changing the translation pattern 8135XXX to use a called party transformation of 50XXX maps inbound calls in the 5XXX of the 813 exchange to number ranges 50000–50999. Similarly, changing the translation pattern 8289XXX to use a called party transformation of 51XXX maps inbound calls in the 9XXX range of the 828 exchange to number ranges 51000–51999.

Insertion of Access Codes in the Received Calls and Missed Calls Menus of Cisco IP Phones

The Cisco IP Phones 7940 and 7960 provide users a **directories** button with several menu items, among them **Missed Calls** and **Received Calls**. When a user receives a call, the phone places the calling number in the **Missed Calls** menu if the user does not answer the call, and the **Received Calls** menu if the user does answer the call.

These menus also provide two soft keys: **Dial** and **EditDial**. Figure 2-14 shows a representation of the **Missed Calls** menu.

Pressing the **Dial** soft key causes the phone to place a new call by dialing the digits of the selected missed call entry. Unfortunately, in many cases, CallManager rejects calls placed using the **Dial** soft key, because a user's calling number is not always the same set of digits that a user must dial to return the call.

Figure 2-14 *Missed Calls Menu of Cisco IP Phone 7960*

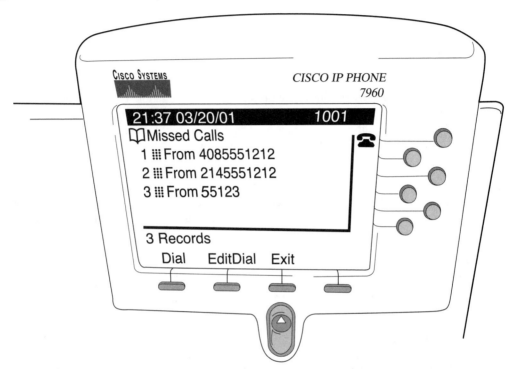

For instance, if a phone in the PSTN with number 408 555 1212 calls a phone controlled by CallManager in the Dallas area, the calling number that the Dallas phone receives is 408 555 1212, and thus the Dallas phone records 408 555 1212 in its **Missed Calls** or **Received Calls** menu. However, practically every enterprise requires an external access code such as 9 to provide access to an external line. Furthermore, in this example, the Dallas's phone return call is a long distance call, which the North American PSTN requires also to start with a 1. So while the phone receives 408 555 1212 as the calling number, to return the call, the Dallas phone must dial 9 1 408 555 1212.

This situation is complicated by the fact that for other types of calls, the return number needs to have just the access code without the 1. For instance, if phone connected to the Dallas PSTN with number 214 555 1212 calls a Dallas phone controlled by CallManager, to return the call, the Dallas phone must use an access code but omit the 1: 9 214 555 1212.

Finally some calls need neither an access code nor PSTN digits added. For instance, if phone 55123 in the Dallas enterprise calls phone 55004 in the Dallas enterprise, 55123 shows up as the calling number in the **Missed Calls** or **Received Calls** menu, and phone 55004 does not need to modify the stored digits at all to return the call.

The IP Phone has no way to predict which digits need to be added for which types of calls, and thus provides an **EditDial** soft key. When a user presses the **EditDial** soft key, the Cisco IP Phone allows the user to edit the stored number before it places the call. This permits the user to insert any necessary access codes and PSTN digits before placing the call. Unfortunately, it requires several additional button presses, which users find quite cumbersome.

Translation patterns can allow you to overcome this limitation, because they give you an opportunity to modify the calling number before CallManager presents a call to an IP Phone. By modifying the calling number, you can insert the appropriate access codes and PSTN digits for calls to IP Phones in your enterprise.

Modifying the calling number does have consequences, though. Modifying the calling number means that when an IP Phone receives an external call, the displayed calling number will contain any access codes and PSTN digits. This solution permits you either to display the pure calling number and require the user to press the **EditDial** soft key for many calls, or to display a modified calling number and allow the user to press the **Dial** soft key for calls. Currently, you cannot have it both ways.

Configuring translations on inbound calls requires two separate steps.

First, you must modify the calling number for calls from the PSTN to CallManager, which causes CallManager to insert the appropriate access codes and PSTN digits.

Second, you must modify the called number for calls from CallManager to the PSTN. This step properly handles the insertion of PSTN digits. In the example above, calls from the PSTN come from both 408 555 1212 and 214 555 1212. In the first case, CallManager needs to prefix 91 for the IP Phone to return the call, and in the second case, CallManager needs to prefix just 9 for the IP Phone to return the call. However, both calls come in over the same gateway, and CallManager cannot look at the calling number to decide which digits to prefix. If CallManager prefixes just 9, the return call to 9 1 408 555 1212 fails because of lack of a required PSTN digit. If CallManager prefixes 91, the return call to 9 214 555 1212 fails because of an excess PSTN digit.

Configuring a translation for calls from CallManager to the PSTN permits you to indiscriminately prefix 91 for calls to CallManager. Then, for calls to the PSTN, you can eliminate the PSTN digit for calls that do not require them.

The following example describes this procedure. Figure 2-15 shows the network that this section has already described, with two phones connected to a CallManager in Dallas, one phone connected to the Dallas PSTN, and one phone connected to the San Jose PSTN.

Figure 2-15 *Sample Network for Access Code Insertion*

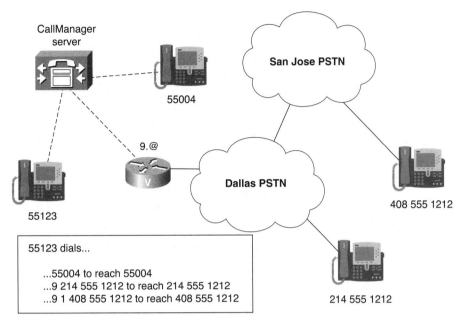

Handling the translations for calls to a Dallas phone relies on the provision of the translation and route patterns in Table 2-48.

Table 2-48 *Patterns for Inserting Access Codes for Calls to a Cisco CallManager Phone*

Configured Route and Translation Patterns	Comments
Partition: InboundTranslations Translation pattern: 55XXX Translation calling search space: CompanyABC Calling party prefix digits: 91	CallManager inserts 91 before the calling number of calls from the PSTN. The translation calling search space CompanyABC contains the partition CompanyABC.
Partition: CompanyABC Route pattern: 55004	55004 is a phone with directory number 55004. This phone has a calling search space that contains partitions CompanyABC, OutboundTranslations, and PSTNGateways.
Partition: CompanyABC Route pattern: 55123	55123 is a phone with directory number 55123. This phone has a calling search space that contains partitions CompanyABC, OutboundTranslations, and PSTNGateways.

continues

Table 2-48 *Patterns for Inserting Access Codes for Calls to a Cisco CallManager Phone (Continued)*

Configured Route and Translation Patterns	Comments
Partition: PSTNGateways Route pattern: 9.@	The gateway to the PSTN is in its own partition, to which phones do not have direct access. The gateway's calling search space contains the partition InboundTranslations.
	Assume for simplicity that the gateway throws away all but the final 5 digits of the called number that the PSTN provides for calls to CallManager.

When IP Phone 55004 dials 55123, CallManager performs the following step:

> The digits 55123 match the directory number 55123 in the CompanyABC partition. CallManager delivers the call directly to IP Phone 55123 with 55004 as the calling number.

When San Jose phone 408 555 1212 dials 214 555 5123, CallManager performs the following steps:

Step 1　The PSTN gateway throws away all but the last five digits of the number the San Jose user dialed, yielding 55123. The calling number that the PSTN provides is 408 555 1212.

Step 2　CallManager uses the calling search space of the gateway to analyze the dialed digits. The digits 55123 match the route pattern 55XXX in the InboundTranslations partition. CallManager applies the calling party prefix digits of 91 to convert the calling number from 408 555 1212 to 9 1 408 555 1212. CallManager does not change the called number at all, because no called party transformations are configured for the translation pattern.

Step 3　CallManager uses the unchanged called number, 55123, for another analysis attempt. This time CallManager uses the calling search space of the translation pattern—CompanyABC—to perform the analysis. The digits 55123 match the directory number 55123 in the CompanyABC partition. CallManager delivers the call to IP Phone 55123 with 9 1 408 555 1212 as the calling number.

When Dallas phone 214 555 1212 dials 214 555 5123, CallManager performs the following steps:

Step 1　The PSTN gateway throws away all but the last five digits of the number that the San Jose user dialed, yielding 55123. The calling number that the PSTN provides is 214 555 1212.

Step 2   CallManager uses the calling search space of the gateway to analyze the dialed digits. The digits 55123 match the route pattern 55XXX in the InboundTranslations partition. CallManager applies the calling party prefix digits of 91 to convert the calling number from 214 555 1212 to 9 1 214 555 1212. CallManager does not change the called number at all, because no called party transformations are configured for the translation pattern.

Step 3   CallManager uses the unchanged called number, 55123, for another analysis attempt. This time, CallManager uses the calling search space of the translation pattern—CompanyABC—to perform the analysis. The digits 55123 match the directory number 55123 in the CompanyABC partition. CallManager delivers the call to IP Phone 55123 with 9 1 214 555 1212 as the calling number.

Figure 2-16 shows the **Missed Calls** menu that results from IP Phone 55123 receiving the three calls just described.

Figure 2-16 *Missed Calls Menu Showing Transformed Numbers*

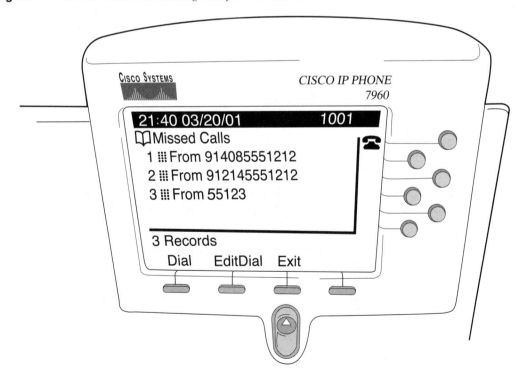

Note that the call from IP Phone 55004 has no prefix digits added, although both of the calls from the PSTN have access code 9 and PSTN digit 1 added. In the case of the call from San Jose, the modified number is identical to the number that the user dials to call the San Jose phone. But in the case of the call from Dallas, the modified number includes PSTN digit 1. If the user dials the number as shown, the Dallas PSTN rejects the call because of the extra digits. Configuring an outbound translation eliminates this problem. Table 2-49 shows the translation pattern required to strip the excess PSTN digit from the local call.

Table 2-49   *Translation Patterns Used to Remove Excess PSTN Digits for Calls to the PSTN*

Configured Route and Translation Patterns	Comments
Partition: OutboundTranslations Translation pattern: 91.214XXXXXXX Translation calling search space: PSTNGateways DigitDiscardingInstructions: PreDot Called Party Prefix Digits: 9	CallManager strips the preceding 91 for calls to the 214 area code and then uses the access code 9. Another way to configure this translation pattern uses route pattern 9.@ and a route filter with clause AREA-CODE == 214. The translation pattern then specifies the digit discarding instruction 11D->10D, which throws away the PSTN Digit 1 while retaining the access code 9.

When IP Phone 55123 presses the **Dial** soft key for the call with digits 9 1 408 555 1212, CallManager performs the following step:

> CallManager uses the calling search space of the IP Phone to analyze the dialed digits 9 1 408 555 1212. These digits match the route pattern 9.@ in partition PSTNGateways. CallManager delivers the call to the PSTN gateway with called number 9 1 408 555 1212.

However, when IP Phone presses the **Dial** soft key for the call with digits 9 1 214 555 1212, CallManager performs the following steps, which remove the extra PSTN digit:

Step 1   CallManager uses the calling search space of the IP Phone to analyze the dialed digits 9 1 214 555 1212. These digits match both the route pattern 9.@ in partition PSTNGateways and the translation pattern 91.214XXXXXXX in partition OutboundTranslations. CallManager applies the digit discarding instructions of PreDot to convert the number from 9 1 214 555 1212 to 214 555 1212, and then CallManager applies the called party prefix digit of 9, yielding 9 214 555 1212.

Step 2   CallManager uses the modified called number, 9 214 555 1212, for another analysis attempt. This time, CallManager uses the calling search space of the translation pattern—PSTNGateways—to perform the analysis. The digits 9 214 555 1212 match route pattern 9.@ in the PSTNGateways partition. CallManager delivers the call to the PSTN gateway with called number 9 214 555 1212.

Multiple Tenant Applications

In a multiple tenant environment, one CallManager or CallManager cluster serves two independent organizations, each with its own numbering plan. The scope of responsibility of the person or organization managing the CallManager cluster can vary dramatically. At the small end of the scale is the landlord who provides the phone service for the tenants in the building (either commercial or residential). This type of deployment is termed *multitenant*. At the large end of the scale is the Internet service provider (ISP) or telephone service provider that manages a network of CallManagers and resells phone services to many companies with separate facilities, who may or may not have PBXs of their own. This type of deployment is called *IP Centrex*. The difference from a routing point of view is simply in amount of configuration; the basic call routing mechanisms used for both types of deployments are essentially the same. This document uses the term *multitenant* rather than *IP Centrex* when describing such deployments, and *service provider* when referring to the person or organization that provides multitenant services.

In a multitenant deployment, the numbering ranges for each organization might be completely isolated from each other, or they might have numbers in common, such as a security desk. Particularly because gateways are simply resources for placing calls to and receiving calls from other networks, two tenants can share gateways.

Extension Mapping for Multiple Tenants

Everything that applies to extension mapping for a single tenant applies for multiple tenants. If an inbound call arrives over a gateway, you must map the full externally published number to the proper internal extension number. Setting a calling search space on the translation pattern is extremely important here, because identical directory numbers that different tenants own must be treated as separate extensions instead of as a shared line appearance.

For example, assume there is a multiple tenant environment in which a service provider uses one CallManager to route calls for company ABC and XYZ. Company ABC has an appearance of line 1000 registered in partition ABC, while company XYZ has an appearance of line 1000 in partition XYZ.

Company ABC's line 1000 is reachable from the PSTN as 828 8000, while company XYZ's line 1000 is reachable from the PSTN as 813 5000. The similar configuration to the one described in the previous section allows inbound calls to reach the appropriate station, though the calling search space must be set appropriately.

For example, assume that company ABC's external numbers are all in the 828 8XXX range, while company XYZ's are all in the 813 5XXX range. By eschewing any transformations in the gateways themselves, you can configure two translation patterns in a partition that only the gateway can see.

The first route pattern, 828 8XXX, uses a called party transformation mask of 1XXX. Furthermore, the translation calling search space for the translation pattern must be set to a calling search space that contains partition ABC but not XYZ.

The second route pattern, 813 5XXX, has an associated called party transformation mask of 1XXX. Its translation calling search space is set to a calling search space that contains partition XYZ but not partition ABC.

Figure 2-17 shows this configuration.

Calls Between Tenants

A wrinkle of multitenant configurations that is not present for single tenant configurations is that of calling between tenants. Independent tenants do not call each other using their internal directory numbers. To each tenant, the other tenant should be indistinguishable from a company that the PSTN serves.

This requirement means that not only the called party must be transformed for intertenant calls, but also the calling party must be transformed. Suppose user A at extension 1000 in company ABC calls user B extension 2000 in company XYZ. If the called party's missed calls display shows the call as coming from calling number 1000, when user B tries to call user A back by dialing 1000, user B instead reaches extension 1000 in user B's own company.

One way to handle this issue is not to handle it at all. When user A dials user B, user A dials user B's external number. If user A is allowed to make outbound calls, this call routes out a gateway to the PSTN, which in turn routes the call right back into the CallManager cluster as an external call. If you have configured extension mapping, user B's display reflects the correct information.

Unfortunately, this configuration wastes gateway resources. Furthermore, the PSTN charges you for a call that the CallManager cluster can connect on its own.

Translation patterns can resolve this problem. For calls among tenants of a cluster, one can define for each tenant translation patterns that transform the calling and called numbers appropriately and extend the call directly to the called party.

Figure 2-17 *Extension Mapping for a Multitenant Configuration*

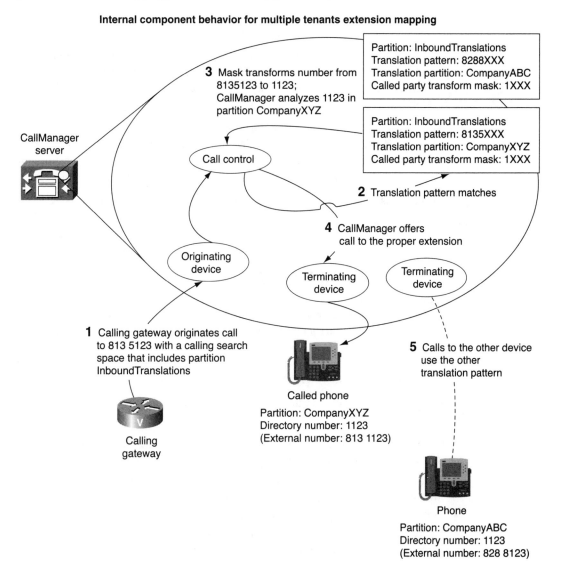

Internal component behavior for multiple tenants extension mapping

Partition: InboundTranslations
Translation pattern: 8288XXX
Translation partition: CompanyABC
Called party transform mask: 1XXX

3 Mask transforms number from 8135123 to 1123; CallManager analyzes 1123 in partition CompanyXYZ

Partition: InboundTranslations
Translation pattern: 8135XXX
Translation partition: CompanyXYZ
Called party transform mask: 1XXX

CallManager server

Call control

2 Translation pattern matches

4 CallManager offers call to the proper extension

Originating device

Terminating device

Terminating device

1 Calling gateway originates call to 813 5123 with a calling search space that includes partition InboundTranslations

5 Calls to the other device use the other translation pattern

Calling gateway

Called phone
Partition: CompanyXYZ
Directory number: 1123
(External number: 813 1123)

Phone
Partition: CompanyABC
Directory number: 1123
(External number: 828 8123)

For example, assume user B's external phone number is 828 2000. User A probably dials this number after first dialing an access code, such as 9. The following steps allow user A's calls to route directly to user B:

Step 1 Define the translation pattern 9 828 2XXX in a partition that is in user A's calling search space.

Step 2   Set the called party transform mask to 2XXX.

Step 3   Set the translation pattern calling search space to a calling search space containing partition XYZ but not ABC.

Step 4   If you have defined external phone number masks for all of your station devices, check the **Use External Phone Number Mask** check box for the translation pattern; otherwise, set a calling party transformation mask of 813 XXXX.

When user A dials user B's external number, the dialed number gets transformed to user B's extension in company XYZ's partition. CallManager uses the results of this transformation for the reanalysis and extends the call directly to user B. The calling party transformation ensures that user B's display reflects user A's external rather than internal number.

User B should have a corresponding translation pattern for calls to company ABC.

Figure 2-18 shows this configuration.

Route Lists and Route Groups

Life is sweet when you have only one gateway for calls to the PSTN. You configure the gateway with the route pattern you wish to use for external calls, and as long as the gateway has an available trunk, it can route calls to the PSTN. But when your network grows beyond the capacity of a single gateway, you are posed with a problem: how do you configure Cisco CallManager so external calls can use both gateways, and how can you make CallManager choose the correct gateway when only one gateway has trunks available?

Route lists and route groups are the answer. This section contains the following subsections:

- "Route List and Group Operation" provides an overview of the process that route lists and route groups use to route calls.

- "Assigning Gateways to Route Groups and Route Groups to Route Lists" discusses the details of assigning gateways and trunks to route groups.

- "Route-Based Calling and Called Party Transformations" discusses how calling and called party transformations on a route list can override the calling and called party transformations you have specified on a route pattern.

Figure 2-18 *Calls Between Tenants*

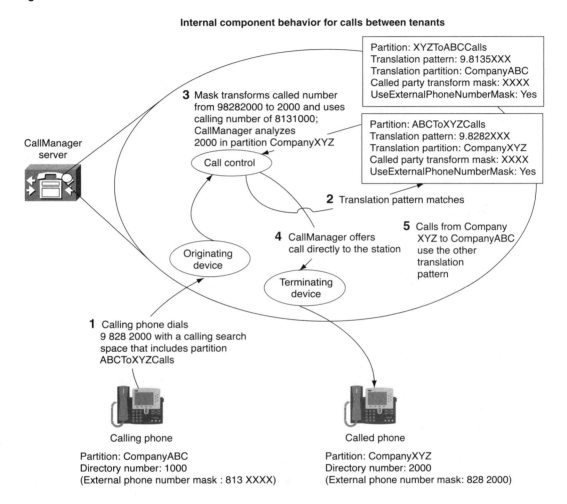

Internal component behavior for calls between tenants

3 Mask transforms called number from 98282000 to 2000 and uses calling number of 8131000; CallManager analyzes 2000 in partition CompanyXYZ

Partition: XYZToABCCalls
Translation pattern: 9.8135XXX
Translation partition: CompanyABC
Called party transform mask: XXXX
UseExternalPhoneNumberMask: Yes

Partition: ABCToXYZCalls
Translation pattern: 9.8282XXX
Translation partition: CompanyXYZ
Called party transform mask: XXXX
UseExternalPhoneNumberMask: Yes

CallManager server

Call control

2 Translation pattern matches

4 CallManager offers call directly to the station

5 Calls from Company XYZ to CompanyABC use the other translation pattern

Originating device

Terminating device

1 Calling phone dials 9 828 2000 with a calling search space that includes partition ABCToXYZCalls

Calling phone
Partition: CompanyABC
Directory number: 1000
(External phone number mask : 813 XXXX)

Called phone
Partition: CompanyXYZ
Directory number: 2000
(External phone number mask: 828 2000)

Route List and Group Operation

The behavior of route lists and route groups is straightforward.

A route group represents several individual trunks and gateways to CallManager as a single high-capacity gateway. A route group is little more than a list. When a route group receives a call, it offers the call to the first device in its list. If the device can accept the call, the route group's job is done. If, however, the device rejects the call (because it is being fully utilized or is out of service), the route group then offers the call to the next device in its list. Only when all devices have rejected the call does the route group reject the call.

Route lists take the abstraction that route groups provide one step further. Although a route group is an ordered list of gateways, a route list is an ordered list of route groups. Where a route group sequentially offers calls to devices in its list, a route list sequentially offers calls to route groups in its list. A route list rejects an outgoing call only when no route groups in its list can accept a call.

Together, route lists and route groups allow you to control which gateways route outgoing calls. They also allow you to order your gateways so that you can route calls over gateways connected to less-expensive service providers before routing calls over gateways to more expensive service providers.

Finally, route lists provide you with additional routing control. The calling and called party transformations on route lists allow you to override, on a route-by-route basis, the calling and called party transformations that you assigned to the route pattern that selected the route list. You may need to override transformations on a particular route basis to properly format a number for the gateway that receives a call.

Figure 2-19 demonstrates these features of a route list.

Figure 2-19 depicts a CallManager that controls two gateways in San Jose and a gateway in Dallas. For routing purposes, the two gateways in San Jose are equivalent—that is, it does not matter which gateway handles a particular call—and they belong to the same route group. The gateway in Dallas belongs in a separate route group.

Both route groups belong to a route list that handles calls from Dallas to San Jose. The route list attempts to provide toll restriction by trying to route the call to the San Jose gateways before the Dallas gateway. The route pattern 9.@ with route filter AREA-CODE == 408 is associated with the route list so that it handles calls to the 408 area code. Furthermore, dialing transformations on the route list convert the 12-digit number that the user dials into a 7-digit number for routing on the San Jose PSTN.

When a user in Dallas dials 9 1 408 555 1212, the route list performs the following steps:

Step 1 First, it attempts to offer the call to the first gateway listed in the San Jose gateways route group. This gateway is an MGCP gateway connected to the San Jose PSTN. Because CallManager manages the state of the trunk interfaces of MGCP gateways, the gateway component can immediately reject the call attempt.

Step 2 Second, it attempts to offer the call to the second gateway listed in the San Jose gateways route group. This gateway is an H.323 gateway, which manages the state of its own trunk interfaces. CallManager offers the call to the gateway, but the gateway rejects the call.

Figure 2-19 *Route List and Route Group Operation*

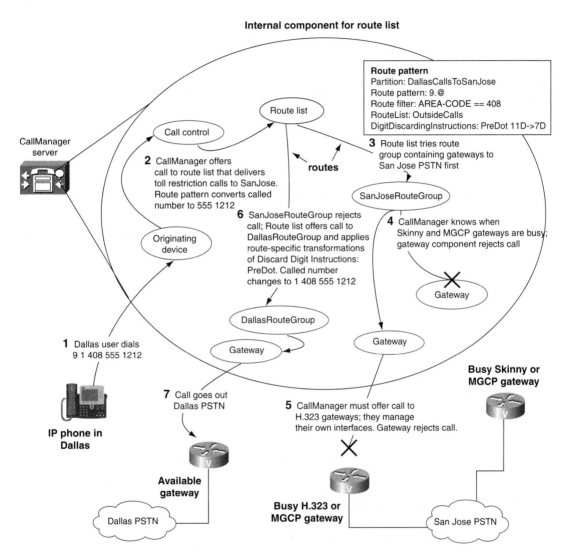

Step 3   The San Jose route group rejects the call that the DallasToSanJose route list extended, so the DallasToSanJose attempts to route the call over the PSTN. It extends the call to the Dallas gateways route group. The transformations that the route pattern applied to the called number to convert it to 555 1212, however, would prevent the call from routing from

Dallas, so dialing transformations on the route override the called party transformations the route pattern applied. The route converts the number to 1 408 555 1212 and then offers the call to the Dallas gateway.

Step 4   The Dallas gateway is available and routes the call over the PSTN.

Assigning Gateways to Route Groups and Route Groups to Route Lists

Route lists are composed of route groups, which, in turn, are composed of gateways. This section describes the process of building the route group and route list structure. It consists of two subsections:

- "Assigning Gateways to Route Groups" defines the criteria by which you determine which gateways should share a route group.
- "Assigning Route Groups to Route Lists" discusses briefly some of the ways that you might choose to place route groups in route lists.

The order of these sections is representative of the way in which you should build your route list structure. First, you start by configuring gateways, which you then place into route groups. Once the route groups are organized, you place them in route lists. Finally, you control routing to these route lists by assigning route patterns.

Assigning Gateways to Route Groups

Each gateway endpoint a CallManager can route to can exist in, at most, one route group. The term *gateway endpoint* is deliberately a bit vague. For purposes of discussing route groups, a gateway endpoint is not necessarily a gateway, nor is it a particular span or channel on the gateway. Rather, an endpoint differs based on the type of gateway.

For example, CallManager has no control over which interface an H.323 gateway, such as the Cisco 2600, routes outbound calls; the H.323 protocol contains no provision for specific interface selection on an H.323 gateway. Rather, the configuration of the Cisco 2600 router determines which interface routes the call. As a result, even if an H.323 gateway contains several individual spans, these spans cannot be added on a span-by-span basis to different route groups. The finest routing granularity that CallManager has for H.323 gateways is the gateway level.

In contrast, CallManager can select individual spans on MGCP gateways with analog interfaces, and as a result, you can place individual spans in different route groups.

Channels of an ISDN or T1 span differ. T1s and E1s are single digital spans that are divided into 23 or 30 logical channels. Although CallManager can route calls to particular channels, it cannot include individual channels in different route groups. You must assign digital interfaces to route groups on a span-by-span basis.

Table 2-50 presents the level of routing granularity CallManager has for each general type of gateway. See Chapter 4 for more information about gateway types.

Table 2-50   *Routing Granularity by Gateway Type*

Gateway Type	Granularity
MGCP gateway analog interfaces	Span
MGCP gateway digital interfaces	Span (but not channel)
H.323 gateways	Gateway

How should you assign interfaces to route groups? The most flexible way is to assign one interface per route group; however, even though the External Route Plan Wizard takes this approach, it is by far the most unwieldy. As a guideline, assuming you do not need to reserve certain interfaces for privileged users, you should place all interfaces that route to the same type of carrier in the same routing area in the same route group.

For instance, assume you have three gateways. Gateway 1 provides access to a PBX. Gateway 2 is hooked up to a local carrier in the PSTN. Gateway 3 is hooked directly to a long distance carrier.

Gateway 1 probably provides access to extensions that the PBX manages. Even if it provides outside access (through trunk interfaces that the PBX manages), it cannot share route group membership with either Gateway 2 or Gateway 3. Because neither Gateway 2 nor Gateway 3 provides access to the PBX extensions, they are not equivalent for routing purposes.

Gateway 2 and Gateway 3 also probably should not share route groups, even though they nominally provide access to the same place.

One reason is that calls to a long distance carrier require only ten digits for long distance calls; long distance carriers that see the initial long distance direct-dial digit reject the call.

In addition, Gateway 3 provides you with less-expensive access for long distance calls, while Gateway 2 provides you with inexpensive local calls. This situation means that you prefer local calls to route first out Gateway 2 and then out Gateway 3 as a last resort, while long distance calls route out Gateway 3 and then Gateway 2 as a last resort. As a route group can list its gateways in only one order, the gateways must be in different route groups to provide you with the behavior you wish.

As a result, Gateway 2 and Gateway 3 are not equivalent for routing purposes, and each must be in its own route group.

If you add a Gateway 4, connected to the PBX, add it to the same route group as Gateway 1, because the gateways are completely equivalent from a routing standpoint.

Assigning Route Groups to Route Lists

Route lists are ordered lists of route groups. Although a given gateway endpoint can exist in at most one route group, a route group can exist in any number of route lists. Figure 2-20 presents a logical view of route lists, route groups, and gateways.

Figure 2-20 *Route Lists, Route Groups, and Gateways*

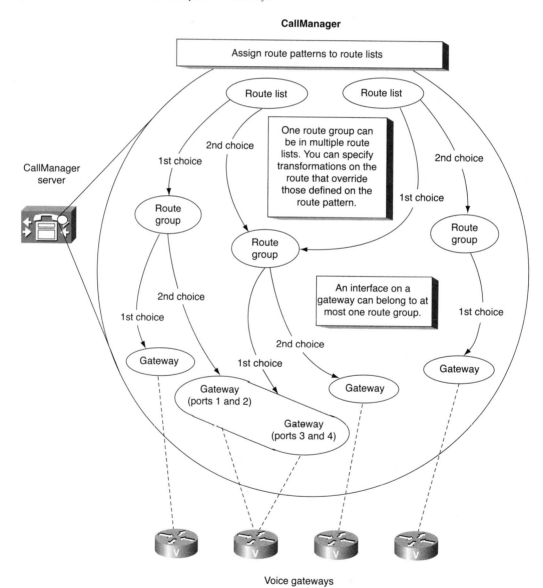

A route list is simply a gateway search pattern. For every unique order in which you wish to attempt to route calls to gateways, you need one route list.

The purpose of a route list is wholly determined by the route pattern you assign to it and the route groups it contains. The External Route Plan Wizard relies heavily on route lists to provide a fine granularity of permission levels for external dialing, and to implement a variety of fallback strategies when gateways are busy or not available. The section "Routing by Geographic Location (or What the External Route Plan Wizard Builds)" describes in detail the way that the External Route Plan Wizard uses route lists for this task.

However, you can use route lists for purposes other than routing based on geographical location. You can use route lists to select outbound gateways based on anticipated cost. For instance, if you have one route group for gateways connected directly to a long distance carrier and another route group for gateways connected to a local carrier, you can define two route lists to route outbound calls accordingly. Figure 2-21 demonstrates such a configuration.

On the first route list, you define a route pattern and route filter that routes local calls. Although the way in which one dials local calls varies among geographical regions in North America, the route pattern 9.@ with route filter AREA-CODE DOES-NOT-EXIST AND LOCAL-AREA-CODE DOES-NOT-EXIST AND INTERNATIONAL-ACCESS DOES-NOT-EXIST AND SERVICE DOES-NOT-EXIST selects all 7-digit calls that a user dials.

For this first route list, you assign as the higher-priority route group the one that contains gateways connected to the local carrier. The lower-priority route group is the one that contains gateways connected to the long distance carrier.

When users dial a number that matches a 7-digit route pattern, CallManager offers the call to the local carrier gateways before trying the long distance carrier gateways.

On the second route list, you define a route pattern and route filter that routes long distance calls, such as 9.@ with route filter AREA-CODE EXISTS OR INTERNATIONAL-ACCESS EXISTS. For this route list, you assign as the higher-priority route group the one that contains gateways connected to the long distance carrier. The lower-priority route group is the one that contains gateways connected to the local carrier.

When users dial a dialed digit string that includes an area code or international access code, CallManager offers the call to the long distance carrier gateways before trying the local carrier gateways.

Figure 2-21 *Route Lists Used for Carrier Selection*

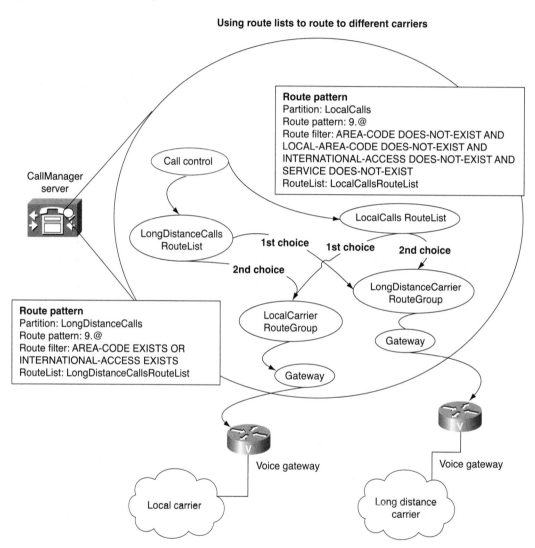

Using route lists to route to different carriers

Route-Based Calling and Called Party Transformations

The association between a route list and one of its route groups is called a *route*. The example in the section "Assigning Route Groups to Route Lists" glosses over a detail about the dialed digits when offering a call to a local carrier versus a long distance carrier.

Elaborating on this detail can demonstrate the way that called party transformations work with routes.

When CallManager offers a long distance call to a local carrier in North America, often the area code must be preceded with a 0 for operator access for a 1 for a direct-dialed call. This is usually not a problem, because users expect to dial these extra digits. On the other hand, when CallManager offers a call to a long distance carrier, any leading 0 or 1 causes the long distance carrier to reject the call.

Also, when CallManager offers a local call to a local carrier, the call is likely to route properly, but when offering a call to a long distance carrier, CallManager must explicitly include the area code as part of the dialed number. In geographical regions with 7-digit dialing, the caller does not dial any area code for calls to local numbers.

When route lists contain route groups that have different requirements for the dialed digits, the calling and called party transformations on the route pattern do not suffice. Instead, CallManager must transform the calling and called parties on a route-by-route basis. When you select a route group from the Route List Configuration screen, Cisco CallManager Administration opens the Route Details Configuration screen, where you can customize the dialing transformations that CallManager applies when it offers a call to the selected route group *from the current route list*.

Each route contains the same calling and called party transformations that exist on the route pattern itself. The calling party transformations are the Prefix Digits, Calling Party Transformation Mask, and the **Use External Phone Number Mask** check box. The called party transformations are the Digit Discarding Instructions, Called Party Transformation Mask, and Prefix Digits.

If all of the calling party transformations for a route are assigned the default values, the calling party transformations of the route pattern take effect. However, if one or both of the calling party transformations on the route is set, the settings on the route take effect, instead of the ones on the route pattern.

Similarly, if all of the called party transformations for a route are assigned the default values, the route pattern's transformations apply. But if any of the settings are assigned on the route, the route's settings take effect instead. To prevent digit discarding instructions from taking effect, the value on the route must be <None>, not NoDigits, which causes the full dialing string to be restored.

Therefore, completing the example begun in the section "Assigning Route Groups to Route Lists" requires specifying, on a route-by-route basis, the called party transformations to apply to the dialed digits.

When a user dials a local call, the user provides a 7-digit number. For the route from the route list to the route group containing gateways to the local carrier, the only transformation that CallManager needs to apply is to discard the PreDot section of the dialed number. However, for the route from the route list to the route group containing long distance gateways, CallManager must not only discard the PreDot section of the dialed number, but also prepend the local area code (for example, 972). (If different calling users can make local calls from different area codes, you must use several route lists.)

When a user dials a long distance call, the user provides an 11-digit number. For the route from the route list to the route group containing gateways to the local carrier, CallManager needs only to discard the PreDot section of the dialed number. However, for the route from the route list to the route group containing long distance gateways, CallManager must discard any leading 0 or 1, as well as the PreDot section of the dialed number. The digit discarding instruction PreDot 11D->10D accomplishes this task. Figure 2-22 presents this configuration.

Calling Search Spaces and Partitions

This section discusses calling search spaces and partitions, a powerful but complex pair of mechanisms by which you can customize dialing restrictions for individual users. Calling search spaces and partitions allow you to administer such policies as routing by geographic location, routing for multiple tenants, and routing by security level of calling user.

The need to configure routing by geographic location occurs because of the nature of VoIP telephony. In an IP network, the location of the endpoints is largely irrelevant. A computer in a cubicle in the United States can connect to a computer in the United Kingdom as easily as it can connect to the computer in the neighboring cubicle. Furthermore, large enterprises can and do interconnect all of their geographically distributed sites so that everyone can access the same data applications. As a result, Cisco CallManager must take into account the fact that two phones controlled by one CallManager may reside in different locations. When one user dials an emergency number, the emergency call may need to route to a different gateway than when a different user dials the same emergency number. In addition, having IP connectivity among all of your enterprise's sites permits you to take advantage of *toll restriction*. Toll restriction is a process by which your enterprise can save money by avoiding routing calls over the PSTN when the endpoints involved in the call are connected by your private data network.

The need to configure routing by organization occurs because you can control devices owned by different companies or departments within a single company using a single CallManager. Perhaps you are an engineer, and your neighbor is in marketing. Because an engineer is likely to require complex computer software packages on the computer, and a marketer is more likely to run standard software, different IS departments might maintain your computers. Customizing call routing by the organization to which a user belongs allows you to set up a common help desk number that users can call when they encounter computer difficulties, but to route those calls to different departments. Taken to an extreme, one CallManager could serve members of completely different companies with completely independent route plans, a configuration termed multitenant or IP Centrex.

Figure 2-22 *Local and Long Distance Route Lists*

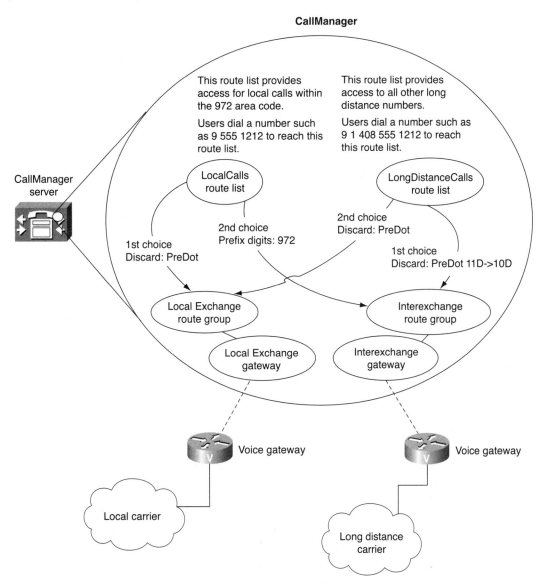

CallManager

This route list provides access for local calls within the 972 area code.

Users dial a number such as 9 555 1212 to reach this route list.

This route list provides access to all other long distance numbers.

Users dial a number such as 9 1 408 555 1212 to reach this route list.

CallManager server

LocalCalls route list

LongDistanceCalls route list

2nd choice
Discard: PreDot

2nd choice
Prefix digits: 972

1st choice
Discard: PreDot

1st choice
Discard: PreDot 11D->10D

Local Exchange route group

Interexchange route group

Local Exchange gateway

Interexchange gateway

Voice gateway

Voice gateway

Local carrier

Long distance carrier

The need to configure routing by security level of calling user occurs because you need to prevent unauthorized users from placing calls that cost your enterprise money. For example, executives within your enterprise might need to make international calls, while office personnel within your enterprise need to be limited to only national numbers, and lobby phones need to be limited to emergency services and internal extensions.

This section contains the following subsections:

- "Calling Search Space and Partitions Analogy" presents an analogy that might clarify how calling search spaces and partitions work.

- "Calling Search Space and Partition Operation" describes the way in which calling search spaces and partitions work. It also presents a simple example and then discusses some unusual aspects of calling search spaces and partitions.

Calling Search Space and Partitions Analogy

Calling search spaces and partitions allow you to configure individualized call routing, because they restrict the route patterns that CallManager can access on behalf of a calling user. When seeking a match for a calling user's dialed number, CallManager restricts its search to only those route patterns that reside in the partitions that are listed in the calling user's calling search space. The following example serves as an analogy that might help explain calling search spaces and partitions.

Figure 2-23 depicts two people, Rita and Dave. Rita wants to call Dave.

For Dave to be called, he must have a phone number. Furthermore, if he wishes people to call him, he needs to list his number in a directory. Assume Dave lists his number in the local white pages. (Whereas in real life, Dave could list his number in multiple directories, for purposes of this analogy, he can choose only one directory in which to list his number.)

To call Dave, Rita needs to know his number. Rita looks for Dave's number by searching through any directories to which she has access.

If she owns the local yellow pages, her little black book, and a copy of the local white pages, when she looks for Dave's number, she finds it in the local white pages. Knowing it, she can dial it, and Dave's phone rings.

Lacking the white pages, however, she is unable to call Dave, because none of the directories she owns lists his number.

The directory in which Dave lists his number is equivalent to the partition in which you list a route pattern, while the list of directories that Rita looks through to find Dave's number is equivalent to the calling search space you assign to calling devices.

Using calling search spaces and partitions allows you to give each device in your network a different picture of the routing landscape. As a result, you can configure your network so that when different users dial the same digit string, CallManager selects different destinations. This ability allows you to solve problems when your users are geographically dispersed, have different calling privileges, and belong to different organizations with independent dial plans. The section "Case Studies" discusses some complex configurations that use calling search spaces and partitions, but first, the section "Calling Search Space and Partition Operation" describes the basics.

Figure 2-23 *Calling Search Space and Partition Analogy*

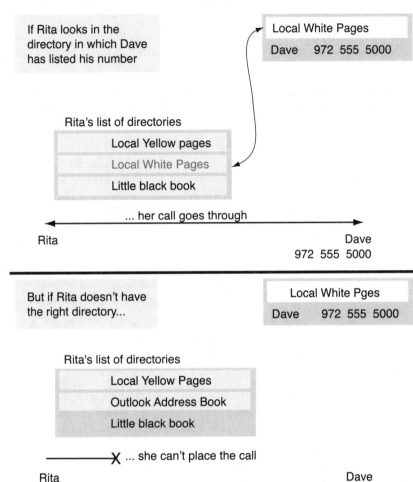

Calling Search Space and Partition Operation

Partitions divide the set of all route patterns into subsets of equally reachable destinations. *Equally reachable* means that a user who can call any single member of the subset can call all members of the subset.

A partition is simply a name you choose to identify a subset. For example, if you need a subset to contain the directory numbers of all user devices in your company (for example, Company ABC), you can create a partition named after your company ("ABC") and then assign the partition to all directory numbers in your system. Any user who can call one of the stations in partition "ABC" can call any of the stations in partition "ABC."

Devices to which you do not assign a partition belong to the **<None>** or *null* partition. Assigning a route pattern to the null partition makes its address visible to every device in the system.

A partition is an attribute of an address. It belongs to *called* entities; it has no bearing on who a device can call. Membership in a partition does not automatically mean that a device can call other devices in the partition. The list of partitions in a device's calling search space is the sole dictator of who it can call.

Partition assignment exists virtually everywhere in CallManager where you assign an address: route patterns, translation patterns, directory numbers, in addition to Meet-Me conference numbers, call park numbers, and so on. The only addresses in CallManager that do not have an associated partition are in the Cisco CallManager Administration **Service Parameters** menu: MessageWaitingOnDN and MessageWaitingOffDN. CallManager places these numbers in the null partition.

Assigning partitions to addresses is not sufficient in itself to allow you to impose dialing restrictions. Partitions merely divide the global address space into meaningful subsets. After assigning partitions, you must assign calling search spaces to your calling users.

A calling search space is nothing more than an ordered list of partitions. A device's calling search space determines the partitions in which it is allowed to look when resolving dialed digit strings to called destinations. Calling search spaces implicitly include the null partition as the last (and thus lowest priority) partition in the list.

Calling search spaces belong to *calling* entities. Naturally, this includes stations and gateways. However, it also includes the CTI interface, which can redirect incoming calls, and call forward, which originates new calls on behalf of a called destination.

Calling search spaces are ordered. However, when analyzing a dialed digit string, the call routing component looks through every partition in the calling search space (including the null partition). Even if the call routing component finds a match in the middle of the routing analysis, closest match routing rules (see the section "Example 2—Closest Match Routing") apply. CallManager seeks the closest match among all the partitions listed, even if the closest match exists in the last partition in a calling search space.

For example, assume that route pattern 1XXX exists in partition A, and the route pattern 1000 exists in partition B. A device with a calling search space that starts with partition A and ends with partition B dials 1000. CallManager extends the call to the device with route pattern 1000, even though 1XXX both matches the dialed number and precedes partition B in the device's calling search space.

Calling search space order comes into play only if two or more partitions contain addresses that match equally closely. In such a case, the call routing component selects the destination from the first partition among the partitions containing a match for the dialed digit string.

To put it another way, CallManager uses the order of partitions in a calling search space only to break ties.

The rest of this subsection covers the following topics:

- "Calling Search Space and Partitions Example" provides a simple example to show how to use calling search spaces and partitions.

- "Calling Search Spaces on Line and on Station" explains why both line and station have calling search space fields.

- "Call Forwarding Calling Search Spaces" describes how the different calling search spaces associated with call forwarding operate.

- "Message Waiting Indicator" describes how CallManager uses calling search spaces and partitions to set voice message waiting indicators.

Calling Search Space and Partitions Example

A multiple tenant installation provides the clearest illustration of how calling search spaces and partitions work. In a multiple tenant environment, one CallManager or CallManager cluster that a single service provider administers serves two independent organizations, each with its own numbering plan. The numbering ranges for each organization may be completely isolated from each other.

Figure 2-24 presents a simple multiple tenant configuration that demonstrates two calls, one that succeeds and one that fails. Company ABC has a station with directory number 1000 and a station with directory number 2000. Company XYZ has a station with directory number 1000 and a station with directory number 3000. Users in Company ABC can call each other but not the users in Company XYZ and vice versa.

Figure 2-24 *Multiple Tenant Example*

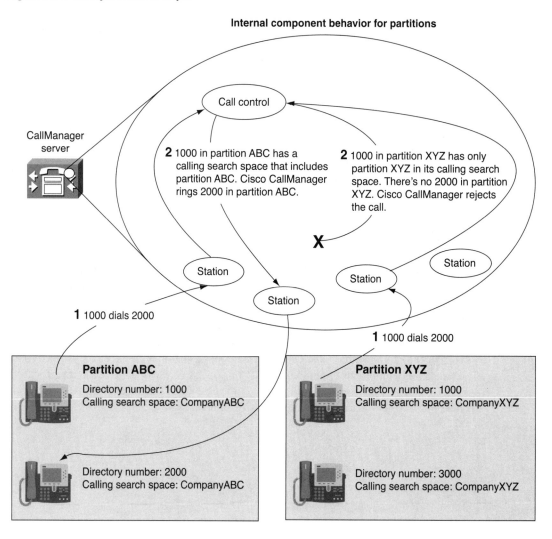

Internal component behavior for partitions

Call control

CallManager
server

2 1000 in partition ABC has a
calling search space that includes
partition ABC. Cisco CallManager
rings 2000 in partition ABC.

2 1000 in partition XYZ has only
partition XYZ in its calling search
space. There's no 2000 in partition
XYZ. Cisco CallManager rejects
the call.

X

Station

Station

Station

Station

1 1000 dials 2000

1 1000 dials 2000

Partition ABC

Directory number: 1000
Calling search space: CompanyABC

Directory number: 2000
Calling search space: CompanyABC

Partition XYZ

Directory number: 1000
Calling search space: CompanyXYZ

Directory number: 3000
Calling search space: CompanyXYZ

In CallManager, no address is complete unless it consists of both a route pattern and a
partition. (Keep in mind that all destinations—directory numbers, call park numbers,
Meet-Me conference numbers—are route patterns.) The previous paragraph, therefore,
commits an egregious error in omitting that the partition is associated with the directory
numbers. If the partition is equivalent to the directory in which one lists a number, it seems
reasonable to list Company ABC's directory numbers in partition ABC and Company
XYZ's directory numbers in partition XYZ. Above all, the stations with directory number

1000 must be listed in different partitions. If you list them in the same directory, they represent a shared line appearance.

Simply setting up the partitions is not enough to complete the routing setup. You must assign each station a calling search space. Because the stations in Company ABC must be able to call other stations in Company ABC, assign them a calling search space that includes partition ABC but not partition XYZ. Assign stations in Company XYZ a calling search space that includes partition XYZ but not ABC.

When the user at directory number 2000 dials 1000, the call routing component looks through the partitions listed in the calling search space to find a match. Because directory number 2000's calling search space contains only partition ABC, the call routing component finds the directory number 1000 in Company ABC. If, on the other hand, the user dials 3000, the call routing component does not find it, and the caller hears reorder tone.

Figure 2-25 presents a modification of the multiple tenant example. Once again, it shows two calls. In this example, users in Company ABC can call not only other Company ABC users, but also Company XYZ users. Users in Company XYZ can still call only Company XYZ users.

Figure 2-25 *Revised Multiple Tenant Example*

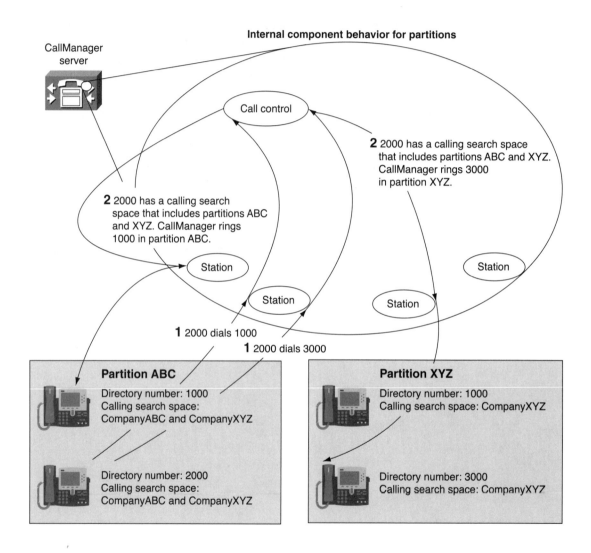

To accomplish this task, the calling search space that users in Company ABC use includes both partition ABC and XYZ. Assume partition ABC is first in the calling search space.

Now, when the user at directory number 2000 dials 1000, the call routing component finds matching route patterns in both partition ABC and XYZ. Because the matches are equal, CallManager still routes the call to the user at directory number 1000 in Company ABC. However, if the user at directory number 2000 dials 3000, the call routing component finds the matching route pattern in partition XYZ and offers a call to the associated destination.

Figure 2-26 revises the example yet again to illustrate closest match routing. Again, the example shows two calls. Assume that the route pattern 3XXX provides Company ABC users access to a PBX through a voice gateway. Because only Company ABC users can dial to the PBX, the route pattern 3XXX is listed in partition ABC.

Figure 2-26 *Revised Multiple Tenant Example*

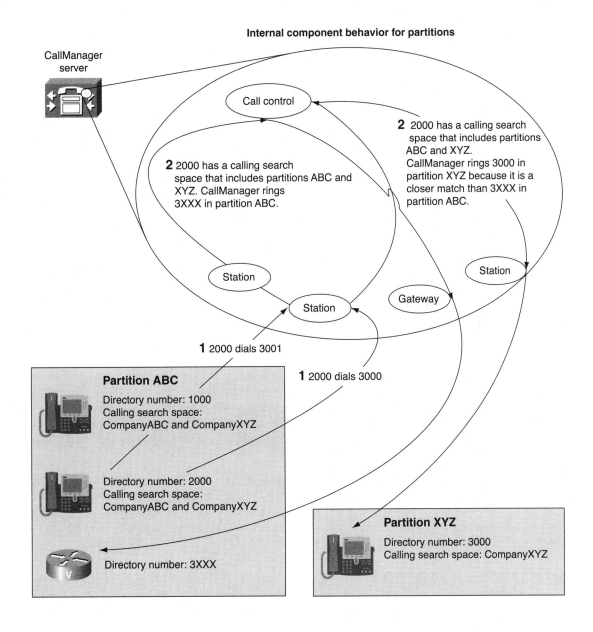

When the user dials directory number 3001, CallManager extends the call to the voice gateway. However, when the user at directory number 2000 dials 3000, the call routes to the user in Company XYZ instead of routing to the PBX, even though the caller's calling search space lists partition ABC before partition XYZ. This behavior occurs because CallManager searches through every listed partition when analyzing dialed digits. Regardless of the order of the partitions in a calling search space, CallManager always delivers a call to the device with the closest matching route pattern.

Calling Search Spaces on Line and on Station

A common question is "Why does a calling search space exist on both the Directory Number Configuration screen and the Phone Configuration screen, and which one should I configure?"

A calling search space exists on the Phone Configuration screen so that different stations with the same line appearance can route differently. Because CallManagers can serve stations that are on different coasts, CallManager must provide a mechanism for routing each station's calls differently. For example, emergency calls from a station in San Jose must route to the San Jose PSTN, even if the San Jose station shares a line appearance with a Dallas station (whose emergency calls must route to the Dallas PSTN).

A calling search space exists on the Directory Number Configuration screen so that different line appearances on a station can route differently. The justification for this configuration is a little more strained. One application is for a security guard desk in a multiple tenant installation. Because different tenants might have phones with identical directory numbers, the security desk needs to be able to place calls to any tenant. As the example in the section "Calling Search Space and Partitions Example" illustrates, calling search space order causes the call routing component to choose from among equal matches to a dialed digit string.

One approach for dealing with the problem is to give the security guard's phone multiple line appearances. When calling one tenant, the guard uses one line appearance; when calling the other, the guard uses the other. If the guard's calling search space was associated solely with the station, such a configuration still would not work. As a result, to have calls from a single station route differently, calling search spaces must also be associated with a line appearance.

If you configure calling search spaces for both a station and a line, CallManager uses both calling search spaces to analyze a dialed digit string. The calling search space associated with the station takes priority when equal matches exist in the station and line calling search spaces.

Call Forwarding Calling Search Spaces

The call forwarding search spaces defined on the Directory Number Configuration screen have some interesting effects. The Directory Number Configuration screen defines three fields that let you set calling search spaces associated with call forwarding: **Call Forward All Calling Search Space**, **Call Forward Busy Calling Search Space**, and **Call Forward No Answer Calling Search Space**.

Using these fields, you can forward a user's calls to destinations the user could not normally call directly. Conversely, you can prevent the user from forwarding calls to certain destinations, even if the user could normally dial such destinations directly. For instance, using call forwarding search spaces, you can prevent a user from forwarding a phone to long distance or international destinations. This sort of configuration prevents a toll-fraud scenario, by which a user call forwards a phone to an international destination and then calls the office phone from home to make a free (to the user but not to your enterprise) long distance call.

The call forward busy and call forward no answer calling search spaces you define always take effect. In particular, when you set the call forward busy or call forward no answer calling search space to **<None>**, CallManager grants the forwarding phone access to only the null partition. The call forward all calling search space operates differently.

If you define a call forward all calling search space that is not **<None>**, it always takes effect. However, if you leave the call forward all calling search space set to **<None>**, when the user forwards the phone from the phone itself or from the user configuration pages, the calling search space that CallManager uses for the call forward is the calling search space that the user uses when placing direct calls.

This behavior allows a user who shares line appearances in different geographical locations (perhaps because the user travels regularly from one location to the other) to forward the phone according to the appropriate geographic location.

Enabling Call Forwarding

CallManager permits you to set up a user's call forward destination from the Directory Number Configuration screen. The user can set up the call forward all destination from the user configuration pages or from the phone itself.

When you set a call forward destination by any of these methods, Cisco CallManager Administration or CallManager do not actually attempt to see whether the destination is valid for call forwarding purposes. For instance, if you have set a call forward busy calling search space that permits only calls to internal extensions, but then you enter a PSTN number in the **Call Forward All Destination** field, CallManager Administration permits you to do so.

When CallManager actually attempts to forward a call when the user is busy, however, the call forward busy calling search space takes effect and prevents the call from routing. The calling user hears reorder.

Calling Search Spaces Interaction with Unified Messaging Systems

Unified messaging systems provide a place where you can centralize your enterprise's data communications. At a minimum, such systems handle the integration of voice mail, e-mail, and fax information. CallManager's direct interaction with such systems is in the voice mail domain. CallManager interacts with unified messaging systems using the following types of interfaces:

- **Skinny Protocol**—Used by unified messaging systems such as Cisco Unity

- **H.323**—Used by unified messaging systems such as Cisco uOne SP

- **Analog gateways managed through a Simple Message Desk Interface (SMDI)**—
  Used by most legacy voice mail systems

All types of unified messaging systems interact with CallManager in essentially the same manner. That is, the nature of the communication between the systems can be boiled down to the following dialog:

- When CallManager offers a call to a unified messaging system, the unified messaging system needs to know to which voice mailbox to redirect the call.

- When a caller has left a message in a voice mailbox, or when a voice mail user deletes all pending messages, CallManager needs to receive a notification from the unified messaging system about which device to notify about the status of pending messages.

The lingua franca of this communication is through directory numbers (from CallManager's point of view) or mailbox numbers (from the unified messaging system's point of view). That is, CallManager delivers a call to a unified messaging system, CallManager provides a mailbox number, and when the unified messaging system delivers a voice mail notification message, the unified messaging system delivers the directory number of the device that should be notified of pending messages. Whether you call it a directory number or a mailbox number, the information the two systems share is simply a number.

CallManager, however, does not deal in bare numbers. Every route pattern and directory number in CallManager's configuration resides in a partition (even if that partition is set to <None>), and when routing calls, CallManager uses the calling search space of the calling device.

Unified messaging systems do not understand calling search spaces and partitions, so CallManager must maintain a calling search space on behalf of the unified messaging system to properly route the message waiting indication. Furthermore, when CallManager has overlapping extensions, as in the case of multitenant installations, it is sometimes necessary to perform number translation to ensure both that messages from two different users do not end up in the same voice mailbox, and that CallManager delivers message waiting notifications to the correct users.

This section covers the following topics:

- "About Cisco Messaging Interface (CMI)" discusses one method that CallManager uses to integrate with voice messaging systems.

- "About Non-SMDI-Based Unified Messaging Systems" discusses another method that CallManager uses to integrate with voice messaging systems.

- "Delivering the Correct Mailbox Number to Unified Messaging" discusses CallManager settings that inform a voice messaging system about which voice messaging box should receive a voice message.

- "Message Waiting Indicator" discusses the CallManager settings that permit a voice messaging system to set message waiting indicators for IP Phones.

About Cisco Messaging Interface (CMI)

Many traditional unified messaging systems connect to CallManager by SMDI. SMDI is a standard protocol specifically designed to permit different telephone systems to integrate with voice mail systems. It uses an RS-232 interface between a telephone system and a voice mail system to communicate information between the systems.

SMDI provides three types of messages:

- Messages about calls from the telephone system to the voice mail system. These messages include the voice messaging box number, whether the call is direct or forwarded, and trunk interface over which the telephone system presents the call.

- Message waiting indications from the voice mail system to the telephone system.

- Error messages between the systems.

CallManager connects to voice messaging systems with the help of the CMI service. The CMI service observes calls from CallManager to a voice mail system and manages the RS-232 SMDI interface between CallManager and the legacy voice mail system.

Figure 2-27 presents a typical connection between CMI and CallManager. When CallManager offers a call to the gateway to the voice mail system, CMI sends an SMDI message to the voice mail system that tells the voice mail system to associate the incoming call with a particular voice messaging box. When the calling user leaves a voice message, the voice mail system, in turn, sends an SMDI message to CMI, which tells CallManager to set the message waiting indicator on the appropriate phone.

Figure 2-27 *SMDI Interaction Between Cisco CallManager and a Legacy Voice Mail System*

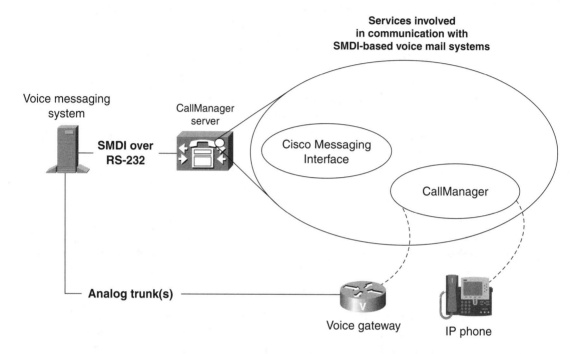

CMI has several service parameters that must be set properly in order to function. CallManager user documentation describes these parameters, but Table 2-51 summarizes the ones that are inextricably intertwined with CallManager call routing settings.

Table 2-51 *CMI Service Parameters Related to Cisco CallManager Routing Settings*

CMI Service Parameter	Description
MWISearchSpace	The calling search space that CMI should use when telling CallManager to set a phone's message waiting indicator. This setting is not a calling search space but rather the list of partitions, separated by colons, that you wish CallManager to search through when seeking a match for the voice messaging box number the voice mail system provides. For instance, if you have two partitions called CompanyABC and CompanyXYZ, specify CompanyABC:CompanyXYZ to have CallManager look through both partitions.
VoiceMailDn	The directory number (or route pattern) associated with the voice mail system. This setting should be identical to the CallManager service parameter VoiceMail.
VoiceMailPartition	The partition associated with the voice mail system. This setting should be identical to CallManager's setting.

About Non-SMDI-Based Unified Messaging Systems

Unified messaging systems that use the Skinny Protocol or H.323 interact directly with CallManager. They do not rely on the CMI service or an RS-232 connection. Rather, when CallManager offers a call to these systems, the call setup message directly provides them with the information that they need to deliver the voice message.

When non-RS-232-based voice messaging systems need to set a message waiting indicator for a particular phone, they do it in a rather unusual manner. CallManager includes a message waiting feature that unified message systems can access by dialing numbers configured in Cisco CallManager Administration.

When a voice messaging system needs to set a message waiting indicator, it calls either the message waiting on or message waiting off directory number and provides the directory number of the phone whose message waiting indicator should change as the calling number. CallManager uses the calling search space you have assigned to the voice messaging system and the calling number that the voice messaging system provides to set the message waiting indicator.

CallManager service parameters control several settings related to voice messaging. Table 2-52 lists these settings.

Table 2-52   *Cisco CallManager Service Parameters Related to Voice Messaging*

Cisco CallManager Service Parameter	Description
MessageWaitingOffDN	The directory number voice messaging systems should dial to extinguish a message waiting indicator.
MessageWaitingOnDN	The directory number voice messaging systems should dial to turn on a message waiting indicator.
MultiTenantMWIMode	When set to T, this setting permits you to use translation patterns to convert voice messaging box numbers back into directory numbers when a voice mail system issues a command to set a message waiting indicator. It defaults to F. The section "Message waiting Indicator" explains this function in more detail.
VoiceMail	The number that Cisco IP Phones should dial when users press the **messages** button.
VoiceMailMaximumHopCount	This value caps the number of times that you can forward one voice mail port to another voice mail port.

Mix and Match

You can mix and match the communication methods between CallManager and your unified messaging system.

For instance, you can run CMI for purposes of delivering the voice message box to the unified messaging system, but have the unified messaging system call CallManager's message waiting numbers to set a phone's message waiting indicator. Or you can have CallManager deliver the voice message box directly over Skinny Protocol or H.323 while delivering the message waiting indicator through SMDI and CMI.

Although in normal cases you would not mix these methods of integration with voice mail, depending on your unified messaging system, mixing these methods may be the only way you can both leave messages in the appropriate mailboxes and receive message waiting indications.

Delivering the Correct Mailbox Number to Unified Messaging

In version 3.1, CallManager introduces a new field on the Directory Number Configuration screen: **Voice Message Box**. Figure 2-28 shows this field.

This field provides a unique voice message box number to the unified messaging system when CallManager needs to deliver a voice message to the user. At the time of this writing, however, not all unified messaging systems handle the voice message box number. The following list describes how CallManager manages the voice message box for different types of unified messaging systems:

- **Skinny Protocol**—Cisco Unity connects to CallManager using the Skinny Client Control Protocol. When CallManager delivers a call to Cisco Unity, it provides both the directory number and voice message box of the phone that received the call. Currently, Cisco Unity determines in which voice message box to leave the caller's message based on the directory number that CallManager provides.

- **H.323**—Cisco uOne SP connects to CallManager using H.323. H.323 provides information about the destination into which a unified messaging system should leave voice mail using the redirecting number information element. If you specify a voice message box for an H.323 endpoint, CallManager uses the voice message box you provide as the redirecting number information element. However, if you leave the **Voice Message Box** field blank, CallManager uses the directory number of the called phone as the redirecting number information element.

  Incidentally, CallManager sets up the redirecting number information element for calls across digital gateways using the same logic. If you connect CallManager to another telephone system with a digital interface, and the other system manages the unified messaging for your enterprise, this behavior can affect the voice message box that the unified messaging receives.

Figure 2-28 *Directory Number Configuration Screen*

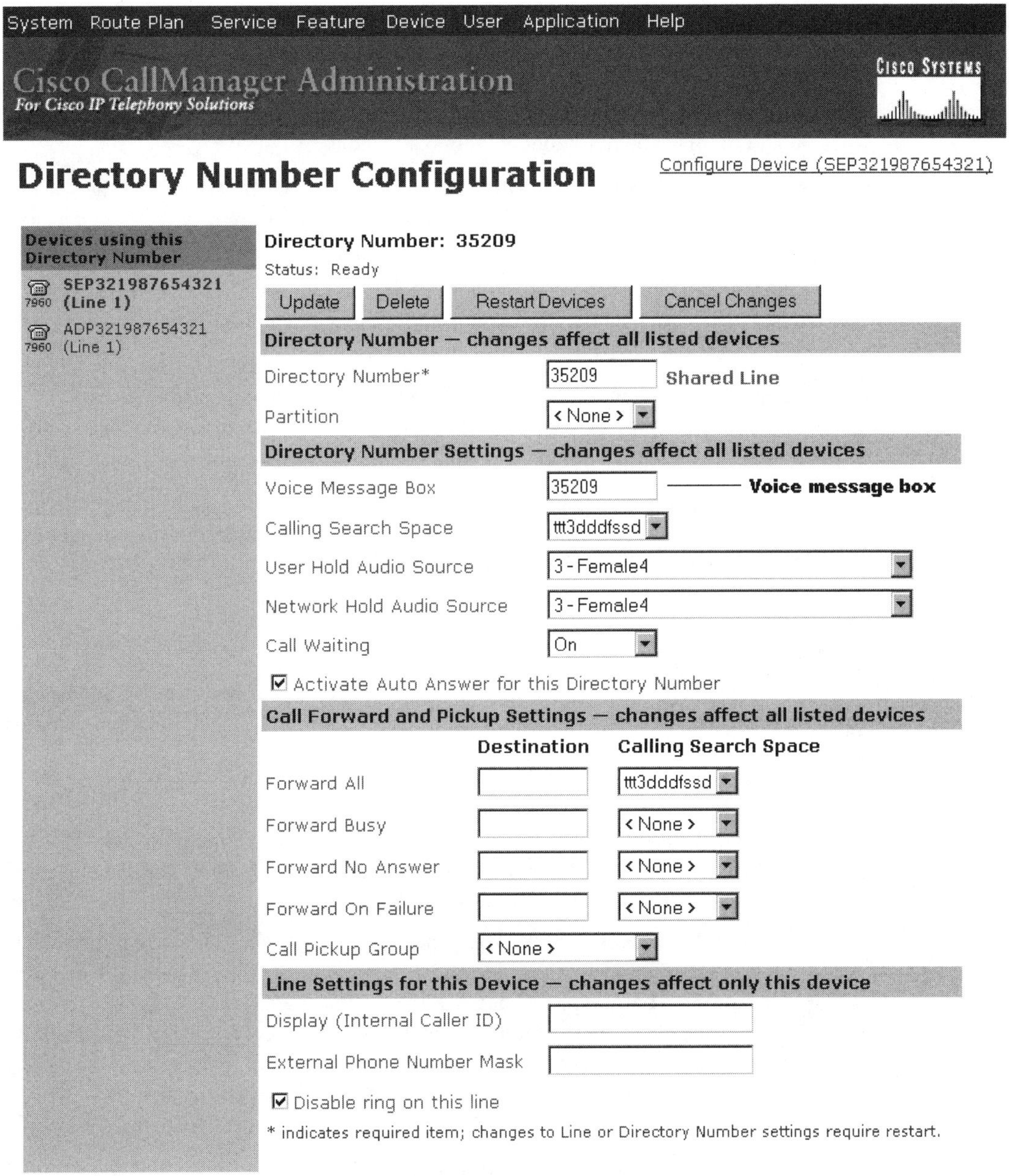

System   Route Plan   Service   Feature   Device   User   Application   Help

Cisco CallManager Administration
For Cisco IP Telephony Solutions

CISCO SYSTEMS

Directory Number Configuration

Configure Device (SEP321987654321)

Devices using this Directory Number

📞 SEP321987654321
7960 **(Line 1)**

📞 ADP321987654321
7960 **(Line 1)**

Directory Number: 35209

Status: Ready

| Update | Delete | Restart Devices | Cancel Changes |

Directory Number — changes affect all listed devices

Directory Number*   35209   **Shared Line**

Partition   < None >

Directory Number Settings — changes affect all listed devices

Voice Message Box   35209 ——— **Voice message box**

Calling Search Space   ttt3dddfssd

User Hold Audio Source   3 - Female4

Network Hold Audio Source   3 - Female4

Call Waiting   On

☑ Activate Auto Answer for this Directory Number

Call Forward and Pickup Settings — changes affect all listed devices

	Destination	**Calling Search Space**
Forward All		ttt3dddfssd
Forward Busy		< None >
Forward No Answer		< None >
Forward On Failure		< None >
Call Pickup Group	< None >	

Line Settings for this Device — changes affect only this device

Display (Internal Caller ID)

External Phone Number Mask

☑ Disable ring on this line

* indicates required item; changes to Line or Directory Number settings require restart.

For instance, if phone 1000 calls phone 2000 controlled by CallManager, and CallManager subsequently forwards the call to the unified messaging system on the other telephone system, the redirecting number information element tells the other system that the call has previously been forwarded so that the voice messaging system can deliver any voice message to the correct voice message box. For the redirecting number, CallManager uses the voice messaging box you have configured for phone 2000, or 2000 if you have not configured a voice message box.

- **Analog gateways connected with CMI and SMDI**—CMI always uses the voice message box you configure when informing a voice messaging system about a call.

The **Voice Message Box** parameter allows you to deal with multiple tenant configurations, because voice messaging systems do not understand calling search spaces or partitions. Without the voice message box information, CallManager can provide only the directory number of a called phone to a voice messaging system.

In a multiple tenant configuration, two users may have the same directory number. CallManager does not provide partition information to voice messaging systems, so how can these systems decide which voice message box to deliver the voice mail message to?

They cannot. Therefore, by providing the **Voice Message Box** field, CallManager permits you to map duplicate directory numbers to unique ones (for example, the external numbers by which users in the PSTN call your enterprise).

Message Waiting Indicator

When a message is left for a user in a voice messaging system, the system tells CallManager to turn on the message waiting indicator for the user by one of the following two methods:

- The voice messaging system sends an SMDI command to CMI containing the voice message box that received a voice message to CMI.

- The voice messaging system calls CallManager's message waiting on and off numbers and provides as the calling number the voice message box of the phone whose message waiting indicator must be changed.

CallManager uses the number that the voice message box provides and the calling search space parameter associated with the voice mail system to locate the phone whose message waiting indicator must be changed. (For CMI, the calling search space CallManager uses for this lookup is the CMI service parameter **MWISearchSpace**. For the message waiting on and off numbers, the calling search space CallManager uses for this lookup is the calling search space of the voice mail interface.) CallManager performs this lookup by using its call routing tables.

When the voice message box and directory number are the same, this lookup locates the number of the appropriate phone. But when the voice message boxes and the directory numbers of your phones differ, as is usually the case in multitenant installations, you must use translation patterns to direct the message waiting indicator to the correct phone. Using translation patterns for this purpose requires that you set the CallManager service parameter **MultiTenantMWIMode** to T. Figure 2-29 shows the behavior that occurs when a voice messaging system attempts to set the message waiting indicator for the phone with voice message box 9725551212. It depicts a scenario that uses the message waiting on number. The same configuration works for the SMDI method of setting the message waiting indicator.

The example relies on the provision of the route and translation patterns in Table 2-53.

Table 2-53 *Patterns for Transforming Voice Messaging Box Numbers to Set Message Waiting Indicators*

Configured Route and Translation Patterns	Comments
Partition: MessageWaiting Translation pattern: 972813XXXX Translation calling search space: CompanyABC Called party transformation mask: XXXX	Translation calling search space CompanyABC contains partition CompanyABC.
Partition: CompanyABC Route pattern: 1212	1212 is a phone with directory number 1212.

When a voice messaging system calls the message waiting on number, CallManager performs the following steps:

Step 1   The voice messaging system calls CallManager's message waiting on directory number (8000) and specifies as the calling number 9725551212: the voice message box of the phone whose message waiting indicator CallManager must set.

Step 2   The message waiting feature takes the information about the calling device (the calling search space and calling party number) and asks the call routing component of CallManager to look up the device. You can think of this process as the message waiting feature placing a special message-waiting-indicator call in which the *calling* party information that the voice messaging system provides becomes the *called* party information for setting the message waiting indicator.

Step 3   The lookup matches the translation pattern 972555XXXX, because the calling party number—9725551212—becomes the called party number for the message-waiting-indicator call. CallManager applies the called party transformation mask XXXX to the number 972555XXXX to convert the called number to 1212.

Figure 2-29 *Transforming Voice Messaging Box Numbers to Set Message Waiting Indicators*

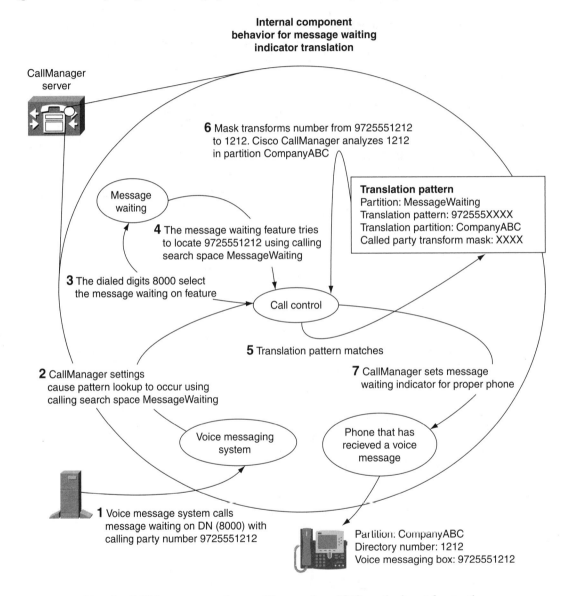

Internal component behavior for message waiting indicator translation

CallManager server

6 Mask transforms number from 9725551212 to 1212. Cisco CallManager analyzes 1212 in partition CompanyABC

Message waiting

Translation pattern
Partition: MessageWaiting
Translation pattern: 972555XXXX
Translation partition: CompanyABC
Called party transform mask: XXXX

4 The message waiting feature tries to locate 9725551212 using calling search space MessageWaiting

3 The dialed digits 8000 select the message waiting on feature

Call control

5 Translation pattern matches

2 CallManager settings cause pattern lookup to occur using calling search space MessageWaiting

7 CallManager sets message waiting indicator for proper phone

Voice messaging system

Phone that has recieved a voice message

1 Voice message system calls message waiting on DN (8000) with calling party number 9725551212

Partition: CompanyABC
Directory number: 1212
Voice messaging box: 9725551212

Step 4   CallManager uses the resulting number, 1212, as the input for another analysis attempt. The calling search space CallManager uses for the analysis attempt is the calling search space of the translation pattern,

CompanyABC. This attempt matches the phone with directory number 1212. CallManager sets the message waiting indicator of the phone with dialed digits of 1212.

Case Studies

This section of the document describes how all of the components described in this chapter—route patterns, route filters, calling and called party transformations, translation patterns, calling search spaces, and partitions—work together to allow you to configure complex routing.

This section covers the following topics:

- "Routing by Class of Calling User" discusses routing by class of calling user. This section shows you how to define three different degrees of external access so that your most trusted users can place all classes of calls, your average users can place a more restrictive class of calls, and your untrusted users can place only the most restrictive calls.

- "Routing by Geographic Location (or What the External Route Plan Wizard Builds)" discusses routing by geographic location in a geographically distributed area. It describes both toll-restriction and scenarios where toll restriction calls must fall back to the PSTN because of fully utilized or nonfunctional gateways.

Routing by Class of Calling User

A common requirement in telephone networks is to be able to restrict the types of calls that users can make. For example, a company executive might have unrestricted dialing privileges: emergency, local, long distance, and international calls are equally accessible. On the other hand, a phone in a lobby might be able to call only internal extensions and emergency numbers. In between these extremes are those phones that you want to prevent from accessing Caribbean area codes and toll services (such as 900 services).

Configuring calling user restrictions uses several of the concepts this chapter introduces:

- Naturally, user restrictions require route patterns.

- Typically, the numbers that you wish to restrict are those in the PSTN. This requirement means that the call routing component must be able to distinguish between types of calls to the PSTN, which, in turn, indicates the use of route filters.

- If you wish to apply different restrictions to different users, you must use calling search spaces and partitions.

Figure 2-30 provides a representative example that you can refer to when configuring your dial plan to deny certain types of calls to certain users. It concerns itself solely with calls to the PSTN.

Figure 2-30 *User Restrictions*

Lobby phone
Can call other internal extensions and
emergency numbers

Office personnel phone
Can call internal extensions,
emergency numbers, and long
distance numbers, but not
international or 900 numbers

Executive phone
Can call internal extensions,
emergency numbers, and long
distance numbers, including
international and 900 numbers

Voice gateway
Provides access to the public
network

Company ABC requires three levels of outside calling privileges. Executives have no
restrictions on calls they can place. Office personnel can place calls to emergency numbers,
local numbers, and long distance numbers, but they cannot place international calls or calls
to 900 numbers. Lobby phones can place calls only to emergency numbers.

Company ABC also has a single gateway, which employees of all levels use for outside
calls. This gateway is not in a route list. The access code for calls to the PSTN is 9, and
Cisco CallManager strips this access code before offering the call to the PSTN.

User-Restriction Configuration Process

The first step in configuring the user restrictions is to define route pattern and filter
combinations for the different levels of PSTN access.

Executives have the simplest route pattern configuration, because they can call all PSTN
numbers. The route pattern is 9.@ (which matches 9 followed by any valid number in the
North American numbering plan). You must strip the initial 9 before CallManager offers the
call to the gateway, so associate digit discarding instructions of PreDot with the route

pattern. Assign this route pattern to partition Executives. Table 2-54 shows the route pattern configuration information for an executive's PSTN access.

Table 2-54   *Executive Access Route Pattern Information*

Field	Value
Partition	Executives
Route pattern	9.@
Route filter	<None>
Digit discarding instructions	PreDot
Route This Pattern	

Office personnel have a more complex route pattern configuration. Office personnel can call some but not all PSTN numbers. This restriction requires the use of route filters.

Office personnel cannot dial two types of numbers. The first type, international numbers, is easy to deal with. Defining the route filter NonInternationalCalls with value INTERNATIONAL-ACCESS DOES-NOT-EXIST and associating it with route pattern 9.@ instructs CallManager to route all PSTN calls that do not contain the North American international access code of 011. This route pattern is assigned to partition OfficePersonnel.

Preventing office personnel from dialing numbers with the area code 900 is trickier. Defining a route filter with value AREA-CODE == 900 does the exact opposite of what is intended: users can dial only those PSTN numbers where the area code is 900. But there is no not-equals operator, so how does one block 900 numbers?

The solution lies in closest match routing. Rather than attempting to configure a single route pattern and filter that accomplishes all of the restrictions, you can define an additional route pattern and route filter to give restricted numbers special treatment. In this case, if you define the route filter 900Numbers with value AREA-CODE == 9XX, associate it with route pattern 9.@ in partition OfficePersonnel, and then check the **Block This Pattern** check box, when an office member dials a number with an area code of 900, closest match routing will cause the restrictive route pattern (9.@ where AREA-CODE == 900) to match in preference to the more general route pattern (which does not constrain AREA-CODE at all). As a result, CallManager applies the blocked treatment. Calls to other area codes, however, do not match the restrictive route pattern at all, so those calls go through just fine. Table 2-55 shows the route pattern configuration information for an office member's PSTN access.

Table 2-55 *Office Personnel Access Route Pattern Information*

Field	Value
Partition	OfficePersonnel
Route pattern	9.@
Route filter	InternationalCalls (INTERNATIONAL-ACCESS DOES-NOT-EXIST)
Digit discarding instructions	PreDot
Route This Pattern	
Partition	OfficePersonnel
Route pattern	9.@
Route filter	900Numbers (AREA-CODE == 900)
Digit discarding instructions	PreDot
Block This Pattern	

Lobby phones have the most restrictive routing restrictions of all; they can call only 911. Defining the route filter 911Calls with value SERVICE == 911 and associating it with route pattern 9.@ instructs CallManager to route all PSTN calls that are specifically intended for 911. You must strip the initial 9 before CallManager offers the call to the gateway, so associate digit discarding instructions of PreDot with the route pattern. Assign the route pattern to partition LobbyPhones. Table 2-56 shows the route pattern configuration information for a lobby phone's public access.

Table 2-56 *Lobby Phone Access Route Pattern Information*

Field	Value
Partition	LobbyPhones
Route pattern	9.@
Route filter	911Calls (SERVICE == 911)
Digit discarding instructions	PreDot
Route This Pattern	

The configuration is not completed. Although the route patterns on the gateway have been configured properly, the calling users have not. You must define calling search spaces for the calling users. Furthermore, it is a good idea to put your phones' extensions within their own partition. For this purpose, define partition ABC for the phones within the enterprise.

Table 2-57 lists all defined partitions and a short description of the types of route patterns each contains.

Table 2-57   *Partitions for User-Restriction Example*

Partition Name	Description
ABC	Contains all phones within the enterprise
LobbyPhones	Contains gateway route patterns that provide access solely to emergency services
OfficePersonnel	Contains gateway route patterns that provide access to noninternational and non-900-number calls
Executive	Contains gateway route patterns that provide access to all external numbers

To complete the configuration, you must define the calling search spaces defined in Table 2-58.

Table 2-58   *Calling Search Spaces for User-Restriction Example*

Calling Search Space	Partitions Contained Within
Executives	ABC, Executives
OfficePersonnel	ABC, OfficePersonnel
LobbyPhones	ABC, LobbyPhones
Gateway	ABC

Calling search space Executives contains partitions ABC and Executives, which permit executive phones to call internal extensions and all PSTN numbers; calling search space OfficePersonnel contains partitions ABC and OfficePersonnel, which permits access to internal extensions and noninternational, nontoll PSTN numbers; calling search space LobbyPhones contains partitions ABC and LobbyPhones, which permits access to internal extensions and emergency PSTN numbers. Finally, it is important not to forget the gateway, which needs to be able to offer PSTN calls to the users. Calling search space Gateway provides access to internal extensions. Assigning the appropriate partition and calling search space to each phone and to the gateway completes the configuration and provides each user with the appropriate level of PSTN access. Figure 2-31 presents a representation of the final configuration.

Figure 2-31 *User Restriction Configuration Diagram*

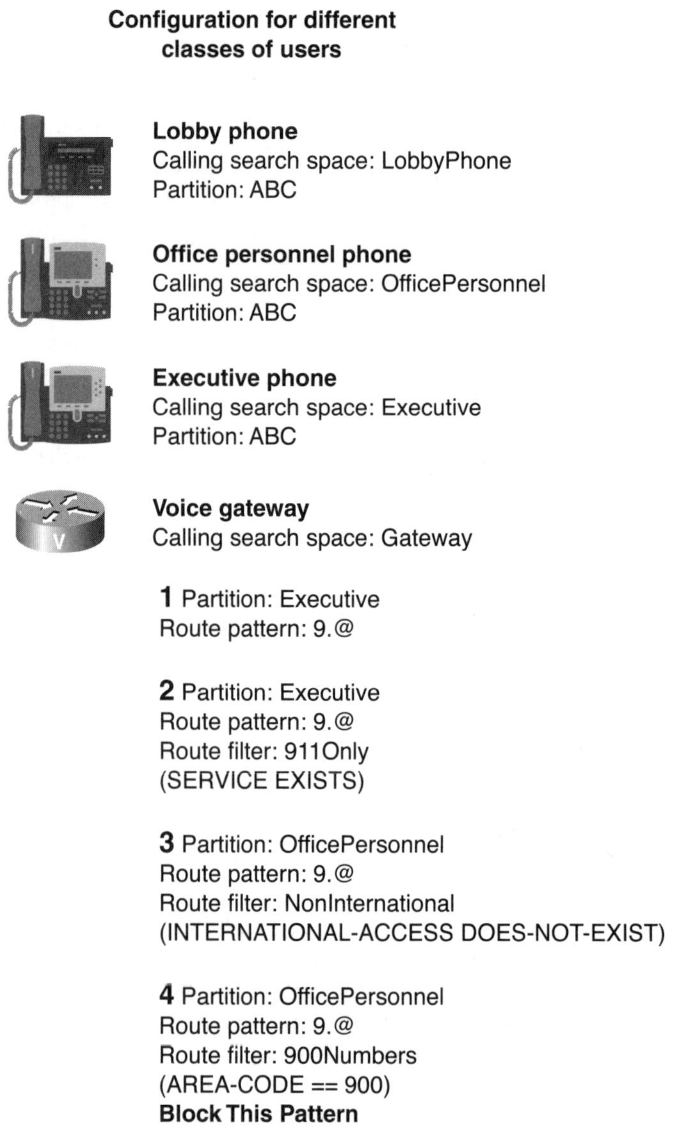

Configuration for different classes of users

Lobby phone
Calling search space: LobbyPhone
Partition: ABC

Office personnel phone
Calling search space: OfficePersonnel
Partition: ABC

Executive phone
Calling search space: Executive
Partition: ABC

Voice gateway
Calling search space: Gateway

1 Partition: Executive
Route pattern: 9.@

2 Partition: Executive
Route pattern: 9.@
Route filter: 911Only
(SERVICE EXISTS)

3 Partition: OfficePersonnel
Route pattern: 9.@
Route filter: NonInternational
(INTERNATIONAL-ACCESS DOES-NOT-EXIST)

4 Partition: OfficePersonnel
Route pattern: 9.@
Route filter: 900Numbers
(AREA-CODE == 900)
Block This Pattern

For explanatory purposes, this section uses a naming convention for the gateway partitions designed to indicate which users can call which route patterns. The section "Routing by Geographic Location (or What the External Route Plan Wizard Builds)" presents a different naming convention that indicates type of call permitted that is more flexible in the long run.

Routing by Geographic Location (or What the External Route Plan Wizard Builds)

A major advantage of routing voice over an IP network is that it allows users served by one Local Access and Transport Area (LATA) to access gateways in a different LATA without actually having to make a call through the PSTN. This can allow you to manage the costs of your telephone network by bypassing the PSTN when possible.

The External Route Plan Wizard is an automated tool that allows you to set up a toll bypass configuration in North America more easily. It is ideal if you have a distributed enterprise connected by a very high bandwidth, very redundant data network with gateways in different call routing areas.

The External Route Plan Wizard asks you about the locations in which your gateways reside and asks you to describe what area codes are local to each gateway. It also asks you general questions about how you want calls to be routed. Given this information, it organizes your gateways into route groups and puts the route groups into many different route lists. With each route list, the External Route Plan Wizard associates a narrow range of calls, for instance, emergency calls or international calls. Then, the External Route Plan Wizard sets up six levels of user access per routing area in your enterprise: emergency calls only; emergency and internal calls only; emergency, internal, and local calls only; emergency, internal, local and toll bypass calls only; emergency, internal, local, and long distance calls only; all calls, including international. Once the External Route Plan Wizard finishes, you can browse to each phone in your enterprise, assign the appropriate calling search space, and expect calls from your phones to route appropriately.

The chief drawback of the External Route Plan Wizard is that it generates immense amounts of data. Each gateway in your organization gets its own route group, each location generates six route lists, and each location generates seven partitions and six calling search spaces.

This section simply describes what the External Route Plan Wizard does to set up a toll bypass configuration. If you are unable to use the External Route Plan Wizard because you run a non-North American site, if you simply want to create a leaner, meaner version of a geographically aware routing plan, if you run a site that manages multiple tenants, or if you simply want an explanation of the prodigious output that the External Route Plan Wizard generates, then keep reading.

A toll bypass configuration draws on almost every one of the components described in this chapter:

- Naturally, a toll bypass configuration requires route patterns.

- A toll bypass configuration requires the dial plan to be able to distinguish types of outside calling. For instance, emergency calls must route out only those gateways local to the calling user. Local calls should preferentially route out gateways local to the calling user. On the other hand, calls to other LATAs where you manage gateways need to route preferentially to those remote gateways. Finally, long distance and international calls can route out any gateway in the network. The need to distinguish between types of PSTN call requires the use of route filters.

- When a user dials a long distance number that routes to a remote gateway, usually the number the user dialed is not a valid number when dialed from the remote gateway itself. From the user's point of view, the number is a long distance number, so CallManager should accommodate a long distance numbering format. For instance, North American users typically dial 11 digits when dialing another geographic region. But the same destination as dialed by a user in the remote location is either seven or ten digits. Allowing the call to route properly once it reaches a remote location requires using called party transformations.

- Calling number is also an issue when a call crosses LATA boundaries. If a user in Boston places a toll bypass call through a gateway in Orlando, how should CallManager represent the calling number? If it presents a Boston calling number, the Orlando central office may complain, because it does not recognize the number of the caller. It is often necessary either to transform the calling number to an attendant number in the remote location or to alias the calling number to a number that is valid in the remote location. These modifications require the use of calling party transformations.

- If locations contain more than one gateway, route lists provide a way to maximize gateway usage.

- Users in different locations need to reach different locations, even if they dial the same digit strings. For instance, a user in Dallas who dials 911 needs to reach Dallas emergency services, while a Boston user needs to reach Boston emergency services. Giving different users different views of the same network requires the use of calling search spaces and partitions.

Geographical Routing Problem Description

Figure 2-32 provides a representative example that you can refer to when configuring your dial plan to handle geographical routing configurations.

Company ABC has two locations, one in Dallas and one in San Jose. A high-bandwidth, highly redundant IP network connects the sites. Each site runs CallManager. The CallManagers are clustered. Where the devices register is not relevant for routing purposes; a San Jose phone registered to the Dallas CallManager still physically resides in San Jose and routes as a San Jose phone.

There are three levels of PSTN access. Lobby phones can dial only internal extensions and emergency numbers. Office personnel can dial local and long distance calls, in addition to internal extensions and emergency numbers. Executives can dial all of the aforementioned types of calls, plus international calls.

Figure 2-32 *Geographical Routing Example*

San Jose devices

30000 and 31100
Office personnel phones that can call internal
extensions and non-toll, non-international PSTN
numbers

31000
Lobby phone that can call only extensions and
emergency numbers

31200
Executive phone that can call internal
extensions and all PSTN numbers

Gateway to San Jose PSTN
San Jose users use this gateway for their emergency
calls and local calls. CallManager prefers to
route their long distance and international calls out
this gateway.

Dallas users use this gateway for calls to the San
Jose public network. They use this gateway as a
backup for their long distance and international calls.

Dallas devices

40000 and 41150
Office personnel phones that can call internal
extensions and non-toll, non-international PSTN
numbers

41050
Lobby phone that can call only extensions and
emergency numbers

41250
Executive phone that can call internal
extensions and all PSTN numbers

Gateway to Dallas PSTN
Dallas users use this gateway for their emergency
calls and local calls. CallManager prefers to
route their long distance and international calls out
this gateway.

San Jose users use this gateway for calls to the Dallas
public network. They use this gateway as a
backup for their long distance and international calls.

The San Jose site has many phones, but this example concentrates on just four phones. 30000 is the attendant (who has office member access privileges), 31000 is a lobby phone, 31100 is an office member phone, and 31200 is an executive phone. One gateway in San Jose provides access to the PSTN. The gateway is connected to the 555 exchange in the 408 area code. The PSTN has assigned a range of 5000–5999 to the San Jose site. For purposes of this example, users in San Jose dial seven digits to make local calls.

The Dallas site also has many phones, but this example only needs to describe four of them. 40000 is the attendant (who has office personnel access privileges), 41050 is a lobby phone, 41150 is an office member's phone, and 41250 is an executive phone. A gateway in Dallas provides access to the PSTN. The gateway is connected to the 555 exchange in the 972 area code. The PSTN has assigned a range of 2000–2999 to the Dallas site. Users in Dallas dial ten digits to make local calls.

Outbound calls route according to Table 2-59.

Table 2-59   *Routing Preferences for Geographical Routing Example*

Calls from San Jose...	
...to a San Jose extension...	...route directly to the extension
...to a Dallas extension...	...route directly to the extension
...to emergency numbers...	...route out the San Jose gateway only
...to local numbers...	...route out the San Jose gateway only
...to Dallas local numbers...	...route out the Dallas gateway, but fall back to the San Jose gateway as a long distance call if the Dallas gateway is busy or not available
...to long distance numbers...	...route out the San Jose gateway, but fall back to the Dallas gateway if the San Jose gateway is busy or not available
...to international numbers...	...route out the San Jose gateway, but fall back to the Dallas gateway if the San Jose gateway is busy or not available
Calls from Dallas...	
...to a San Jose extension...	...route directly to the extension
...to a Dallas extension...	...route directly to the extension
...to emergency numbers...	...route out the Dallas gateway only
...to local numbers...	...route out the Dallas gateway only
...to San Jose local numbers...	...route out the San Jose gateway, but fall back to the Dallas gateway as a long distance call if the San Jose gateway is busy or not available

Table 2-59   *Routing Preferences for Geographical Routing Example (Continued)*

Calls from Dallas...	
...to long distance numbers...	...route out the Dallas gateway, but fall back to the San Jose gateway if the Dallas gateway is busy or not available
...to international numbers...	...route out the Dallas gateway, but fall back to the San Jose gateway if the Dallas gateway is busy or not available

Building a toll bypass configuration occurs in two phases.

- The section "Outbound Dialing" describes how to build the route groups and route lists for external access, how to create route filters for different levels of user access and routing by geographical region, how to transform the calling and called parties, and how to assign calling search spaces.

- The section "Inbound Dialing" describes how to build translation patterns to map external phone numbers to internal extensions and how to assign calling search spaces to control the destinations inbound gateway calls can reach.

Outbound dialing

Configuring outbound dialing consists of the following steps:

- "Route Group and Route List Creation" describes how to assign the gateways to route groups and how to build route lists to provide varied access to the route groups.

- "Route Filter Creation and Route Pattern Assignment" describes the route patterns and filters you must assign to the route lists to ensure that a calling user's call routes out the proper gateways.

- "Applying Calling and Called Party Transformations" describes the transformations you must apply to the calling and called numbers for the PSTN to properly process your calls.

- "Calling Search Space Creation, Calling Search Space Assignment, and Phone Configuration" describes how to assign calling search spaces to each user so that each user has the proper level of external access.

Route Group and Route List Creation

This subsection describes the first step in creating a toll bypass network: creation of the route groups and route lists that the toll bypass network uses.

Defining the route groups is simple. One gateway provides access to the San Jose PSTN; the other provides access to the Dallas PSTN. Each needs its own route group. Assign the San Jose gateway to route group SanJoseGateways and the Dallas gateway to route group DallasGateways.

Before defining the route lists, a concept introduced in Table 2-59 must be discussed. Table 2-59 introduces a concept that the External Route Plan Wizard uses, *fallback*. Fallback is the process of offering a call to a less desirable gateway after all desirable gateways have been exhausted.

The External Route Plan Wizard uses three types of fallback:

- *Local call fallback* is the strangest of the bunch. The External Route Plan Wizard prefers to route local calls from a given location only out gateways that reside in that location. If local call fallback is enabled, after all local gateways have been tried, CallManager routes local calls to gateways in different geographic locations. This process transforms a local call into a long distance call, potentially an expensive proposition.

- *Toll bypass fallback* is more straightforward. If a caller makes a call to a remote geographic location and CallManager can determine that a gateway in the IP network resides in that location, CallManager prefers to route calls over the IP network to the remote gateway, rather than routing calls to a local gateway that must route them through the PSTN. This process is called *toll bypass*, and it requires turning a long distance call into a local call. But if all remote gateways are busy or not available, toll bypass fallback tells CallManager to go ahead and route the call out a local gateway.

- *Long distance and international fallback* extends the External Route Plan Wizard's default option for routing long distance and international calls. The External Route Plan Wizard prefers to route long distance and international calls out a gateway that is local to the calling user. Long distance and international fallback allows CallManager to try gateways in remote locations if the local gateways are busy or not available.

Table 2-59 describes toll bypass fallback and long distance and international fallback, but not local fallback. Some calls fall back from Dallas gateways to San Jose gateways, while others fall back from San Jose gateways to Dallas gateways. Other types of calls do not fall back at all.

Each type of fallback selects route groups somewhat differently. Every time that route group selection order must vary, one must create a route list. If different routes need different transformations, more route lists may be required. Table 2-60 shows which route lists need to be created as a result of the fallback strategy.

Table 2-60 *Route List Requirements*

Calls from San Jose...	Description
...to emergency numbers route out the San Jose route group only	These calls require no route-specific transformations.
...to local numbers route out the San Jose route group only	**Action:** Create route list SanJoseLocal, which contains only the San Jose route group.
...to Dallas local numbers route out the Dallas route group, but fall back to the San Jose route group as a long distance call if the Dallas route group is busy or not available	This call requires route-specific transformations. When a user dials an 11-digit Dallas number, the call must be converted to a local call before it routes out the Dallas gateway, but if it falls back to the San Jose gateway, all 11 digits must be sent.
	In addition, if a toll bypass call from a San Jose calling number routes out a Dallas gateway, it is sometimes necessary to provide a Dallas calling number so that the local carrier does not reject the call. The Dallas attendant number can serve this purpose.
	Action: Create route list TollBypassToDallas, which contains the Dallas route group followed by the San Jose route group.
...to long distance numbers route out the San Jose route group, but fall back to the Dallas route group if the San Jose route group is busy or not available ...to international numbers route out the San Jose route group, but fall back to the Dallas route group if the San Jose route group is busy or not available	These calls require route-specific transformations. If a long distance call from a San Jose calling number routes out a Dallas gateway, it is sometimes necessary to provide a Dallas calling number so that the local carrier does not reject the call. The Dallas attendant number can serve this purpose. **Action:** Create route list SanJoseLongDistance, which contains the San Jose route group followed by the Dallas route group.

continues

Table 2-60 *Route List Requirements (Continued)*

Calls from Dallas...	Description
...to emergency numbers route out the Dallas route group only	These calls require no route-specific transformations.
...to local numbers route out the Dallas route group only	**Action:** Create route list DallasLocal, which contains only the Dallas route group.
...to San Jose local numbers route out the San Jose route group, but fall back to the Dallas route group as a long distance call if the San Jose route group is busy or not available	This call requires route-specific transformations. When a user dials a 7-digit San Jose number, the call must be converted to a local call before it routes out the San Jose gateway, but if it falls back to the Dallas gateway, CallManager must convert the dialed number to 11 digits to route the call across the PSTN. In addition, if a toll bypass call from a Dallas calling number routes out a San Jose gateway, it is sometimes necessary to provide a San Jose calling number so that the local carrier does not reject the call. The San Jose attendant number can serve this purpose. **Action:** Create route list TollBypassToSanJose, which contains the San Jose route group followed by the Dallas route group.
...to long distance numbers route out the Dallas route group, but fall back to the San Jose route group if the Dallas route group is busy or not available ...to international numbers route out the Dallas route group, but fall back to the San Jose route group if the Dallas route group is busy or not available	These calls require route-specific transformations. If a long distance call from a Dallas calling number routes out a San Jose gateway, it is sometimes necessary to provide a San Jose calling number so that the San Jose local carrier does not reject the call. The San Jose attendant number can serve this purpose. **Action:** Create route list DallasLongDistance, which contains the Dallas route group followed by the San Jose route group.

Route Filter Creation and Route Pattern Assignment

The enterprise rules listed in Table 2-59 describe seven types of calls:

- Emergency calls: These are the same whether dialed from San Jose or Dallas.
- Local calls in San Jose: These consist of 7-digit calls to the San Jose PSTN.
- Local calls in Dallas: These consist of 10-digit calls to the Dallas PSTN.
- Toll bypass calls to Dallas: These consist of 11-digit calls from San Jose to the Dallas area codes.
- Toll bypass calls to San Jose: These consist of 11-digit calls from Dallas to the San Jose area code.
- Long distance calls: These are the same whether dialed from San Jose or Dallas.
- International calls: These are the same whether dialed from San Jose or Dallas.

Table 2-61 presents the list of route filters to create, their values, and a description of their purposes.

Table 2-61   *Route Filters for Geographical Routing Example*

Route Filter	Value	Description
Emergency	SERVICE EXISTS	Network services such as information (411) and emergency services (911)
SanJoseLocal	OFFICE-CODE EXISTS AND LOCAL-AREA-CODE-DOES-NOT-EXIST AND AREA-CODE DOES-NOT-EXIST	7-digit calls, which represent local calls in the San Jose area
DallasLocal	LOCAL-AREA-CODE == 972 OR LOCAL-AREA-CODE == 214	10-digit calls to area codes 214 and 972, which are local calls in the Dallas area
TollBypassToDallas	AREA-CODE == 972 OR AREA-CODE == 214	Long distance calls to area codes 214 and 972
TollBypassToSanJose	AREA-CODE == 408	Long distance calls to area code 408
LongDistance	AREA-CODE EXISTS	Long distance calls to area codes that no gateways in the enterprise network serve
International	INTERNATIONAL-ACCESS EXISTS	Calls to international destinations

In all cases, the route pattern is 9.@. The enterprise rules define two locations and three levels of outside calling. This argues for six different partitions for outside dialing. An additional partition can handle calls between extensions. Create the following partitions in Table 2-62.

Table 2-62 *Partitions for Geographical Routing Example*

Partition	Description
ABC	This partition contains the directory numbers of internal extensions.
SanJoseEmergency	This partition contains the route pattern that San Jose users access for their emergency calls.
SanJoseLocalAndLongDistance	This partition contains the route patterns that San Jose users access for local, toll bypass, and long distance calls.
SanJoseInternational	This partition contains the route patterns that San Jose users access for international calls.
DallasEmergency	This partition contains the route pattern that Dallas users access for their emergency calls.
DallasLocalAndLongDistance	This partition contains the route patterns that Dallas users access for local, toll bypass, and long distance calls.
DallasInternational	This partition contains the route patterns that Dallas users access for international calls.

Having created the route filters and partitions, assign the partitions, route patterns, and filters according to Table 2-63. Remember that the route lists control the gateway access order. For example, route list SanJoseLocal selects only those gateways connected directly to the San Jose PSTN, while route list DallasInternational first selects gateways connected to the Dallas PSTN, but then uses gateways connected to the San Jose PSTN if the Dallas gateways are busy or unavailable.

Table 2-63 *Route Pattern and Filter to Route Lists for Geographical Routing Example*

Partition	Pattern	Filter	Route List
SanJoseEmergency	9.@	Emergency	SanJoseLocal
SanJoseLocalAndLongDistance	9.@	SanJoseLocal	SanJoseLocal
SanJoseLocalAndLongDistance	9.@	TollBypassToDallas	TollBypassToDallas
SanJoseLocalAndLongDistance	9.@	LongDistance	SanJoseLongDistance
SanJoseInternational	9.@	International	SanJoseInternational
DallasEmergency	9.@	Emergency	DallasLocal
DallasLocalAndLongDistance	9.@	DallasLocal	DallasLocal
DallasLocalAndLongDistance	9.@	TollBypassToSanJose	TollBypassToSanJose

Table 2-63 *Route Pattern and Filter to Route Lists for Geographical Routing Example (Continued)*

Partition	Pattern	Filter	Route List
DallasLocalAndLongDistance	9.@	LongDistance	DallasLongDistance
DallasInternational	9.@	International	DallasInternational

Applying Calling and Called Party Transformations

Having defined the route lists and assigned the route patterns and filters, you must handle route-specific and non-route-specific transformations. Table 2-60 describes which routes require route-specific transformations.

Assign non-route-specific Digit Discarding Instructions according to Table 2-64. Non-route-specific digit discarding instructions belong directly on the route pattern.

Table 2-64 *Non-Route-Specific Transformations*

Partition	Route Pattern	Route Filter	Digit Discarding Instruction
SanJoseEmergency	9.@	SERVICE EXISTS	PreDot
SanJoseLocal	9.@	OFFICE-CODE EXISTS AND LOCAL-AREA-CODE-DOES-NOT-EXIST AND AREA-CODE DOES-NOT-EXIST	PreDot
DallasEmergency	9.@	SERVICE EXISTS	PreDot
DallasLocal	9.@	AREA-CODE == 972 OR AREA-CODE ==214	PreDot

Assign route-specific called party transformations according to Table 2-65. To assign route-specific called party transformations, click specific route groups within the context of a given route list.

Table 2-65 *Route-Specific Transformations*

Route List	Route Group	Digit Discarding Instructions	Calling Party Transform Mask	Use External Phone Number Mask
TollBypassToDallas	DallasGateways	PreDot 11D->10D	972 555 0000	No
TollBypassToDallas	SanJoseGateways	PreDot		Yes

continues

Table 2-65 *Route-Specific Transformations (Continued)*

Route List	Route Group	Digit Discarding Instructions	Calling Party Transform Mask	Use External Phone Number Mask
TollBypassToSanJose	SanJoseGateways	PreDot 11D->7D	408 555 0000	No
TollBypassToSanJose	DallasGateways	PreDot		Yes
SanJoseLongDistance	SanJoseGateways	PreDot		Yes
SanJoseLongDistance	DallasGateways	PreDot	972 555 0000	No
DallasLongDistance	DallasGateways	PreDot		Yes
DallasLongDistance	SanJoseGateways	PreDot	408 555 0000	No

Calling Search Space Creation, Calling Search Space Assignment, and Phone Configuration

This final stage is simple. You must create the calling search spaces and then assign them to the calling devices. With two locations and three levels of external access, you require six calling search spaces. Create calling search spaces according to Table 2-66.

Table 2-66 *Outbound Calling Search Spaces for Geographical Routing Example*

Calling Search Space	Contains Partitions	Description
SanJoseLobbyPhone	ABC, SanJoseEmergency	Provides access to internal extensions and PSTN services only
SanJoseOfficePersonnel	ABC, SanJoseEmergency, SanJoseLocalAndLongDistance	Provides access to internal extensions, PSTN services, and local, toll bypass, and long distance calls
SanJoseManager	ABC, SanJoseEmergency, SanJoseLocalAndLongDistance, SanJoseInternational	Provides access to internal extensions and all PSTN numbers
DallasLobbyPhone	ABC, DallasEmergency	Provides access to internal extensions and PSTN services only
DallasOfficePersonnel	ABC, DallasEmergency, DallasLocalAndLongDistance	Provides access to internal extensions, PSTN services, and local, toll bypass, and long distance calls.
DallasManager	ABC, DallasEmergency, DallasLocalAndLongDistance, DallasInternational	Provides access to internal extensions and all PSTN numbers

After defining the calling search spaces, assign them according to Table 2-67. External phone number masks result from the exchange number and phone number range the phone company has assigned Company ABC in San Jose and Dallas. Finally, assign directory numbers for all phones to partition ABC.

Table 2-67   *Assignment of Calling Search Spaces*

Extension	Calling Search Space	External Phone Number Mask
San Jose Phones		
30000	SanJoseOfficePersonnel	408 555 5XXX
31000	SanJoseLobbyPhone	408 555 5XXX
31100	SanJoseOfficePersonnel	408 555 5XXX
31200	SanJoseManager	408 555 5XXX
Dallas Phones		
40000	DallasOfficePersonnel	972 555 2XXX
41050	DallasLobbyPhone	972 555 2XXX
41150	DallasOfficePersonnel	972 555 2XXX
41250	DallasManager	972 555 2XXX

Inbound Dialing

For inbound dialing in a toll bypass scenario, it is theoretically possible to have a phone be reachable by inbound dialing from any gateway in any geographical location. Such a configuration means that every internal number would have several external phone numbers. For example, if station 41050 was dialable from the San Jose gateway, in addition to 41050's Dallas address of 972 555 2050, 41050 would also have a San Jose external address of 408 555 5050. This type of configuration would very quickly consume any spare numbers you bought from the PSTN, as well as being rather cumbersome to implement.

As a result, this example concerns itself with making Dallas extensions available from Dallas gateways and San Jose extensions available from San Jose gateways. This problem is therefore not truly related to a toll bypass configuration, but it does provide some guidance for inbound dialing.

Inbound dialing configuration consists of performing the tasks in the following sections:

- "Define Translation Patterns" recaps how to use translation patterns to map external phone numbers to internal extensions.

- "Define and Assign Inbound Calling Search Spaces" describes how to assign calling search spaces to control the destination's inbound calls through gateways can reach.

Define Translation Patterns

Although this example permits the use of gateway called party transformations to convert an inbound phone number to an extension number, configuring the map using translation patterns saves some reconfiguration effort if you ever purchase another phone number range from the phone company.

San Jose gateways and Dallas gateways need individualized translation patterns. Define the translation patterns defined in Table 2-68.

Table 2-68 *Translation Patterns*

Partition	Translation Pattern	Translation Partition	Called Party Transformation Mask
SanJoseTranslations	408 555 5XXX	ABC	31XXX
DallasTranslations	972 555 2XXX	ABC	41XXX

Define and Assign Inbound Calling Search Spaces

After defining the translation patterns, you must create calling search spaces and assign them to the gateways. Create the calling search spaces Table 2-69.

Table 2-69 *Inbound Calling Search Spaces for Geographical Routing Example*

Calling Search Space	Contains Partitions	Description
SanJoseTranslations	SanJoseTranslations	Provides access to the extension mapping tables when the PSTN offers calls to CallManager over San Jose gateways
DallasTranslations	DallasTranslations	Provides access to the extension mapping tables when the PSTN offers calls to CallManager over Dallas gateways

Assign calling search space SanJoseTranslations to the San Jose gateway and calling search space DallasTranslations to the Dallas gateway.

Note that calling search spaces and partitions, when assigned this way, prevent tandem calls from one gateway to another. However, users can transfer or forward (unless you are also using call forward calling search spaces) inbound calls out gateways.

Geographical Routing Summary

Although configuring CallManager for geographical routing requires a complex configuration, the complexity stems from the fact that the call routing tasks CallManager must perform are themselves complex.

Configuring geographical routing requires the following steps:

Step 1   Think about the users in your network and how you want CallManager to treat their calls. What types of calls are permitted? Do you want toll restriction? What types of fallback routing do you wish to permit?

Step 2   Configure your outbound dialing.

— Provision your gateways.

— Define route groups to contain gateways that connect to the same network.

— Create one route list for each unique route group search pattern that your network needs. Assign route groups to each route list appropriately.

— Define route filters that properly describe the levels of external access you wish to permit. Provide outside access by narrowly tailoring these route lists to permit just one class of external call. For instance, if your network provides two levels of outside access, national numbers and unlimited access, define one route filter that defines access to national numbers only and another that defines access to international numbers only. By providing your most privileged users access to route patterns with both route filters, you give them unlimited access.

— Define partitions for each unique level of external access you wish to provide. Define a partition for internal extensions.

— Assign partitions, route patterns, and route filters with the appropriate route lists.

— Set up the appropriate dialing transformations. This means using a combination of dialing transformations on the route pattern and dialing transformations on the routes themselves, when fallback or toll restriction means that certain route groups must receive a specific set of called digits.

— Build calling search spaces for each level of external access and assign them to the phones in your enterprise.

Step 3 Configure your inbound dialing.

— Define translation patterns that map the external number ranges that the PSTN assigns you to the internal ranges that your network requires.

— Define calling search spaces for the gateways in each of your geographic locations and assign them to the gateways in these locations.

Miscellaneous Solutions

This section contains some miscellaneous solutions that did not fit well in any other section of this chapter. It includes the following sections:

- "Insertion of Access Codes in the Placed Calls Menu of Cisco IP Phones" describes how to keep a user's dialed digit string intact so that the user can use the **Dial** soft key to redial previously placed calls.

- "Authorization and Account Codes" describes how to secure external calling and associate billing accounts with specific external calls.

- "One-to-One Station-to-Trunk Mapping" describes a common small PBX requirement, mapping calling users to specific outbound analog trunks, and vice versa.

- "Fallback Routing to Another PBX" describes a way to ease migration of users from an existing phone system to Cisco CallManager.

- "Multiple Call Appearances" describes how you can emulate a traditional PBX feature in which the same directory number appears on multiple lines.

- "Enhanced 911 Support" describes considerations for providing the proper calling number for emergency services in North America.

Insertion of Access Codes in the Placed Calls Menu of Cisco IP Phones

The **Placed Calls** menu of Cisco IP Phones 7940 and 7960 permits a user to quickly redial numbers that the user has previously dialed from the phone. However, the number that the phone stores is not always exactly the number that the user has dialed, because the phone stores the number after the call routing component has applied dialing transformations.

Typically, this means that the numbers in the **Placed Calls** menu lack any enterprise outside access code that you have provisioned, because the called party transformations on the route pattern usually strip off outside access codes.

Users who employ the **Placed Calls** menu can use the **Edit Dial** soft key to edit the stored number before placing the call, but users find this process cumbersome.

You can retain the access code for placed calls, however, by deferring your application of called party transformations until later in the call routing process. Instead of applying called party transformations in the Route Pattern Configuration screen, assign your outbound gateways to a route group and perform the called party transformations there. This configuration hides the called party transformations from the calling phone and ensures that the **Placed Calls** menu contains the untransformed number. (Note, however, that the CDR records that CallManager logs will contain the access code, as well.)

Authorization and Account Codes

CallManager does not provide explicit support for authorization codes and account codes.

Authorization codes require users to dial a specific sequence of dialed digits before they can place external calls. Account codes require users to dial a specific sequence of dialed digits before they can place external calls; these digits show up in the call detail record (CDR) so that you can later charge the call to a specific account.

A quick-and-dirty implementation of authorization codes is to use an obscure access code at the beginning of route patterns that select external calls. This provides only a minimal level of security, however, because the dialed account code shows up in the **Placed Calls** menu of the Cisco IP Phones 7940 and 7960.

Using the same technique, however, does provide a mechanism for you to assign account codes to external calls your users make. Figure 2-33 shows this configuration.

Figure 2-33 *Account Codes Implementation*

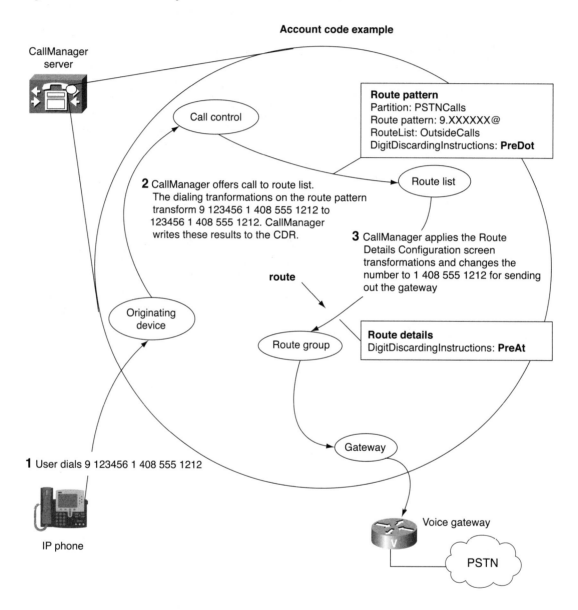

Account code example

CallManager
server

Call control

Route pattern
Partition: PSTNCalls
Route pattern: 9.XXXXXX@
RouteList: OutsideCalls
DigitDiscardingInstructions: **PreDot**

2 CallManager offers call to route list.
The dialing tranformations on the route pattern
transform 9 123456 1 408 555 1212 to
123456 1 408 555 1212. CallManager
writes these results to the CDR.

Route list

3 CallManager applies the Route
Details Configuration screen
transformations and changes the
number to 1 408 555 1212 for sending
out the gateway

route

Originating
device

Route group

Route details
DigitDiscardingInstructions: **PreAt**

Gateway

1 User dials 9 123456 1 408 555 1212

IP phone

Voice gateway

PSTN

Assume that external calls are matched by the route pattern 9.@. You would like to see an
account code show up in the CDR. Assume also that the account code is a 6-digit number.

When CallManager logs a CDR, the called party digits are those that the called party transformations on the route pattern generate. Dialing transformations that CallManager applies after the route pattern's dialing transformations do not show up in the CDR records. (CallManager has five opportunities to transform calling and called numbers. See the section "Dialing Transformations" for more information.)

Integrating the account code into the route pattern and then making sure that the called party transformations do not strip it ensures that the account code shows up as part of the called number in the CDR. Therefore, to get a 6-digit account code into a CDR, define a route pattern such as 9.XXXXXX@ and apply digit discarding instructions of PreDot. The first six digits of the called number in the CDR are the account code that the calling user dials.

However, you must strip the account code before the call can route out any external gateways. To accomplish this procedure, associate the route pattern with a route list that provides external access. Then, on the routes to the gateways, define digit discarding instructions of PreAt rather than PreDot. The digit discarding instructions on a route supersede those of the route pattern, and they strip the account code before the call routes out an external gateway.

This solution does not address inbound calls, and CallManager does not prompt users to enter their account code in any way, but it is a partial solution.

If you want to safeguard against the entry of an invalid account code, or you wish to secure Cisco IP Phone 7910s (which have no **Placed Calls** menu) using authorization codes, a variation on this method permits it. Figure 2-34 demonstrates this configuration.

In this configuration, for each valid account or authorization code, you assign a specific route pattern to the route list that provides access to external gateways. For instance, if your valid account codes are 123456 and 135791, you define route patterns 9.123456@ and 9.135791@.

In itself, this configuration ensures that for users to be able to dial out to the PSTN, they must enter the correct code. This configuration works fine for account codes, but for authorization codes, it means that users can discover the outside access code through exploration, because CallManager rejects a user's call attempt when it knows that there is no chance for an eventual match. For instance, given the example authorization codes, an exploring user could dial 9, then 1, and then 4. When CallManager applies reorder tone after the 4, the exploring user knows that authorization codes exist that start with a 1 but for which 4 is not a legal second digit. Through repeated attempts, a user can quickly discover authorization codes in this manner.

Figure 2-34 *Authorization Codes Implementation*

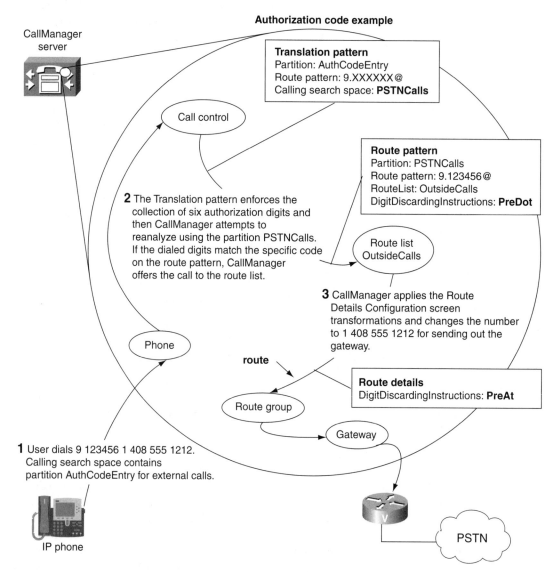

Authorization code example

CallManager server

Translation pattern
Partition: AuthCodeEntry
Route pattern: 9.XXXXXX@
Calling search space: **PSTNCalls**

Call control

Route pattern
Partition: PSTNCalls
Route pattern: 9.123456@
RouteList: OutsideCalls
DigitDiscardingInstructions: **PreDot**

2 The Translation pattern enforces the collection of six authorization digits and then CallManager attempts to reanalyze using the partition PSTNCalls. If the dialed digits match the specific code on the route pattern, CallManager offers the call to the route list.

Route list OutsideCalls

3 CallManager applies the Route Details Configuration screen transformations and changes the number to 1 408 555 1212 for sending out the gateway.

Phone

route

Route group

Route details
DigitDiscardingInstructions: **PreAt**

1 User dials 9 123456 1 408 555 1212. Calling search space contains partition AuthCodeEntry for external calls.

IP phone

Gateway

PSTN

You can prevent this type of exploration by using a translation pattern such as 9.XXXXXX@ in a partition designed specifically for collection of a full access code plus 6-digit account code plus external number. Then, when CallManager collects the entire dialed digit string, it attempts to reanalyze the number using the calling search space that the translation pattern specifies. This calling search space provides access directly to the route list that provides external access. If the account code matches one of the specific route patterns you have configured on the route list, CallManager routes the call, but if it does not, CallManager rejects the call. Although users can still discover account codes through exhaustive exploration, this method greatly increases the number of attempts that users must make before they succeed.

One-to-One Station-to-Trunk Mapping

Small PBXs associate calling stations to specific analog trunks, and vice versa. The service parameter **MatchingCgpnWithAttendantFlag** (see the section "Dialing Transformations") provides a quick way to ensure that a given calling station's external calls route over a specific analog trunk.

However, if you have several analog gateways, to ensure that the calling user's call is presented to the correct gateway, you must put all of your analog gateways in a route list to successfully use the **MatchingCgpnWithAttendantFlag**. If you have more than a few gateways, this configuration is not efficient, because CallManager attempts to offer external calls to each analog interface one at a time until CallManager finds the analog interface with an **Attendant DN** that matches the calling number.

Calling search spaces and partitions offer a solution, if a cumbersome one. For inbound calls, you can use the same field as the gateways with analog interfaces do: configure the associated phone's directory number as the **Attendant DN** setting for the analog port.

For external dialing, however, provision each external trunk with its own @ pattern (or other external dialing pattern) and then assign each route pattern a unique partition. A calling user includes one of the unique partitions in the calling search space, which causes the calling user's outbound calls always to route to one specific trunk.

For example, assume you have two users, Alice, with directory number 1000, and Bill, with directory number 2000. In addition, you have an MGCP gateway with two loop start trunks. Inbound calls from the first trunk route to Alice, and Alice's outbound calls route out the first trunk. Inbound calls from the second trunk route to Bill, and Bill's outbound calls route out the second trunk.

To route the inbound calls correctly, you must simply assign Alice's directory number (1000) as the **Attendant DN** of the first port and Bill's directory number (2000) as the **Attendant DN** of the second port.

Routing outbound calls requires that you use calling search spaces and partitions. Create two partitions, CallsFromAlice and CallsFromBill. Create the route pattern 9.@ in partition CallsFromAlice and associate it with the first trunk. Then create the route pattern 9.@ in partition CallsFromBill and associate it with the second trunk. Finally, assign Alice a calling search space that includes partition CallsFromAlice and assign Bill a calling search space that includes partition CallsFromBill.

When Alice dials an external number such as 9 1 408 555 1212, her dialed digit string matches the 9.@ pattern associated with the first trunk, because her analysis request can only see the route patterns defined in partition CallsFromAlice. On the other hand, when Bill dials an external number, his dialed digit string matches the 9.@ pattern associated with the second trunk. Figure 2-35 presents this behavior.

Fallback Routing to Another PBX

If you migrate users from another telephone system to CallManager, which is connected to the other telephone system by a gateway, you might wish to maintain the directory numbers of those users who have moved.

When you migrate users from one system to another, directory numbers within a directory number range are often spread between both systems. For example, if your directory number range is 8000 to 8999, CallManager might serve directory numbers 8101, 8301, and 8425, while the other telephone system serves all other extensions in the range.

Maintaining the routing between the two systems would be a very difficult task if you had to enter all of the extensions that the other phone system manages into the CallManager database one by one.

Using closest match routing, you can define a pattern, such as 8XXX, on the gateway to the other system. When a user that CallManager serves dials an extension that CallManager also serves, closest match routing causes specific pattern to match; whereas, if a user dials a number that CallManager does not control, route pattern XXXX sends the call to the other system.

For example, assume CallManager serves directory numbers 8101, 8301, and 8425. Route pattern XXXX corresponds to the gateway to the other phone system. If a user dials 8101, CallManager offers the call to the phone it controls, but if a user dials 8500, CallManager routes the call to the gateway to the other phone system.

If that was all there was to it, this configuration would not deserve its own section. However, what if the other phone system does not control any phone with directory number 8500? If the other phone system is configured to route unknown directory numbers to the CallManager, the two systems will play table tennis with the call. The call forwards from system to system until it consumes all trunk resources between the systems. The call clears at that point, but the situation ties up all of the trunks temporarily. If the systems are connected by nonphysical resources such as intercluster trunks, CallManager bounces the calls between the systems indefinitely.

Calling search spaces and partitions allow you to break the routing loop. If you put the fallback pattern XXXX in a partition that is not included in the gateway's calling search space, when the other telephone system routes the outgoing call to 8500 back into CallManager, CallManager does not find any matches for the dialed number and rejects the call before the routing loop consumes all the gateway resources.

Figure 2-35 *One-to-One Trunk-to-Station Mapping*

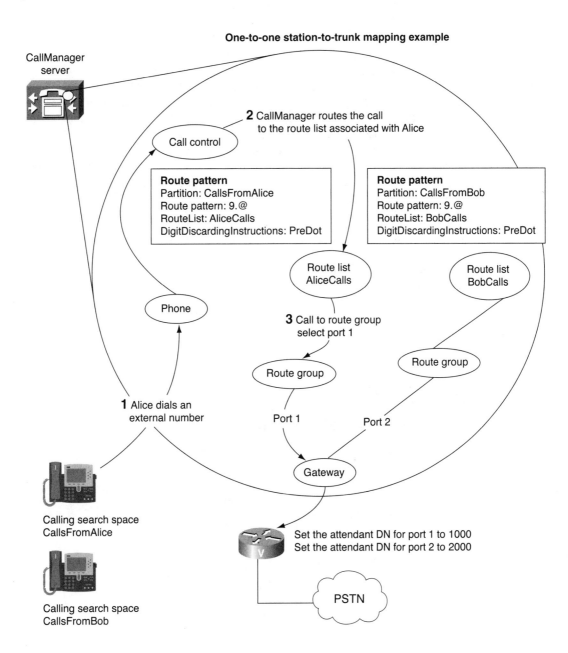

One-to-one station-to-trunk mapping example

Multiple Call Appearances

Traditional PBX phones provide users with a one- or two-line display and rows of buttons next to LEDs. The limited user interface means that providing complex user features is quite a challenge.

Users of PBX phones, especially administrative assistants, require the ability to take numerous calls at a single number. In addition, users need to be able to transfer individual calls to other destinations, no matter how many calls currently terminate on the line. Traditional PBX phones accomplish this by permitting multiple appearances of the same directory number to appear on a single phone. These multiple appearances are termed *call appearances*. As new calls arrive at a phone with multiple call appearances, traditional PBXs offer them to unoccupied call appearances. By selecting different call appearances, a user at a phone can move from call to call and transfer individual users.

CallManager does not support multiple call appearances. If you assign a particular directory number to a line on a particular IP Phone, CallManager Administration will not allow you to assign it to another line on that phone. However, using calling search spaces and partitions, you can emulate traditional call appearances very closely. Figure 2-36 shows an IP Phone configured with multiple call appearances.

Figure 2-36 *Multiple Call Appearances on an IP Phone*

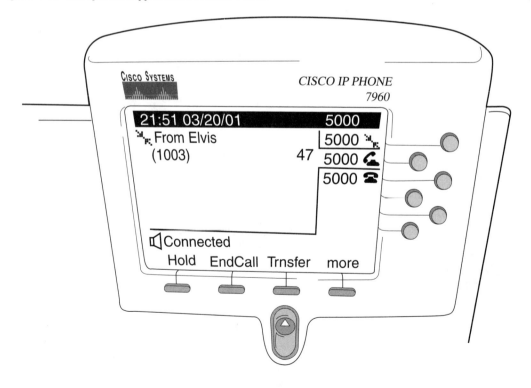

This functionality relies on the fact that, to CallManager, identical directory numbers in different partitions are different destinations. Because partition names do not show up on IP Phone displays, to the user at 5000, it appears that there are three call appearances of directory number 5000.

Assume that you wish to configure a phone with directory number 5000 with three line appearances. Create the partitions in Table 2-70.

Table 2-70 *Partitions for Multiple Call Appearances*

Partition	Description
Standard	Assigned to the first call appearance of the IP Phone, this partition represents the partition to which you normally assign your phone users
Line2	Assigned to the second call appearance of the IP Phone
Line3	Assigned to the third call appearance of the IP Phone

When a call arrives for directory number 5000, if the first call appearance is busy, you want CallManager to forward the call to the second call appearance; likewise, if the second call appearance is busy, you want CallManager to forward the call to the third line appearance. Finally, if the third call appearance is busy, CallManager forwards the call to voice mail. Assume that the voice mail pilot number is 5050.

If the user is not present at the phone, CallManager rings the phone until the call forward no answer timer expires. Whether the call is ringing at the first, second, or third call appearance, if the user does not answer, CallManager should forward the call to voice mail.

Making the call forward from line appearance to line appearance means using some call forward calling search spaces. Configure the calling search spaces in Table 2-71.

Table 2-71 *Calling Search Spaces for Multiple Call Appearances*

Calling Search Spaces	Partitions	Description
Standard	Varies	This calling search space includes whatever partitions the users need to place their day-to-day calls. At the very least, this calling search space typically includes the ability to call other internal extensions, emergency services, and voice mail.
Line2	Line2	This calling search space permits a user to call any call appearance assigned to the Line2 partition.
Line3	Line3	This calling search space permits a user to call any call appearance assigned to the Line3 partition.

Given these calling search spaces and partitions, you can configure phone 5000 according to Table 2-72.

Table 2-72 *Directory Number Configuration Screens for Multiple Call Appearances*

First Call Appearance

Setting	Value		Description
Directory Number	5000		
Partition	Line1		
Calling Search Space	Standard		Provides access to all numbers the user is permitted to dial
Call Forward Busy	Destination	Calling Search Space	Forwards the call to line 2 when line 1 is busy
	5000	Line2	
Call Forward No Answer	Destination	Calling Search Space	Forwards the call to voice mail when line 1 does not answer
	5050	Standard	

Second Call Appearance

Setting	Value		Description
Directory Number	5000		
Partition	Line2		
Calling Search Space	Standard		Provides access to all numbers the user is permitted to dial
Call Forward Busy	Destination	Calling Search Space	Forwards the call to line 3 when line 2 is busy
	5000	Line3	
Call Forward No Answer	Destination	Calling Search Space	Forwards the call to voice mail when line 2 does not answer
	5050	Standard	

Third Call Appearance

Setting	Value		Description
Directory Number	5000		
Partition	Line3		

Table 2-72 *Directory Number Configuration Screens for Multiple Call Appearances (Continued)*

Third Call Appearance

Setting	Value		Description
Calling Search Space	Standard		Provides access to all numbers the user is permitted to dial
Call Forward Busy	Destination	Calling Search Space	Forwards the call to voice mail when line 3 is busy
	5050	Standard	
Call Forward No Answer	Destination	Calling Search Space	Forwards the call to voice mail when line 3 does not answer
	5050	Standard	

Enhanced 911 Support

This section describes some aspects of emergency call handling in North America, but it is by no means a complete treatise on the subject. Rather, it informs you of some of the issues you may need to consider when configuring emergency call routing for your enterprise. Furthermore, legal requirements for emergency calls differ from state to state, so the information and example configuration that this section presents may not be valid in your enterprise's locale. At the time of this writing, at least seven states have legal requirements relating to emergency calls: Kentucky, Illinois, Mississippi, Tennessee, Texas, Vermont, and Washington.

In North America, the number for emergency services is 911. Local carriers route 911 calls to Public Safety Answering Points (PSAPs). PSAPs are staffed with trained personnel and equipment that can properly handle emergency calls.

The North American PSTN treats calls to 911 very specially. Unlike other calls to the PSTN, after a call reaches the switches owned by the local carrier, calls to 911 usually route over an independent telephone network. Unlike a traditional call, the PSTN routes 911 calls based on the number of the caller, not the dialed digits. Note that different trunk interfaces deliver the calling number in different ways, and some trunk interfaces cannot deliver a calling number at all. For these latter trunk interfaces, the PSTN manages the calling number.

Users directly connected to the PSTN who dial 911 cause the local carrier to perform several database lookups when it handles the call. The piece of information that starts the lookups is the calling number of the user. Using this calling number, the local carrier looks in several databases to find the emergency service number (ESN), which indicates which PSAP needs to handle the call, and the automatic location identification (ALI), which provides a street address associated with the calling user. The PSAP informs the authorities of this address when dispatching medical, police, or fire safety personnel to aid the caller.

Clearly, it is important to ensure that this address enables officials to actually locate the person in trouble. If your enterprise serves more than a few users, you should take special pains to ensure that the calling number you provide allows the local carrier to return an ALI that locates the caller's position accurately; one approach is to reserve some enterprise numbers specifically for the purpose of providing a calling number for 911 calls that can identify a caller's area to within a few thousand square feet, including building and floor number. (Having such a number is essential for extensions in your enterprise, such as lobby phones, that may not have external phone numbers.) Customizing the ALI database entry for a particular calling number typically requires that you contact the local carrier and public safety authorities.

Complicating the problem is that if the local carrier routes an emergency call to the incorrect PSAP because of incorrect calling number information, the PSAP is usually unable to redirect the call to the appropriate PSAP, because the tandem trunk networks over which 911 calls typically do not directly connect one PSAP to another.

CallManager supports basically two approaches to handling emergency calls.

- First, you can route emergency calls to a dedicated attendant station, along with the extension number of the calling user. In turn, the attendant contacts emergency personnel, usually remaining conferenced in on the call to assist if necessary.

- Second, you can route emergency calls directly to the local carrier by routing the call to a gateway connected to the local carrier and providing the digits 911. You must provide the appropriate calling number to the local carrier so that the carrier can route the call to the correct PSAP and provide the required ALI.

Figure 2-37 presents a small example network that demonstrates a 911 configuration. It depicts a distributed enterprise. One CallManager serves users in Dallas and in Richardson (a Dallas suburb). The enterprise has gateways connected to both the Dallas and the Richardson PSTN. Both the Dallas and the Richardson offices have an attendant whose directory number provides a good calling number to present to the PSTN for 911 calls; the attendant's location is reasonably close to the locations of users in the branch office.

The configuration supports three types of calls to the PSTN:

- 911 calls from Richardson users route to the gateway connected to the Richardson PSTN with the calling number of the Richardson attendant.

- 911 calls from Dallas users route to the gateway connected to the Dallas PSTN with the calling number of the Dallas attendant.

- All other calls route to the Dallas gateway first and to the Richardson gateway if the Dallas gateway is unavailable. (Note that despite this example to the contrary, it is an excellent idea to reserve a gateway or at least an interface on a gateway specifically for 911 calls. This way, you can guarantee that a caller in trouble can reach the PSTN.)

Figure 2-37 *Example Network for 911 Routing*

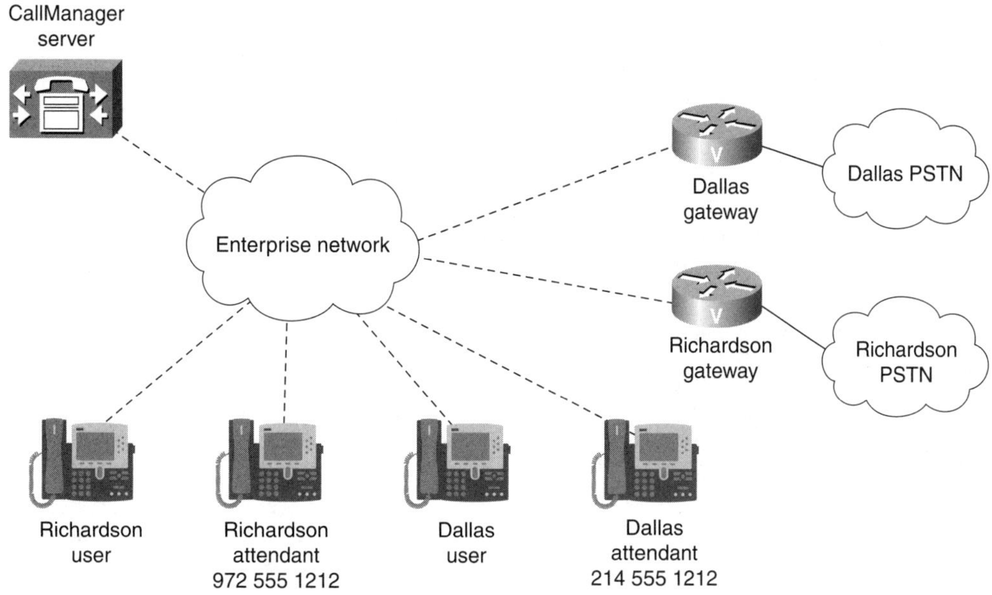

The configuration defines three different gateway access methods, which calls for the use of a route list. Assuming that you have already provisioned the gateways, you need to create the route groups in Table 2-73.

Table 2-73 *Route Groups for 911 Routing*

Route Group Name	Gateways Contained
DallasGateways	DallasGateway
RichardsonGateways	RichardsonGateway

You have three different search algorithms. The first, used for 911 calls from Richardson, selects just the gateways connected to the Richardson PSTN. The second, used for 911 calls from Dallas, selects just the gateways connected to the Dallas PSTN. The last, used for all other external calls, selects the Dallas gateways first and the Richardson gateways next. Three search algorithms require three route lists, which Table 2-74 lists.

Table 2-74 *Route Lists for 911 Routing*

Route List Name	Route Groups Contained
Richardson911Calls	RichardsonGateways
Dallas911Calls	DallasGateways
PSTNCalls	DallasGateways, RichardsonGateways

Distinguishing 911 calls from other calls requires using a route filter. The route filter that Table 2-75 lists selects only 911 calls from the North American numbering plan.

Table 2-75 *Route Filter for 911 Routing*

Route Filter Name	Value
911Calls	SERVICE == 911

The sample configuration requires individualized routing. CallManager routes calls from Dallas users who dial 911 differently from calls from Richardson users who dial 911. Individualized routing requires the creation of partitions and calling search spaces. Table 2-76 contains the partitions that this example requires, and Table 2-77 contains the calling search spaces that this example requires.

Table 2-76 *Partitions for 911 Routing*

Partition Name	Description
PSTNCalls	Contains route patterns that grant PSTN access to all enterprise users
Dallas911	Contains the route pattern that grants 911 access to Dallas users
Richardson911	Contains the route pattern that grants 911 access to Richardson users

Table 2-77 *Calling Search Spaces for 911 Routing*

Calling Search Space	Contains Partitions	Description
DallasUsers	Dallas911, PSTNCalls	Provides customized PSTN access for Dallas users
RichardsonUsers	Richardson911, PSTNCalls	Provides customized PSTN access for Richardson users

Then, assign route patterns to the route lists. Table 2-78 lists the route patterns to define.

Table 2-78 *Route Patterns for 911 Routing*

Route Pattern	Description
Partition: PSTNCalls Route Pattern: 9.@ Route List: PSTNCalls Use External Phone Number Mask: Yes Digit Discarding Instructions: PreDot	Provides general access to the PSTN. CallManager strips the 9 from the called number before extending the call to the PSTN. CallManager uses the external phone number mask that you configure on the calling user's Directory Number Configuration screen as the calling number.

Table 2-78   *Route Patterns for 911 Routing (Continued)*

Route Pattern	Description
Partition: PSTNCalls Route Pattern: 9.@ Route Filter: 911Calls Route List: Richardson911Calls Use External Phone Number Mask: No Calling Party Transformation Mask: **9725551212** Digit Discarding Instructions: PreDot	Contains the route pattern that grants 911 access to Richardson users. Closest match routing rules ensure the CallManager selects this route pattern when a Richardson user dials 911. CallManager strips the 9 from the called number and substitutes the Richardson attendant's number for that of the caller.
Partition: PSTNCalls Route Pattern: 9.@ Route Filter: 911Calls Route List: Dallas911Calls Use External Phone Number Mask: No Calling Party Transformation Mask: **2145551212** Digit Discarding Instructions: PreDot	Contains the route pattern that grants 911 access to Dallas users. Closest match routing rules ensure the CallManager selects this route pattern when a Dallas user dials 911. CallManager strips the 9 from the called number and substitutes the Dallas attendant's number for that of the caller.

Finally, make sure that you assign the calling search space DallasUsers to phones in Dallas and RichardsonUsers to phones in Richardson, and set up the external phone number mask for each phone.

The North American Numbering Plan

The call routing component of Cisco CallManager is extensible. In previous sections, the @ wildcard has always been described in the context of the North American numbering plan. As described in the section "@ Wildcard," the @ wildcard is a macro that, based on the numbering plan you select, adds many route patterns on your behalf. Currently, CallManager Administration permits you to select only **North American Numbering Plan** from the **Numbering Plan** drop-down list.

The list of route patterns that CallManager adds is available in an administrator-accessible file. In the installation directory of CallManager is a subdirectory called dialPlan. (The CallManager service parameter **DialPlanPath** tells CallManager where to look for the numbering plan file.) When CallManager initializes, it looks in this subdirectory for information about the North American numbering plan. When you configure an @ pattern from the Route Pattern Configuration or Translation Pattern Configuration screens, you are instructing CallManager to expand the @ wildcard according to the file called "NANP" in this subdirectory.

File Format

The file is a little more complex than just a list of route patterns, however, because for CallManager to correctly apply digit discarding instructions and route filters, you need to tell it what substrings of a given number are meaningful for routing purposes. For example, the 7-digit North American numbering plan route pattern [2-9]XX XXXX contains two meaningful substrings, an office code and a subscriber.

As described in the section "Tags," these meaningful substrings are called *tags*. The tags defined for a given numbering plan dictate which tags are available on the Route Filter Configuration screen and which parts of a dialed number can be discarded using digit discarding instructions.

Following is a short excerpt from the NANP file that describes a long distance number preceded by a request for a particular long distance carrier:

```
# 101 XXXX 1 [2-9]XX [2-9]XX [2-9]XX
P: 101          TRANSIT-NETWORK-ESCAPE
P: XXXX         TRANSIT-NETWORK
P: 1            LONG-DISTANCE-DIRECT-DIAL
P: [2-9]XX      AREA-CODE
P: [2-9]XX      OFFICE-CODE
P: XXXX         SUBSCRIBER
T: N
```

Each route pattern in a numbering plan is represented as several lines of text followed by a blank line. The first character on each line of text defines one of five types of records:

- **#:** A line beginning with # is treated as a comment line. The call routing component ignores these lines when expanding an @ wildcard.

- **P:** This type of line is by far the most important. In this line, you describe a substring for a particular route pattern. This type of line has one mandatory argument and an optional argument. The first argument is a description of the substring itself, in pattern notation (see the section "Route Patterns and Route Filters"). The second argument, if present, describes the tag name you wish to associate with this substring. The tag name can be anything you want, though it can contain only alphabetic characters and hyphens. Most route patterns consist of several P lines that together define the entire route pattern.

- **T:** A line beginning with "T:" specifies whether the type of number represents an international number or a national number. When followed by an *N*, the route pattern is considered national; when followed by an *I*, it is considered international. Digital signaling interfaces such as PRI require CallManager to characterize a dialed number when it offers a call to the PSTN for the call to route correctly. When you set the

Called Party IE Number Type option to **Cisco CallManager** on any digital gateway configuration screen, you tell CallManager to set up the called number based on this value in the numbering plan file.

- **U:** A line beginning with "U:" specifies that a route pattern is urgent. When a route pattern is urgent, if the user dials a string that matches the route pattern, all interdigit timing is circumvented. When followed by a *Y* (for yes), the route pattern is considered urgent; when followed by an *N* or if the line is not present at all, it is considered normal. The NANP file characterizes the information and emergency services as urgent route patterns so that you do not accidentally hamper access to emergency services by creating an extension such as 9110.

- **W:** A line beginning with "W:" specifies associated information. This line is not currently used, but it should be used for setup of the network-specific facilities information element in ISDN. CallManager associates any information following the tag with the route pattern, and the destination device can use this information to make decisions. In the case of the current NANP file, operator calls are followed with a "W:" line that specifies OP or OP/P so that PRI code can configure the outbound called number information as an operator call. CallManager currently ignores this line.

Replacing the North American Numbering Plan

If you are industrious and knowledgeable, you can replace the North American numbering plan with one for another country. Changing the file means that when CallManager expands the @ wildcard, instead of adding a set of route patterns that correspond with well-formed addresses on the North American network, CallManager expands the @ wildcard according to different rules. What this means is that although you might configure a route pattern using the @ wildcard and choose North American numbering plan as the numbering plan, CallManager will instead add the route plan of your choosing.

A replaced numbering plan is not seamless, however. The Route Filter Configuration screen allows you to limit the number of route patterns CallManager adds when it expands the @ wildcard, and the digit discarding instructions that CallManager applies are tailored to North American needs. If you are careful, however, you can map your own country's numbering plan to tags in the North American numbering plan. For instance, if your country's numbering plan uses city codes, by tagging the city code portion of an entry in the NANP file as AREA-CODE, you can use the AREA-CODE tag in the Route Filter Configuration screen to control access to different cities.

An example might better demonstrate how you can replace the North American numbering plan. The numbering plan for the Netherlands is a reasonably uniform one, but it does not achieve the uniformity of the North American numbering plan. The site www.opta.nl/download/telecom/nummerplan/Np-ISDN-tw.pdf provides an overview of the numbering plan for the Netherlands (in Dutch).

The Dutch numbering plan has the following basic features:

- Numbers beginning with 00 provide access to international numbers. Following the 00 is a country code, followed by the national number.

- Numbers beginning with 01, 02, 03, 04, 05, and 07 provide access to different areas within the Netherlands. Area codes are either two or three digits long. The total length of national number is almost always ten digits, so when an area has a 2-digit area code, the subscriber number is seven digits long, but when an area has a 3-digit area code, the subscriber number is six digits long.

- Numbers in the 06, 08, and 09 ranges are used for services varying from telex, mobile, voice mail, and pay services. The length of these numbers varies from 3 to 11 digits.

- Numbers beginning with 11 are 3-digit network services, such as emergency services, and numbers beginning with 12 are 4-digit network services.

- Numbers beginning with 2, 3, 4, 5, 6, 7, or 8 are either 6- or 7-digit subscriber numbers for calling within a particular (3-digit or 2-digit) numbering area.

The rest of this section explains representative samples of the numbering plan in the order described above:

- "International Calls" presents numbering plan records for one particular international numbering zone.

- "National Calls" presents numbering plan records for both 2- and 3-digit area codes.

- "Miscellaneous Service Calls" presents some sample miscellaneous service numbering plan records.

- "Network Services" presents the network services numbering plan records

- "Local Numbers" presents strategies for coping with the variable-length subscriber numbering ranges.

International Calls

The ITU-T standard defines the world's country codes. Country codes vary from one to three digits long, and there is not much rhyme or reason as to which codes are of a particular length. In the Netherlands numbering plan, 00 provides access to the international network. After 00, users dial the country code to which they wish to place their call, followed by a variable-length national number.

World numbering zone 3 includes the countries in Table 2-79.

Table 2-79   *Countries in World Numbering Zone 3*

Country	Country Code	Country	Country Code
Greece	30	Iceland	354
Netherlands	31	Albania	355
Belgium	32	Malta	356
France and Monaco	33	Cyprus	357
Spain	34	Finland	358
Gibraltar	350	Bulgaria	359
Portugal	351	Hungary	36
Luxembourg	352	Yugoslavia	38
Ireland	353	Italy	39

Country codes starting with 35 are 3-digit country codes, while country codes in other ranges are 2-digit country codes. The following numbering plan records set up international dialing to country codes in zone 3:

```
# 00 3[0234689] ! #
P: 00           INTERNATIONAL-ACCESS
P: 3[0234689] COUNTRY-CODE
P: !            NATIONAL-NUMBER
P: #            END-OF-DIALING
T: I

# 00 35X ! #
P: 00           INTERNATIONAL-ACCESS
P: 35X          COUNTRY-CODE
P: !            NATIONAL-NUMBER
P: #            END-OF-DIALING
T: I
```

The first record describes calls to all of the 2-digit country codes in zone 3 (excluding the Netherlands itself), while the second record describes calls to the 3-digit country codes in zone 3. Both records describe the type of call as international, and both records require the user to dial # at the end of international numbers before CallManager routes the call.

A chief point to note is that the expression 3[0234689] in the first record and 35X in the second record describe different numbering ranges. The first expression deliberately excludes digit strings starting with 35, while the second includes only those digit strings starting with 35. Preventing overlap between patterns in a numbering plan is essential to eliminate interdigit timing.

National Calls

Numbers beginning with 01, 02, 03, 04, 05, and 07 provide access to different areas within the Netherlands. The cities in Table 2-80 are in the listed codes in the 02 numbering range.

Table 2-80   *Cities in the Netherlands in the 02 Numbering Range*

City	City Code	City	City Code
Amsterdam	020	Nijmegen	024
Den Burg	0222	Beverwijk	0251
Den Helder	0223	Hillegom	0252
Schagen	0224	Ijmuiden	0255
Noord Scharwoude	0226	Arnhem	026
Middenmeer	0227	Weensp	0294
Enkhuizen	0228	Uithoorn	0297
Hoorn	0229	Purmerend	0299
Haarlem	023		

The initial 0 indicates access to a different numbering area, which means that city codes are either two or three digits long. When a city code is two digits long, the subscriber number that follows is seven digits long. When a city code is three digits long, the subscriber number that follows is six digits long.

Building numbering plan records for the city uses the same logic that building numbering plan records for country codes does. Explicit enumeration of each range that starts with a unique set of initial digits makes the task straightforward. The following numbering plan records set up dialing within the Netherlands to city codes that begin with 2:

```
# 020, 023, 024, 026
P:   0                  LONG-DISTANCE-DIRECT-DIAL
P:   2[0346]            AREA-CODE
P:   [2-8]XXXXXX        SUBSCRIBER
T:   N

# Rest of 022
P:   0                  LONG-DISTANCE-DIRECT-DIAL
P:   22[2-46-9]         AREA-CODE
P:   [2-8]XXXXX         SUBSCRIBER
T:   N

# Rest of 025
P:   0                  LONG-DISTANCE-DIRECT-DIAL
P:   25[125]            AREA-CODE
P:   [2-8]XXXXX         SUBSCRIBER
T:   N

# Rest of 029
P:   0                  LONG-DISTANCE-DIRECT-DIAL
P:   29[479]            AREA-CODE
P:   [2-8]XXXXX         SUBSCRIBER
T:   N
```

The numbering plan records tag the initial zero as LONG-DISTANCE-DIRECT-DIAL so that by defining a route filter such as LONG-DISTANCE-DIRECT-DIAL DOES-NOT-EXIST, you can exclude all intercity calls. The city code itself is mapped to area code, and the 6- or 7-digit subscriber number is tagged as SUBSCRIBER.

Miscellaneous Service Calls

Numbers beginning with 06 in the Netherlands numbering plan represent miscellaneous services, such as mobile, videotex, and data services. The number length varies significantly in this range; the records are either six, nine, or ten digits long.

The following records show the 06 range of special services:

```
# 061/062/065 (mobile)
P:  0                   LONG-DISTANCE-DIRECT-DIAL
P:  6[125]              SERVICE
P:  XXXXXXX             SUBSCRIBER
T:  N

# 066 (semafonie)
P:  0                   LONG-DISTANCE-DIRECT-DIAL
P:  66                  SERVICE
P:  XXXXXXX             SUBSCRIBER
T:  N

# 067 (videotex & data services)
# 6 digits except 067281, 067284 and 067364 which are 10
P:  0                   LONG-DISTANCE-DIRECT-DIAL
P:  67                  SERVICE
P:  [^*#23]XX           SUBSCRIBER
T:  N

P:  0                   LONG-DISTANCE-DIRECT-DIAL
P:  67                  SERVICE
P:  2[^*#8]X            SUBSCRIBER
T:  N

P:  0                   LONG-DISTANCE-DIRECT-DIAL
P:  67                  SERVICE
P:  28[^*#14]           SUBSCRIBER
T:  N

P:  0                   LONG-DISTANCE-DIRECT-DIAL
P:  67                  SERVICE
P:  28[14]XXXX          SUBSCRIBER
T:  N

P:  0                   LONG-DISTANCE-DIRECT-DIAL
P:  67                  SERVICE
P:  3[^*#6]X            SUBSCRIBER
T:  N

P:  0                   LONG-DISTANCE-DIRECT-DIAL
P:  67                  SERVICE
P:  36[^*#4]            SUBSCRIBER
T:  N
```

```
P:  0                   LONG-DISTANCE-DIRECT-DIAL
P:  67                  SERVICE
P:  364XXXX             SUBSCRIBER
T:  N
```

There are two interesting things to note about these records. First, they demonstrate one of the weaknesses of reusing the North American tags. It might be nice to further subclassify the 06 numbering range into mobile, semafonie, videotex, and data calls based on the initial digits. By mapping these services to other tags (such as TRANSIT-NETWORK), you might be able to accomplish this task, but the results would make for some rather unusual route filters.

The other interesting thing to note about these records is the use of the ^ wildcard in some of the expressions. The expression [^*#4] means that the particular character matches all digits that are not *, #, or 4—in other words, [0-35-9].

Network Services

In the Netherlands, users access network services by dialing numbers beginning with 11 or 12. The following numbering plan records handle this numbering range:

```
# 112 - Emergency service
P:  112                 SERVICE
T:  N
U:  Y

# 11x - Other 3 digit services (like 118)
P:  11X                 SERVICE
T:  N

# 12XX - Other 4 digit services
P:  12XX                SERVICE
T:  N
```

This set of records demonstrates the U: tag, which marks the route pattern as urgent in the macro expansion that CallManager performs. Marking the route pattern as urgent means that CallManager will route the call the moment a calling user dials a digit string that matches the route pattern. Urgent route patterns cancel the interdigit timer.

Local Numbers

The final class of numbers in the Netherlands numbering plan introduces an instance where configuration of overlapping route patterns cannot be avoided, local dialing. In the Netherlands numbering plan, subscriber numbers are either six digits or seven digits. The problem that occurs is that users in a 6-digit dialing area must wait for the interdigit timer to expire before CallManager routes their call, if the numbering plan also includes a 7-digit route pattern.

If you know that you are deploying a system in an area with 6-digit dialing, one approach to handling this problem is not to encode the 7-digit subscriber number. Although this approach works, a chief advantage that IP telephony offers is geographical independence. One CallManager can control phones that reside in different dialing areas. Users in 6-digit dialing areas need the 6-digit numbering plan record, and users in 7-digit dialing areas need the 7-digit dialing record.

The North American numbering plan has exactly this issue with 7-digit and 10-digit local dialing areas. It gets around this problem by defining both numbering plan records and then relying on the administrator to selectively suppress the longer numbering plan record for those users in the shorter numbering area. The North American numbering plan permits this by applying a tag to the longer record that the administrator can use a route filter to suppress.

The following two records handle local dialing in the Netherlands:

```
# 7 digit local subscriber, 3 digit local area code
P:  [2-8]        LOCAL-AREA-CODE
P:  XXXXXX       SUBSCRIBER
T:  N

# 6 digit local subscriber, 4 digit local area code
P:  [2-8]XXXXX   SUBSCRIBER
T:  N
```

The LOCAL-AREA-CODE on the longer numbering plan record provides the handle that a route filter needs to eliminate interdigit timing for users in a 6-digit dialing area. If you define and apply the route filter LOCAL-AREA-CODE DOES-NOT-EXIST, CallManager includes all of the numbering plan records that this section has defined except the 7-digit record. Thus, users in 6-digit dialing areas need not experience interdigit timing.

Troubleshooting

This section covers some problems commonly encountered relating to call routing in Cisco CallManager.

Cisco CallManager Applies Outside Dial Tone Too Late

This problem always occurs because a pattern exists that overlaps with the route pattern to which you want CallManager to apply outside dial tone. Usually, through inspection, you can discover another route pattern, directory number, translation pattern, or feature-related number that begins with the same sequence of digits as the route pattern in question.

Check all other route patterns in the system to see if any of them begin with the same digit sequence as the pattern for which you expect outside dial tone. CallManager only applies outside dial tone when all possible matching route patterns have had their **Outside Dial Tone** box checked. Patterns such as directory numbers and features cause the suppression of outside dial tone when their range overlaps with that of a route pattern. See the section "Outside Dial Tone" for more details.

In very rare cases, the problem occurs because SQL Server contains an erroneous route plan record that causes the overlapping pattern. In this case, only directly editing the route plan tables in SQL Server can solve the problem.

Cisco CallManager Applies Outside Dial Tone Too Early

This problem occurs when you are using outside access codes that are longer than a single digit. Because of the way that CallManager's outside dial tone logic works, you must configure a separate route pattern that specifically suppresses outside dial tone until the digit that you wish. Note particularly that the location of the . wildcard in a route pattern has no effect on when CallManager applies outside dial tone.

To delay the application of outside dial tone, add a route pattern that represents just your outside access code, but leave the **Outside Dial Tone** check box unchecked. This configuration will cause CallManager to suppress outside dial tone until all digits of the access code have been dialed, because the access code itself, for which outside dial tone is not applied, suppresses the application of outside dial tone. See the section "Outside Dial Tone" for details about outside dial tone.

7-Digit Calls to the North American PSTN Wait Ten Seconds Before Routing

Because some geographical regions use 7-digit dialing and others use 10-digit dialing, the North American numbering plan that ships with CallManager must accommodate both types of dialing. Furthermore, because the IP network allows stations in different geographical locations to register with the same CallManager, CallManager must support both types of dialing simultaneously.

Applying the route filter **7-Digit Dialing** prevents CallManager from adding the numbering plan record in the North American numbering plan that routes 10-digit local calls.

Phone A Can Call Phone B, but Not Vice Versa

This problem usually, but not always, is related to calling search spaces and partitions. In the most common scenario, the partition in which station B is listed is in station A's calling search space, but not vice versa. You might be encountering this problem if CallManager applies reorder while phone B is dialing phone A, or if CallManager applies reorder immediately on collecting all the digits of phone A.

See the section "Calling Search Spaces and Partitions" for more information about calling search spaces and partitions.

Route Pattern 9 XXX XXXX and Route Pattern 9.@ Are Defined, but Cisco CallManager Never Selects Route Pattern 9 XXX XXXX

The @ pattern causes CallManager to add many specific patterns, some of which may match a dialed digit string more closely than the ones you configure.

You can either more narrowly tailor the route pattern you add or use route filters on the @ pattern to eliminate the more closely matching route pattern. See the section "@ Wildcard" for more information about how closest match routing and the @ wildcard interact.

Digit Discarding Instructions on a Route Pattern Are Defined, but the Digit Discarding Instructions Are Not Taking Effect

There are two common causes of this problem.

The first main cause is that digit discarding instructions generally apply only to @ patterns. It is particularly tempting for users who configure patterns such as 0!# to attempt to configure the digit discarding instruction trailing-#. Unfortunately, this digit discarding instruction simply removes the END-OF-DIALING terminator as specified in the North American numbering plan. To discard trailing-# from a non-@ pattern, configure the StripTrailingPound service parameter.

The second main cause occurs when route lists are in operation. If you configure the digit discarding instructions NoDigits instead of <None> on a particular route, you instruct CallManager to ignore the digit discarding instructions defined on the route pattern and instead apply the ones defined on the route. In this case, the digit discarding instruction NoDigits tells CallManager to restore the original dialed digit string.

CPU Usage on a Cisco CallManager Server Rises to 100 Percent, Memory Usage Escalates, and Ultimately Cisco CallManager Restarts

If you can trace this problem to a particular phone call that a user makes, it might be due to a call routing loop. When a phone loses its registration to CallManager, CallManager purges the directory number entry associated with the phone. Normally, this causes no problem, but if you have multiple clusters or a gateway to another PBX, you have configured a generic route pattern such as 8XXX to route calls to extensions that CallManager does not handle to the other system.

If the other system also has such a generic route pattern, when CallManager routes the call to it, the other system does not find any phone to which to extend the call. As a result, its logic sends the call back to CallManager, which again forwards the call to the other system. The call loops indefinitely, consuming CPU and memory until the CallManager cannot cope anymore. (In traditional circuit-switched systems, this problem can occur but is less serious, because at some point, all of the circuits between the systems are exhausted and the call tears down.)

Eliminating this problem means making sure that when a call arrives from another system, CallManager cannot immediately forward that call out another gateway connection. To accomplish this task, give the gateway from the other system a calling search space that does not include the partition in which the gateway itself resides. See the section "Calling Search Spaces and Partitions" for more information.

All Users Receive Immediate Reorder When They Go Off-Hook

This problem can occur if you have mistakenly added a translation pattern of **<None>** in the null partition with no called party transformations or calling search space. Accidentally creating one is easy to do: if you go to the Translation Pattern Configuration screen and click **Insert**, Cisco CallManager Administration adds an empty translation pattern.

Translation patterns are always urgent patterns, which means that as soon as a user dials a number that matches them, CallManager applies the transformations and attempts to reanalyze the resulting digits. When the **Translation Pattern** field is **<None>** and the **Partition** field is <None>, CallManager matches the translation pattern the instant anyone takes any phone off-hook.

A translation pattern of **<None>** is, in itself, not a bad thing. Hotline functionality relies on empty translation patterns (see the section "Hotline Functionality" for more information). But when the translation pattern applies no called party transformations or specifies no calling search space, CallManager's reanalysis causes CallManager to select the same translation pattern. After ten iterations, CallManager detects the translation pattern loop and returns reorder to the caller.

Fix the problem by removing the errant translation pattern.

Summary

This chapter has covered all aspects of call routing in Cisco CallManager. It has discussed route patterns and route filters, CallManager's fundamental call routing concept.

From discussing route patterns, it moved on to dialing transformations, the means by which you effect the calling and called numbers that CallManager presents as part of offering calls.

Translation patterns provide a way to alias other route patterns. This powerful tool provides you with the opportunity to modify the calling and called numbers and select new destinations based on the resulting digits.

Route lists and route groups allow you to set up search patterns across your enterprise's gateways to ensure that you fully utilize the most cost-efficient gateways in your enterprise.

The sections about calling search spaces and partitions discussed a mechanism by which you can customize routing on a user-by-user basis. Using calling search spaces and partitions, you can route calls by the type or geographic location of the calling user.

Several case studies and miscellaneous examples described how all of the call routing fundamental concepts work together to solve complex problems. Although none of the case studies represents a complete solution to the most complex enterprises, by studying the approaches these examples described, you can apply the proposed solutions to your enterprise's specific problems.

One section of this chapter discussed CallManager's treatment of the North American numbering plan and described how you can replace it if you so choose, though this task is not for the meek.

Finally, a troubleshooting section summarized common problems that administrators encounter with CallManager's call routing capabilities and proposed solutions.

## CHAPTER 3

Station Devices

This chapter discusses the station protocols Cisco CallManager uses to communicate with the Cisco station devices. CallManager contains several signaling layers, each of which has distinct functions. For example, the Call Control Layer handles all of the call signaling that controls call setup, teardown, and call routing, and the Protocol/Aggregation Layer handles all protocol-specific signaling required for specific devices.

This chapter describes the various station devices that CallManager supports. It contains the following main sections:

- **Definition of Station Devices**—Introduces the station device in the context of CallManager

- **System Devices**—Introduces other devices in CallManager that serve the user

- **Overview of Station Devices Supported by Cisco CallManager**—Differentiates users from stations and categorizes the station devices by protocol

- **Skinny Station Devices**—Describes the functionality of the devices that support the Skinny Client Control Protocol (SCCP) and explains the protocol that supports the devices

- **Computer Telephony Interface (CTI) Devices**—Describes the interface support for devices that connect to CallManager through CTI

- **H.323 Endpoint Devices**—Describes the H.323 endpoints and CallManager's H.323 protocol support

- **Implementation of Trivial File Transfer Protocol (TFTP) for Station Devices**—Provides a detailed description of how station devices use Trivial File Transfer Protocol (TFTP)

Figure 3-1 shows the block structure of CallManager.

The darker shading in Figure 3-1 highlights the software layers and blocks within CallManager that this chapter describes in detail. Other blocks are highlighted with lighter shading. They are part of the station signaling path, but this chapter does not cover them in as much detail.

Figure 3-1 *Cisco CallManager Block Structure Diagram*

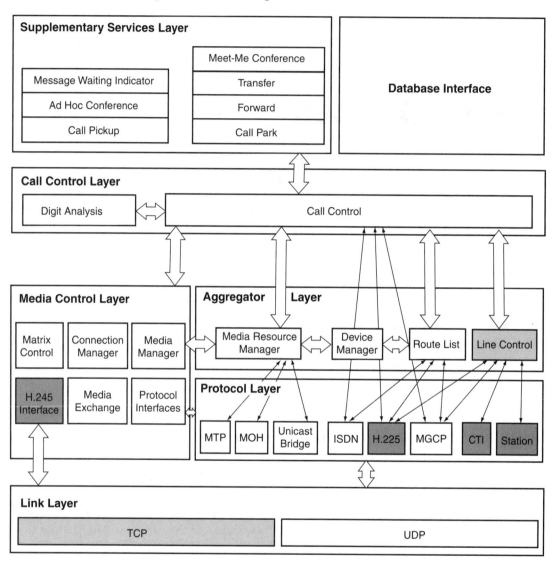

The software in the Media Control Layer handles all media connections CallManager makes between devices. Whereas the Call Control Layer sets up all of the signaling connections between call endpoints and CallManager, the Media Control Layer directs the devices to establish streaming connections. The Media Control Layer can insert other media-processing devices into a call and create appropriate streaming connections to those devices without the Call Control Layer knowing about them.

The blocks in the Protocol/Aggregation Layer control the media-processing devices. They provide the device interface and handle all communication between the devices and CallManager.

Definition of Station Devices

A *station device*, as opposed to a gateway device, is any device that is characterized as a terminal endpoint. A *terminal endpoint* is a device or software application that provides real-time, two-way communication for a single user. The remainder of this chapter often refers to a station device as a *station*.

Software applications that act as station devices include Cisco applications, third-party applications, Cisco Interactive Voice Response (IVR), auto attendant, and voice mail/unified messaging.

Contrast a station device with a gateway device. A *gateway* provides real-time, two-way communication between the packet-based network and other stations on either another packet-based network or a switched network. A gateway provides service for multiple users or provides access connections for simultaneous use by multiple users. A gateway can provide protocol support to terminate multiple stations attached to the gateway device. Gateways can also be used to terminate trunks attached to the Public Switched Telephone Network (PSTN) or to a corporate switch, such as a Private Branch eXchange (PBX).

In contrast, a station usually supports a single user at a time, though one station can support multiple users who log in and out of the station at different times. Whereas, a station may consist of multiple lines and might have the capability of terminating multiple connections, stations typically have only a single connection active at a time and provide only a single media stream to a user. Figure 3-2 shows examples of various stations and a sample gateway device.

Overview of Station Devices Supported by Cisco CallManager

This section summarizes the various station devices that CallManager supports and differentiates a user from a station for the purposes of the discussion. This section categorizes station devices by protocol and then subdivides them by device capabilities.

Figure 3-3 shows the station devices that are part of CallManager. These station devices include H.323 stations, voice mail/unified messaging, IP Phones, Unicast conference devices, transcoders, and voice applications such as Cisco IP SoftPhone. Chapter 5, "Media Processing," discusses conference devices and transcoders in detail.

Figure 3-2 *Station Devices*

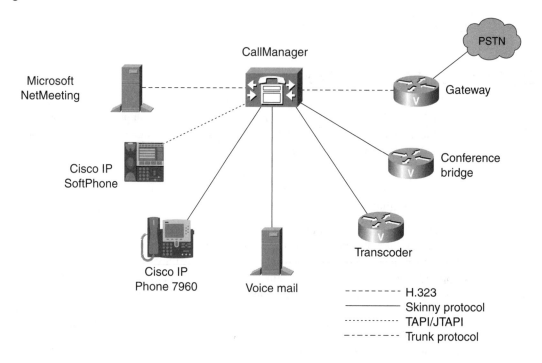

This chapter focuses on the communication between station devices and CallManager. The three basic protocols CallManager uses for this communication are Skinny Client Control Protocol (SCCP, or simply Skinny Protocol), H.323, and Computer Telephony Interface (CTI).

CTI provides Telephony Application Programming Interface (TAPI) and Java TAPI (JTAPI) application layer support. Although stations can reside on the other side of a gateway, the stations discussed in this chapter are limited to those that communicate directly with CallManager. Refer to Chapter 4, "Trunk Devices," for gateway communication and protocols such as Media Gateway Control Protocol (MGCP).

User/Station Distinction

This section describes the concept of a user and differentiates a user from a station for the purpose of eliminating confusion.

A *user* is a person or software application that uses a station to communicate with another user. For the purposes of this chapter, a user has one or more directory numbers that can be dialed to communicate with the user. You can associate one directory number with one or more stations.

Figure 3-3 *System Station Devices*

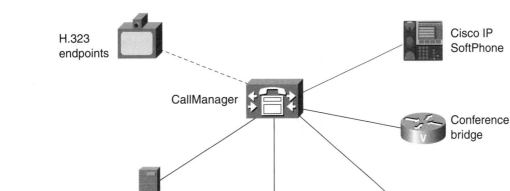

In a typical installation, you assign each user a directory number, or more simply, a phone number. When a user wants to call another user, the called user's directory number is the means by which the calling user specifies the called user. CallManager's model for directory numbers on stations closely resembles the model PBXs use to support digital telephones.

All stations have at least one directory number. When a user selects a directory number, CallManager rings all stations that have an appearance of that directory number. If the directory number appears on multiple stations, the call can be answered at any station with that line appearance.

This capability is typically referred to as *shared line appearances*. Using this feature, users can have stations in multiple places (main office, remote office, home, and so on) with the same line appearance and can receive calls at any of these locations.

Users communicate over a media path, typically audio, that is established between two stations during a call. CallManager allows devices with dissimilar protocols to establish a connection and communicate. The protocol of the caller might be the Skinny Protocol, for example, whereas the protocol of the destination might be H.323.

Figure 3-4 shows three stations. Each station has a unique directory number. Station 3 also has a second directory number. This allows the station to answer calls directed to either station 2 or station 3 (directory number 1002 or 1003). This capability is typically referred to as *multiple line appearances*. When a caller dials directory number 1002, both stations 2 and 3 indicate an incoming call, and the call can be answered at either station.

Figure 3-4   *Station Devices and Directory Numbers*

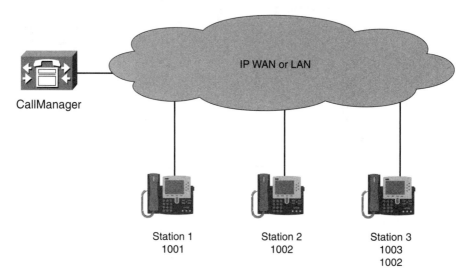

Role of Cisco CallManager for Stations

CallManager provides call control on behalf of stations or gateways. In the case of stations, stations indicate requests for service to CallManager, and CallManager acts on the requests for service. The requests for service include such tasks as device initialization, device configuration information, call origination, call acceptance, call termination, call information, media statistics, and feature activation. CallManager provides the call control engine for the devices that are configured as part of CallManager.

The signaling from CallManager to the station is the call signaling path. The media path for the exchange of media between stations does not pass through CallManager. The stations stream media directly between the stations or directly from a station to a media processing device, such as a Unicast conferencing device or a transcoder.

The protocols that this section discusses include the H.323 protocol (as it relates to stations), Skinny Protocol, and CTI.

Skinny Station Overview

This section provides an overview of the Skinny Protocol device category.

Skinny Protocol is a lightweight, simple, stimulus protocol. The signaling path is a TCP/IP connection that the station establishes to CallManager. The message set for the control of the station encompasses three basic areas: registration and station management, call control, and media stream (audio) control. CallManager directs the establishment of the media connection, but the station and device to which the station is connected establish the media stream directly to each other.

Computer Telephony Interface (CTI) Overview

This section describes the CTI protocol device category. This section also includes an introduction to how TAPI and JTAPI interact with CallManager.

CTI provides a common interface into CallManager. Both JTAPI and TAPI make use of CTI communication with CallManager. The CTI protocol is specific to communication between the Cisco TAPI service provider and CallManager. TAPI applications communicate with the TAPI service provider and have no knowledge of the CTI protocol.

Microsoft's TAPI for Windows simplifies telephony application development. The interface abstracts the telephony services from the actual hardware and software infrastructure of CallManager. Applications developed with TAPI are more portable and less subject to change as the infrastructure changes.

JTAPI is a Java-based interface that provides similar abstraction for Java-based development. JTAPI also abstracts the application development from the CallManager infrastructure. JTAPI extends application portability to include not only independence from CallManager infrastructure, but also independence from any particular operating system.

Figure 3-5 shows the role of the CTI protocol in the application infrastructure of CallManager.

H.323 Endpoint Overview

This section describes the H.323 endpoint protocol device category. An *H.323 endpoint* is a device or software application that communicates with CallManager with the H.323 protocol specification. The Microsoft NetMeeting software application is an example of an H.323 endpoint.

Figure 3-5   *CTI Protocol*

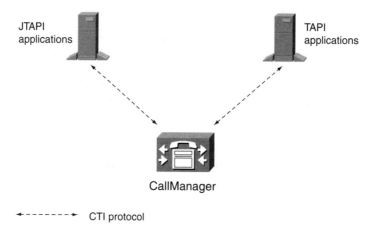

JTAPI
applications

TAPI
applications

CallManager

←-------→   CTI protocol

The H.323 Recommendation from the International Telecommunication Union
Telecommunication Standardization Sector (ITU-T) contains a set of very complex
interlocking protocols. These protocols (for example, H.225.0 and H.245) manage the
connection and the media for a communication session. The frame structure for the
multiplex layer allows for a vast multitude of services. However, the complexity is more
extensive than is required for simple voice communications. H.323 stations must maintain
state information for a call and thus are relatively complex. By contrast, the Skinny Protocol
provides both features and services for relatively low-cost user stations that require no
protocol state processing.

Figure 3-6 shows the relationship of the protocols under the H.323 umbrella specification.

Skinny Station Devices

This section describes the Skinny Protocol devices. The Cisco family of IP Phones has
evolved from the 12SP+ and the 30VIP to the 7900 series IP Phones. The interface to the
full family of Cisco IP Phones uses the same Skinny Protocol. As the Cisco IP Phone family
evolved to include the Cisco 7900 series IP Phones, Skinny Protocol expanded, but the
interface is backward-compatible to support the earlier 12SP+ and 30VIP IP Phones.

Figure 3-6   *H.323 Protocol Specification*

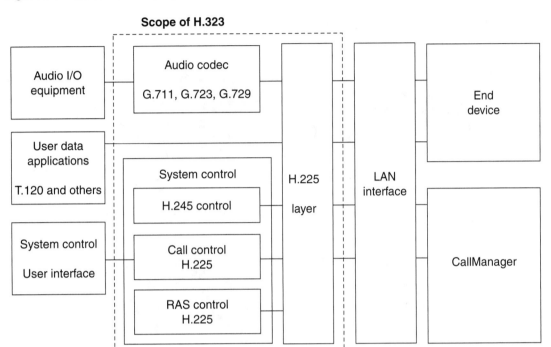

IP Phones

This section describes the original IP Phone capability and interface. The Cisco IP Phone family includes Cisco IP Phone 12SP+, Cisco IP Phone 30VIP, and Cisco IP Phones 7960, 7940, 7935, and 7910. Figure 3-7 shows these Cisco IP Phones and the Cisco IP SoftPhone.

The Cisco IP Phone model 12SP+ is an IP telephone targeting the office user. This voice instrument supports 12 programmable line and feature buttons, an internal two-way speakerphone, and microphone mute. The Cisco 12SP+ also features a two-line liquid crystal display (LCD) capable of displaying 20 characters per line for information such as date and time, calling party name, calling party number, and digits dialed. An LED associated with each of the 12 features indicates the line status and line buttons.

Figure 3-7 *Cisco IP Phones*

Cisco IP Phone 7960

Cisco IP Phone 7910

Cisco IP Phone 7940

Cisco IP Phone
Conference Station 7935

Cisco IP Phone 12SP+

Cisco IP Phone 30VIP

The Cisco IP Phone model 30VIP voice instrument provides more functionality required by executives and managers. It provides 26 programmable line and feature buttons, an internal two-way speakerphone with microphone mute, and a dedicated transfer feature button. The 30VIP provides a 40-character LCD, consisting of two lines of 20 characters each. The display provides functionality such as date and time, calling party name, calling party number, and digits dialed. An LED associated with each of the 30 feature and line buttons provides feature and line status.

The Cisco IP Phone 7910 is a single-line phone with a smaller display, but with a similar look and functionality to the more feature-rich 7940. The Cisco 7935 is a speaker set with similar functionality as the 7910.

Cisco SoftPhone is different than the Cisco IP Phones in that it is software that runs on a PC and uses JTAPI to communicate with CallManager. Cisco SoftPhone provides a similar user interface as the 7960, but offers additional functionality by the graphical user interface (GUI).

The Cisco IP Phones 7940 and 7960 are more-capable IP Phones that use a larger screen, soft keys, and allow Web-based applications to be launched from the **services** button. The user interaction for making calls, phone setup and configuration, and use of features is enhanced by the use of the larger display and more user-friendly interface.

Capabilities and Interface of Cisco IP Phones 7960 and 7940

This section describes the capabilities and interface of Cisco IP Phones 7960 and 7940. Figure 3-8 shows Cisco IP Phone 7960.

Figure 3-8   *Cisco 7960 IP Phone*

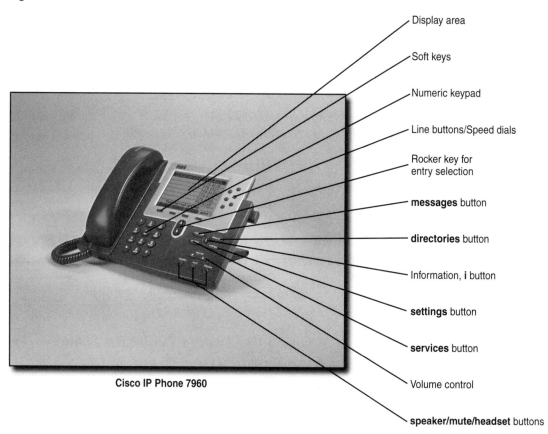

Display area

Soft keys

Numeric keypad

Line buttons/Speed dials

Rocker key for
entry selection

messages button

directories button

Information, **i** button

settings button

services button

Volume control

speaker/mute/headset buttons

Cisco IP Phone 7960

The Cisco IP Phones 7960 and 7940 both include the following:

- Display area—Provides visual information to the user based on the button selected.
- **messages** button—Provides access to voice mail.
- **i** button—Provides additional help functionality.
- **services** button—Allows access to Web-based applications to extend the capability of the phone.

- **directories** button—Provides access to the directory capabilities of the phone, which include calls received, calls placed, and calls missed. Personal and corporate directories can also be added to the directory functionality.

- **settings** button—Gives access to phone-related settings, such as screen contrast and brightness, and phone configuration.

- Four soft key buttons—Provide access to call processing-related features.

- Numeric keypad.

- Up/down entry selection.

- Volume control.

- Programmable line or speed-dial buttons—Six on the 7960 and two on the 7940.

- **speaker**, **mute**, and **headset** buttons.

The **i** button, **directories** button, and **services** button have an associated URL. A URL allows access to a particular entry, such as a file, in a directory that can exist on any machine accessible in the network. A standard default URL is installed with CallManager and is downloaded to the phone. You can override the URL to allow the phone capabilities to be extended. The section under the heading "Cisco IP Phone Services" describes how you can use the **services** button to extend capabilities.

Cisco IP Phone Registration

Cisco IP Phones register with CallManager. The phones must first determine a prioritized list of CallManager nodes with which to register. Once a phone determines a list, the phone attempts to register with the first CallManager node. If successful, that CallManager node is responsible for handling the Skinny Protocol for the IP Phone. The IP Phone also establishes and maintains a connection to a secondary CallManager node, with which it registers in the event that the primary CallManager node is no longer available.

The phone uses Domain Name Server (DNS), Dynamic Host Configuration Protocol (DHCP), and TFTP to determine initially the IP address of the prioritized list of CallManager nodes to which the phone can register. Although each of the above services can ease implementation, they are not all required.

DNS, for example, is not required if CallManagers use IP addresses for their names; for networks not running DHCP, you can use static IP addressing. Figure 3-9 shows the interaction of the phone with DNS, DHCP, TFTP, and CallManager during the initial registration.

Figure 3-9 *Cisco IP Phone Initialization*

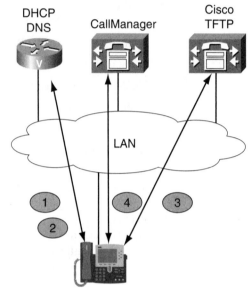

1 Get IP address, mask, DNS

  •Static or DHCP

2 Get TFTP server address (use any one of these)

  •Static address
  •Option 150 (single IP address)
  •Option 66 (first IP address or DNS name)
  •Lookup CiscoCM1.your.domain

3 Get configuration from CallManager TFTP

  •XML file or .cnf file with list of up to three CallManager servers
  •If XML file, verify firmware version. If version update is required, get the new firmware load.

4 Register with the Cisco CallManager server. If using the .cnf file and the version is not confirmed with the XML file, then request and verify the version information. If a version update is required, unregister, get the new version, and reregister.

DHCP is a service provided with the Microsoft Windows 2000 server or the Cisco Network Registrar that automatically assigns IP addresses to devices on the network. Cisco IP Phones are DHCP-enabled by default. If DHCP is not in use, use the **settings** button on the phone to disable DHCP and manually configure the IP address of the phone and the TFTP server address. Disabling DHCP and manually configuring the IP addresses prevents mobility of the phone. Assuming DHCP, DNS, and TFTP services are running, the phone goes through the following sequence of events to register initially with a CallManager node:

1 The phone requests an IP address from the DHCP service.

2 As part of the DHCP response, the DHCP server returns the TFTP server address to the phone.

3 Once the phone receives the TFTP address, the phone requests its configuration information from the TFTP server. The configuration information includes a prioritized list of up to three CallManager nodes. The configuration information can be in the form of an extensible markup language (XML) file or a configuration (.cnf) file. Release 3.1 versions of the IP phones make use of the XML file. The XML file contains additional information, including the phone load version.

4 The phone establishes communication with the highest CallManager node in the prioritized list and sends a registration request. If the phone requested a configuration file and not an XML file, the phone also sends a version request and checks the phone load version. If the phone firmware version matches the current phone firmware version, the phone continues with the registration process. If the phone needs a new firmware version, the phone aborts the registration process and downloads a new version of the phone firmware from the TFTP server. Once the phone loads the new firmware, the phone restarts the registration process. If the phone processed an XML file for the configuration information, the version has already been verified and is not requested from CallManager.

5 Once the phone has successfully registered, the DHCP and TFTP communications are not repeated, unless the phone experiences a hard reset through a power off/on sequence or by a reset from Cisco CallManager Administration.

The "Implementation of TFTP for Station Devices" section at the end of this chapter contains more information about TFTP-specific details.

Call Signaling

Skinny Protocol is a simple stimulus interface between the Cisco IP Phone and CallManager. The communication takes place over a TCP/IP connection that the phone establishes to CallManager on port 2000. Once established, the connection remains as long as the phone is capable of initiating or accepting calls. Figure 3-10 shows the basic Skinny Protocol call signaling for a call between Cisco IP Phones. Figure 3-10 illustrates the sequence of events detailed in Table 3-1.

Figure 3-10 *Making a Call Between IP Phones*

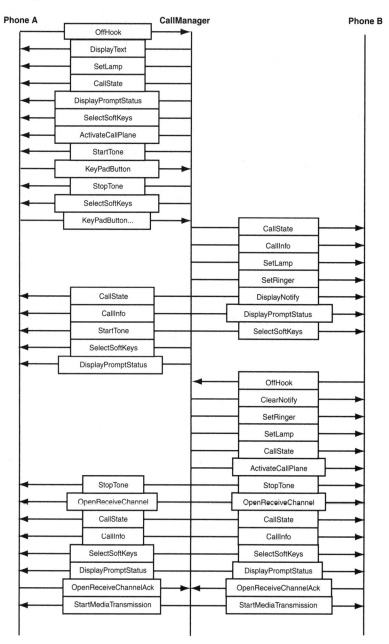

Table 3-1   *Making a Call Between IP Phones*

Phone A	Cisco CallManager	Phone B	Description
OffHook -->			When you lift the handset of IP Phone A, the phone reports off-hook to CallManager.
	DisplayText <--		CallManager sends the text to update the display of a limited-display phone, such as the 30VIP.
	SetLamp <--		CallManager sends the information required to set the line lamp of the line used for the call. The 12SP+ and the 30VIP have a line lamp that is lit.
	CallState <--		CallManager sends the CallState information, which the Cisco IP Phones 7960 and 7940 use to update call state information. The IP Phones use this information to update the icon of the appropriate line as a visual indication of call state.
	DisplayPromptStatus <--		CallManager sends the DisplayPromptStatus to update the prompt line, which is the display line just above the soft key text line on the Cisco IP Phones 7960 and 7940. This initial prompt is "Enter number." The prompt message is associated with a particular line. If a different line is selected, the prompt will change to the prompt associated with the selected line.
	SelectSoftKeys <--		CallManager sends SelectSoftKeys to activate a set of soft keys and a mask to select which soft keys are enabled and which keys are disabled. The Cisco IP Phones 7960 and 7940 use the soft keys.

continues

Table 3-1 *Making a Call Between IP Phones (Continued)*

Phone A	Cisco CallManager	Phone B	Description
	ActivateCallPlane <--		CallManager sends ActivateCallPlane to activate the call plane for the specified line. In this case, the call is line 1 as the default because no specific line was selected. The Cisco IP Phones 7960 and 7940 use the ActivateCallPlane command.
	StartTone <--		CallManager directs the phone to play a dial tone. The phone internally generates a dial tone.
KeyPadButton -->			As you enter the number of the desired destination—Phone B in this case—the phone sends a KeyPadButton for each digit dialed. The KeyPadButton messages continue until CallManager determines that you have entered the required number of digits to reach your destination. Once CallManager determines the called party—Phone B in this case—CallManager initiates the message sequence to Phone B to extend the call to Phone B.
	CallState -->		CallManager sends the CallState information, which the Cisco IP Phones 7960 and 7940 use to update the call state information and the icon of the appropriate line as a visual indication of call state. In this case, the call state indicates an incoming call.

Table 3-1   *Making a Call Between IP Phones (Continued)*

Phone A	Cisco CallManager	Phone B	Description
	CallInfo -->		CallManager sends CallInfo to the station to provide the specific information about the call, which includes calling and called party name and number, the line number for the call, and the type of call (inbound, outbound, or forwarded). In this case, the call type is inbound. The name might not be provided in all cases. A gateway call, for example, might not provide calling party name.
	SetLamp -->		CallManager sends the information required to set the line lamp of the line used for the call. Cisco IP Phones 12SP+ and 30VIP have a line lamp that can be lit.
	SetRinger -->		CallManager sends the SetRinger to Phone B to cause the phone to ring, indicating an incoming call. The ring type is InsideRing, as distinguished from OutsideRing, because this is an internal call from Phone A to Phone B.
	DisplayNotify -->		CallManager sends DisplayNotify to Phone B to indicate an incoming call and has an associated timeout that defaults to 10 seconds. DisplayNotify updates the display immediately and is not associated with a particular line.
	CallState <--		CallManager updates the call state of Phone A to indicate that Phone B is now ringing.

continues

Table 3-1 *Making a Call Between IP Phones (Continued)*

Phone A	Cisco CallManager	Phone B	Description
	DisplayPromptStatus -->		CallManager sends DisplayPromptStatus to Phone B to update the display associated with the particular line of the incoming call. This display persists for the selected line until it is changed by another DisplayPromptStatus message.
	CallInfo <--		CallManager sends CallInfo to Phone A to provide the specific information about the call, which includes calling and called party name and number, the line number for the call, and the type of call. Because Phone A originated the call, the call is outbound.
	SelectSoftKeys -->		CallManager sends SelectSoftKeys to Phone B to activate the appropriate soft keys.
	StartTone <--		CallManager sends StartTone to Phone A to initiate the ringback tone to the caller at Phone A. The tone is generated internally by Phone A.
	SelectSoftKeys <--		CallManager sends SelectSoftKeys to Phone A to activate the appropriate soft keys for the ringing call.
	DisplayPromptStatus <--		CallManager sends DisplayPromptStatus to Phone A to display the prompt appropriate for the updated soft keys.
		OffHook <--	When you lift the handset of Phone B, the phone reports off-hook to CallManager.
	ClearNotify -->		CallManager clears the notify message rather than waiting for the timeout. The display then reverts to the prompt display associated with the line being answered.

Table 3-1 *Making a Call Between IP Phones (Continued)*

Phone A	Cisco CallManager	Phone B	Description
	SetRinger -->		CallManager turns off the ringer because the call has been answered.
	SetLamp -->		CallManager sets the line lamp of the line answered on Phone B.
	CallState -->		CallManager updates the call state information for the call because it has changed from ringing to answered.
	ActivateCallPlane -->		CallManager activates the call plane for the line that was answered.
	StopTone <-- -->		CallManager stops the ringback tone on Phone A and the ringer tone on Phone B.
	OpenReceiveChannel <-- -->		CallManager sends OpenReceiveChannel to both Phone A and B to cause the phone to begin receiving audio sent from the other phone. This is only half of the audio path, and because neither phone is transmitting at this point, the connection is not yet fully established.
	CallState <-- -->		The call state is updated to connected for both Phone A and B.
	CallInfo <-- -->		The call info is updated for both Phone A and B.
	SelectSoftKeys <-- -->		The soft keys are updated on both Phone A and B.

continues

Table 3-1   *Making a Call Between IP Phones (Continued)*

Phone A	Cisco CallManager	Phone B	Description
	DisplayPromptStatus <-- -->		The prompt line is updated on both Phone A and B.
OpenReceive ChannelAck -->		OpenReceive ChannelAck <--	Both phones have responded with an OpenReceiveChannelAck, indicating that they are ready to receive media transmission.
	StartMediaTransmission <-- -->		CallManager sends StartMediaTransmission to both Phone A and B to cause the phone to begin sending audio to the other phone. Because both phone are transmitting and receiving audio at this point, the connection is now fully established.

Cisco IP Phone Services

This section describes the functionality of the flexible and extensible services provided by the Cisco IP Phones 7960 and 7940. These phones are able to deploy customized client services. The services make use of the keypad, soft keys, and display to interact with the user. The services are deployed using the HTTP protocol. This protocol is available on standard Web servers such as Microsoft Internet Information Server (IIS).

The **services** button initiates the services. The URL is set for the phone, but you can change it. This section describes the service capabilities of Cisco IP Phones 7940 and 7960 to help you understand the flexibility they offer.

Overview of Cisco IP Phone Services

When the user pushes the **services** button, the display provides a list of services that have been configured for the phone. The user can select a menu item using either the scroll and entry selector on the phone or the keypad to enter the numeric value of the selection.

Each user can control the services that are displayed by changing the user configuration from the Cisco IP Phone Configuration Web interface. The Cisco IP Phone Configuration page allows you not only to set speed-dial numbers and call forward but also to enable Cisco IP Phone Services from a drop-down list of available services.

Once the user selects a menu item, the phone uses its HTTP client to send the HTTP request to the Web server that the URL address specifies. The phone is not a Web browser and is not able to parse HTML. The response to the HTTP request is either plain text or packaged in specifically defined XML wrappers. The phone receives the object returned by the Web server and interacts with the user as specified by the text or XML data type supported by the phone.

Phone-Supported XML Data Types

When progressing through the data page returned by the Web server, the phone simply processes the text or XML data types to update the display and process user input as directed.

The following pages discuss each of the six XML data types supported by the phone. Several of the XML data types described here have optional **Title** and **Prompt** fields. These fields behave identically, so this paragraph describes them and the remainder of this chapter does not repeat the description.

Text defined in the **Title** field is displayed at the top of the page. If the data page specifies no **Title** field, the IP Phone displays the **Name** field of the last selected MenuItem in the **Title** field.

The **Prompt** field defines text to be displayed at the bottom of the display page. If the data page specifies no **Prompt** parameter, the prompt area of the display is cleared.

Menu

```
<CiscoIPPhoneMenu>
  <Title>Title text goes here</Title>
  <Prompt>Prompt text goes here</Prompt>
  <MenuItem>
    <Name>The name of each menu item</Name>
    <URL>The URL associated with the menu item</URL>
  </MenuItem>
</CiscoIPPhoneMenu>
```

The XML type CiscoIPPhoneMenu simply lists text items, one per line. Users select individual menu items either by using the scroll and entry selector or by number from the numeric keypad. The XML format allows you to specify a menu **Title** and **Prompt**, followed by up to 32 MenuItems. Each MenuItem has a name and an associated URL. Once the user selects a menu option, the phone sends an HTTP request based on the URL associated with the menu item selected.

Text

```
<CiscoIPPhoneText>
  <Title>Title text goes here</Title>
  <Text>The text to be displayed as the message body goes here</Text>
  <Prompt>The prompt text goes here</Prompt>
</CiscoIPPhoneText>
```

The XML type CiscoIPPhoneText displays text on the phone display. The text should contain no control characters other than carriage return, line feed, or tab. The phone provides pagination and word-wrap to fit the text to the phone display. Plain text can be delivered either through this XML type or as plain text through HTTP. Text delivered as type text/HTML behaves the same as type CiscoIPPhoneText, except for the inability to include a **Title** or **Prompt**.

Image

```
<CiscoIPPhoneImage>
  <Title>Image title goes here</Title>
  <LocationX>Position information of graphic</LocationX>
  <LocationY>Position information of graphic</LocationY>
  <Width>Size information for the graphic</Width>
  <Height>Size information for the graphic</Height>
  <Depth>Number of bits per pixel</Depth>
  <Data>Packed Pixel Data</Data>
  <Prompt>Prompt text goes here</Prompt>
</CiscoIPPhoneImage>
```

The Cisco IP Phones 7960 and 7940 have a bitmapped display that is 133 by 65 pixels. Each pixel has four grayscale settings. The CiscoIPPhoneImage is used to render graphics on the Cisco IP Phone 7960 or 7940 display. The values specified by parameters LocationX and LocationY control the position of the graphic. These values specify the location, in pixels, of the upper left corner of the graphic. The values 0, 0 position the graphic at the upper left corner of the display. The values -1, -1 instruct the phone to center the graphic in the display area.

Width and **Height**, used to control those two dimensions, must be matched up properly with the pixel stream in the **Data** field to produce the desired results. **Depth** specifies the number of bits per pixel, which currently must be set to 2.

The Data tag delimits a string of hexadecimal digits that contain the packed value of pixels in the display. In the Cisco IP Phones 7960 and 7940, each pixel has only three possible states, allowing 4 pixels packed per byte. Each byte is specified as 2 hex digits.

Table 3-2 shows how the hex digits are packed to specify the pixel values, 2 bits per pixel. A contiguous stream of hex digits, with no separators or spaces, specifies the entire display. The stream is (width x height + 3)/4 characters in length. The phone display is cleared at the time the graphic is displayed.

Table 3-2   *Data Tag Digits*

Pixels	1	3	2	0
Binary Value	01	11	10	00
Hex Digits	7		8	
Packed Value	78			

GraphicMenu

```
<CiscoIPPhoneGraphicMenu>
  <Title>Menu title goes here</Title>
  <LocationX>Position information of graphic</LocationX>
  <LocationY>Position information of graphic</LocationY>
  <Width>Size information for the graphic</Width>
  <Height>Size information for the graphic</Height>
  <Depth>Number of bits per pixel</Depth>
  <Data>Packed Pixel Data</Data>
  <Prompt>Prompt text goes here</Prompt>
  <MenuItem>
    <Name>The name of each menu item</Name>
    <URL>The URL associated with the menu item</URL>
  </MenuItem>
</CiscoIPPhoneGraphicMenu>
```

Graphic menus, like text menus, allow a user to select a menu item. The graphic menu allows a graphic to be used instead of text for the menu items. The menu item is presented as a bitmapped graphic. The user enters a menu selection by using the keypad to enter a number that selects the menu item. The XML tags for GraphicMenu are identical to the tag definitions for CiscoIPPhoneImage and CiscoIPPhoneMenu.

Directory

```
<CiscoIPPhoneDirectory>
  <Title>Directory title goes here</Title>
  <Prompt>Prompt text goes here</Prompt>
  <DirectoryEntry>
    <Name>The name of the directory entry</Name>
    <Telephone>The telephone number for the entry</Telephone>
  </DirectoryEntry>
</CiscoIPPhoneDirectory>
```

CiscoIPPhoneDirectory XML data type is used for directory type operations. The directory entry is selected just like menu items. In addition, the Cisco IP Phones 7960 and 7940 display the appropriate soft keys that are needed to initiate a call to the selected number. One soft key is **Edit Dial**, which allows the user to insert an access code or other necessary digits before dialing. The **DirectoryEntry** field is repeated as many times as is necessary to send all of the entries to the phone.

Input

```
<CiscoIPPhoneInput>
  <Title>Directory title goes here</Title>
  <Prompt>Prompt text goes here</Prompt>
  <URL>The target URL for the completed input goes here</URL>
  <InputItem>
    <DisplayName>Name of the input field to display</DisplayName>
    <QueryStringParam>The URL query parameter</QueryStringParam>
    <InputFlags></InputFlags>
    <DefaultValue>Value</DefaultValue>
  </InputItem>
</CiscoIPPhoneInput>
```

In response to a CiscoIPPhoneInput, the phone builds and displays the input form. The input form prompts the user for specific data. Once the user enters the data, the phone collects that data according to the input form specifications and sends the data to the target URL. The URL tag specifies the URL to receive the results. The HTTP request sent to the server is the URL with a list of parameters appended as a query string. The parameters are name/value pairs, one pair for each input item. The Cisco IP Phones 7960 and 7940 do not support the HTTP POST method. POST is an HTTP method for submitting data to a Web server.

The InputItem tag delimits each of the lists of input items. Each item has a DisplayName, a QueryStringParam, a DefaultValue, and a set of InputFlags. The DisplayName specifies the prompt that is written to the display for the input list item. The QueryStringParam provides the parameter name used in the URL that is returned to the server when the input is complete. The DefaultValue tag, if specified, denotes the default value to be displayed. The set of InputFlags controls the input to be used for the input item. The input types include

- A—Plain ASCII text. The dual tone multifrequency (DTMF) keypad is used to enter text consisting of uppercase and lowercase letters, numbers, and special characters.

- T—Telephone number. DTMF digits are the only acceptable input for this field. This includes numbers, the pound key (#), and the asterisk key (*).

- N—Numeric. Numbers are the only acceptable input.

- E—Equation. This includes numbers and special math symbols.

- U—Uppercase. This is only uppercase letters.

- L—Lowercase. This is only lowercase letters.

- P—Password field. Individual characters are displayed as they are keyed in using the standard keypad-repeat entry mode. As soon as each character is accepted, it is converted to an asterisk, allowing for privacy of the entered value.

Soft Keys

During the entry of the text, the Cisco IP Phones 7960 and 7940 display soft keys that are intended to help the data-entry process. The following soft keys are used:

- **Submit**—This indicates that the form is complete and the resulting URL should be sent by HTTP.
- **<<**—Backspace within a field.
- **Cancel**—Cancels the current Input.

Field-to-field navigation can be performed with the vertical scroll button used to navigate menus.

An excellent white paper, "Cisco IP Phone Services Application Development Notes," contains more detailed information and can be found at the following link:

```
www.cisco.com/univercd/cc/td/doc/product/voice/sw_ap_to/devguide/
index.htm
```

Computer Telephony Interface (CTI) Devices

This section describes CallManager's application interface implementation and the underlying CTI. CTI is the internal interface to CallManager, on which the standard interfaces, such as TAPI and JTAPI, are supported. CTI communication from the application platform to CallManager is through TCP/IP.

CTI Application Architecture Overview

This section provides an overview of the application architecture that provides a means of controlling call behavior from external applications. CallManager provides already-developed applications and a development infrastructure to allow third-party application development.

Figure 3-11 shows the CallManager infrastructure that supports the applications. The applications run on the application platform and make use of the application services. Applications provide a high-level functionality that is usually specific to a particular need, such as IP Contact Center, voice messaging/unified messaging, and so on. The applications might have media termination functionality or might simply control stations that actually terminate the media. The application platform and services provide the application programming interface (API), call-control protocols, administration and serviceability functionality, and directory and database interfaces.

Figure 3-11 *Cisco CallManager Application Infrastructure*

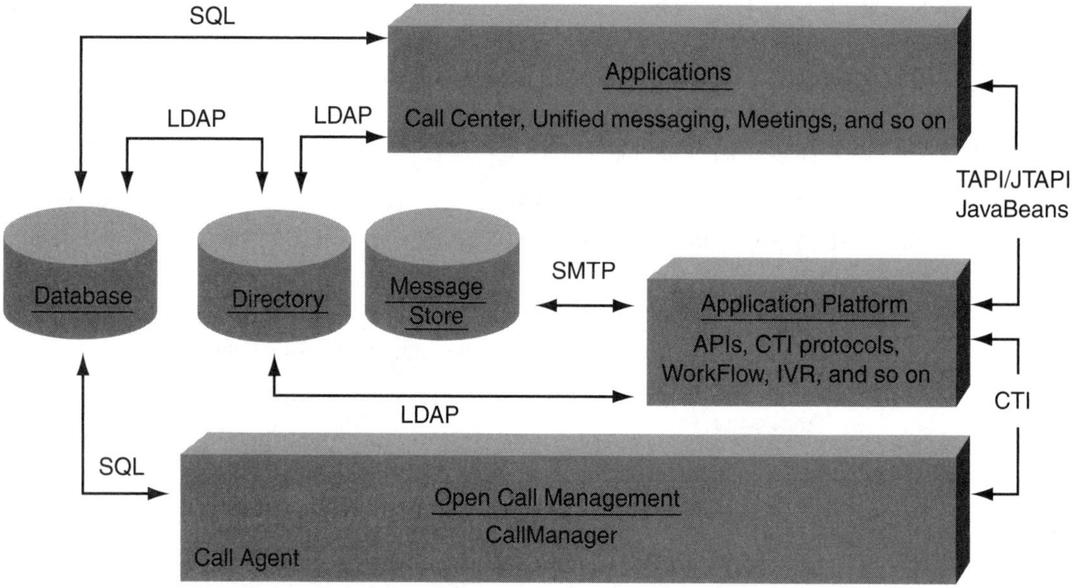

Application Layers External to Cisco CallManager

This section describes the layers external to CallManager that allow an application to interface to CallManager. The two primary application service APIs supported by CallManager are TAPI and JTAPI. These two APIs enable developers to extend the capabilities of CallManager to meet specific enterprise needs. The choice of TAPI or JTAPI is based on the particular needs and preferences of the corporation.

Microsoft's TAPI for Windows was initially used for first-party device control for devices that were co-resident, such as controlling modems. The application would initiate a modem connection from the software running on the personal computer to a destination provided by the application. TAPI was extended to include a telephony server for third-party remote control, such as PBX devices. The TAPI framework abstracts the telephony services from the CallManager infrastructure. The applications are more portable and insulated from the effect of changes as new releases of CallManager are released.

Figure 3-12 illustrates the components that make up the TAPI architecture and reside in the PC running the telephony application. The TAPI architecture is an abstraction layer between the TAPI applications and the underlying hardware and transport protocols of CallManager. The TAPI application accesses the device-specific controls for communications and call processing through a dynamic link library (DLL). Each TAPI application is a separate process that communicates using TAPI with Tapi32.dll or Tapi3.dll, provided by Microsoft. Tapi32.dll and Tapi3.dll communicate with the TAPISRV.EXE process using a private remote-procedure call (RPC) interface. TAPISRV.EXE is a Microsoft process that runs as a service in Windows NT and Windows 2000. TAPISRV.EXE communicates with the telephony service provider (TSP) using Telephony Service Provider Interface (TSPI). The Cisco TAPI Service Provider (Cisco TSP) is a DLL that runs under the TAPISRV.EXE process. The Cisco TSP communicates with CallManager through a TCP/IP interface known as CTIQBE. The Quick Buffer Encoding (QBE, pronounced "cube") format is based loosely on Microsoft's TAPI buffer format. QBE defines C-language structures that can be byte-copied directly to or from an input/output stream. The Cisco TSP allows developers to create customized IP telephony applications for CallManager.

The Cisco TSP supports first-party call control or third-party call control. In first-party call control, the application terminates the audio stream. With third-party call control, the application controls the audio stream of some other audio stream-terminating device. The device can be a particular station or a group of stations for which the application is responsible. CallManager for TAPI currently supports 2.1, not 3.*x*.

Figure 3-12 *Cisco TAPI Architecture*

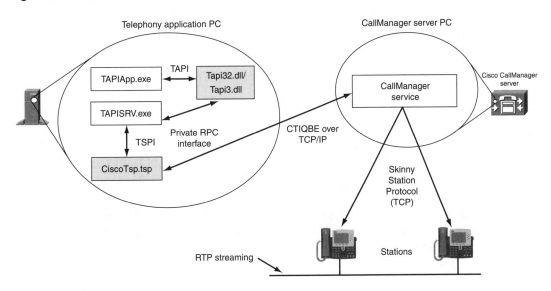

JTAPI provides similar functionality for Java-based applications development. JTAPI supports call control and primitive media support. JTAPI is more OS-independent than TAPI. CallManager for JTAPI currently supports JTAPI 1.2, not 1.3. CallManager provides the following packages:

- Core Package (Make Call, Answer, Disconnect, all events)
- Call Control Package (Hold, Conference, Transfer, Accept, Redirect, many events)
- Call Center Package (Routing)
- Media Package (DTMF detection, generation)

CallManager also provides the following extensions:

- API usability (Transfer/Conference meta-information)
- Media termination (Media terminal registration, RTP stream events)
- Device roaming (Terminal/Address IN_SERVICE/OUT_OF_SERVICE events)
- CallManager value add (call reason codes, such as FORWARD_NO_ANSWER)

CallManager also provides the following RTP Termination extensions:

- Special CallManager device types (CTI ports) can be registered by applications.
- Devices must be pre-provisioned (no programmatic creation).
- An application specifies its codec capabilities, and CallManager selects the codec to be used for each call.
- An application must implement an RTP stack, although Java Media Framework (JMF) is allowed for client applications.

CTI Layer

This section describes the CTI Layer within CallManager that provides a generic interface to the application layer. The CTI Layer is the means by which the CallManager-specific capabilities of the application layer are implemented.

Figure 3-13 shows the CTI functionality within CallManager. CTI communicates with the application platforms through the TCP/IP layer to provide the CTI functionality of CallManager. The CTI Layer is an integral part of CallManager.

Figure 3-13 *Cisco CallManager CTI Functionality*

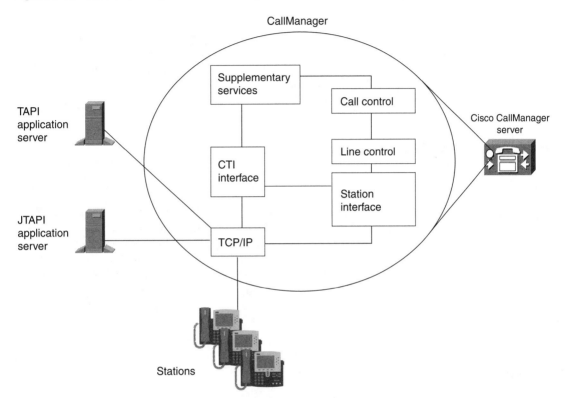

CTI interacts with the other CallManager components through the Signal Distribution Layer that Chapter 1, "Cisco CallManager Architecture," describes. CTI works together with the station module to provide the signals from a CTI device. If a station device such as a Cisco IP Phone is being controlled by an application, CTI interacts with the station module in CallManager responsible for the particular station being controlled.

The application also needs information about activity at a selected station. CTI receives notification about station activity, known as *events*, from the station components for stations that the application is monitoring.

CTI also interacts with the supplementary services component to provide additional call control capabilities, such as transfer and conference. The CTI component can invoke supplementary services on behalf of stations being controlled or directly for CTI application devices. CTI also sends event notifications of supplementary service activity for selected stations being monitored by an application.

H.323 Endpoint Devices

This section describes the concept of an H.323 endpoint. An H.323 endpoint is a station device that communicates with CallManager using the H.323 protocol specification. The H.323 protocol in CallManager supports both gateways and endpoints, as well as Registration, Admission, and Status (RAS) protocol, for communication with a gatekeeper. The gatekeeper provides address translation and controls access to the network for H.323 devices based on bandwidth availability.

H.323 Protocol Support

This section provides a detailed description of the H.323 capability that is supported and the limitations and restrictions on what is specifically not supported for H.323 endpoints.

Figure 3-14 shows the H.323 protocol components that CallManager supports. The audio compression components known to CallManager are Global System for Mobile Communications (GSM), G.711, G.723, and G.729. CallManager supports the capabilities negotiation for these audio compression types. CallManager provides the system control components for H.245 for media setup, H.225 for call control, and H.225 RAS for gatekeeper communication, if a device is configured for gatekeeper control.

Figure 3-14 *H.323 Protocol Components*

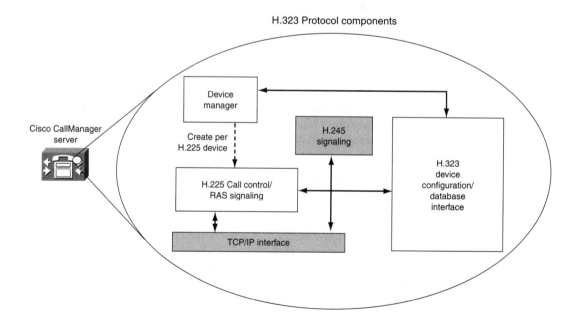

The H.323 specification encompasses several specifications. The particular implementation in CallManager includes H.225 and H.245 signaling for proper operation of the H.323 endpoint. It provides for call control, capability exchange, signaling of commands and indications, and messages to open and fully describe the content of logical channels for media streams. CallManager terminates the H.225 signaling originated by any H.323 device defined in the database and directed to CallManager. The call can terminate at any endpoint, gateway, or cluster accessible by CallManager, regardless of the protocol of the terminating device. Likewise, CallManager extends, by H.225 signaling, a call to any H.323 device defined in the database from any endpoint, gateway, or cluster accessible by CallManager, regardless of the protocol of the originating device. The H.225 and H.245 signaling is always between CallManager and the H.323 endpoint. As with other station protocols, the media streaming uses RTP for the media, and the media streaming is done directly between the two devices and does not go through CallManager.

H.323 Device Configuration

Use Cisco CallManager Administration to configure all H.323 endpoint devices that communicate with CallManager. CallManager implementation uses directory numbers for all endpoint access, including H.323 endpoints. You must also assign all configured H.323 endpoint devices a directory number. Other users use the directory number to extend a call to the H.323 endpoint. No advantage exists in having an H.323 endpoint under gatekeeper control as in the case of an H.323 gateway because they are endpoint devices that support a single call to or from a CallManager-controlled device. Refer to Chapter 4 for a detailed discussion of gatekeeper control for H.323 gateway devices.

Gatekeeper Functionality

H.323 endpoints can be configured as gatekeeper controlled. If an endpoint is gatekeeper controlled, the gatekeeper is identified as part of the H.323 device configuration. CallManager registers the H.323 endpoint with the gatekeeper when it initializes. The specified gatekeeper controls all calls made to or from the H.323 endpoint. The H.323 gatekeeper signaling is RAS, as defined in the H.323 protocol specification.

H.225 Signaling

This section describes the details of CallManager's implementation of H.225. The section provides the signaling detail of a call from an H.323 endpoint to a station, and also a call from a station to an H.323 endpoint, to allow a detailed discussion of CallManager's H.225 and H.245 implementation. For purposes of this description, the call is not gatekeeper controlled. The following section illustrates additional RAS signaling for gatekeeper-controlled calls.

Figure 3-15 shows the signaling for a call from an H.323 endpoint to an IP Phone.

The procedure is as follows:

Step 1 To originate a call from an H.323 endpoint, the endpoint establishes a TCP/IP connection to CallManager at the well-known port address 1720, to use for H.225 call signaling. The means by which the H.323 endpoint knows the IP address of CallManager is a function of the particular H.323 endpoint implementation. To originate a call from Microsoft NetMeeting, for example, the call is made to a directory number, and the call is specified as gatekeeper controlled, with CallManager specified as the gateway.

Figure 3-15 *Call Originating from an H.323 Endpoint to a Station*

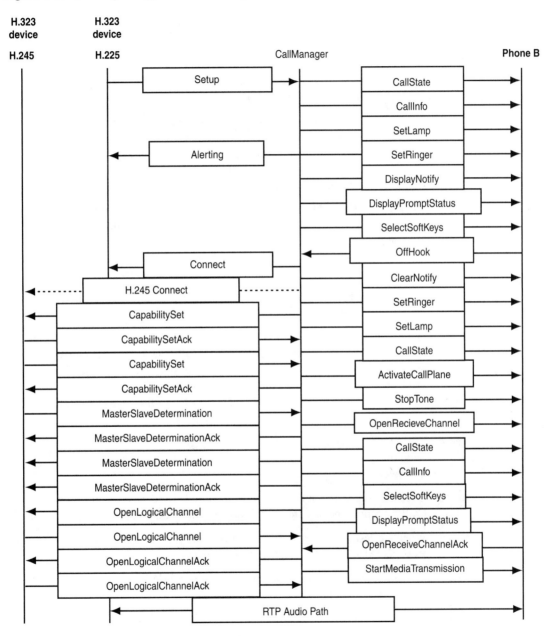

Step 2   Once the H.323 endpoint establishes the TCP/IP connection to CallManager, it sends the first H.225 signal to CallManager: Setup. Selected setup fields follow with comments about the specific implementation details of CallManager.

— **H245Address**—The **H245Address** field contains the specific transport address to be used to establish the H.245 signaling channel.

— **source Address**—The **source Address** field can contain either the alias address, which CallManager uses as the display name when it extends the call to the station, or the E.164 address. CallManager uses the E.164 address, if provided, as the calling party number when it extends the call to the station.

— **destinationAddress**—CallManager uses the **destinationAddress** field for routing purposes, if provided, only if it contains an E.164 address. The field must specify an E.164 address in either the destination address element or the Q.931 called party information element for CallManager to route the call to be routed.

— **fastStart**— CallManager does not currently use the **fastStart** field. It might be made available in a future release.

Step 3   Once CallManager receives the Setup message, it creates a process to handle the H.225 protocol for this particular call. The process, unique to the call, handles all of the H.225 signaling for the duration of the call. The H.225 process is active from the time of the setup until the call is terminated and the TCP/IP connection is closed. If either side closes the TCP connection prematurely, the call is dropped.

Step 4   When CallManager decodes the Setup message, it extends the call to the directory number, as specified by the E.164 address in the Setup message.

Step 5   Once CallManager determines the destination is valid, it sends an H.225 CallProceeding message to the originating H.225 device.

Step 6   When the destination device reaches an alerting state, CallManager sends an H.225 Alerting to the originating H.225 device.

Step 7   Once the destination device answers the call, CallManager begins the media connection process.

Step 8   The media connection requires CallManager to establish a TCP/IP connection to the originating H.323 device for H.245 protocol.

Step 9   Once CallManager establishes the TCP/IP connection, CallManager initiates the H.245 signaling with the H.323 originating device.

Step 10 The H.245 signaling includes master/slave determination, capabilities exchange, and logical channel signaling to start the media stream. Because the destination device in this example is a station, which uses Skinny Protocol, only a single H.245 session between CallManager and the originating H.323 endpoint is required. If the destination device is also an H.323 device, CallManager establishes a separate additional H.245 session to the destination H.323 device.

Step 11 Once the open logical channel has completed and the media stream is established in both directions, CallManager sends the H.225 Connect message to the H.323 originating endpoint, and the call is established.

Step 12 The media streaming is sent directly between the H.323 endpoint and the station. CallManager is not involved in the media stream, only in the call signaling to establish and terminate the call.

Figure 3-16 shows the call signaling for terminating a call from an H.323 endpoint to a station.

Once a call is established, either side can end the call. The following steps describe the signaling for a call that is terminated by the IP Phone:

Step 1 To release the call, either the endpoint or the station indicates that the call is completed. If the IP Phone releases the call, the station sends an OnHook to CallManager.

Step 2 CallManager sends a ReleaseComplete message to the H.323 endpoint.

Step 3 CallManager sends the messages required to return the phone displays and keys and tones to a clean state.

Step 4 CallManager then signals the station that the call is complete and directs the station to stop media streaming.

Step 5 CallManager also originates a CloseSession H.245 message to stop streaming at the H.323 endpoint.

Step 6 At the same time, the H.323 endpoint sends a CloseSessionConfirm to CallManager.

Step 7 On receipt of the CloseSessionAck, CallManager closes the H.245 TCP/IP connection.

Step 8 Once the H.323 endpoint sends the ReleaseComplete message, the endpoint closes the TCP/IP connection and the call is terminated.

As you can see from this description, the H.323 protocol uses a fairly complex message set that requires multiple TCP/IP connections to establish a call. TCP/IP and CallManager processor resources required for an H.323 call are greater than those for a direct station-to-station call or a call involving MGCP.

Figure 3-16 *Call Termination from an H.323 Endpoint to a Station*

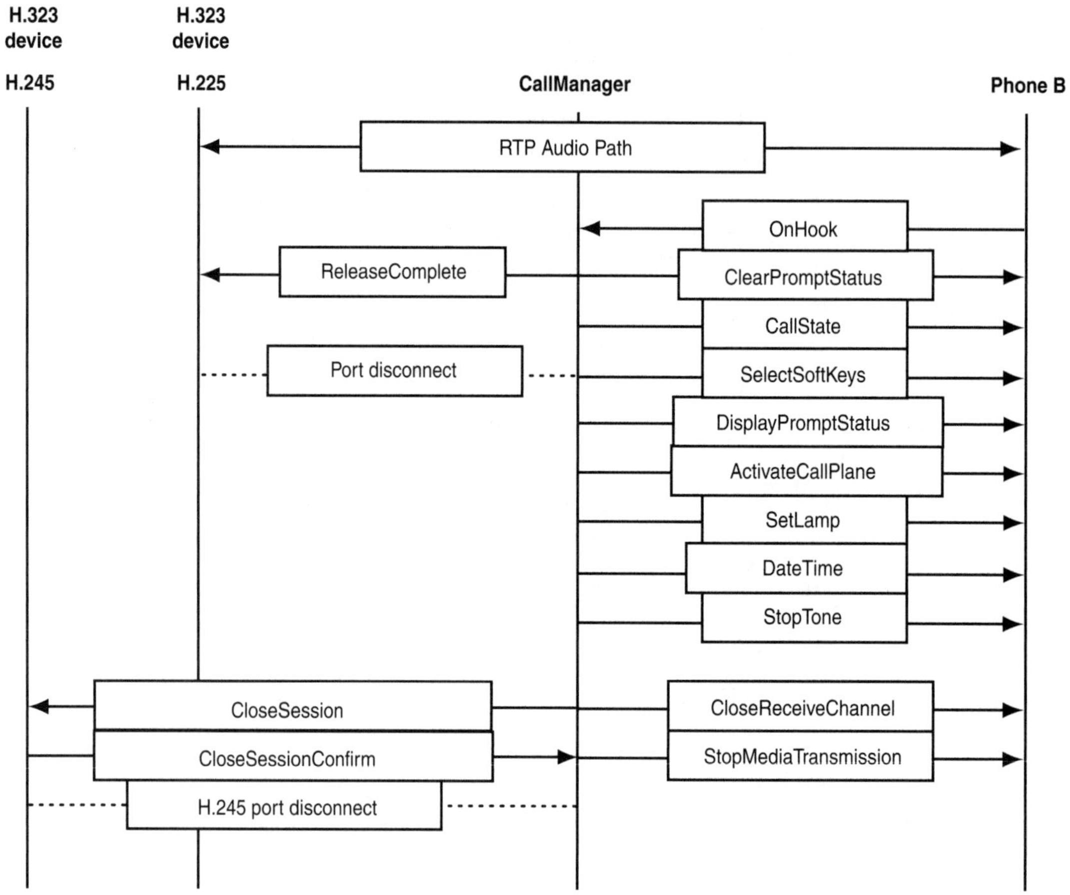

RAS Protocol Support for Gatekeeper Control

This section provides a detailed description of the RAS protocol supported in CallManager for H.323 endpoint devices. This section includes the RAS messages and message sequence.

The RAS signaling shows the communication from CallManager to the gatekeeper on behalf of the H.323 endpoint. When CallManager initializes, it scans the database for configured H.323 devices. If the H.323 device is configured as gatekeeper controlled, CallManager registers the endpoint with the gatekeeper on behalf of the H.323 device. Figure 3-17 shows the registration sequence. CallManager sends a Registration Request

(RRQ) to the gatekeeper. The gatekeeper responds with a Registration Confirm (RCF) to accept the registration. As mentioned previously, although the H.323 endpoints can be configured as gatekeeper controlled, they are seldom configured as such because they are endpoint devices that support a single call to or from a CallManager-controlled device. There is no advantage in having an H.323 endpoint under gatekeeper control as there is in the case of an H.323 gateway. Refer to Chapter 4 for a detailed discussion of gatekeeper control for H.323 gateway devices.

Figure 3-17 *H.323 RAS Signaling*

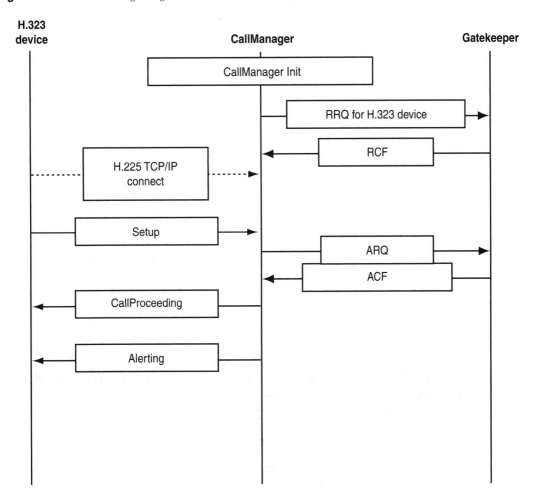

CallManager performs additional signaling on behalf of the H.323 endpoint device for each call. As shown in Figure 3-17, when the H.323 endpoint initiates the call with a Setup message, CallManager issues an Admission Request (ARQ) to the gatekeeper. The gatekeeper can allow or deny the request. The request is typically denied when there is insufficient bandwidth between the two endpoints to allow the call. In Figure 3-17, the gatekeeper responds with an Admission Confirm (ACF) and allows the call to be extended.

Implementation of TFTP for Station Devices

This section provides a detailed description of the TFTP functionality for stations.

Understanding TFTP

The phones have an order of preference that they use to select the address of the TFTP server. If the phone receives conflicting or confusing information from the DHCP server, the phone uses the following sequence to determine what information is valid:

1 You can configure the phone with a TFTP server address through the phone configuration.

This manually configured address overrides the TFTP address sent by the DHCP server.

The phone always tries to resolve the DNS name CiscoCM1.

2 If the name CiscoCM1 is resolved, it overrides the information sent by the DHCP server. It is not necessary to name the TFTP server CiscoCM1, but you must enter a DNS name record to associate CiscoCM1 with the address or name of the TFTP server.

3 The phone uses the value of Next-Server in the boot process. This DHCP configuration parameter has traditionally been used as the address of the TFTP server. When configuring BOOTP servers, this field is typically referred to as the address of the TFTP server. This information is returned in the **siaddr** field of the DHCP header. You should always use this option, if available, because some DHCP servers will place their own IP address in this field if it is not configured. Note: You shouldn't always use this option. It is an option, and one that the user should be aware of, but it is in no way preferable to option 066 or option 150, described in the following steps.

4 The phone uses the site-specific option 150. This option overcomes the issue of Microsoft Windows 2000 or NT servers not allowing the Next-Server configuration parameter. Microsoft Windows 2000 and NT servers only allow access to the Next-Server parameter when IP addresses are statically assigned.

5 The phone also accepts the Optional Server Name parameter. This DHCP configuration parameter is the DNS name of a TFTP server. You should not use a dotted decimal IP address.

6 The phone accepts the 066 option, which is the name of the boot server.

Option 066 normally replaces the **Name** field when option overloading occurs. This **Name** field can contain a DNS name or a dotted decimal IP address.

You should *not* use the 066 option with the 150 option. If the options are sent together, the phone prefers the IP address to the name given by the 066 option. However, if both a dotted decimal IP address and a 150 option are sent, the order of preference is dependent on the order that they appear in the option list. The phone chooses the last item in the option list. Therefore, option 066 and option 150 should be considered mutually exclusive.

Summary

This chapter covered the concepts of endpoints, stations, and users. It included signaling protocol details for H.323, Skinny Protocol, and CTI support for TAPI and JTAPI. It described in detail the phone services application development capability. It described specific Cisco IP Phones, including their features and capabilities. It also covered the process by which the phones get configuration data, register, and signal for calls.

## CHAPTER 4

Trunk Devices

This chapter discusses the gateway protocols that Cisco CallManager uses to communicate with Cisco gateway devices. CallManager contains several signaling layers, each of which has distinct functions. For example, the Call Control Layer handles the call signaling that controls call setup, teardown, and call routing, and the Protocol and Aggregator Layers handles all protocol-specific signaling required for specific devices.

This chapter includes the following sections:

- Overview of Trunk Devices
- H.323 Gatekeeper and Gateway
- H.323 Features
- MGCP Gateways
- Cluster-to-Cluster Communication
- Initialization, Recovery, and Device Registration
- ISDN Timers
- H.323 Implementation Details
- Troubleshooting
- Summary

Figure 4-1 shows the block structure of CallManager. This chapter covers the shaded parts of Figure 4-1.

In Figure 4-1, the software layers and blocks within CallManager that this chapter describes in detail are indicated with the darker shading. Other blocks that this chapter touches on lightly are indicated with lighter shading because they are part of the gateway signaling path.

The software in the Media Control Layer handles all media connections that CallManager makes between devices. The Call Control Layer sets up signaling connections between call endpoints and CallManager. The Media Control Layer directs the devices to establish streaming connections between themselves, and it can insert other media processing devices into a call and create appropriate streaming connections to those devices without the Call Control Layer knowing about them.

Figure 4-1 *CallManager Block Structure Diagram*

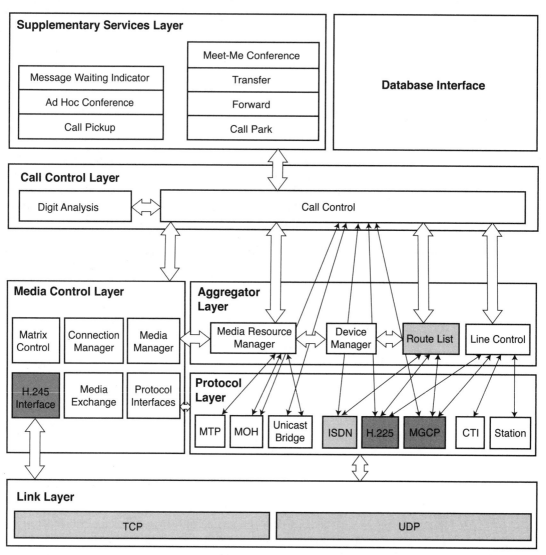

The blocks in the Protocol and Aggregator Layers control the media processing devices. They handle all communication between the devices and CallManager.

Gateway devices enable communication between CallManager and the Public Switched Telephone Network (PSTN). As shown in Figure 4-2, gateways provide a bridge between CallManager and the PSTN. Gateway devices connect to the IP network on one side and the PSTN on the other side, allowing CallManager to connect to users throughout the

PSTN. The gateway bridges the gap between the packet-switched network and the circuit-switched network.

Figure 4-2 *Gateway Trunking Devices*

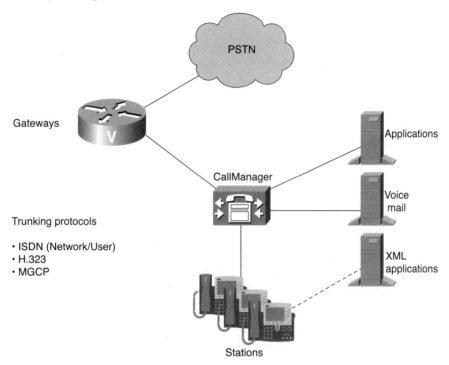

The communication from CallManager to gateway devices includes numerous protocols. From the perspective of CallManager, gateway devices are characterized by the particular protocols that gateways support and the ability of gateways to support multiple simultaneous active calls.

CallManager clusters communicate with other CallManager clusters using the H.323 protocol. The H.323 protocol between clusters is the same protocol that CallManager uses to communicate with H.323 gateway devices connected to the PSTN. This chapter also describes H.323 intercluster communication.

The gateway protocols that this chapter covers include both Media Gateway Control Protocol (MGCP) and H.323. This chapter describes gateway and intercluster communication and how they relate to the H.323 model. The discussion of H.323 includes H.323 gatekeepers and their relationship to call admission control. In addition, to more fully detail CallManager signaling models, this chapter describes both the signaling between CallManagers within a cluster and the signaling between clusters.

Overview of Trunk Devices

Cisco CallManager supports several protocols for gateway devices, including H.323 and MGCP. MGCP supports both direct MGCP signaling and the Q.931 associated signaling.

H.323 Call Model Overview

The H.323 recommendation from the International Telecommunication Union Telecommunication Standardization Sector (ITU-T) is an umbrella specification that describes terminals, gateways, and other entities that provide communication services over packet-based networks. The specification is called an umbrella specification because it references other specifications for the call control, media control, and coding and decoding control specifications. Of particular interest in the discussion in this chapter are the H.225 recommendation for call signaling; the H.245 recommendation for multimedia control; audio speech coding and decoding recommendations G.711, G.723.1, G.729a, and GSM; and the H.450 series recommendations for feature functionality.

The generic H.323 protocol model includes many control mechanisms. This section identifies the specific control model that CallManager uses for intercluster communication and communication with H.323 Cisco gateways connected to the PSTN.

Figure 4-3 identifies the H.323 protocol entities. The H.323 entities that are part of CallManager include the H.323 communication stack, the H.323 Cisco gateways, and the H.323 Cisco gatekeeper. This collection of H.323 devices interoperates to form an H.323 infrastructure that allows communication between CallManager and the PSTN and communication between CallManager clusters.

Figure 4-3   *H.323 Protocol Entities*

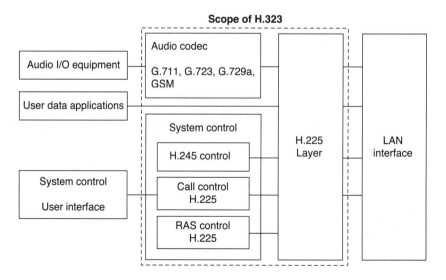

H.323 Call Signaling Protocol Support Overview

This section provides an overview of the H.225 call signaling support in CallManager and how it fits in with the architecture of CallManager. The H.225 recommendation defines the call signaling protocol that establishes a call from one H.323 device to another.

The H.323 devices that communicate with CallManager use an H.225 protocol session for the call signaling. The H.225 signaling is sent in the form of packets over a TCP/IP connection. The call initiator establishes the TCP/IP connection. If CallManager extends a call to an H.323 gateway, CallManager establishes the H.225 session. If the H.323 gateway extends a call to a device controlled by CallManager, the gateway establishes the H.225 session.

Opening a TCP/IP connection between the H.323 gateway and CallManager establishes an H.323 session. The originating device knows the IP address and port of the destination. The H.225 recommendation identifies the well-known port as port 1720. Specifically, if CallManager extends a call to the H.323 gateway, CallManager makes a TCP/IP connection to the gateway using the IP address of the gateway and port 1720. The H.225 protocol stack on the gateway listens for new connections and accepts them. Once CallManager establishes (or accepts) the connection, CallManager and the H.323 gateway exchange call control packets to establish the call.

Figure 4-4 shows the basic call control signaling between CallManager and a gateway. CallManager sends an H.225 Setup message to the H.323 gateway. If the gateway has available PSTN ports and can extend the call to the PSTN, the gateway responds with a CallProceeding message. Once the gateway extends the call to the PSTN, and the PSTN alerts the destination device of a call, the gateway sends an Alerting message back to CallManager. Once the recipient answers the call, the gateway sends a Connect message to CallManager, and when CallManager receives that message, CallManager starts an H.245 session to establish the media connection and allow the two endpoints to establish an audio path. CallManager and the gateway maintain the H.225 call signaling session until the end of the call. When one of the end users hangs up, CallManager or the gateway sends ReleaseComplete to tear down the call.

If the gateway device originates a call, the gateway establishes a TCP/IP connection with CallManager using the IP address of CallManager and port 1720. CallManager listens for new connections on port 1720 and accepts the connection. The gateway sends the Setup message and CallManager responds with CallProceeding, Alerting, and Connect messages as the call progresses and is answered.

All basic calls to and from an H.323 gateway to a destination endpoint that CallManager controls use this same H.323 call model, unless you have configured a gatekeeper to enforce call admission control.

Figure 4-4 *H.225 Basic Call Signaling*

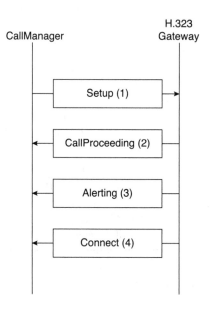

RAS Protocol Support for Gatekeeper Control Overview

An H.323 gatekeeper is a central resource that maintains knowledge of the addresses of H.323 devices, including H.323 endpoints and other gatekeepers. It responds to requests for the location of particular H.323 devices by name or directory number (such as an E.164 address). CallManager registers its IP address on behalf of the H.323 devices associated with it. The gatekeeper also allows or denies calls, as H.323 devices that are gatekeeper-controlled request permission before extending each call. This allows the gatekeeper to control bandwidth by limiting the number of calls between locations with limited bandwidth. Gatekeeper-controlled calls use the same basic call signaling with the addition of messages to and from the gatekeeper for admission control and location information.

The H.225 gatekeeper messages are Registration, Admission, and Status (RAS) messages. RAS messages allow the gatekeeper, which is tracking available bandwidth and the location of registered H.323 entities, to allow or deny a call to be placed. This section provides an overview of the H.225 RAS gatekeeper support and the gatekeeper support that CallManager provides.

Location service is provided by the gatekeeper by registration of H.323 entities. To identify the gatekeeper to CallManager, configure the gatekeeper in Cisco CallManager Administration. The CallManager cluster registers with the gatekeeper at initialization if configured for gatekeeper control. Once the CallManager cluster registers, the gatekeeper knows about the cluster and can route calls to CallManager from other clusters that are registered with the same gatekeeper.

CallManager uses the manual gatekeeper discovery process to determine the specific gatekeeper to use for registration. An additional discovery method not currently supported by CallManager is automatic discovery and is included here for completeness.

- Manual discovery
    - Statically configured in CallManager Administration.
    - CallManager knows the gatekeeper name and address.
- Automatic discovery
    - H.323 entity does not know the gatekeeper name or address.
    - H.232 entity uses RAS discovery messages to find a gatekeeper.

The discovery protocol is a series of RAS messages that allow an H.323 entity to find the gatekeeper.

Figure 4-5 shows the discovery protocol messaging to allow an H.323 entity to find the gatekeeper.

Figure 4-5   *Gatekeeper Discovery*

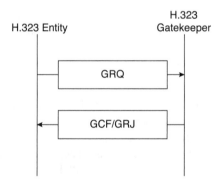

An H.323 entity sends a Gatekeeper Request (GRQ) to the gatekeeper's multicast address, 224.0.1.41, to request a gatekeeper. If a gatekeeper responds with a Gatekeeper Confirm (GCF), the H.323 entity has found a gatekeeper and can begin registering. The Gatekeeper Reject (GRJ) simply means that the responding gatekeeper does not want the H.323 entity to register with it.

When a call is made to an H.323 device and the gatekeeper is configured to provide admission control, CallManager sends RAS messages, allowing the gatekeeper to control the bandwidth. This control makes sure that the number of calls does not exceed the available bandwidth and degrade the voice quality of the calls. The means by which the gatekeeper limits the calls is the RAS Admission Request (ARQ) message.

Figure 4-6 shows the messaging that occurs for an H.323 call using the gatekeeper for call admission control.

Figure 4-6 *Call Signaling with Gatekeeper Control*

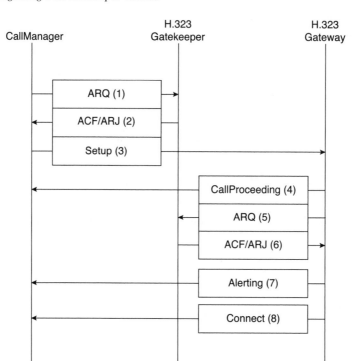

Before CallManager extends a call to an H.323 gateway, it queries the gatekeeper by sending an ARQ to the gatekeeper. If bandwidth is available, the gatekeeper responds with an Admission Confirm (ACF) indicating that CallManager may extend the call. If the required bandwidth is not available, the gatekeeper responds with an Admission Reject (ARJ), and CallManager does not place the call. If CallManager receives an ARJ, it applies the no-circuits-available call treatment.

If you configure a route list that contains alternate routes, the no-circuits-available call treatment causes CallManager to reroute the call. If all additional routes are busy or no additional routes are available, CallManager sends a reorder tone (also known as *fast busy*) to the originator indicating that the call could not be placed.

Assuming that the gatekeeper returns an ACF to allow the call to be extended, the gateway, if configured for gatekeeper control, sends another ARQ to the gatekeeper before it accepts the call. The gateway sends the ARQ to the gatekeeper after sending the CallProceeding message to CallManager, but before the gateway extends the call to the PSTN or IP WAN and sends the Alerting message to CallManager. If the gatekeeper responds with an ACF, the call proceeds normally. If the gatekeeper returns an ARJ, the gateway sends a

ReleaseComplete message to CallManager indicating that the call cannot be completed. CallManager then proceeds with the no-circuits-available call treatment.

H.323 Gatekeeper and Gateway

This section describes the role of H.323 gateways, the capabilities that they support, and the role of the gatekeeper as it relates to H.323 gateway calls.

Figure 4-7 shows the role of H.323 gatekeeper-controlled gateways for call admission control and routing between Cisco CallManager clusters.

Figure 4-7 *Gatekeeper Control*

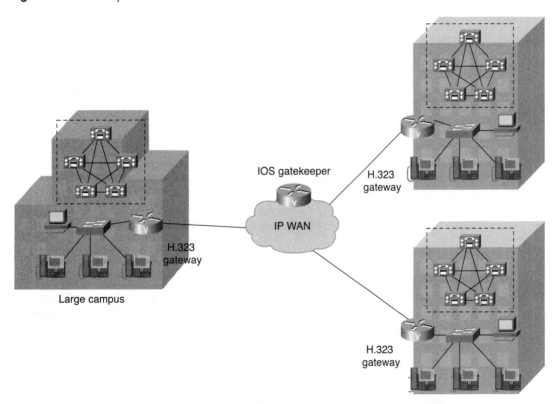

Gatekeeper provides call admission control and routing for calls to another cluster.

H.323 Gateways

This section describes H.323 gateways. This description includes which gateways CallManager supports and which capabilities and features CallManager supports.

Cisco H.323 gateways allow CallManager to communicate with the PSTN. The connection from the Cisco H.323 gateway to the PSTN can be through either analog or digital connections.

The analog connections include Foreign Exchange Station (FXS) and Foreign Exchange Office (FXO) trunks. FXS ports provide connection to loop-start or ground-start telephone lines, Private Branch eXchange (PBX) ports, and other analog telephone devices. FXO ports provide connection to central office ports or PBX extensions. The digital connections allow connection to the central office or PBX with digital Primary Rate Interface (PRI) lines or digital T1 connections.

CallManager provides very little feature support to endpoints terminated by the H.323 gateways either directly or through the PSTN. H.323 gateways can initiate or receive calls but are limited in their ability to invoke features. CallManager permits IP Phone users to place calls to H.323 gateways on hold and resume them either to the same party or to another party.

The empty capability set support in CallManager and in the gateway allows H.323 endpoints to be participants in CallManager features such as hold, transfer, call park, and Ad Hoc conference, though they cannot in themselves initiate such features. H.323 gateways can participate in CallManager features that users can invoke merely by providing dialed digits. Thus, H.323 gateways can join existing Meet-Me conferences and retrieve parked calls. CallManager offers a full range of services to an IP Phone user, even if the user's call connects through a Cisco gateway.

The CallManager H.245 protocol stack enables the redirection of media streams between two devices involved in a call. When an H.323 call is established, an H.245 session is established to control the media between the two endpoints. Part of the H.245 media control includes exchanging capability sets to determine a voice encoding scheme (codec) that is common to both endpoints in the call. Once the endpoints establish this media, it remains unless there is a need to change the media path in response to a feature request from one of the endpoints.

When the invoked feature requires the interruption of the media stream, as in the case of hold, CallManager stops the media streaming by modifying the existing media session and specifying new capabilities. When the new capability set contains no entries, which nominally means that the two endpoints involved in the call share no codecs in common, the endpoints involved in the call cease streaming media to each other.

When the invoked feature requires that the media stream be resumed or redirected, CallManager sends the existing media session a new non-empty set of capabilities (and a new streaming address, if needed). Because the two endpoints now have a codec in common, they resume the media stream with each other or begin streaming to a new destination.

H.323 Gatekeepers

This section provides a description of the functionality of the H.323 gatekeeper. This description includes the role of the gatekeeper, CallManager support of external gatekeepers, and the role of the gatekeeper in the CallManager environment.

H.323 gatekeepers provide address resolution and call admission control. The gatekeeper is especially important when communication between two clusters is provided over a limited-bandwidth WAN.

If the number of calls traversing the WAN exceeds the bandwidth that the WAN provides, voice quality can degrade for all calls that traverse the WAN. Therefore, the gatekeeper provides a method by which you can restrict the number of calls that traverse the WAN and thus maintain voice quality.

The gatekeeper also allows you to provision a centralized dial plan to provide address resolution. A centralized dial plan can reduce CallManager configuration requirements for a large network with numerous remote clusters. In this configuration, each CallManager cluster registers with the gatekeeper. The gatekeeper is then able to not only handle the call admission control, but also provide the address resolution based on its internal dial plan for calls between CallManager clusters. The specific means of controlling the bandwidth and address resolution capabilities vary based on the specific gatekeeper and are beyond the scope of this book's focus on CallManager.

When H.323 calls or intercluster calls are gatekeeper-controlled and configured properly, CallManager processes the **destCallSignalAddress** in the gatekeeper response to the ARQ to determine the destination cluster address. The configuration that allows CallManager to connect dynamically to the destination address specified by the gatekeeper is referenced as *anonymous device configuration*. If the anonymous device configuration is not used, CallManager uses the address configured in CallManager Administration as the destination address and ignores the **destCallSignalAddress** field.

Gatekeeper Controls

CallManager allows control of the gatekeepers through the use of configuration settings. A few of the most commonly used settings that apply to gatekeeper control are shown in Table 4-1. **TerminalType** allows CallManager to register as a terminal or as a gateway. Calling party selection controls the directory number sent on an outbound call; Originator—send the directory number of the calling device, First Redirect Number—send the directory number of the redirecting device, Last Redirect Number—send the directory number of the last device to redirect the call.

Table 4-1 *Gatekeeper Controls*

Gatekeeper Setting	Selections
TerminalType	terminal
	gateway
Calling party selection	Originator
	First Redirect Number
	Last Redirect Number

H.323 Features

This section describes Cisco CallManager signaling for features that involve H.323.

H.323-Originated Features

H.323 relies on the H.450 standard to allow H.323 endpoints to initiate features such as transfer. CallManager does not support H.450, so H.323 gateways cannot initiate most call features. H.323 gateways can access CallManager features by two methods.

First, H.323 endpoints can access features for which CallManager provides access solely through the use of dialed digits. Thus, H.323 endpoints can retrieve parked calls and join already established Meet-Me conferences.

Second, CallManager supports the carriage of hookflash through the H.245 **userInfoIndication** field. If an H.323 device sends a hookflash followed by a directory number during an active call, CallManager transfers the existing call to the new directory number.

H.323-Terminated Features

This section provides a detailed description of the messaging that occurs when an IP Phone invokes a feature during a call with an H.323 gateway. As described previously, CallManager can start and stop the media stream to the H.323 gateway and allow the H.323 gateway to be controlled by the features of CallManager.

CallManager features require the core ability to stop and restart a media stream to the same or a different endpoint. To provide this capability, CallManager uses the H.245 empty capability set to stop the media streaming. Most Cisco gateways support the H.245 empty capability set. Such gateways can resume streaming to the same or to a different endpoint when CallManager provides a new capability set, and the H.245 media negotiation is again completed. This stop and restart streaming can occur as many times during a call as required by feature control.

The empty capability set provides a way to redirect Real-Time Transport Protocol (RTP) streams. The following example includes the H.245 sequence and describes how the RTP streams are redirected. Figure 4-8 shows the use of the empty capability set for this example.

Figure 4-8   *H.245 Empty Capability Set*

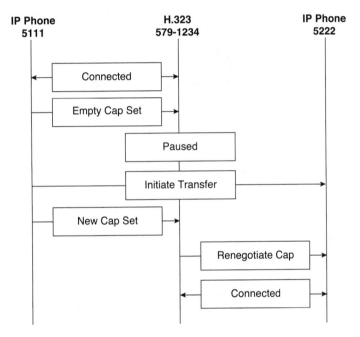

In this example, party 5111, an IP Phone, is connected to party 579-1234 on the H.323 gateway and wishes to transfer 579-1234 to party 5222, another IP Phone.

After CallManager establishes a logical channel between party 5111 and the H.323 that controls party 579-1234, party 5111 sends an H.245 Empty Capability Set message to party 579-1234.

When the gateway receives the Empty Capability Set message, party 579-1234 closes the previous logical channel opened with party 5111 and moves to a Pause state, waiting for a new Capability Set message.

After party 5111 completes the call transfer, party 579-1234 receives a new Cap Set message. After receiving the new Cap Set message with a non-empty set of capabilities, party 579-1234 moves to the beginning of Phase B (initial communication and capability exchange). Phase B includes capability exchange (Renegotiate Cap), master-slave determination, and a new Open Logical Channel message to open a new logical channel with another endpoint, in this case party 5222. All of the RTP streams are then sent to the new endpoint.

If the H.323 gateway does not support the empty capability set to stop and resume streaming, you can configure the H.323 gateway to insert a media termination point (MTP). Chapter 5, "Media Processing," describes MTPs. The MTP provides a bridge for the media between the H.323 gateway and the desired endpoint. MTP terminates the H.323 gateway media for the duration of the call, while allowing the other destination to stop, change, and restart the media connection to allow feature control for H.323 gateways that do not support the H.245 empty capability set renegotiation.

Although MTP can only support calls that use the G.711 codec, empty capability set allows codec negotiation across regions through capability exchange with the new endpoint. The empty capability set is implemented as an H.323 enhancement in Cisco IOS release 12.0(6)T and Cisco CallManager release 3.0.

MGCP Gateways

This section describes the role of Media Gateway Control Protocol (MGCP) gateways and the capabilities they support. The description contrasts MGCP and H.323 gateways.

MGCP Gateway Protocol

This section describes in detail MGCP and the capabilities it supports. MGCP is a draft of the Internet Engineering Task Force (IETF) and is not a standard. Many companies, including Cisco, have chosen to support the IETF draft and have interoperability among products. The Cisco gateways that support MGCP include the VG200, 3620, 3640, and 3660. The PSTN connections supported include FXS, FXO, PRI, and T1-CAS.

MGCP is a simple text-based protocol. MGCP messages are sent over a User Datagram Protocol (UDP) connection, rather than a TCP/IP connection as used in H.323. The audio media transmission is RTP, which is the same for all CallManager-supported protocols, including H.323.

The primary elements that MGCP uses are endpoints, commands, and events or signals. An endpoint is the same as in the other protocols. Endpoints can originate or terminate an audio media stream. The Cisco VG200 gateway, for example, has multiple ports, either FXS or FXO. Each Cisco VG200 port represents an endpoint.

MGCP commands are a means of requesting and reporting requested activity to and from the gateway. A summary of commands is shown in Table 4-2.

Table 4-2   *MGCP Command Summary*

Command Code	Command	Description
RQNT	Notification request	Requests gateway to send notifications of specified events and to apply a specific signal to an endpoint
NTFY	Notify	Allows a gateway to report the occurrence of the requested events
CRCX	Create connection	Requests the gateway to create a connection or to apply a specific signal to endpoint with an existing connection
MDCX	Modify connection	Modifies an existing gateway connection
DLCX	Delete connection	Deletes a gateway connection
AUEP	Audit endpoint	Audits the characteristics of an endpoint, including connection state, codecs, and so on
AUCX	Audit connection	Audits a connection to get the call ID
RSIP	Restart in progress	Allows a gateway to notify CallManager that a restart has occurred

Events are occurrences at an endpoint. The common events for MGCP gateways are off-hook, on-hook, hookflash, dual tone multifrequency (DTMF) keypad digits, and operation complete. CallManager requests notification of events that should be reported. Signals are specifically applied to an endpoint at the request of CallManager. The signal can be of three types:

- On/off signals—Last until they are turned off
- Timeout signals—Last until the signal is either turned off or times out
- Brief signals—Stop on their own

Common signals include dial tone, ring back tone, ringing, DTMF, and busy tone.

MGCP Interaction

This section summarizes the capabilities of CallManager's support of MGCP gateways over and above those of H.323 gateways. The additional capabilities include

- Automatic switchover by MGCP gateways from a failed CallManager to a secondary CallManager

- Call survival through a switchover to a secondary CallManager

- Voice mail support through an MGCP interface to an FXS port on the gateway

This chapter discusses MGCP gateway initialization later in the "Initialization, Recovery, and Device Registration" section.

Cluster-to-Cluster Communication

This section describes the intercluster communication capabilities of Cisco CallManager in version 3.1. This section includes a description of the intercluster trunks and the use of a transcoding device.

Figure 4-9 shows the H.323 communication between CallManager clusters.

Figure 4-9 *Cluster-to-Cluster Communication*

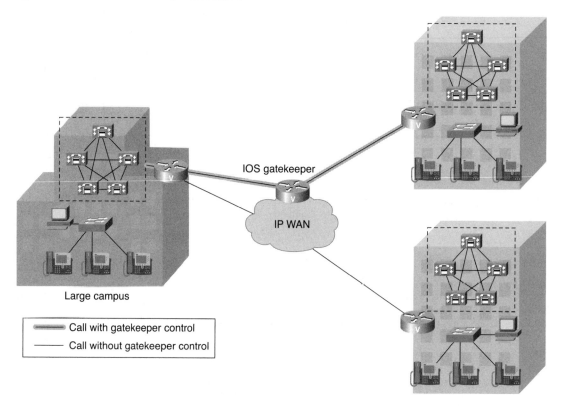

H.323 Intercluster Trunking

This section describes the trunking capabilities and limitations of an H.323 intercluster trunk.

H.323 gateways allow CallManager to communicate to the PSTN. In the case of intercluster signaling, CallManager sends H.323 protocol signaling directly to a CallManager in another cluster without the involvement of an intervening gateway and using whatever TCP/IP connection path is available between the two clusters.

The intercluster signaling protocol is essentially identical to the CallManager-to-gateway protocol that the section "H.323 Call Signaling Protocol Support Overview" describes. The CallManager node that serves the caller establishes a TCP/IP connection to a CallManager node in the destination cluster. CallManager in the originating cluster sends the Setup message, and CallManager in the destination cluster responds with the CallProceeding, Alerting, and Connect messages as the call progresses and is answered.

The signaling path can be either WAN or LAN and might be gatekeeper controlled. Regardless of the intercluster trunk topology, the H.323 signaling protocol between CallManager clusters is the same. Chapter 1, "Cisco CallManager Architecture," describes the supported network topologies in detail. For each topology that requires intercluster signaling, the H.323 intercluster signaling model is used.

The supported topologies are as follows:

- Single-site model
    - When one CallManager cluster can support the number of devices in your enterprise, no intercluster signaling is required.
    - When the number of users in a single campus exceeds 10,000 users, you need to deploy more than one cluster and must configure intercluster trunks between the clusters. However, because the campus is usually a LAN environment, you usually do not need to configure call admission control to regulate network bandwidth.
- Multiple-site IP WAN model with distributed call processing
    - Typically, CallManager clusters are geographically separated.
    - This is usually a WAN connection with limited bandwidth, and call admission control is required.
- Multiple-site model with centralized call processing
    - Remote devices do not require a dedicated CallManager at the remote site or branch office.

— Typically, this network topology uses location-based call admission control for the remote IP Phones that are registered to the central CallManager cluster.

— No intercluster signaling is required because the phones are registered to the central CallManager cluster.

- Combined multiple-site model

    — The combined multiple-site model combines the characteristics of the multiple-site IP WAN model with distributed call processing and the multiple-site model with centralized call processing. You need to configure call admission control between clusters, but you can use locations-based call admission control within a cluster.

Transcoder Usage with an Intercluster Trunk

CallManager requires transcoding when the two devices being connected do not support a common codec such as G.711 or G.729a. The Cisco DSP resource is a shared resource device that provides transcoding from one codec to another. It terminates media from two endpoints with dissimilar media types, such as G.711 and G.723. It is most commonly used when the media is sent across a restricted-bandwidth WAN and does not allow G.711. If the media can terminate at a device that only supports G.711, such as an application or voice mail, then a transcoder is required. Further details are provided in Chapter 5.

Initialization, Recovery, and Device Registration

Gateway devices register with Cisco CallManager based on the gateway configuration information. Once the gateway determines the IP address of CallManager, the gateway establishes a communication path with CallManager and sends a registration request to CallManager. This section describes the registration process for H.323 and MGCP gateways.

To set up the H.323 gateway, configure the gateway in Cisco CallManager Administration. CallManager initializes the H.323 gateway device process at initialization. In CallManager Administration, configure the H.323 gateway device with a prioritized list of CallManager nodes in the device group for the H.323 gateway device. When CallManager initializes, it creates a process to handle the H.323. The H.323 process is created on each node in a cluster, allowing any CallManager to handle H.323 gateway calls. If the H.323 gateway device is gatekeeper controlled, CallManager registers the gateway with the gatekeeper as described in the section "RAS Protocol Support for Gatekeeper Control Overview." The H.323 gateway device must also be configured appropriately in IOS to reach CallManager.

The MGCP gateway establishes a TCP/IP connection to CallManager. The MGCP gateway initializes and sends the Restart in Progress (RSIP) message to CallManager. CallManager responds with a Notification Request (RQNT), requesting to be notified of off-hook events from each configured endpoint on the MGCP gateway. CallManager then sends Audit Endpoint (AUEP) messages to the gateway, and the gateway responds with the idle, busy, and out-of-service status of each endpoint. The MGCP gateway, once initialized, maintains existing calls and starts the initialization sequence with the secondary CallManager node in the case of a failure of the primary. The secondary CallManager node determines the idle, busy, and out-of-service status of the endpoints and does not allow new calls to busy or out-of-service ports.

After the gateway sends the registration to CallManager, CallManager creates a device process to handle the gateway communication and then informs the device manager process of the gateway registration. The device manager propagates the device registration information to all CallManager servers in the cluster so that the route list information is accurate for all CallManagers in the cluster. Gateways are high-traffic devices, so each CallManager maintains control of calls that are originated locally in each CallManager node.

Figure 4-10 shows the device registration sequence for two gateways registering to two separate CallManager nodes. The device registration information is propagated to all CallManager nodes in the cluster.

Figure 4-10 *Gateway Registration*

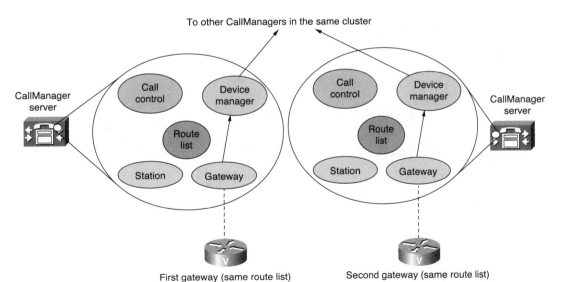

Figure 4-11 shows that any gateway device is available for use by any CallManager in the cluster.

Figure 4-11 *Gateway Call*

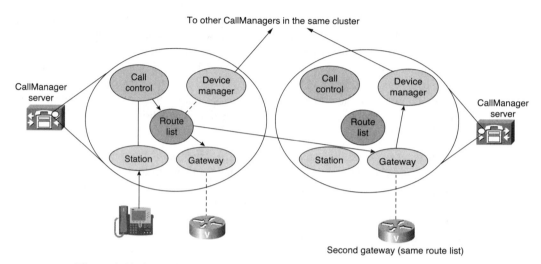

Figure 4-12 shows that a gateway device has a list of CallManager servers and registers with the next CallManager server in the list when the primary server is not available.

Figure 4-12 *Gateway Device Recovery*

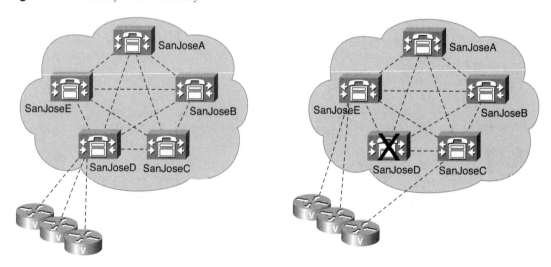

ISDN Timers

This section describes the ISDN Layer 2 and 3 configurable timers and parameters used in Cisco CallManager and gateways.

Layer 2 Timers

Timers permit Cisco gateways to recover from errors on the Q.921 interface. This section describes the configurable Q.921 Layer 2 timers and parameters used in Cisco gateways. Table 4-3 shows the configurable timers and parameters that CallManager passes to the gateway Layer 2 Q.921 processing. MGCP gateways handle all Layer 2 Q.921 signaling. Default values are provided for each parameter, but parameters are user-configurable.

Table 4-3   *Layer 2 Timers and Parameters*

Parameter	Default Duration	Description
TimerT200	1 second	Retransmission time indicating the number of seconds until the retransmission of a message
TimerT203	10 seconds	KeepAlive time indicating the time between KeepAlive messages
Timer T1Frame	2 seconds	T1 frame timer
L2RetriesN200	3	Number of retries before declaring the data link down
OutstandingIFramesK	7	The maximum number of outstanding I-frames that are acknowledged
AbleToEstablishMF	1	Send the SABME at startup instead of waiting for the distant end to do it
MaxErrorsToReport	3	The number of errors to report per data link establishment
TimeToDelayBeforeSendingAn Ack	0	The time to wait to send an RR acknowledgement on a given non-poll I-frame; a value of 0 means send immediately
MaxNumberOfReceivedIFrames BeforeAcking	4	The number of I-frames to be received before responding with an RR for an acknowledgement
PollInterval	1200	Polling interval in 250 millisecond increments; default value of 1200 is 5 minutes
ClearCallsWhenDatalinkGoes Down	1	Value of 1 indicates that calls are not cleared when data link goes down; a value of 0 indicates that calls are cleared

Layer 3 Timers

Timers permit CallManager to recover from errors in the Q.931 interface. This section describes the ISDN Q.931 timers that CallManager uses. Table 4-4 shows the configurable timers that CallManager uses for gateway Layer 3 Q.931 processing. Default values are provided for each parameter, but parameters are user-configurable.

Table 4-4   *Layer 3 Timers*

Parameter	Default Duration	Timer Description
TimerT301	180 seconds	User—(Call Delivered) Alerting received
		Network—(Call Received) Alerting received
TimerT302	10 seconds	User—(Overlap Sending) Setup Ack sent
		Network—(Overlap Sending) Setup Ack sent
TimerT303	10 seconds	User—Setup sent
		Network—Setup sent
TimerT304	20 seconds	User—(Overlap Sending) Setup Ack received
		Network—(Overlap Sending) Setup Ack received
TimerT305	30 seconds	User—(Disconnect Request) Disconnect Sent
		Network—(Disconnect Indication) Disconnect without progress sent
TimerT306	30 seconds	Network—(Disconnect Indication) Disconnect with progress sent
TimerT307	180 seconds	Network—(NULL) Suspend Ack sent
TimerT308	4 seconds	User—(Release Request) Release sent
		Network—(Release Request) Release sent
TimerT309	90 seconds	User/Network—Data link lost
TimerT310	20 seconds	User—(Outgoing Call Proceed) Call proceed received
		Network—(Incoming Call Proceed) Call proceed received
TimerT313	4 seconds	User—(Connect Request) Connect sent
TimerT316	120 seconds	(Restart request) Restart sent
TimerT317	300 seconds (5 minutes)	(Restart) Restart received
TimerT321	30 seconds	D-Channel failure
TimerT322	4 seconds	Status inquiry sent

H.323 Implementation Details

This section describes in detail the H.323 protocol messages and fields that Cisco CallManager supports and elaborates on what capabilities CallManager does not support for H.323 gateway devices. This information is provided for the reader who is interested in H.323 interoperability with CallManager and needs the specific details of the protocol support provided in CallManager H.323 protocol stack. You might want to skip this section if the H.323 interoperability details are not important to you.

Figure 4-13 shows the trunking devices that signal CallManager when using the H.323 signaling protocol. The devices include H.323 gateways and other CallManager clusters.

Figure 4-13 *H.323 Trunking Devices*

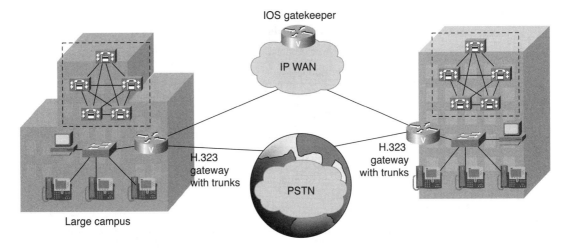

H.323 Call Signaling Protocol Support

This section describes in detail the H.323 call signaling protocol that CallManager supports for H.323 gateway devices. It includes sufficient detail to allow you to determine which capabilities CallManager supports, including H.323 protocol versions, message types, and information elements (IEs).

The H.323 messages, including the call signaling messages, follow the ITU-T Q.931 recommendation as specified in H.323. In H.323, the user-user information element (UUIE) conveys the H.323-related information. The H.323 user information protocol data unit (PDU) is ASN.1-encoded. The ASN.1 is encoded using the basic aligned variant of the packed encoding rules as specified in X.691. The ASN.1 structure begins with H323-UserInformation.

The call signaling protocol that is supported in the H.323 protocol umbrella is H.225. H.225 includes the call signaling messages and the RAS messages. This section covers the specific details of the call signaling messages.

Table 4-5 lists each H.225 message and provides the specific UUIE fields of the H.225 call signaling messages that CallManager exchanges with an H.323 gateway (GW in table). Table 4-5 lists each field, along with a brief description of the field usage and support as implemented by CallManager.

Table 4-5 *H.225 Call Signaling Message Details: UUIE Fields*

Message	Field Name	Comments
Alerting Direction: From GW	protocolIdentifier	Assumes v2; only v2 fields are processed
	destinationInfo	Not used
	h245Address	Used if present
	callIdentifier	Not required
	h245SecurityMode	Not supported
	Tokens	Not supported
	cryptoTokens	Not supported
	FastStart	Not supported
Alerting Direction: To GW	protocolIdentifier	Set to v2
	destinationInfo	Endpoint type terminal
	h245Address	If present at alerting, contains the IP address and port of the CallManager H.245 transport address
	callIdentifier	Unique call identifier
	h245SecurityMode	Not supported
	Tokens	Not supported
	cryptoTokens	Not supported
	FastStart	Not supported

Table 4-5 *H.225 Call Signaling Message Details: UUIE Fields (Continued)*

Message	Field Name	Comments
CallProceeding Direction: From GW	protocolIdentifier	Assumes v2; only v2 fields are processed
	destinationInfo	Not used
	h245Address	Used if present
	callIdentifier	Not used
	h245SecurityMode	Not supported
	Tokens	Not supported
	cryptoTokens	Not supported
	FastStart	Not supported
CallProceeding Direction: To GW	protocolIdentifier	Set to v2
	destinationInfo	Endpoint type terminal
	h245Address	If present at CallProceeding, contains the IP address and port of CallManager H.245 transport address
	callIdentifier	Unique call identifier
	h245SecurityMode	Not supported
	Tokens	Not supported
	cryptoTokens	Not supported
	FastStart	Not supported
Connect Direction: From GW	protocolDiscriminator	Assumes v2; only v2 fields are processed
	h245Address	Used if present; required if not present in previous message
	destinationInfo	Not used
	conferenceId	Required
	callIdentifier	Not used
	h245SecurityMode	Not supported
	Tokens	Not supported

continues

Table 4-5 *H.225 Call Signaling Message Details: UUIE Fields (Continued)*

Message	Field Name	Comments
	cryptoTokens	Not supported
	FastStart	Not supported
Connect Direction: to GW	protocolDiscriminator	Set to v2
	h245Address	Contains the IP address and port of CallManager H.245 transport address
	destinationInfo	Endpoint type terminal
	conferenceId	Unique conference identifier
	callIdentifier	Unique call identifier
	h245SecurityMode	Not supported
	Tokens	Not supported
	cryptoTokens	Not supported
	FastStart	Not supported
UserInformation Direction: From GW	protocolIdentifier	Assumes v2; only v2 fields are processed
	callIdentifier	Not used
UserInformation Direction: To GW	protocolIdentifier	Set to v2
	callIdentifier	Unique call identifier
Progress Direction: From GW	protocolIdentifier	Assumes v2; only v2 fields are processed
	destinationInfo	Not used
	h245Address	Used if present; required if not present in previous message
	callIdentifier	Not used
	h245SecurityMode	Not supported
	Tokens	Not supported
	cryptoTokens	Not supported
	FastStart	Not supported

Table 4-5   *H.225 Call Signaling Message Details: UUIE Fields (Continued)*

Message	Field Name	Comments
Progress Direction: To GW	protocolIdentifier	Set to v2
	destinationInfo	Endpoint type terminal
	h245Address	Contains the IP address and port of CallManager H.245 transport address
	callIdentifier	Unique call identifier
	h245SecurityMode	Not supported
	Tokens	Not supported
	cryptoTokens	Not supported
	FastStart	Not supported
ReleaseComplete Direction: From GW	protocolIdentifier	Assumes v2; only v2 fields are processed
	Reason	Reason for disconnect
	callIdentifier	Not used
ReleaseComplete Direction: To GW	protocolIdentifier	Set to v2
	Reason	Reason for disconnect
	callIdentifier	Unique call identifier
Setup Direction: From GW	protocolIdentifier	Assumes v2; only v2 fields are processed
	h245Address	Contains the IP address and port of CallManager H.245 transport address
	SourceInfo	Not used
	sourceAddress	Source address if provided
	destinationIAddress	Not used; E.164 address is in the Q.931 Called Party Number IE

continues

Table 4-5 *H.225 Call Signaling Message Details: UUIE Fields (Continued)*

Message	Field Name	Comments
	destinationCallSignalAddress	Not used
	destExtraCallInfo	Not used
	destExtraCRV	Not used
	ActiveMC	Not used
	conferenceId	Unique conference identifier
	conferenceGoal	Not used
	callServices	Not used
	CallType	Not used
	sourceCallSignalAddress	Not used
	remoteExtensionAddress	Not used
	callIdentifier	Unique call identifier
	h245SecurityCapability	Not supported
	Tokens	Not supported
	cryptoTokens	Not supported
	FastStart	Not supported
	mediaWaitForConnect	Used if present; defaults to false if not present
	canOverlapSend	Not used
Setup Direction: To GW	protocolIdentifier	Set to v2
	h245Address	Contains the IP address and port of CallManager H.245 transport address
	SourceInfo	Endpoint type terminal
	sourceAddress	Source address as E.164 address, H.323 alias, or both

Table 4-5   *H.225 Call Signaling Message Details: UUIE Fields (Continued)*

Message	Field Name	Comments
	destinationIAddress	E.164 address present here and also included in the Q.931 Called Party Number IE
	destinationCallSignalAddress	Not used
	destExtraCallInfo	Not used
	destExtraCRV	Not used
	ActiveMC	Not used
	conferenceId	Unique conference identifier
	conferenceGoal	Set to create
	callServices	Not used
	CallType	Point to point
	sourceCallSignalAddress	Not used
	remoteExtensionAddress	Not used
	callIdentifier	Unique call identifier
	h245SecurityCapability	Not supported
	Tokens	Not supported
	cryptoTokens	Not supported
	FastStart	Not supported
	mediaWaitForConnect	Set to false
	canOverlapSend	Set to false

RAS Protocol Support for Gatekeeper Control

This section describes in detail the RAS protocol that CallManager supports. It includes sufficient detail for you to determine what is supported, including RAS protocol version, specific message types, and information elements.

H.225 includes both the call signaling messages and the RAS messages. This section covers the specific details of the H.225 RAS messages that CallManager exchanges with gatekeepers (GK in table). The RAS message support provided by CallManager is the H.225 version 2 protocol.

Tables 4-6 through 4-13 describe the specific fields. The tables are arranged alphabetically by message type.

H.323 entites uses the RAS discovery messages to find a gatekeeper. CallManager does not currently support RAS discovery messages, but they are included here for completeness. An H.323 entity sends a GatekeeperRequest (GRQ) to find a gatekeeper. If an H.323 entity does not find a gatekeeper in response to the GRQ, it resends the GRQ at periodic intervals. Table 4-6 shows the fields that an H.323 entity uses to discover the gatekeeper.

Table 4-6 *H.225 RAS Terminal and Gateway Discovery Message Details: UUIE Fields*

Message	Field Name	Comments
GatekeeperRequest GRQ Direction: To GK	RequestSeqNumber	Not used in CallManager 3.11
	ProtocolIdentifier	
	NonStandardData	
	RasAddress	
	endpointType	
	gatekeeperIdentifier	
	callServices	
	endpointAlias	
	alternateEndpoints	
	Tokens	
	cryptoTokens	
	authenticationCapability	
	algorithmsOIDs	
	Integrity	
	integrityCheckValue	
GatekeeperConfirm GCF Direction: From GK	requestSeqNumber	Allowed, but ignored if received
	protocolIdentifier	
	nonStandardData	
	gatekeeperIdentifier	
	RasAddress	
	alternateGatekeeper	

Table 4-6   *H.225 RAS Terminal and Gateway Discovery Message Details: UUIE Fields (Continued)*

Message	Field Name	Comments
	authenticationMode	
	Tokens	
	cryptoTokens	
	algorithmsOIDs	
	Integrity	
	integrityCheckValue	
GatekeeperReject GRJ Direction: From GK	requestSeqNumber	Allowed but ignored when received
	protocolIdentifier	
	nonStandardData	
	gatekeeperIdentifier	
	rejectReason	
	AltGKInfo	
	Tokens	
	cryptoTokens	
	integrityCheckValue	

CallManager uses registration messages to register with the gatekeeper that the manual or automatic discovery process identifies. CallManager attempts to register with the gatekeeper and, if not successful, retries the registration at configurable intervals. If successful, CallManager sends the registration request at an interval, configurable in minutes, to refresh the registration. Table 4-7 shows the fields that CallManager uses to register with the gatekeeper.

Table 4-7   *H.225 RAS Registration Message Details: UUIE Fields*

Message	Field Name	Comments
RegistrationRequest RRQ Direction: To GK	requestSeqNumber	Unique sequence number that is incremented for each new request
	protocolIdentifier	Set to v2
	nonStandardData	Not used

continues

Table 4-7   *H.225 RAS Registration Message Details: UUIE Fields (Continued)*

Message	Field Name	Comments
	discoveryComplete	Set to false
	callSignalAddress	Set to the IP and port of the call signaling address
	rasAddress	Set to the IP and port of the RAS signaling address
	terminalType	Set to indicate terminal or gateway device
	terminalAlias	No alias set
	gatekeeperIdentifier	Gatekeeper ID set
	alternateEndpoints	No alternates set
	timeTolive	Set to configuration value; defaults to 60
	Tokens	Not supported
	cryptoTokens	Not supported
	integrityCheckValue	Not supported
	keepAlive	Set to true if this is a refresh registration
	endpointIdentifier	Endpoint ID set
	willSupplyUUIEs	Not set
RegistrationConfirm RCF Direction: From GK	requestSeqNumber	Unique sequence number
	protocolIdentifier	Assumes v2; only v2 fields are processed
	nonStandardData	Not used
	callSignalAddress	Use the IP address to specify the call signaling address
	terminalAlias	Not used
	gatekeeperIdentifier	Not used
	endpointIdentifier	Endpoint identifier
	alternateGatekeeper	Not used
	timeTolive	Time to live duration

Table 4-7 *H.225 RAS Registration Message Details: UUIE Fields (Continued)*

Message	Field Name	Comments
	Tokens	Not supported
	cryptoTokens	Not supported
	integrityCheckValue	Not supported
	willRespondToIRR	Not used
	pregrantedARQ	Not used
RegistrationReject RRJ Direction: From GK	requestSeqNumber	Unique sequence number
	protocolIdentifier	Assumes v2; only v2 fields are processed
	nonStandardData	Not used
	rejectReason	Reject reason
	gatekeeperIdentifier	Not used
	altGKInfo	Not used
	Tokens	Not supported
	cryptoTokens	Not supported
	integrityCheckValue	Not supported

CallManager uses unregistration messages to unregister with the gatekeeper when a gatekeeper-registered device is stopped. Table 4-8 shows the fields that CallManager uses to unregister with the gatekeeper.

Table 4-8 *H.225 RAS Unregistration Message Details: UUIE Fields*

Message	Field Name	Comments
UnregistrationRequest URQ Direction: To GK	requestSeqNumber	Unique sequence number that is incremented for each new request
	callSignalAddress	Set to the IP and port of the call signaling address
	endpointAlias	Not set
	nonStandardData	Not used

continues

Table 4-8 *H.225 RAS Unregistration Message Details: UUIE Fields (Continued)*

Message	Field Name	Comments
	endpointIdentifier	Not set
	alternateEndpoints	Not used
	gatekeeperIdentifier	Not set
	tokens	Not supported
	cryptoTokens	Not supported
	integrityCheckValue	Not supported
	reason	No reason set
UnregisterConfirm UCF Direction: From GK	requestSeqNumber	Allowed but ignored when received
	nonStandardData	
	tokens	
	cryptoTokens	
	integrityCheckValue	
UnregisterReject URJ Direction: From GK	requestSeqNumber	Allowed but ignored when received
	rejectReason	
	nonStandardData	
	altGKInfo	
	tokens	
	cryptoTokens	
	integrityCheckValue	

CallManager uses call admission control to determine whether enough bandwidth exists for CallManager to place the call. CallManager requests call admission before establishing a call. Table 4-9 shows the fields that CallManager uses to exchange call admission control messages with the gatekeeper.

Table 4-9   *H.225 RAS Admission Message Details: UUIE Fields*

Message	Field Name	Comments
AdmissionRequest ARQ Direction: To GK	requestSeqNumber	Unique sequence number that is incremented for each new request
	CallType	Set to point-to-point
	CallModel	Not set
	endpointIdentifier	Set to endpoint ID
	destinationInfo	Up to 16 E.164 addresses
	destCallSignalAddress	Not set
	destExtraCallInfo	Not set
	SrcInfo	If present, a list of up to 16 E.164 addresses
	srcCallSignalAddress	Set to the IP and port of the call signaling address
	bandwidth	Requested bandwidth to be used
	callReferenceValue	Set to call reference value for this call
	nonStandardData	Not used
	callServices	Set to None
	conferenceId	Unique conference identifier
	activeMC	Set to false for no MC
	answerCall	Set to true if call is incoming, false otherwise
	canMapAlias	Set to false
	callIdentifier	Unique call identifier
	srcAlternatives	Set to None
	gatekeeperIdentifier	Not set
	tokens	Not supported
	cryptoTokens	Not supported
	integrityCheckValue	Not supported
	transportQOS	Not supported
	willSupplyUUIEs	Not set

continues

Table 4-9 *H.225 RAS Admission Message Details: UUIE Fields (Continued)*

Message	Field Name	Comments
Admissionconfirm ACF Direction: From GK	requestSeqNumber	Unique sequence number
	bandWidth	Not used
	callModel	Not used
	destCallSignalAddress	Uses the IP address to specify the call signaling address; used if configured for anonymous device; ignored otherwise
	irrFrequency	Used to specify the InfoRequestResponse (IRR) frequency while on the call
	nonStandardData	Not used
	destinationInfo	Not used
	destExtraCallInfo	Not used
	destinationType	Not used
	remoteExtensionAddress	Not used
	alternateEndpoints	Not used
	tokens	Not supported
	cryptoTokens	Not supported
	integrityCheckValue	Not supported
	transportQOS	Not supported
	willRespondToIRR	Not used
	uuiesRequested	Not used
AdmissionReject ARJ Direction: From GK	requestSeqNumber	Unique sequence number
	rejectReason	Used only for ARJ trace display

Table 4-9   *H.225 RAS Admission Message Details: UUIE Fields (Continued)*

Message	Field Name	Comments
	nonStandardData	Not used
	altGKInfo	Not used
	tokens	Not supported
	cryptoTokens	Not supported
	callSignalAddress	Not used
	integrityCheckValue	Not supported

CallManager does not use bandwidth control messages. This chapter lists them for completeness. These messages might be used in a future release. Table 4-10 shows the bandwidth message fields. CallManager does not use these messages in release 3.1.

Table 4-10   *H.225 RAS Bandwidth Message Details: UUIE Fields*

Message	Field Name	Comments
BandwidthRequest BRQ Direction: To GK	requestSeqNumber	Not used in CallManager release 3.1
	endpointIdentifier	
	conferenceID	
	callReferenceValue	
	callType	
	bandWidth	
	nonStandardData	
	callIdentifier	
	gatekeeperIdentifier	
	tokens	
	cryptoTokens	
	integrityCheckValue	
	answeredCall	

continues

Table 4-10 *H.225 RAS Bandwidth Message Details: UUIE Fields (Continued)*

Message	Field Name	Comments
BandwidthConfirm BCF Direction: From GK	requestSeqNumber	Allowed but ignored if received
	bandWidth	
	nonStandardData	
	tokens	
	cryptoTokens	
	integrityCheckValue	
BandwidthReject BRJ Direction: From GK	requestSeqNumber	Allowed but ignored if received
	rejectReason	
	allowedBandWidth	
	nonStandardData	
	altGKInfo	
	tokens	
	cryptoTokens	
	integrityCheckValue	

CallManager does not use location messages in release 3.1. This chapter lists them for completeness. CallManager might use them in a future release. Table 4-11 shows the location request message fields.

Table 4-11 *H.225 RAS Location Request Message Details: UUIE Fields*

Message	Field Name	Comments
LocationRequest LRQ Direction: To GK	requestSeqNumber	Not used in Cisco CallManager release 3.1
	endpointIdentifier	
	destinationInfo	

Table 4-11   *H.225 RAS Location Request Message Details: UUIE Fields (Continued)*

Message	Field Name	Comments
	nonStandardData	
	replyAddress	
	sourceInfo	
	canMapAlias	
	gatekeeperIdentifier	
	tokens	
	cryptoTokens	
	integrityCheckValue	
LocationConfirm LCF Direction: From GK	requestSeqNumber	Allowed but ignored if received
	callSignalAddress	
	rasAddress	
	destinationInfo	
	destExtraCallInfo	
	destinationType	
	remoteExtensionAddress	
	alternateEndpoints	
	tokens	
	cryptoTokens	
	integrityCheckValue	
LocationReject LRJ Direction: From GK	requestSeqNumber	Allowed but ignored if received
	rejectReason	
	nonStandardData	
	altGKInfo	
	tokens	
	integrityCheckValue	

Gatekeepers use disengage messages to force a call to be dropped. CallManager uses disengage messages to indicate that an endpoint is being dropped. Table 4-12 shows the fields that CallManager uses to exchange disengage messages with the gatekeeper.

Table 4-12   *H.225 RAS Disengage Message Details: UUIE Fields*

Message	Field Name	Comments
DisengageRequest DRQ Direction: To or from GK	requestSeqNumber	Unique sequence number
	endpointIdentifier	Endpoint identifier
	conferenceID	Unique conference identifier
	callReferenceValue	Call reference value
	disengageReason	If sent, set to reason; if received, used to set the release complete reason
	nonStandardData	Not used
	callIdentifier	Unique call identifier
	gatekeeperIdentifier	Not used
	tokens	Not supported
	cryptoTokens	Not supported
	integrityCheckValue	Not supported
	answeredCall	Not used
DisengageConfirm DCF Direction: To or from GK	requestSeqNumber	Unique sequence number
	nonStandardData	Not used
	tokens	Not supported
	cryptoTokens	Not supported
	integrityCheckValue	Not supported
DisengageReject DRJ Direction: From GK	requestSeqNumber	Unique sequence number

Table 4-12 *H.225 RAS Disengage Message Details: UUIE Fields (Continued)*

Message	Field Name	Comments
	rejectReason	Reason for reject
	nonStandardData	Not used
	altGKInfo	Not supported
	tokens	Not supported
	cryptoTokens	Not supported
	integrityCheckValue	Not supported

The gatekeeper sends information request messages to request status information. CallManager responds to information request messages from the gatekeeper, but CallManager does not send unsolicited information request messages to the gatekeeper. Table 4-13 shows the fields that CallManager uses to exchange information request messages with the gatekeeper.

Table 4-13 *H.225 RAS Information Request Message Details: UUIE Fields*

Message	Field Name	Comments
InfoRequest IRQ Direction: From GK	requestSeqNumber	Unique sequence number
	callReferenceValue	Call reference value
	nonStandardData	Not used
	replyAddress	Not used
	callIdentifier	Not used
	tokens	Not supported
	cryptoTokens	Not supported
	integrityCheckValue	Not supported
	uuiesRequested	Not used
InfoRequestResponse IRR Direction: To GK	nonStandardData	Not used
	requestSeqNumber	Unique sequence number

continues

Table 4-13 *H.225 RAS Information Request Message Details: UUIE Fields (Continued)*

Message	Field Name	Comments
	endpointType	Set to the value of the endpoint type to indicate either terminal or gateway and set value to NoMC and not undefined node
	endpointIdentifier	Endpoint identifier
	rasAddress	Set to the IP and port of the RAS signaling address
	callSignalAddress	Not present
	endpointAlias	Not present
	perCallInfo	See the following entries
	PerCallInfo.nonStandardData	Not used
	PerCallInfo.callReferenceValue	Call reference value
	PerCallInfo.conferenceId	Unique conference ID
	PerCallInfo.originator	Set to false
	PerCallInfo.audio	Not set
	PerCallInfo.video	Not set
	PerCallInfo.data	Not set
	PerCallInfo.h245	Set to false
	PerCallInfo.callSignaling	Not present
	PerCallInfo.callType	Point to point
	PerCallInfo.bandwidth	Set to 1280
	PerCallInfo.callModel	Set to direct
	PerCallInfo.callIdentifier	Call ID
	PerCallInfo.tokens	Not supported
	PerCallInfo.cryptoTokens	Not supported
	PerCallInfo.substituteConfIDs	Not supported
	PerCallInfo.pdu	Not supported
	tokens	Not supported
	cryptoTokens	Not supported
	integrityCheckValue	Not supported
	needResponse	Not supported

Table 4-13   *H.225 RAS Information Request Message Details: UUIE Fields (Continued)*

Message	Field Name	Comments
InfoRequestAck IACK Direction: From GK	requestSeqNumber	Allowed but ignored if received
	nonStandardData	
	tokens	
	cryptoTokens	
	integrityCheckValue	
InfoRequestNak INAK Direction: From GK	requestSeqNumber	Allowed but ignored if received
	nonStandardData	
	nakReason	
	altGKInfo	
	tokens	
	cryptoTokens	
	integrityCheckValue	

Troubleshooting

This section describes common problems with trunking devices, describes tools useful for troubleshooting, and provides general recommendations for troubleshooting.

Troubleshooting MGCP Gateways

Useful trace data is available for the MGCP gateways. For the Computer Telephony Interface (CTI) trace data, set user mask 13 to provide trace data. The MGCP gateway itself also provides useful trace information. The following MGCP gateway commands are useful debug commands:

```
debug mgcp [all | errors | events | packets | parser]
debug ccm-manager [backhaul-events | errors | events | packets]
```

Only **events** is recommended during normal traffic.

The following is sample output of the **show ccm-manager** command as shown from the IOS gateway:

```
Total number of host: 3
Priority       Status                Host
=============================================================
Primary        Registered            100.20.71.30
First backup   Backup ready          100.20.71.26
Second backup  Idle                  100.20.71.47

Current active Call Manager:    100.20.71.30
Current backup Call Manager:    100.20.71.26
Redundant link port:            2428
Failover Interval:              30 seconds
Keepalive Interval:             15 seconds
Last keepalive check:           00:00:00
Last MGCP traffic time:         00:00:32
Last switchover time:           None
Switchback mode:                Immediate
```

Microsoft Performance also provides data regarding the MGCP gateways and analog ports. If Microsoft Performance shows no gateway connection, the following checks might help isolate the problem:

• Make sure the hostname.domainName matches in CallManager and the MGCP gateway.

• Check the call agent IP address from the MGCP gateway.

If an FXS port on the MGCP gateway has no dial tone, check to make sure that the gateway is connected to CallManager. If connected, reset the port from the MGCP configuration terminal by using the **voice-port**, **shut**, and **no shut** commands. From CallManager Administration, reset the MGCP member.

Troubleshooting H.323 Gateways

Useful trace data is available for H.323 gateways. You can enable the trace data for H.323 devices to include expanded output of the UUIEs for the H.225 signaling. This trace data allows you to investigate specific protocol-related problems between CallManager and H.323 gateway devices. The H.225 trace data includes not only H.225 signaling messages, but also RAS messaging between CallManager and the gatekeeper.

Summary

This chapter provided a description of the role of gateways in the Cisco CallManager architecture. Gateways bridge the gap between the packet-switched network and the circuit-switched network. The chapter included details about the H.323 and MGCP protocol support CallManager provides for gateway communication. It detailed the role of the gatekeeper and the H.323 gatekeeper communication protocol. It also covered the H.323 communication between CallManager clusters, including feature support between clusters.

## CHAPTER 5

Media Processing

This chapter discusses everything you ever wanted to know about media processing resources and media connection processing, but were afraid to ask. It might not answer all the questions you have on the subject, but it should at least discuss the salient points and provide insight into how media streams are controlled and handled by Cisco CallManager. There are two signaling layers within CallManager. Each signaling layer has distinct functions. The Call Control Layer handles all of the normal call signaling that controls call setup, teardown, and call routing. The second signaling layer is the Media Control Layer, which handles all media connection signaling required to connect the voice paths or media streams of the calls.

This chapter is divided into two major sections:

- Media Processing Overview—The first section provides a general overview of media processing devices and how media connections are established between them. It also covers media resource allocation and control.

- Architecture and Functionality of the Media Control Layer—The second section contains more detailed information on the architecture and functionality of media processing and the related devices in CallManager. It goes into detail about each type of device and how it is connected and used by CallManager. It also covers call preservation, which is the ability to maintain media connections (voice paths) in the event of failures.

NOTE   Call control signaling is discussed in Chapter 3, "Station Devices," and Chapter 4, "Trunk Devices." These chapters cover both phones and gateways.

Figure 5-1 shows the block structure of CallManager.

Figure 5-1 *Cisco CallManager Block Structure Diagram*

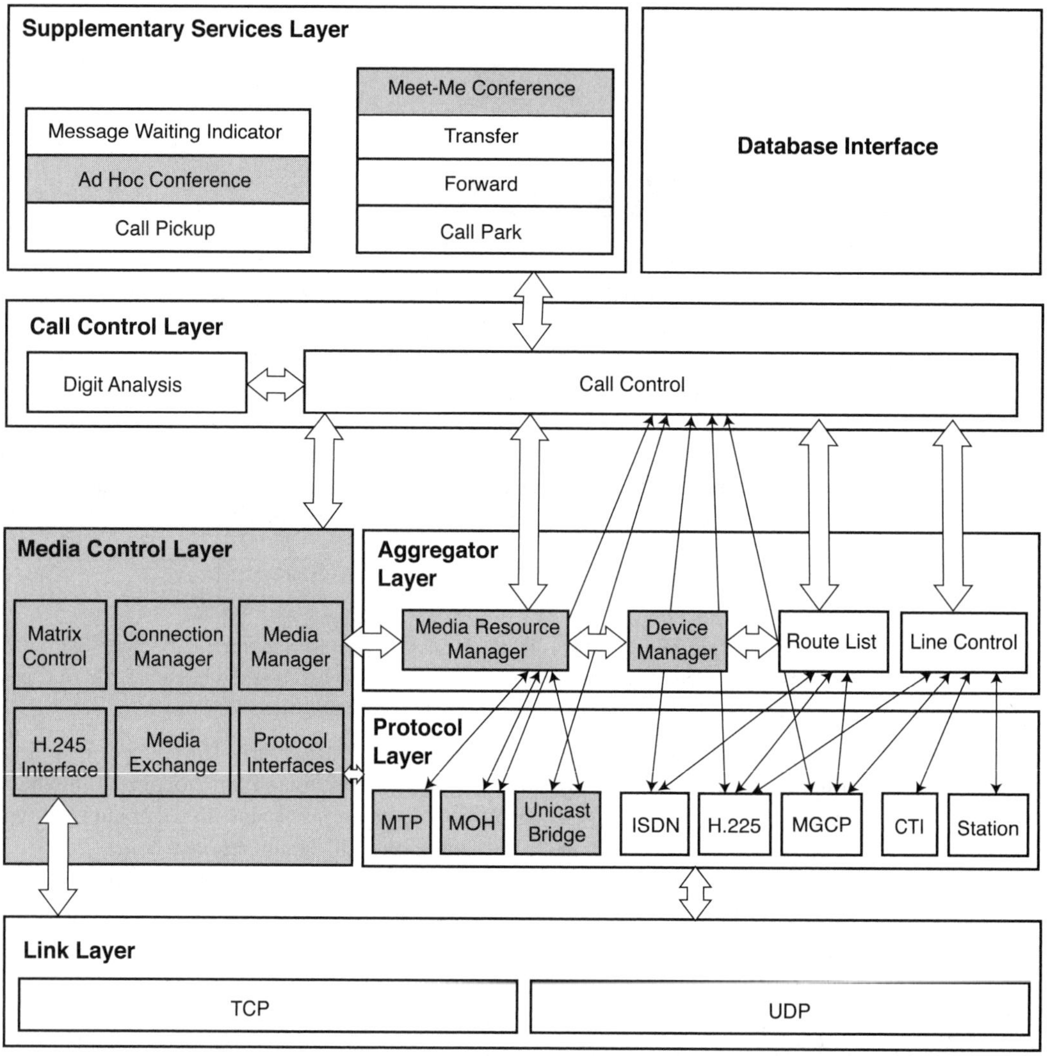

Figure 5-1 highlights the software layers and blocks within CallManager that are described in detail in this chapter. Other blocks are touched on lightly but are not highlighted because they are not covered in detail here.

The software in the Media Control Layer handles all media connections that are made between devices in CallManager. The Call Control Layer sets up and controls all of the call signaling connections between call endpoints and CallManager. The Media Control Layer directs the devices to establish streaming connections among themselves. It can insert other necessary media processing devices into a call and create appropriate streaming connections to those devices without the Call Control Layer knowing about them.

The Media Control Layer becomes involved in a call when the Call Control Layer notifies the Media Control Layer that a call has been connected between two endpoints. The Media Control Layer then proceeds to establish the media streaming connections between the endpoints as required to set up the voice path for that call.

The blocks highlighted in the Protocol/Aggregation layers of Figure 5-1 are those that control the media processing devices. They provide the device interface and handle all communication between the devices and CallManager.

The *Media Resource Manager* (MRM) handles all resource allocation and de-allocation. When call processing or a supplementary service determines that a media processing resource of a particular type is needed, the request is sent to the MRM. The MRM finds an available resource of the requested type, allocates the resource, and returns the resource identification information to the requestor.

Media Processing Overview

Cisco CallManager controls the voice paths or media connections of all calls handled by Cisco CallManager. The *Media Control Layer* (MCL) is responsible for making all of these connections through the underlying network (LAN or WAN). The MCL is a signaling layer that signals between CallManager and the endpoint devices and instructs the devices on how to set up appropriate media streaming connections. The MCL itself does not process or handle the actual media streams. This is important because CallManager nodes do not get bogged down by processing all of the streaming data from the thousands of calls being processed.

The system administrators and, to a lesser extent, the users of the system are directly aware and have control over some endpoints. They are only indirectly aware or not aware at all of other endpoints that might be involved in a call. The user, for example, is directly aware of IP Phones as endpoints in a call, indirectly aware of conference bridges and *music on hold* (MOH) servers, and not aware at all of transcoders, *media termination points* (MTPs), gateways, and other such devices. In many cases, only the MCL is actually aware of all devices that are involved a particular call and how the devices are connected. These connections between the devices create the voice path for a call.

The major topics for this section are

- Definition of Common Terms and Concepts Used in Voice over IP
- Media Processing Resource Types
- Understanding Media Processing Resources
- Controlling the Allocation and Usage of Media Processing Resources

Definition of Common Terms and Concepts Used in Voice over IP

This definition section is not exhaustive, but it covers the most important concepts and terms relevant to this chapter.

Logical Channels

A *logical channel* is a streaming data connection between two endpoints. A logical channel, in effect, is a pipeline through the data network between two endpoints that carries streaming data. When creating a logical channel, the creating entity specifies parameters that establish what kind of data is transported through that logical channel, which direction it is transported, the size of the datastream, and so forth. All voice data streams are transported through logical channels. Multiple logical channels can exist between any two given endpoints.

CallManager itself does not create logical channels. Instead, it instructs the endpoints in a call to establish either one or two simplex (one way) logical channels between them. One logical channel carries the voice data stream from the calling party to the called party, and the other carries the voice data stream from the called party back to the calling party. CallManager sometimes instructs an endpoint device, such as a Cisco IP Phone, to create a logical channel between itself and a media processing resource, such as a conference bridge or a transcoder. This is the mechanism used to create conferences and to provide MOH and other similar applications.

Voice Codecs

A *voice codec* is either a hardware or a software entity that converts an analog audio source into a digitized data stream, and vice versa. The codec packages the digitized data into a stream of data packets, each of which contains digitized voice data and is generated or sent at regular intervals. When silence suppression is enabled, variable numbers of bytes of data per interval can be generated, and it is possible that no packets of data are generated during silence. The interval at which codecs create and send data packets is dependent on the configuration of the packet sizes for each codec. You can set these configuration parameters through the Service Parameters screen in Cisco CallManager Administration (**System > Service Parameters select a server > Cisco CallManager**). Table 5-1 defines the service parameters for controlling codec packet generation and their possible values in milliseconds.

Table 5-1   *Codec Packet Size*

Service Parameter	Set of Possible Values	Default Value
PreferedG711MillesecondPacketSize	10 ms, 20 ms, 30 ms	20 ms
PreferedG729MillesecondPacketSize	10 ms, 20 ms, 30 ms, 40 ms, 50 ms, 60 ms	20 ms
PreferedG723MillesecondPacketSize	30 ms, 60 ms	30 ms

NOTE   Changing the packet size that a codec generates can have both positive and negative effects on the system. In general, the smaller the packet size, the less latency you have in the voice stream, and the more bandwidth and processing power it takes to handle the increased packet load. The larger the packet size, the more latency you have in the voice stream, and the less bandwidth and processing power it takes to process the data stream.

In this chapter, all information about capacities for media processing devices such as conference bridges, bandwidth consumed in the network, and so forth is based on the default packet size for the codecs. Cisco recommends that you do not change these values.

Codecs normally exist in endpoint devices such as IP Phones, gateways, and so forth. The codec in a given IP Phone converts the caller's voice from analog audio into a stream of data packets referred to as a *voice data stream* or a *media stream*. This stream of data packets is then routed to the other endpoint through a logical channel that has previously been established.

There are different voice codecs. Each codec follows a specific algorithm to convert analog voice into digital data. CallManager supports five different codec types: G.711, G.729a, GSM, G.723, and Wideband. Each of these codecs produces a different set of digital data. G.723, G.729a, and GSM are classed as low-bandwidth codecs, and G.711 and Wideband are considered high-bandwidth codecs.

Table 5-2 presents a list of some common voice codecs used in the packet-switched world and describes the amount of bandwidth each consumes.

Table 5-2 *Bandwidth Consumption by Codec Type*

Type of Codec	Bandwidth Used for Data Packets Only	Bandwidth Used per Call (Including IP Headers) with 30 ms Data Packets	Bandwidth Used per Call (Including IP Headers) with 20 ms Data Packets
G.711	64 kbps	80 kbps	88 kbps
G.721	32 kbps	48 kbps	56 kbps
G.723	6 kbps	22 kbps	Not applicable
G.728	16 kbps	32 kbps	40 kbps
G.729a	8 kbps	24 kbps	32 kbps
GSM	13 kbps	29 kbps	37 kbps
Wideband*	256 kbps	272 kbps	280 kbps

*Wideband is not the same as G.722.

The most popular voice coding standards for telephony and packet voice include

- **G.711 (A-law and μ-law)**—G.711 codecs encode the voice stream in the correct format for digital voice delivery in the public phone network. The processing requirements for encoding and decoding G.711 are very low, which makes it suitable for software-only implementations.

- **G.729a**—G.729a provides near toll-quality voice and provides a compressed stream bit rate of 8 kbps.

- **GSM**—GSM is a codec that is predominant in European wireless telephone systems. It provides a compressed stream rate of 13 kbps.

- **Wideband**—Wideband is a proprietary Cisco codec and is not the same as G.722. It produces a high-fidelity stream rate of 256 kbps. This codec is supported on Cisco IP Phones, software conference bridges, and MOH servers.

- **G.723.1**—G.723.1 is a low bit rate codec that provides good quality sound and has a stream rate of either 5.3 kbps or 6.3 kbps.

Silence Suppression

Silence suppression is the ability to suppress or reduce the RTP packet flow on the network when silence is detected during a phone call. Silence suppression may also be called *voice activity detect* (VAD). When enabled, endpoints, such as Cisco IP Phones or gateways, detect periods of silence or pauses in voice activity and either stop sending normal RTP packets or reduce the number of packets sent during these pauses in a phone conversation.

This reduces the number of RTP packets on the network and, thus, bandwidth consumed during the call.

To mask the silence suppression, the endpoint can play comfort noise. *Comfort noise* is also called white noise or background noise and is meant to make the user feel more comfortable that the call is still active while audio is being suppressed. Without comfort noise, the user might hear total silence. Some endpoints are capable of generating *pink noise,* which is background noise that resembles the background sounds from the current call.

There are two service parameters that control silence suppression, as shown in Table 5-3.

Table 5-3 *Service Parameters That Control Silence Suppression*

Service Parameter	Set of Possible Values	Default Value	Definition
SilenceSupression SystemWide	True or False	True	Determines whether silence suppression is disabled for all devices on a systemwide basis
SilenceSuppression WithGateways	True or False	True	Determines whether silence suppression is disabled for all gateways

If users complain about the silence during a phone call or the comfort noise generated to replace it, you can disable silence suppression by setting the service parameters to false (**System > Service Parameters > select a server > Cisco CallManager**), and the calls will sound more natural. However, the calls will consume more bandwidth.

IP Phone

An *IP Phone* in CallManager refers to a telephone device that contains, among other things, a *Digital Signal Processor (DSP),* and another processor chip such as an ARM Risc processor. An IP Phone can be plugged directly into an RJ-45 connector and looks like a standard network device to the network. It has an IP address, a Media Access Control (MAC) address, and it is able to use Dynamic Host Configuration Protocol (DHCP) and other standard network facilities.

During a call that is connected between two IP Phones, each IP Phone uses its codec (DSP) to create its own outgoing voice data stream. The voice data stream is sent through a logical channel to the other IP Phone or other device to which it is connected. The IP Phones also use their codecs (DSPs) to process the incoming voice data stream from the other IP Phone or other endpoint device.

CallManager instructs each of the two IP Phones to create a Transmit Logical Channel and a Receive Port between itself and the other IP Phone in the call. The Transmit Logical Channel of one IP Phone is connected to the Receive Port of the other IP Phone.

Media Termination Point

A *media termination point (MTP)* is a software-based media processing resource that accepts two full-duplex G.711 stream connections. It bridges the media streams between the two connections and allows the streaming connections to be set up and torn down independently.

Transcode

To *transcode* is to convert a voice data stream from one codec type to another codec type. For example, transcoding G.729a to G.711 means to convert the G.729a data stream produced by one codec into a G.711 data stream consumed by another codec.

Transcoder

A *transcoder* is a hardware-based device capable of doing a transcode operation. It also supports the functionality of an MTP, and in addition, it supports other stream types besides G.711. The stream types supported depend on the particular transcoder.

Call Leg

The term *call leg* is used when referring to a call signaling connection between two entities. In CallManager, the term refers to a call signaling connection between CallManager and an endpoint device. In a standard call (one that does not involve any media processing devices) between two IP Phones for example, there are two call legs: one between the originating IP Phone and CallManager, and the other between CallManager and the destination IP Phone.

This chapter does not discuss call legs because media connections are made point-to-point between two endpoints. They do not follow the call legs in that there are no media connections established between CallManager and the endpoints in a call. The MCL establishes all media connections, and it is not aware of the call signaling connections being processed in the Call Control Layer of CallManager.

Media Processing Resource Types

CallManager provides access to a variety of media resources. All media resources that are registered to any CallManager node in the cluster are made available to all CallManager nodes within the cluster.

A media processing resource is a software-based or hardware-based entity that performs some media processing function on the voice data streams that are connected to it. Media processing functions include mixing multiple streams to create one output stream, passing the stream from one connection to another, or transcoding the data stream from one codec type to another, and so forth.

CallManager allocates and uses four types of media resources:

- Unicast conferencing resources
- MTP resources
- Transcoding resources
- MOH resources

This section discusses each of these resource types. It explains their basic operation and purpose in the system.

Unicast Conferencing Resources

A *Unicast conference bridge* is a device that accepts multiple connections for a given conference. It can accept any number of connections for a given conference, up to the maximum number of streams allowed for a single conference on that device. There is a one-to-one correspondence between full duplex media streams connected to a conference and participants connected to the conference. The conference bridge mixes the input streams together and creates a unique output stream for each connected party. The output stream for a given party is usually the composite of the input streams from all connected parties minus their own input stream. Some conference bridges mix only the three loudest talkers on the conference and distribute that composite stream to each participant (minus their own input stream if they were one of the talkers).

A Unicast conference server supports more than one conference bridge and is either hardware-based or software-based. CallManager allocates a conference bridge from a conference server that is registered with the cluster. Both hardware-based and software-based conference servers can be registered with CallManager at the same time, and CallManager can allocate and use conference bridges from both of them. Hardware-based and software-based conference servers have different capabilities. Some hardware-based conference servers are able to conference streams from different codecs together, although other hardware-based conference servers are not. A software conference server is only able to conference streams from G.711 and wideband codecs.

The system does not distinguish between the types of conference bridges when a conference-allocation request is processed. CallManager cannot specifically allocate a hardware conference bridge or a software conference bridge directly. It simply allocates a conference bridge from the pool of conference resources available to the device for which the conference bridge is being allocated.

The CallManager system administrator has control over the types of conference resources that are in the pool of resources available to a particular device. This is covered in detail in the section, "Controlling the Allocation and Usage of Media Resources." If the CallManager administrator knows that a particular endpoint, such as a gateway, normally needs a hardware conference bridge to take advantage of its mixed stream conferencing capabilities, the administrator could configure the system so that the gateway only has access to hardware conference resources. The same thing applies to any particular group of devices that would normally need a particular resource type. The system administrator could also configure the device, or set of devices, so that it has access to software conference resources only after all hardware conference resources were allocated, or any other arrangement that seems appropriate.

CallManager allocates a Unicast conference bridge when a user presses the **Confrn** or **MeetMe** soft key on the phone. If no conference resources are available to that phone when the soft key is pressed, the button press is ignored and no conference is started. Unicast conference bridges can be used for both Ad Hoc and Meet-Me conferences.

Software-Based Unicast Conference Bridge

A software Unicast bridge is a standard conference mixer and is capable of mixing G.711 and wideband audio streams. Both G.711 A-law and G.711 μ-law streams can be connected to the same conference. The number of parties that can be supported on a given conference depends on the server where the conference bridge software is running and the configuration for that device. Because G.711 μ-law is the most common format, wideband and G.711 A-law streams are converted to G.711 μ-law before being sent to the mixer. The output streams from the mixer are converted back into G.711 μ-law or wideband as required for a particular endpoint.

Hardware-Based Unicast Conference Bridge

A hardware conference bridge has all of the capabilities of a software conference bridge. In addition, some hardware conference bridges can support multiple low bit-rate stream types such as G.729a, GSM, or G.723. This allows some hardware conference bridges to handle mixed-mode conferences. In a mixed-mode conference, the hardware conference bridge transcodes G.729a, GSM, and G.723 streams into G.711 streams, mixes them, and then encodes the resulting stream into the appropriate stream type for transmission back to the user. Some hardware conference bridges support only G.711 conferences.

Media Termination Points (MTPs)

An MTP is an entity that accepts two full duplex stream connections. The streaming data received from the input stream on one connection is passed to the output stream on the other connection, and vice versa. In addition, software-based MTPs transcode A-law to μ-law, and vice versa, and adjust packet sizes as required by the two connections. Hardware-based MTPs (transcoders) also are able to transcode data streams between two different codec types when needed.

Figure 5-2 illustrates the connections to and usage of an MTP. MTPs are used to extend supplementary services to H.323 endpoints that do not support empty capability sets. When needed, an MTP is allocated and connected into a call on behalf of an H.323 endpoint. When it is inserted, the media streams are connected between the MTP and the H.323 device and are not torn down for the duration of the call. The media streams connected to the other side of the MTP can be connected and torn down as needed to implement features such as hold, transfer, and so forth.

Figure 5-2 *MTP*

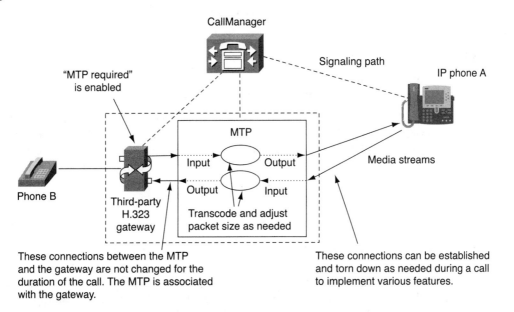

There are both hardware- and software-based MTPs. Hardware MTPs are really transcoders being used as MTPs.

Software-Based MTP

A software-based MTP is a device that is implemented by installing the Cisco IP Voice Media Streaming Application on a server. When the installed application is configured as an MTP application, it registers with a CallManager node and tells CallManager how many MTP resources it supports.

A single software-based MTP device can handle many more calls than its hardware counterpart, but it can only handle G.711 and Wideband codecs.

Hardware-Based MTP

A hardware-based MTP is a device that is implemented on a hardware blade that is plugged into a hardware-switching platform, such as a Catalyst 6000 or a Catalyst 4000. It is really a transcoder being used as an MTP, because transcoders have MTP capabilities. The device registers with a CallManager node as a transcoder and tells CallManager how many resources it supports. Some hardware-based MTPs can also support transcoding operations between connected endpoints. Transcoders when used as MTPs have the capability of handling more codecs, such as G.729, G.723, and GSM. The codecs supported by a given hardware-based MTP vary depending on its transcoding capabilities.

Transcoders

A transcoder is a device that takes the output stream of one codec and converts it in real time (transcodes it) into an input stream for a different codec type.

For example, it takes an output stream from a G.711 codec and transcodes it into a G.729a input stream accepted by a G.729a codec. Transcoders in release 3.1 will transcode between G.711, G.723, GSM, and G.729a codecs (transcoders do not support Wideband codecs in release 3.1). In addition, a transcoder also provides the capabilities of an MTP and can be used to enable supplementary services for H.323 endpoints when required.

Music on Hold (MOH) Resources

MOH resources are provided by software-based MOH servers that register with CallManager as MOH servers. MOH servers are configured through CallManager Administration, as are the other media processing devices. Each MOH server is capable of supplying up to 500 Unicast output streams of audio and 204 Multicast streams simultaneously. Up to 51 different audio sources can be configured on the MOH servers. All MOH servers in the cluster have the same MOH source configuration. This allows the CallManager to connect a held device to any MOH server in the cluster, and it receives the same audio source regardless of which server provides it. A given IP Phone can be connected to any available MOH output stream port, and the MOH server will connect that output stream to the source specified in the connect request. The MOH server can have up to 50 different source files on its disk for each codec type that it supports, and when a particular source is requested, it streams the audio data from the source file through the designated output stream connections. It is possible to connect all 500 MOH output streams to the same audio source.

One fixed source is always identified as source 51. Source 51 is connected to a fixed source, usually a sound card, in the server. Any sound source that can be attached to the sound card can then provide the audio stream for source 51.

Figure 5-3 illustrates a cluster of two CallManagers with media resources.

Figure 5-3   *A Cluster of Two Cisco CallManagers with Media Resources*

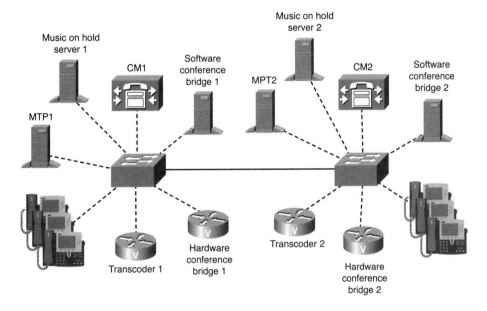

All resources are accessible by both CM1 and CM2.

In Figure 5-3, a complement of media processing resources is registered with each of the CallManager nodes. Figure 5-3 illustrates that there can be both hardware-based media resources and software-based media resources in the same cluster and on the same CallManager node. All resources are available to both CallManager nodes, regardless of which one they are registered with.

Understanding Media Processing Resources

To understand media processing resources, you must understand how voice data is generated and transported in VoIP networks. You also need to understand some of the basic components of the system, such as codecs, logical channels, endpoints, and so forth. This section assumes that you now have a general understanding of how the voice data streams are created and transported using these basic components.

NOTE   The basics of VoIP are explained in Chapter 1, "Cisco CallManager Architecture."

Media processing devices in general do not support call signaling. Within the CallManager software, the device control process for a media processing device handles all of the call signaling from the Call Control Layer for these devices, and none of the call signaling is actually sent to the devices. The media processing resources do understand media connection signaling. Media connection signaling is the signaling required to establish and control logical channels, media streams, and so forth. The media processing resources are treated as standard devices as far as media connections are concerned, and media connection signaling is sent to the devices.

There are two categories of media processing resources:

- Software-based media processing resources
- Hardware-based media processing resources

Software-Based Media Processing Resources

A software-based media processing resource is typically a Microsoft Windows 2000 server that is running the Cisco IP Voice Media Streaming Application. The Cisco IP Voice Media Streaming Application can be configured to operate and register with CallManager as three different device types. Each type of device provides a specific function or set of functions to CallManager. The three device types are

- Software conference bridge
- MTP
- MOH server

Each of these device types is discussed in detail in later sections.

The physical location of the Cisco IP Voice Media Streaming server is not significant to CallManager, as long as the server is accessible to all of the CallManager nodes in the cluster.

Hardware-Based Media Processing Resources

Hardware-based media processing resources are resources that run on hardware blades that plug into a network switching platform, such as a Cisco Catalyst 6500 or another similar device. Hardware-based resources have a complement of DSPs and other processors that give them additional capabilities that are not available on software-based resources. These devices register with CallManager as a particular type of device. Each type of device provides a certain set of functions to CallManager. The two types of hardware-based media processing devices are

- Hardware conference bridge
- Transcoder

Each of these device types is discussed in detail in later sections.

Advantages and Disadvantages of Hardware and Software Media Processing Resources

Software-based resources generally provide fewer processing-intensive features than do their hardware counterparts. Table 5-4 shows you recommendations based on various goals.

Table 5-4 *Recommendations for Choosing Software-Based or Hardware-Based Media Processing Resources*

Goal	Recommendation	Reason
Process high number of G.711 voice streams	Software	Software-based media processing resources are capable of processing many more voice data streams than hardware-based resources.
		Software-based media processing resources can only process G.711 voice streams.
Reduced cost for processing G.711 streams	Software	Software-based media processing resources are less expensive per stream than their hardware-based counterparts.
No additional switching platform requirements	Software	Software-based media processing resources generally require their own Windows 2000 server in all but very small installations, but they do not require that hardware be installed on a switching platform.
Ability to process streams from multiple codecs	Hardware	Hardware-based media processing resources can handle G.711, G.729a, and G.723 voice data streams. Some devices can handle GSM streams. Wideband is not supported.
		For example, a hardware-based conference bridge is capable of running a mixed-mode conference (one with different stream types).

continues

Table 5-4 *Recommendations for Choosing Software-Based or Hardware-Based Media Processing Resources (Continued)*

Goal	Recommendation	Reason
No additional server requirements	Hardware	Hardware-based media processing resources require hardware to be installed on a switching platform, but they do not require any network server support.

Media Resource Registration

All media processing resources currently register and communicate with CallManager using the Skinny Client Control Protocol (SCCP). All Cisco IP Phones also use this protocol. Third-party IP Phones that connect to a CallManager node can use Skinny Protocol, but there are also H.323 phones that connect to CallManager. The device registration is similar, but not identical, for all device types that use Skinny Protocol. Media processing resources do not use most of the protocol elements of Skinny Protocol. Media devices in general use some of the registration elements and the media control elements from this protocol.

Media Resource Device Registration Sequence

CallManager receives a registration request from a device. The registration request contains the device name and the device type. CallManager then attempts to look up the device in the database. If the lookup attempt is successful, all configuration information associated with this device is retrieved from the database, and the device is allowed to continue registering. Each device tells CallManager during the registration sequence how many full duplex media streams it can support. CallManager creates appropriate resources to support that device based on its device type.

On the device side, each media resource is given a list of CallManager nodes in priority order to which it should attempt to register. The first CallManager in the list is its primary CallManager. If the primary CallManager fails or is not available for any reason, it attempts to register with the next available CallManager in its list. Each device can register with only one CallManager at a time. The device always registers with its primary CallManager if that node is available, and it reregisters with the primary CallManager when it becomes available again after a failure. CallManager can have multiple devices of the same type registered. Each of these devices might be registered to a different CallManager node or to the same CallManager node as configured by the system administrators.

The Media Control Layer

The *Media Control Layer (MCL)* is a layer of software within CallManager that controls all media streaming connections between endpoints or devices in the CallManager system.

The MCL directs the construction of the voice path through the network for each call that is processed by CallManager.

This book does not discuss the elements that compose the underlying data network. It discusses only the logical connections made between the devices and endpoints that compose the CallManager system. All signaling and data streams are carried through an IP data network, and it is assumed for purposes of this discussion that the MCL is able to make all TCP/IP or UDP connections requested, and that the underlying network is able to carry all VoIP traffic as needed.

Users of the system are directly or indirectly aware of the endpoints in the call. For this discussion, consider the VoIP devices to be the endpoints in a call, and not the actual persons involved. Thus, if you pick up your phone and call another person, consider your phone as the originating endpoint of the call, and the called person's phone as the terminating endpoint of the call. Think of the voice stream as being created by your phone, traveling through the network, and being terminated by the called phone. You, a user, are aware of these two endpoints, because you directly used them by picking up one and dialing the other.

Figure 5-4 depicts the signaling and streaming connections made between two endpoints, in this case, Cisco IP Phones and CallManager. MCL directs the phones to open two logical channels, one in each direction between the two phones.

Figure 5-4 *Calls Between Two Endpoints*

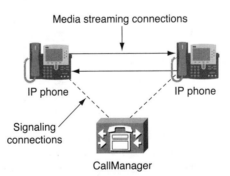

In some cases, it is not as simple as it seems at first glance. If the called party does not have an IP Phone that is on the CallManager system directly, such as when you call home from your IP Phone at the office, even though you can think of your voice traveling from your IP Phone directly to the phone at home, in fact there are other endpoints or devices in the call as far as CallManager is concerned. In this case, the endpoints in the call are really your IP Phone as the originating endpoint and a VoIP gateway as the terminating endpoint. The gateway connects directly to the public switched telephone network (PSTN), and the PSTN then carries the voice the remainder of the way. In this case, you are only indirectly aware of the endpoints. Figure 5-5 depicts that scenario.

Figure 5-5 depicts the signaling and streaming connections made between two endpoints, in this case, a Cisco IP Phone and an IP gateway. The MCL directs the IP Phone and the IP gateway to open two logical channels, one each direction between the IP Phone and the IP gateway.

All endpoints are not apparent to the users of the system. Sometimes the MCL inserts media processing entities into the voice data stream path without the user's knowledge. MTPs and transcoders are examples of these devices.

Figure 5-5   *Call Between a Cisco IP Phone and a Non-IP Phone*

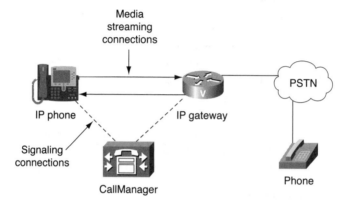

Figure 5-6 depicts the signaling and streaming connections made between three endpoints, in this case, two Cisco IP Phones and a transcoder. MCL instructs IP Phone A and Transcoder A to create two logical channels between themselves. It also instructs Transcoder A and IP Phone B to create two logical channels between themselves, making a total of four logical channels. The IP Phones are not aware of the transcoder, and each phone believes that it has established a connection with another phone in the network. The two phones are logically connected, but the actual connections run through a transcoder.

Some devices, such as conference bridges, are inserted at the user's request, and the user has indirect knowledge and control of their insertion. The control is indirect because you cannot directly select the conference bridge you wish to insert, but you indirectly select a conference bridge by pressing the conference button on the phone.

No audio data travels between endpoints in the CallManager system without the MCL first instructing the endpoints involved in the call to establish media connections between them.

Figure 5-6 *Calls Between Two Cisco IP Phones Using a Transcoder*

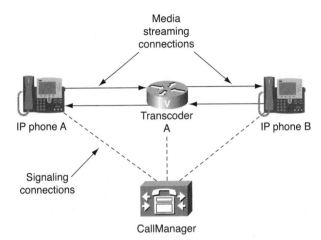

Controlling the Allocation and Usage of Media Resources

The CallManager system administrator has great flexibility in controlling where resources register in the cluster and which endpoints can use the resource. The administrator can organize the system based on geographical boundaries, on the structure of the underlying network infrastructure, or any other way desired. The topics covered in this section are

- Reasons to control the allocation of media resources
- Media resource default configuration
- How to control media resource allocation

Reasons to Control the Allocation of Media Resources

When allocating a media processing resource, it is important to be able to select which resource or set of resources can be used by a particular endpoint. If you have a geographically dispersed network, such as one that covers both Dallas and San Jose, and you have gateways in both Dallas and San Jose to handle local calls, it becomes very important where the media processing devices inserted into a call are physically located on the network. If CallManager inserts a media resource that is physically located in Dallas into a San Jose local call, the voice data for that call streams from the IP Phone in San Jose to a media resource in Dallas and back to the gateway in San Jose, before going out over the PSTN for the local call. This is a very inefficient use of bandwidth and resources.

Because all media resources that are registered with CallManager are available to all CallManager nodes within the cluster, any CallManager node in the cluster can select and insert any available resource into a call, no matter where the device physically resides or the CallManager node to which it is registered. CallManager system administrators have complete flexibility to configure the system any way they desire. The administrator can associate media processing resources with endpoints so that if an endpoint requires a media resource such as a conference bridge, CallManager knows which set of conference bridge resources are available to that endpoint.

If the system is configured correctly, and you are making a local call from an IP Phone in San Jose that requires a media resource, the CallManager controlling the call selects a media resource from a pool of local resources in San Jose.

Media Resource Default Configuration

In the absence of any configuration defined by CallManager Administration, all media resource devices are available to any endpoint in the system. The resources are used in the order that they were read from the database, and no attempt is made to associate a media processing resource with any particular endpoint. This arrangement is usually fine for small installations in a single location. If the system is large or geographically dispersed, the CallManager administrator will probably need to control media resource allocation.

How to Control Media Resources Allocation

This section discusses Media Resource Groups (MRGs), Media Resource Group Lists (MRGLs), and how they are used to control the allocation and usage of media processing resources. It also explains the algorithms used during the resource allocation process. The main topics are

- Media Resource Group (MRG) definition
- Media Resource Group List (MRGL) definition
- The order of precedence for MRGL assignments
- Media resource allocation through Media Resource Manager (MRM)
- Organizing resource allocation using MRGs and MRGLs

Media Resource Group Definition

All media processing resources belong at least one *Media Resource Group* (MRG). An MRG is essentially a list of media processing resources that are made available as a group. If a media processing resource is not explicitly assigned to an MRG, it belongs to the Null MRG.

The Null MRG is the default MRG that exists even when no MRGs have been explicitly created through CallManager Administration. When CallManager is first installed, the default configuration includes only the Null MRG and does not have any MRGLs defined. All media processing devices that register with a CallManager node are therefore assigned to the Null MRG by default. Once MRGs have been created through CallManager Administration, media processing devices can be assigned to them as desired.

An MRG can contain one or more media processing resources of the same type. The same media processing resource can be a member of as many MRGs as are necessary to achieve the desired configuration. In release 3.1, the types of media processing resources are

- Software conference bridge
- Hardware conference bridge
- MTP
- Transcoder
- MOH server

An MRG can contain one or more types of media processing resources. You can specify media processing resources of different types in any order, because their order is not a primary concern in the MRG.

Figure 5-7 illustrates the resources in the Null MRG. When multiple resources of the same type are in an MRG, they are grouped together. This figure shows devices of each type and how they are grouped within the MRG. Notice that the MTP group includes both MTPs and transcoders. The conference resources contain both hardware- and software-based resources. They are allocated in the order that they appear in the list.

Media Resource Group List Definition

After an MRG is created, you can add it to a *Media Resource Group List* (MRGL). An MRGL is an ordered list of MRGs. An MRGL can have one or more MRGs in its list. When you create an MRGL, if it contains more than one MRG, specify the list in priority order. The list is searched from first to last when looking for an available media processing resource. When looking for a resource of a specific type, all resources of that type that are available in the first MRG from the list are allocated before any resources of that type are used from the second and subsequent MRGs in the list.

Figure 5-8 illustrates some characteristics of both MRGs and MRGLs. The same devices exist in more than one MRG, and the Music MRG exists in more than one MRGL. With this arrangement, the phones on CM1 get media resources in a different order than the phones on CM2.

Figure 5-7 *Resources in the Null MRG*

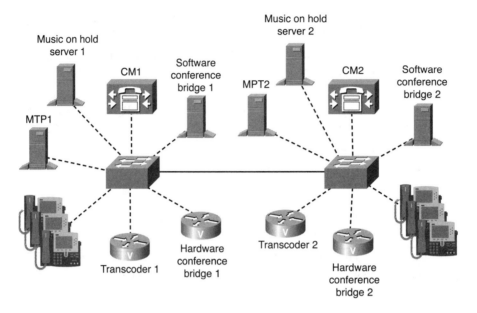

MTP	Transcoding	Conference	MOH
MTP1	Transcoder 1	Software conference bridge 1	Music on hold server 1
MTP2	Transcoder 2	Hardware conference bridge 1	Music on hold server 2
Transcoder 1		Software conference bridge 2	
Transcoder 2		Hardware conference bridge 2	

Resource allocation on CM1 is as follows:

- **Conference allocation**—When a conference is needed by the phones on CM1, they get either a software conference resource or a hardware conference resource. This continues until there are no more conference resources.

- **MTP allocation**—Both transcoders and MTPs are allocated when an MTP is requested.

- **Transcoder allocation**—Only transcoders are allocated until there are no more.

- **MOH allocation**—Both MOH servers are used, and the load is balanced across both of them.

Figure 5-8   *Media Resource Group and List Structures*

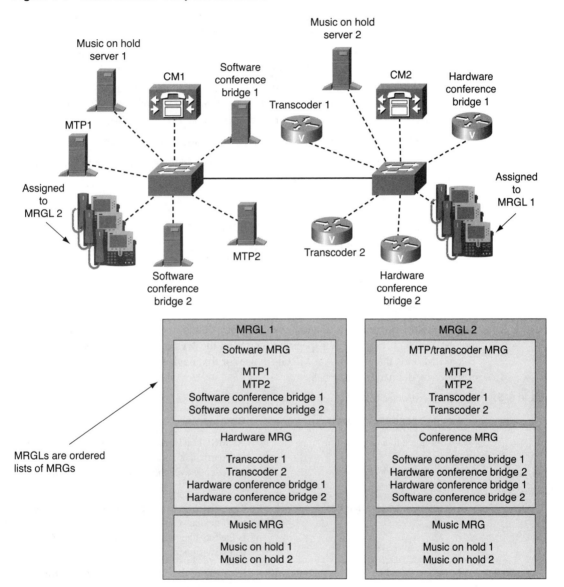

Resource allocation on CM2 is as follows:

- **Conference allocation**—The phones on CM2 always get a software conference bridge until there are no more software conference resources in the cluster. Then they get hardware conference resources until software resources are available again. Software resources always have priority over hardware conference resources.

- **MTP Allocation**—Software MTPs are allocated until there are no more software MTPs. Transcoders are allocated only when there are no software MTPs available. Software MTPs always have priority over transcoders.

- **Transcoder allocation**—Only transcoders are allocated until there are no more.

- **MOH allocation**—Both MOH servers are used, and the load is balanced across both of them.

The Order of Precedence for MRGL Assignments

Each endpoint device can have an MRGL associated with it. The two levels at which a system administrator can assign an MRGL are

- The Device Level
- The Device Pool Level

When a CallManager needs a media resource for an endpoint during a call, CallManager requests a media resource of a specified type from the *Media Resource Manager* (MRM). The MRM finds the appropriate MRGL to use for that device by following the order of precedence, defined in Table 5-5.

Table 5-5   *MRGL Precedence Levels*

Order of Precedence Levels	Comments
MRGL assigned to a device	An MRGL assigned to a device applies only to that particular device. The device MRGL has precedence over the MRGL assigned to the Device Pool.
MRGL assigned to a Device Pool	The MRGL assigned to a Device Pool applies to all devices that are in that Device Pool. This is the most general level at which an MRGL can be assigned.
No MRGL assigned to the Device Pool or the device	If neither of these two entities have an MRGL assigned, CallManager uses the Null MRG for all media resource allocations required.

Media Resource Allocation Through Media Resource Manager (MRM)

CallManager uses a simple two-step process to select a resource for a given allocation request once the MRGL is identified. Each step executes a simple algorithm. The interaction of these two algorithms makes control of the resource allocations very flexible.

The two-step allocation process is as follows:

Step 1 Get an MRG from the MRGL.

Step 2 Find a resource within that MRG, if one is available.

If the MRM finds an available resource of the specified type, it is returned to the requestor.

If the selected MRG has no resources of the requested type, or the existing ones are not available, the MRM repeats this two-step sequence (perhaps multiple times) until either an available resource is found or all of the MRGs in the MRGL have been searched.

Only if the MRM cannot find a resource of the specified type after searching all groups in the entire MRGL does it return an error indicating that no resources of that type are available.

Selecting an MRG from the MRGL

This algorithm selects and returns the next MRG from the list contained in the MRGL in priority order from top to bottom. The list is processed only once on each allocation request.

Selecting a Resource Within an MRG

Resources within an MRG are organized so that all resources of each given type are in a list together in the order presented in the MRG. In other words, it contains a set of lists, one for each type of resource that is present in that MRG.

This algorithm performs the following steps:

Step 1 Find the resource list for the type of resource requested.

Step 2 Once the list is found, allocate the next available resource using a least-used algorithm on the list. The least-used allocation begins at the point in the list where the previous allocation request ended.

Step 3 If an available resource is found, allocate it and return it to the requestor. If one is not found, notify the MRM that one is not available in this MRG.

Figure 5-9 illustrates the allocation order within an MRG. All resources are contained in the MRG. For calls that require a transcoder, the allocation order is illustrated. Note that they are allocated in least-used fashion.

Allocating a resource is accomplished by finding a device in the list that appears to have resources available. The device control process maintains the resource status for each device, so the MRM sends an allocation request to the device control process and attempts to allocate a resource. If one is available and the device status is good, a resource is allocated and returned to the MRM. If one is not available or the device status is bad (not available), the MRM is notified that no resource is available on that device. This is illustrated in Figures 5-10, 5-11, and 5-12.

Figure 5-9 *Allocation Order Within an MRG*

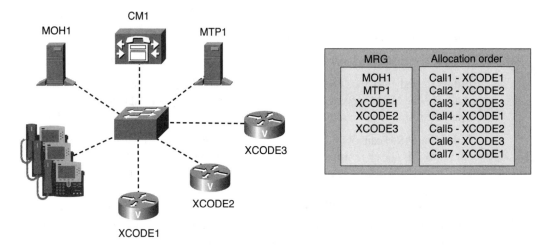

MRG	Allocation order
MOH1	Call1 - XCODE1
MTP1	Call2 - XCODE2
XCODE1	Call3 - XCODE3
XCODE2	Call4 - XCODE1
XCODE3	Call5 - XCODE2
	Call6 - XCODE3
	Call7 - XCODE1

Figure 5-10 shows the order of processing for resource allocation. The MRM gets a device name from the MRG and then sends a device look up request to the device manager. The device manager responds with the location of the device controller, whereupon the MRM sends an Allocation Request to the device controller. If the device controller has available resources, it responds with a Resource Allocation Response message, which is then returned to the requestor.

Figure 5-10 *Normal Resource Allocation Sequence*

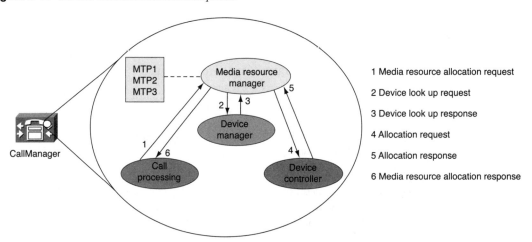

1 Media resource allocation request

2 Device look up request

3 Device look up response

4 Allocation request

5 Allocation response

6 Media resource allocation response

Figure 5-11 shows the allocation sequence when the first device is not registered. The MRM selects another device from the MRG and makes another request to the device manager. The sequence then proceeds normally.

Figure 5-11 *Device Is Not Registered or Out of Service*

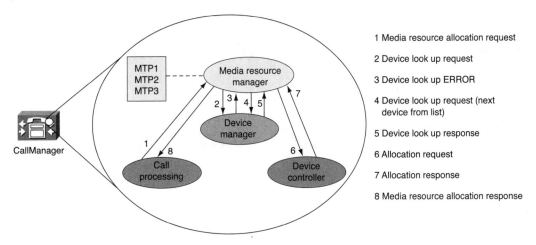

1 Media resource allocation request

2 Device look up request

3 Device look up ERROR

4 Device look up request (next device from list)

5 Device look up response

6 Allocation request

7 Allocation response

8 Media resource allocation response

Figure 5-12 shows the sequence when the device controller has no resources available for the device. In this case, the MRM must select another device from the MRG, request the location of the device controller, and then ask that device controller if it has a resource. The device controller responds with a Resource Allocation Response, and the Resource Allocation Response is returned to the requestor.

When the MRM has exhausted the list of devices in the MRG and subsequently in the MRGL, it notifies the requestor that no resources of the requested type are available.

HINT   If you want the processing load for a given resource type spread across several media resource servers, put all media resource servers of a given type in the same MRG. Within a single MRG, a resource of a given type is allocated in a least-used fashion. This does not guarantee that it will spread the load evenly, but it will spread the load. If you want to force the system to allocate resources from the same server until there are no more resources available on that server, you must put each resource server of the same type in a separate MRG, and organize the MRGs in the MRGL in the order that you want the resource servers used.

Figure 5-12 *Device Controller Has No Resources Available*

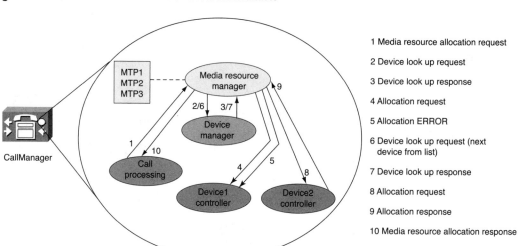

1 Media resource allocation request

2 Device look up request

3 Device look up response

4 Allocation request

5 Allocation ERROR

6 Device look up request (next device from list)

7 Device look up response

8 Allocation request

9 Allocation response

10 Media resource allocation response

Organizing Resource Allocation Using MRGs and MRGLs

The resource allocation tools provided allow a great deal of flexibility in determining how CallManager allocates media processing resources. Several different arrangements are shown in this section. This is not an exhaustive set, but perhaps it is enough to spark some ideas and to help you understand how MRGs and MRGLs can be used effectively.

The first arrangement configures the resources so that they are allocated almost exactly as they would be in release 3.0 systems.

Figure 5-13 illustrates a possible arrangement of media resources within a CallManager cluster. In this example, different departments are homed on separate CallManager nodes. This arrangement forces phones in Sales to use resources from the Sales group, phones in Marketing to use resources in the Marketing group and so forth. In this case, the resources are registered with the same CallManager node as the phones and gateways. See Figure 5-14 for another possible arrangement.

Figure 5-13 *Media Resource Group Cluster Overview*

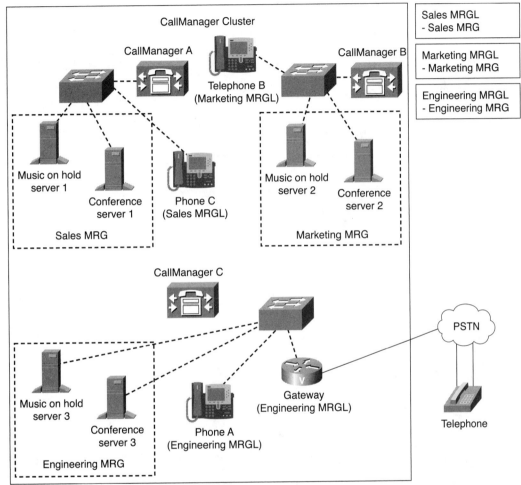

Figure 5-14 illustrates the fact that media resources are available throughout the cluster and do not have to be registered with the same CallManager from which they are used. All IP Phones and the gateway in this figure have full access to media processing resources, even though in some instances the IP Phones are registered to CallManager nodes that do not have any media processing resources registered to them. This arrangement still forces the IP Phones on CallManagers A or B to use only resources from MRG 1. The devices on CallManager C or D can use all resources, but they use the resources from MRG2 first. When those are exhausted, they can use the resources from MRG1.

Figure 5-14 *Media Resource Group System Overview*

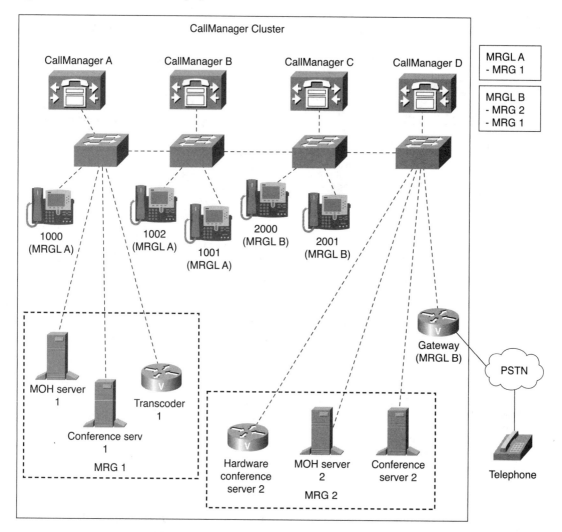

Figure 5-15 illustrates a possible arrangement for restricting access to media processing resources.

Figure 5-15 *Using an MRGL to Restrict Access to Media Resources*

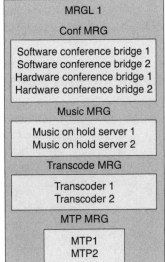

You can assign all resources to four groups as shown (no resources are left in the default group). Then create an MRGL called EMPTY_LIST and do not assign an MRG to it. In the phone configuration, for the phones homed on CM1, assign the EMPTY_LIST as their MRGL. These phones cannot use any media resources when they are configured this way.

You can use the same concept to restrict any particular device or type of devices from groups of users. For example, if you want to restrict phones on CM1 from using any conference resources, create an MRGL, add all other groups except conference MRG to it, and assign that MRGL to those phones. Now they cannot access conference bridges.

Architecture and Functionality of the Media Control Layer

This section contains more detail on the devices and functions handled by the MCL. You can skip this section if you are not interested in such detail, or dive in if you really like this sort of thing. These are the major topics of discussion in this section:

- Conferencing and transcoding DSP resources
- Conference resource basic architecture
- Transcoding resource basic architecture
- MOH basic architecture
- Call preservation during system failures

Conferencing and Transcoding DSP Resources

The Catalyst 6000 WS-X6608-T1, Catalyst 6000 WS-X6608-E1, and Catalyst 4000 WS-X4604-GWY voice modules provide hardware conferencing and transcoding resources for Cisco CallManager. Other DSP resource farms will be available in the future, and their processing capabilities and limits are expected to be similar to the Catalyst 4000 WS-X4604-GWY module. Table 5-6 provides configuration information and limits for the current modules.

NOTE   A *transcoding session* is defined as one full-duplex codec translation between two different codecs. When a transcoder is used as an MTP, it also counts as one transcoding session.

Table 5-6 *DSP Resource Configuration Table*

Catalyst Voice Modules	Conference Participants per Physical Port	MTPs/Transcoders per Port
Catalyst 4000 WS-X4604-GWY (This device can be configured to support either conferencing or transcoding, or both.)	**G.711 only** (**Note:** If other codecs, such as G.729a, are involved in a conference, they will be routed through a transcoder first and then connected to the conference.) 24 conference participants per physical port. Maximum of 4 conferences with 6 participants in each. **Note:** This conference bridge mixes the 3 loudest talkers.	**G.729a to G.711** 16 MTPs or transcoders
Catalyst 6000 WS-X6608-T1 WS-X6608-E1 (Each module has 8 physical ports. Each of the ports can be configured as either a conferencing resource or a transcoding resource.)	**G.711** **G.723** **G.729a** **GSM / FR** 32 conference participants per physical port. 256 conference participants total per module. Maximum conference size of 6 participants. (This is a marketing restriction because both the hardware and the software will support up to 32 participants.) **GSM / EFR** 24 conference participants per physical port. 192 conference participants per module. **Note:** This conference bridge mixes all conference participants.	These capacities apply to both transcoders and simultaneous transcode and conference sessions (a G.729a connection to a conference bridge, for example): **G.723.1 to G.711** **G.729a to G.711** **GSM / FR to G.711** **GSM / EFR to G.711** 24 transcoders per physical port. 192 transcoders per module. **G.729a to G.723.1** **GSM / FR to G.723.1** **GSM / FR to G.279** **GSM / EFR to G.723.1 or G.729a** 12 transcoders per physical port. 96 transcoders per module.

Limitations on Conferencing and Transcoding Resources

Table 5-6 does not describe all possible combinations. For example, you might have one or more G.711 conferences running at the same time as one or more G.729a conferences. The resource allocation matrix for a media resource device is not visible to CallManager, and CallManager has no visibility into the allocation and usage of DSP resources by these devices. These devices depend on DSP resources being available when they are needed, and the devices use varying amounts of DSP resources depending on the codecs being used in the active calls. G.729a requires more DSP support than does G.723 or G.711, for example, so the Catalyst 6000 modules register only 24 resources with CallManager, which should cover the worst-case processing requirements.

Conference Resource Basic Architecture

This section describes the architecture of all conferencing resources in CallManager and the components that form the basis of control and operation of the conferencing subsystem. This includes the Supplementary Services Layer, the Call Control Layer, the Protocol Layer, and the Media Control Layer.

Supplementary Services Layer

The Supplementary Services Layer in CallManager implements the feature operation as seen from a user perspective. It controls the operation of the feature and processes all soft key and button presses from the user after a feature has been activated. The Supplementary Services Layer in CallManager implements all features that exist in CallManager itself. For the conferencing features, it maintains all the conference information, such as which conferences are active and who the participants are for each one. This layer of processing is the one that ignores or processes button presses from the phones. It ignores conference requests when it cannot allocate a conference resource and processes them otherwise.

Supplementary Services Layer interfaces directly with the Call Control Layer. It can communicate with the Protocol Layer only through Call Control.

Protocol Layer

The Protocol Layer receives and handles the device registration. It also handles all communication with the device.

This layer also handles conference bridge device failures. Device failures and the subsequent handling for active conferences are both described in the section, "Call Preservation During System Failures."

Creating and Managing Conference Bridge Resources

All conference bridge servers use SCCP to communicate with CallManager. This is true of both hardware-based conference servers and software-based servers.

When a conference bridge server registers with CallManager, it provides several pieces of information needed by CallManager to communicate with the device and control conference allocation and usage on that device. The important ones for this discussion are

- Device name (conference bridge server name)
- Total number of streams (conference participants) that it can support (it takes one stream to support each conference participant)
- The number of streams that are currently active (normally set to 0)
- Number of streams (participants) that can be part of a single conference (this is an optional parameter)
- IP address of the device
- Device type

CallManager uses the device name provided at registration time to look up the device configuration information in the database. If the device is not configured in the database, the device is not allowed to register with CallManager. If the device is found in the database, it is allowed to complete registration, and CallManager creates a control process that communicates with the device and keeps track of the resources available for that device.

The device control process computes the number of conference resources that the device can support by taking the total number of streams that the device can support from the device registration message, and creating one conference bridge resource for every three streams that the server supports. Thus, if a conference bridge supports 32 streams, CallManager creates 10 conference resources to support this device.

If the device provides the maximum number of participants that can be part of a single conference at registration time, CallManager uses that value to compute how many conference bridge resources to create. For example, if the device supports 6 conference participants per conference and the device can support 24 participants total, CallManager creates four conference bridge resources.

The control process registers the device with the Device Manager, which makes its resources available for allocation by the MRM.

HINT	The number of conference bridge resources determines the number of conference bridges available on that device and, thus, the number of conferences that can be active simultaneously. Each conference bridge supports one active conference.
	Also, there is a one-to-one correspondence between the number of streams a device supports and the number of conference participants it supports.

Conference Resource Allocation and Control

The section contains a more detailed description of how conferencing resources are controlled and allocated by CallManager.

Allocating a Conference Bridge Resource

The conference supplementary service allocates one conference bridge resource for each conference that it starts. The conference bridge allocation is released when the conference is terminated. When the conference supplementary service needs a conference bridge for a new conference, it allocates a conference bridge using the MRM. The MRM does not attempt to distinguish between software-based conference bridges and hardware-based conference bridges when they are being allocated. It therefore allocates the next available conference bridge following the normal media resource allocation process. The allocated bridge can be either a hardware- or software-based conference bridge, depending on how conferencing resources are configured for that endpoint.

Mixed-Mode Conference Support

CallManager supports mixed-mode conferences. This means that a single conference can consist of users with different codecs, such as G.729a, G.723, and G.711 codecs, in the same conference. This is supported directly by some hardware-based conference bridges. Some hardware conference bridges automatically provide any transcoding that is required, based on the codec type of the connected participant within the transcoding capabilities of that conference bridge device.

HINT	Hardware conference bridges do not all support the same set of codecs, so when you purchase hardware and configure the system, you should make sure that the conference bridge devices and transcoders in your system support the codecs that are required.
	Not all hardware conference bridges support mixed-mode conferences. If a conference bridge does not support mixed-mode conferences itself, CallManager allocates and inserts transcoders as required by the conference participants of a given conference. This is true for both software-based conference bridges and hardware-based conference bridges.

Table 5-7 provides information about which codecs are supported by which devices.

Table 5-7   *Codec Support by Device Type*

Device Type	Codecs Supported
Catalyst 6000 WS-X6608-T1	G.711 (A-law and μ-law)
Catalyst 6000 WS-X6608-E1	G.723
	G.729a
	GSM / FR
	GSM / EFR
Catalyst 4000 WS-X4604-GWY	G.711 (A-law and μ-law)
(Note: This device supports only G.711	G.729a
conferences. Transcoders support the listed	GSM / FR
codecs.)	GSM / EFR
Software Conference Bridge	G.711 (A-law and μ-law)
(Cisco IP Voice Media Streaming Application)	Wideband
Software MTP	G.711 (A-law and μ-law)
	Wideband

Mixed-Mode Conference Support for Catalyst 6000 Conference Bridges

Mixed-mode conferences on Catalyst 6000 WS-X6608-T1 and WS-X6608-E1 voice modules use DSPs to perform the transcoding operations for conferences. The conference mixers on the Catalyst 6000-based hardware conference bridges only mix G.711 streams and do not use a DSP for mixing. If a conference participant is using some other codec, such as a G.729a codec, the incoming stream is transcoded from G.729a to G.711 automatically before being sent to the mixer, and the output stream from the mixer is transcoded from G.711 to G.729a before being output to the conference participant. All such transcoding is handled transparently on the Catalyst 6000 voice modules.

When setting up a conference on this type of device, you are guaranteed a minimum of three streams available. You cannot extend the conference unless additional streams are available on the device when you attempt to extend the conference.

Mixed-Mode Conference Support for Software Conference Bridges   Software
conference bridges support G.711 A-law, G.711 μ-law, and Wideband codecs. If a software conference bridge requires mixed-mode support for any other codecs, CallManager allocates and inserts transcoders as needed to handle the transcoding operations. Software conference bridges cannot transcode for any other codec type.

When setting up a conference on this type of device, you are guaranteed a minimum of three streams available. You cannot extend the conference unless additional streams are available on the device when you attempt to extend the conference.

Mixed-Mode Conference Support for Catalyst 4000 Conference Bridges   The Catalyst 4000 WS-X4604-GWY devices do not directly support mixed-mode conferences. Their conference mixers also only support G.711 A-law and μ-law. If mixed-mode conference support is needed when using these devices, CallManager will allocate and insert transcoders as needed.

Each conference on this device is mixed in a DSP. This limits the size of the conference to six participants but has the advantage of guaranteeing that you can always have up to six participants in each conference.

Large Conference Support

There currently is no way to request a conference bridge of a particular size or type. Some conference bridge servers support larger conferences than others, but there is no way to specifically allocate a bridge by size. Cisco does not officially support conference bridges larger than six participants, but the software conference bridges, and in some cases, the hardware conference bridges, actually support larger conferences.

If you know that a particular device is always used to set up large conferences and you want to use particular devices, such as Catalyst 6000 WS-X6608-T1 (up to 32 participants) or a software conference bridge (up to 48 conference participants), you could configure an MRGL for this device, and structure the MRGs with the appropriate devices in them in the order that you want them used. This would force the device to allocate from a resource pool that supports large conferences. (Conversely, you could construct another MRG and MRGL set with small conference resources in it and force another set of devices to use only those resources.)

HINT   Software conference bridges can support much larger conferences if they are installed on a dedicated server. Cisco does not recommend or officially support larger configurations, but CallManager and the Cisco IP Voice Media Streaming Application are both capable of supporting much larger configurations. Larger configurations might stress the limits of the underlying network, so if you want to experiment with them, you should consider the network implications also.

Extending Existing Conferences

CallManager does not guarantee that resources will be available to extend the conference on hardware- or software-based conference resources. It is possible to allocate a conference bridge on a device that has plenty of additional streams available to extend the conference at the time it was allocated and still have those streams all used in other conferences by the time you attempt to extend your conference. It is also possible to allocate a conference on a device that only has sufficient streams available to establish the conference. In this case, the conference cannot be extended, even though it would normally be allowed to grow. Some devices, by their implementation, guarantee that at least six participants can join any conference.

Controlling the Usage of Conference Bridge Servers

CallManager provides flexible and powerful mechanisms to control the allocation of conference bridges and other media resources. Which conference server to use when allocating a conference bridge depends first on the system configuration relating to media resource allocation, and second on which device is controlling the conference. Conference servers can be included in an MRG. MRGs are assigned to one or more MRGLs. Each device in the system might have an MRGL assigned to it, either by default or explicitly when the device is configured through Cisco CallManager Administration.

NOTE	Conference bridge servers are handled through MRGs and MRGLs the same as any other media processing resource. To understand how to configure and use MRGs and MRGLs to control conference bridge allocation, see the section, "How to Control Media Resources Allocation."

HINT	CallManager allocates all conference resources based on the device and directory number the conference controller is using to set up the conference. The conference controller is the one who sets up the conference.

When CallManager determines that a conference bridge is needed, it allocates a conference bridge, using the MRGL assigned to the directory number that the conference controller is using on this call. If an MRGL is not assigned to the directory number explicitly, CallManager uses the MRGL assigned to the conference controller's device. Failing that, CallManager uses the MRGL assigned to the Device Pool. If there is no MRGL assigned to the Device Pool, CallManager uses the conference servers that are available in the Null MRG. This group contains all servers that are not explicitly assigned to at least one MRG. If no conference servers are in the Null MRG, conferencing is not available for this call.

Default Configuration for Conference Servers

The initial system configuration does not have any MRGs defined. This initial configuration causes all media resource servers registered with CallManager to be in the Null MRG. It also forces all devices to use the Null MRG for all media resources allocation requests. This is the simplest configuration and makes every conference server that registers with

CallManager available to all devices that are registered to CallManager. This configuration is sufficient for small- or medium-sized installations, where there is no requirement to assign media processing resources to particular groups of devices.

Device Registration and Initialization

Each conference device has a list of CallManager nodes with which it is allowed to register. The list is in priority order. In general, each conference device attempts to register with its primary CallManager node, which is the first node in its list. If it cannot register with that CallManager node for some reason, it attempts to register with each of the other CallManager nodes in its list, from highest priority to lowest priority, until it successfully registers with one of them. Because conference devices use the SCCP, their switchover and switchback characteristics are similar to other station type devices and are not covered in detail here.

NOTE   The conference devices will attempt to keep calls active in the event of failures. This along with their switchover and switchback algorithms is covered in the section, "Call Preservation During System Failures."

A Look at Device Registration from the Side of Cisco CallManager

A CallManager administrator controls device registration in the CallManager cluster. Every device that is allowed to register with the cluster must first be defined in the configuration database through Cisco CallManager Administration. The only exception to this is when phones are configured to auto-register, which requires that the administrators enable auto-registration. When the system administrator defines media processing resources, those resources are given a name and device type. Depending on the device being defined, there are other parameters and information required, such as the maximum stream count for that device. Specific configuration parameters for each device are covered in the device-specific section.

The media processing device registration sequence is as follows:

1   CallManager receives a registration request from a device, followed by a Station IP Port message that identifies the port that CallManager is to use when communicating with this device. The registration request contains the device name and the device type, among other things. CallManager then attempts to look up the device in the database using the device name. If the lookup attempt is successful, all configuration information associated with this device is retrieved from the database, and the device is allowed to continue registering.

NOTE	See the section, "Creating and Managing Conference Bridge Resources" for more details on what information is passed to CallManager on device registration.

2 CallManager sends a Register Ack message, followed by a Capabilities Request message.

3 The device sends a Version Request, and CallManager responds with a Version Response.

4 The device sends a Capabilities Response message, followed by a KeepAlive message. The Capabilities Response message informs CallManager what codecs the device supports for incoming and outgoing media streams.

5 CallManager responds with a KeepAlive Ack, and the device registration is complete.

6 The device can send a StationMediaResourceNotificationMessage at any time following registration to inform CallManager of any changes in its stream processing capabilities, or to inform CallManager about its specific conference configuration. This message contains

— Maximum streams per conference

— Number of streams in service

— Number of streams out of service

7 CallManager uses the maximum number of streams per conference to compute the number of conference resources that this device can support. The message is also used to decrease or increase the number of streams that the device can support at the current time (which can also change the number of resources that the device can support). This message is used whenever the device experiences an event that changes its processing capabilities, such as a non-recoverable DSP failure and so forth.

After the device is registered, all of the CallManager nodes in the cluster have access to it and can allocate and use the media processing resources of that device.

Conferencing Limitations and Configuration Notes

CallManager in general has a "stream-centric" view of conferencing resources that are registered with it. This view is consistent with the implementation of both the software conference bridges and the Catalyst WS-6608-T1 and WS-6608-E1 hardware modules. When dealing with standard G.711 conferences, the view is accurate and complete. In these cases, CallManager creates one conference bridge resource for each set of three streams that are registered by these devices. It requires at least three participants to set up an Ad Hoc conference. These devices support conference sizes ranging from three up to the maximum number of streams supported by the device. This means that CallManager has complete control over the streams registered and can establish any number of conferences of varying sizes, as long as the total number of streams used in the conferences does not exceed the number of streams registered by the device. The conference sizes are, of course, limited by the maximum sizes configured through CallManager Administration.

For example: The device registers 32 streams. It does not limit the maximum number of conference participants per conference at the device level, and the maximum participants for a conference at the system level is set at 32. In this case, CallManager creates 10 conference resources to support this device, which allows CallManager to set up a maximum of 10 simultaneous conferences on this device. The device can support from 1 to 10 simultaneous conferences using the 32 streams. Some of the possible configurations that CallManager could set up are

- A single conference with 32 participants
- Two conferences with 16 participants each
- Three conferences, one with 20 participants, one with 9 participants and the other with 3 participants
- Eight conferences with three participants each and two conferences with four participants each
- Ten conferences with three participants each
- Any other combination, as long as the total number of conference participants does not exceed 32 and the maximum number of simultaneous conferences does not exceed ten

Some DSP farms used for conference bridges, such as the Catalyst 4000 WS-X4604-GWY, are not implemented in the same manner. These devices are more "DSP-centric" in that they implement each conference on a separate DSP. This means that a single conference is limited in size to the maximum number of streams that can be processed by one DSP. In this case, even though the device might register 24 streams, for example, the largest conference it can support is six participants, because each DSP can handle a maximum of six streams. When these devices register, they also supply the optional parameter "Max Streams Per Conference," which informs CallManager about this configuration. When this parameter is provided, CallManager divides the registered stream count by this parameter to compute the number of conference resources to create for that device. If the device registers 24 streams and 6 streams maximum per conference, CallManager creates four conference resources for this device.

For example, one of these devices registers 24 streams and a maximum per-conference stream limit of six. The maximum participants for a conference set through CallManager Administration is six. CallManager creates four conference resources for this device, which in turn allows CallManager to create four simultaneous conferences. CallManager could then use the 24 streams to set up conferences in the following configurations:

- Four conferences with six participants each
- Four conferences, each having between three and six participants each

- Four conferences with three participants each
- Any other combination, as long as the total number of conferences does not exceed four and the maximum participants per conference does not exceed six

---

HINT   When using hardware that mixes conferences on the DSPs and the same device registration parameters as in the previous example, it is possible to use all the conference resources and still have half of the streams unused, by setting up four conferences. This occurs when each conference has only three participants, which is the downside. The upside is that each conference has three more streams that are guaranteed to be available, and thus each conference can add three more participants, if desired.

Unicast Conference Bridge Application (Software)

The Cisco IP Voice Media Streaming Application used to support Unicast conferences is a Cisco software application that installs on a server during the CallManager installation process. In the installation, the component is called the Cisco IP Voice Media Streaming App and is common to the MTP, MOH, and the conference bridge applications. The Cisco IP Voice Media Streaming Application runs as a service under Microsoft Windows 2000.

Ad Hoc Conferencing

An Ad Hoc conference is established by using the **Confrn** soft key or button on the phone. The person who sets up the conference is referred to as the conference controller. The conference controller adds each participant to the conference, and therefore has complete control over who joins the conference. Once the conference controller adds a participant to the conference, the participant cannot be forced to leave the conference. The conference participants can drop out of the conference any time they desire by hanging up the phone, thus terminating the call. As long as there are two or more participants remaining in the conference, the conference bridge is still active, and the conference is maintained. When an Ad Hoc conference has only one remaining participant, the conference call is terminated, and the remaining participant is disconnected.

There are several variations on the basic method of setting up a conference, but a conference controller always establishes an Ad Hoc conference. The conference controller sets up the conference by pressing the conference button during a call, calling a third person, and then pressing the conference button a second time. The first conference button press allocates the conference bridge for this conference. The second conference button press creates the conference and connects all three participants to it. The conference controller can continue to add additional participants to the conference until either the conference bridge being used is out of resources, or the maximum number of participants as specified in system configuration is reached.

To add additional conference participants to the conference, the conference controller presses the **Confrn** soft key or button on the phone. CallManager provides a dial tone to the controller, the conference controller then calls the person to be added, and presses the **Confrn** soft key or button again. The controller rejoins the conference, and the new participant is added to the conference.

Meet-Me Conferencing

A Meet-Me conference is established by using the **MeetMe** soft key or button on the phone. The person who sets up the conference is referred to as the conference controller. Unlike in an Ad Hoc conference, the conference controller does not have complete control over who joins the conference. The Meet-Me conference controller selects one of the Meet-Me conference numbers from the range specified for the CallManager node that is controlling the call. The conference controller then establishes the conference using that Meet-Me conference number. After the conference is established, anyone who calls that particular Meet-Me conference number is immediately connected to the conference.

Meet-Me Feature Operation

Two separate operations are involved in a Meet-Me conference call:

- A user must establish a Meet-Me conference by pressing the **MeetMe** soft key or button on the phone and then dialing a Meet-Me number from range of numbers available for that particular CallManager node.

- Once the conference is established, each conference participant places a call to that particular Meet-Me conference number and is immediately connected into the conference.

HINT   If more control is desired over who can participate in a Meet-Me conference, participants can be instructed to dial into an operator or attendant who then transfers them to the conference number and announces their joining.

Conference Configuration

A CallManager administrator can enable Ad Hoc or Meet-Me conferencing in CallManager by completing the following steps:

Step 1   Install and configure one or more hardware conference bridges in the cluster. It is not important which CallManager node the conference bridge registers with, as long as the CallManager node is in the cluster. All conference and other media resources are shared across the entire cluster.

or

During the system installation, install the Cisco IP Voice Media Streaming Application and configure it as a software conference bridge. When the IP Voice Media Streaming Application is installed, the software conference bridge, MTP, and MOH devices are automatically created in the Cisco CallManager Administration database with default settings.

Step 2 If you are configuring Ad Hoc conferencing, set "Max # of users in one Ad Hoc Conference" to the maximum number of participants you wish to allow in an Ad Hoc conference. If you are configuring Meet-Me conferencing, set "Max # of users in one Meet-Me Conference" to the maximum number of participants you wish to allow in a Meet-Me conference.

NOTE These are both system-wide parameters and are normally set to six. You can set them to a higher number, but some conference bridge devices are limited to six participants in a single conference.

Step 3 Configure the new conference devices.

What Happens When Conference Resources Are Not Available

If you attempt to create or extend an Ad Hoc conference or create a Meet-Me conference when the necessary conference resources are not available, the conference will not be created or extended. The behavior that the conference controller or the potential participants sees will vary depending on what conference resource is not available, and when that was determined. The following behaviors might be observed.

Out of Resources When Creating a Conference

When you attempt to create a conference and a conference bridge is not available, CallManager does not respond to the **MeetMe** or **Confrn** soft key. In other words, the button presses are ignored. Some of the possible reasons for this condition are

- The conference bridge server has not registered with the system yet.
- The conference bridge server failed for some reason.
- All available conference bridges in the Null MRG are in use.
- No conference bridge servers are in the Null MRG.
- All available conference servers in the MRGL assigned to the conference controller are full.
- No conference servers in the MRGL are assigned to the conference controller.

Out of Streams When Extending an Ad Hoc Conference

When a conference is already active, the conference controller attempts to add another participant to the conference, but there are no more streams available for this conference, the user is left on hold, and the conference controller is joined back into the conference.

Out of Streams When Extending a Meet-Me Conference

When a Meet-Me conference is active and no more streams are available, a user dialing the Meet-Me conference number will hear reorder tone (sometimes referred to as fast busy) and will not be connected to the conference.

Maximum Number of Participants in an Ad Hoc Conference Exceeded

When a conference already has the maximum number of participants allowed in an Ad Hoc conference and the conference controller attempts to add another participant to the conference, CallManager ignores the **Confrn** soft key or button press, and the conference controller stays connected to the conference.

Maximum Number of Participants in a Meet-Me Conference Exceeded

When a Meet-Me conference is active and the maximum conference participant count has been reached, a user dialing the Meet-Me conference number will hear reorder tone and will not be connected to the conference.

Maximum Number of Conference Bridges Supported

The maximum number of conference bridges supported by the device can be different than the number of conference resources created in CallManager.

If the device does not provide the maximum number of participants that can be part of a single conference, CallManager creates one resource for each set of three streams. If the device supports 24 participants total and does not tell CallManager that it supports six participants per conference, for example, CallManager will create eight conference resources for that device, even though it can only support four conferences.

In this case, when CallManager attempts to connect the fifth concurrent conference to the device, the conference controller can set up the conference. When the conference controller presses the **Confrn** button for the second time, the three calls will be terminated, and the participants in the conference will hear reorder tone because of the conference failure.

Unicast Conference Performance Statistics

Performance counters are available that monitor the usage of Unicast conference resources. All performance statistics are monitored through Microsoft Windows 2000 counters. You can monitor these counters in the Admin. Serviceability Tool in Cisco CallManager Serviceability. Table 5-8 contains the available counters and their meaning.

Table 5-8 *Unicast Conference Counters per Cisco CallManager Node*

Counter	Description
UnicastHardwareConfResourceActive	Indicates the total number of Unicast hardware conference resources that are in use on all hardware conference devices that are registered with this CallManager node.
UnicastHardwareConfResourceAvailable	Indicates the total number of Unicast hardware conference resources that are not in use and are available to be allocated on all hardware conference devices that are registered with this CallManager node.
UnicastHardwareConferenceActiveParticipants	Indicates the number of participants that are in all active conferences that are using a hardware conference bridge allocated from this CallManager node.
UnicastHardwareConferenceCompleted	Indicates the number of Unicast conferences that used a hardware conference bridge allocated from this CallManager node and have been completed, which means that the conference bridge has been allocated and released.
UnicastHardwareConferenceOutOfResources	Indicates the number of times CallManager attempted to allocate a Unicast hardware conference resource from those that are registered to this node when none were available, either because they were all in use or none were registered.
UnicastSoftwareConfResourceActive	Indicates the total number of Unicast software conference resources that are in use on all software conference devices that are registered with this CallManager node.
UnicastSoftwareConferenceActiveParticipants	Indicates the number of participants that are in all active conferences that are using a software conference bridge allocated from this CallManager node.

continues

Table 5-8 *Unicast Conference Counters per Cisco CallManager Node (Continued)*

Counter	Description
UnicastSoftwareConferenceCompleted	Indicates the number of Unicast conferences that used a software conference bridge allocated from this CallManager node and have been completed, which means that the conference bridge has been allocated and released.
UnicastSoftwareConfResourceAvailable	Indicates the total number of Unicast software conference resources that are not in use and are available to be allocated on all software conference devices that are registered with this CallManager node.
UnicastSoftwareConferenceOutOfResources	Indicates the number of times CallManager attempted to allocate a Unicast software conference resource from those that are registered to this CallManager node when none were available, either because they were all in use or none were registered.

MTP and Transcoding Resource Basic Architecture

This section describes the architecture of transcoding resources in CallManager. This includes a description of the Protocol Layer, the Media Control Layer, and device registration. Although the architecture is the same in many respects as conference resource architecture, there are important differences because transcoding resources are not signaling entities and are not known by the signaling layers.

Why to Use an MTP

An MTP is inserted on behalf of H.323 endpoints, such as Microsoft NetMeeting clients that are involved in a call, to enable supplementary services to those endpoints. Supplementary services include such features as hold, transfer, conference, and so forth. To implement these features, the logical channels to the endpoint must be closed and reopened again. Sometimes the logical channels are opened to another endpoint that is different than the first to implement a feature such as transfer.

Figures 5-16, 5-17, and 5-18 illustrate the streaming connections created and torn down during a consultation transfer.

Figure 5-16 shows the initial call from Phone B to IP Phone A. It goes through a third-party H.323 gateway that requires an MTP, so the MCL inserted an MTP into the media stream. It illustrates both the signaling and the media streaming connections.

Figure 5-16 *Call Transfer Initiation*

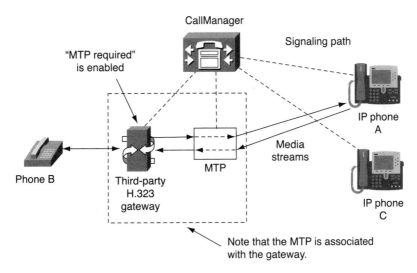

Figure 5-17 illustrates the connections that exist after the user on IP Phone A pressed the **Trnsfer** soft key and called Phone C. Note that the media streams between the MTP and the H.323 gateway are still connected, so as far as the gateway knows, it is still connected to Phone A. The logical channels between the MTP and IP Phone A have been closed, and a new set of logical channels have been created between IP Phone A and IP Phone C. These two parties are talking to each other. After a short conversation, the user on IP Phone A presses the **Trnsfer** soft key again and completes the transfer.

Figure 5-18 shows the final signaling and streaming connections that exist when the transfer has been completed. Logical channels have been connected between IP Phone C and the MTP. As far as call control signaling layers and the users involved know, IP Phone C is connected to Phone B. The use of the MTP is transparent to the users. If the MTP was not inserted into the call when it was required, supplementary services would not be available on that call.

Figure 5-17 *IP Phone A Transfers Phone B to Phone C*

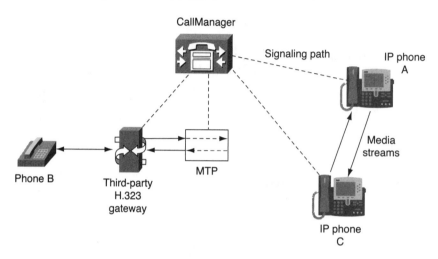

Figure 5-18 *Transfer Completion*

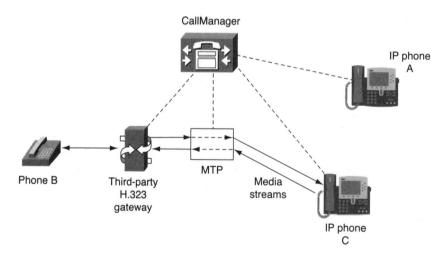

CallManager uses one of two basic methods to prevent the endpoint from tearing down the call when the media streams are closed. They are as follows:

- Send the device a capability set with zero capabilities in it, and the device closes its media streaming connections

- Insert an MTP into the media stream on behalf of the endpoint so that the media streams to the device are never closed

If the endpoint supports empty capability sets, when CallManager desires to close the media streams, it sends the device a set of capabilities that has no capabilities in it. The device, on receiving that set of capabilities, closes all logical channels, but it does not tear down the call. CallManager can now establish a connection with another device. It sends the H.323 device another capability set with appropriate capabilities in it and then opens new logical channels to the new destination. H.323 v1 endpoints do not allow empty capability sets. If an endpoint does not support empty capability sets, it is not possible to extend any features to that endpoint directly. This is because the logical channels must be closed in order to implement any of the supplementary services such as those mentioned. As soon as the logical channels are closed, the H.323 endpoint tears down the call, even though it has not been instructed to do so through the signaling channels. In H.323 v2, the concept of empty capability sets was implemented. If the device is using H.323 v2, it allows CallManager, for example, to send a capability set to the H.323 device, which has no capabilities specified in it (an empty capability set). When the H.323 device receives these capabilities, it closes the logical channels and waits for a new capability set. All Cisco H.323 gateways support zero capability sets and thus do not require MTPs.

When an MTP Is Inserted

The MCL inserts an MTP on behalf of H.323 endpoints, such as Microsoft NetMeeting clients, and H.323 gateways only if the MTP Required flag is enabled through CallManager Administration for that device. MTPs are used only in support of H.323 endpoints and are not used for any other type of endpoint.

The MCL follows the steps in Figure 5-19 to determine whether an MTP is required.

Figure 5-19 *MTP Allocation Flowchart*

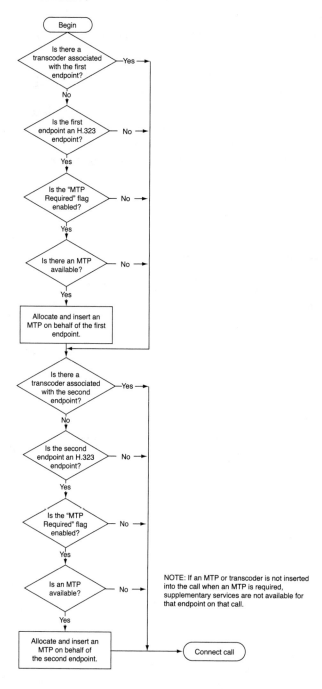

Figure 5-19 illustrates the processing steps in the MCL to determine whether to insert an MTP. When the MCL determines that an MTP should be inserted, it allocates an MTP resource from the resource pool specified by the MRGL associated with that device. The MCL inserts the MTP resource into the call on behalf of an H.323 endpoint. The MTP resource use is not visible to either the users of the system or the endpoint on whose behalf it was inserted.

Why to Use a Transcoder

Transcoders are used to connect calls whose endpoints do not have a common codec. A transcoder can be used as an MTP if an endpoint in the call requires an MTP and none are available. Transcoders are allocated and inserted into a call automatically by the MCL. The use of a transcoder resource is not visible to either the users of the system or the endpoint on whose behalf the transcoder was inserted.

It is possible that the endpoint devices in the call have common codecs available, but they cannot use them because CallManager restricts their usage. Regions are commonly used to restrict the bandwidth between endpoints, which in turn limits the codecs that can be used by the two endpoints. If the region specifications require a low-bandwidth codec be used between the two endpoints, and the two endpoints do not have a common low-bandwidth codec, a transcoder will be inserted, if it is available. For example, if one endpoint supports only G.723 and the other supports only G.729a for low-bandwidth usage, a transcoder is required. Another example occurs when a call is transferred to voice mail and that voice mail system requires a G.711 input stream. If a low-bandwidth caller cannot use a G.711 codec (possibly because of region restrictions), a transcoder will be inserted on behalf of the voice mail port to transcode the media stream from a low-bandwidth stream to a higher-bandwidth G.711 stream.

Figure 5-20 illustrates an example of how the system is configured when transcoders are needed. Transcoders are invoked only if matching codecs do not exist at the endpoints of a call.

Figure 5-20 *The Insertion of a Transcoder into a Call*

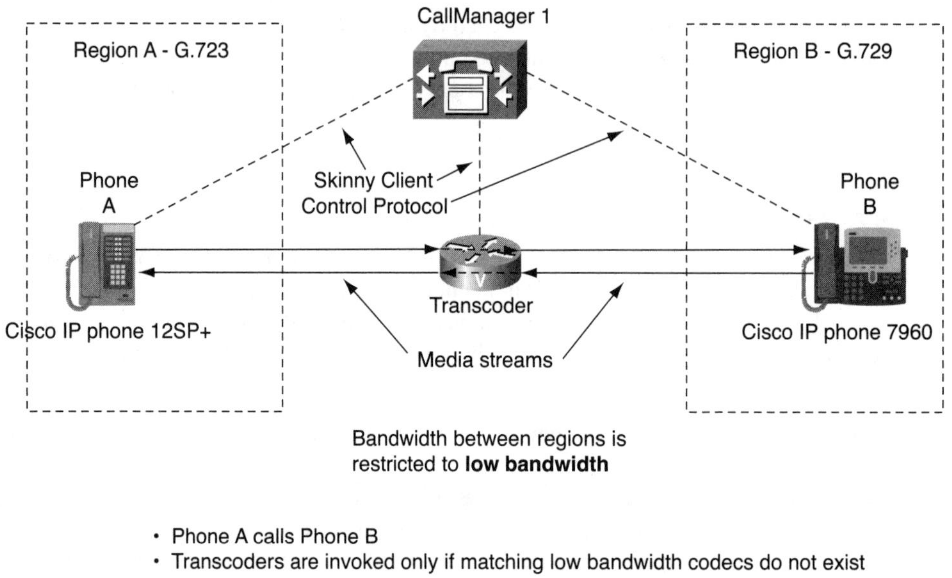
CallManager 1
Region A - G.723
Region B - G.729
Phone A
Phone B
Skinny Client Control Protocol
Transcoder
Cisco IP phone 12SP+
Cisco IP phone 7960
Media streams
Bandwidth between regions is restricted to low bandwidth
• Phone A calls Phone B
• Transcoders are invoked only if matching low bandwidth codecs do not exist

What Happens When Transcoders or MTPs Are Not Available When Needed

CallManager always attempts to connect calls whenever it can, and then provides supplementary services, if possible. Thus, if the choice is to connect the call without supplementary services or not to connect the call at all, CallManager always chooses to connect the call, even with diminished capabilities. CallManager follows these two rules:

- If an MTP is required in a given call and neither an MTP nor a transcoder (to act as an MTP) is available at that point in time, CallManager connects the call directly, and supplementary services are not available on that call. The user is not notified but will find out when trying to use a feature that requires an MTP. CallManager does not respond to the button presses.
- If a transcoder is required, that means that the two endpoints do not have matching codecs and cannot communicate with each other directly. In this case, CallManager attempts to connect the call, which causes the call to terminate without ever establishing a media connection.

Rules for Inserting Transcoders and MTPs When They Are Available

As far as the MCL is concerned, a call is a connection between two parties. If the call is a conference call, for example, the MCL is not aware of the conference. To the MCL, a conference call is a series of individual calls. The fact that the second party in all of those individual calls is a conference bridge is of no particular interest to the MCL. The MCL simply makes connections between two parties as directed by call control. In the case of a conference call, the conference supplementary service is the only entity within CallManager that knows that there is a conference call being set up. In a conference call, each person connected to the conference bridge appears to the MCL as a separate call between the caller and the conference bridge. Because each party is individually connected to the conference bridge, the MCL inserts an MTP or transcoder only if one is required for that call. Thus, many MTPs or transcoders might be involved in a single conference, or none at all, depending on the requirements of each connection that is part of the conference.

The rules for inserting transcoders and MTPs apply to each individual call and can be quite complex in some instances. Provided first is a simple set of rules that will suffice for understanding how, in general, the selection is made. A more in-depth explanation follows for those interested in greater detail.

In any single call, MCL inserts a maximum of two MTPs. If a transcoder is required, normally only one transcoder is inserted within a given CallManager cluster.

The MCL first obtains the capabilities of both endpoints involved in the call. The MCL does not attempt to make a connection until it has received the capabilities from both endpoints in the call.

Figure 5-21 shows the configuration where phones at a remote site call each other using G.711 both at the central office and at the remote office. The communication link between the remote site and the central campus is a low-bandwidth connection, so the calls over that link are restricted to G.723.

Figure 5-21 *Intercluster Calls with Restricted Bandwidth*

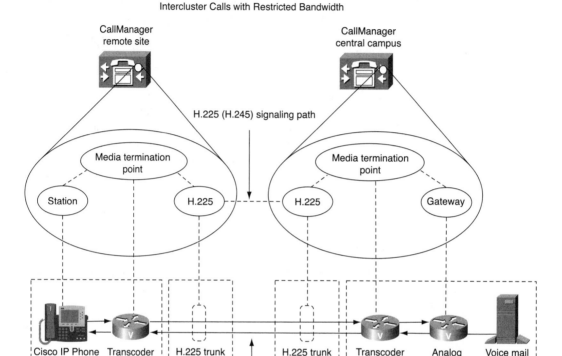

Intercluster Calls with Restricted Bandwidth

Bandwidth between region A and region B is G.723   Bandwidth between region C and region D is G.723

- H.225 trunk between CallManager clusters is used to connect all calls between clusters. In this configuration, transcoders are invoked because there is no common codec between the endpoint devices and the H.225 trunk due to region matrix specification.

NOTE: Because intercluster trunks are direct connections from CallManager to CallManager, no separate H.225 device physically resides on the LAN. Nevertheless, CallManager treats intercluster trunks as virtual gateways and routes call signaling and media control through them.

In this example, two transcoders are required because the region matrix forces a G.723 codec between the endpoints and the trunk devices. (The bandwidth between Region A and Region B is set to G.723, and the bandwidth between Regions C and D is set to G.723). Within Regions A and D, the bandwidth is set to G.711. The CallManager node at the central campus inserts a transcoder between voice mail and the H.225 trunk, because the bandwidth between Region C and Region D is G.723 and voice mail does not support that codec. The CallManager node at the remote site inserts a transcoder between the phone and the H.225 trunk, because the Cisco IP 7960 does not support the G.723 codec.

CallManager automatically inserts a transcoder when one is needed because of lack of a common codec between endpoints in a call. CallManager allocates a transcoder based on the capabilities of the endpoints involved in the call and the region matrix that is applicable to the respective endpoints.

Table 5-9 describes MCL actions when determining whether to insert MTPs or transcoders.

Table 5-9   *Rules for Inserting MTPs and Transcoders Within a Single Cisco CallManager Cluster*

Current Resources Allocated in the Call	MCL Actions
No resources allocated	Match capabilities between two parties. If capabilities do not match, allocate a transcoder whose capabilities match at least one available codec on each endpoint.
	If both parties require an MTP, allocate an additional MTP for the other party.
No resources allocated	Match capabilities between two parties. If capabilities do not match and no transcoder is available whose capabilities match at least one available codec on each endpoint, terminate the call. (Not all transcoders support all capabilities of the endpoints.)
No resources allocated	Match capabilities between two parties. If capabilities match, check both parties to see whether they require an MTP.
	Allocate an MTP for each of the two parties that require one. If none are required, connect the call direct without any MTPs or transcoders.
One MTP	Match capabilities between MTP and the other party. If capabilities do not match, allocate a transcoder.
One MTP	Match capabilities between MTP and the other party. If capabilities match and MTP is required for other party, allocate another MTP.
One transcoder	If MTP is required for other party, allocate an MTP.
One transcoder and one MTP	No additional resource required.
Two MTPs	Match capabilities between the two MTPs. If capabilities do not match, allocate a transcoder.

H.323 devices do not always require an MTP or transcoder, so the MCL does not allocate one unless the H.323 device has the MTP Required flag set. The Cisco H.323 gateways support all of the low-bandwidth codecs supported by Cisco IP Phones, so it usually comes down to configuring the right codec on the gateway to work with the phones. If this is not adequate because of various regions and third-party devices, you can explicitly invoke an MTP by enabling MTP Required for the gateway. If MCL determines that a transcoder is needed because of a capabilities mismatch, it will automatically insert one.

Device Control and Operation

The device control process maintains device status, resource availability, and other such information about the device. It is also responsible for device registration and all communication to and from the device. When the MRM is allocating resources, it always queries the device control process for available resources once a potential device is selected.

Device Registration and Initialization

Normally, when a device registers with a CallManager node, it has all its resources available. If the device was previously registered with a CallManager node that failed, and the MTP device had active calls at the time of the failure, the device still attempts to register with its backup CallManager node. Calls that are active on the server at the time it lost communication with its primary CallManager node are maintained in an active state. In other words, CallManager attempts to maintain all calls that are in an active state when a CallManager node fails. See the section, "Call Preservation During System Failures" for more details on how calls are preserved.

MTP and Transcoder Configuration

A CallManager administrator can enable MTPs and transcoders by completing the following steps:

Step 1 Install and configure one or more hardware transcoders in the cluster. It is not important which CallManager node the transcoder registers with, as long as the CallManager node is in the cluster. All transcoder and MTP resources are shared across the entire cluster.

or

During the system installation, install the Cisco IP Voice Media Streaming Application and configure it as an MTP. When the IP Voice Media Streaming Application is installed, an MTP device is automatically created in the Cisco CallManager Administration database with default settings.

Step 2   Configure the new transcoder devices, or modify the MTP device configuration as desired.

MTP and Transcoder Performance Statistics

A number of performance counters are available to monitor the usage of MTPs and transcoders. All performance statistics are monitored through Microsoft Windows 2000 counters. You can monitor these counters in the Admin. Serviceability Tool in Cisco CallManager Serviceability. Table 5-10 contains the available counters and their meaning.

Table 5-10   *MTP and Transcoder Counters per Cisco CallManager Node*

Counter	Description
MediaTermPointsResourceActive	Indicates the total number of MTPs that are in use on all MTP devices registered with this CallManager node. An MTP in use is one MTP resource that has been allocated for use in a call.
MediaTermPointsResourceAvailable	Indicates the total number of MTPs that are not in use and are available to be allocated on all MTP devices that are registered with this CallManager node.
MediaTermPointsOutOfResources	Indicates the number of times CallManager attempted to allocate a MTP resource from one of the MTP devices that is registered with this node when none were available, either because they were all in use or none were registered. This also means that no transcoders were available to act as MTPs.
TranscoderResourceActive	Indicates the total number of transcoders that are in use on all transcoder devices registered with this CallManager node. A transcoder in use is one transcoder resource that has been allocated for use in a call.
TranscoderResourceAvailable	Indicates the total number of transcoders that are not in use and are available to be allocated on all transcoder devices that are registered with this CallManager node.
TranscoderOutOfResources	Indicates the number of times CallManager attempted to allocate a transcoder resource from one of the transcoder devices that is registered to this CallManager node when none were available, either because they were all in use or none were registered.

Music on Hold (MOH)

For callers to hear MOH, the MOH server must be installed. This is normally done during the CallManager installation process. When the MOH server is installed, it sets up a default configuration that will support the basic MOH functionality. The MOH feature has two different aspects. The feature requires an MOH server to provide the MOH audio stream sources, and the feature also requires CallManager to be configured to use the MOH streams provided by the MOH server when a call is placed on hold. This section describes both aspects of the feature:

- Configuring MOH servers
- Configuring Cisco CallManager to use MOH

Configuring MOH Servers

An MOH server is a software application that runs on a Microsoft Windows 2000 server. It is installed as a plug-in during CallManager installation. If MOH server is installed on a dedicated server, it can support up to a total of 500 MOH Unicast streaming connections between all of its audio sources. All MOH servers in a cluster have the same audio source file configuration. This means that audio source 1 provides the same audio source on all MOH servers, audio source 2 provides the same audio source on all MOH servers, and so forth. One audio source on an MOH server can support from 1 to 500 MOH output streaming connections. In other words, the users connected to all 500 MOH output streams could be listening to the same music or audio source at the same time.

MOH servers support a total of 51 audio sources, 50 of which come from audio files on the disk. One audio source, source 51, is a fixed source usually connected to a sound card. An audio source file on disk can be encoded in one of several different formats for the supported codecs. Each of those 51 sources can support both Unicast and Multicast connections at the same time, and the source can be streamed for all supported codecs simultaneously. In release 3.1, the MOH servers support G.711 (A-law and μ-law), G.729a, and wideband audio codecs.

The IP Voice Media Streaming Application implements the MOH server. The IP Voice Media Streaming Application is the same application software that implements software Unicast conference bridges and MTPs. Each source stream is essentially a nailed-up conference with a fixed identifier called an *audio source ID*. It has a single input stream that is streaming audio data from a data source, and one or more output streams that transport the streaming data to the devices that are connected to MOH. The source stream audio source IDs range from 1 to 51, with 51 being reserved for the single fixed data source that is usually from the sound card.

Figure 5-22 illustrates phones with particular source assignments and how the MOH server handles the connections.

Figure 5-22 *MOH Stream Connections*

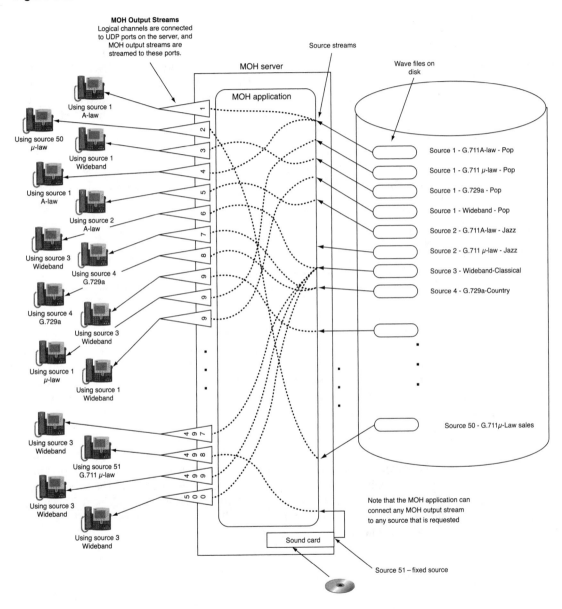

Figure 5-22 illustrates the basic architecture of the MOH subsystem. In this drawing, it is assumed that the MOH source assignment for each phone was already determined, and it is shown below the phone. A held device can be connected to any of the 500 possible MOH output streams and receive its specified audio source. When the logical channel is connected to the MOH server, the MOH server looks at the codec type being specified and the audio source ID supplied. It then connects the correct source to the port where that logical channel was connected.

Note that there is a source file on the disk for each of the codec types. This means that for source 1, which is Pop music, there are four files with the same music in them, but each of them is formatted for one of the different codecs. The MOH server selects the right source file to use based on the audio source ID supplied and the codec type specified in the logical channel connection. When the held device closes the logical channel to the MOH server, the MOH server stops the stream for that port as well.

Many logical channels can receive music from the same source file at the same time. As long as one logical channel is receiving music from a given source file, the MOH server continues streaming that source file. When there are no more connections to that source file, the MOH server stops streaming that source.

NOTE   The details of determining the source assignment for a particular call will be explained in the section, "Configuring Cisco CallManager to Use MOH."

MOH Server Audio Source and Audio Source ID

An audio source can be either a file or a fixed audio source. The source files must be in either G.711 A-law or μ-law formats, recorded at a sampling rate of 8 KHz, G.729a, or wideband. These data sources are disk files containing audio data that has been transcoded or formatted for the particular codec type before being loaded onto the disk of the MOH server. There is a one-to-one correspondence between audio sources and audio source IDs.

The fixed data source is provided by the Windows audio input that is normally linked to the local sound card. This allows radios, CD players, or any other compatible sound source to be used. The stream from the fixed data source is transcoded in real time to support the codec that was configured through Cisco CallManager Administration. The fixed data source can be transcoded into G.711 A-law and μ-law, G.729a, and wideband. This is the only data source that is transcoded in real time. G.729 will consume about 5 to 7 percent of your total CPU time in this transcoding operation.

Using the MOH Audio Translator

When the CallManager administrator desires to add a new audio source or to update an existing one, the new audio source must be transcoded and converted to the proper format, then copied to the proper location, where the TFTP server can pick it up and send it to all MOH servers when requested. The MOH Audio Translator is used to accomplish this task.

To add a new audio source to the MOH servers, copy the source file into the Audio Source Input Directory as specified by the service parameter **MOHSourceDirectory**. The default directory path for this directory is c:\Cisco\DropMOHAudioSourceFilesHere. Valid input files are most standard .wav and .mp3 files. It takes about 30 seconds to convert a 3-MB .mp3 file.

When the file is dropped into this directory, the Audio Translator service detects the file and automatically processes it, creating the audio source files needed for all supported codecs. The files are then moved to the output directory, along with all transcoded files that were created. The path for this directory is specified by the service parameter **DefaultTFTPMOHFilePath**. Whatever directory path is specified, \MOH will be appended to it. All transcoded files are stored in this MOH directory.

When the CallManager administrator configures a particular audio source for a particular codec, CallManager Administration copies the files from the output MOH directory where they are stored to the TFTP file path directory.

The path names used for these two directories can be changed by changing the values of the two service parameters at **System > Service Parameters >** *select a server* **> MOH Audio Translator**.

WARNING	If Audio Translator is installed on the same server as CallManager and files are translated, CallManager might experience errors or slowdowns. This process consumes all available CPU cycles until it is done with the conversion. Cisco recommends that you do not install this service on a CallManager node.

Table 5-11 contains the service parameters used by the MOH servers and Audio Translator service.

Table 5-11 *Service Parameters for Audio Translator and MOH Server*

Service Parameter	Service it Applies to	Definition
MOHSourceDirectory	MOH Audio Translator	Defines the directory where new audio sources are dropped so that they will be transcoded for the supported codecs. This parameter applies servicewide.

continues

Table 5-11 *Service Parameters for Audio Translator and MOH Server (Continued)*

Service Parameter	Service it Applies to	Definition
DefaultTFTPMOHFilePath	MOH Audio Translator	Defines the directory path for the TFTP source directory. \MOH is appended to this path name to create the output directory. This parameter applies on a server-by-server basis.
DefaultTFTPMOHIPAddress	Media Streaming App	IP address or computer name of the server where the transcoded audio source files are located. This parameter applies on a server-by-server basis.
DefaultMOHCodec	Media Streaming App	Defines the codecs that are supported in this installation. The possible values are: G.711 μ-law, G.711 A-law, G.729, wideband. This parameter applies servicewide.

MOH Source Stream Play Mode

The CallManager administrator configures the source play mode to one of two settings

- Continuous
- One shot

CallManager is not aware of the play mode.

Continuous Play Mode   Continuous play mode causes the MOH server to stream the data from the audio source file in a loop. This means that as soon as it has streamed the file from start to finish, it immediately begins streaming from the start again. This continues for as long as this audio source is being streamed. The MOH server keeps track of how many MOH output streams are connected to each audio source, and when the count reaches zero, the audio source streaming is stopped. The fixed audio source is always played continuously and is not stopped.

If Multicast support is selected for this audio source, the audio source is played continuously, because the MOH server does not know when held devices are listening at a Multicast point.

One Shot Play Mode   One shot play mode, as it is currently implemented, is designed to support one connection at a time. It works as long as only one user is connected to a given audio source. The connected user always hears the complete audio clip from the beginning exactly one time. When the clip ends, the user hears silence until being retrieved from hold.

If any other users are connected to that audio source while the first user is still connected, they hear the clip starting wherever it was at the time the user was connected. If the clip is finished, they hear silence, just like the first caller. For example, if the first user already listened to half of the one shot audio clip when the second user was connected to the same audio source, the second user would only hear the second half of the clip, starting wherever the clip was in its playback when the user was connected.

When all users are disconnected from the one shot audio source, the cycle starts again for the next user that is connected to the one shot source.

Handling MOH Stream Connections Errors

Table 5-12 shows what happens when the audio streams are not configured correctly in the system, and what will happen to the MOH stream connection if that error occurs.

Table 5-12   *Stream Connection Errors*

Error	Actions Taken
Audio source is not configured	If an audio source is selected that is not connected to an audio source file, the held devices will hear silence.
Connection to the CallManager is lost	The MOH server terminates all current output stream connections. This is done because CallManager cannot disconnect the streams because it cannot talk to the MOH server. The callers that were hearing MOH will now hear silence.

MOH Server Initialization

When an MOH server is initialized, it checks the date and time stamp for its audio source files against the values stored in the CallManager Administration database. If they differ, the new files will be obtained from the default TFTP client as specified by the service parameter **DefaultTFTPMOHIPAddress**. After the transfer is completed, the date and times on the MOH server are updated for each file that was transferred.

The same process is followed when the MOH server receives a change notification for the selected audio source. If the audio source is currently being streamed and a change is noted, the new audio source is retrieved and used when the current audio source is no longer active.

Summary of MOH Server Capabilities

The following are the current capabilities of the MOH servers:

- Supports at least 500 one-way Unicast audio output streams and 51 Multicast audio source streams at the same time. All the output connections can be connected to one source stream or any combination of source streams. Note that a Multicast connection does not take any extra stream resources from the MOH server.

- Fifty audio source IDs, each of which is assigned to an audio source, can be specified.

- One fixed audio source (from sound card) can be used (audio source ID 51).

- An audio source can be configured to play in a continuous loop or one shot. If a source stream has the Multicast option selected, the data source is automatically played in a continuous loop, because the MOH server does not know when devices are connected to the Multicast points. The MOH server makes the assumption that someone is always connected to the MOH Multicast point. If the Multicast option is not selected, but the source stream is configured to play in a continuous loop, the music source is only played when output streams are connected to the audio source stream.

- G.711 A-law, G.711 μ-law, G729a, and wideband audio codecs are supported.

- Unicast and Multicast output is supported for each audio source.

HINT   It is possible that the MOH server can support more than 500 output streams simultaneously, but this has not yet been confirmed. As new server hardware becomes available with faster processors, this stream count will likely increase. These limits are the limits set for release 3.1.

MOH Multicast Configuration

Cisco CallManager Administration configures each MOH server with a Multicast base address and port, and it specifies whether the port or the IP address is to be incremented to create a range of Multicast IP addresses as required. Each MOH server must be configured with a different range of Multicast addresses. This prevents multiple servers from streaming audio to the same Multicast address.

It is not necessary for all MOH servers to support Multicast streams. One server can provide all 51 streams to 51 different Multicast addresses for each enabled codec. If all codecs are enabled, it would require 204 different Multicast addresses.

HINT   It might be useful to configure two or more servers for Multicast so that if one server fails, Multicast is still available.

The MOH servers can provide each audio source as a Unicast stream and a Multicast stream. If Multicast output is desired, the **Multicast** check box for that source must be checked in the audio source configuration, and the MOH server must be configured for Multicast, as well.

MOH Server Usage and Performance Monitoring

All performance and usage monitoring statistics are provided in the Admin. Serviceability Tool in Cisco CallManager Serviceability. You can also monitor these statistics in Microsoft Performance Monitor. They are in the form of counters provided under base objects.

The Cisco MOH server is an object that can be selected. The MOH server counters are for the specific MOH server device that you selected. These counters are from the view of a particular MOH server and have their counters broken out by CallManager node.

MOH Server Counters   Each MOH server maintains statistics about each CallManager node to which it has made a primary connection. All of the statistics maintained by the MOH server are initialized when the MOH server initializes.

Each of the following counters is available for each individual CallManager node in that MOH server's CallManager list. In other words, the MOH server maintains statistics for each CallManager node with which it is allowed to register. The MOH server also maintains a total for all of the CallManager nodes with which it is allowed to register. Table 5-13 has a list of the counters available.

Table 5-13   *MOH Server Counters Available*

Counter	Description
Connection State	This counter indicates which CallManager is primary and which is secondary:
	1 = primary
	2 = secondary
	0 = not connected

continues

Table 5-13 *MOH Server Counters Available (Continued)*

Counter	Description
NumberOfActiveSources	Indicates the total number of active audio sources. For this counter, each codec type for each audio source ID is counted as an active audio source when a user is connected with that codec type.
	For example, if two calls are connected to the MOH server, both requesting Audio Source ID 1, and one specified G.711 μ-law and the other specified G.729a, the MOH server would stream two versions of the same music at the same time (one for each codec type). That counts as two active audio sources.
NumberOfActiveStreams	Tells you the total number of active streams. This includes all active Unicast streams and potentially an additional Multicast stream for each codec type.
NumberOfAvailableStreams	Indicates the total number of simplex streams available; the total is the total number of available streams in the device driver for all devices.
NumberOfLostConnections	Indicates the number of times a connection has been lost to the corresponding CallManager node.
TotalNumberOfStreams	Indicates the total number of streams that have been processed.

Configuring Cisco CallManager to Use MOH

MOH is configured through Cisco CallManager Administration. Once an MOH server is configured in the database, it can be added to one or more MRGs. An MOH server is a standard media processing resource. Its usage can be controlled and configured the same as any other media processing resource by using MRGs and MRGLs.

Hold Types in Cisco CallManager

There are two different types of hold. They are

- User hold
- Network hold

User hold is invoked when a user directly places a call on hold by pressing the **Hold** soft key on a Cisco IP Phone.

Network hold is invoked when a caller is placed on hold by some other feature, such as a transfer. The user presses the **Trnsfer** soft key on a Cisco IP Phone, and as a result, CallManager places the user on network hold until the transfer is completed.

How a Stream Source Is Selected When a User Is Placed on Hold

The stream source that a given held call hears depends on how both the device that originated the hold and the device being held are configured. The device that originated the hold determines which audio source is played to the user being held, and the device that is being held determines which MOH server will be used to supply the source audio stream. Figure 5-23 illustrates these connections.

Figure 5-23 illustrates a possible configuration of a cluster with two CallManager nodes in one location and a PSTN connection. The following examples use this configuration.

Example 1: Caller on 5000 Is Placed on Hold

Scenario: PSTN phone 5000 calls 3001 at PWI Brokerage Inc., and 3001 answers the call. 3001 places 5000 on hold.

In this example, 5000 is connected to MOH server MOH 1 because the gateway is assigned to MRGL1. MRGL1 has Hold Group 1 in its list. The caller is listening to the stream source 2 because the user hold stream for 3001 is set to stream source 2, which just happens to be a sales infomercial about new account types and services. The user on phone 5000 listens to a great sales pitch.

Figure 5-23 *How MOH Streams Are Selected*

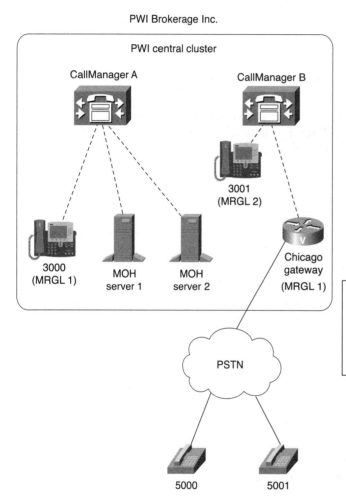

PWI Brokerage Inc.

PWI central cluster

CallManager A

CallManager B

3001
(MRGL 2)

3000
(MRGL 1)

MOH
server 1

MOH
server 2

Chicago
gateway
(MRGL 1)

PSTN

5000

5001

MOH configuration

MOH server configuration

Stream source 1 - Classical
Stream source 2 - Sales info
Stream source 3 - Pop
Stream source 4 - Country

Media resource groups

Hold group 1
- MOH server 1

Hold group 2
- MOH server 2

Media resource group lists

MRGL1
- Hold group 1

MRGL2
- Hold group 2

Stream sources configured for DN 3000
User hold stream source   - 1 Classical
Network hold stream source - 4 Country

Stream sources configured for DN 3001
User hold stream source   - 2 Sales info
Network hold stream source - 3 Pop

Example 2: Caller on 5001 Is Placed on Network Hold and then on User Hold

Scenario: PSTN phone 5001 calls 3000 at PWI Brokerage Inc. A stockbroker at 3000 answers and finds out that the caller wants to set up a new account. The stockbroker then transfers the caller to 3001 in new accounts.

When the stockbroker presses the **Trnsfer** soft key on the phone, the caller is placed on network hold. The caller then hears stream source 4, which is playing country music because the Network Hold Stream Source for 3000 is set to stream source 4, Country. The music is delivered from server MOH 1 because the gateway is assigned to MRGL1.

After a minute or two, the new account representative answers on 3001, but is extremely busy and puts the caller on 5001 on hold. Now the caller hears a nice sales pitch on all of the new accounts and services being offered. This occurs because the User Hold Stream Source for 3001 is set to stream source 2, Sales Info. The Sales Info stream is provided from MOH 1 because the gateway is assigned to MRGL1.

Finally, the new account representative retrieves the call from hold and sets up the new account.

MOH and Conferences

Conference is a special case for MOH. MOH is never played directly into a conference. If a conference participant places the conference on hold, CallManager recognizes this as a special case and does not connect that held call to MOH. The conference hears silence from that participant until the conference call is resumed.

Configuring MOH in Cisco CallManager

Configuring and using MOH in CallManager can be very simple or very complex, depending on the requirements for your installation.

Initial MOH Configuration   MOH is disabled when CallManager is installed and IP Voice Media Streaming Application is not installed. In this configuration, CallManager plays Tone on Hold when a caller is placed on hold for any reason, if the endpoint device associated with that user is capable of generating Tone on Hold. If not, the caller hears silence.

Simplest MOH Configuration   The MOH server is installed when the IP Voice Media Streaming Application is installed during the CallManager installation process. When an MOH server is installed, it automatically installs a default sound source file, and it creates and configures an MOH device in the database. Once MOH is installed, all devices have access to MOH as soon as the MOH server registers with a CallManager node. All callers hear audio source 1 from the MOH server anytime a call is placed on hold.

In this case, all devices are getting their MOH server through the Null MRG where the MOH server is declared by default because it is not part of any MRG. The Hold Stream Source defaults at the system level are set to audio source 1. This continues until the CallManager administrator changes the configuration by putting the MOH server into an MRG.

More Complex MOH Configurations   If a more complex configuration is needed, creating MRGs and MRGLs and assigning MRGLs to various devices in the system can achieve it. When you configure an MRG with a MOH server in it, you must also configure the Multicast/Unicast flag for that MRG.

The MOH User Hold Stream Source and the MOH Network Stream Source can be set to any MOH stream source that is configured on the MOH servers. If either User Hold Stream Source or Network Hold Stream Source is set to an audio source that has not yet been configured on the MOH servers, the callers will hear silence when connected to MOH.

A Multicast flag is in the MRG. If the **Multicast** box is not checked, Unicast streams are used for all MOH connections. If the **Multicast** box is checked, MOH allocation attempts try to allocate and use a Multicast stream connection. If Multicast MOH streams are not available, the held calls hear Tone on Hold, if their endpoint device supports it. Otherwise, they hear silence.

Order of Precedence of MOH Music Stream Source Assignments

MOH stream source assignments follow a defined order of precedence. When CallManager processes a hold request, it decides which MOH audio source stream to use based on the MOH stream source assignments in order of precedence, with 1 being the highest precedence. Table 5-14 defines the MOH source assignment order of precedence for both user hold and network hold.

Table 5-14 *MOH Stream Source Assignment Precedence*

MOH Source Assignment Order of Precedence	Comments
1. Assigned at the directory number level	The MOH stream source assigned at the directory number level applies only to that particular directory number and has precedence over all other MOH source assignments, if any, that are on the device level or Device Pool level.
2. Assigned at the device level	An MOH stream source assigned at the device level applies only to that particular device. The device level MOH stream source assignment has precedence over the MOH source assigned at the Device Pool level.
3. Assigned at the Device Pool level	The MOH stream source assigned at the Device Pool level applies to all entities that are assigned to that Device Pool. It has precedence over the system defaults.
4. Default system assignments	This is the most general level at which a MOH stream sources can be assigned, and it applies when CallManager cannot find any other MOH stream source assignment that applies for a particular call based on the device and directory number used.

Cisco CallManager MOH Usage and Performance Monitoring

All performance monitoring provided by CallManager is through Microsoft Windows 2000 counters. You can monitor these counters in the Admin. Serviceability Tool in Cisco CallManager Serviceability. CallManager provides two sets of counters that are maintained by each CallManager node:

- MOH counters per CallManager node
- Counters per MOH server from a CallManager node's perspective

Counters per Cisco CallManager Node

Each of the following counters is for an individual CallManager. They represent the total for all MOH servers that are registered with that CallManager node (see Table 5-15).

Table 5-15 *MOH Counters per Cisco CallManager Node*

Counter	Description
MOHMulticastResourceActive	Indicates the total number of active Multicast MOH connections on all MOH servers that are registered with this CallManager node.
MOHMulticastResourceAvailable	Indicates the total number of Multicast MOH connections that are not being used on all MOH servers that are registered with this CallManager node.
MOHTotalMulticastResources	Indicates the total number of Multicast MOH resources or connections provided by all MOH servers that are currently registered with this CallManager node.
MOHUnicastResourceActive	Indicates the total number of active Unicast MOH connections on all MOH servers that are registered with this CallManager node.
MOHUnicastResourceAvailable	Indicates the total number of Unicast MOH connections that are not being used on all MOH servers that are registered with this CallManager node.
MOHTotalUnicastResources	Indicates the total number of Unicast MOH resources or streams provided by all MOH servers that are currently registered with this CallManager node.
MOHOutOfResources	Indicates the number of times that the MRM attempted to allocate an MOH resource when either all available connections on all MOH servers registered with this CallManager node were active, or none were registered.

Counters per MOH Server from a Cisco CallManager Node's Perspective

Each MOH server registers with a CallManager node independently, and CallManager maintains statistics about each MOH server that is registered. Table 5-16 contains the counters that are maintained for each registered MOH server.

Table 5-16 *Counters per Registered MOH Server*

Counters	Description
MOHMulticastResourceActive	Indicates the number of currently active Multicast connections to Multicast addresses served by this MOH server.
MOHMulticastResourceAvailable	Indicates the number of MOH Multicast connections to Multicast addresses served by this MOH server that are not active and are still available to be used at the current time.
MOHTotalMulticastResources	Indicates the total number of MOH Multicast connections allowed to Multicast Addresses served by this MOH server.
MOHUnicastResourceActive	Indicates the number of active Unicast connections to this MOH server.
MOHUnicastResourceAvailable	Indicates the number of MOH Unicast connections that are not active and are still available to be used at the current time on this MOH server.
MOHTotalUnicastResources	Indicates the number of MOH Unicast connections allowed by this MOH server.
MOHOutOfResources	Indicates the number of times the MRM attempted to allocate an MOH resource from this MOH server and failed, either because all available connections of the type requested are in use, or because this device was unregistered at the time of the request.
MOHHighestActiveResources	Indicates the largest number of simultaneously active MOH connections on this MOH server, including both Multicast and Unicast connections.

Call Preservation During System Failures

Call preservation refers to the ability of the CallManager to maintain call connections during failure conditions on either the underlying network or the components within CallManager. Call preservation was greatly enhanced in release 3.1 of Cisco CallManager. This section describes the processing involved in call preservation and covers failure conditions for all major components. Call Preservation is included in the media processing section because when a failure occurs, it is the media streaming that must be maintained to keep the call connected.

General Overview of Call Preservation

CallManager consists of a cluster of CallManager nodes, Cisco IP Phones, gateways that provide connections to the PSTN, and various media processing resources such as conference bridges, transcoders, MTPs and so forth. It can also support numerous other voice applications, such as call centers and Interactive Voice Response (IVR) systems. Any of these entities can be involved in a call being processed by CallManager.

CallManager nodes provide call processing services and call connection control for all calls processed by a device. Once a device has created media streaming connections to other devices under the direction of CallManager, the devices themselves control all aspects of the media streams and connections until directed to terminate the media streaming connections.

Each CallManager node maintains primary call state information for all calls that it controls. If a CallManager node is not involved in a given call, it has no knowledge of that call. If a CallManager node does not control a call but controls devices that are involved in the call, that CallManager node maintains only call state information relating to the devices registered to itself that are part of that call, and not the call itself. Because the various endpoint devices and media processing resources can be registered with different CallManager nodes in the cluster, the entities involved in a given call can be, and usually are, controlled by more than one CallManager node.

NOTE   Normally without call preservation, each call that is controlled by a CallManager node that fails, or any call that involves a device that is controlled by a node that fails, would terminate immediately on the failure of any node or device involved in the call. This happens either because the other node or nodes involved in the call recognize the node or device failure and disconnect their end of the call (which ends media streaming), or because the devices themselves recognize that the CallManager node to which they are registered has failed. In that case, the device normally closes its media streaming connections and reregisters with another CallManager node.

With the enhanced call preservation in release 3.1, the users are generally able to continue their conversations without call processing support. This means that while the call is still active, no supplementary services are available, and the call configuration cannot be changed for the duration of the call. Hanging up will clear the call.

Call preservation involves complex processing in both CallManager and the devices that register with CallManager. Many communication links of various types are involved in calls being processed. This creates complex recovery scenarios, because any one signaling path or any combination of paths might be broken.

The failure of any given device or CallManager node creates some interesting and complex failure and recovery scenarios. This section explores some of the failure possibilities and identifies recovery algorithms used by CallManager and the devices. The following topics are covered:

- Failure and recovery objectives
- Handling system and device failures
- Device recovery and call preservation algorithms
- Call preservation during device failure and recovery

Failure and Recovery Objectives

In several failure cases, the signaling path for call processing is interrupted, but the media streaming connections are not necessarily affected. When a CallManager node fails, for example, the media streams between devices are not affected. It is also possible that when communication between a CallManager node and a device fails, the streaming connections between devices are not affected. In this case, a CallManager node involved in the call might have communication with other devices that are in the call. It becomes the responsibility of all CallManager nodes involved in the call to clear down the signaling paths that are related to the failure, without instructing the devices with which they still have communication to clear the call as they would in normal circumstances when the signaling path is cleared.

CallManager does not know whether the streaming connections between the devices have been interrupted. In failure conditions, it becomes the responsibility of the devices involved in a call to maintain the streaming connections that are already established. This is true even when the signaling path between the device and its CallManager node has failed.

If communication between a device and its CallManager node did not fail, it is the device's responsibility to inform its CallManager node when the streaming connections have been closed in the same manner as they do in normal call processing.

When handling failure scenarios, CallManager attempts to accomplish the following objectives:

- Maintain all active streaming connections that existed at the time of the failure so that no active call is interrupted
- Clear all calls that are in the call setup phase at the time of the failure and were affected by the failure
- Maintain communication with all devices that are still accessible after the failure
- Recover all devices that were registered to a failed CallManager node

- Minimize downtime for CallManager nodes and devices involved in or affected by a failure
- Maintain normal system operation as much as possible during the failure

Handling System and Device Failures

Endpoint and media processing devices have responsibility for and control over media connections and media streams, once the streams have been established under the direction of CallManager. Maintaining them in a failure condition is primarily the devices' responsibility, but it also requires close cooperation with CallManager.

Failures present unique and sometimes difficult situations that must be handled correctly to maintain active calls through the system.

The recognized failure cases are

- Cisco CallManager node failure
- Media processing device failure
- Endpoint device failure
- Cisco CallManager-to-device communication failure
- Node-to-node communication failure within a cluster
- Device-to-device communication failure

The main causes for each of these failure cases are defined, and some of the failure scenarios are discussed in this section.

Cisco CallManager Node Failure

CallManager node failures can be caused by a CallManager software error, by a server failure, or by a network failure. If the failure is caused by a software error or a server failure, the failure causes call processing functions on that node to stop, and all communication with that node is lost.

When this failure occurs, all devices registered to that CallManager node recognize that their current CallManager node has failed. Similarly, the other CallManager nodes in the cluster detect the failure of that node. When a node failure occurs, all remaining CallManager nodes immediately execute a call preservation teardown of all calls that they are processing that involve the failed node. A call preservation teardown is the same as a normal teardown, except that all devices involved in the call are not notified that the call has been torn down, and the device control processes in CallManager for each of the devices involved in the call maintain low-level state information about the call so that they know the device is involved in a call without call signaling support. No new calls are extended to devices that are in a call preservation mode. The affected devices involved in a call maintain all active calls until the end user hangs up or the devices can determine that the media connection has been closed. No call processing features can be invoked on the preserved calls.

If the failure is caused by a network failure, call processing functions are still intact, but communications between that CallManager node and some or all of the devices registered with that node, as well as communication with other nodes in the cluster, might be lost. When communication with a node or device is lost, that device or node is treated as though it has failed.

A CallManager node recognizes that another node has failed when the TCP/IP link to the other CallManager node returns an error that indicates a link failure. If the communication link fails, the other node is considered to have failed.

A CallManager node recognizes that a device has failed in one of two ways: either the TCP/IP link to the device returns an error that indicates the link has failed, or no KeepAlive request has been received from the device within its prescribed KeepAlive interval. Whether the device actually failed or just the link failed is not significant, because either case is treated the same.

Similarly, a device recognizes that its CallManager node has failed when CallManager fails to respond to its KeepAlive requests within the prescribed time. If the communication link has failed, the device recognizes the error when it receives an error from its TCP/IP stack that indicates the link has failed. Whether the CallManager node actually failed or only the communication link failed is not significant, because either case is treated the same.

Media Processing Device Failure

Typical media processing devices are conference bridges, MTPs, and transcoders.

CallManager recognizes device failures when a KeepAlive timeout for that device occurs. The failure can be caused by a device software error, a server failure, or a network failure, but to CallManager it makes no difference. When a device fails for any reason, the result is a loss of communication with the device. Because all communication is lost, the device must execute its own failure and recovery algorithms. CallManager's responsibility in this case is to release its own call processing resources as appropriate without terminating the call or calls being handled by the device.

If the device truly failed, call streaming through the device also stops, and other devices involved in the call must detect the streaming failure and clear the call. The device's active CallManager node recognizes the device failure and clears call processing entities within CallManager that are associated with calls in the failed device.

If the device loses communication with CallManager while media streaming connections are active, the device assumes all responsibility for and control over all active connections and media streams. It must also find another CallManager node with which it can register.

The device itself decides when and if it will register with CallManager while it has streaming connections active.

Endpoint Device Failure

Typical endpoint devices are Cisco IP Phones, other IP Phones, gateways, and so forth. Device failures and loss of communication with a device are considered the same failure.

Cisco CallManager-to-Device Communication Failure

A communication failure to a device, regardless of the cause of the failure, is treated as a device failure. CallManager recognizes a device failure when a KeepAlive timeout occurs. CallManager also recognizes a device failure when the TCP/IP socket connection to the device is broken. When a device fails, all call processing resources associated with that device are released, and call signaling is cleared.

Node-to-Node Communication Failure Within a Cluster

A CallManager cluster is fully meshed between all CallManager nodes in the cluster, which means that there is a TCP/IP connection from each CallManager node to every other CallManager node in the cluster. If, for any reason, the TCP/IP link from any given CallManager node to any other CallManager node fails, the other node to which it is connected is considered to have failed. An appropriate call preservation teardown will occur for all calls associated with the failed node.

Device-to-Device Communication Failure

Device-to-device communications are usually in the form of logical channels or, in other words, media streaming connections that are carrying audio streaming data. When the communication path breaks, the error is detected as a media streaming error, and the CallManager node to which the device is registered is notified. Device-to-device call preservation is implemented completely in the devices, and the CallManager nodes involved in the call have little or no ability to help or influence the processing, other than making sure that CallManager does not clear the call. This allows the devices to handle processing in the best way they can and to report to CallManager when the call clears, if they are still registered.

Call Preservation Examples

The following two examples illustrate some of the complexities that exist even in these relatively simple configurations.

Example 1: Call Between Two Phones, Each Registered to a Different Node

Figure 5-24 shows a single node failure when two CallManager nodes are involved in a call.

Figure 5-24 *Single Node Failure When Two Cisco CallManager Nodes Are Involved in a Call*

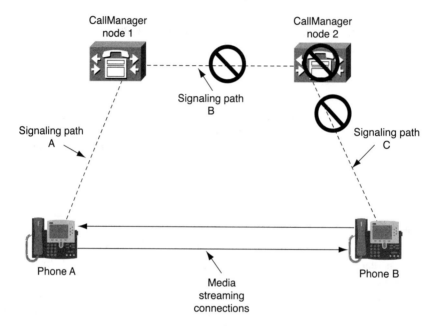

Note that Phone A is registered to CallManager node 1 and Phone B is registered to CallManager node 2. Phone A calls Phone B, and the call is connected successfully.

If CallManager node 2 fails, CallManager node 1 recognizes that signaling path B has failed, and it does a call preservation call teardown for Phone A. Signaling path C also fails, and that failure is recognized by Phone B. This leaves only signaling path A and the media streaming connections still active. There is no call processing support available for the remainder of this call, but the devices can continue streaming data to each other indefinitely. The phones tear down the media streaming connections when they are placed on-hook, thus terminating the call. Phone A reports the on-hook to CallManager node 1. Phone B will then register with its backup CallManager node.

If CallManager node 1 fails, the same process occurs, with the actions on the two phones being reversed.

If the signaling path B fails, each CallManager node does a call preservation teardown for its respective phone. There is no call processing support for the remainder of the call. When either phone goes on-hook, the call is terminated. Both phones report the termination to their respective CallManager nodes, and each CallManager node will release all remaining low-level resources associated with the call.

Example 2: A Conference Call   Figure 5-25 illustrates the connections that are present for a conference call that was set up by Phone A. This example will explain what happens to the call in call preservation situations caused by failures of various devices and communication links. Not all of the possibilities are discussed, but enough are discussed to illustrate how call preservation works.

Figure 5-25 *Call Preservation for Conference Call*

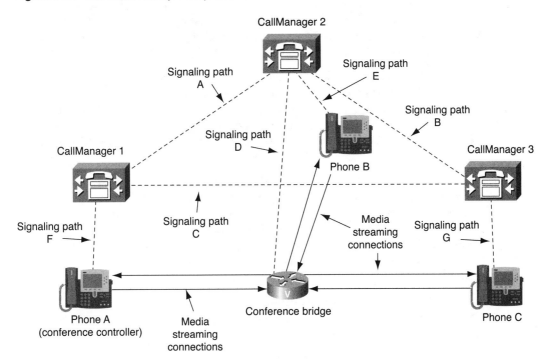

Phone A sets up a conference, which includes A, B, and C. Several different scenarios could occur because of failures on this conference call. If CallManager 1 fails, signaling paths A, C, and F fail, and call processing for Phone A, who is the conference controller, is lost. The conference continues, but it cannot be extended to any other parties. When Phone A is placed on-hook, it terminates its media streaming connections to the conference bridge and registers with another CallManager node. The other participants in the conference terminate the conference normally. They are unaffected by the failure.

If CallManager 2 fails, signal paths A, B, D, and E fail, and call processing for the conference bridge and Phone B is lost. The conference can continue only if the conference bridge allows the media connections to remain active even though it cannot communicate with CallManager. No call processing functions are available on this conference call. Even though the conference controller is still active, the conference cannot be extended, because there is no communication between CallManager and the conference bridge. When Phone B is placed on-hook, it terminates its media streaming connections to the conference bridge and registers with another CallManager node. As soon as either Phone A or C hangs up, the conference terminates and the conference bridge registers with another CallManager node.

If CallManager 3 fails, signaling paths B, C, and G fail. The conference can continue, but Phone C has no call processing functions available. The conference can also be extended because the conference controller and the conference bridge are unaffected by the failure. When Phone C is placed on-hook, it terminates its media streaming connections to the conference bridge and registers with another CallManager node.

If Phone A's network connection fails, signaling path F and the media streaming connections to Phone A are lost. This causes a normal call teardown for Phone A. The conference bridge recognizes the failure of the media streams and closes the media connections, leaving Phone B and Phone C in the conference. The conference cannot be extended because the conference controller is lost. Phone A registers with CallManager again when its network connection is restored.

If Phone B's or Phone C's network connection fails, signaling path E or G, respectively, and the media streaming connections to Phone B or Phone C are lost. This causes a normal call teardown for the affected phone. The conference bridge recognizes the failure of the media streams and closes the media connections to the lost phone, leaving Phone A and either Phone B or Phone C in the conference. Phone A can extend the conference, if desired, because the rest of the conference is not affected. The lost phone registers with CallManager again when its network connection is restored.

If signaling path A fails, it causes a call preservation teardown for all phones, because Cisco CallManager 1 was controlling the conference and each of the calls. Because Cisco CallManager 1 cannot talk to the conference bridge because of the signaling path failure, the entire conference goes into call preservation mode. The conference can continue without call processing support.

If signaling path B fails, it has no effect on the conference call.

If signaling path C fails, it causes a call preservation teardown for Phone C, because CallManager 1 was controlling the call from Phone C to the conference bridge, and the communication link to Phone C is lost. The conference continues, but Phone C does not have call processing support. The conference can be extended, if desired.

Combinations of failures can occur, resulting in even more complex recovery scenarios.

Recovering Devices After a Failure

CallManager is a multinode system, which provides redundancy for CallManager nodes that handle all call processing. All devices are not redundant, meaning, for example, if a Cisco IP Phone fails, there is no backup phone to take over. In the case of gateways, there might be redundancy, depending on the implementation of CallManager. Call processing redundancy is implemented in CallManager by creating a cluster of CallManager nodes, some of which serve as backups for other CallManager nodes in the event of a node failure.

All devices are intelligent endpoints and are responsible for finding a CallManager node with which to register. Redundant call processing support for devices is implemented by assigning each device an ordered list of CallManager nodes with which it is to register. The list is in priority order from first to last and is referred to as the *CallManager list*. The device registers with the first CallManager node that is in its list and currently available. The first CallManager in its list is often referred to as its *primary CallManager*. During failure conditions, a device registers with the CallManager node that is highest on its list and available when its primary CallManager fails. The process of unregistering with one CallManager node and registering with a CallManager node that is lower on the list is referred to as *switchover*. Devices reregister with a CallManager node that is higher on their list during recovery from the failure. A failure recovery occurs when the primary CallManager node or another node higher on the list returns to service, or node-to-device communications are restored. The process of unregistering with one CallManager node and registering with a CallManager node that is higher on the list is known as *switchback*.

Devices and Applications That Support Call Preservation

The following list of devices and applications are known to support call preservation:

- Cisco IP Phones
- Software conference bridge (Service)
- MTP (Service)
- Hardware conference bridge (Cisco Catalyst 6000 WS-X6608-T1 and WS-X6608-E1 gateway modules, Cisco Catalyst 4000 WS-X4604-GWY gateway module)
- Transcoder (Cisco Catalyst 6000 WS-X6608-T1 and WS-X6608-E1 gateway modules, Cisco Catalyst 4000 WS-X4604-GWY gateway module)
- Non-IOS EVVBU gateways using MGCP PRI Backhaul (Cisco Catalyst 6000 WS-X6608-T1 and WS-X6608-E1 gateway modules, Catalyst 6000 WS-X6624-FXS, DT24+, DE30+)
- IOS MGCP gateways (VG200, Catalyst 4000 WS-X4604-GWY gateway module, Cisco 2620, Cisco 3620, Cisco 3640, Cisco 3660, Cisco 3810)
- Cisco WebAttendant

Devices and Applications That Do Not Support Call Preservation

The following devices and applications do not support call preservation in release 3.1:

- H.323 devices
- CTI applications
- TAPI applications
- JTAPI applications

Call Preservation Algorithms

The next sections describe the switchover and switchback algorithms used by devices that are involved in active calls at the time of a failure. These algorithms do not specify how the device should decide to switchover or switchback, but rather the actions that must take place once the device has made the decision to switch.

Switchover Algorithms

Two algorithms are used by devices to determine when to switch over to a CallManager node that is lower on their list. Each device that is capable of maintaining calls in failure situations is required to implement either one or both of the algorithms. If the device implements both of the algorithms, the administrator configures the device to use the one desired by the administrator.

Graceful Switchover   This algorithm allows the device to delay switchover to another CallManager node until the device stops all active streaming connections. The device determines when to terminate the streaming connections based on the disconnect supervision options supported by that device. A Cisco IP Phone, for example, terminates its streams when the user hangs up the phone, or when it detects an error in transmission to the other endpoint in the call.

If no CallManager is lower in its list and is available when the device initiates a switchover attempt, the device can reregister with the primary CallManager node if it is available, or another CallManager node that is higher in its list.

If no CallManager node is available when the device initiates a switchover, the device terminates the active streaming connections after attempting to locate an available CallManager node for a reasonable amount of time. It continues looking for an available CallManager node to which it can register.

Immediate Switchover   This algorithm allows the device to switchover immediately to a CallManager that is lower in its list. When this device registers with the new CallManager node, it tells CallManager during registration how many connections it supports and how many of them are active at the time of registration. Thereafter, the device informs CallManager each time one of the active streams is closed.

When a device initiates a switchover attempt, it is possible that no backup or lower-order CallManager node is available. In this case, the device can choose to reregister with the original primary or other CallManager higher in its list. This is exactly the same as a switchover with a subsequent switchback.

If no CallManager node is available when the device initiates a switchover, the device terminates the active streaming connections after attempting to locate an available CallManager node for a reasonable amount of time. It continues looking for an available CallManager node to which it can register.

Switchback Algorithms

Each device implements one or more of the following switchback algorithms. If the device supports more than one switchback algorithm, the system administrator configures which algorithm it uses. Only one configuration is active at any given time. A switchback does not occur because of an error condition directly. It is a recovery operation when some or all of the failure conditions have cleared. The device, therefore, has the opportunity to choose when it will switchback to its primary CallManager. Table 5-17 documents all allowed switchback algorithms.

Table 5-17   *Switchback Algorithms*

Switchback Algorithms	Description
Graceful Algorithm	The device delays registering with a CallManager node that is higher in its list until all of its active streaming connections are stopped. This prevents any disruption to existing calls.
Immediate Algorithm	The device immediately registers with a CallManager node that is higher in its list as soon as communications with that node are established. The registering device communicates the status of all active connections to the selected CallManager. It also notifies CallManager when each of the active connections is closed as the calls are cleared. When using this algorithm, all calls in progress at the time go into call preservation mode and do not have access to call processing services for the duration of the call.
Schedule-Time Algorithm	In this case, the administrator sets a configurable timer. The timer must be set to expire within 24 hours from when it is set. On timer expiration, the Immediate algorithm is then invoked. This algorithm allows the system administrator to schedule a time when the device will switchback. If it is a phone, for example, it might be scheduled to switchback at 2 a.m. when it is not likely to be used.

continues

Table 5-17 *Switchback Algorithms (Continued)*

Switchback Algorithms	Description
Uptime-Delay Algorithm	On detection that a CallManager node that is higher in its list is available, a user-configurable timer is set. On timer expiration, the Immediate algorithm is invoked. Basically the same as Schedule-Time algorithm, except that the user has control of the timer.
Graceful with Guard Timer	A guard timer is set. This guard timer can be statically implemented in the device or user-configurable. The Graceful algorithm is invoked. If the guard timer expires before switchback has been initiated per the Graceful algorithm, the Immediate algorithm is invoked.
	This basically says to wait until all calls are finished and the device is idle before executing a switchback. If this does not occur within a prescribed time, it forces a switchback. (Some devices might never go idle.)

HINT The Immediate option leaves the active maintained calls connected but without call processing support for remainder of their calls. The users cannot change the configuration of their calls and do not have access to features such as hold, transfer, conference, and so forth. This option also drops any calls that are in the process of being established. Only the calls that are already connected at the time of switchback are maintained. Because there is no CallManager node failure or communication failure condition in this case, the Immediate option is the least desirable of all the algorithms, as it affects active calls and is visible to the user.

Call Attempts During Switchover and Switchback

It is possible that a new call setup is initiated from the device during the switchover or the switchback time frame. The call attempt is handled in the following manner.

During the process of switchover or switchback, when the device is not registered with a CallManager node, any new call setup request initiated from the device is ignored until the device has completed its registration with the CallManager node.

If the configured switchback algorithm is other than Immediate, registration with a CallManager node that is higher in its list can be delayed. During this time, the current CallManager node is still the active node and is capable of processing calls.

During any switchback delay introduced by a switchback option, the device processes new call setup attempts normally until the delay condition is satisfied and switchback can be initiated.

Cisco IP Phone Unregistration Sequence Requirements

Unregister requests from Cisco IP Phones are used when the phone is registered to a CallManager node lower in its list and a CallManager node that is higher in its list returns to service. When CallManager receives an unregister request, it checks for pending calls or connections to that phone, such as held calls, transfers in progress, call park in progress, and so forth. These calls can exist in CallManager without the Cisco IP Phone having an active media connection for that call. If CallManager determines that there are pending calls for the device, CallManager returns an unregister acknowledgement with a NAK**,** indicating that the device is not permitted to unregister at that time.

If CallManager determines that there are no pending calls for the device, it returns an unregister acknowledgement with an ACK**,** indicating that the Cisco IP Phone is free to register with the higher CallManager node.

Active Connection Management in Device Modules on Device Registration

Some devices can register with a CallManager node while involved in active connections. The following sections detail requirements that CallManager must satisfy to restore active connections and manage their release during call tear down.

Hardware Conference Bridge and Transcoders   When a hardware conference bridge or transcoder registers with CallManager, it reports the number of streams that it supports and the number of streams that are currently active on that device. CallManager notes the number of active streams, and it does not make these resources available for allocation until the device notifies CallManager that the stream is no longer active. The stream is then added to the available pool.

MGCP Gateway Device Modules   On MGCP gateway registration, the CallManager node sends the Audit Endpoint message to each endpoint of each PSTN interface of the registering gateway.

When the endpoint returns a connection identifier in the Audit Endpoint Response, the device control process in CallManager marks the device endpoint active. This allows the gateway to control when the resource is released and ready for use.

For each connection identifier returned in the Audit Endpoint Response, the device module that is managing the gateway interfaces in the CallManager node marks the endpoints active to allow the endpoint to control release sequence.

For interfaces that use MGCP call control signaling and support either end-user or media streaming failure disconnect supervision, CallManager sends a Request Notify command to the gateway to have the gateway report call termination events to the CallManager node. As the calls are terminated, the endpoints are made available for use again.

There are specific requirements for MGCP gateways using MGCP call control signaling. MGCP call control signaling is supported for the following interfaces and platforms:

- FXO/FXS on IOS VG200 gateways
- T1-CAS on IOS VG200 gateways

There are specific requirements for MGCP gateways using PRI-backhaul call control signaling. PRI-backhaul signaling is supported for the following interfaces and platforms:

- T1-PRI on EVVBU non-IOS (Catalyst 6000 WS-C6608-T1 and DT24+ gateways) and IOS VG200 gateways
- E1-PRI on EVVBU non-IOS (Catalyst 6000 WS-C6608-E1 and DE30+ gateways) and IOS VG200 gateways
- FXS/FXO on non-IOS EVVBU gateways
- T1-CAS on Catalyst 6000 WS-C6608-T1 and Catalyst 6000 WS-C6608-E1 gateways

For each of the active connections, the device control process that is managing the gateway ports in the CallManager node sets the ports in an active call state. When working with the PRI protocol, the device control process needs the Q.931 call reference value.

During normal call setup, the CallManager node includes the Q.931 call reference value in the Call ID parameter of the Create Connection command for each connection associated with the PRI interface.

MGCP protocol provides the Audit Connection sequence to relay active connection information from the gateway to the CallManager node.

Media Streaming Failure Disconnect Supervision Handling

Devices that support media streaming failure disconnect supervision report media failure signals to the CallManager node on detection of the failure. If the associated call is in a preserved state, it should be cleared (from a call control perspective) toward the device. Otherwise, it is assumed that the call will be cleared through normal means.

Summary

In this chapter, basic VoIP concepts and terms were presented and their relationship to media processing devices was explained. Four basic types of media processing resources are available to Cisco CallManager in release 3.1:

- Conferencing resources
- MTPs
- Transcoders
- MOH resources

Release 3.1 adds the capability of sharing these resources across the entire cluster. This allows more efficient use of resources and eliminates the need to have all resource types registered to each Cisco CallManager node. In addition, these resources can now be associated with endpoint devices on a geographical basis or on any other grouping that seems appropriate. Resource sharing also provides the capability of restricting the use of media processing resources so that certain endpoints or groups of endpoints do not have access to one or more types of resources. Release 3.1 also allows both hardware- and software-based resources to be registered with a given CallManager node at the same time. Their usage can be organized such that the load is distributed across all resources of a given type, or it can be ordered such that the hardware or software resources are used before the other type of resource is used. The grouping and ordering of the resources is very flexible and allows the administrators a great deal of control over how media processing resources are registered and used within the cluster.

This chapter discussed the differences between hardware- and software-based resources, and the advantages and disadvantages of each.

The MOH feature was added in release 3.1, and the MOH server was introduced. This server is based on the Cisco IP Voice Media Streaming Application and can be installed and configured in the same manner as the Unicast conference bridge and MTP. The MOH servers provide a minimum of 500 simultaneous one-way audio streams.

Call preservation was introduced and explained. Call preservation attempts to maintain call connections that are active during failure conditions. In most instances, a call connection can be maintained as long as the endpoint devices involved in the call did not fail. When CallManager fails with calls active, the calls are maintained, but they have no call processing support. This means that they cannot place the call on hold or activate any other feature for the duration of that call. CDR billing information for these calls is not recorded. The algorithms used to recover failed devices were also explained.

After reading this chapter, you should understand the media processing resources that are available and the configuration options that are available through Cisco CallManager Administration. You should have a good comprehension of MRGs and MRGLs and the power they give system administrators in configuring the media resources in their systems. You should also have an understanding of the basic architecture and support for all media type devices.

## CHAPTER 6

Manageability and Monitoring Tools

Cisco provides tools that can make managing your Cisco CallManager system simpler and faster. The Bulk Administration Tool (BAT) helps you manage large add, update, and delete operations by performing single transactions in which large number of users or devices are affected. The Administrative Reporting Tool (ART) helps you manage billing records, among many other tasks. In addition to these manageability tools, there are several monitoring tools. Monitoring your system with the tools described in this chapter can help you make sure your system is running efficiently and pinpoint the cause of problems when they arise. The vast majority of problems encountered with the CallManager system are the result of misconfiguration. The tools described here will assist you in determining the cause of the problem; they can also be used to help you plan for expansion and ensure quality of service (QoS). The following products are discussed in this chapter:

- Bulk Administration Tool (BAT)
- Administrative Reporting Tool (ART)
- Cisco CallManager Serviceability
- Event Viewer
- Terminal Services Client
- CiscoWorks2000
- Simple Network Management Protocol (SNMP) Management Information Bases (MIBs)
- Microsoft Performance
- Remote Serviceability
- Cisco Discovery Protocol (CDP)
- Q931 Translator

The shaded blocks in Figure 6-1 illustrate the software layers and blocks within CallManager that contain manageability- and monitoring-related functionality. Unlike the other block diagrams in this book, Figure 6-1 is completely shaded. Because virtually every component in CallManager logs alarms, constructs CDR information, receives provision information through BAT, logs trace information, or sets CallManager counters, not a single CallManager layer or block escapes manageability and monitoring.

Figure 6-1 *CallManager Block Structure Diagram*

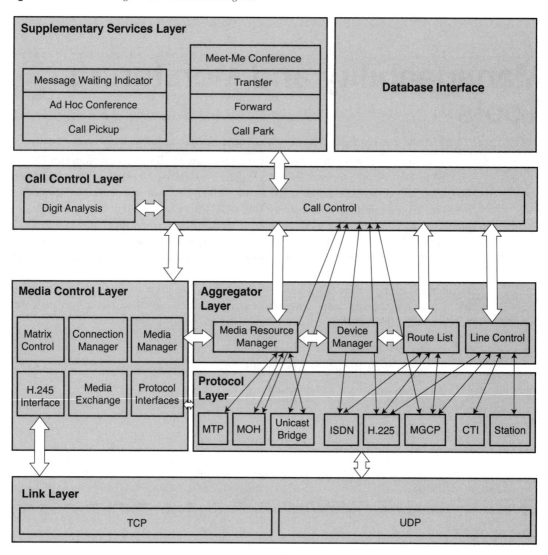

Manageability Tools

Manageability tools ease the burden of managing a large system. BAT and ART are discussed in this section.

Using these tools, you can perform bulk transactions, where large number of users or devices are added, updated, or deleted from the Cisco CallManager database. In addition, you can run reports on the system to generate information about billing, traffic, gateways, and QoS statistics.

Bulk Administration Tool (BAT)

BAT lets you perform bulk add, update, and delete operations on the CallManager database. This means that for large systems, you can configure or update your CallManager database faster and with less manual entry. Different versions of BAT provide different features. This discussion focuses on BAT release 4.2, which coincides closely with CallManager release 3.1.

With BAT release 4.2, you can perform the following bulk operations on the CallManager database:

- Add phones (including Computer Telephony Interface [CTI] ports and Cisco IP Conference Station 7935), Cisco IP Phone 7914 Expansion Modules, Cisco IP Phone services, speed dials, users, Cisco VG200 gateways, and Foreign Exchange Station (FXS) ports on Cisco Catalyst 6000 gateways
- Update phones, lines, and FXS ports on Cisco Catalyst 6000 gateways
- Delete phones, Cisco VG200 gateways, and all FXS ports on Cisco Catalyst 6000 gateways

Using special BAT templates in combination with comma separated value (CSV) files that you create, you can effect basic database changes that previously required labor-intensive manual entries in CallManager Administration. With BAT, instead of adding 100 phones one at a time in CallManager Administration, you can create a BAT template and a CSV file (both of which are reusable for future bulk add transactions) and add the same 100 phones in one transaction. BAT provides sample templates and CSV files for each kind of transaction (phones, ports, gateways, users) that you can modify for each bulk transaction.

To help ensure against performance degradation on CallManager, BAT provides a formula to compute roughly how long it takes to complete a bulk transaction. This is useful information to know before you perform the transaction, because you can determine whether system performance will be impacted. If performance is an issue, simply perform the bulk transaction when the system is not heavily used.

All releases of BAT up to and including release 4.2 are downloaded from Cisco Connection Online (CCO, www.cisco.com). Later releases of BAT will be available as a plug-in application to CallManager Administration (**Application > Install Plugins**).

NOTE   Depending on the number of records you are adding, updating, or deleting to the CallManager database during the bulk transaction, BAT can consume a great deal of system resources. Therefore, Cisco recommends that BAT be used only during off-peak hours to minimize impact on CallManager performance.

Reasons to Use BAT

BAT's goal is to save you time by reducing repetitive labor-intensive manual data entry tasks. This goal remains the same whether you are installing a new CallManager system or already have an existing system. BAT also combines tasks by allowing you to add users and devices (phones, gateways, or CTI ports) and associate users with their devices, all in one bulk transaction.

Setting Up a New System or Installing New Devices

BAT is most useful when you are first setting up a system. You can bulk-add devices, speed dials, and users. Using BAT to set up your CallManager database saves you time and money by reducing the amount of effort required to add or update devices or users. The information you provide in the BAT template (described in the section "Bulk Adds") and CSV file (described in the section "CSV Files") can be as specific or generic as you want. If the information is generic, you can always update the device or user information in CallManager Administration later.

A common problem with new systems is misconfiguration. This problem can be because of incomplete understanding of how a feature works; often it is simply a data entry mistake. With BAT, if you add devices, for example, and then realize after doing so that there is an error in the device configuration, you can simply modify the same CSV file to correct the error. You can then use it and the same BAT template to update the same set of devices. In this example, you would have to delete the misconfigured devices first before you could add them again, but you can do that using BAT, as well.

You might find that you want to restrict long distance dialing on certain phones in your company, such as lobby phones, conference room phones, or other phones that are located in common areas. You can use BAT to add or update that set of phones with a calling search space that blocks long distance dialing.

Working with an Existing System

BAT is also useful when you have an established system for which you need to add a new block of users or devices or make the same update to many devices or users. For example, if you plan to delete a device pool, all phones currently using that device pool must be updated with a new device pool before the old one can be deleted from CallManager Administration. You can quickly update all phones using the existing device pool with the new one by running a bulk update on all phones using the old device pool.

Perhaps you want to change the voice mail access number, add a new voice mail access number, or add a speed dial to the Human Resources department for all phones. BAT lets you update all phones that have a common characteristic, such as device pool, location, or calling search space.

In another example, you could set up all of the phones used by salespeople in your company with a special set of Cisco IP Phone services. Phone services are extensible markup language (XML) services that you can configure using the Cisco IP Phone Productivity Services software development kit (Cisco XML SDK) (see Appendix A, "Feature List," for more information). Perhaps you have services that tie in directly to a database showing current sales goals or a list of reference account contacts. Although this information is critical to salespeople, it might not be of much interest to anyone else in your company. You can add all phones belonging to the sales staff with a specific set of phone services so that only their phones provide this service when the **services** button on a Cisco IP Phone 7960 or 7940 is pressed. Likewise, if you have a common service that you want to appear on all phones in your company, such as your company's stock quote or a calendar showing paid holidays, you can specify this when adding the phones in BAT.

Figure 6-2 shows the Insert Phones/Users screen (**Configure > Phones / Users**) where you can perform three functions at once: adding users, adding phones, and associating the user to the phone.

Figure 6-2 *Bulk Administration Tool*

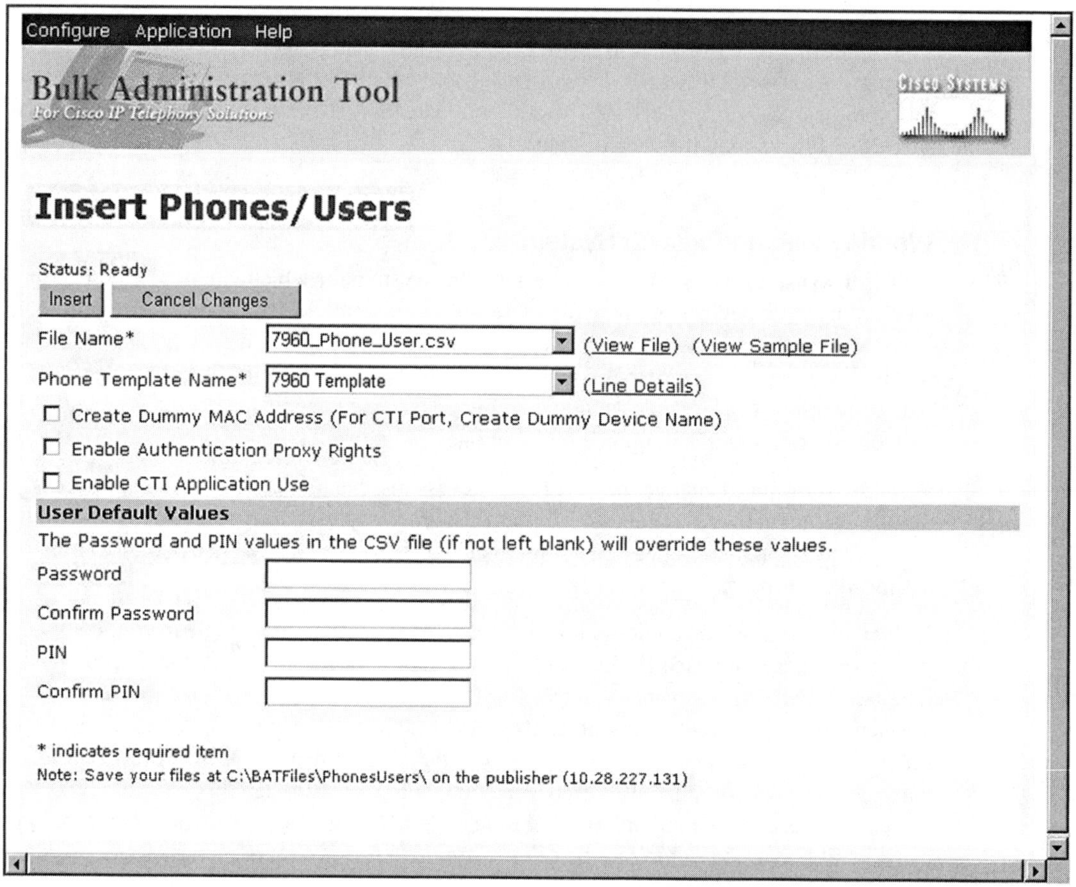

CSV Files

BAT's strength lies in its ability to allow you to make large device or user changes to the database without compromising customization of the devices or users. Using the CSV file, you can specify as much detail as you like about the devices you plan to add. For example, for phones you can supply directory numbers, Media Access Control (MAC) addresses, call forward no answer directory number, and more. Once all of the data is entered in the CSV file, and you have created a BAT template, you can insert the data from CSV files and BAT templates into CallManager Administration. When the phones are plugged into the network, they will be able to register with CallManager and find their device settings based on the information inserted into the database from the CSV file.

You can use the sample Microsoft Excel spreadsheet template (provided for you during BAT installation) to create the CSV file for each type of bulk transaction. A different tab is provided for users and each type of device: phones, gateways, gateways ports, and so on. Figure 6-3 shows a spreadsheet containing sample information; in this case, it contains all new hires for the month of June. You can indicate as much detail as you like, including manager's user ID, description, location, directory number, display, and so on.

Figure 6-3 *Example Excel Spreadsheet for Adding Phones and Users Combined*

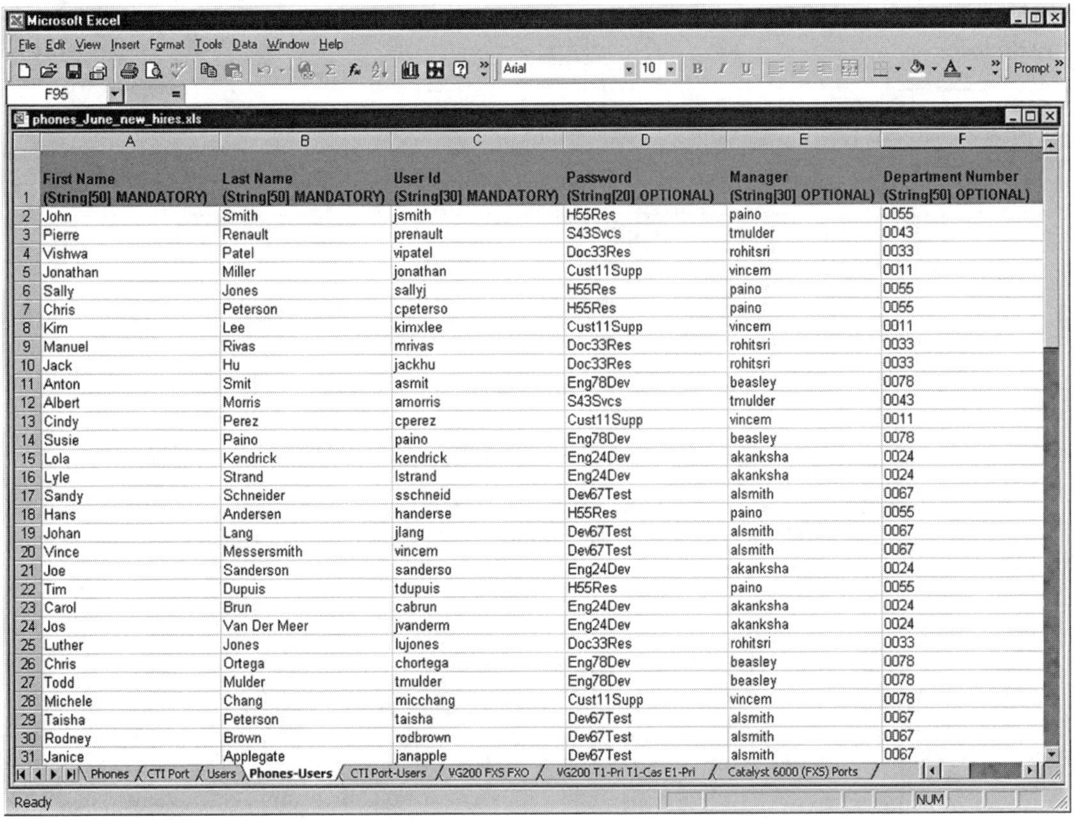

	A	B	C	D	E	F
1	First Name (String[50] MANDATORY)	Last Name (String[50] MANDATORY)	User Id (String[30] MANDATORY)	Password (String[20] OPTIONAL)	Manager (String[30] OPTIONAL)	Department Number (String[50] OPTIONAL)
2	John	Smith	jsmith	H55Res	paino	0055
3	Pierre	Renault	prenault	S43Svcs	tmulder	0043
4	Vishwa	Patel	vipatel	Doc33Res	rohitsri	0033
5	Jonathan	Miller	jonathan	Cust11Supp	vincem	0011
6	Sally	Jones	sallyj	H55Res	paino	0055
7	Chris	Peterson	cpeterso	H55Res	paino	0055
8	Kim	Lee	kimxlee	Cust11Supp	vincem	0011
9	Manuel	Rivas	mrivas	Doc33Res	rohitsri	0033
10	Jack	Hu	jackhu	Doc33Res	rohitsri	0033
11	Anton	Smit	asmit	Eng78Dev	beasley	0078
12	Albert	Morris	amorris	S43Svcs	tmulder	0043
13	Cindy	Perez	cperez	Cust11Supp	vincem	0011
14	Susie	Paino	paino	Eng78Dev	beasley	0078
15	Lola	Kendrick	kendrick	Eng24Dev	akanksha	0024
16	Lyle	Strand	lstrand	Eng24Dev	akanksha	0024
17	Sandy	Schneider	sschneid	Dev67Test	alsmith	0067
18	Hans	Andersen	handerse	H55Res	paino	0055
19	Johan	Lang	jlang	Dev67Test	alsmith	0067
20	Vince	Messersmith	vincem	Dev67Test	alsmith	0067
21	Joe	Sanderson	sanderso	Eng24Dev	akanksha	0024
22	Tim	Dupuis	tdupuis	H55Res	paino	0055
23	Carol	Brun	cabrun	Eng24Dev	akanksha	0024
24	Jos	Van Der Meer	jvanderm	Eng24Dev	akanksha	0024
25	Luther	Jones	lujones	Doc33Res	rohitsri	0033
26	Chris	Ortega	chortega	Eng78Dev	beasley	0078
27	Todd	Mulder	tmulder	Eng78Dev	beasley	0078
28	Michele	Chang	micchang	Cust11Supp	vincem	0078
29	Taisha	Peterson	taisha	Dev67Test	alsmith	0067
30	Rodney	Brown	rodbrown	Dev67Test	alsmith	0067
31	Janice	Applegate	janapple	Dev67Test	alsmith	0067

After you have entered the data in the spreadsheet, click the **Export To BAT Format** button in the spreadsheet. A dialog box displays the default file name and location to which the file will be saved. The default file name is PhonesUsers#timestamp.txt, for example, PhonesUsers#06272001093545.txt. This file name indicates that this file was created on June 27, 2001 at 9:35:45 a.m. You can overwrite the default name with something more memorable, such as June_new_hires.txt. You should save CSV files in the \BatFiles subdirectory created during BAT installation. Figure 6-4 shows the CSV file after it has been exported from Excel.

Figure 6-4   *Example CSV File for Phones and Users Combination after Export from Spreadsheet*

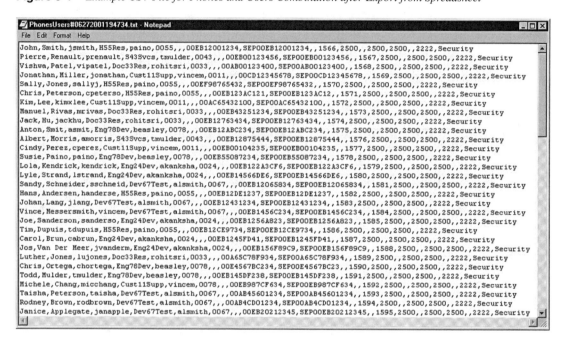

You can easily insert the data in the CSV file into the CallManager database using BAT.

In the CSV file you can specify individual MAC addresses for each phone or use a dummy MAC address. If the dummy MAC address option is used, the address can be updated later using Tools for Auto-Registered Phone Support (TAPS).

Tool for Auto-Registered Phone Support (TAPS)

TAPS is an optional component of BAT that requires Cisco IP Interactive Voice Response on the Cisco Customer Response Applications Server. Auto-registration must be enabled in CallManager for the TAPS feature to work. With TAPS, you can enter dummy MAC addresses in the CSV file. Later, when the Cisco IP Phone is plugged in, the user can retrieve device information for the new phone simply by dialing a TAPS directory number and entering his or her phone number. This is particularly useful when you want to configure devices for a group of users who are as yet undefined, such as new employees. TAPS is also useful when an existing user replaces his or her phone because of damage or defect. When the user receives the new phone (same model), the user can simply dial the TAPS directory number and then their current directory number, and TAPS downloads device information configured for the previous phone to the new phone.

BAT: Looking Forward

Future releases of BAT might include the ability to bulk add, update, or delete Cisco Unity mailboxes.

Learn More About BAT

Detailed information about BAT is available at the following location:

www.cisco.com/univercd/cc/td/doc/product/voice/sw_ap_to/admin/bulk_adm/index.htm

Administrative Reporting Tool (ART)

ART, a Web-based application, provides reports about QoS, gateway usage, traffic details, user call details, and more. Cisco CallManager provides information about each call in Call Detail Records (CDRs) and Call Management Records (CMRs), collectively known as CDR data. This CDR data serves as the basic information source for ART. This discussion focuses on ART release 1.1, which coincides closely with CallManager release 3.1.

All releases of ART up to and including release 1.1 can be downloaded from Cisco Connection Online (CCO, www.cisco.com). Later releases of ART will be available as a plug-in application to CallManager Administration (**Application > Install Plugins**).

Reasons to Use ART

ART helps you manage CallManager in terms of QoS statistics and system capacity by generating reports that give information about voice quality. ART generates reports on the performance of the gateways and is also useful to associate calls to users and reconcile phone billing with usage. ART can also be used for troubleshooting. For example, if several users report dropped calls when dialing in to retrieve voice mail messages, you can run a voice mail utilization report in ART to see whether the voice mail server is receiving more requests than it can process. The information in this report can help you determine whether to add another voice mail server to your system.

ART provides reporting features for three levels of users:

- ART administrators
- Managers
- Individual users

ART administrators can use all of the features of ART. Managers can monitor call details for the various groups and individuals in the company. Individual users can view details about their calls. Numerous reports are available in either detail or summary format.

ART administrators can use ART as a tool for monitoring QoS. For example, reports generated in ART can help you detect QoS problems in the system and, to some extent, diagnose and isolate QoS problems. Other reports provide metrics on traffic, system overview, gateways, voice mail utilization, conference bridge utilization, Cisco IP Phone services, and more.

Managers can use ART to generate reports about usage for their department or select users to view top usage by cost or call duration. This can be useful to keep watch over expenses or to determine ongoing budgeting for departmental phone usage. Managers can also run detailed reports that help determine whether any unauthorized calls have been made by their department or select users.

Individuals can use ART to generate summary or detail reports for calls they made. This can be useful for tracking phone numbers, call duration, and billing purposes.

NOTE   Users must be given the URL for ART before they can access the system. Authentication is handled by the user ID established in the Global Directory in CallManager Administration. See the ART documentation for more information.

Figure 6-5 shows the QOS Summary screen in ART (**System Reports > QoS Reports> QoS Summary**). In this screen, you can specify the types of calls to include in the summary report and the timeframe that the report examines.

Figure 6-5   *User-Configured QoS Summary Report*

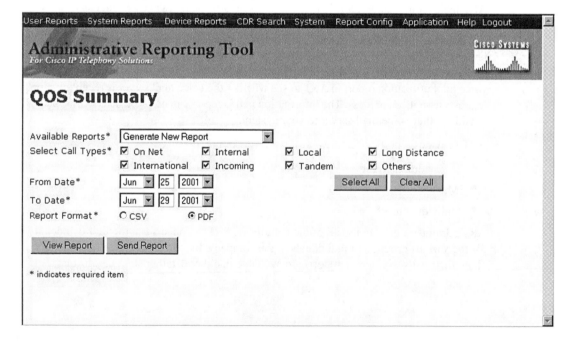

You can also view monthly summary reports by selecting the report in the **Available Reports** list box (shown in Figure 6-5). Figure 6-6 shows an example of the QoS monthly summary report for a fictitious company named CSR, Inc.

Figure 6-6 *QoS Monthly Summary Report*

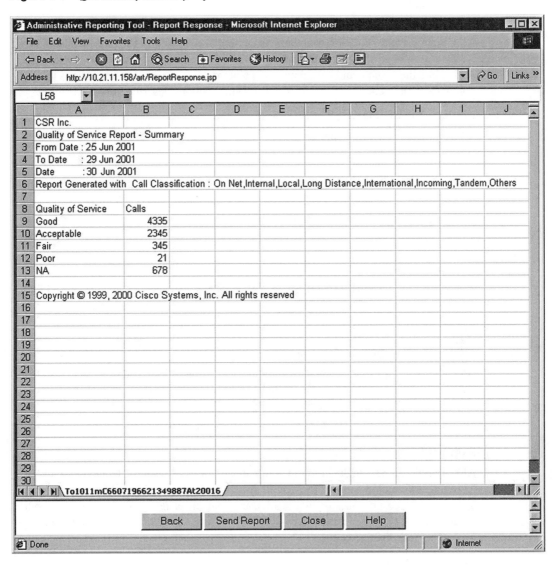

NOTE	ART consumes a great deal of system resources. Therefore, Cisco recommends that ART be used only during off-peak hours to minimize the impact to CallManager performance.

ART Features

ART provides all of the reports already discussed, plus access for the three levels of users. ART allows you to schedule automatic generation of reports, the time that CDR data is loaded into the system, and ART database maintenance. You can also set up alerts to notify you when certain conditions occur. The following sections describe the ART features:

- Loading CDR Data
- Automatic Report Generation
- Reports
- ART Database Maintenance
- Alerts

Descriptions of these features follow.

Loading CDR Data

ART lets you specify when CDR data (CDR and CMR records) is loaded into the ART database. You can schedule the loading of data at the non-peak hours of CallManager.

Automatic Report Generation

ART allows reports to be generated automatically at a user-specified time. This results in reports being automatically generated and stored for future use. You can view these reports quicker than reports that are generated on demand.

Reports

ART reports can be scheduled to run automatically or to be used on demand to track incoming or outgoing call quality, overall system performance, individual or group call usage (such as cost or duration of all calls), and gateway usage details, among many other functions. ART reports are displayed in PDF form using Acrobat Reader. Reports generated by ART include the following:

- User reports
- Call reports
- Traffic summary reports

- Gateway reports
- QoS reports
- System overview reports
- CDRs

Reports can be generated for viewing, printing, or e-mail distribution to interested parties by using the **Send Report** button in ART.

User Reports   User reports (**User Reports > Bills**) provide information to let users monitor their own calling records. Reports about user calls can be sent to relevant personnel (managers, high-usage users, and so on) to inform them of possible anomalies in their usage patterns.

You can also generate a report detailing the users who have a CTI port enabled.

Call Reports   This report is used to analyze the calls based on destinations, users, and calls. Call reports can be generated by charge or by duration. The various call reports are as follows:

- Top N users in the organization or group who have incurred maximum charge or have used the phone for the maximum duration

- Top N destinations to which the organization or group has incurred maximum charge or spent maximum time

- Top N calls from the organization or group that incurred maximum charge or were for the maximum duration

Traffic Summary Reports   The traffic summary report (**System Reports > Traffic Summary**) displays network usage patterns on an hourly and daily basis. This report helps you determine if too much or too little equipment is deployed on the network.

Gateway Reports   Gateway reports (**Device Reports > Gateway Reports**) provide gateway traffic details to help you analyze the performance of gateways. The following information describes some of the available gateway reports:

- Gateway detail is a report on the performance of the various gateways in the enterprise and provides the date, origination time, termination time, duration, origination number, destination number, origination codec, destination codec, origination IP, and QoS of calls that used the gateway. It can be generated on demand by specifying the call classification, QoS grades, gateways, and date range.

- Gateway summary is a report that shows a summary of the performance of the various gateways. It presents a matrix of the number of calls of various call classifications and QoS through a gateway. It also gives the total number of calls and the duration under each of the categories. The report is scheduled for generation every month and can also be generated on demand by specifying the call classification and date range.

QoS Reports   You can use ART to gather information on voice quality and manage CallManager QoS statistics and system capacity (**System Reports > QoS Reports**). Calls are categorized into a voice quality category based on the information in the CDR data and the QoS parameters you provide. QoS reports provide information about the quality of calls for all phones in the network. This helps you determine whether there are any possible issues in the network. Reports include codec type, packets lost, jitter, and latency.

- QoS summary report helps managers and administrators analyze CallManager performance. It can be scheduled for automatic generation every month or run on demand for a specified date range and provides a pie chart of the number of calls under various QoS grades.

- QoS detail is a report on the voice quality grades achieved for calls. You can use this report to analyze CallManager performance for various manager groups or for the entire organization. It provides the origination time, termination time, duration, origination number, destination number, call classification, origination codec, destination codec, origination IP, origination span, and QoS. The QoS detail report is scheduled for generation daily, or you can generate a report on demand by specifying the call classification, QoS grades, date range, and users (if desired).

System Overview Reports   The system overview report (**System Reports > System Overview**) provides a composite report consisting of call reports, the QoS summary report, and the gateway summary report. This report gives a broad picture of the overall system performance, and it can be scheduled for automatic generation every month or generated on demand for any selected date range.

CDR   **CDR Search** allows you to view CDR data from the CallManager database based on a specified date, gateway, or extension number. The results display the CDR data fields for records that match the selection criteria.

ART Database Maintenance

You can configure ART to notify you when the ART or CDR database is reaching capacity (**System > Database >** *select the alert for ART or CDR*). You can then manually purge the selected database (**System > Database > Database Purge**). You can also schedule automatic purging of records in the ART database when its database size exceeds the specified limit.

Alerts

You can configure ART to alert you when any of the following conditions occur:

- ART or the CDR database size exceeds a limit you specify.
- QoS parameters go beyond a predefined limit.
- A user exceeds the daily charge limit.

Alerts are sent to the e-mail ID you specify when configuring the alert.

Learn More About ART

Detailed information about ART is available through the online help documentation contained within the ART application or at the following location:

www.cisco.com/univercd/cc/td/doc/product/voice/sw_ap_to/admin/admin_rp/index.htm

Monitoring Tools

This section describes the tools that can be used to monitor CallManager and your network:

- Cisco CallManager Serviceability
- Event Viewer
- Terminal Services Client
- CiscoWorks2000
- SNMP MIBs
- Microsoft Performance
- Remote Serviceability
- Cisco Discovery Protocol (CDP)
- Q931 Translator

Cisco CallManager Serviceability

CallManager Serviceability provides alarms, traces, component version information, and real-time monitoring of Cisco AVVID IP Telephony components in a CallManager cluster. CallManager Serviceability is a Web-based application installed with CallManager and accessible from CallManager Administration by clicking **Application > Cisco CallManager Serviceability**. You can access CallManager Serviceability by browsing to the CallManager server by IP address or Domain Name System (DNS) host name, if applicable.

CallManager Serviceability, shown in Figure 6-7, provides the following features:

- Alarm configuration and detailed alarm definitions
- Trace configuration, analysis, and collection
- Component version information
- Control center for starting and stopping services
- Admin. Serviceability Tool (AST) for real-time system monitoring, device monitoring, and configurable alerts

Figure 6-7 *Example of a Screen in CallManager Serviceability*

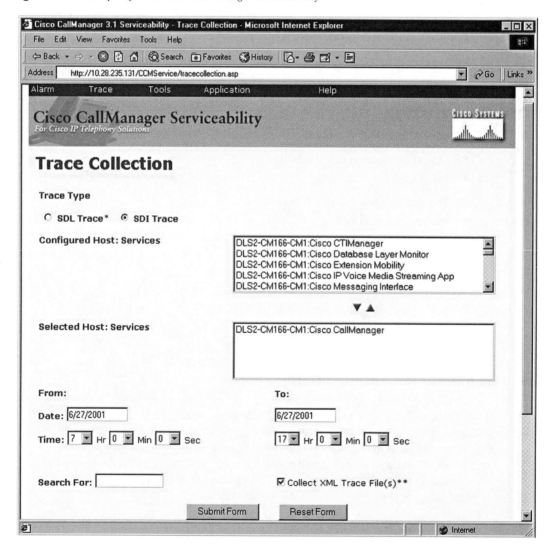

Security

A user must have a valid username and password to access CallManager Serviceability features. When you access CallManager Serviceability, you are authenticated as a user through the Internet Information Server (IIS) authentication method of the Web virtual directory. CallManager Administration uses the same authentication method.

Alarm Configuration

The CallManager system generates alarms to notify you of various events. The alarms are categorized into different levels, as described in Table 6-1. You can configure the system to have alarms forwarded to selected monitors, and for each monitor, you can also choose to capture alarms of certain levels. These settings are configured in the Alarm Configuration screen in CallManager Serviceability for each service (such as Cisco CallManager, Cisco TFTP, and so on). Alarm Configuration also allows you to apply a given configuration to all nodes in the CallManager cluster. The monitors to which alarms can be forwarded include:

- SDI Trace Log—View the alarms in the .txt or .xml trace files
- SDL Trace Log (Cisco CallManager alarms only)—View the alarms in the .txt or .xml trace files
- Event Viewer—View the alarms in Event Viewer; see "Event Viewer" later in this chapter for more information about viewing CallManager alarms in Event Viewer
- Syslog—Specify the IP address of the CiscoWorks2000 server and then view the alarms in CiscoWorks2000 (some configuration is also required in CiscoWorks2000)

Table 6-1 *Alarm Event Levels*

Level	Description
Emergency	The system is unusable.
Alert	Indicates a condition that warrants immediate action.
Critical	Indicates a critical condition.
Error	Indicates an error.
Warning	Indicates a warning condition.
Notice	Indicates a normal but significant condition.
Informational	Provides information messages only.
Debug	Provides detailed messages for use in debugging by Cisco engineers.

Alarm Definitions

You can view detailed alarm descriptions in CallManager Serviceability. Click **Alarm > Definitions** to view these definitions. A simple search dialog box is provided that allows you to search for and view alarms, their descriptions, and recommended actions. Once a search has returned a list of alarms, you can click any part of the alarm description to see detailed information about that alarm. The detailed information also includes an explanation of any reason codes that are given as part of the alarm. For example, an alarm generated by a transient device will have a reason code that explains why the device is considered a transient device. This can help in diagnosing and solving problems in the CallManager system.

Figure 6-8 shows the Alarm Detail screen after a specific alarm, in this case, BChannelISV, has been clicked from the Alarm Message Definitions screen. You can view detailed alarm information for any alarm by clicking on it from the Alarm Message Definitions screen.

Figure 6-8   *Alarm Details Window*

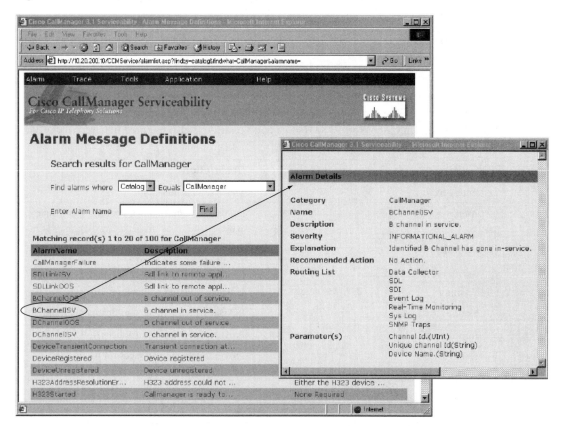

Tracing

Traces are diagnostic tools that can help you determine the cause of a problem. Running a trace can generate information you might need to identify or isolate the source or symptoms of a problem. The path to problem resolution becomes much simpler once you can point to the cause of the problem.

There are two kinds of traces:

- SDI trace, which is also known as Cisco CallManager trace (CCM trace)
- SDL trace

NOTE   To generate good, usable trace information, all clocks should match on all CallManager-related devices. CallManager automatically installs the Network Time Protocol Daemon (xNTPD). xNTPD provides a consistent time for all devices that poll it. To ensure time-matching on all CallManager-related devices, you must set the server time so that all servers are within 15 minutes of the actual time, to allow the times on all devices to converge properly. This results in trace data that accurately reflects a single time across the system.

SDI Traces

SDI traces (also known as CCM traces) are useful for diagnosing most problems you might encounter with the CallManager system. SDI traces log different types of run-time events related to CallManager—including device names, their IP addresses, alarms, and other general information—to help you determine the origin of the problem. You can specify a set of devices for tracing so that the trace log will contain only events that originate from the selected devices. The Cluster ID and nodeID appear in the trace files to help you determine which trace files belong to which node of the cluster.

For example, a user reports that a dialed number will not connect. You can turn on SDI trace and trace only the phone and gateway involved to learn why CallManager cannot connect the user's call. This could show a problem with a conflicting route pattern that might be preventing the dialed number from being routed. In another example, a user reports that calls are being dropped. You can turn on SDI trace on the gateways to help identify the reason that the call is dropping and determine whether the problem lies within the CallManager system or in the Public Switched Telephone Network (PSTN).

You can choose to log SDI traces in XML format or in standard text-based format. When XML trace formatting is selected, the resulting trace logs can be used with Trace Analysis. Trace Analysis is a powerful tool that lets you filter trace information so only the pertinent data you specify is returned. This allows you to focus on only the information you need in the log file.

NOTE   SDI tracing is enabled by default and turned on when you configure and run the trace in CallManager Serviceability.

SDI Trace Output   SDI traces generate files (for example, CCM000000000) that store traces of CallManager activities. These traces provide information about the CallManager initialization process, registration process, call flow, digit analysis, and related devices, such as Cisco IP Phones, gateways, gatekeepers, and more. This information can help you isolate problems when troubleshooting CallManager.

The trace files are stored in the following default location:

C:\Program Files\Cisco\Trace

If a trace is enabled, a new trace file is started each time CallManager restarts or when the designated number of lines or minutes has been reached.

To avoid performance degradation on the server, be sure that you turn off SDI tracing after the trace has been captured.

SDL Traces

The Cisco Technical Assistance Center (TAC) and Cisco engineers use SDL traces to diagnose difficult problems. The only time you should change the SDL trace configuration is when directed to do so by TAC. SDL trace logs state transitions only for CallManager and Cisco CTI Manager. Cisco engineers use SDL traces to find the cause of an error. You are not expected to understand the information contained in an SDL trace. However, while working with TAC, you might be asked to change the SDL trace configuration and provide the resulting trace files to TAC. To avoid any performance degradation on the server, be sure that you turn off SDL tracing after the trace has been captured.

NOTE   Before gathering any SDL traces in CallManager Serviceability, you must enable SDL tracing in CallManager Administration. The Cisco TAC representative requesting the trace can advise you on how to enable SDL tracing.

Trace Considerations for Performance Impact and Disk Space

Traces can be very detailed depending on the level of trace enabled. Therefore, they can consume a large amount of disk space and can also impact CallManager performance. For this reason, Cisco advises you to turn on tracing for a specific amount of time, review the trace information that was generated, and then turn off the trace. SDL traces typically are much more detailed and more likely to impact CallManager performance. SDL traces should be run only when the impact will not affect CallManager performance.

Trace Configuration

Trace configuration allows you to specify the criteria for SDI tracing. Click **Trace > Configuration** to select the server you want to trace, and then select the service on that server, such as Cisco CallManager, the Database Layer, CTI Manager, and so on. Figure 6-9 shows the Trace Configuration screen with the default values selected.

You can custom configure the trace by selecting the level of trace, the trace fields, and device names (if applicable). Table 6-2 provides a list of the debug trace level settings.

Table 6-2   *Debug Trace Levels*

Level	Description
Error	Use this level for all traces generated in abnormal paths, such as coding errors or other errors that normally should not occur.
Special	Use this level for all informational, nonrepetitive messages, such as process startup messages, registration messages, and so on. All system and device initialization traces are at this level.
State Transition	Use this level to trace call processing events or normal events traced for the subsystem (traces for signaling layers).
Significant	Use this level to trace media layer events.
Arbitrary	Use this level to generate low-level debug traces. This level is best suited for a testing setup or for debugging difficult problems in a subsystem.
Detailed	This level should not be enabled during normal system operation. It is used for detailed debug information or highly repetitive messages that are primarily used for debugging, including KeepAlives and responses.

CallManager Serviceability provides the option of device-based filtering. This is useful when a certain problem is known to be occurring on a specific device and you want to only view trace information relating to that device. You select device name-based tracing in the Trace Configuration screen. Selecting the devices and then running the trace returns results for any events involving the selected devices.

By default, trace results are saved in a file. You can choose to save traces in .txt format, where up to 10,000 lines can be saved and the file can be viewed in any text editor, or you can choose to save the results in XML format. Only the XML-formatted traces can be used with Trace Analysis, which makes trace output easier to analyze and provides more post-filtering control than text-based traces. However, XML-formatted trace files are limited to less than 2000 lines.

After a trace starts, it continues until you turn it off. When tracing reaches its limit in the trace files, it begins to overwrite trace data, starting with the earliest trace files/lines. To view an XML trace, you can use Trace Analysis (see the following section, "Trace Analysis"). To view a text-based trace, open the trace in a text editor.

Figure 6-9 *Trace Configuration Screen*

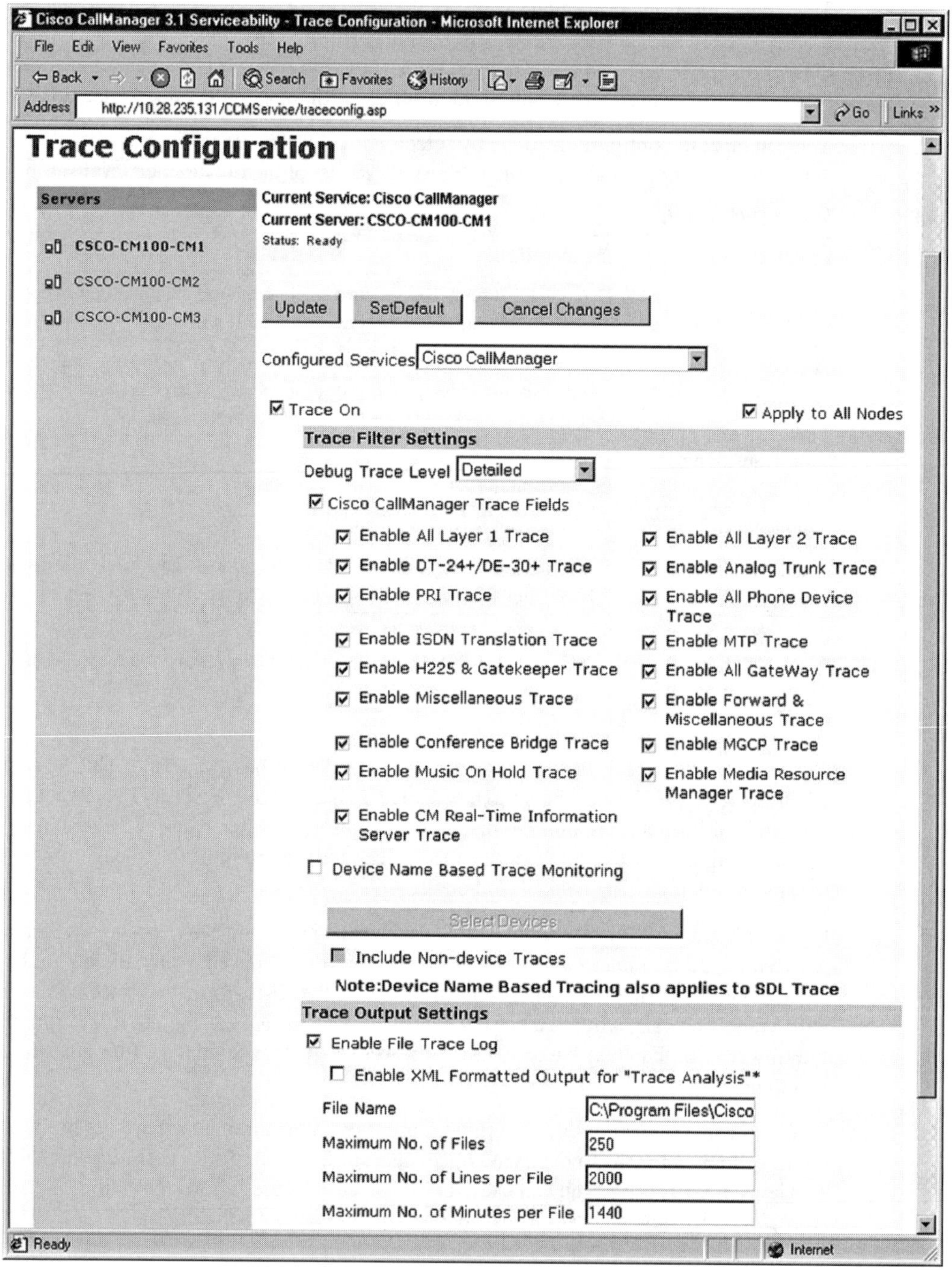

Figure 6-10 shows trace output as it appears when viewed in a text editor such as Notepad. Figure 6-11 shows trace output (before Trace Analysis) when viewed in XML format on a Web browser. In Figure 6-13, you can see XML trace output results after Trace Analysis.

Figure 6-10 *Traditional Trace Output Viewed in a Text Editor*

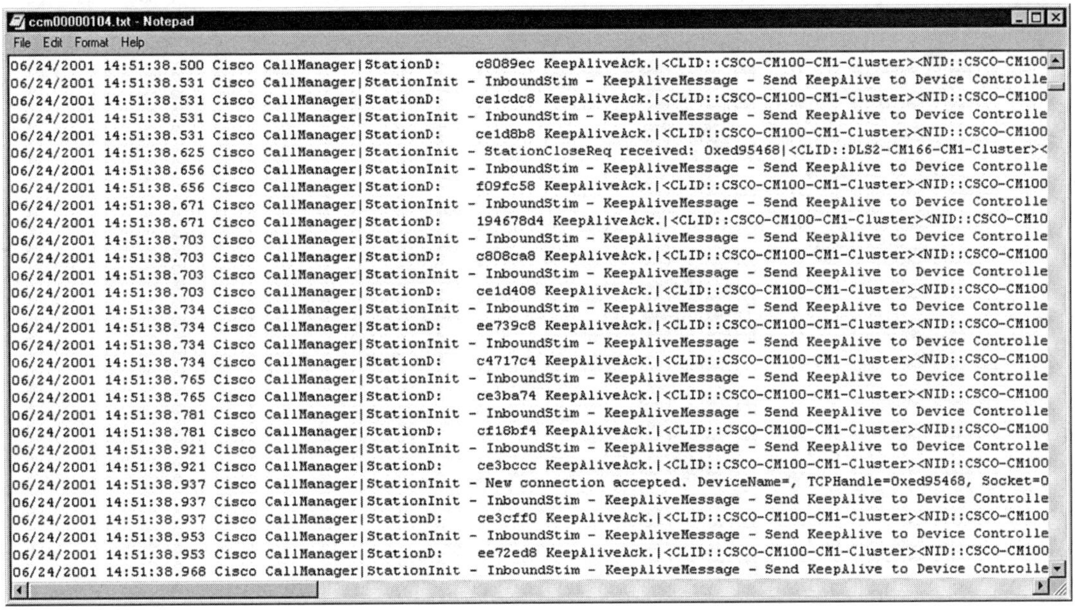

```
ccm00000104.txt - Notepad
File Edit Format Help
06/24/2001 14:51:38.500 Cisco CallManager|StationD:    c8089ec KeepAliveAck.|<CLID::CSCO-CM100-CM1-Cluster><NID::CSCO-CM100
06/24/2001 14:51:38.531 Cisco CallManager|StationInit - InboundStim - KeepAliveMessage - Send KeepAlive to Device Controlle
06/24/2001 14:51:38.531 Cisco CallManager|StationD:    ce1cdc8 KeepAliveAck.|<CLID::CSCO-CM100-CM1-Cluster><NID::CSCO-CM100
06/24/2001 14:51:38.531 Cisco CallManager|StationInit - InboundStim - KeepAliveMessage - Send KeepAlive to Device Controlle
06/24/2001 14:51:38.531 Cisco CallManager|StationD:    ce1d8b8 KeepAliveAck.|<CLID::CSCO-CM100-CM1-Cluster><NID::CSCO-CM100
06/24/2001 14:51:38.625 Cisco CallManager|StationInit - StationCloseReq received: 0xed95468|<CLID::DLS2-CM166-CM1-Cluster><
06/24/2001 14:51:38.656 Cisco CallManager|StationInit - InboundStim - KeepAliveMessage - Send KeepAlive to Device Controlle
06/24/2001 14:51:38.656 Cisco CallManager|StationD:    f09fc58 KeepAliveAck.|<CLID::CSCO-CM100-CM1-Cluster><NID::CSCO-CM100
06/24/2001 14:51:38.671 Cisco CallManager|StationInit - InboundStim - KeepAliveMessage - Send KeepAlive to Device Controlle
06/24/2001 14:51:38.671 Cisco CallManager|StationD:    194678d4 KeepAliveAck.|<CLID::CSCO-CM100-CM1-Cluster><NID::CSCO-CM10
06/24/2001 14:51:38.703 Cisco CallManager|StationInit - InboundStim - KeepAliveMessage - Send KeepAlive to Device Controlle
06/24/2001 14:51:38.703 Cisco CallManager|StationD:    c808ca8 KeepAliveAck.|<CLID::CSCO-CM100-CM1-Cluster><NID::CSCO-CM100
06/24/2001 14:51:38.703 Cisco CallManager|StationInit - InboundStim - KeepAliveMessage - Send KeepAlive to Device Controlle
06/24/2001 14:51:38.703 Cisco CallManager|StationD:    ce1d408 KeepAliveAck.|<CLID::CSCO-CM100-CM1-Cluster><NID::CSCO-CM100
06/24/2001 14:51:38.734 Cisco CallManager|StationInit - InboundStim - KeepAliveMessage - Send KeepAlive to Device Controlle
06/24/2001 14:51:38.734 Cisco CallManager|StationD:    ee739c8 KeepAliveAck.|<CLID::CSCO-CM100-CM1-Cluster><NID::CSCO-CM100
06/24/2001 14:51:38.734 Cisco CallManager|StationInit - InboundStim - KeepAliveMessage - Send KeepAlive to Device Controlle
06/24/2001 14:51:38.734 Cisco CallManager|StationD:    c4717c4 KeepAliveAck.|<CLID::CSCO-CM100-CM1-Cluster><NID::CSCO-CM100
06/24/2001 14:51:38.765 Cisco CallManager|StationInit - InboundStim - KeepAliveMessage - Send KeepAlive to Device Controlle
06/24/2001 14:51:38.765 Cisco CallManager|StationD:    ce3ba74 KeepAliveAck.|<CLID::CSCO-CM100-CM1-Cluster><NID::CSCO-CM100
06/24/2001 14:51:38.781 Cisco CallManager|StationInit - InboundStim - KeepAliveMessage - Send KeepAlive to Device Controlle
06/24/2001 14:51:38.781 Cisco CallManager|StationD:    cf18bf4 KeepAliveAck.|<CLID::CSCO-CM100-CM1-Cluster><NID::CSCO-CM100
06/24/2001 14:51:38.921 Cisco CallManager|StationInit - InboundStim - KeepAliveMessage - Send KeepAlive to Device Controlle
06/24/2001 14:51:38.921 Cisco CallManager|StationD:    ce3bccc KeepAliveAck.|<CLID::CSCO-CM100-CM1-Cluster><NID::CSCO-CM100
06/24/2001 14:51:38.937 Cisco CallManager|StationInit - New connection accepted. DeviceName=, TCPHandle=0xed95468, Socket=0
06/24/2001 14:51:38.937 Cisco CallManager|StationInit - InboundStim - KeepAliveMessage - Send KeepAlive to Device Controlle
06/24/2001 14:51:38.937 Cisco CallManager|StationD:    ce3cff0 KeepAliveAck.|<CLID::CSCO-CM100-CM1-Cluster><NID::CSCO-CM100
06/24/2001 14:51:38.953 Cisco CallManager|StationInit - InboundStim - KeepAliveMessage - Send KeepAlive to Device Controlle
06/24/2001 14:51:38.953 Cisco CallManager|StationD:    ee72ed8 KeepAliveAck.|<CLID::CSCO-CM100-CM1-Cluster><NID::CSCO-CM100
06/24/2001 14:51:38.968 Cisco CallManager|StationInit - InboundStim - KeepAliveMessage - Send KeepAlive to Device Controlle
```

Figure 6-11 *XML Trace Output Viewed in a Browser*

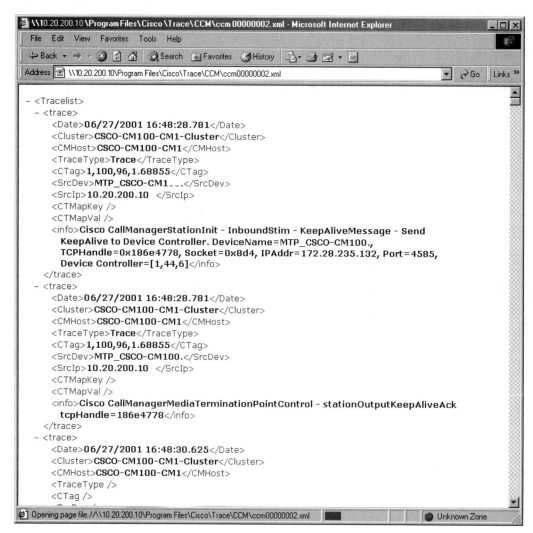

Trace Analysis

Trace Analysis allows you to perform post-filtering on an XML trace file so that only the relevant information is displayed. Because trace files can be large and encompass so much information, the ability to reduce and sort that information is extremely useful. You must know which trace file you want to analyze to use Trace Analysis. Click **Trace > Analysis** to choose a trace file and specify the selection criteria and the fields you want displayed in the Trace Analysis results.

Figure 6-12 shows the Trace Analysis window, which simplifies the trace selection process for you. With Trace Analysis, you can specify collection criteria such as

- Cisco CallManager host
- Device name
- IP address
- Trace type
- MGCP endpoint

Figure 6-12 *Trace Analysis Screen*

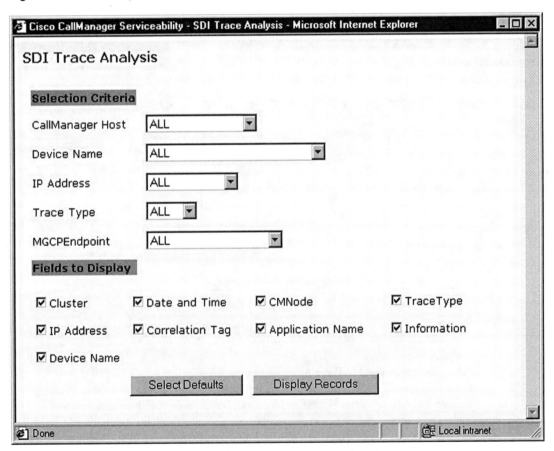

You can filter the trace so that only the pertinent information is displayed. The following information can be displayed or filtered out of the trace:

- Cluster
- Date and time

- CallManager node
- Trace type
- IP address
- Correlation tag
- Application name
- Information
- Device name

Figure 6-13 shows the results after Trace Analysis.

Figure 6-13 *XML Trace Output After Trace Analysis*

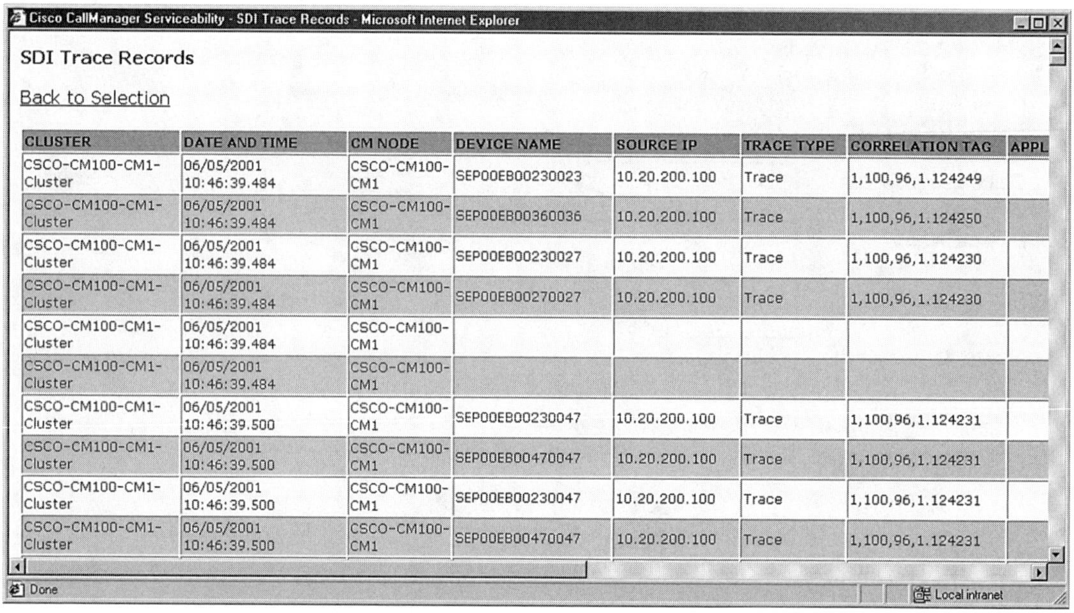

CLUSTER	DATE AND TIME	CM NODE	DEVICE NAME	SOURCE IP	TRACE TYPE	CORRELATION TAG	APPL
CSCO-CM100-CM1-Cluster	06/05/2001 10:46:39.484	CSCO-CM100-CM1	SEP00EB00230023	10.20.200.100	Trace	1,100,96,1.124249	
CSCO-CM100-CM1-Cluster	06/05/2001 10:46:39.484	CSCO-CM100-CM1	SEP00EB00360036	10.20.200.100	Trace	1,100,96,1.124250	
CSCO-CM100-CM1-Cluster	06/05/2001 10:46:39.484	CSCO-CM100-CM1	SEP00EB00230027	10.20.200.100	Trace	1,100,96,1.124230	
CSCO-CM100-CM1-Cluster	06/05/2001 10:46:39.484	CSCO-CM100-CM1	SEP00EB00270027	10.20.200.100	Trace	1,100,96,1.124230	
CSCO-CM100-CM1-Cluster	06/05/2001 10:46:39.484	CSCO-CM100-CM1					
CSCO-CM100-CM1-Cluster	06/05/2001 10:46:39.484	CSCO-CM100-CM1					
CSCO-CM100-CM1-Cluster	06/05/2001 10:46:39.500	CSCO-CM100-CM1	SEP00EB00230047	10.20.200.100	Trace	1,100,96,1.124231	
CSCO-CM100-CM1-Cluster	06/05/2001 10:46:39.500	CSCO-CM100-CM1	SEP00EB00470047	10.20.200.100	Trace	1,100,96,1.124231	
CSCO-CM100-CM1-Cluster	06/05/2001 10:46:39.500	CSCO-CM100-CM1	SEP00EB00230047	10.20.200.100	Trace	1,100,96,1.124231	
CSCO-CM100-CM1-Cluster	06/05/2001 10:46:39.500	CSCO-CM100-CM1	SEP00EB00470047	10.20.200.100	Trace	1,100,96,1.124231	

Performance Impact   Trace Analysis runs as a low-priority task so that it does not disrupt higher priority CallManager functions. However, it should be used judiciously because it can be resource-intensive. Memory impact on the CallManager system is minimal, as long as only a few concurrent users run analysis at any given time. If possible, run Trace Analysis only when the CallManager system is not busy. Because traces are being collected and merged into an output file, the tool continuously accesses the disk. Also, be certain the CallManager system has enough disk space for the temporary output files. Currently, no user interface is available to clean up these temporary files, but the tool does automatically recycle them.

Trace Collection

Trace Collection is a post-processing tool that lets you gather trace logs collected in different files and on different CallManager nodes within the cluster based on the date and time range you select. This is useful when you do not know which file you want to analyze or when you have an error you cannot pinpoint. If the traces are logged in XML format, you can then perform post-filtering to analyze the trace logs captured during the time range you specified. For example, if a user complains that a call was cut off, you can collect traces for the time period in which the dropped call occurred (say, yesterday morning between 7:45 a.m. and 8:15 a.m.). After all of the traces for the specified time period have been collected, you can use Trace Analysis to filter the pertinent trace information to help you pinpoint the cause of the dropped call.

Control Center

CallManager Serviceability allows you to start and stop services by clicking **Tools > Control Center**. The Control Center allows you to start or stop services (such as Cisco CallManager, Cisco Telephony Call Dispatcher, Cisco TFTP, and so on) on one CallManager or all CallManager nodes within a cluster. The Control Center indicates whether the services on the CallManager nodes are currently running or stopped.

Component Version Information

You can check the versions of installed components by clicking **Help > Component Versions**. This is useful when you are trying to verify whether you have the latest version of an installed component.

Admin. Serviceability Tool (AST)

CallManager Serviceability provides real-time monitoring of your CallManager system through the Admin. Serviceability Tool (AST) (**Tools > Admin. Serviceability Tool**). AST provides real-time performance monitoring and device monitoring. You can monitor CallManager and Windows 2000 performance objects and counters in chart view or table view using the **Performance** tab in AST. You can also set thresholds and generate alerts that can be sent to you as e-mail or pop-up messages. Alerts can be configured for CallManager on a per-node basis, or on phones, gateways, ports, Cisco TFTP, and much more.

NOTE	The AST Web page must be open and running for alerts to be sent.

The **Devices** tab in AST provides monitoring information about devices in the CallManager cluster, their IP addresses, their real-time status (such as whether they are successfully registered to CallManager and to which CallManager node), and other useful device information. For devices that support an HTTP server, such as phones and gateways, you can right-click the specific device information to open an HTTP connection to the selected device. You can then browse information stored locally on the device, such as network configuration and statistics information. You can also launch related screens in CallManager Administration by right-clicking a device type (phone, gateway, voice mail, and so on).

Clicking the icons on the lower-right corner of the AST window provides quick links to the following features or information:

- Preferences, where you can create pop-up message alerts or e-mail alerts for devices or CallManager
- CallManager cluster information
- Resource usage information
- AST version information
- Online help for AST
- Catastrophic alerts

NOTE   AST is a Web-based Java applet that runs on the browser. Real-time performance and device monitoring does consume system resources and, if run on a CallManager node, will impact CallManager performance. Cisco advises that you run the AST applet from a separate machine browsing into the CallManager cluster.

Figure 6-14 shows eight counters in chart view in the AST window that are used to monitor call activity: one each in five panes and three active lines together in the sixth pane.

With AST you can select and monitor real-time performance counters that you specify in your CallManager cluster. The window provides six panes per category, accommodating up to 18 counters. You can add counters to the panes by double-clicking them from the list of counters. You can also drag and drop counters to layer up to three counters in a single pane. You can add new categories to monitor additional counters. For example, you might have eight T1 lines and are capacity-planning to determine whether to acquire additional T1 lines. You can monitor the counters associated with T1 gateways to determine when usage is approaching the limit. Another example is for load balancing. You can monitor the same counters from two different CallManager nodes in the cluster and put them on the same chart to see if one CallManager is more heavily loaded than the other. You might decide to change the configuration to balance the load better.

Figure 6-14 *Monitoring Call Activity in CallManager*

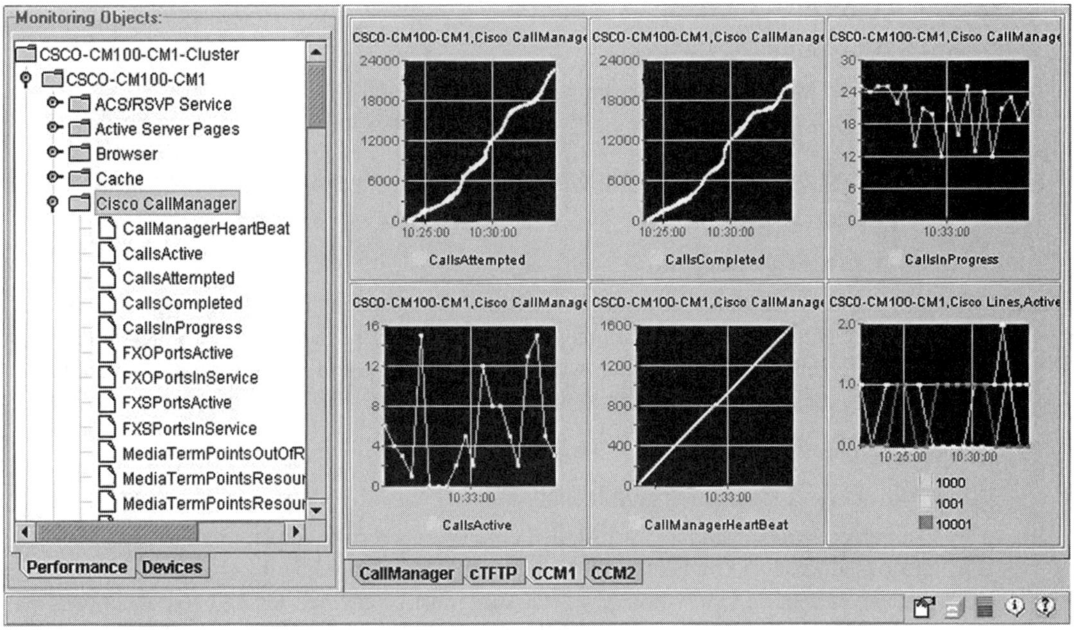

NOTE   The information in the following tables is provided for your reference. New features and bug fixes cause the counters and objects to be routinely updated. Check AST for the latest objects and counters.

The following is a list of CallManager objects available in either AST or Microsoft Performance:

- Cisco CallManager
- Cisco CTI Manager
- Cisco H.323
- Cisco Lines
- Cisco Media Streaming Application
- Cisco Media Termination Point
- Cisco Messaging Interface
- Cisco MGCP FXO Device
- Cisco MGCP FXS Device
- Cisco MGCP Gateways

- Cisco MGCP PRI Device
- Cisco MGCP T1 CAS Device
- Cisco Music on Hold Device
- Cisco Music on Hold Server
- Cisco Phones
- Cisco Software Conference Bridge
- Cisco TFTP
- Cisco WebAttendant

Many objects and counters, in addition to those described in this section, are shown in AST. Some are generated by applications you have installed (such as Cisco IP IVR), whereas others are generated by the Windows 2000 operating system. For information about these counters, consult the documentation for those products.

Objects and Counters Availability

Counters are only available for installed components. For example, to view Cisco CallManager counters, CallManager must be installed on the computer that you are attempting to monitor. Also, statistics must be enabled for AST to collect data. Statistics are enabled by default in CallManager and can be turned on or off in the Service Parameters Configuration screen in CallManager Administration (**System > Service Parameters >** *StatisticsEnable parameter set to **True** to enable or **False** to disable statistics*).

Cisco CallManager Objects and Counters

You can see descriptions of every counter by right-clicking the counter and selecting **Properties**. Descriptions for Cisco CallManager counters are provided for your convenience in the following sections. This book may provide some additional information than that provided by right-clicking a counter in CallManager Serviceability or in Microsoft Performance.

Cisco Analog Access Counters   The counters in this section provide port and call information about Analog Access gateways.

Table 6-3 provides a list of all counters in the Cisco Analog Access object and a description of what each counter represents.

Table 6-3   *Cisco Analog Access Counters*

Counter	Description
OutboundBusyAttempts	The total number of times that a call was attempted through the Analog Access when all ports were busy.
PortsActive	The number of ports that are currently in use.
PortsOutOfService	The number of ports that are currently out of service. Applies to Loop Start and Ground Start trunks only.

Cisco CallManager Counters   The counters in this section allow you to monitor CallManager activity in real time, which is particularly useful for troubleshooting or monitoring the general health of the system.

Table 6-4 provides a list of all counters in the Cisco CallManager object and a description of what each counter represents.

Table 6-4   *Cisco CallManager Counters*

Counter	Description
CallManagerHeartBeat	The heartbeat of CallManager. This is an incremental count that indicates that CallManager is alive and running. If the count does not increment, this means CallManager is down (dead).
CallsActive	The number of calls that actually have a voice path connected on this CallManager.
CallsAttempted	The number of attempted calls. This number increments with each call attempt. Any time a phone goes off-hook and back on-hook, it is considered an attempted call, regardless of whether any digits were dialed or if it connected to a destination. Some call attempts are made by the system during feature operations (such as transfer and conference) and are considered attempted calls.
CallsCompleted	The number of calls that were actually connected (a voice path was established) through this CallManager. This number increments when the call is terminated.

continues

Table 6-4 *Cisco CallManager Counters (Continued)*

Counter	Description
CallsInProgress	The number of calls currently in progress on this CallManager. This includes all active calls. When all calls that are attempted have connected, the number of CallsInProgress and the number of CallsActive are the same.
FXOPortsActive	The number of FXO ports that are in an active call on this CallManager.
FXOPortsInService	The number of FXO ports that are in service in the system.
FXSPortsActive	The number of FXS ports that are in an active call on this CallManager.
FXSPortsInService	The number of FXS ports that are in service in the system.
MediaTermPointsOutOfResources	The number of times CallManager attempted to allocate an MTP resource from one of the MTP devices that is registered with this CallManager when none were available, either because they were all in use or none were registered. This also means that no transcoders were available to act as MTPs.
MediaTermPointsResourceActive	The total number of MTPs that are in use on all MTP devices registered with this CallManager. An MTP in use is one MTP resource that has been allocated for use in a call.
MediaTermPointsResourceAvailable	The total number of MTPs that are not in use and are available to be allocated on all MTP devices that are registered with this CallManager.
MOHMulticastResourceActive	The total number of active Multicast MOH connections on all MOH servers registered with this CallManager.
MOHMulticastResourceAvailable	The total number of Multicast MOH connections that are not being used on all MOH servers that are registered with this CallManager.

Table 6-4   *Cisco CallManager Counters (Continued)*

Counter	Description
MOHOutOfResources	The number of times that the Media Resource Manager (MRM) attempted to allocate an MOH resource when either all available connections on all MOH servers registered with this CallManager were active, or none were registered.
MOHTotalMulticastResources	The total number of Multicast MOH resources or connections provided by all MOH servers that are currently registered with this CallManager.
MOHTotalUnicastResources	The total number of Unicast MOH resources or streams provided by all MOH servers that are currently registered with this CallManager.
MOHUnicastResourceActive	The total number of active Unicast MOH connections on all MOH servers that are registered with this CallManager.
MOHUnicastResourceAvailable	The total number of Unicast MOH connections that are not being used on all MOH servers registered with this CallManager.
PRIChannelsActive	The number of PRI voice channels that are in an active call on this CallManager.
PRISpansInService	The number of PRI spans that are in service in the system.
RegisteredAnalogAccess	The number of Cisco Access Analog gateways that are registered with this system. This does not include the number of Cisco Analog Access ports.
RegisteredDigitalAccess	The number of Cisco Access Digital gateways that are registered with this system. This does not include the number of Cisco Digital Access ports.
RegisteredHardwarePhones	The number of Cisco IP Phones that are currently registered in the system.
Registered MGCPGateway	The number of registered MGCP gateways.
RegisteredOtherStationDevices	The number of Skinny Protocol-based devices currently registered in the system. This device type includes Cisco IP SoftPhones, Cisco uOne ports, and Cisco Unity voice mail ports.

continues

Table 6-4 *Cisco CallManager Counters (Continued)*

Counter	Description
T1ChannelsActive	The number of T1 CAS voice channels that are in an active call on this CallManager.
T1SpansInService	The number of T1 CAS spans that are in service in the system.
TranscoderResourceActive	The total number of transcoders that are in use on all transcoder devices registered with this CallManager. A transcoder in use is one transcoder resource that has been allocated for use in a call.
TranscoderResourceAvailable	The total number of transcoders that are not in use and are available to be allocated on all transcoder devices that are registered with this CallManager.
TranscoderOutOfResources	The number of times CallManager attempted to allocate a transcoder resource from one of the transcoder devices that is registered to this CallManager when none were available, either because they were all in use or none were registered.
UnicastHardwareConfResourceActive	The total number of Unicast hardware conference resources that are in use on all hardware conference devices (Cisco Catalyst 6000, Cisco Catalyst 4000, Cisco VG200) that are registered with this CallManager. A Unicast conference is considered active when one or more calls are connected to a Unicast bridge.
UnicastHardwareConferenceActiveParticipants	The number of participants that are in all active conferences that are using a hardware conference bridge allocated from this CallManager node.
UnicastHardwareConfResourceAvailable	The number of Unicast hardware conference resources that are not in use and are available to be allocated on all hardware conference devices (such as Cisco Catalyst 6000, Cisco Catalyst 4000, Cisco VG200) that are registered with this CallManager. Each conference resource represents the availability of three available full-duplex streams on this CallManager.

Table 6-4   *Cisco CallManager Counters (Continued)*

Counter	Description
UnicastHardwareConferenceCompleted	The number of Unicast conferences that used a hardware conference bridge (hardware-based conference devices such as Cisco Catalyst 6000, Cisco Catalyst 4000, Cisco VG200) allocated from this CallManager and have been completed, which means that the conference bridge has been allocated and released. A Unicast conference is activated when the first call is connected to the bridge. The conference is completed when the last call disconnects from the bridge.
UnicastHardwareConferenceOutOfResources	The number of times CallManager attempted to allocate a Unicast hardware conference resource from those that are registered to this CallManager when none were available, either because they were all in use or none were registered.
UnicastSoftwareConfResourceActive	The total number of Unicast software conference resources that are in use on all software conference devices registered with this CallManager. A Unicast conference is considered active when one or more calls are connected to a Unicast bridge.
UnicastSoftwareConferenceActiveParticipants	The number of participants that are in all active conferences that are using a software conference bridge allocated from this CallManager.
UnicastSoftwareConfResourceAvailable	The number of new software-based Unicast conferences that can be started at this point in time for this CallManager. A minimum of three streams must be available for each new conference.
UnicastSoftwareConferenceCompleted	The number of Unicast conferences that used a software conference bridge allocated from this CallManager and have been completed, which means that the conference bridge has been allocated and released. A Unicast conference is activated when the first call is connected to the bridge. The conference is completed when the last call disconnects from the bridge.

continues

Table 6-4 *Cisco CallManager Counters (Continued)*

Counter	Description
UnicastSoftwareConferenceOutOfResources	The number of times CallManager attempted to allocate a Unicast software conference resource from those that are registered to this CallManager when none were available, either because they were all in use or none were registered.

Cisco CtiManager Counters   The counters in this section supply information including the number of CTI-controlled devices, lines, and connections that have been established with this CallManager. CTI connections include the Applications Server, WebAttendant, Cisco IP SoftPhone, and any other third-party TAPI- or JTAPI-controlled device.

Table 6-5 provides a list of all counters in the Cisco CTI Manager object and a description of what each counter represents.

Table 6-5 *Cisco CtiManager Counters*

Counter	Description
NumOfActiveCmLink	The total number of active CallManager links
NumOfCtiConnection	The total number of CTI connections at a given time
NumOfOpenDevices	The total number of open devices
NumOfOpenLines	The total number of open lines
QbeVersion	The CtiManager QBE protocol version

Cisco H.323 Counters   The counters in this section provide information about H.323 devices. H.323 devices include station devices such as NetMeeting and Symbol phones and H.323-compliant gateways such as Cisco 2600, 3600, or 5300. Each H.323 device is listed by name. The name is obtained from CallManager Administration.

Table 6-6 provides a list of all counters in the Cisco H.323 object and a description of what each counter represents.

Table 6-6   *Cisco H.323 Counters*

Counter	Description
CallsAttempted	The number of calls that have been attempted on this device. This includes both successful and unsuccessful call attempts.
CallsInProgress	The number of calls currently in progress on this device.

Cisco Line Counter   The counters in this section provide information about lines. A line includes all dialable directory numbers but does not include route patterns. The directory number identifies the line; for example, a line assigned directory number 1234 is referred to as Line 1234.

Table 6-7 provides the counter in the Cisco Lines object and a description of what it represents.

Table 6-7   *Cisco Lines Counter*

Counter	Description
Active	The state of the line: either active or not active. If the number here is greater than 0, the line is active and the number represents the number of calls currently in progress on that line. A maximum of two calls can be active at one time. If more than one call is active, this indicates that a call is on hold either because of being placed on hold specifically, or because a transfer is in progress and it is on transfer hold. Applies to all directory numbers assigned to any device.

Cisco Media Streaming App Counters   The counters in this section provide information about software Media Termination Points (MTPs), software conference bridge, and Music On Hold (MOH) and are generated by the Cisco IP Voice Media Streaming Application.

Table 6-8 provides a list of all counters in the Cisco Media Streaming App object and a description of what each counter represents.

Table 6-8 *Cisco Media Streaming App Counters*

Counter	Description
HeartBeat	The heartbeat of the process. This is an incremental count that indicates that the Cisco IP Voice Media Streaming Application is alive and running. If the count does not increment, this means that the Cisco IP Voice Media Streaming Application is down (dead).
IOCTL Errors	The number of Input/Output control (IOCTL) errors. The count increments when an application has trouble communicating with the Media Streaming Application kernel mode driver.
Missing Device Driver Errors	The number of missing device driver errors.
Out of Streams	The number of times a stream was requested but not available.
StartTime	The time in milliseconds that the Cisco IP Voice Media Streaming Application service started. This time is based on the real-time clock in the computer, which is simply a reference point that indicates the current time and the length of time that has elapsed, in milliseconds, since the service started. The reference point is midnight, January 1, 1970.

Cisco Media Termination Point Counters   For software media termination points, the counters in this section provide information about the availability of streams and the connection state.

Table 6-9 provides a list of all counters in the Cisco Media Termination Point object and a description of what each counter represents.

Table 6-9 *Cisco Media Termination Point Counters*

Counter	Description
ConnectionState	The current connection state to CallManager; 1 = primary, 2 = secondary
NumberOfActiveConnections	The number of active connections
NumberOfActiveStreams	The number of active streams
NumberOfAvailableStreams	The number of available streams

Table 6-9   *Cisco Media Termination Point Counters (Continued)*

Counter	Description
NumberOfLostConnections	The total number of times a CallManager connection was lost
TotalNumberOfConnections	The total number of connections
TotalNumberOfStreams	The total number of streams

Cisco Messaging Interface Counters   The counters in this section provide communication information between CallManager and Cisco Messaging Interface (CMI) for voice mail systems using SMDI.

Table 6-10 provides a list of all counters in the Cisco Messaging Interface object and a description of what each counter represents.

Table 6-10   *Cisco Messaging Interface Counters*

Counter	Description
24-hour Outbound SMDI Message Count	The running count of outbound SMDI messages in a 24-hour period.
24-hour Inbound SMDI Message Count	The running count of inbound SMDI messages in a 24-hour period.
HeartBeat	The heartbeat of the CMI process. This is an incremental count that indicates CMI is alive and running. If the count does not increment, this means CMI is down (dead).
Inbound SMDI Message Count	The running count of inbound SMDI messages.
Outbound SMDI Message Count	The running count of outbound SMDI messages.
StartTime	The time in milliseconds that the CMI service started. This time is based on the real-time clock in the computer, which is simply a reference point that indicates the current time and the length of time that has elapsed, in milliseconds, since the service started. The reference point is midnight, January 1, 1970.

Cisco MGCP FXO Device Counters   The counters in this section provide status information for MGCP-based analog (FXO) trunks.

Table 6-11 provides a list of all counters under the Cisco MGCP FXO Device object and a description of what each counter represents.

Table 6-11 *Cisco MGCP FXO Device Counters*

Counter	Description
CallsCompleted	The number of successful calls made from this device
OutboundBusyAttempts	The number of times a call through this device was attempted when there were no voice channels available
PortStatus	The status of the FXO port associated with this MGCP device

Cisco MGCP FXS Device Counters   The counters in this section provide status information for MGCP-based analog (FXS) stations (such as fax machines).

Table 6-12 provides a list of all counters under the Cisco MGCP FXS Device object and a description of what each counter represents.

Table 6-12 *Cisco MGCP FXS Device Counters*

Counter	Description
CallsCompleted	The number of successful calls made from this device
OutboundBusyAttempts	The number of times a call through this device was attempted when there were no voice channels available
PortStatus	The status of the FXS port associated with this MGCP device

Cisco MGCP Gateways Counters   The counters in this section provide information about the ports, spans, and channels in MGCP gateways.

Table 6-13 provides a list of all counters under the Cisco MGCP Gateways object and a description of what each counter represents.

Table 6-13   *Cisco MGCP Gateways Counters*

Counter	Description
FXOPortsActive	The number of FXO ports that are active in a call on the gateway
FXOPortsInService	The number of FXO ports that are in service in the gateway
FXSPortsActive	The number of FXS ports that are active in a call on the gateway
FXSPortsInService	The number of FXS ports that are in service in the gateway
PRIChannelsActive	The number of PRI voice channels that are active in a call on the gateway
PRISpansInService	The number of PRI spans that are in service in the gateway
T1ChannelsActive	The number of T1 CAS voice channels that are active in a call on the gateway
T1SpansInService	The number of T1 CAS spans that are in service in the gateway

Cisco MGCP PRI Device Counters   The counters in this section provide call and channel status information for MGCP PRI gateways.

Table 6-14 provides a list of all counters under the Cisco MGCP PRI Device object and a description of what each counter represents.

Table 6-14   *Cisco MGCP PRI Device Counters*

Counter	Description
CallsCompleted	The number of successful calls made from this device.
Channel 1 Status	The status of the indicated B-Channel associated with this MGCP device. Valid values are 1, 2, 3, or 4:
Channel 2 Status	1 (out of service) indicates that this channel is not available for use.
Channel 3 Status	
Channel 4 Status	2 (idle) indicates that this channel has no active call and is ready for use.
Channel 5 Status	3 (busy) indicates an active call on this channel.
Channel 6 Status	4 (reserved) indicates that this channel has been reserved for use as
Channel 7 Status	a D-channel, or for use as a Synch-Channel for E1.
Channel 8 Status	

continues

Table 6-14 *Cisco MGCP PRI Device Counters (Continued)*

Counter	Description
Channel 9 Status	
Channel 10 Status	
Channel 11 Status	
Channel 12 Status	
Channel 13 Status	
Channel 14 Status	
Channel 15 Status	
Channel 16 Status	
Channel 17 Status	
Channel 18 Status	
Channel 19 Status	
Channel 20 Status	
Channel 21 Status	
Channel 22 Status	
Channel 23 Status	
Channel 24 Status	
Channel 25 Status	
Channel 26 Status	
Channel 27 Status	
Channel 28 Status	
Channel 29 Status	
Channel 30 Status	
Channel 31 Status	

Table 6-14   *Cisco MGCP PRI Device Counters (Continued)*

Counter	Description
DataLinkInService	The state of the Data Link (D-Channel) on the corresponding Cisco Digital Access gateway. It is set to 1 if the Data Link is up (in service) or 0 if the Data Link is down (out of service).
OutboundBusyAttempts	The number of times a call through this device was attempted when there were no voice channels available.

Cisco MGCP T1CAS Device Counters   The counters in this section provide call and channel status information for MGCP T1 CAS gateways.

Table 6-15 provides a list of all counters under the Cisco MGCP T1CAS Device object and a description of what each counter represents.

Table 6-15   *Cisco MGCP T1CAS Device Counters*

Counter	Description
CallsCompleted	The number of successful calls made from this device.
Channel 1 Status	The status of the indicated B-Channel associated with this MGCP device. Valid values are 1, 2, 3, or 4:
Channel 2 Status	
Channel 3 Status	1 (out of service) indicates that this channel is not available for use.
Channel 4 Status	2 (idle) indicates that this channel has no active call and is ready for use.
Channel 5 Status	3 (busy) indicates an active call on this channel.
Channel 6 Status	4 (reserved) indicates that this channel has been reserved for use as a D-channel, or for use as a Synch-Channel for E1.
Channel 7 Status	
Channel 8 Status	
Channel 9 Status	
Channel 10 Status	

continues

Table 6-15 *Cisco MGCP T1CAS Device Counters (Continued)*

Counter	Description
Channel 11 Status	
Channel 12 Status	
Channel 13 Status	
Channel 14 Status	
Channel 15 Status	
Channel 16 Status	
Channel 17 Status	
Channel 18 Status	
Channel 19 Status	
Channel 20 Status	
Channel 21 Status	
Channel 22 Status	
Channel 23 Status	
Channel 24 Status	
OutboundBusyAttempts	The number of times a call through this device was attempted when there were no voice channels available.

Cisco MOH Device Counters   The counters in this section provide information about music on hold (MOH) resource availability. MOH is a component of the Cisco IP Voice Media Streaming Application.

Table 6-16 provides a list of all counters under the Cisco MOH Device object and a description of what each counter represents.

Table 6-16 *Cisco MOH Device Counters*

Counter	Description
MOHHighestActiveResources	The largest number of simultaneously active MOH connections on this MOH server. This includes both Multicast and Unicast connections.
MOHMulticastResourceActive	The number of currently active Multicast connections to Multicast addresses served by this MOH server.

Table 6-16 *Cisco MOH Device Counters (Continued)*

Counter	Description
MOHMulticastResourceAvailable	The number of MOH Multicast connections to Multicast addresses served by this MOH server that are not active and are still available to be used at the current time.
MOHOutOfResources	The number of times the Media Resource Manager (MRM) attempted to allocate an MOH resource from this MOH server and failed, either because all available connections of the type requested are in use, or because this device was unregistered at the time of the request.
MOHTotalMulticastResources	The total number of MOH Multicast connections allowed to Multicast addresses served by this MOH server.
MOHTotalUnicastResources	The number of MOH Unicast connections allowed by this MOH server.
MOHUnicastResourceActive	The number of active Unicast connections to this MOH server.
MOHUnicastResourceAvailable	The number of MOH Unicast connections that are not active and are still available to be used at the current time on this MOH server.

Cisco Music on Hold (MOH) Server Counters   The counters in this section provide stream information on a per-CallManager basis. These counters apply to this MOH server only.

Table 6-17 provides a list of all counters under the Cisco Music on Hold object and a description of what each counter represents.

Table 6-17 *Cisco Music on Hold Counters*

Counter	Description
ConnectionState	The current connection state to CallManager; 1 = primary, 2 = secondary
NumberOfActiveAudioSources	The number of active audio sources for this MOH server
NumberOfActiveStreams	The number of active streams
NumberOfAvailableStreams	The number of currently available streams

continues

Table 6-17 *Cisco Music on Hold Counters (Continued)*

Counter	Description
NumberOfLostConnections	The total number of times that a CallManager connection was lost
TotalNumberOfStreams	The total number of streams that have connected to the MOH server

Cisco Phones Counters   The counters in this section can be used to determine the total number of calls that have been made per device (not per line) since the system started.

Table 6-18 lists the counter under the Cisco Phones object and a description of what it represents.

Table 6-18 *Cisco Phones Counters*

Counter	Description
CallsAttempted	The number of attempted calls. Each time the phone goes off-hook and then on-hook, it is considered an attempted call. This number is incremented for each call attempt on a per-device basis and includes all call attempts, whether or not they were successful.

Cisco SW Conference Bridge Counters   The counters in this section provide stream information on a per-CallManager basis for software-based conferences.

Table 6-19 provides a list of all counters in the Cisco SW Conference Bridge object and a description of what each counter represents.

Table 6-19 *Cisco SW Conference Bridge Counters*

Counter	Description
ConnectionState	The current connection state to CallManager; 1 = primary, 2 = secondary
NumberOfActiveConferences	The number of active (currently in use) conferences
NumberOfActiveStreams	The number of active streams
NumberOfAvailableStreams	The number of available streams
NumberOfLostConnections	The total number of times that a CallManager connection was lost

Table 6-19   *Cisco SW Conference Bridge Counters (Continued)*

Counter	Description
TotalNumberOfConferences	The total number of conferences
TotalNumberOfStreams	The total number of streams

Cisco Tftp Counters   The counters in this section show database changes processed by the Cisco TFTP server and the disposition of those change requests. Information in these counters applies to this Cisco TFTP server only.

Table 6-20 provides a list of all counters in the Cisco Tftp object and a description of what each counter represents.

Table 6-20   *Cisco Tftp Counters*

Counter	Description
HeartBeat	The heartbeat of the TFTP server. This count increments when Cisco TFTP is alive and running. If the count does not increment, this means Cisco TFTP is down (dead).
StartTime	The time in milliseconds that the TFTP server started. This time is based on the real-time clock in the computer, which is simply a reference point that indicates the current time and the length of time that has elapsed, in milliseconds, since the service started. The reference point is midnight, January 1, 1970.
TotalChangeNotifications	The total number of database change notifications handled by the TFTP server.
TotalSegmentsAcknowledged	The total number of segments acknowledged by the TFTP server. Files are broken into segments for transmission over the network.
TotalSegmentsSent	The total number of segments sent by the TFTP server.
TotalTftpRequests	The total number of requests handled by the TFTP server. The total of the next four counters should equal this count.
TotalTftpRequestsAborted	The total number of TFTP requests aborted by the TFTP server.
TotalTftpRequestsLocal	The total number of TFTP requests handled by the TFTP server.

continues

Table 6-20 *Cisco Tftp Counters (Continued)*

Counter	Description
TotalTftpRequestsNotFound	The total number of Not Found TFTP requests handled by the TFTP server.
TotalTftpRequestsOverFlow	The total number of TFTP requests rejected because the maximum request count is exceeded.

Cisco WebAttendant Counters   The counters in this section describe the types of data collected by the Telephony Call Dispatcher service (TcdSrv). The TCD service is the server-side component for all the WebAttendant client applications. TCD provides call control and line state service to WebAttendant clients. It also provides hunt group functionality.

Table 6-21 provides a list of all counters in the Cisco WebAttendant object and a description of what each counter represents.

Table 6-21 *Cisco WebAttendant Counters*

Counter	Description
CcmLineLinkState	Indicates the line state. Valid values are 0, 1, 10, or 11: 0 means that the TCD service has not registered or has not received line link state from CallManager. 1 means that the TCD service has registered and is receiving line state information. 10 means that the TCD service has logged into CTI but has not registered or has not received line link state from CallManager. 11 means that the TCD service has logged into CTI and has registered and is receiving line state information.
HeartBeat	The heartbeat of the TCD service. This is an incremental count that indicates that the TCD service is alive and running. If the count does not increment, this means the TCD service is down (dead).

Table 6-21   *Cisco WebAttendant Counters (Continued)*

Counter	Description
StartTime	The time in milliseconds that the TCD service started. This time is based on the real-time clock in the computer, which is simply a reference point that indicates the current time and the length of time that has elapsed, in milliseconds, since the service started. The reference point is midnight, January 1, 1970.
TotalActiveCalls	The total number of active calls in progress. This counter is useful, for example, if you are planning to stop the TCD service or CallManager so that you can monitor this counter to see how many calls will be affected.
TotalActiveLines	The total number of lines that are currently active. An active line is any line state other than idle.
TotalCalls	The total number of calls that have been made since the TCD service started.
TotalClients	The total number of WebAttendant clients that are currently registered with TCD.
TotalCtiRoutePoints	The total number of CTI route points that are open by this TCD service.
TotalIdleLines	The total number of lines that are currently idle. An idle line is any line that is on-hook and not currently receiving a call.
TotalLines	This counter should not be used. Information in this counter may not accurately reflect the total number of lines.
TotalOnlineClients	The total number of Cisco WebAttendant client applications online. This number increments and decrements for each instance of WebAttendant that goes online or offline.
TotalRedirectedCalls	The total number of redirected calls for this TCD service. This number increments every time a pilot point receives a phone call and redirects it to a member in a hunt group.

continues

Table 6-21 *Cisco WebAttendant Counters (Continued)*

Counter	Description
TotalRegisteredClients	The total number of registered clients for this TCD service. This number increments with each new registration of a WebAttendant client (when the client application goes online).
Version	The version of the TCD service.

Learn More About Cisco CallManager Serviceability

Detailed information about CallManager Serviceability is available at the following location:

www.cisco.com/univercd/cc/td/doc/product/voice/c_callmg/3_1/service/index.htm

Event Viewer

Microsoft Event Viewer helps identify problems at the system level. For example, a group of users cannot make calls in a system with one gateway. You can use Event Viewer to look for events about the gateway (such as registration or unregistration events) to pinpoint the problem. Event Viewer starts automatically when Windows 2000 is started and records events in three kinds of logs:

- Application log—Contains events logged by applications or programs, such as CallManager.

- System log—Contains events logged by the Windows 2000 system components, such as the failure of a system component.

- Security log—Contains records of security events. CallManager events do not display in this log.

Event Viewer displays the following types of events:

- Error—A significant problem, such as loss of data or loss of functionality. For example, if a problem occurs with a device that is registered with CallManager, an error event would provide device information and error details to help you isolate the problem.

- Warning—An event that is not necessarily significant but might indicate a possible future problem. For example, warning events can include CallManager services that have stopped or started.

- Information—An event that describes system information, such as host name or IP address and the version of the database layer in use.

By default, CallManager alarms are sent to the Event Viewer at the Error level. You can change the Alarm Event Level in the Alarm Configuration screen in CallManager Serviceability (**Alarm > Configuration >** *select a server > select a service*).

Figure 6-15 shows the details of an Information message that indicates that the gateway has registered with CallManager.

Figure 6-15 *Event Viewer Information Message*

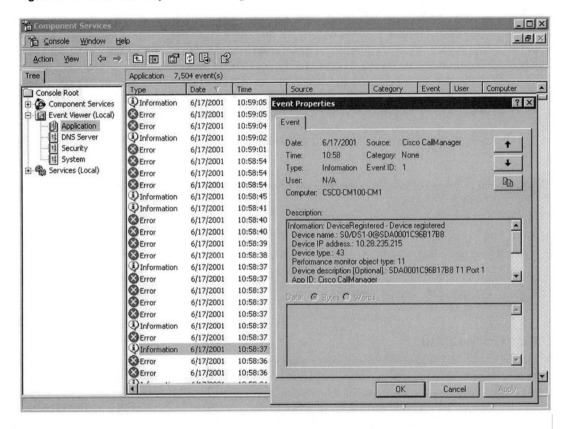

You can access Event Viewer by clicking **Start > Programs > Administrative Tools > Event Viewer**.

Learn More About Event Viewer

Detailed information about Event Viewer is available in Microsoft Windows 2000 documentation.

Terminal Services Client

Terminal Services Client, part of Windows 2000 server, allows you to export a remote desktop to your PC. It is particularly useful because it allows you access to the remote PC as though you were local to the machine. You must have valid permissions that allow you to access the remote server.

Installing and Accessing Terminal Services Client

To install Terminal Services Client, you must first create floppy disks containing the application. From the Cisco CallManager server, click **Start > Programs > Administrative Tools > Terminal Services Client Creator**. Use the Terminal Services Client Creator to create floppy disks; then install Terminal Services on any PC using the floppy disks. When installed on the PC, you can use Terminal Services by clicking **Start > Programs > Terminal Services Client** and designating the IP address or host name of the remote server you want to access.

NOTE   You must have the Terminal Services service started on the CallManager node to which you want to connect.

Learn More About Terminal Services

Online help is available by clicking the **Help** button in Terminal Service. For additional information, consult your Windows 2000 documentation.

CiscoWorks2000

CiscoWorks2000 is the network management system (NMS) of choice for all Cisco devices, including the Cisco CallManager system. CiscoWorks2000 provides the ability to manage diagnostic and troubleshooting information collected from your Cisco AVVID IP Telephony installation. CiscoWorks2000 is not bundled with CallManager and must be purchased separately.

Using CiscoWorks2000, you can configure and produce reports on log messages collected from CallManager nodes and other IP telephony devices. CiscoWorks2000 provides a common system log for applications in the multihost and multiplatform Cisco AVVID IP Telephony Solutions environment. In addition, with help from SNMP, CiscoWorks2000 can provide additional information on each device from which the log messages originate.

Each time a device is added to the CiscoWorks2000 device inventory, a new database is created. After the device is added to the list, CiscoWorks2000 gathers some device information over SNMP. You can read and use this information for system maintenance and problem solving.

The CiscoWorks2000 family of Web-based products supports maintenance of Cisco enterprise networks and devices. The products include Resource Management Essentials, Campus Manager, and Voice Health Monitor, which provide Syslog Analysis, Topology Services, Path Analysis, User Tracking, Fault Management, and other network management services.

System Log Management

The Syslog Analysis tools are Syslog Collector and Syslog Analyzer. They are offered with CiscoWorks2000 as part of the Resource Management Essentials package. Syslog output from CallManager can alternatively be adapted for use with other NMSs that support the standard syslog format:

- The Syslog Collector keeps common system logs that record messages reported to the CallManager system.
- The Syslog Analyzer controls and displays all events so they can easily be read, interpreted, and used for system maintenance and problem solving.

Using the reporting and managing capabilities of these tools, you can monitor and manage a wide range of events and error messages concurrently on each CallManager node and other Cisco devices.

Cisco Syslog Collector

Syslog Collector gathers log messages from a CallManager cluster or node at any network installation. The service collects a wide range of significant event messages that reflect system status. After validating the events or error messages collected, Syslog Collector passes them to the Syslog Analyzer. When this process is complete, you can use Syslog Analyzer to analyze the log messages.

Cisco Syslog Analyzer

Syslog Analyzer, which resides on a CiscoWorks2000 server, receives the messages collected from multiple applications by the Syslog Collector. When a collection of data is received, the Syslog Analyzer parses and stores the results in the CiscoWorks2000 database. This interface allows you to access and manage whatever data is collected from the system's managed devices.

With Syslog Analyzer, you can examine the event log reports from each Cisco CallManager system, including the description and recommended actions for each log message. In addition to a cluster of Cisco CallManagers, a network installation can also have some voice equipment, routers, gateways, and other devices generating log messages. After you have set up your system, you can access all of this information through one server.

IP Path Analysis Interface

PathTool is one of a suite of tools included in Cisco Campus Manager, which is offered with CiscoWorks2000. PathTool is designed to define your CallManager system paths in the form of maps, trace logs, or discovery tables.

PathTool traces connectivity between two specified points on your network. It analyzes both physical and logical paths (Layers 2 and 3) taken by packets flowing between those points. This makes it possible to trace activity among all of the devices in your Cisco IP Telephony solutions architecture.

Learn More About CiscoWorks2000

Detailed information about CiscoWorks2000 is available at the following locations:

www.cisco.com/univercd/cc/td/doc/pcat/wrnemns1.htm

www.cisco.com/univercd/cc/td/doc/product/rtrmgmt/cw2000/

SNMP MIBs

A *Management Information Base (MIB)* is a structured set of data variables, called objects, in which each variable represents some resource to be managed. Simple Network Management Protocol (SNMP) MIB conceptual tables organize and distribute the information gathered from your IP telephony system.

SNMP allows CallManager to be managed with standard network management applications, such as CiscoWorks2000 or HP OpenView. Windows 2000 server provides an extensible SNMP agent that can be installed and run as a service. Cisco extension agents (dynamic link library, or DLL) support Cisco MIBs, which provides support for CallManager-specific data.

Compaq Insight Agent

For CallManager nodes that run on Compaq servers, the network management application can get system information from the Compaq Insight Agent through CPQHOST-MIB. There is no trap provided in this MIB, so the management application needs to poll the information that it is interested in periodically and generate its own trap when it reaches a certain threshold value.

CCM MIB Extension Agent

SNMP objects and traps are defined in CISCO-CCM-MIB. The CCM MIB extension agent implements the Cisco CallManager MIB. This MIB exports the data in the CallManager database and in other data sources. A *trap* is an unsolicited message sent by an agent to a management station in an asynchronous manner. The purpose is to notify the management station of some unusual event. The traps are sent to trap-receiving hosts configured in the Windows 2000 SNMP service. Network management applications such as Cisco Voice Health Manager (VHM) can gather data that can be used for fault management and analysis purposes. Although the design of the MIB and trap is tied to CiscoWorks2000 applications, it does not limit you from developing network management applications by using third-party software.

The SNMP extension agent for the CISCO-CCM-MIB is packaged as a DLL file and bundled in the CallManager installation.

End User Interface

The end user interface is through a network management application, such as the CiscoWorks2000 VHM application. The CallManager SNMP extension agent uses the Windows Event Log to report debug trace messages.

CDP MIB Extension Agent

The CDP MIB extension agent implements all of the variables related to the tell side of Cisco Discovery Protocol (CDP). The MIB variables implemented are cdpInterfaceTable, cdpGlobalRun, cdpGlobalMessageInterval, and cdpGlobalDeviceId. This is the minimum CDP SNMP support that network management applications such as CiscoWorks2000 need to discover the CallManager server. The variable cdpGlobalDeviceId is of type DisplayString (meaning an alphanumeric string) and will return the same value that CDP reports in its CDP advertisement messages.

Updating the CISCO-CCM-MIB Information

The Cisco RIS Data Collector is primarily responsible for updating the information used by the SNMP agents, and it buffers the CISCO-CCM-MIB information that the agents process.

At startup, the Cisco RIS Data Collector updates all of the relevant information by periodically fetching data from CallManager or the CallManager database. This updated information is based on interaction with CallManager and other CallManager-associated services.

Updating the CISCO-CDP-MIB Information

At startup, the CDP SNMP extension agent interacts with the CDP driver, fetching and buffering CDP-related information.

Read-Only Access

Unless otherwise specified, all traps and objects have read-only access.

Downloading the Latest MIBs

New features and bug fixes cause the CISCO-CCM-MIB to be routinely updated. You can download the latest MIB from the following location:

```
ftp.cisco.com/pub/mibs
```

This site provides detailed information about hundreds of MIBs, including CISCO-CDP-MIB and other MIBs that may be of interest to you.

CISCO-CCM-MIB

The Cisco CallManager MIB, CISCO-CCM-MIB, is used to export CallManager data. A CallManager system can be composed of multiple regions, with each region potentially consisting of several CallManager nodes. The MIB can be used by CallManager to present provision and statistics information. This section describes the objects in the CISCO-CCM-MIB.

CallManager Group Table (ccmGroupTable)

The CallManager Group Table lists the Cisco CallManager groups in the system. The table is indexed by ccmGroupIndex. Table 6-22 provides information about the CallManager Group table.

Table 6-22 *ccmGroupTable Objects*

Object	Type	Description
CcmGroupIndex	A numeric value with a range of 1 to 4294967295	An arbitrary integer, selected by the local CallManager, that uniquely identifies a Cisco CallManager group. The local CallManager is the server where CallManager is running.

Table 6-22 *ccmGroupTable Objects (Continued)*

Object	Type	Description
ccmGroupName	The CallManager group name, up to 128 alphanumeric characters	The name of the CallManager group.
ccmGroupTftpDefault	A Boolean value, either yes or no	Indicates whether this is the default TFTP server group.

Cisco CallManager Table (ccmTable)

This table lists all CallManager nodes registered. This list of CallManager nodes is the same one that is passed to the devices during the registration process. The table is indexed by ccmIndex. Table 6-23 provides information about ccmTable objects.

Table 6-23 *ccmTable Objects*

Object	Type	Description
CcmIndex	A numeric value with a range of 1 to 4294967295.	An arbitrary integer, selected by the local CallManager, that uniquely identifies a CallManager in a system.
CcmIndexOrZero	A numeric value with a range of 0 to 4294967295.	This textual convention is an extension of the CcmIndex convention. The latter defines a number greater than 0 to identify an entry of the CCM MIB table in the managed system. This extension permits the additional value of 0. The value 0 is object-specific and must be defined as part of the description of any object that uses this syntax.
ccmName	An alphanumeric string with a range of 0 to 128 characters.	The name or IP address of CallManager.
ccmDescription	An alphanumeric string with a range of 0 to 255 characters.	The description for CallManager.
ccmVersion	An alphanumeric string with a range of 0 to 24 characters.	The CallManager version number.

continues

Table 6-23 *ccmTable Objects (Continued)*

Object	Type	Description
ccmStatus **Note:** ccmStatus has been updated for CallManager release 3.1	A numeric value where 1 = Unknown: Current status of CallManager is unknown. 2 = Up: CallManager is running and can communicate with other CallManager nodes. 3 = Down: CallManager is down or the Agent cannot communicate with the local CallManager.	The current status of CallManager. CallManager is up if the SNMP agent received a system up event from the local CallManager system.
ccmInetAddressType **Note:** ccmInetAddressType is new for CallManager release 3.1	A value that represents a type of Internet address. Valid values are 0 = Unknown: An unknown address type. This value must be used if the value of the corresponding InetAddress object is a zero-length string. It can also be used to indicate an IP address that is not in one of the following formats: 1 = IPv4: An IP version 4 address as defined by the InetAddressIPv4 textual convention. 2 = ipv6: An IP version 6 address as defined by the InetAddressIPv6 textual convention. 16 = DNS: A DNS domain name as defined by the InetAddressDNS textual convention.	The IP address type of ccmInetAddress.
CcmInetAddress **Note:** ccmInetAddress is new for CallManager release 3.1	A generic Internet address.	The last known IP address of the CallManager system.

Table 6-23 *ccmTable Objects (Continued)*

Object	Type	Description
ccmClusterID **Note:** ccmClusterID is new for CallManager release 3.1	An alphanumeric string with a range of 0 to 128.	The ID of the cluster to which CallManager belongs.

Cisco CallManager Group Mapping Table (ccmGroupMappingTable)

This table lists all CallManager-to-group mappings in a CallManager system. The table is indexed by ccmGroupIndex and ccmIndex. Table 6-24 provides information about ccmGroupMappingTable.

Table 6-24 *ccmGroupMappingTable*

Object	Type	Description
ccmGroupMappingCMPriority	A 32-bit number that can only be positive	The priority of the CallManager in the group. Sets the order of the CallManager in the list.

Region Table (ccmRegionTable)

This table lists all geographically separated regions in a CallManager system. Regions are used to limit the bandwidth usage between devices that are assigned to different (or the same) regions. The table is indexed by ccmRegionIndex. Table 6-25 provides information about ccmRegionTable objects.

Table 6-25 *ccmRegionTable Objects*

Object	Type	Description
ccmRegionIndex	A 32-bit number that can be positive	An arbitrary integer, selected by the local CallManager, that uniquely identifies a region name in the table
ccmRegionName	The region name, up to 128 alphanumeric characters	The name of the region

Cisco CallManager Region Pair Table (ccmRegionPairTable)

This table lists all geographical region pairs in a CallManager system. The pair consists of the Source region and Destination region. The table is indexed by cmRegionSrcIndex and ccmRegionDestIndex. Table 6-26 provides information about ccmGroupRegionPairTable.

Table 6-26 *ccmRegionPairTable*

Object	Type	Description
ccmRegionAvailableBandwidth	A number where 1 = Unknown: Unknown bandwidth 2 = Other: Unidentified bandwidth 3 = bwG723: For low bandwidth using G.723 codec 4 = bwG729: For low bandwidth using G.729 codec 5 = bwG711: For high bandwidth using G.711 codec	The maximum available bandwidth between the two regions. If the bandwidth is 1000 kbps or more, the link is considered to be a high/unlimited bandwidth link, and the calls between the regions will use either G.711 or G.723 standards. (They attempt to use G.711 first.) If the bandwidth is 56 kbps, it is considered to be a low-bandwidth link, and G.723 will be used for calls between those regions.

Time Zone Group Table (ccmTimeZoneTable)

This table lists the time zone groups configured in a CallManager system. The phones use the time zone information to display the time for their region. The table is indexed by ccmTimeZoneIndex. Table 6-27 provides information about ccmTimeZoneTable objects.

Table 6-27 *ccmTimeZoneTable Objects*

Object	Type	Description
ccmTimeZoneIndex	A 32-bit number that can be positive	An arbitrary integer, selected by the local CallManager, that uniquely identifies a time zone group entry in the table
ccmTimeZoneName	The time zone group name, up to 128 alphanumeric characters	The name of the time zone group
ccmTimeZoneOffset	A 32-bit number that can be either positive or negative with a range of –12 to 12	The offset of the time zone group's time zone from Greenwich Mean Time (GMT)

Device Pool Table (ccmDevicePoolTable)

This table lists device pools configured in a CallManager system. Each device in the CallManager system belongs to only one device pool. This determines the region and time zone for the devices in the pool. A device pool contains region, date/time group, and CallManager group criteria that is common among many devices. The table is indexed by ccmDevicePoolIndex. Table 6-28 provides information about ccmDevicePoolTable objects.

Table 6-28   *ccmDevicePoolTable Objects*

Object	Type	Description
ccmDevicePoolIndex	A 32-bit number that can be positive.	An arbitrary integer, selected by the local CallManager, that uniquely identifies a device pool entry in the table.
ccmDevicePoolName	The device pool name, up to 128 alphanumeric characters.	The name of the device pool.
ccmDevicePoolRegionIndex	A 32-bit number that can be either positive or zero. A value of 0 indicates that the index to the Region table is Unknown.	The ID of the device region to which this device pool maps. A positive value of this index is used to identify the region to which this device pool entry belongs.
CcmDevicePoolTimeZone-Index	A 32-bit number that can be either positive or zero. A value of 0 indicates that the index to the TimeZone table is Unknown.	The ID of the time zone group to which this device pool belongs. A positive value of this index is used to identify the time zone to which this device pool entry belongs.
ccmDevicePoolGroupIndex	A 32-bit number that can be positive or zero. A value of 0 indicates that the index to the CallManager group table is Unknown.	The index of the CallManager group to which this device pool is tagged. A positive value of this index is used to identify the CallManager group to which this device pool entry belongs.

Phone Detail Info Table (ccmPhoneTable)

This table lists IP phones that have registered to the local CallManager system at least once. The table is indexed by phoneIndex.

NOTE	For CallManager release 3.1, IpAddress has been replaced with InetAddress and InetAddressType. The ccmPhoneTable contained the deprecated IpAddress object type. In CallManager release 3.1, these tables have been updated to use the new object types for supporting IP version 6 addresses, as defined in the RFC 2851.

Table 6-29 provides information about ccmPhoneTable objects.

Table 6-29 *ccmPhoneTable Objects*

Object	Type	Description
ccmPhoneIndex	A 32-bit number that can be positive.	An arbitrary integer, selected by the local CallManager, that uniquely identifies a phone within CallManager.
ccmPhonePhysicalAddress	The phone's MAC address.	The hardware-dependent MAC address of the phone.
ccmPhoneType	A numeric value where. 1 = unknown phone type. 2 = unidentified phone type. 3 = Cisco IP Phone 30SP+ (obsolete). 4 = Cisco IP Phone 12SP+. 5 = Cisco IP Phone 12SP (obsolete). 6 = Cisco IP Phone 12S (obsolete). 7 = Cisco IP Phone 30VIP. 8 = Cisco IP Phone 7910. 9 = Cisco IP Phone 7960. 10 = Cisco IP Phone 7940. 11 = Cisco IP SoftPhone. 12 = Cisco IP Conference Station 7935.	The phone model.
ccmPhoneDescription	The phone description, up to 255 alphanumeric characters.	The description of the phone. When the phone is configured in CallManager, the user can enter a description for the phone.

Table 6-29 *ccmPhoneTable Objects (Continued)*

Object	Type	Description
ccmPhoneUserName	The user name, up to 255 alphanumeric characters.	The user name assigned to the phone. When the phone is not in use, the name refers to the last known user assigned to the phone.
ccmPhoneIpAddress	The phone's IP address, typically in IP version 4 dotted-decimal format.	The last known IP address of the phone.
ccmPhoneStatus	A numeric value where. 1 = Unknown: Unknown status. 2 = Active: Active and registered with the local CallManager. 3 = Lost Contact: Lost contact or is no longer registered with the local CallManager.	The state of the phone. The state of the phone changes from Unknown to Active when it registers with the local CallManager.
ccmPhoneTimeLastRegistered	The date and time.	The time in milliseconds when the phone last registered with CallManager.
ccmPhoneE911Location	The E911 location, up to 255 alphanumeric characters.	The E911 location of the phone.
ccmPhoneLoadID	The load ID, up to 128 alphanumeric characters.	The phone's firmware load ID.
ccmPhoneLastError	A 32-bit number that can be either positive or negative with a range from -1 to 65535. A positive value or 0 indicates the last error reported by the phone. A value of -1 indicates that the last error reported is Unknown.	The error ID of the last error reported by the phone.
ccmPhoneTimeLastError	The date and time.	The amount of time elapsed since the last phone error occurred. The reference point for this time is the time the last error occurred, as reported by the local CallManager.

continues

Table 6-29 *ccmPhoneTable Objects (Continued)*

Object	Type	Description
cmPhoneDevicePoolIndex **Note:** This object is new for CallManager release 3.1	A positive number. A value of 0 indicates that the index to the Device Pool table is Unknown.	A positive value of this index is used to identify the Device Pool to which this Phone entry belongs.
ccmPhoneInetAddressType **Note:** This object is new for CallManager release 3.1.	A value that represents a type of Internet address. Valid values are 0 = Unknown: An unknown address type. This value must be used if the value of the corresponding InetAddress object is a zero-length string. It can also be used to indicate an IP address that is not in one of the following formats: 1 = IPv4: An IP version 4 address as defined by the InetAddressIPv4 textual convention. 2 = IPv6: An IP version 6 address as defined by the InetAddressIPv6 textual convention. 16 = DNS: A DNS domain name as defined by the InetAddressDNS textual convention.	Represents the type of address stored in ccmPhoneInetAddress.
ccmPhoneInetAddress **Note:** This object is new for CallManager release 3.1.	A generic Internet address.	The phone's last known IP address.

Phone Extension Table (ccmPhoneExtensionTable)

This table lists the IP phone extensions configured in a CallManager system. The table is indexed by CcmPhoneIpAddress and CcmPhoneExtensionIndex.

NOTE   For CallManager release 3.1, IpAddress has been replaced with InetAddress and InetAddressType. The ccmPhoneExtensionTable contained the deprecated IpAddress object type. In CallManager release 3.1, these tables have been updated to use the new object types for supporting IP version 6 addresses, as defined in the RFC 2851.

Table 6-30 provides information about ccmPhoneExtensionTable objects.

Table 6-30   *ccmPhoneExtensionTable Objects*

Object	Type	Description
ccmPhoneExtensionIndex	A 32-bit number that can be positive.	An arbitrary integer, selected by the local system, that uniquely identifies a phone extension within CallManager.
ccmPhoneExtension	Any number between 0 and 24.	The extension number for the phone extension.
ccmPhoneExtensionIpAddress	The phone's IP address, typically in IP version 4 dotted-decimal format.	The IP address of the phone.
ccmPhoneExtensionMultiLines	A 32-bit number that can only be positive.	The number of multiline appearances for each phone extension.
ccmPhoneExtensionInet-AddressType **Note:** This object is new for CallManager release 3.1.	A value that represents a type of Internet address. Valid values are 0 = Unknown: An unknown address type. This value must be used if the value of the corresponding InetAddress object is a zero-length string. It can also be used to indicate an IP address that is not in one of the following formats: 1 = IPv4: An IP version 4 address as defined by the InetAddressIPv4 textual convention. 2 = IPv6: An IP version 6 address as defined by the InetAddressIPv6 textual convention. 16 = DNS: A DNS domain name as defined by the InetAddressDNS textual convention.	The type of address stored in ccmPhoneExtensionInet-Address.

continues

Table 6-30 *ccmPhoneExtensionTable Objects (Continued)*

Object	Type	Description
CcmPhoneExtensionInet-Address **Note:** This object is new for CallManager release 3.1.	A generic Internet address.	The IP address of the extension.

ccmPhoneFailedTable Object

This table lists all initialization failures that occurred with respect to an IP phone that attempted to register to the local CallManager. Each entry of this table is stored only for the duration specified in the ccmPhoneFailedStorePeriod object. When this interval is set to 0, all table entries are deleted and no new entries are created. Reasons for these failures might include configuration error, maximum number of phones has been reached, lost contact, and so on. These failures are recorded for both Cisco IP Phones and Cisco IP SoftPhones. Table 6-31 provides information about ccmPhoneFailedTable objects.

Table 6-31 *ccmPhoneFailedTable Object*

Object	Type	Description
ccmPhoneFailedIndex	A 32-bit number that can be positive.	An arbitrary integer, selected by the local CallManager, that is incremented with each new entry in the ccmPhoneFailedTable. This integer value will wrap if needed.
ccmPhoneFailedTime	The date and time.	A time stamp for when the phone failed to register with CallManager.
ccmPhoneFailedName	The phone name, up to 64 alphanumeric characters.	The name assigned to the phone when it was added to CallManager. It contains an ASCII form of the phone's MAC address.

Table 6-31   *ccmPhoneFailedTable Object (Continued)*

Object	Type	Description
ccmPhoneFailedInetAddress-Type	A value that represents a type of Internet address. Valid values are 0 = Unknown: An unknown address type. This value must be used if the value of the corresponding InetAddress object is a zero-length string. It can also be used to indicate an IP address that is not in one of the following formats: 1 = IPv4: An IP version 4 address as defined by the InetAddressIPv4 textual convention. 2 = IPv6: An IP version 6 address as defined by the InetAddressIPv6 textual convention. 16 = DNS: A DNS domain name as defined by the InetAddressDNS textual convention.	InetAddress Type of ccmPhoneInetAddress.
ccmPhoneFailedInetAddress	A generic Internet address. A value of all zeros indicates that the IP address of a device is unavailable.	The last known IP address of the phone experiencing a communication failure.

continues

Table 6-31 *ccmPhoneFailedTable Object (Continued)*

Object	Type	Description
ccmPhoneFailCauseCode	A numeric value where 1 = Unknown: Unknown error cause. 2 = NoEntryInDatabase: The device is not configured in the system. 3 = DatabaseConfigurationError: There is some device configuration error in the database. 4 = DeviceNameUnresolveable: CallManager tried to get the device's IP address based on the device name, but cannot find it in its internal table. 5 = MaxDevRegExceeded: The maximum number of this device has been exceeded. 6 = ConnectivityError: CallManager cannot establish communication with the device during the registration process. 7 = InitializationError: There is an error when CallManager tries to initialize the device.	The reason for the device communication error.

ccmPhoneStatusUpdateTable Object

This table lists phone status updates, including when the phone lost contact or registered with CallManager. This table provides only the historical information of when these update events occurred; it does not provide the details of the phone itself. For the management application to get the detailed phone information, it must make a cross-reference to the ccmPhoneTable using the ccmPhoneIndex provided in this table. Cisco IP SoftPhone's status changes are not recorded in this table. Only hard phones such as Cisco IP Phone 12SP+, 30VIP, 7960, 7940, 7910 and so on are reported when their statuses change. Each entry of this table is stored only for the duration specified in the ccmPhoneStatusUpdateStorePeriod object. When this interval is set to 0, all table entries are deleted and no new entries are created. Table 6-32 provides information about ccmPhoneStatusUpdateTable objects.

Table 6-32   *ccmPhoneStatusUpdateTable Object*

Object	Type	Description
ccmPhoneStatusUpdateIndex	A 32-bit number that can be positive.	An arbitrary integer, selected by the local Cisco CallManager, that is incremented with each new entry in the ccmPhoneStatusUpdateTable. This integer value will wrap if needed.
ccmPhoneStatusPhoneIndex	A 32-bit number that can be either positive or negative. A value of 0 indicates that the index to the ccmPhoneTable is Unknown.	A positive value of this index is used to identify an entry in the ccmPhoneTable.
ccmPhoneStatusUpdateTime	The date and time.	The time of the phone's registration status change.
ccmPhoneStatusUpdateType	A numeric value where 1 = Unknown: Unknown error cause. 2 = phoneRegistered: The phone has registered with CallManager. 3 = phoneLostContact: The phone has lost contact with CallManager.	The type of status updates.

Gateway Info Table (ccmGatewayTable)

This table lists gateways that have registered with the local CallManager at least once. The table is indexed by the ccmGatewayIndex.

NOTE   For CallManager release 3.1, a new column was added at the end of the ccmGatewayTable object to include the Inet address and Inet address type of the gateway in this table.

Table 6-33 provides information about ccmGatewayTable objects.

Table 6-33 *ccmGatewayTable Objects*

Object	Type	Description
ccmGatewayIndex	A 32-bit number that can be positive.	The index of the entry in the table.
ccmGatewayName	The gateway name, up to 128 alphanumeric characters.	The name assigned to the gateway in CallManager Administration. This name is assigned when a new device of type *Gateway* is added to the CallManager database.
ccmGatewayType	A numeric value where 1 = Unknown: Unknown gateway type. 2 = Other: Unidentified gateway type. 3 = Cisco Analog Access. 4 = Cisco Digital Access PRI. 5 = Cisco Digital Access T1. 6 = Cisco Digital Access PRI Plus. 7 = Cisco Catalyst 6000 E1 (WS-X6608). 8 = Cisco Catalyst 6000 T1 (WS-X6608). 9 = Cisco Catalyst 6000 FXS (WS-X6624). 10 = Cisco MGCP gateway. 11 = Cisco DT-30+ Digital Access E1. 12 = Cisco DT-24+ Digital Access T1. 13 = Cisco Catalyst 6000 PRI (WS-X6608). 14 = Cisco Catalyst 6000 FXO (WS-X6612). 15 = Cisco MGCP trunk. 16 = Cisco VG200. 17 = Cisco Catalyst 26xx series. 18 = Cisco 362x series. 19 = Cisco 364x series. 20 = Cisco 366x series.	The gateway model.

Table 6-33 *ccmGatewayTable Objects (Continued)*

Object	Type	Description
ccmGatewayDescription	The gateway description, up to 255 alphanumeric characters.	The gateway description. The gateway was given its description when it was added or configured in CallManager Administration.
ccmGatewayStatus	A numeric value where 1 = Unknown: Gateway status is unknown. 2 = Registered: The gateway is active and registered with the local CallManager. 3 = Lost Contact: The gateway lost contact with or is no longer registered with the local CallManager.	The state of the gateway. The gateway status changes from Unknown to Registered when the gateway registers with the local CallManager.
ccmGatewayDevicePool Index	A numeric value. A value of 0 indicates that the index to the Device Pool table is Unknown.	A positive value of this index is used to identify the Device Pool to which this gateway entry belongs.
ccmGatewayInet-AddressType **Note:** This object is new for CallManager release 3.1.	A value that represents a type of Internet address. Valid values are 0 = Unknown: An unknown address type. This value must be used if the value of the corresponding InetAddress object is a zero-length string. It can also be used to indicate an IP address that is not in one of the following formats: 1 = IPv4: An IP version 4 address as defined by the InetAddressIPv4 textual convention. 2 = IPv6: An IP version 6 address as defined by the InetAddressIPv6 textual convention. 16 = DNS: A DNS domain name as defined by the InetAddressDNS textual convention.	Represents the type of address stored in ccmGatewayInetAddress.

continues

Table 6-33 *ccmGatewayTable Objects (Continued)*

Object	Type	Description
ccmGatewayInet-Address **Note:** This object is new for CallManager release 3.1.	A generic Internet address. A value of all zeros indicates that the IP address is not available.	The last known IP address of the gateway.

Gateway Trunk Table (ccmGatewayTrunkTable)

NOTE   The ccmGatewayTrunkTable is obsolete in CallManager release 3.1. The gateway trunk information is available directly from the gateway itself. It is presented here only for reference for systems before release 3.1.

This table lists the registered endpoints in the gateways and their status. The information about the trunks is only partial and complementary to the information that can be obtained from the VOICE-IF-MIB and VOICE-ANALOG-IF-MIB that are implemented by the IOS gateways. The table is indexed by ccmGatewayTrunkIndex. Table 6-34 provides information about ccmGatewayTrunkTable objects.

Table 6-34   *ccmGatewayTrunkTable Objects*

Object	Type	Description
CcmGatewayTrunkIndex	A 32-bit number that can be positive.	An arbitrary integer, selected by the local CallManager, that uniquely identifies a gateway trunk within the scope of CallManager.

Table 6-34 *ccmGatewayTrunkTable Objects (Continued)*

Object	Type	Description
CcmGatewayTrunkType	A numeric value where 1 = Unknown: Unknown trunk type. 2 = Other: Unidentified trunk type. 3 = Ground Start trunk: Provides far-end disconnect supervision. 4 = Loop Start trunk: Provides no far-end disconnect supervision. 5 = DID trunk: Direct Inward Dial. 6 = POTS. 7 = E&M Type 1. 8 = E&M Type 2. 9 = E&M Type 3. 10 = E&M Type 4. 11 = E&M Type 5. 12 = Analog. 13 = PRI. 14 = BRI.	The type of the endpoint.
CcmGatewayTrunkName	The gateway trunk name, up to 128 alphanumeric characters.	The name of the trunk as defined in CallManager Administration.
CcmTrunkGatewayIndex	A 32-bit number that can be either positive or negative. A value of 0 indicates that the index to the gateway table is Unknown.	A positive value of this index is used to identify the gateway to which this trunk entry belongs.

continues

Table 6-34 *ccmGatewayTrunkTable Objects (Continued)*

Object	Type	Description
CcmGatewayTrunkStatus	A numeric value where 1 = Unknown: Unknown state of trunk. 2 = Up: The trunk is up and running and is idle with no calls. 3 = Busy: The trunk is in a busy state. 4 = Down: The trunk is down.	The state of the trunk. The trunk status changes from Unknown to Up when it registers with the local CallManager.

SNMP Objects

The following SNMP objects are provided for phones and gateways:

- ccmActivePhones—This SNMP object has a count of the number of active phones (registered and sending KeepAlives) for CallManager. This variable is of type Counter32.

- ccmInActivePhones—The number of phones that are registered but lost contact with CallManager. The phones are considered to have lost contact with CallManager if CallManager does not receive any KeepAlives. This variable is of type Counter32.

- ccmActiveGateways—The number of gateways configured with this CallManager and actively in communication (by KeepAlives) with CallManager. This variable is of type Counter32.

- ccmInActiveGateways—The number of gateways that have registered but lost contact with CallManager. The gateways are considered to have lost contact if CallManager does not receive any KeepAlives. This variable is of type Counter32.

ccmMediaDeviceTable

This table lists media devices that have registered with the local CallManager at least once. Table 6-35 provides information about ccmMediaDeviceTable objects.

Table 6-35 *ccmMediaDeviceTable Objects*

Object	Type	Description
ccmMediaDeviceIndex	A 32-bit number that can be positive.	An arbitrary integer, selected by the local CallManager, that identifies a media device entry in the table.

Table 6-35 *ccmMediaDeviceTable Objects (Continued)*

Object	Type	Description
ccmMediaDeviceName	The media device name, up to 128 alphanumeric characters.	This is the device name assigned to the media device. This name is assigned when a new device of this type is added to CallManager Administration.
ccmMediaDeviceType	A numeric value where 1 = Unknown device type. 2 = WS-X6608 media termination point. 3 = WS-X6608 software conference bridge.	The media device type.
ccmMediaDeviceDescription	The media device description, up to 128 alphanumeric characters.	The description assigned to the media device when it is configured in CallManager Administration.
ccmMediaDeviceStatus	A numeric value where 1 = Unknown: Unknown state of the media device. 2 = Registered: The media device is configured and registered with CallManager. 3 = Lost contact: The media device is in Configured state initially but has not sent KeepAlives for a while.	The state of the media device. The status changes from Unknown to Registered when it registers with the local CallManager.
ccmMediaDeviceDevicePool-Index	A 32-bit number that can be either positive or negative. A value of 0 indicates that the index to the Device Pool table is Unknown.	A positive value of this index is used to identify the device pool to which this media device entry belongs.

continues

Table 6-35 *ccmMediaDeviceTable Objects (Continued)*

Object	Type	Description
ccmMediaDeviceInetAddress Type	A value that represents a type of Internet address. Valid values are	Represents the type of address stored in ccmMediaDeviceInetAddress.
	0 = Unknown: An unknown address type. This value must be used if the value of the corresponding InetAddress object is a zero-length string. It can also be used to indicate an IP address that is not in one of the following formats:	
	1 = IPv4: An IP version 4 address as defined by the InetAddressIPv4 textual convention.	
	2 = IPv6: An IP version 6 address as defined by the InetAddressIPv6 textual convention.	
	16 = DNS: A DNS domain name as defined by the InetAddressDNS textual convention.	
ccmMediaDeviceInetAddress	A generic Internet address. A value of all zeros indicates that the IP address is Unknown.	The last known IP address of the media device.

ccmGatekeeperTable

This table lists gatekeepers that have registered to the local CallManager at least once. Table 6-36 provides information about ccmGatekeeperTable objects.

Table 6-36 *ccmGatekeeperTable Objects*

Object	Type	Description
ccmGatekeeperIndex	A 32-bit number that can be positive.	An arbitrary integer, selected by the local CallManager, that identifies a gatekeeper entry in the table.

Table 6-36   *ccmGatekeeperTable Objects (Continued)*

Object	Type	Description
ccmGatekeeperName	The gatekeeper name, up to 128 alphanumeric characters.	The gatekeeper name assigned to the gatekeeper. This name is assigned when the gatekeeper is added in CallManager Administration.
ccmGatekeeperType	A numeric value where 1 = Unknown gatekeeper. 2 = Unidentified gatekeeper. 3 = Terminal. 4 = Gateway.	The type of gatekeeper.
ccmGatekeeperDescription	The gatekeeper description, up to 128 alphanumeric characters.	The description assigned to the gatekeeper when it was configured in CallManager Administration.
ccmGatekeeperStatus	A numeric value where 1 = Unknown: Unknown state of gatekeeper. 2 = Registered: The gatekeeper is configured and registered with CallManager. 3 = Lost Contact: The gatekeeper has been configured but has not sent KeepAlives for a while.	The state of the gatekeeper. The gatekeeper status changes from Unknown to Registered when it registers with the local CallManager.
ccmGatekeeperDevicePool-Index	A 32-bit number that can be either positive or negative. A value of 0 indicates that the index to the Device Pool table is Unknown.	A positive value of this index is used to identify the Device Pool to which this gatekeeper entry belongs.

continues

Table 6-36 *ccmGatekeeperTable Objects (Continued)*

Object	Type	Description
ccmGatekeeperInetAddress-Type	A value that represents a type of Internet address. Valid values are	Represents the type of address stored in ccmGatekeeperInetAddress.
	0 = Unknown: An unknown address type. This value must be used if the value of the corresponding InetAddress object is a zero-length string. It can also be used to indicate an IP address that is not in one of the following formats:	
	1 = IPv4: An IP version 4 address as defined by the InetAddressIPv4 textual convention.	
	2 = IPv6: An IP version 6 address as defined by the InetAddressIPv6 textual convention.	
	16 = DNS: A DNS domain name as defined by the InetAddressDNS textual convention.	
ccmGatekeeperInetAddress	A generic Internet address. A value of all zeros indicates that the IP address is Unknown.	The last known IP address of the gatekeeper.

ccmCTIDeviceTable

This table lists Computer Telephony Interface (CTI) devices that have registered to the local CallManager at least once. Table 6-37 provides information about ccmCTIDeviceTable objects.

Table 6-37 *ccmCTIDeviceTable Objects*

Object	Type	Description
ccmCTIDeviceIndex	A 32-bit number that can be positive.	An arbitrary integer, selected by the local CallManager, that identifies a CTI device entry in the table.

Table 6-37   *ccmCTIDeviceTable Objects (Continued)*

Object	Type	Description
ccmCTIDeviceName	The CTI device name, up to 64 alphanumeric characters.	The name of the CTI device that is assigned when this device is added to CallManager Administration.
ccmCTIDeviceType	A numeric value where 1 = Unknown CTI device. 2 = Unidentified CTI device. 3 = CTI Route Point. 4 = CTI Port.	The type of the CTI device.
ccmCTIDeviceDescription	The CTI device description, up to 128 alphanumeric characters.	The description of the CTI device. This description is given when the CTI device is added or configured in CallManager Administration.
ccmCTIDeviceStatus	A numeric value where 1 = Unknown: Unknown state of the CTI device. 2 = Registered: The CTI device is active and registered with CallManager. 3 = Lost Contact: The CTI device has lost contact or is no longer registered with CallManager.	The state of the CTI device.
ccmCTIDevicePoolIndex	A 32-bit number that can be either positive or zero. A value of 0 indicates that the index to the Device Pool table is Unknown.	A positive value of this index is used to identify the Device Pool to which this CTI device entry belongs.

continues

Table 6-37 *ccmCTIDeviceTable Objects (Continued)*

Object	Type	Description
ccmCTIDeviceInetAddress-Type	A value that represents a type of Internet address. Valid values are 0 = Unknown: An unknown address type. This value must be used if the value of the corresponding InetAddress object is a zero-length string. It can also be used to indicate an IP address that is not in one of the following formats: 1 = IPv4: An IP version 4 address as defined by the InetAddressIPv4 textual convention. 2 = IPv6: An IP version 6 address as defined by the InetAddressIPv6 textual convention. 16 = DNS: A DNS domain name as defined by the InetAddressDNS textual convention.	Represents the type of address stored in ccmCTIDeviceInetAddress.
ccmCTIDeviceInetAddress	A generic Internet address. A value of all zeros indicates that the IP address is Unknown.	The IP address of the host where this CTI device is running.
ccmCTIDeviceAppInfo	An alphanumeric string with a range of 0 to 64 characters.	The appinfo string that indicates the application name or type of this CTI device. This information might not be available, especially when the application uses TAPI.

ccmCTIDeviceDirNumTable

This table lists directory numbers assigned to CTI devices that are configured in a CallManager system. Table 6-38 provides information about ccmCTIDeviceDirNumTable objects.

Table 6-38   *ccmCTIDeviceDirNumTable Objects*

Object	Type	Description
ccmCTIDeviceDirNumIndex	A 32-bit number that can be positive	An arbitrary integer, selected by the local system, that identifies a directory number of a CTI device registered to the local CallManager
ccmCTIDeviceDirNum	The CTI device directory number, up to 24 characters	The directory number of this CTI device

CISCO-CCM-MIB Traps and Objects

A *trap* or *notification* is an unsolicited message sent by an SNMP agent to a management station in an asynchronous manner. The purpose is to notify the management station of some unusual event. Some SNMP traps and their supporting objects are introduced in the CISCO-CCM-MIB to support event notification.

Configuration of SNMP Trap Receiver   The SNMP community strings and the SNMP trap receiver settings are configured through the Windows SNMP Service properties. Refer to the Windows online help for instructions on how to configure these settings.

Trap Enabling/Disabling Objects   The SNMP objects described in Table 6-39 are used to enable or disable the traps that are defined in the CISCO-CCM-MIB. This SNMP object allows only one setting for enabling or disabling traps in the system, therefore; the setting applies to all of the trap receivers where multiple trap receivers exist.

NOTE   This object provides read-write access.

Table 6-39 *Trap Enabling or Disabling Objects*

Object	Type	Description
ccmCallManagerAlarmEnable	A numeric value where 1 = True: Enabling this object allows the CallManager agent to generate the following alarms: ccmCallManagerFailure. ccmMediaResourceList-Exhausted. ccmRouteListExhausted. 2 = False: This is the default value.	Allows the generation of traps in response to CallManager general failures
ccmGatewayAlarmEnable	True or False, where 1 = True: Enabling this object allows the CallManager agent to generate the following: ccmGatewayFailed. ccmGatewayLayer2change notifications. 2 = False: This is the default value.	Allows the generation of alarms in response to gateway failures of which CallManager is aware

ccmPhoneFailedConfig Objects   These objects show the minimum interval time between the sending of ccmPhoneFailed trap notification and how long the failure information is kept in the ccmPhoneFailedTable. The ccmPhoneFailed trap is generated when the trap interval time has expired and at least one entry is in the ccmPhoneFailedTable. This method eliminates the need for the management application to poll the ccmPhoneFailedTable periodically, thereby reducing the amount of traffic. The management application needs to retrieve the failure information from ccmPhoneFailedTable only when it receives such a trap, provided that the store period has not expired. Therefore, the ccmPhoneFailedStorePeriod should be set to a higher value than the ccmPhoneFailedAlarmInterval. Note that the setting of the objects applies to all the trap receivers, and it will be made available only in the host where the agent resides.

Setting the ccmPhoneFailedAlarmInterval trap to zero can disable the trap notification in cases where the management application chooses to poll the ccmPhoneFailedTable periodically. Table 6-40 provides information about ccmPhoneFailedConfig objects.

Table 6-40 *ccmPhoneFailedConfig Objects*

Object	Type	Description
CcmPhoneFailedAlarm Interval	A number of seconds with a range from 0 seconds to 1 hour (3600 seconds) in 30-second increments. The default value is 0 seconds.	The minimum interval (in seconds) between sending of the ccmPhoneFailed notification. The ccmPhoneFailed notification is sent only when at least one entry is in the ccmPhoneFailedTable and the notification has not been sent for the last ccmPhoneFailedAlarmInterval defined in this object.
ccmPhoneFailedStorePeriod	A number of seconds with a range from 0 second to 1 hour (3600 seconds), in 60-second increments. The default value is 0 seconds.	The time duration in seconds for storing the failure information. This information is stored in the ccmPhoneFailedTable object. This value should ideally be set to a higher value than the value set in ccmPhoneFailedAlarmInterval object.

ccmPhoneStatusUpdateConfig Objects   These objects show the minimum interval time between the sending of ccmPhoneStatusUpdate trap notification and how long the status update information is kept in the ccmPhoneStatusUpdateTable. The ccmPhoneStatusUpdate trap is generated when the trap interval time has expired and at least one entry is in the ccmPhoneStatusUpdateTable. This method eliminates the need for the management application to poll the ccmPhoneStatusUpdateTable periodically, thereby reducing the amount of traffic. The management application needs to retrieve the information from ccmPhoneStatusUpdateTable only when it receives such a trap, provided the store period has not expired. Therefore, the ccmPhoneStatusUpdateStorePeriod should be set to a higher value than the ccmPhoneStatusUpdateTrapInterval. Note that the setting of the objects applies to all the trap receivers, and it will be made available only in the host where the agent resides.

NOTE   These objects have read-write access.

Setting the ccmPhoneStatusUpdateTrapInterval to zero can disable the trap notification in cases where the management application chooses to poll the ccmPhoneStatusUpdateTable periodically. Table 6-41 provides information about ccmPhoneStatusUpdateConfig objects.

Table 6-41 *ccmPhoneStatusUpdateConfig Objects*

Object	Type	Description
ccmPhoneStatusUpdateAlarm Interv	A number in seconds with a range from 0 seconds to 1 hour (3600 seconds) in 30-second increments. The default value is 0 seconds.	The minimum interval between sending of the ccmPhoneStatusUpdate notification in seconds. The ccmPhoneStatusUpdate notification is sent only when at least one entry is in the ccmPhoneStatusUpdateTable and the notification has not been sent for the last ccmPhoneStatusUpdateAlarm Interv defined in this object. A value of 0 indicates that the alarm notification is disabled.
ccmPhoneStatusUpdateStore-Period	A number in seconds with a range from 0 seconds to 1 hour (3600 seconds) in 60-second increments. The default value is 0 seconds.	The time duration for storing the phone status update information in seconds. This information is stored in the ccmPhoneStatusUpdateTable object. This value should ideally be set to a higher value than the value in the ccmPhoneStatusUpdateAlarm Interv object.

MIB Objects Used by CallManager Notifications/Alarms   Table 6-42 contains a list of objects that are used by the various CallManager notifications and alarm MIBs. Table 6-42 provides information about CallManager notification and alarm object MIBs.

Table 6-42   *CCM Notifications and Alarm MIB Objects*

Object	Type	Description
ccmAlarmSeverity	A numeric value where. 1 = Emergency: The system is unusable. 2 = Alert: Immediate response is needed. 3 = Critical: Critical condition. 4 = Error: Error condition. 5 = Warning: Warning condition. 6 = Notice: Normal but significant condition. 7 = Informational: Informational situation.	The alarm severity code.

continues

Table 6-42 *CCM Notifications and Alarm MIB Objects (Continued)*

Object	Type	Description
ccmFailCauseCode	A numeric value where 1 = Unknown: Unknown. 2 = heartBeatStopped: CallManager stopped generating a heartbeat. 3 = routerThreadDied: CallManager detected the death of the router thread. 4 = timerThreadDied: CallManager detected the death of the timer thread. 5 = criticalThreadDied: CallManager detected the death of one of its critical threads. 6 = deviceMgrInitFailed: CallManager failed to start its device manager subsystem. 7 = digitAnalysisInitFailed: CallManager failed to start its digit analysis subsystem. 8 = callControlInitFailed: CallManager failed to start its call control subsystem. 9 = linkMgrInitFailed: CallManager failed to start its link manager subsystem. 10 = dbMgrInitFailed: CallManager failed to start its database manager subsystem. 11 = msgTranslatorInitFailed: CallManager failed to start its message translation manager subsystem. 12 = suppServicesInitFailed: CallManager failed to start its supplementary services subsystem.	The cause code of the failure. This cause is derived from a monitoring thread in CallManager or from a heartbeat monitoring process.

Table 6-42   *CCM Notifications and Alarm MIB Objects (Continued)*

Object	Type	Description
ccmPhoneFailures	A 32-bit number that can only be positive.	The count of the phone initialization or communication failures that are stored in the ccmPhoneFailedTable object.
ccmPhoneUpdates	A 32-bit number that can only be positive.	The count of the phone status changes that are stored in the ccmPhoneStatusUpdateTable object.
ccmGatewayFailCauseCode	See the list of values in the CcmFailCauseCode object.	The reason for a gateway device communication error.
ccmMediaResourceType	A numeric value where 1 = Unknown: Unknown resource type. 2 = Media termination point. 3 = Transcoder. 4 = Conference bridge. 5 = Music on hold.	The resource types in a CallManager system.
ccmMediaResourceListName	The media resource list name, up to 128 alphanumeric characters.	The name of a media resource list. This name is assigned when a new media resource list is added to CallManager.
ccmRouteListName	The route list name, up to 128 alphanumeric characters.	The name of a route list. This name is assigned when a new route list is added in CallManager Administration.
ccmGatewayPhysIfIndex	A numeric value with a range up to 2147483647 characters.	The identifier of an interface in a gateway that has registered with the local CallManager. On a DS1/E1 interface, this should be the same as the ifIndex value in the gateway.
ccmGatewayPhysIfL2Status	A numeric value where 1 = Unknown status. 2 = Up: Interface is up. 3 = Down: Interface is down.	The Layer 2 status of a physical interface in a gateway that has registered with the local CallManager.

Notifications

Table 6-43 contains a list of notifications that are used by various CallManager objects and provides information about the notification MIBs.

Table 6-43 *Notification MIBs*

Notification	Object	Description
ccmCallManagerFailed	ccmAlarmSeverity ccmFailCauseCode	The CallManager process detected a failure in one of its critical subsystems. It can also be detected from a heartbeat/event monitoring process.
ccmPhoneFailed	ccmAlarmSeverity ccmPhoneFailures	Within the time interval specified in ccmPhoneFailedAlarmInterval, at least one phone has attempted to register or communicate with CallManager and failed.
ccmPhoneStatusUpdate	ccmAlarmSeverity ccmPhoneUpdates	Within the time interval specified in ccmPhoneStatusUpdateAlarm Interv, at least one phone has successfully registered with CallManager or has lost contact with CallManager.
ccmGatewayFailed	ccmAlarmSeverity ccmGatewayName ccmGatewayInetAddressType ccmGatewayInetAddress ccmGatewayFailCauseCode	At least one gateway has attempted to register or communicate with CallManager and failed.
ccmMediaResourceList-Exhausted	ccmAlarmSeverity ccmMediaResourceType ccmMediaResourceListName	CallManager has run out of a certain specified type of resource.
ccmRouteListExhausted	ccmAlarmSeverity ccmRouteListName	CallManager could not find an available route in the indicated route list.

Table 6-43   *Notification MIBs (Continued)*

Notification	Object	Description
ccmGatewayLayer2Change	ccmAlarmSeverity ccmGatewayName ccmGatewayInetAddressType ccmGatewayInetAddress ccmGatewayPhysIfIndex ccmGatewayPhysIfL2Status	A state change has been detected in the D-Channel/ Layer 2 of an interface in a Skinny Protocol gateway that has registered with CallManager.

Additional SYSAPPL-MIB Support

In CallManager release 3.0, an SNMP subagent was implemented to support SYSAPPL MIB. It included Cisco CallManager, Cisco TFTP, and Cisco CallManager database layer (DBL) applications for a CallManager system. These applications are presented in the sysApplInstallPkgTable, and each has one or more associated elements in the sysApplInstallElmtTable. In CallManager release 3.1, the SYSAPPL support has been extended to include the items in Table 6-44.

You can get complete information in the SYSAPPL-MIB. See "Downloading the Latest MIBs" earlier in this chapter for more information.

Table 6-44   *Additional SYSAPPL-MIB Support*

Entry Name	Type	Associated To
Cisco CTIManager	sysApplInstallElmtEntry and sysApplElmtRunEntry	Cisco CallManager
Cisco IP Voice Media Streaming Application	sysApplInstallElmtEntry and sysApplElmtRunEntry	Cisco CallManager
DC Directory Service	sysApplInstallPkgEntry and sysApplRunEntry	N/A
CCM Database Publisher	sysApplInstallPkgEntry and sysApplRunEntry	N/A
CCM Database Subscriber	sysApplInstallPkgEntry and sysApplRunEntry	N/A
Cisco RIS Data Collector	sysApplInstallPkgEntry and sysApplRunEntry	N/A
Cisco MOH Audio Translator	sysApplInstallPkgEntry and sysApplRunEntry	N/A
Cisco Messaging Interface	sysApplInstallPkgEntry and sysApplRunEntry	N/A

continues

Table 6-44 *Additional SYSAPPL-MIB Support (Continued)*

Entry Name	Type	Associated To
Cisco Syslog Collector	sysApplInstallPkgEntry and sysApplRunEntry	N/A
Cisco Web Attendant Server	sysApplInstallPkgEntry and sysApplRunEntry	N/A

Microsoft Performance

Microsoft Performance is a Windows 2000 Administrative Tool that monitors and logs resource counters from CallManager nodes in the network. Microsoft Performance shows CallManager-specific status information and Windows 2000 system information in real time. Statistical information is gathered by the CallManager system and fed into Microsoft Performance by way of objects and counters. For example, you can monitor the number of calls in progress at any time, or the number of calls currently passing through a specific Cisco gateway.

Microsoft Performance can collect data from multiple systems at once and compile it into a single log file. The logged information can be viewed in Microsoft Performance and then exported to tab separated value (TSV) or comma separated value (CSV) file format that can be viewed with most spreadsheet applications.

Microsoft Performance lets you view statistical data in graphical, histogram, and report form. You can access Microsoft Performance by clicking **Start > Programs > Administrative Tools > Performance**.

Customizing Microsoft Performance

Like the Admin. Serviceability Tool provided in CallManager Serviceability (discussed earlier in this chapter in the section "Cisco CallManager Serviceability"), you use Microsoft Performance to monitor various real-time conditions in a CallManager system. For example, you can discover the number of calls in progress on a particular CallManager system at any time, or the number of calls currently being attempted in a CallManager cluster. This information can be useful for capacity planning, network planning and design, load balancing, and troubleshooting, among other uses.

Each object includes counters that keep track of statistics such as the number of registered MGCP gateways or the number of registered hardware phones. These counters define current conditions within groups of related information. Each group of related information can be considered an object that contains multiple counters, such as Cisco CallManager or Cisco Software Conference Bridge, and each of these objects can have more than one instance. Objects and counters are automatically added when CallManager or the related component (such as Conference Bridge) is installed. Using objects and counters, you can retrieve detailed, relevant, and timely system information. Microsoft Performance can also be customized to track Cisco applications such as the IP IVR or Windows 2000 system objects and counters. Object and counter descriptions are provided in the section "Admin. Serviceability Tool (AST)."

Data Availability

Microsoft Performance data is available only for installed components. For example, to view Cisco CallManager counters, CallManager must be installed on the computer you are attempting to monitor. Also, statistics must be enabled in CallManager Administration for Microsoft Performance to collect data. Statistics are enabled by default. They can be turned on or off in the Service Parameters Configuration screen in CallManager Administration (**System > Service Parameters** > *StatisticsEnable parameter set to* **True** *to enable or* **False** *to disable statistics*).

Learn More About Microsoft Performance

Detailed information about Microsoft Performance is available in Microsoft Windows 2000 documentation.

Remote Serviceability

Remote Serviceability tools are used by Cisco Systems Engineers (SEs) to gather system and debug information when troubleshooting or diagnostic help is needed for your Cisco CallManager system.

Cisco Bridged Telnet

Bridged Telnet provides transparent firewall access to CallManager servers for remote diagnostic and troubleshooting assistance. This is useful when you want to call in problems that require diagnosis of a remote CallManager server by an SE. Bridged Telnet works by enabling a Telnet client to connect to a Telnet daemon behind a firewall at your site. Using an external proxy machine, the system relays TCP/IP communications from behind your firewall to a host behind another firewall at the Cisco Technical Assistance Center (TAC). This relay server maintains the integrity and configuration of both firewalls, yet supports secure communication between each of the shielded remote systems. No modifications to your firewall are necessary. Cisco Systems cannot telnet into your system without permission and assistance from your site.

Figure 6-16 shows the customer site on the left and the TAC on the right. In the center connecting the two systems is the relay server, which connects the two systems transparently, allowing the same access as if the machine was being used locally, and maintaining firewall configuration and security for both sites.

Figure 6-16 *Bridged Telnet System*

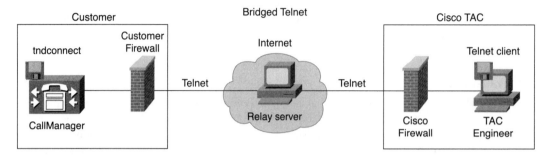

Bridged Telnet requires your network administrator to work in conjunction with an SE to set up the bridged Telnet system. When set up, Bridged Telnet provides communication with any CallManager node at your site. The requests and responses exchanged between your site and the Cisco TAC can be viewed onscreen in real time. In addition, all Telnet exchanges generate logs that can be reviewed later.

Learn More About Bridged Telnet

Additional information about Bridged Telnet is available at the following location:

```
www.cisco.com/univercd/cc/td/doc/product/voice/c_callmg/3_0/service/index.htm
```

Cisco Discovery Protocol (CDP)

CDP allows CallManager to advertise itself to other Cisco devices on the network by sending periodic messages to a well-known Multicast address monitored by other neighbor devices. Network operators and analysts use this information for configuration monitoring, topology discovery, and fault diagnosis purposes.

With CDP support, CallManager periodically sends out CDP messages or Protocol Data Units (PDUs) on the active physical interfaces. These messages contain CallManager information such as the device ID, interface name, system capabilities, and so on. Any Cisco devices with CDP support can discover CallManager by listening to these periodic messages.

Q931 Translator

Q931 Translator filters Integrated Services Digital Network (ISDN) Layer 3 protocol messages produced by the CallManager system in SDI trace files, then parses and translates them into Cisco IOS-equivalent messages. These messages can be useful in diagnosing and troubleshooting connectivity problems in CallManager installations. Because you can use Trace Analysis in CallManager Serviceability to filter out unwanted information from SDI trace files, the Q931 Translator has been rendered nearly obsolete. However, the tool is still available, should you want to use it.

Figure 6-17 displays the messages in the Q931 Translator interface.

Figure 6-17 *SDI Trace in Q931 Message Translator*

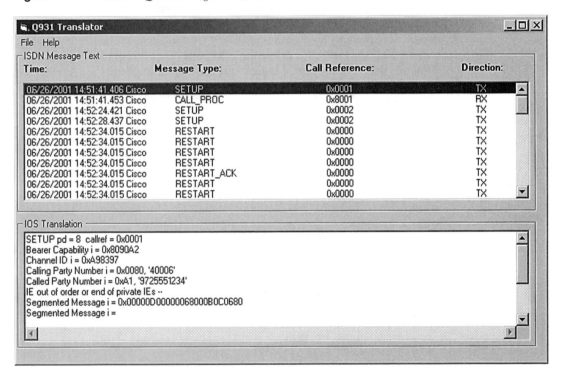

When generating SDI trace files using CallManager Serviceability, be advised that Q931 Translator can successfully translate only trace files that have been saved in text (.txt) format. XML-formatted trace files cannot be used with Q931 Translator.

Q931 Translator is available in the \Cisco\bin directory. Double-click **Q931Transaltor.exe** to launch the application.

Learn More About Q931 Translator

Online help about Q931 Translator is available through the **Help** menu in Q931 Translator.

Summary

This chapter provided information about two applications to assist with managing your network, BAT and ART. The important thing to consider is whether the tools described can help in your daily operations. In most cases, either BAT or ART (or both tools) can save you considerable time (and, therefore, money) in configuring, managing, and diagnosing your Cisco CallManager system.

Several monitoring applications were discussed, including CallManager Serviceability, which can assist in monitoring your system. You should understand how to use the features in CallManager Serviceability because these will help you with troubleshooting the system. In particular, the XML-formatted traces and the Trace Analysis tool help you simplify trace output by filtering traces for only those criteria relevant to your problem.

The CISCO-CCM-MIB and the Cisco AVVID IP Telephony objects and counters were provided in detail for your reference.

## CHAPTER 7

Call Detail Records

Cisco CallManager produces two types of records: Call Detail Records (CDRs) and Call Management Records (CMRs). CDRs are data records that contain information about each call that was processed by Cisco CallManager. CMRs are sometimes referred to as *diagnostic records*. In this chapter, both CDRs and CMRs together are referred to as *CDR data*. CDR data provides a record of all calls that have been made or received by users of the CallManager system. CDR data is useful primarily for generating billing records, but it can also be used for tracking call activity, diagnosing certain types of problems, and evaluating the quality of service of calls through the system.

This chapter includes a general overview of the CDR facilities provided in release 3.1 of CallManager. The first three sections give a general understanding of the CDR data, the facilities provided for controlling the generation and usage of the data, and a description of what happens to CDR data in failure scenarios. The first three sections are

- Overview of CDR Data
- Creation and Usage of CDR Data
- Storage and Maintenance of CDR Data

The remaining sections contain more detailed information that is useful to those who are writing or integrating post-processing packages for CDR data, or those who are interested only in the details. The remaining sections are

- Understanding Field Data in CDRs
- Understanding Field Data in CMRs
- Identifying CDR Data Generated for Each Call Type
- Accessing CDR Data in the Central CDR Database
- Hints on Processing CDR Data
- Troubleshooting CDR Data Generation and Storage

Figure 7-1 shows the blocks within CallManager. The shaded blocks are those that contain the software discussed in this chapter.

Figure 7-1 *Blocks Within Cisco CallManager*

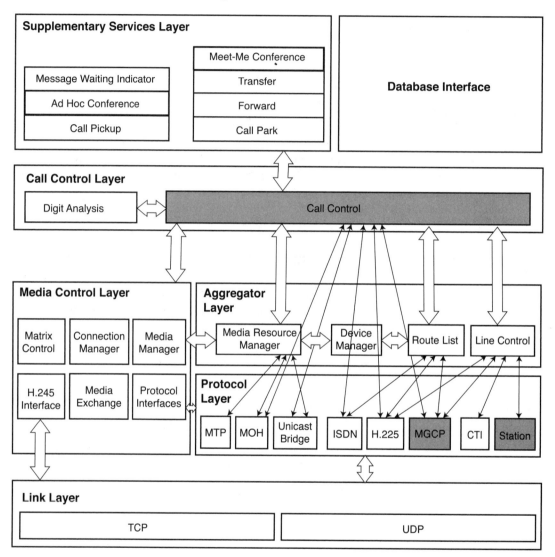

Overview of CDR Data

CDRs contain information about the call origination, the call destination, the date and time the call was started, the time it actually connected, and the time it ended. A call is considered started or originated when the caller goes off-hook. The call is considered ended when either the caller or the called party goes on-hook. CDRs are generated in the Call Control block (see Figure 7-1).

CMRs contain information about the amount of data sent and received, jitter, latency, and lost packets. CMRs are generated in the Station and Media Gateway Control Protocol (MGCP) blocks within the Protocol and Aggregator layers (see Figure 7-1).

CDR data is written when significant changes occur to a given call, such as the following:

- Ending a call
- Transferring a call
- Redirecting a call
- Parking a call
- Creating a conference
- Joining a conference

CDR data is stored in a central CDR database. It can be retrieved by billing software or viewed by an administrator as soon as it has been written into the central database. The process of gaining access to the data is described later in this chapter in the section "Accessing CDR Data in the Central CDR Database." Figure 7-1 illustrates the blocks within CallManager that contain the software that generates CDR data. Call Control generates CDR records from data that is collected from other layers of software during normal call processing. Most of it comes from the Protocol and Aggregator layers, and some of it comes from the Supplementary Services layer.

Contents and Generation of CDRs

A CDR for a call contains information about the call origination, the call destination, and the call duration. It also indicates whether the call has been forwarded, and it contains information used to link all CDRs and CMRs related to a given call. CallManager writes only one CDR for each normal call that CallManager processes. A normal call is one in which a user calls another user directly and does not use any features. If a user utilizes any features during the call, such as call park, transfer, or conference, CallManager might generate more than one CDR for that call. CallManager is a highly distributed system, which means that more than one CallManager node in the cluster can be involved in processing a single call. More than one CallManager node is involved, for example, when a call is placed from a phone that is registered on one CallManager node to a phone that is registered on another CallManager node. One CallManager node is always in charge of a call and is responsible for generating the CDR records as soon as a significant change happens to the call. The CallManager node in charge of a call is usually the CallManager node where the phone or device that originated the call is registered. However, this rule has several exceptions. Some examples are

- If the phone is part of a multiline, the CallManager node where the first phone of the multiline registered will be the controlling CallManager for all calls originated from the multiline.

- The same CallManager node that controls the conference controller's call, controls all calls that are part of a conference.

- The same CallManager that controls the original call, controls all call connections that are part of the transfer.

Contents and Generation of CMRs

CMRs contain information supplied by the phones or gateways that were used in a call. You can use the data to evaluate the quality of service for that call; to gather information on network congestion; and to discover network configuration problems, device errors, and device performance issues. Not all devices can provide this data. In CallManager release 3.1, only Cisco IP Phones and MGCP controlled gateways can supply this data. When a call ends, CallManager writes a CMR for each endpoint in the call that provides the CMR data. If the endpoint device does not provide CMR data, CallManager does not request the data from the device and does not write a CMR. Calls from IP Phone to IP Phone cause two CMRs to be written for each call. If a call was transferred, CallManager might write three or four CMRs, depending on the type of transfer. When a conference call ends, CallManager writes a CMR for each party in the conference that is from an IP Phone or through an MGCP-controlled gateway.

HINT   CallManager writes CMR data only for Cisco IP Phones and gateways that use MGCP to interface with CallManager. When a call ends, CallManager requests the data from these devices and generates a CMR when the data is received. When a call involves other endpoints besides Cisco IP Phones and MGCP-controlled gateways, the diagnostic data is not available, so the number of CMRs written for a given call varies accordingly.

CMRs contain data from the perspective of the device that provided the data. Each CMR contains information on the amount of voice data sent and received and the number of packets lost, jitter, and latency, which can be used to determine quality of service on a call. A CMR also contains information that links it back to the CDR for that call. If two CMRs exist for a given call, they need to have corresponding data. However, it is possible that one of the endpoints experienced problems with voice quality caused by latency, jitter, or lost packets, while the other endpoint did not. In those cases, the packet and octet counts in associated CMRs might not correspond.

Creation and Usage of CDR Data

You can enable and disable CDR and CMR processing through Cisco CallManager Administration. Select the desired service parameters from the list in Table 7-1, set their values appropriately, and save them. When you modify the CDR-related service parameters, the specified Cisco CallManager node changes its processing accordingly within a short time, usually within a few seconds. Table 7-1 lists the service parameters that control the generation of CDR data.

Table 7-1   *CDR and CMR Service Parameters*

Parameter Name	Definition	Possible Values
CdrEnabled	Enables and disables the generation of CDR data for the specified CallManager only	T—CDRs are generated F—No CDRs are generated (default)
CallDiagnosticsEnabled	Enables and disables the generation of CMR data for the specified CallManager only	T—CMRs are generated F—No CMRs are generated (default)
CdrLogCallsWithZero DurationFlag	Enables and disables the logging of CDR data for calls that were not connected or were connected for less than 1 second for the specified CallManager only	T—CDRs for unconnected calls are generated F—No CDRs for unconnected calls are generated (default)

Enabling and Disabling CDR Data Generation

The **CdrEnabled** parameter either enables or disables the generation of CDR data. CDR data generation is disabled by default when the system is installed because some users do not need CDR data and do not have processing to handle it. This setting prevents the creation of the data (which saves processing time and disk space) unless you explicitly enable its generation. You must enable CDR data generation if you desire CDR data. You can enable or disable CDR data generation through the Service Parameters screen in CallManager Administration (**System > Service Parameters**).

HINT   When you change the setting of **CdrEnabled**, it only applies to the CallManager node selected. You should configure it to be the same for all CallManager nodes in the cluster to get consistent and predictable results. If you set the configuration differently on different CallManager nodes, some CDR data is not logged. This parameter must be enabled before CallManager recognizes any other CDR-related service parameter.

Logging or Not Logging Calls with Zero Duration

The **CdrLogCallsWithZeroDurationFlag** parameter enables and disables the generation of CDRs for calls that were never connected or were connected for less than a second. Two common examples are

- When a user takes a phone off-hook and places it back on-hook without completing a call.

- When a user completes a blind transfer. (The consultation call does not connect.)

CallManager distinguishes between calls that have a duration of 0 seconds and terminate normally and calls that do not connect because of an error condition. Calls that terminate normally are those that have one of the following termination cause codes:

- 0—No error

- 16—Normal call clearing

- 31—Normal, unspecified

CallManager always generates CDR data for calls that have a duration of 0 seconds and terminate because of an error condition of some sort, regardless of the setting of **CdrLogCallsWithZeroDurationFlag**. Calls to busy destinations or with a bad destination are examples of this type of call. The duration of these calls is 0 because they were never connected, but their CDRs are generated anyway.

CallManager does not generate CDR records for calls that terminate normally and have a duration of 0 seconds, unless **CdrLogCallsWithZeroDurationFlag** is enabled. When CDR generation is enabled, CallManager generates a CDR for each call that was connected for 1 second or more.

HINT   **CdrLogCallsWithZeroDurationFlag** service parameter is valid only when the **CdrEnabled** service parameter is enabled. If CDR generation is disabled, this flag has no significance.

Enabling and Disabling CMR or Diagnostic Data Generation

You can enable and disable the generation of CMR data through the Service Parameters screen in CallManager Administration (**System > Service Parameters**). You control CMR data generation by enabling both the **CdrEnabled** service parameter and the **CallDiagnosticsEnabled** service parameter. CMR data generation is disabled by default when the system is installed. The system generates CMRs only when both CDR and CMR generation are enabled.

HINT	When you change the setting of **CallDiagnosticsEnabled**, it only applies to the CallManager node selected. You should configure it to be the same for all CallManager nodes in the cluster. CallManager nodes generate CMRs only when you enable both CDR and CMR data generation, but they generate CDRs without having CMR data generation enabled.

Storage and Maintenance of CDR Data

The Cisco CallManager cluster stores all CDR data in a central CDR database. This section describes how the database collects and stores CDR data and how the architecture provides fault tolerance and redundancy. Topics include

- Why to use a central database
- What happens when the central database is not available
- What happens to CDR data when a CallManager node fails

This section reviews some design goals and history relating to the current architecture. It describes what happens when a CallManager node loses its link to the central CDR database and how the database layer recovers the data and makes it available.

Why to Use a Central Database

All CallManager nodes in a cluster form what is essentially one large system. Therefore, it is essential that all data is collected and treated as if it is a single system. This section reviews the design decisions and tradeoffs that were made and why.

In previous versions of the software, CallManager wrote CDR data into comma-delimited files and stored them on the local disks. One file contained each day's records. Each CallManager was a complete system, as clustering technology was not available in versions 2.x and before.

Cisco's design team decided to enhance the system to make it a distributed fault-tolerant and redundant system. Based on the design goals of creating a distributed system that is fault-tolerant and redundant, the team decided that having CDR data scattered on different servers did not fit well into the architecture for the new system. The team considered three major design goals when creating the current architecture of the system:

- Prevent the loss or unavailability of CDR data
- Store the CDR data in a fault-tolerant, redundant facility
- Make the data accessible from a single location

The team decided that putting the CDR data into a central database was the best way to meet these design goals, and that the central database architecture is inherently more robust and secure. A central database can be either backed up or replicated as required to create a fault-tolerant and redundant storage facility. The database can be made as secure as requirements for a particular customer demand.

When a CallManager node crashes, it does not affect the accessibility of the CDR data for calls handled by that node. Each node maintains a TCP/IP connection to the central CDR database server. Maintaining links to other servers in the cluster is a normal cluster operation, so the necessary support was already in place.

The new clustering technology supports a significant number of CallManager nodes. Release 3.1 supports a single cluster of six CallManager nodes. As the number of nodes in a cluster grows, the collection and processing of CDR data becomes increasingly complex for a call management application, if the data must be collected and processed from each node in the cluster. In this architecture, the cluster looks and functions like a single system.

Storing the CDR data in a central database provides a single location where all CDR data can be retrieved and processed. Software billing packages do not have to gather data from individual CallManager nodes, and, therefore, they are not sensitive to the particular configuration of CallManager.

CallManager stores CDR data in the database through database access routines known as the database layer. The database layer provides quick access to data in the database without having to know the database schema or exactly where or how the data is stored. The database layer decides where to write the data initially and when and how the data will be transferred to the central CDR database. From the CallManager perspective, after it writes the CDR into the database by calling an access routine in the database layer, the data is secure. CallManager nodes themselves do not know where the data is stored.

The two service parameters that control CDR functions in the database layer are listed in Table 7-2.

Table 7-2   *CDR Database Control Parameters*

Parameter Name	Definition	Possible Values
CDRMoveIntervalInSeconds	Defines the interval at which CDR data is moved from individual CallManager nodes to the central CDR database.	Specified in seconds Default value = 60 seconds
MaxCdrRecords	Specifies the maximum number of CDR records to keep in the database. If the number of CDR records reaches this maximum number, the oldest records are deleted and an alarm is generated. This check occurs once a day.	Range up to 10,000,000 records Default value = 1,500,000 records

What Happens When the Central Database Is Not Available

As in any distributed system, it is possible to lose a link between any of the nodes in the cluster and a central data storage facility.

The design team faced three major challenges in handling this contingency:

- How do you handle CDR data when the link between a CallManager node and the central database has been lost?
- How do you make the data secure on local drives in a cost-effective manner?
- How do you handle the CDR data when the amount of data during peak traffic periods from all CallManager nodes exceeds the capabilities of the database?

To resolve these challenges, the team decided to have all CDR data written to the local database on the CallManager node as soon as it is generated. The data is then transferred to the central CDR database in background mode at regular specified intervals. The interval is configurable and can be set by going to CallManager Administration (**System > Service Parameters > Cisco Database Layer Monitor**) and setting **CDRMoveIntervalInSeconds** to the desired number of seconds. The default value is 60 seconds. After transferring the data successfully to the central CDR database, the database layer removes the local copy.

HINT

The database layer makes the decisions on where or how to write the CDR data, and the decisions can vary depending on the conditions in the cluster at a given moment. If the database layer loses its link to the central CDR database, for example, it alters the processing to compensate.

If the link to the central database is lost for any reason, CallManager stores the data on the local drives until the link is restored. The local drives on CallManager servers are mirrored drives so that no data will be lost when a drive fails. This minimizes the potential loss of data until the database layer transfers the data to the central database. When the link is restored, the database layer transfers the data in background mode to the central database. After transferring the data successfully, the local copy is removed.

Historical Background

The initial implementation caused all CDR data to be written directly into the central database. Losing the link to the central database caused the database layer to write the CDR data into the local database on the CallManager node. When the link was recovered, the database layer transferred the CDR data to the central CDR database in background mode. After successfully transferring the data to the central database, the database layer removed the local copy.

During stress tests, the integration team discovered that the central database could not handle the volume of CDR data being generated within the cluster during peak traffic loads. This caused a design change so that the database layer would write all CDR data to the local database on the CallManager node first. The database layer then transferred the data to the central database in background mode. This design change enabled handling the peak traffic periods for the cluster, as writing the data was now spread across multiple databases. This was essentially the original failure-processing mode with a few tweaks.

What Happens to CDR Data When a CallManager Node Fails

When a CallManager node fails, it loses all CDR data for all calls that it is controlling that are currently in progress but not completed. The calls remain active even after CallManager fails, but there is no way to collect CDR data for those calls. Partial CDRs are never written.

When a CallManager node fails but the server that the CallManager node is running on does not fail, the database layer continues transferring CDR data from the local disks to the central database until all local CDR data has been moved. If the server itself crashes, the local CDR data is not accessible until the server is brought back online and the system transfers the data to the main database.

Understanding Field Data in CDRs

The remainder of this chapter contains detailed information about the contents of each data record. Those who are interested in a general understanding of CDRs or are involved only as administrators on the system can skip the remainder of this chapter. If you use CDR data for diagnostic purposes, creating post-processing applications, such as billing systems, call management systems, or any other use that requires detailed information, the following sections are for you.

The topics in this section include

- General information about the data types used
- Field data conversions
- Notes on other field types
- CDR record field definitions

NOTE   To understand and use the data from the CDR records, you need to understand both the type of the data as it is used in CallManager and the data type used to store the field value in the database. The two types are not always the same. The database field types are adequate to store the data, but the correct interpretation of the data must, in some cases, take into account the field types used by CallManager.

General Information About the Data Types Used

A fundamental difference exists in the data types used for handling and storing numeric data between CallManager and the Microsoft SQL database. CallManager always uses an unsigned integer as a type for all numeric CDR data fields, whereas the database always uses a signed integer field to store the data. The difference in the two data types causes the data in certain fields to appear inconsistent or even erroneous when viewed as a database record. The values displayed are sometimes negative and sometimes positive, but the real value is always a 32-bit positive number. You will notice this most often in fields that contain IP addresses. Always convert the value contained in a numeric database field to an unsigned integer value before interpreting the data.

HINT   When processing field data values from CDR data, you must interpret or use the high order bit, or sign bit, correctly because the value represented is a positive 32-bit number. All numeric fields contain 32-bit unsigned integer values but are stored in the CDR data as 32-bit signed integers. There are no negative numbers in CDR data. The sign bit is part of the value contained in the field.

Default Values for Unused Fields

Not all fields contain valid data in every CDR or CMR record. If the field is unused, the software sets it to its default value. The default values are

- Zero for numeric fields
- Blank for character fields

Field Data Conversions

The following sections define the conversion information for basic field types and explain what the types represent. Also covered is how to convert field types from their stored format to a more useful format that you can use when creating billing records and other reports.

Time Values

The database stores and displays all time values as signed integers, but the values are actually 32-bit unsigned integers. All time fields contain a value that is obtained from the Windows 2000 system routines. The value is the number of seconds since midnight (00:00:00) January 1, 1970, Greenwich mean time (GMT). The value is not adjusted for time zones or daylight savings time. All time values in a CDR are from the CallManager node that wrote the CDR. The node ID of the CallManager node that wrote the CDR is found in the **globalCallID_callManagerId** field.

IP Addresses

IP addresses are normally written as four octets (8-bit groups) separated by periods, with each octet expressed as a decimal number. This is known as *dotted decimal notation* (for example, 192.150.23.45). Because the database displays IP addresses as signed decimal integers, they sometimes appear as negative numbers. You can convert the signed decimal value to an IP address by first converting the value to an unsigned 32-bit hex (or binary) number.

A 32-bit number consists of four octets. Because the data is from an Intel-based machine, the four octets are in the reverse order of the four octets of an IP address. You must, therefore, reverse the order of the octets and then convert each octet to a decimal number. The resulting four octets are the four octet fields of the IP address. The following examples illustrate this conversion sequence.

HINT   The database displays an IP address as a negative number when the low octet of the IP address has a value greater than or equal to 128.

Example: Conversion of an IP Address Displayed as a Negative Number

IP address value from CDR record: -1139627840

HINT   If you use a calculator to convert the value, enter the decimal number as a negative number and then convert it to hex or binary.

Figure 7-2 illustrates how to convert a signed integer value to an unsigned integer value. Negative and positive values are essentially the same, but negative values have the high order bit set. It is interpreted as a sign bit and displayed accordingly. Signed integers are 32-bit numbers and contain a 31-bit value plus a high order sign bit. Unsigned integers are 32-bit numbers and contain a 32-bit value that is assumed to be a positive number.

Figure 7-2 *Convert Negative Signed Integer Value to Unsigned Integer Value*

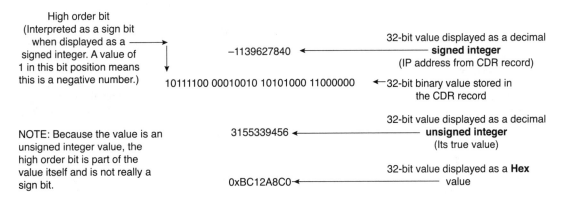

Figure 7-3 shows the steps needed to convert a 32-bit number into an IP address. As illustrated, the IP address from a CDR record can be either a positive integer or a negative integer. When you look at it as a 32-bit binary value, it has four octets.

Figure 7-3 *How to Convert a 32-Bit Decimal Number to an IP Address*

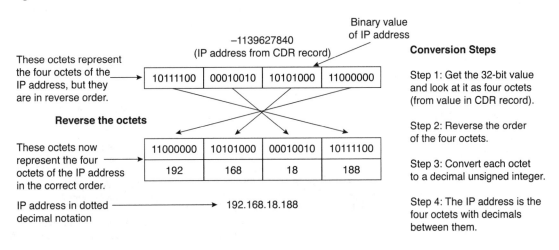

The following example illustrates the conversion process for a number that is positive.

Example: Conversion Example Using a Positive Number

IP Address value from CDR record: 991078592

Figure 7-4 illustrates how to convert a signed integer value to an unsigned integer value. Negative and positive values are essentially the same, but positive values have the high order bit cleared. It is interpreted as a sign bit and displayed accordingly. Because this is a positive integer, it is the same in both signed and unsigned displays.

Figure 7-4   *Convert Positive Signed Integer Value to Unsigned Integer Value*

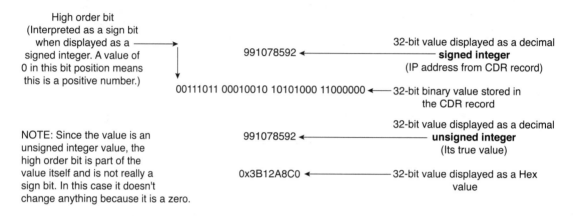

Figure 7-5 shows the steps needed to convert a positive integer number into an IP address. The IP address from a CDR record can be either a positive integer or a negative integer. When you look at it as a 32-bit binary value, it has four octets.

Figure 7-5   *How to Convert a 32-Bit Positive Decimal Number to an IP Address*

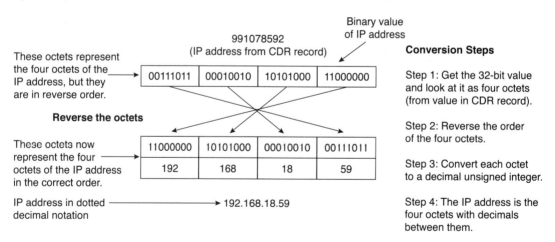

Notes on Other Field Types

This section contains useful information about some of the fields or types of fields contained in the CDR records that need explanation about their contents. This information should add to your understanding of how to use the data contained in these fields. In some cases, it might help to understand what the data actually represents and how it is used in CallManager.

Global Call Identifiers (GCIDs)

Historical Background

A global call identifier is usually referred to as a *global call ID* (GCID). GCIDs were originally created for use by the Computer Telephony Interface (CTI). The Java Telephony Application Programming Interface (JTAPI) dictated the requirement for GCID. The JTAPI call model requires a common identifier that identifies all call legs that are part of the same call. GCIDs have since been included in CDR data and are used to help identify CDRs related to a given call. Other fields also help identify the set of records that are needed.

CallManager uses a global call identifier (GCID) to tag calls that are related to each other in some way and are logically part of the same call, as defined by CTI. The GCID does not tag all of the calls that are related from a CDR or billing perspective. The GCID in CDR data consists of two fields:

* globalCallID_callManagerId
* globalCallID_callId

GCID Structure within CallManager

CallManager combines **globalCallID_callManagerId** and **globalCallID_callId** into a 64-bit unsigned integer structure that is known as the GCID. In CDR data, the GCID is stored in two separate numeric fields because the database cannot store a single 64-bit unsigned integer. The value in the **globalCallID_callId** field contains a 24-bit unsigned integer value that begins at 1 each time that Cisco CallManager is restarted. (Note: This field can be expanded to a 27-bit value.)

The following examples illustrate the usage of GCIDs.

Example: GCID Usage in a Call Transfer

A call transfer creates three separate calls and thus, three CDRs. If user A calls user B, and then user A transfers user B to user C, the calls created are

- GCID 1—Call from A to B
- GCID 2—Call from A to C to announce the transfer
- GCID 1—Call from B to C when the transfer is completed

In this case, CallManager assigns calls 1 and 3 the same GCID, and the second call is considered a separate call that is not necessarily related to the other two calls. Each call generates a CDR. In addition, the system logs four CMRs.

Example: GCID Usage in a Conference Call

A conference call consists of many separate but related calls. Each party that joins the conference is a separate call. In an Ad Hoc conference, when the conference controller presses the button to complete the conference, CallManager connects each of the three users to the same conference bridge and assigns each of their separate calls the same GCID. The calls created are

- GCID 1—Call from A to B, original call; conference always gets this GCID
- GCID 2—Call from A to C
- GCID 1—Call from A to conference bridge
- GCID 1—Call from B to conference bridge
- GCID 1—Call from C to conference bridge

The system generates five CDRs, and each CDR has the GCID as noted. CallManager also logs five CMRs.

The section "Identifying CDR Data Generated for Each Call Type" later in this chapter identifies the set of records created for the illustrated call examples.

You can use GCIDs to help link all CDR data related to a given call. A GCID is unique across a cluster as long as you do not restart a CallManager node in that cluster. When you restart a CallManager node, the GCID restarts at the same value that it had when that CallManager node was originally started after installation. This is not a problem for online processing, as CallManager requires a GCID to be unique across all calls in the cluster for the duration of the call to which it is assigned. When you restart CallManager, the call signaling is lost for calls currently in progress. When new calls begin after the restart, they all have new GCIDs that are unique within the cluster at that point in time, even though they are duplicates of GCIDs previously used. Therefore, the GCIDs are not unique across time.

Each time you restart a CallManager node, it creates the same set of GCIDs as the previous execution of the CallManager software.

Even though a CallManager node restart does not create any issues for online processing, it does create a problem for CDRs. CDR data that has the same GCID as the CDRs from the newly restarted CallManager node might exist. Thus, if a search is made in the database for all records with a given GCID, unrelated records might show up in the search results. When this occurs, the date and time stamps will be different and can be used to determine whether records are related.

Call Leg Identifiers

Call leg identifiers are usually referred to as *call leg IDs*. CallManager uses call leg IDs internally and includes them in the CDR data to help link CDR and CMR data records and CDR records related to the same call. You can also use call leg IDs in tracking call-related problems by using them as a hook into trace data generated by the system.

CallManager uses a call leg ID to identify a single call leg. Each complete call consists of two call legs. When you originate a call by going off-hook, the connection between your phone and CallManager is a *call leg*. When you dial a directory number that identifies a destination, the connection between CallManager and the destination is another call leg. Both call legs together form a complete call.

CallManager views each call as two separate call legs and each call leg has a call leg ID that is unique within the cluster for the duration of that call. It is not unique across time, because when you restart a CallManager node for any reason, the call leg IDs start again with the same value that they had after the last restart of that CallManager node. The call leg ID is a 32-bit unsigned integer that consists of a 24-bit unsigned integer value, which begins at 1 each time CallManager is restarted, and the node ID for that CallManager.

Directory Numbers

CallManager can perform translations on digits that are dialed by a user. The translated number, and not the original dialed digits, is populated into the CDR record. The gateways can also perform further modifications to a directory number before it is output through the gateway. These modifications are not included in the CDR record.

If the dial plan allows callers to use the pound (#) key for speed dialing, the pound (#) key is populated into the database when it is used. For example, the **finalCalledPartyNumber** field might contain a value such as 12087569174#.

Partitions

Directory numbers referenced within a CDR are identified uniquely by a combination of the directory number and its partition, if partitions are defined. When partitions exist, both values are required to fully identify a directory number because the same directory number might be used in more than one partition. The **callingPartyNumberPartition** field is empty when a call originates through a gateway. When a call terminates through a gateway, the **finalCalledPartyNumberPartition** field shows the partition to which the gateway belongs.

Duration

The **duration** field is an unsigned integer value that represents the number of seconds that the call was connected. The **duration** field is usually nonzero, except in two cases:

- The **CdrLogCallsWithZeroDurationFlag** is enabled (T), the call duration is 0 seconds, and the call terminates normally. This happens mainly when a user took a phone off-hook and put it back on-hook without attempting a call.

- The call duration is 0 seconds, and one of the call termination cause codes in the CDR is not a normal termination code. This indicates that some error or special processing occurred.

CDR Record Field Definitions

Table 7-3 provides information about each field in a CDR. Each record consists of 50 individual fields. The information provided for each field is as follows:

- The field name or the column names from the database record
- The field data type
- The field definition

The fields are arranged here to facilitate an understanding of the information available and are not in the same order that they appear in the actual record.

HINT   All numeric fields in the CDR data are actually unsigned integers in CallManager.

All character fields in CDR data are defined as 50-character fields, except the **origDeviceName and destDeviceName** fields, which are 129-character fields. All character fields are of varying lengths in CallManager.

Table 7-3   *Field Definitions for a CDR*

Field Name	Field Type	Field Definition
cdrRecordType	numeric	Specifies the type of this specific record. It will be set to End call record (1).

Table 7-3 *Field Definitions for a CDR (Continued)*

Field Name	Field Type	Field Definition
globalCallId_ClusterID	character	The name assigned to this cluster. It will be unique so that if records are collected from multiple clusters, those from a given cluster can be identified.
globalCallID_callManagerId	numeric	Half of the GCID. It represents the Node ID of the node that controlled the call corresponding to this record. This should be used with the second half of the GCID.
globalCallID_callId	numeric	The second half of the GCID. It is a value that starts at 1 and is serially incremented for each GCID.
origDeviceName	character	The name of the device from which this call originated. For IP Phones and some other devices, the name contains the MAC address. The names are the device names from the Cisco CallManager Administration database. This field contains up to 129 characters.
origIpAddr	numeric	Contains the IP address of the signaling connection on the device from which the call originated.
origIpPort	numeric	Contains the IP port of the signaling connection on the device from which the call originated.
callingPartyNumber	character	The directory number of the device from which the call originated. For transferred calls, this is the transferred party.
callingPartyNumberPartition	character	This field contains the partition associated with the directory number from which the call originated.
origLegCallIdentifier	numeric	The call leg ID for the origination leg of this call.

continues

Table 7-3   *Field Definitions for a CDR (Continued)*

Field Name	Field Type	Field Definition
dateTimeOrigination	numeric	Represents the time that the device originating the call went off-hook, or the time that an outside call was first recognized by the system. (It received the Setup message through a gateway.) The value is a GMT value and is the number of seconds since midnight (00:00:00) January 1, 1970.
origNodeId	numeric	Represents the node within the Cisco CallManager cluster where the device that was used to originate the call was registered at the time of this call.
origSpan	numeric	Contains the originator's port or span number if the call originated through a gateway. If the call originated through an H.323 trunk (H.225), this field contains the call leg ID of the corresponding call leg. If neither of these two cases is true, this field contains zero.
origCause_location	numeric	Contains the ISDN location value from the cause information element for the originator's leg of the call. See Table 7-5 for a definition of the possible values for this field.
origCause_value	numeric	Represents why the call leg to originating device was terminated. In the case of transfers, forwards, and so forth, the cause of call termination might be different for the originating device and the termination device. Thus, two cause fields are associated with each call. Usually, they will be the same. See Table 7-6 for a definition of the possible values for this field.
origMediaTransportAddress_IP	numeric	The destination IP address that the media stream from the originator was connected to.

Table 7-3   *Field Definitions for a CDR (Continued)*

Field Name	Field Type	Field Definition
origMediaTransportAddress_port	numeric	The destination port to which the media stream from the originator was connected.
origMediaCap_payloadCapability	numeric	Contains the codec type that the originator used on the sending side during this call. It might be different than the codec type used on its receiving side. See Table 7-4 for a definition of possible values for this field.
origMediaCap_maxFramesPer Packet	numeric	Contains the number of milliseconds of data per packet sent to the destination by the originator of this call. The actual data size depends on the codec type used to generate the data.
origMediaCap_g723BitRate	numeric	Defines the bit rate to be used by G.723. There are two bit rate values: 1 for 5.3 K bit rate, and 2 for 6.3 K bit rate.
origCallTerminationOnBehalfOf	numeric	Identifies which feature or other entity caused the origination call leg to be terminated. See Table 7-7 for possible values.
lastRedirectDn	character	The directory number of the last device that redirected this call. This field applies only to calls that were redirected, such as conference calls, call forwarded calls, and so forth, but is primarily used to identify who last forwarded the call.
lastRedirectDnPartition	character	The partition of the last device that redirected this call. This field applies only to calls that were redirected, such as conference calls, call forwarded calls, and so forth, but is primarily used to identify who last forwarded the call.
lastRedirectRedirectOnBehalfOf	numeric	Identifies which feature caused the last redirection. See Table 7-7 for possible values. *continues*

Table 7-3 *Field Definitions for a CDR (Continued)*

Field Name	Field Type	Field Definition
lastRedirectRedirectReason	numeric	Contains the reason code identifying why the last redirect occurred. See Table 7-8 for possible code values.
JoinOnBehalfOf	Numeric	Identifies the feature that caused the join to occur. See Table 7-7 for possible code values.
destDeviceName	character	The device name of the device on which this call terminated. For IP Phones and some other devices, the name contains the MAC address. The names are the device names from the Cisco CallManager Administration database. This field contains up to 129 characters.
destLegIdentifier	numeric	The call leg ID for the destination leg of this call.
destNodeId	numeric	Contains the node ID of CallManager where the destination device was registered at the time of this call.
destSpan	numeric	Contains the destination port or span number if the call was terminated through a gateway. If the call terminated through an H.323 trunk (H.225), this field contains the call leg ID of the corresponding call leg. If neither of these two cases is true, this field contains a zero.
destIpAddr	numeric	Contains the IP address of the signaling connection on the device that terminated the call.
destIpPort	numeric	Contains the IP port of the signaling connection on the device that terminated the call.
destCallTerminationOnBehalfOf	numeric	Identifies which feature caused the destination call leg to be terminated. See Table 7-7 for possible values.

Table 7-3   *Field Definitions for a CDR (Continued)*

Field Name	Field Type	Field Definition
destConversationId	numeric	Contains the conversation ID associated with the destination side of this call. A conversation ID is sometimes referred to as the Conference ID. Typically, this field will be filled in only for conference calls.
originalCalledPartyNumber	character	Contains the directory number to which the call was originally extended, based on the digits dialed by the originator of the call. If the call completes normally (the call was not forwarded), this directory number must always be the same as the number in the **finalCalledPartyNumber** field. If the call was forwarded, this field contains the original destination of the call before it was forwarded.
originalCalledPartyNumber Partition	character	Contains the partition associated with the originally called party number.
origCalledPartyRedirectReason	numeric	Contains the reason code identifying why the originally called party was redirected. See Table 7-8 for redirect reason codes.
origCalledPartyRedirectOnBehalf Of	numeric	Identifies which feature caused the originally called party to be redirected. See Table 7-7 for possible values.
finalCalledPartyNumber	character	Contains the directory number to which the call was actually extended. If the call completes normally (the call was not forwarded), this directory number must always be the same as the number contained in the **originalCalledPartyNumber** field. If the call was forwarded, this field contains the directory number of the final destination of the call after all forwards were completed.

continues

Table 7-3 *Field Definitions for a CDR (Continued)*

Field Name	Field Type	Field Definition
finalCalledPartyNumberPartition	Character	Contains the partition associated with the destination to which the call was actually extended. In a normal call, this field should be the same as the partition contained in the **originalCalledPartyNumber Partition** field. If the call was forwarded, this field contains the partition of the final destination of the call after all forwards were completed.
destCause_location	numeric	The ISDN location value from the destination cause information element. See Table 7-5 for a definition of possible values in this field.
destCause_value	numeric	This cause represents why the call to the termination device was terminated. In the case of transfers, forwards, and so forth, the cause of call termination might be different for the recipient of the call and the originator of the call. Thus, two cause fields are associated with each call, which usually are the same. When an attempt is made to extend a call to a busy device that is forwarded, the cause code reflects "Busy," even though the call was connected to a forward destination. See Table 7-6 for a definition of possible values in this field.
destMediaTransportAddress_IP	numeric	The originator's IP address to which the media stream from the destination was connected.
destMediaTransportAddress_Port	numeric	The originator's port to which the media stream from the destination was connected.

Table 7-3 *Field Definitions for a CDR (Continued)*

Field Name	Field Type	Field Definition
destMediaCap_payloadCapability	numeric	Contains the codec type that the destination used on its sending side during this call. It might be different than the codec type used on its receiving side. See Table 7-4 for the definition of the possible values in this field.
destMediaCap_maxFramesPer Packet	numeric	Contains the number of milliseconds of data per packet sent to the originator by the destination of this call. The actual data size depends on the codec type used to generate the data.
destMediaCap_g723BitRate	numeric	Defines the bit rate to be used by G.723. There are two bit rate values: 1 for 5.3 K bit rate, and 2 for 6.3 K bit rate.
dateTimeConnect	numeric	The date and time that the call was connected between the originating and terminating devices. The value is a GMT value and is the number of seconds since midnight (00:00:00) January 1, 1970. This field is zero if the call was not connected.
dateTimeDisconnect	numeric	The time that the call was disconnected between the originating and terminating devices. The value is a GMT value and is the number of seconds since midnight (00:00:00) January 1, 1970. This field is zero if the call was not connected.
duration	numeric	The number of seconds that the call was connected. It is the difference between the date/time of connect and the date/time of disconnect. It will be zero for all calls that were not connected, and also for calls that were connected for less than 1 second. *continues*

Codec Types

Table 7-4 provides a list of codecs used in the system. These are all of the possible values for the **destMediaCap_payloadCapability** field and the **origMediaCap_payloadCapability** field.

Table 7-4 *Codec Types*

Value	Description
1	Nonstandard
2	G.711 A-law 64 k
3	G.711 A-law 56 k
4	G.711 μ-law 64 k
5	G.711 μ-law 56 k
6	G.722 64 k
7	G.722 56 k
8	G.722 48 k
9	G.7231
10	G.728
11	G.729
12	G.729AnnexA
13	Is11172AudioCap
14	Is13818AudioCap
15	G.729AnnexB
16	G.729 Annex AwAnnexB
18	GSM Full Rate
19	GSM Half Rate
20	GSM Enhanced Full Rate
25	Wide Band 256 k
32	Data 64 k
33	Data 56 k
80	GSM
81	Cisco Unity
82	G.726_32 K
83	G.726_24 K
84	G.726_16 K

Cause Location Definitions

Table 7-5 contains the possible values for the **origCause_location** and the **destCause_location** fields.

Table 7-5   *Cause Location Values*

Code	Description
0	User (U)
1	Private network serving the local user (LPN)
2	Public network serving the local user (LN)
3	Transit network (TN)
4	Public network serving the remote user (RLN)
5	Private network serving the remote user (RPN)
7	International network (INTL)
10	Network beyond interworking point (BI)
All other values are reserved	

Cause Code Definitions

Table 7-6 contains the definition of the cause code values for the **origCause_value** field and the **destCause_value** field. The clearing cause values are per ITU specification Q.850. For OnNet call legs, CallManager determines the cause value. For OffNet call legs, or those that pass through a gateway, the cause value is determined by the terminating switch or device.

Table 7-6   *Cause Code Definitions*

Code	Description
0	No error
1	Unallocated (unassigned) number
2	No route to specified transit network (national use)
3	No route to destination
4	Send special information tone
5	Misdialed trunk prefix (national use)
6	Channel unacceptable
7	Call awarded and being delivered in an established channel
8	Pre-emption
9	Pre-emption—circuit reserved for reuse
16	Normal call clearing

Table 7-6   *Cause Code Definitions (Continued)*

Code	Description
17	User busy
18	No user responding
19	No answer from user (user alerted)
20	Subscriber absent
21	Call rejected
22	Number changed
26	Nonselected user clearing
27	Destination out of order
28	Invalid number format (address incomplete)
29	Facility rejected
30	Response to STATUS ENQUIRY
31	Normal, unspecified
34	No circuit/channel available
38	Network out of order
39	Permanent frame mode connection out of service
40	Permanent frame mode connection operational
41	Temporary failure
42	Switching equipment congestion
43	Access information discarded
44	Requested circuit/channel not available
46	Precedence call blocked
47	Resource unavailable, unspecified
49	Quality of service not available
50	Requested facility not subscribed
53	Service operation violated
54	Incoming calls barred
55	Incoming calls barred within Closed User Group (CUG)
57	Bearer capability not authorized
58	Bearer capability not presently available
62	Inconsistency in designated outgoing access information and subscriber class

Table 7-6   *Cause Code Definitions (Continued)*

Code	Description
63	Service or option not available, unspecified
65	Bearer capability not implemented
66	Channel type not implemented
69	Requested facility not implemented
70	Only restricted digital information bearer capability is available (national use)
79	Service or option not implemented, unspecified
81	Invalid call reference value
82	Identified channel does not exist
83	A suspended call exists, but this call identity does not
84	Call identity in use
85	No call suspended
86	Call having the requested call identity has been cleared
87	User not member of CUG
88	Incompatible destination
90	Nonexistent CUG
91	Invalid transit network selection (national use)
95	Invalid message, unspecified
96	Mandatory information element is missing
97	Message type nonexistent or not implemented
98	Message is not compatible with the call state, or the message type is nonexistent or not implemented
99	An information element or parameter does not exist or is not implemented
100	Invalid information element contents
101	The message is not compatible with the call state
102	The call was terminated when a timer expired and a recovery routine was executed recover from the error
103	Parameter nonexistent or not implemented—passed on (national use)
110	Message with unrecognized parameter discarded
111	Protocol error, unspecified
125	Out of bandwidth (this is a Cisco-specific code)

continues

Table 7-6   *Cause Code Definitions (Continued)*

Code	Description
126	Call split (this is a Cisco-specific code). It is used when a call is terminated during a feature operation indicating why the call leg was terminated. This occurs on transfers when the call leg was split off and terminated. (It was not part of the final transferred call.) This can help determine which calls were terminated as part of a feature operation
127	Interworking, unspecified

Legend for the **OnBehalfOf** Fields

Table 7-7 defines the possible values of the **OnBehalfOf** fields. These fields are intended to help identify all records that are part of a feature call. These fields note the feature that is responsible for the call termination on each half of a call. They also note which feature caused the originator to be redirected, and which feature was the last feature to cause the call to be redirected.

When a device terminates a call, the **OnBehalfOf** field is set to **Device**, which is the value that is used for all calls that do not involve a supplementary service.

Table 7-7   *Legend for the **OnBehalfOf** Fields*

Value	Feature
0	Unknown
1	CctiLine
2	Unicast Shared Resource Provider
3	Call Park
4	Conference
5	Call Forward
6	Meet-Me Conference
7	Meet-Me Conference Intercepts
8	Message Waiting
9	Multicast Shared Resource Provider
10	Transfer
11	SSAPI Manager
12	Device
13	Call Control

Reason for Redirect

Table 7-8 defines the possible values of the redirect reason codes. These codes are sent to the CTI interface to identify for third-party applications why a call has been redirected.

Table 7-8   *Reason for Redirect Codes*

Reason Code	Redirect Reasons
0	No Reason
1	Call Forward Busy
2	Call Forward No Answer
3	Call Transfer
4	Call Pickup
5	Call CPE Out of Order
6	Call Forward
7	Call Pickup
15	Call Forward Unconditional

Understanding Field Data in CMRs

This section contains a list of all fields contained in a diagnostic record. The field definitions include some basic information about the quality of service fields, such as jitter and latency.

The topics are as follows:

- Fields contained in the CMR
- How to identify the CDR associated with a CMR

Fields Contained in the CMR

Table 7-9 provides information about each field in a CMR. Each record consists of 17 individual fields. The information provided about each field is as follows:

- The field name or the column names from the database record
- The field type
- The field definition

The fields in Table 7-9 are arranged to facilitate understanding of the data that is available in the CMR record. They are not in the same order as the actual database record.

HINT   All numeric fields in the CMR data are actually unsigned integers in CallManager.

All character fields in CMR data are defined as 50-character fields, except the **deviceName** field. All character fields are of varying lengths in CallManager.

Table 7-9   *Field Definitions for a CMR*

Field Name	Field Type	Field Definition
cdrRecordType	numeric	Specifies the type of this specific record. It is set to CMR record (2).
globalCallId_ClusterID	character	The name assigned to this cluster. It is unique so that if records are collected from multiple clusters, those from a given cluster can be identified.
deviceName	character	The name of the device from the CallManager Administration database. This field contains up to 129 characters.
globalCallID_callManagerId	numeric	Half of the GCID. It represents the node ID of the node that controlled the call corresponding to this record. This should be used in conjunction with the second half of the GCID.
globalCallID_callId	numeric	The second half of the GCID. It is a value that starts at 1 and is serially incremented for each GCID.
nodeId	numeric	The node within the CallManager cluster where the device from which these diagnostics were collected was registered.
callIdentifier	numeric	A call leg ID that identifies to which call leg this record pertains.
directoryNum	character	The directory number of the device from which these diagnostics were collected.
directoryNumPartition	character	The partition of the directory number in this record.

Table 7-9   *Field Definitions for a CMR (Continued)*

Field Name	Field Type	Field Definition
dateTimeStamp	numeric	Represents the approximate time that the device went on-hook. The time is put into the record when the device responds to a request for diagnostic information. The value is a GMT value and is the number of seconds since midnight (00:00:00) January 1, 1970.
numberPacketsSent	numeric	The total number of RTP data packets transmitted by the device since starting transmission on this connection. If the connection mode was "receive only," the value is zero.
numberOctetsSent	numeric	The total number of payload octets (not including header or padding) transmitted in RTP data packets by the device since starting transmission on this connection. If the connection mode was "receive only," the value is zero.
numberPacketsReceived	numeric	The total number of RTP data packets received by the device since starting reception on this connection. The count includes packets received from different sources if this is a Multicast call. If the connection mode was "send only," the value is zero.
numberOctetsReceived	numeric	The total number of payload octets (not including header or padding) received in RTP data packets by the device since starting reception on this connection. The count includes packets received from different sources, if this is a Multicast call. If the connection mode was "send only," the value is zero.

continues

Table 7-9 *Field Definitions for a CMR (Continued)*

Field Name	Field Type	Field Definition
numberPacketsLost	signed integer	The total number of RTP data packets that have been lost since the beginning of data reception on this connection. This number is defined to be the number of packets expected less the number of packets actually received, where the number of packets received includes any that are late or duplicates. Thus, packets that arrive late are not counted as lost, and the loss might be negative if there are duplicates. The number of packets expected is defined to be the extended last sequence number received less the initial sequence number received. If the connection mode was "send only," the value is zero.
jitter	numeric	An estimate of the statistical variance of the RTP data packet interarrival time measured in milliseconds and expressed as an unsigned integer. The interarrival jitter is defined to be the mean deviation (smoothed absolute value) of the difference in packet spacing at the receiver compared to the sender for a pair of packets. If the connection mode was "send only," the value is zero.
latency	numeric	This value is an estimate of the network latency, expressed in milliseconds. This is the average value of the difference between the Network Time Protocol (NTP) time stamp indicated by the senders of the RTP messages and the NTP time stamp of the receivers, measured when these messages are received. The average is obtained by summing all the estimates, and then dividing by the number of RTP messages that have been received.

How to Identify the CDR Record Associated with a CMR Record

You cannot use any set of CDR data fields to guarantee a positive link between CMR and CDR data if you depend on an exact match between corresponding fields. You can, however, figure it out by using the combination of the GCID, call leg IDs, **globalCallId_ClusterID**, and the date/time fields that exist in each of the records. The **globalCallId_ClusterID** field was added to make the records unique across multiple clusters. The combination of the GCID fields and the call leg ID is not unique across time on the same cluster because their values are reset whenever a CallManager node is restarted. If you also consider the **dateTimeDisconnect** field in the CDR and the **dateTimeStamp** field in the CMR, it will make a positive match. The date/time field in a CMR might not match exactly the date/time of disconnect in the CDR because they are written separately.

Before the CMR can be written, CallManager must request the data for the CMR from the endpoint device. Some time exists lapse during this request cycle, and if the system clock ticks over a second boundary, the times will differ by a second. If the records have the same GCIDs and call leg IDs and the specified date/time values are within a few seconds of each other, the records are definitely related. It takes CallManager a minimum of 10 seconds to come online after a restart, and it usually takes much longer, depending on the number of devices that are in the database for that system. Given that the IDs match, and the time is not off by more than 10 seconds, the records are related to the same call.

Identifying CDR Data Generated for Each Call Type

Each type of call creates a set of CDR data records. This section identifies the records that form the set for each type of call. Many types of calls produce multiple CDRs and CMRs. It helps to identify the expected set of records for a given call before processing the data for that call. This section does not provide an exhaustive set of call types and examples. It does, however, contain a representative sample of different types of calls and the records produced. The assumption is made that CDR generation is enabled, and **CdrLogCallsWithZeroDurationFlag** is disabled.

Calls Between Two Endpoints

A standard call is a call between two endpoints that does not involve any features. The endpoints can be either phones or gateways. These calls generate one CDR and two CMRs if they are between Cisco IP Phones or between Cisco IP Phones and MGCP-controlled gateways. If an endpoint involved in a call is not a Cisco IP Phone or an MGCP-controlled gateway, no CMR data will be written for that endpoint. This section illustrates the following two topics:

- CDR data for a call between two IP phones
- CDR data for calls involving a gateway

HINT   The **originalCalledPartyNumber** field always contains the same directory number as the **finalCalledPartyNumber** field in a normal call.

CDR Data for a Call Between Two IP Phones

Each normal call between two IP phones logs one CDR at the end of the call. Each CDR contains all fields identified in Table 7-3. Not all fields in a CDR or CMR record are used for a given call. If the field is not used it contains the default value for that field type. CallManager also writes one CMR per endpoint that is involved in the call. In a standard call between two parties that are each using a Cisco IP Phone, the system writes two CMRs, one each for the originator and the destination of the call. In this case, the call will have a duration greater than 0 seconds, and the **originalCalledPartyNumber** field and the **finalCalledPartyNumber** field both contain the same information.

CDR Values for Calls Involving a Gateway

When a call involves a gateway as one of the endpoints, the IP address for that endpoint is the IP address of the gateway, even though the call might not actually terminate there. The call can pass through the gateway to a real endpoint on the PSTN. Calls that involve a gateway have a nonzero value for a span number in one or both of the span fields (**origSpan** or **destSpan**). The fields **origDeviceName** or **destDeviceName** contain the device names of the terminating devices. Thus, you have the name of the gateway through which the call passed. When you both originate and terminate a call through a gateway, the software writes a nonzero number into both span fields. The span is normally the port or channel on that gateway used for that call. In the case of an H.323 trunk call, the span fields contain the call leg ID for the call leg going through that gateway.

Abandoned Calls

An abandoned call is defined as any call that terminates before it actually connects to a destination. Abandoned calls will always have a duration of 0 seconds, and the **origCause_value** field indicates why the call was terminated. If the call has any cause termination value that is not a normal call termination (that is, not 0, 16, or 31), the CDR is logged for that call. Abandoned calls each generate one CDR and one CMR.

Some ways you can create abandoned calls include

- Take a phone off-hook and place it back on-hook without dialing any digits. (CDR is not normally logged for this call type.)
- Take the phone off-hook and dial a partial or invalid number and then hang up. (CDR is logged.)
- Call a phone where the user did not answer and it was not forwarded. (CDR is logged.)
- Call a busy phone that did not forward on busy. (CDR is logged.)
- Call an invalid number. (CDR is logged.)

CallManager does not distinguish between calls that you abandon on purpose and calls that do not connect because of some network or system error condition. If the cause of termination is anything but a normal call termination, the CDR is logged.

Short Calls

A short call is a call with a duration of less than 1 second. It appears as a zero duration call in the CDRs. These can be differentiated from failed calls by the **dateTimeConnect** field, which shows the actual connect time of the call. For failed calls (which have never connected), this value is zero. If you want to see these calls, you need to enable **CdrLogCallsWithZeroDurationFlag**.

Cisco IP Phone Failures During a Call

When a Cisco IP Phone is unplugged, there is no immediate physical indication to CallManager. CallManager relies on a TCP-based KeepAlive signaling mechanism to detect when a Cisco IP Phone is disconnected. The KeepAlive interval is normally set to 30 seconds, and for this discussion, it is assumed that the interval is set at its default value.

Every 30 seconds, each Cisco IP Phone sends a KeepAlive message to CallManager, and CallManager responds with an acknowledgment. Both parties then know that the other is functioning properly. When a Cisco IP Phone is unplugged, it fails to send this KeepAlive message. CallManager waits for three KeepAlive intervals (by default, this is about 90 seconds) from the time of the last KeepAlive message before assuming that the IP Phone is no longer functioning. The implication to billing is that when a Cisco IP Phone is unplugged, the duration of the call reflected in the CDR can be up to three KeepAlive intervals (about 90 seconds) longer than the actual speech time experienced by the user. This value, 90 seconds, is worst-case, assuming that the default KeepAlive interval of 30 seconds is not changed. When two KeepAlives are missed, the call is terminated at the next KeepAlive interval. Calls that fail in this manner might be identified by a cause value of 41

(Temporary Failure). It is possible for this cause value to occur in other circumstances because external devices such as gateways can also generate this cause value.

Forwarded or Redirected Calls

The fields in the CDRs for both forwarded calls and redirected calls are the same as those for normal calls, except for the **originalCalledPartyNumber** field and the **originalCalledPartyNumberPartition** field. These two fields contain the directory number and partition of the original destination for this call. When you forward a call, the **finalCalledPartyNumber** and the **finalCalledPartyNumberPartition** fields are updated to contain the directory number of the final destination of the call. The **lastRedirectDn** and **lastRedirectDnPartition** fields contain the directory number and partition of the last phone that forwarded or redirected this call, and the **lastRedirectRedirectOnBehalfOf** field identifies which feature or entity caused the call to be redirected. In the case of forwarding, the **lastRedirectRedirectReason** field identifies why the call was forwarded.

HINT   If the call is forwarded more than one hop, the intermediate forwarding parties are not recorded in the CDR.

Features such as conference and call pickup redirect calls to implement the feature operation.

Transferred Calls and Examples

Calls that are transferred have additional records logged for them. The three calls that are logged are as follows:

- Original call from party A to party B
- Call from the transferring party (party A or B) to the transfer destination (party C)
- Call from the transferred party (party A or B) to the destination (party C)

If the transfer is a blind transfer—in which the user did not wait for the transfer destination to answer before completing the transfer—the record logged has a duration of 0 seconds and the **origCause_Value** and **destCause_Value** fields set to 126 (Call Split).

The following examples are not an exhaustive set and are intended to illustrate the records that are generated under the stated circumstances. The examples help clarify what records are generated on transferred calls, parked calls, and conference calls. These examples assume that you did not enable **CdrLogCallsWithZeroDurationFlag**.

Transferred Call Example 1: A Calls B, A Transfers B to C

The call scenario is as follows:

1 A calls B.

2 B answers the call.

3 A presses **Trnsfer**.

4 A calls C.

5 C answers the call.

6 A presses **Trnsfer** again.

7 When B and C are done talking, one or both hang up.

Three CDRs and four CMRs are generated for this call:

- CMR for A—Logged when A initiates the transfer.

- Three records are logged when A completes the transfer (second button press):
  - CDR for call from A to B—Original call
  - CDR for call from A to C—Consultative call, where A announces the transfer of B to C
  - CMR for A

- Three records are logged when either B or C hangs up:
  - CDR for call from B to C—Active call after transfer is complete
  - CMR for B
  - CMR for C

This call is a consultation transfer because the call from A to C was actually connected. The **originalCalledPartyNumber** and **finalCalledPartyNumber** field values are the same in the CDRs for this call.

Transferred Call Example 2: A Calls B, B Transfers A to C

The call scenario is as follows:

1 A calls B.

2 B answers the call.

3 B presses **Trnsfer** button.

4 B calls C.

5 C answers the call.

6 B presses **Trnsfer** button again.

7 When A and C are done talking, one or both hang up.

Three CDRs and four CMRs are generated for this call. The records logged are

- CMR for B—Logged when B presses the **Trnsfer** button.
- Three records are logged when B presses the **Trnsfer** button the second time:
  — CDR for call from A to B—Original call
  — CDR for call from B to C—Consultative call where B announces the transfer of A to C
  — CMR for B
- Three records are logged when either A or C hangs up:
  — CDR for call from A to C—Active call after transfer is complete
  — CMR for A
  — CMR for C

Transferred Call Example 3: A Calls B, A Transfers B to C on a Blind Transfer

The call scenario is as follows:

1 A calls B.

2 B answers the call.

3 A presses **Trnsfer**.

4 A calls C.

5 C does not answer yet.

6 A presses **Trnsfer** again.

7 C answers the call.

8 When B and C are done talking, one or both hang up.

Three CDRs and four CMRs are generated for this call:

- CMR for A—Logged when A pressed the **Trnsfer** button.

- Three records are logged when A presses the **Trnsfer** button the second time:
  — CDR for call from A to B

  — CMR for A

  — CDR for call from A to C (zero duration and termination cause of 126 [Call Split])
- Three records are logged when either B or C hangs up:
  — CDR for call from B to C

  — CMR for B

  — CMR for C

Because the call was a blind transfer, the call from A to C has a duration of 0 seconds and the **origCause_Value** and **destCause_Value** set to 126 (Call Split). The call is logged because of the Call Split cause code.

Transferred Call Example 4: A Calls B, B Transfers A to C on a Blind Transfer

The call scenario is as follows:

1 A calls B.

2 B answers the call.

3 B presses **Trnsfer**.

4 B calls C.

5 C does not answer yet.

6 B presses **Trnsfer** again.

7 C answers the call.

8 When A and C are done talking, one or both hang up.

Three CDRs and four CMRs are generated for this call:

- CMR for B—Logged when B pressed the **Trnsfer** button.
- Three records are logged when B presses the **Trnsfer** button the second time:
  — CDR for call from A to B

  — CMR for B

  — CDR for call from B to C (zero duration and termination cause of 126 [Call Split]).
- Three records are logged when either A or C hangs up:
  — CDR for call from A to C

— CMR for A

— CMR for C

Because the call was a blind transfer, the call from B to C has a duration of 0 seconds and the **origCause_Value** and **destCause_Value** set to 126 (Call Split).

Transferred Call Example 5: A Calls B, B Transfers A to C on a Blind Transfer, and C Is Forwarded to D

The call scenario is as follows:

1 Set Call Forward All on phone C to phone D.

2 A calls B.

3 B answers the call.

4 B presses **Trnsfer**.

5 B calls C (C is forwarded to D).

6 D does not answer yet.

7 B presses **Trnsfer** again.

8 D answers the call.

9 When A and D are done talking, one or both hang up.

Three CDRs and four CMRs are generated for this call:

- CMR for B—Logged when B pressed **Trnsfer** button.
- Three records are logged when B presses the **Trnsfer** button the second time:
  — CDR for call from A to B
  — CMR for B
  — CDR for call from B to C (which was forwarded to D)
- Three records are logged when either A or D hangs up:
  — Call from A to D
  — CMR for A
  — CMR for D

This call was a blind transfer, and the call from B to C has a duration of 0 seconds and the **origCause_Value** and **destCause_Value** set to 126 (Call Split). Because the destination C was forwarded to D, the call logged from A to D will have the

originalCalledPartyNumber field set to "C," and the **finalCalledPartyNumber** field set to "D."

Parked Call Example: A Calls B, A Parks B, and C Picks Up B

The call scenario is as follows:

1 A calls B.

2 B answers the call.

3 A presses **Park** (call was parked on a Park Number).

4 C calls B's Park Number.

5 When B and C are done talking, one or both hang up.

Two CDRs and three CMRs are generated for a parked call:

- CMR for A—Logged when A pressed the **Park** button.
- CDR for call from A to B (original call)—Logged when A pressed the **Park** button.
- Three records are logged when either B or C hangs up:
  - CDR for call from C to B (the final call when C picked it up)
  - CMR for B
  - CMR for C

Conference Calls and Examples

CallManager allows two types of conferences, Ad Hoc and Meet-Me. CallManager creates a different set of records for each of these conference types.

Ad Hoc Conference Example: A Calls B, A Calls C, A Sets Up Conference Among A, B, and C

The call scenario is as follows:

1 A calls B.

2 B answers the call.

3 A presses **Confrn** button.

4 A calls C.

5 A presses **Confrn** again.

6 When A, B, and C are done talking, two or more hang up.

Five CDRs and five CMRs are generated for a three-party Ad Hoc conference:

- CMR for A—Logged when A pressed the **Confrn** button.
- CDR for call from A to B—Logged when A pressed the **Confrn** button.
- CDR for call from A to C—Logged when A pressed the **Confrn** button the second time.
- CMR for A—Logged when A pressed the **Confrn** button the second time.
- Six records are logged when the conference is terminated. The CDRs are logged in the order that the participants hang up:
    - CDR for call from A to conference bridge
    - CDR for call from B to conference bridge
    - CDR for call from C to conference bridge
    - CMR for A
    - CMR for B
    - CMR for C

In an Ad Hoc conference, each additional participant added causes four additional records to be generated. In this case, the call scenario to add another participant is as follows:

1 A presses **Confrn** button.

2 A calls D.

3 D answers the call.

4 A presses **Confrn** button again (D joins the conference).

Two CDR and two CMR records would be logged:

- CMR for A when A pressed the **Confrn** button to begin the conference addition
- CDR for call from A to D logged when A pressed the **Confrn** button the second time
- CDR for call from D to conference bridge logged when the conference is terminated
- CMR for D logged when conference was terminated

Meet-Me Conference Example: A Sets Up Meet-Me Conference, B and C Call into Conference

The call scenario is as follows:

1 A goes off-hook.

2 A presses **MeetMe** button.

3 A dials Meet-Me number (A is connected to the conference).

4 B calls Meet-Me number (B is connected to the conference).

5 C calls Meet-Me number (C is connected to the conference).

6 When A, B, and C are done talking, they hang up.

Three CDRs and three CMRs are generated for a three-party Meet-Me conference. The CDR and CMR for each call into the conference are logged when that participant hangs up. The records are as follows:

- CDR for call from A to Meet-Me conference
- CMR A
- CDR for call from B to Meet-Me conference
- CMR B
- CDR for call from C to Meet-Me conference
- CMR C

For each additional participant in a Meet-Me conference, one CDR record is logged and one CMR record is logged.

Held Calls Example

This illustrates what happens when calls are placed on hold and resumed again.

The call scenario is as follows:

1 A calls B.

2 A presses **Hold**.

3 A presses **Resume**.

4 A presses **Hold**.

5 A presses **Resume**.

6 B presses **Hold**.

7 B presses **Resume**.

8 A presses **Hold**.

9 A presses **Resume**.

10 B presses **Hold**.

11 B presses **Resume**.

12 A or B hangs up.

Held calls create one CMR for each time you put a call on hold. They also create only one CDR for the entire call, which includes the talk time and hold time from the time the call originally connected to the time of the final disconnect. CMRs are generated in order each time a user presses the **Hold** button.

- CMR for A—B placed on hold
- CMR for A—B placed on hold again
- CMR for B—A placed on hold
- CMR for A—B placed on hold
- CMR for B—A placed on hold
- CDR for call from A to B

Calls with Busy or Bad Destinations

A call with a busy or bad destination is logged with all relevant fields containing data. Which fields contain data is dependent on what caused the call to terminate. The **destCause_value** field contains a cause code indicating why the call was not completed.

One CDR is logged and possibly one CMR is logged for each of these calls.

If you abandoned the call without dialing any digits, the cause will be NO_ERROR (0), and the duration will always be 0 seconds. These calls are not logged unless **CdrLogCallsWithZeroDurationFlag** is enabled. If the call is logged, one CDR is logged and possibly one CMR is logged.

Accessing CDR Data in the Central CDR Database

Cisco CallManager stores all CDR data in the central CDR database. In some cases, it is not the same database as the CallManager Administration database. You can access all tables in the database in a read-only fashion and the CDR and CMR tables in a read/write fashion.

When you are processing CDR data, you might want to read other tables in the CallManager Administration database to obtain information about the type of device for which this CDR was written. The device name is provided in the CDR record, but the device type and other information is not.

CallManager uses the Microsoft SQL Server 7.0 database. You can gain direct access to the database with Open DataBase Connectivity (ODBC).

Gaining Access to Database Tables

The easiest way to read data from the SQL database is to use ODBC. The following example illustrates what a good connection string looks like:

```
DRIVER={SQL Server};SERVER=machineX;DATABASE=CCM0300
DRIVER={SQL Server};SERVER=machineX;DATABASE=CDR
```

You must be sure to use the correct database name. Previous versions of the product had the CDR tables in the CCM0300 database. The tables have been moved to the CDR database. If a new version of the CCM0300 database is installed over an older version of the database, both databases still exist. The highest-numbered database should be used. You can find the primary database (machine and name) currently in use by the cluster by selecting **Help > About Cisco CallManager** and clicking the **Details** button.

The registry on servers hosting a database can also be checked. Look at the following registry key for DBConnection0:

\\HKEY_LOCAL_MACHINE\Software\Cisco Systems Inc.\DBL

The DBConnection0 string item contains a connection string similar to the preceding with the machine name and database name of the primary database. Also, the CDR database name is stored in a local registry key.

\\HKEY_LOCAL_MACHINE\Software\Cisco Systems Inc.\DBL\PrimaryCdrServer

---

HINT   You will need access to both the configuration database and CDR database to properly resolve the CDR information.

CallManager uses SQL Users to control access to the database. Table 7-10 specifies the two UserIDs and associated passwords that you can use to access the CallManager database.

Table 7-10 *SQL UserIDs for Accessing the Main Database*

Database	Tables	SQL UserID	Password	Capability
CDR	CallDetailRecord, CallDetailRecord Diagnostic	CiscoCCMCDR	dipsy	Read/write
CCM0300	(All other tables)	CiscoCCMReader	cowboys	Read only

Performance Issues Related to Processing and Removing CDR Data

Keep the following performance guidelines in mind when you consider how to process CDR data. If the database is on the same server as CallManager, CDR processing during normal to heavy call activity might have a significant impact on system performance. Cisco recommends that no CDR processing should be done on the data in the CDR table except to move the data to a separate machine. This is the best way to ensure that CDR analysis will not impact system performance. The following are additional tips for processing CDR data:

- Partner's software and databases should never reside on the MCS platform and should be placed on a separate physical system.

- Do not use database triggers on CallManager tables.

- Do not use database-stored procedures on CallManager tables.

- If a partner does not want CDR data written to the CallManager Administration database, a Data Source Name (DSN) entry on CallManager can be changed so that CDR data is written to the separate server. If a large memory cache is made available on the separate server, these actions should improve CallManager performance.

- When moving CDR data from the CallManager CDR database to a separate database or machine, activate a low-priority thread to offload CDR data from CallManager to the separate server during low-volume periods.

- If bulk pulling CDR data from the database, a rule of thumb is to pull no more than 10 K records at a time.

Maintaining CDR/CMR Record Data in the Database

CallManagers within the cluster generate CDR data and write it into the database. In general, the system does not make any attempt to process the data or remove the data when it has been processed except those actions necessary to preserve system integrity. The section "System Actions and Limits on Record Storage" covers the actions taken to preserve system integrity.

Administrator's Responsibility

CallManager relies on third-party or user-supplied software packages to post-process the CDR data and remove it when processing is complete. The administrator has the responsibility either to ensure that the post-processing software removes the data when all processing of the data has been completed, or to establish and execute other procedures to remove the data. CallManager removes data as necessary to enforce a limit on disk usage if the data store grows too large. This preserves system integrity, but it can result in lost CDR data if it has not been processed.

The database layer creates a protective shield around the database to prevent altering configuration data except through Cisco CallManager Administration. You must have write access into the database to remove data, as this involves modifying the database. Two SQL UserIDs provided allow access to the CDR data. To gain write access into the database and remove the data, you must use the CiscoCCMCDR SQL UserID.

When CDR data is removed from the database after analysis is completed, all related CMR records should also be removed. If either CMR data or CDR data is not removed when the corresponding records have been removed in the other table, no particular harm is done, except that the data is not available and takes up disk space.

It is recommended that you do regular backups on your CDR database. If you do regular backups, no further action needed.

System Actions and Limits on Record Storage

The CallManager server platforms ship with sufficient disk storage to safely store approximately 10 million CDRs and their associated CMRs. Once a day, the system checks the number of CDRs currently stored in the database against a configured maximum value. If the number of records contained in the CallDetailRecord table exceeds this maximum value, the system takes the following actions to ensure that sufficient disk space is maintained to safely operate the cluster:

- If CDR records accumulate to a configured maximum, the oldest CDRs are removed, along with related CMRs, once a day. The CDR data count is reduced back to the configured maximum.

- When records are removed from the database, an alarm is generated that says, "Local CDR tables grew too large. Records were deleted." This alarm is routed to the Event Viewer and to trace files.

HINT   The configured maximum number of CDR records is set to 1.5 million when the system is shipped. CallManager makes no attempt to intelligently remove data, so if CallManager is required to remove CDR data, it is possible to remove part of the CDR data for a given call but not all of it.

HINT   You should remove records more often than once a day or per week in large systems. Queries to remove records consume CPU time and transaction log space relative to the size of the table. The smaller the table, the quicker your query runs. Removing significant quantities of records from the database during normal system operation might have a severe performance impact on CallManager.

Hints on Processing CDR Data

There are issues with the CDR data that CallManager generates. The CallManager database contains all configuration information needed to operate the system, but it does not contain enough information to satisfy all requirements from third-party call accounting software packages. This section identifies the known problem areas and gives a few suggestions on how you might resolve these issues.

Additional Configuration Data Needed

The CDR data contains IP addresses and device names for the endpoints of a call. This provides the necessary information for most endpoints; however, in the case of gateways, the post-processing software must collect some additional configuration data when the post-processing system is installed or configured. Some typical configuration data that the post-processing software might need are

- Identification of gateways by name or IP address
- Gateway physical location
- Gateway span configuration
- Gateway type or usage
- Billing rates

Only directory numbers assigned to devices on CallManager are in the database. You will have to make processing assumptions when the directory number is not found in the database. The following section provides clues about some typical assumptions you might need to make.

OnNet Versus OffNet

This is a really thorny issue when trying to generate accurate billing information, because it is difficult to determine whether the call stayed completely on the IP network or was terminated on the public network. One clue you can use is to check the device type on both ends of the call. If both are phones that are defined in the database, you can assume that it stayed OnNet. If the call terminated on a gateway, it is more difficult.

You might have different types of gateways configured on the system. Cisco Access Analog gateways might have station ports with standard analog phones attached to them. Typically, these devices are considered OnNet. The Cisco Access Analog gateway might be connected to analog phone lines and used as an access into the PSTN. Calls terminating on those ports went OffNet. Other gateways have similar situations that must be accounted for. You can also look at the called party number to see if the number dialed is defined in the CallManager database. If you do not find it there, or it does not match a dial plan for OnNet calls, it likely went OffNet.

To process calls that terminate in the PSTN, you need to have information about the physical location of the gateway. A given directory number can be either local or long distance, depending on where the gateway is located.

Gateway Directory Number Processing

If you make a call that routes through a gateway and terminates on the PSTN somewhere, the digits you dialed to get to the gateway might not be the digits that were actually sent to the PSTN. The gateways have the capability of modifying the directory number further by stripping digits or adding additional digits and so forth. Whether the gateway modifies numbers or not depends on how you configure the gateway. The gateways can modify both incoming and outgoing digit strings. In either case, Call Control does not know about any modifications that are made to the digit strings by the gateways themselves. On the incoming side, the modified directory number is received from the gateway, but Call Control does not know whether any modifications were made by the gateway, or whether the number was just received by the gateway and passed through to Call Control. CDR data reflects any changes made by a gateway on the incoming side because that is the number that was processed by Call Control. The CDR data does not reflect any changes that are made by the gateways on the outgoing side because that information is not returned to Call Control.

Troubleshooting CDR Data Generation and Storage

This section documents some common problems and errors and suggests possible solutions. This is not an exhaustive list, so you should check the Cisco Press Web site (www.ciscopress.com) for any updates to this chapter if you are experiencing problems that are not covered here.

No CDR Records Are Written to the Central Data Store

Possible Cause: CallManager is shipped with CDR data generation disabled. The most common problem in this area is that you have not enabled CDR data generation.

Solution: Set the **CdrEnabled** service parameter to "T" on all CallManager nodes in the cluster. If you also want CMR data, you should enable the **CallDiagnosticsEnabled** service parameter.

CDR Data Is Logged for Some Calls, but Not for Others

Possible Cause: If you enable CDR data generation by setting the **CdrEnabled** service parameter equal to "T" on some CallManager nodes in the cluster and not on other ones, the system logs CDR data only from the CallManager nodes where you enabled CDR data generation.

Solution: Set the **CdrEnabled** service parameter to be the same on all CallManager nodes in the cluster.

No CMRs Are Written to the Central Data Store

Possible Cause: The system does not generate CMR data unless both the **CdrEnabled** service parameter and the **CallDiagnosticsEnabled** service parameter are enabled. Usually, one or the other of these two service parameters is not enabled.

Solution: Enable both the **CdrEnabled** and the **CallDiagnosticsEnabled** service parameters on all CallManager nodes in the cluster.

CMR Data Is Logged for Some Cisco IP Phones and MGCP Gateways, but Not for Others

Possible Cause: The current setting of both the **CallDiagnosticsEnabled** and **CdrEnabled** service parameters is not the same on all CallManager nodes in the cluster. The system logs CMR data only from the CallManager nodes where both parameters are enabled. It might be possible that some MGCP gateways do not support diagnostic data.

Solution: Set both the **CdrEnabled** service parameter and the **CallDiagnosticsEnabled** service parameter to be the same on all CallManager nodes in the cluster. If you want CMR data, you must enable both service parameters. If a particular gateway does not support diagnostic data, it will not be available for that gateway.

Summary

Two record types are included in CDR data: CDRs, which contain information needed to create billing records, and CMRs, which contain information that can be used to evaluate the quality of service for a given call. Together, they can be used for tracking call activity, diagnosing certain types of problems, and evaluating the quality of service of calls through the system. Both records are stored in a central SQL database in separate tables.

With Cisco CallManager release 3.1, device names and other important information is now available directly from the CDR data and no longer requires additional external processes to obtain this information.

Calls such as transfers and conference calls produce a set of records that must be identified and processed as a set to properly bill for the calls. Extensive field data information and examples have been provided in the hope of being useful in the development of billing packages, call activity tracking, and other reporting tools.

With this information, a system administrator should have a good understanding of the CDR facilities that CallManager provides and learns how to manage and control those facilities, how to obtain access to CDR data, and how to process the CDR data.

Feature List

This appendix provides a list of Cisco CallManager features. Features that are new to CallManager with release 3.1 are indicated.

Both phone and CallManager features are detailed in this appendix. Features include the functions of the soft keys or buttons on a Cisco IP Phone in addition to administration functions for CallManager.

Cisco CallManager Feature List

The following features are available in CallManager release 3.1:

- Administrative Reporting Tool (ART)
- Answer/Release
- Auto Answer
- Broadcast Paging Support
- Context-Sensitive Help on Phone
- Bulk Administration Tool (BAT)
- Call Connection
- Call Detail Records (CDRs)/Call Management Records (CMRs)
- Call Forward Reason Codes
- Call Forwarding
- Call Forwarding Support for Third-Party Applications
- Call Park
- Call Pickup/PickUp
- Call Preservation to MGCP Gateways
- Call Status per Line
- Call Waiting/Retrieve
- Calling Line Identification (CLID)

- Calling Party Name Identification (CNID)
- Centralized System Administration
- Cisco CallManager Administration Enhancements for Large System Administration
- Cisco CallManager Administration Support for Cisco MGCP Gateways
- Cisco CallManager Failover Interoperability with Cisco Catalyst Gateways
- Cisco CallManager Serviceability
- Cisco H.323 Gateway Support
- Cisco IP Phone 7960, 7940, and 7910 Support
- Cisco IP Phone Conference Station 7935 Support
- Cisco IP Phone User Options Web Page
- Cisco IP Phone Expansion Module 7914 Support
- Cisco IP Phone Productivity Services (by XML API)
- Cisco IP SoftPhone Support
- Cisco Personal Address Book
- Cisco VG200 FXS/FXO Support Through MGCP
- Cisco VG200 Hookflash Transfer Support
- Cisco WebAttendant
- CISCO-CCM-MIB Updates
- Click to Dial from Cisco IP Phone Models 7960 and 7940
- Conference/Confrn
- CTI API Enhancements
- CTI Support for Cisco Applications and Software Development Kit (SDK)
- Database API
- Database Automated Change Notification
- Date/Time Display Format Configurable per Phone
- Debug Information to Common Syslog File
- Device Change to Database Does Not Require Cisco CallManager Restart
- Device Downloadable Feature Upgrade
- Device Mapping Tool—IP Addresses to MAC Addresses
- Device Pool
- Device Search in Cisco CallManager Administration

- Device Wizard
- DHCP IP Assignment for Phones and Gateways
- Dial Plan Partitions and Calling Search Spaces
- Dialed Number Translation Table (Inbound and Outbound Translation)
- Direct Inward Dial
- Direct Outward Dial
- Directories
- Directory Dial from Phone
- Directory on Cisco IP Phone 7960 and 7940
- Disable Visual and Audio Indication of Ringing Line
- Distinctive Ring—Internal vs. External
- Distinctive Ring per Cisco IP Phone 79*xx*
- Distributed Cisco CallManager
- Distributed Resource Sharing
- DSP Resource Alignment
- Embedded Directory for User Data
- Emergency 911 Service (E911)
- EndCall
- Extension Mobility
- External Route Plan Wizard
- FXS Support for Cisco Catalyst 6000 (WS-6624) 24 Port Gateways
- Gain Attenuation for Audio Levels on Cisco Catalyst 6000 E1/T1-PRI (WS-6608-x1) 8 Port Gateways, Cisco Catalyst 6000 FXS (WS-6624) 24 Port Gateways, and Cisco Access DT-24+/DE-30+ Gateways
- Group Call Pickup/GPickUp
- GSM-EFR/FR Support Through Use of Hardware Transcoder
- H.323-Compliant Interface to H.323 Clients, Gateways, and Gatekeepers
- Hold/Resume
- HTTPD Server
- Integrated Call Distributor
- JTAPI Computer Telephony Interface (CTI)
- LDAPv3 Directory Interface
- Line

- Media Resource Group List Support
- Meet-Me Conference/MeetMe
- Message Waiting Indicator
- Messages
- Microsoft NetMeeting
- Multiple Line Appearances per Phone
- Music on Hold
- Mute
- NewCall
- Off-Hook Dialing
- Outbound Hookflash Support to Adjunct PBXs from H.323 Clients
- Overlap Sending
- Paperless Phone
- Performance Monitoring
- Privacy
- QoS Statistics for the Phone
- Redial/REDL
- Remote Site Survivability
- Scalability Enhancements Through H.323 Gatekeeper (Beyond Ten Sites)
- Select Specified Line Appearance
- Serviceability Enhancements Through SNMP, CDP, CiscoWorks2000
- Services on Cisco IP Phone Models 7960 and 7940
- Settings
- Shared Line Appearance on Multiple Phones
- Single CDR per Cluster
- Single Point for System/Device Configuration
- Speakerphone/SPKR
- Speed Dial
- Supplementary Services to Cisco IOS H.323 Gateways Without Media Termination Point (MTP)
- System Event Reporting
- T1/E1 PRI Support for Cisco Catalyst 6000 (WS-6608-x1) 8 Port Gateways

- T1-CAS Support on Cisco Digital Access DT-24+ and Cisco Catalyst 6000 T1 Interfaces
- TAPI CTI
- TAPI/JTAPI Interface and Applications Support (Cisco IP Contact Center, Cisco IP IVR, Cisco IP AA, Cisco IP SoftPhone)
- TAPI/JTAPI Redundancy Support
- Time Zone Configuration
- Tone on Hold
- Transfer/XFER
- Unicast Conference
- Vendor-Specific MGCP Information Configuration
- Visual Indicator of Ringing Phone
- Volume Controls
- Wideband Stereo Codec on 79xx
- Year 2000 Compliance
- Zero Cost Automated Phone Moves
- Zero Cost Phone Adds

Administrative Reporting Tool (ART)

The Administrative Reporting Tool (ART), a Web-based application, provides reports that can help simplify departmental billing, administration for diagnostics and Call Detail Records (CDRs), and quality of service (QoS) and traffic monitoring, among other features. Refer to Chapter 6, "Manageability and Monitoring Tools," for detailed information about ART.

Answer/Release

Answer/Release is available for Cisco IP Phone models 12SP+, 30VIP, 7960, and 7940. The following sections describe how Answer/Release works for each Cisco IP Phone model.

Answer/Release on Cisco IP Phone Models 12SP+ and 30VIP

Answer/Release is used in conjunction with a headset, so the user can press a button on the headset apparatus to answer and release (disconnect) calls. The phone's handset must be off-hook to use Answer/Release.

Answer/Release can be configured on the button template for Cisco IP Phone models 12SP+ or 30VIP. To answer a call when using a headset, the user presses the **Answer/Release** button and is connected to the caller. To disconnect, the user presses the **Answer/Release** button again.

Answer/Release on Cisco IP Phone Models 7960 and 7940

Answer is a soft key used to answer a ringing line. To release a call, you can press **EndCall** or toggle the **HEADSET** button on the phone if you're using a headset. On Cisco IP Phone models 7960 and 7940, the **Answer** and **Resume** soft keys are automatically available.

Auto Answer

Auto Answer is a feature available for Cisco IP Phone models 12SP+ or 30VIP only. Auto Answer can be configured on the button template and allows the user to have incoming calls answered automatically by speakerphone. When this feature is programmed on the button template, it causes the phone to go off-hook (on speakerphone) automatically when an incoming call is received.

Broadcast Paging Support

Broadcast paging support is achieved through configuration of one or more Foreign Exchange Station (FXS) gateway ports configured within CallManager with specific directory numbers on each port. A third-party product attached to the FXS ports automatically answers the calls and distributes the audio to broadcast speakers.

Context-Sensitive Help on Phone

Cisco IP Phone models 7960 and 7940 provide help for phone features using the **i** button. Help displays on the screen.

Bulk Administration Tool (BAT)

The Bulk Administration Tool (BAT), a Web-based application, can be used to perform bulk add, update, and delete operations on the CallManager database. For large systems, BAT can significantly reduce the manual labor involved in creating or maintaining the CallManager database. BAT is accessed from the **Application** menu in Cisco CallManager Administration. Refer to Chapter 6 for detailed information about BAT.

Call Connection

CallManager provides phone-to-phone call connection.

Call Detail Records (CDRs)/Call Management Records (CMRs)

CDRs provide billing information about calls. CMRs provide diagnostic information about calls. You can learn more about these features in Chapter 7, "Call Detail Records."

Call Forward Reason Codes

NOTE   This is a new feature for CallManager release 3.1.

CallManager provides reason codes that describe whether the call forwarded unconditionally, because of no response, or because of a busy subscriber to the voice mail system. The following interfaces are supported:

- Skinny Protocol
- Cisco Messaging Interface (by simplified message desk interface [SMDI])
- ISDN
- Telephony Application Programming Interface (TAPI)/Java TAPI (JTAPI)
- H.323

Call Forwarding

Calls placed to a phone that has a call forwarding designation are forwarded to the specified number. Calls can be forwarded on three conditions:

- When the user designates a number to which all calls should be forwarded
- When the line is busy
- When the phone is not answered

Forward All/CFwdAll

This feature is known as Forward All or CFwdAll, depending on the phone model in use.

- For Cisco IP Phone models 12SP+, 30VIP, or 7910, the feature is called Forward All.
- For Cisco IP Phone models 7960 or 7940, the feature is called CFwdAll.

Forward All on Cisco IP Phone Models 12SP+, 30VIP, and 7910

Forward All can be configured on the button template for Cisco IP Phone models 12SP+, 30VIP, and 7910. To forward all calls, the user presses the **Forward All** button, hears two tones, and then dials the number (internal, or external if permitted) to which the user wants all calls forwarded. If the dialed number is valid, two confirmation tones are heard. The Forward All light remains lit when call forwarding is set. To disable Forward All, the user presses the **Forward All** button again, hears two tones, and the forwarding request is cancelled.

CFwdAll on Cisco IP Phone Models 7960 and 7940

To forward all calls, the user presses the **CFwdAll** soft key, hears two tones, and then dials the number (internal, or external if permitted) to which the user wants all calls forwarded. The display shows the number to which all calls are being forwarded. To cancel forwarding all calls, the user presses the **CFwdAll** button again, hears two tones, and the forwarding request is cancelled. The user can also configure this feature in the Cisco IP Phone User Options Web page (see "Cisco IP Phone User Options Web Page" later in this appendix). The **CFwdAll** soft key is automatically available.

Table A-1 provides information about Call Forwarding service parameters.

Table A-1 *Forward All/CFwdAll Values*

Value/Definition	Default	Range	Cisco CallManager Administration Location
AdvanceCallForwardHopFlag Determines whether CallManager will skip the busy or unregistered voice mail port when selecting the next voice mail port.	F	True (T) or False (F) If this flag is set to True, CallManager skips any busy or unregistered voice mail ports and routes the call to an available voice mail port. If this flag is set to False, CallManager extends the call to the voice mail ports in order, regardless of whether any are busy or unregistered. When a call is extended to a busy or unregistered voice mail port, the call will be rejected and forwarded to the next consecutive voice mail port.	Service Parameters Configuration screen (**Service > Service Parameters** > *select server* > **Cisco CallManager**)
ForwardMaximumHopCount The maximum number of attempts to extend a forwarded call.	12	Any number 1 or greater	Service Parameters Configuration screen (**Service > Service Parameters** > *select server* > **Cisco CallManager**)

Table A-1   *Forward All/CFwdAll Values (Continued)*

Value/Definition	Default	Range	Cisco CallManager Administration Location
MaxForwardsToDn This parameter applies only to intercluster calls and calls from the PSTN. A value of 0 disables this feature and there is no limit on the number of forwards. Designates the maximum number of times a call can be forwarded. When the value specified in MaxForwardsToDn is reached, the call terminates and the caller hears a reorder tone.	0	3 to 20; if 1 or 2 is entered, it will be forced to 3.	Service Parameters Configuration screen (**Service** > **Service Parameters** > *select server* > **Cisco CallManager**)
ToneOnCallForward When you are already on an active line, this parameter determines whether to play some type of tone when a call is being forwarded.	T	T (play tone) or F (do not play tone)	Service Parameters Configuration screen (**Service** > **Service Parameters** > *select server* > **Cisco CallManager**)

Call Forward Busy

Call Forward Busy forwards calls only when the line is busy. This feature is available for all Cisco IP Phone models and must be configured by the system administrator. You can configure call forward busy in the Directory Number Configuration screen of CallManager Administration (**Device** > **Phone** > *select phone* > *select line*).

Call Forward No Answer

Call Forward No Answer forwards calls when the phone is not answered. This feature is available for all Cisco IP Phone models and must be configured by the system administrator.

The default length of time before an unanswered call rolls over to the designated directory number is 12 seconds. To change the time, you must configure the ForwardNoAnswerTimeout service parameter (see Table A-2). You configure the Call Forward No Answer number in the Directory Number Configuration screen of CallManager Administration (**Device > Phone** > *select phone* > *select line*).

Table A-2 provides information about the Call Forward No Answer service parameter.

Table A-2   *Call Forward No Answer Value*

Value/Definition	Default	Range	Cisco CallManager Administration Location
ForwardNoAnswerTimeout The number of seconds to wait before forwarding a call that has not been answered	12 seconds	Any number of seconds greater than 1	Service Parameters Configuration screen (**Service > Service Parameters** > *select server* > **Cisco CallManager**)
MaxForwardsToDn The maximum number of times to extend a forwarded call	0 (disabled)	3 to 20	Service Parameters Configuration screen (**Service > Service Parameters** > *select server* > **Cisco CallManager**)

Call Forwarding Support for Third-Party Applications

NOTE	This is a new feature for CallManager release 3.1.

Using JTAPI, you can execute the **Forward All** command in third-party applications.

Call Park

Call Park allows a user to store a call on a specific directory number so that any other user on the system can retrieve it. It is configured in CallManager Administration and implemented by the user from any Cisco IP Phone on the system.

For example, a user receives a call but wants to take it in a conference room where it is possible to speak privately. Transferring the call to the conference room is not an option, because the conference room it is transferred to might be in use, or the user is unable to walk to the conference room in time to answer the call. The user can use Call Park to place the call at a specific directory number and then retrieve the call on reaching the conference room. Figure A-1 illustrates the call park operation.

Figure A-1   *Call Park Operation*

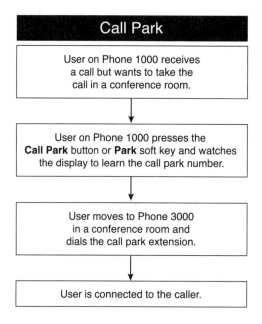

Configuration of Call Park

To use Call Park, one or more directory numbers must be configured in CallManager Administration as call park numbers. You can define either a single directory number or a range of directory numbers for use as call park extensions. Only one call at a time can be parked on each call park extension.

Call park is available to the user during an active call on all Cisco IP Phone models, if configured. For Cisco IP Phone models 7960 and 7940, the **Park** soft key is automatically available. For Cisco IP Phone models 12SP+, 30VIP, or 7910, you must configure one **Call Park** button on the button template used by those phones. To use the feature, the user simply presses the **Call Park** button or **Park** soft key during an active call. The display indicates that the call is parked at the specified extension, and the call park reversion timer begins. The user has the length of time specified in the CallParkReversionTimeout service parameter to retrieve the call from any phone on the CallManager system that has access to the directory number to which the call is parked. To retrieve the call, the user goes off-hook and dials the extension at which the call was parked. The user is then connected to the other party. If the call is not retrieved within the specified time, the call is automatically returned to the phone from which it was parked and placed on hold.

The length of time that a call remains parked is determined by the CallParkReversionTimeout value set in the Service Parameters Configuration screen (**Service > Service Parameters >** *select server* **> Cisco CallManager**) of CallManager Administration. You can configure up to 100 Call Park extensions at a time (for example, 35*xx*), or individually configure specific Call Park extensions (3500, 3501, and so on). Table A-3 provides information about the Call Park service parameter.

Table A-3   *Call Park Value*

Value	Default	Range	Cisco CallManager Administration Location
CallParkReversionTimeout The number of seconds to wait before reverting a parked call to the call parker.	60 seconds	Any numeric value in seconds	Service Parameters Configuration screen (**Service > Service Parameters >** *select server* **> Cisco CallManager**)

Call Pickup/PickUp

Call Pickup allows users to pick up incoming calls within their group. The appropriate call pickup group number is dialed automatically when a user presses the button or soft key on the phone. Call pickup is available for all Cisco IP Phone models. On Cisco IP Phone models 12SP+, 30VIP, and 7910, the button is called **Call Pickup** and must be configured on the button template. On Cisco IP Phone models 7960 and 7940, the soft key is called **PickUp** and is automatically available.

For call pickup to be operational, you must configure the call pickup group in the Call Pickup Configuration screen in CallManager Administration (**Feature > Call Pickup**). The call pickup group is composed of directory numbers. Only directory numbers that have a call pickup group designated in their line properties can use the call pickup feature. The appropriate call pickup group number must be configured in the Directory Number Configuration screen of CallManager Administration (**Device > Phone >** *find and select phone > click line number*) for each directory number that should be able to use the call pickup feature.

To use call pickup, the user goes off-hook and presses the **Call Pickup** button or **PickUp** soft key when the user hears an incoming call ringing on another phone. This causes the ringing call to be redirected to the user's phone. Figure A-2 illustrates the call pickup operation.

Figure A-2   *Call Pickup Operation*

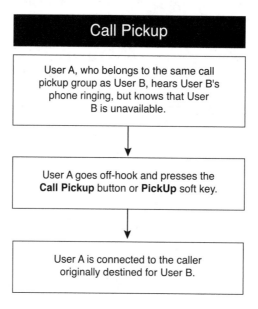

Call Preservation to MGCP Gateways

NOTE	This is a new feature for CallManager release 3.1.

Call preservation ensures that active calls will not be interrupted if CallManager nodes fail or when communication between a device and its CallManager node fails. Calls are preserved even during failure if both parties are connected through one of the following devices:

- Cisco IP Phones
- Software conference bridge (service)
- Software media termination point (service)
- Hardware conference bridge
- Transcoder
- Media Gateway Control Protocol (MGCP) Primary Rate Interface (PRI) gateways including Cisco Catalyst 6000, Cisco Digital Access DT-24+ or DE-30+, and Cisco Analog Access gateways
- Cisco IOS MGCP gateways

Active calls are maintained until the end user hangs up or the devices can determine that the media connection has been released. When a CallManager node fails or communication fails between a device and the CallManager node that controls it, the call processing function for any calls that were set up through it is lost.

Call Status per Line

All Cisco IP Phone models provide basic call status on a per-line basis. The display indicates the connected state, the number, and a timer showing the call duration.

Call Waiting/Retrieve

When a call is received on the secondary line of the directory number currently in use, a tone sounds and the display shows the call information for the waiting call. The user can retrieve the new incoming call by disconnecting or placing the current call on hold. All Cisco IP Phone models provide call waiting on each line, if enabled. You do not need two lines configured on the phone to use the call waiting feature (see "Line" later in this appendix for more information). Table A-4 provides information about the call waiting service parameter.

Table A-4   *Table A-4 Call Waiting Value*

Value	Default	Range	Cisco CallManager Administration Location
CallWaitingEnable Enables or disables Call Waiting for the system	T	T (enabled) or F (disabled)	Service Parameters Configuration screen (**Service > Service Parameters >** *select server* **> Cisco CallManager**)
CallWaitingTimeout Designates the number of seconds that a caller hears ring back (alerting tone) when the person being called is in one of these states: • Internal to the Cisco AVVID (Architecture for Voice, Video and Integrated Data) IP Telephony system • On the phone • Has Call Waiting enabled • Does not have forwarding enabled	180 seconds	Any numeric value in seconds	Service Parameters Configuration screen (**Service > Service Parameters >** *select server* **> Cisco CallManager**)

Calling Line Identification (CLID)

Calling Line Identification (CLID or Caller ID) provides the phone number of an incoming call. Table A-5 provides information about Caller ID service parameters.

Table A-5   *Caller ID Values*

Value	Default	Range	Cisco CallManager Administration Location
UnknownCallerId The directory number to be displayed for caller ID purposes. This can be any numeric value representing a general number for your system (if you wish to provide caller ID functionality to called parties).		Any valid telephone number	Service Parameters Configuration screen (**Service > Service Parameters** > *select server* > **Cisco CallManager**)
UnknownCallerIdFlag This parameter determines whether the value in the UnknownCallerId parameter will be used. Cisco strongly recommends that you use the default setting.	T	T (use value in UnknownCallerId parameter) F (disregard any value in the UnknownCallerId parameter)	Service Parameters Configuration screen (**Service > Service Parameters** > *select server* > **Cisco CallManager**)
UnknownCallerIdText The text to be displayed to called parties having caller ID capability.	Unknown	The first line allows 20 characters and the second line allows 14 characters. Use a string of text that looks acceptable in the display when broken into two lines with the specified number of characters per line.	Service Parameters Configuration screen (**Service > Service Parameters** > *select server* > **Cisco CallManager**)

Calling Party Name Identification (CNID)

CallManager provides the user's phone number to the party receiving the call.

Centralized System Administration

Cisco CallManager Administration, a Web-based application, provides centralized databases that can be accessed by CallManager servers. CallManager cluster configuration is stored in a collection of multiple databases. One database is designated as the Publisher (master) database. All other databases in the cluster are designated as Subscriber databases. All CallManager nodes communicate to the database through an abstraction layer called the database layer. When you work in CallManager Administration, you are making changes to the configuration of the system. Those changes are immediately posted to the Publisher database. Replication software automatically reposts the change to the Subscriber databases. This design allows for improved system redundancy and enhances overall system availability. CallManager Administration is essentially a collection of Web pages that are connected through a Web server with access to the Publisher database.

Cisco CallManager Administration Enhancements for Large System Administration

CallManager allows you to locate devices in a large system by finding and listing phones, gateways, and other devices using filtering criteria.

Cisco CallManager Administration Support for Cisco MGCP Gateways

CallManager Administration supports Cisco Media Gateway Control Protocol (MGCP) gateways, including Cisco 362*x*, 364*x*, and 366*x* gateways.

Cisco CallManager Failover Interoperability with Cisco Catalyst Gateways

CallManager now provides redundant capabilities with Cisco IOS H.323 gateways (includes gateway models 26*xx*, 36*xx*, 53*xx*, 65*xx*, and 7*xx*).

Cisco CallManager Serviceability

NOTE	This is a new feature for CallManager release 3.1.

CallManager Serviceability, a Web-based application, provides detailed alarm definitions and configuration; trace configuration, analysis, and collection; component version information; and real-time monitoring of Cisco AVVID IP Telephony components in a CallManager cluster. It is available from the **Application** menu in CallManager Administration. Chapter 6 provides detailed information about CallManager Serviceability.

Cisco H.323 Gateway Support

CallManager supports the H.323 protocol.

Cisco IP Phone 7960, 7940, and 7910 Support

CallManager supports Cisco IP Phone models 7960, 7940, and 7910. The following sections describe the phone models.

Cisco IP Phone 7960

Cisco IP Phone 7960 provides a nine-line display screen, four soft key buttons to access various features, six line or speed dial buttons, and a cluster of additional buttons providing access to voice mail, directories, services, phone settings, volume controls, headset, mute, and speakerphone. Additional features are described in the following list:

- Security is provided in the form of a lock on the configuration settings of the phone, so only system administrators who know how to unlock the phone can make changes. See the section "Settings" for more information.

- Comprehensive help is available for all phone features. See the section "**i** Button Help—7960" for more information.

- The display indicates when a call has been missed and provides the number of the missed call. See the section "Directories" for more information.

- A headset button provides easy access to on-hook and off-hook states when using a headset with the phone.

i Button Help—7960

For information, press the **i** button. You can use the **i** button in three ways:

- Press the **i** button and then any other key about which you would like information.

- With a feature selected, press the **i** button twice quickly to display help for that feature. For example, press the **settings** button. A menu displays several options. If you press the **i** button twice quickly, the help for the selected option is displayed.

- Press the **i** button twice quickly during an active call to view network statistics about the call.

Cisco IP Phone 7940

Cisco IP Phone 7940 provides a nine-line display screen, four soft key buttons to access various features, two line buttons or one line and one speed dial button, and a cluster of additional buttons providing access to voice mail, directories, services, phone settings, volume controls, headset, mute, and speakerphone. Additional features are described in the following list:

- Security is provided in the form of a lock on the configuration settings of the phone, so only system administrators who know how to unlock the phone can make changes. See the section "Settings" for more information.

- Comprehensive help is available for all phone features. See the section "i Button Help—7940" for more information.

- The display indicates when a call has been missed and provides the number of the missed call. See the section "Directories" for more information.

- A headset button provides easy access to on-hook and off-hook states when using a headset with the phone.

i Button Help—7940

For information, press the **i** button. You can use the **i** button in three ways:

- Press the **i** button and then any other key about which you would like information.

- With a feature selected, press the **i** button twice quickly to display help for that feature. For example, press the **settings** button. A menu displays several options. If you press the **i** button twice quickly, the help for the selected option is displayed.

- Press the **i** button twice quickly during an active call to view network statistics about the call.

Cisco IP Phone 7910

Cisco IP Phone 7910 provides a one-line display screen, six configurable buttons on the faceplate of the phone, in addition to one line button and three features accessible by soft keys on the phone's display. Additional features are described in the following list:

- Security in the form of a lock on the configuration settings of the phone, so only system administrators who know how to unlock the phone can make changes. See the section "Settings" for more information.

- Hands-free dialing.

- Help for settings information.

- Headset connects in the handset jack when handset is disconnected (third-party headset must provide on/off functionality).

- Line button toggles for on-hook and off-hook states.

On-Screen Help

Cisco IP Phone model 7910 provides on-screen help for phone features.

Cisco IP Conference Station 7935 Support

CallManager supports Cisco IP Phone 7935, an IP-based, full-duplex, hands-free conference station that utilizes state-of-the-art conference room speakerphone technology from Polycom. Features include redial, hold, transfer, mute, Ad Hoc and Meet-Me conferencing, call park, call pickup, and more.

- The configuration settings are password-protected, so only system administrators who know the password to unlock the phone can make changes. Changes can be made on the Web or directly on the phone.
- Hands-free dialing.
- Line button toggles for on-hook and off-hook states.

Cisco IP Phone User Options Web Page

The Cisco IP Phone User Options Web page allows users to program their speed dial buttons, change their PIN (for extension mobility), change their password, configure phone services, set call forwarding directives, and configure address book entries in the Cisco Personal Address Book. See "Cisco Personal Address Book" for more information about the Cisco Personal Address Book. See Appendix B, "Cisco Integrated Solutions" for more information about Cisco IP Phone User Options Web Page.

Cisco IP Phone Expansion Module 7914 Support

NOTE	This is a new feature for CallManager release 3.1.

CallManager supports the Cisco IP Phone Expansion Module 7914, an add-on module to Cisco IP Phone model 7960. The Expansion Module 7914 extends the base phone functionality by providing additional line appearance or speed dial buttons. These buttons can be configured as either line or speed dial buttons under the care of the base phone. CallManager supports a maximum of 34 lines, or any combination of lines and speed dial buttons (at least one line is required). Up to two Cisco IP Phone Expansion Modules can be added to a Cisco IP Phone 7960.

Cisco IP Phone Productivity Services (by XML API)

NOTE	This is a new feature for CallManager release 3.1.

An extensible markup language (XML) application programming interface (API) works in conjunction with Cisco IP Phone models 7960 and 7940 to offer custom-configured services. This API includes the services and directory functionality previously available in Cisco IP Phones 7960 and 7940. Existing XML primitives have been expanded to include the ability to override soft key set definitions. This allows for re-mapping of the existing functionality and labels to different keys and adding new keys with associated URLs for application control. A mechanism such as an icon is also provided to indicate to the user that an instant message has been received.

Chapter 3, "Station Devices," provides more information about the XML functionality available in the form of an XML software development kit (SDK).

Cisco IP SoftPhone Support

CallManager provides support for Cisco IP SoftPhone, a virtual telephone that runs on the user's desktop. Using virtual private networks (VPNs), you can use any Internet connection while on the road to handle calls on your extension as if you were in the office. The Cisco IP SoftPhone has all of the features of a desktop business telephone, including hold, transfer, mute, Ad Hoc and Meet-Me conferencing, redial, caller ID display, voice mail integration, dial pad by keyboard or on-screen, context-sensitive online help, and more. The Cisco IP SoftPhone is available in English, French, and German versions.

Cisco IP SoftPhone Support for Microsoft NetMeeting

Cisco IP SoftPhone can launch the following applications for Microsoft NetMeeting if a collaborative PC is configured:

- Application sharing
- Chat
- File transfer
- Video
- White board

Refer to Microsoft documentation for more information about each of these features.

Cisco Personal Address Book

NOTE   This is a new feature for CallManager release 3.1.

Cisco Personal Address Book is an IP phone application that lets users store and retrieve their personal address book entries from their IP phone. Personal Address Book consists of two IP phone services to which users can subscribe. The **PersonalAddressBook** service allows users to search and view their address book entries. Once an entry is selected using the **services** button on the Cisco IP phone, the user can dial the corresponding directory number from the Cisco IP phone. The **PersonalFastDials** service is similar to a speed dial button on the IP phone. When the service is selected using the **services** button on the Cisco IP phone, a list of fast dial entries is displayed in menu format. The user can select a menu item by entering the index number on the IP phone's keypad. The corresponding directory number is then automatically dialed.

A Cisco Address Book utility allows users to synchronize their Microsoft Outlook and Outlook Express address book entries with Cisco Personal Address Book. The Cisco IP Phone Synchronizer performs the synchronization process on the user's desktop.

This feature works with Cisco IP Phone models 7960 and 7940 only and requires configuration in CallManager Administration. For users to have access to the Personal Address Book services, you must first configure the **PersonalAddressBook** and **PersonalFastDials** services in CallManager Administration (**Feature > Cisco IP Phone Services**). To allow users access to the Synchronization utility, you must install the plug-in (**Application > Install Plugins**).

Users can subscribe to Cisco Personal Address Book services on the Cisco IP Phone User Options Web page. They can also synchronize their contact information there, as well as configure their Personal Address Book.

Cisco VG200 FXS/FXO Support Through MGCP

CallManager provides hookflash support through MGCP on Cisco VG200 gateways.

Cisco VG200 Hookflash Transfer Support

Cisco VG200 gateways provide hookflash transfer support.

Cisco WebAttendant

Cisco WebAttendant allows a company to post one or more live attendants to answer and handle inbound and outbound calls that are not serviced by Direct Inward Dial (DID), Direct Outward Dial (DOD), or automated attendant functions. WebAttendant is a client/server application. The WebAttendant is the client application used by the live attendant (receptionist). Telephony Call Dispatcher (TcdSrv) is the server application that extends telephony services to WebAttendant clients and performs the hunt group routing function. Line State Server (LSS) monitors line and device status in the cluster and is one of the functions of the Telephony Call Dispatcher.

WebAttendant provides the following features:

- Busy or available indication
- Call status (date, duration, number)
- Direct station select
- Drag-and-drop transfer
- Headset compatibility
- Left- or right-hand access
- Log-on and log-off
- Web browser interface

WebAttendant provides support for CallManager redundancy.

Longest Idle Support

NOTE	This is a new feature for CallManager release 3.1.

WebAttendant supports longest idle call routing for CallManager release 3.1. Longest idle allows the incoming call load to be more evenly distributed among a group of directory numbers.

WebAttendant uses hunt group lists to determine the destination number for a call. In each hunt group, there is an inherent order for each member in the group. The longest idle feature, if enabled, overrides the inherent order of members and creates a new virtual hunt group each time a call arrives. This new virtual group is ordered by the length of time that each directory number has been idle. In the case of the user/line number pairs, the pair would be translated to a directory number that could then be tracked for length of time idle.

Table A-6 provides information about Cisco WebAttendant service parameters.

Table A-6   *Cisco WebAttendant Values*

Value	Default	Range	Cisco CallManager Administration Location
CCM Line State Port Designates the port number of the TCP/IP port in Cisco CallManager that is used by the line state server to register and receive line and device information	3223	Cisco recommends that the default value be used; however, any port can be used as long as it has been properly configured in all instances.	Service Parameters Configuration screen (**Service > Service Parameters >** *select server* **> Cisco Telephony Call Dispatcher**)
LSS Access Password Designates the default password used at registration to authenticate line state server	private	Any range of alphanumeric characters.	Service Parameters Configuration screen (**Service > Service Parameters >** *select server* **> Cisco Telephony Call Dispatcher**)
LSS Listen Port Designates the TCP port where Cisco WebAttendant clients register with TcdSrv for line and device state information	3221	Cisco recommends that the default value be used; however, any port can be used as long as it has been properly configured in all instances.	Service Parameters Configuration screen (**Service > Service Parameters >** *select server* **> Cisco Telephony Call Dispatcher**)
TCDSrv Listen Port Designates the TCP port where Cisco WebAttendant clients register with TcdSrv for call control	4321	Cisco recommends that the default value be used; however, any port can be used as long as it has been properly configured in every instance of WebAttendant and TCD.	Service Parameters Configuration screen (**Service > Service Parameters >** *select server* **> Cisco Telephony Call Dispatcher**)

CISCO-CCM-MIB Updates

NOTE   This feature has been updated for CallManager release 3.1.

Simple Network Management Protocol (SNMP) Management Information Base (MIB) tables organize and distribute the information gathered from your company site. Additional objects have been added to the CISCO-CCM-MIB tables for CallManager release 3.1. Chapter 6 provides detailed information about SNMP MIBs. You can also view the MIBs at the following location:

```
ftp://ftp.cisco.com/pub/mibs/v2/CISCO-CCM-MIB.my
```

Click to Dial from Cisco IP Phone Models 7960 and 7940

Cisco IP Phone models 7960 and 7940 provide directory access and call initiation from a list of missed, received, and placed calls.

Conference/Confrn

NOTE	CallManager provides two types of conferences: Ad Hoc and Meet-Me. Ad Hoc conferences require the conference controller to include attendees to the conference by calling them individually. Meet-Me conferences allow attendees to dial into the conference after the conference controller has established the conference. Ad Hoc conferences are identified simply by the term *Conference*, while Meet-Me conferences are identified by the term *Meet-Me*. This section describes the Conference feature. Meet-Me is covered in this appendix in the section "Meet-Me Conference/MeetMe."

Conference allows a user to establish a conference, call individual attendees, and connect them to that conference. Conference is available for all Cisco IP Phone models. On Cisco IP Phone models 12SP+, 30VIP, and 7910, the button is called **Conference** and must be configured on the button template. On Cisco IP Phone models 7960 and 7940, the soft key is called **Confrn** and is automatically available during an active call. The **Conference** button is not used to participate in a conference call, only to initiate one. For the Conference feature to be available to users, you must configure the Conference parameters. This can be done in the Conference Bridge Parameters screen in CallManager Administration on a conference bridge that has already been configured (**Service > Conference Bridge > Conference Bridge Parameters**).

To establish a conference, the user, known as a *conference controller*, calls the first conference attendee. Once connected to that user, the conference controller presses the **Conference** button or the **Confrn** soft key. The called party is placed on hold, and the conference controller hears a dial tone. At the dial tone, the conference controller dials the next conference participant and, after connecting to that user, presses the **Conference/ Confrn** button again to connect all three parties and establish the conference. The conference controller can continue to add attendees in this fashion until the specified maximum number of users is reached or until there are no more bridge ports available.

Conference attendees and the conference controller can depart the conference at any time. As long as there are two conference attendees, the conference will remain in effect, but without the conference controller, no additional attendees can be added. Figure A-3 illustrates the Conference operation.

Figure A-3   *Conference Operation (Ad Hoc)*

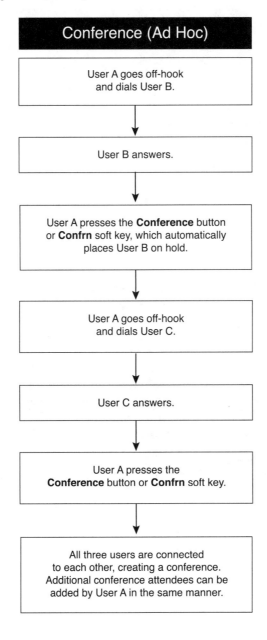

You can learn more about this feature in Chapter 5, "Media Processing."

CTI API Enhancements

NOTE This is a new feature for CallManager release 3.1.

The following enhancements to CallManager functionality are made possible by enhancements to the CTI API. Each feature is described in its own section in this appendix.

- CTI Redundancy with CTI Manager
- Auto-Answer with Zip Tone
- Cisco Personal Assistant Support
- Forward on Failure Support

CTI Redundancy with CTI Manager

NOTE This is a new feature for CallManager release 3.1.

The CTI API supports redundancy.

CTI Manager is now a separate service from CallManager. This allows applications to connect to a single CTI to obtain access to resources and functionality of all CallManager nodes in the cluster. CTI provides recovery of failure conditions resulting from a failed CallManager node within a cluster that includes CallManager and the CTI Manager service. Recovery and survivability are available for the following devices:

- CTI Port/Route Point
- Cisco IP Phones
- CTI Manager
- Applications

Auto-Answer with Zip Tone

NOTE	This is a new feature for CallManager release 3.1.

The CTI API supports auto-answer.

Auto-answer allows the user to have an incoming call announced by a beep (also called a *zip tone*) and then automatically connected if the user is not already on an active call. This feature eliminates the time it takes to answer a call, which allows more calls to be handled in the same amount of time. Auto-answer with zip tone requires the use of a headset and is compatible with Cisco IP Phone models 7960 and 7940 only.

The **Activate Auto-Answer for this Directory Number** check box on the Directory Number Configuration screen in CallManager Administration (**Device > Phone >** *find and select phone > click line number*) allows the auto-answer feature to be turned on or off on a per-line basis. If enabled, the directory number is auto-answered when the **HEADSET** button is in use. This feature is not supported for shared line appearances.

Auto-answer does not engage if the headset is not in use or if the user is on an active call; instead, the phone rings as usual or plays the call waiting tone, allowing the user the choice of answering or allowing the call to roll to voice mail, if configured.

Cisco Personal Assistant Support

NOTE	This is a new feature for CallManager release 3.1.

The CTI API supports Cisco Personal Assistant.

Personal Assistant allows end users to customize how they wish to be contacted depending on various criteria, such as time of day, caller ID, and meeting schedules. Personal Assistant does this by intercepting a call before it is extended to an endpoint. This allows Personal Assistant to reroute the call to the final destination based on a set of rules specified by the user. System administrators can turn this feature on or off using CallManager Administration.

Call Forward on Failure

Call Forward on Failure forwards calls when a phone connected by CTI route point or CTI port is not registered. If the phone did not register with Cisco CallManager, and the call was not intercepted, then the caller would hear a reorder tone. With Call Forward on Failure, Cisco CallManager detects the unregistered phone and, instead of dropping the call, sends it to the specified directory number. This feature is automatically available for all Cisco IP Phone models.

CTI Support for Cisco Applications and Software Development Kit (SDK)

Upgrades to CallManager provide stability for CTI. CallManager is able to deploy and support TAPI and JTAPI applications, in addition to the CTI SDK. Applications affected by the upgrade include:

- Cisco WebAttendant
- Cisco IP Contact Center
- Cisco Automated Attendant
- Low-End Interactive Voice Response
- Low-End Call Center
- Cisco IP SoftPhone
- TAPI SDK
- JTAPI SDK

Database API

NOTE   This is a new feature for CallManager release 3.1.

CallManager provides an XML interface to the CallManager database. This allows add, update, delete, and retrieval of phones, users, and lines (including forwarding of lines).

Database Automated Change Notification

Any changes made in CallManager Administration cause a change notification request to be sent to all affected CallManager nodes in the cluster. This ensures that each CallManager in the cluster has the most current database.

Change notification is the process by which changes you make through CallManager Administration get applied to running Cisco AVVID IP Telephony services. Different Cisco AVVID IP Telephony services respond to database updates through CallManager Administration differently, but there are three basic approaches.

- Automatic update—When you change the database, the service updates immediately.
- Polled update—The service polls the database periodically and refreshes its settings.
- Manual update—The service requires manual intervention to update its settings. In some cases, this means restarting the service, while in others, it means that you must initiate a reset of a component related to the service from CallManager Administration.

Table A-7 shows the types of change notification used by different Cisco AVVID IP Telephony services.

Table A-7 *Change Notification by Service*

Service	Change Notification
Cisco TFTP	Polled update every 5 minutes
Cisco IP Voice Media Streaming Application	Automatic update
Cisco Messaging Interface	Polled update every 5 minutes
RIS Data Collector	Automatic update
Telephony Call Dispatcher	Polled update every 3 minutes
CTI Manager	Manual update
Database Layer Monitor	Polled update every 5 minutes
Cisco MOH Audio Translator	Polled update every 5 minutes

CallManager change notification mechanisms are more complex than those in Table A-7. Changes with no user impact usually get applied automatically; changes that could affect a call require you to manually initiate a device reset (so that you can choose a time when the disruption will be minimal). Table A-8 provides general guidelines about the type of change notification that different changes use.

Table A-8 *Change Notification Guidelines*

Type of Change	Change Notification
Cisco CallManager groups	Automatic
Voice mail port	Automatic

continues

Table A-8   *Change Notification Guidelines (Continued)*

Type of Change	Change Notification
Gatekeeper settings	Requires manual reset from CallManager Administration
Gateway or trunk settings	Requires manual reset from CallManager Administration
Phone settings	Requires manual reset from CallManager Administration
Phone button template	Requires manual reset from CallManager Administration of all devices using that template
Line settings	Requires manual reset from CallManager Administration of all devices sharing that line
Route pattern	Automatic reset of devices associated with the pattern
Route list and route group	Automatic
Translation pattern	Automatic
Calling search space, partition, route filter	Requires manual reset of all affected devices from CallManager Administration
Regions	Requires reset from CallManager Administration
Device Pool	Requires manual reset of all affected devices from CallManager Administration
Enterprise parameters	Automatic
Service parameters	Automatic
Locations	Automatic
Date-time devices	Manual reset of all affected devices

Date/Time Display Format Configurable per Phone

Devices belong to a Device Pool that designates the appropriate date format and time zone. All Cisco IP Phone models display the date and time according to their designated device pool.

Debug Information to Common Syslog File

Trace and alarm data can be generated in syslog format and output to a syslog interface, where it can be collected and processed.

Device Change to Database Does Not Require Cisco CallManager Restart

Changes to devices in CallManager Administration require only a reset of the device that received the change. CallManager does not need to be restarted for device changes to take effect.

Device Downloadable Feature Upgrade

You can upgrade firmware by downloading a new version on device initialization. You can download upgrades for the following devices:

- Cisco IP Phones
- Cisco IP Conference Phone 7935
- Transcoder resource
- Conference bridge resource
- Cisco Catalyst 6000, Cisco Analog Access, and Cisco Digital Access gateways

Device Mapping Tool—IP Addresses to MAC Addresses

CiscoWorks2000 provides a user-tracking utility to map IP addresses to devices using the device's Media Access Control (MAC) address. See Chapter 6 for more information about CiscoWorks2000.

Device Pool

Device pools (**System > Device Pool**) reduce administration time for a large system by allowing you to specify criteria that are common among many devices. The following criteria are specified in a device pool:

- Cisco CallManager Group
- Date/Time Group
- Region
- Media Resource List (optional)
- User Hold Music on Hold Audio Source (optional)
- Network Hold Music on Hold Audio Source (optional)
- Calling Search Space (optional)

Device Search in Cisco CallManager Administration

CallManager Administration provides a device search by name, description, directory number, calling search space, or device pool to make locating a specific device in a large system simpler. A complete list of all devices is also available at the user's discretion.

Device Wizard

CallManager Administration provides a Device wizard (**Device > Add a New Device**) that makes adding new devices to CallManager a simple process.

DHCP IP Assignment for Phones and Gateways

Cisco IP Phones and gateways can use Dynamic Host Configuration Protocol (DHCP) for IP address assignment.

Dial Plan Partitions and Calling Search Spaces

Partitions and calling search spaces are an extremely powerful but complex pair of mechanisms by which you can customize dialing restrictions for individual users. Partitions and calling search spaces allow you to administer such policies as routing by geographic location, for multiple tenants, and by security level of the calling user. You can learn more about this feature in Chapter 2, "Call Routing."

Dialed Number Translation Table (Inbound and Outbound Translation)

CallManager can translate dialed or received digits.

Direct Inward Dial

Direct Inward Dial (DID) allows a caller outside a company to call an internal extension directly, without the assistance of an operator or attendant.

Direct Outward Dial

Direct Outward Dial (DOD) allows a user to call an external number directly, without the assistance of an operator or attendant. Usually an access digit, such as 9, is dialed first to indicate an external call, followed by the external number.

Directories

The **directories** button on Cisco IP Phone models 7960 and 7940 provides access to the following features:

- Missed Calls
- Received Calls
- Placed Calls
- Corporate Directory

Missed Calls

Missed Calls displays a list of up to 16 calls that have been received by the phone but not answered. Selecting a call from the list and pressing the **Dial** soft key automatically speed dials the telephone number of the missed call.

Received Calls

Received Calls displays a list of up to 16 calls that have been answered by the phone. Selecting a call from the list and pressing the **Dial** soft key automatically speed dials the telephone number of the received call.

Placed Calls

Placed Calls displays a list of up to 16 calls that have been placed from the phone. Selecting a call from the list and pressing the **Dial** soft key automatically speed dials the telephone number of the previously placed call.

Corporate Directory

Corporate Directory provides a search feature for users based on first name, last name, or number. You can enter letters or numbers using the dial pad and then press the **Search** soft key to return a list of users most closely matching the criteria you entered. You can then select a user in the list and press the **Dial** soft key to call that person. User information is pulled from your currently configured Lightweight Directory Access Protocol (LDAP) directory.

Directory Dial from Phone

Using the **directories** button, users can speed dial the number of a missed, placed, or received call on a Cisco IP Phone model 7960 or 7940. See the section "Directories" for more information.

Directory on Cisco IP Phone 7960 and 7940

Cisco IP Phone models 7960 and 7940 provide a global directory by way of the **directories** button on the phone. The global directory can be integrated with CallManager through CallManager Administration (**User > Global Directory**).

Disable Visual and Audio Indication of Ringing Line

CallManager Administration allows you to turn off the ring sound on a per-line basis on Cisco IP Phones. Turning off the ring sound on Cisco IP Phone models 7960, 7940, and 7910 also disables the strobe light on the handset and body.

Distinctive Ring—Internal vs. External

All Cisco IP Phone models provide a distinction in the ringer sound for internal and external calls. Internal calls generate one ring, while external calls generate two rings with a very short pause between the rings. No configuration is required.

Distinctive Ring per Cisco IP Phone 79*xx*

Cisco IP Phone models 7960 and 7940 provide multiple different ringer sounds, allowing the user to choose a preferred ring or to differentiate the phone from a neighboring user's ringer sound. Cisco IP Phone 7910 provides two ring tones. System administrators can limit the number of available rings in the ringlist.dat file.

Distributed Cisco CallManager

Multiple redundant CallManager servers can exist across one or more locations to create a distributed environment. You can learn more about this feature in Chapter 1, "Cisco CallManager Architecture."

Distributed Resource Sharing

NOTE	This is a new feature for CallManager release 3.1.

CallManager release 3.1 provides a Media Resource Manager (MRM) that is responsible for maintaining a list of available and in-use resources. When a resource request is received, the MRM can allocate resources across the cluster as needed to complete various feature requests. Complete information about resource management is provided in Chapter 5.

DSP Resource Alignment

NOTE This is a new feature for CallManager release 3.1.

CallManager provides support for Digital Signal Processor (DSP) -centric devices. When a resource allocation for a DSP-centric device is received, CallManager checks to see if the number of parties has exceeded the MaxStreamPerConf service parameter. If not, CallManager allows the new party to join the conference if the DSP still has streaming capability. An error message is returned if the DSP is out of streams.

Embedded Directory for User Data

CallManager servers provide an LDAP directory for user information.

Emergency 911 Service (E911)

CallManager and supporting components provide a complete E911 solution. CallManager provides a sophisticated and flexible solution for E911 call routing and reporting. Its partitioned dial plan allows multiple distributed sites to share a common dial pattern for emergency services (such as 911 in the United States) while allowing the calls to that pattern to be routed out through local site gateways. Callback information and information required by local E911 agents to resolve phone location in the event of an emergency services call is delivered through PRI ISDN trunks or Centralized Automatic Message Accounting (CAMA) trunks. The CAMA solution is achieved through a Cisco IOS-based FXS gateway and a third-party product that translates Calling Line ID information on the FXS ports to CAMA signaling. You can learn more about routing emergency numbers in Chapter 2.

EndCall

The **EndCall** soft key on Cisco IP Phone models 7960 and 7940 allows the user to disconnect a call with the touch of a soft key. This is particularly useful when using a headset. The soft key is automatically available and there are no configuration requirements.

Extension Mobility

NOTE	This is a new feature for CallManager release 3.1.

Extension mobility allows a user to configure any IP phone to appear as that user's phone temporarily. By logging into an IP phone, the user can temporarily convert the phone to adopt his or her line numbers, speed dials, services, and other user-specific properties of an IP phone. This feature is particularly useful in situations where users are not permanently assigned physical phones.

In the past, only system administrators could change phone settings using CallManager Administration. With extension mobility, users can achieve the same effect by way of a user login service on the phone. This service provides an interface by which applications can log users in and out. The login service enforces a variety of policies, including duration limits on phone configuration and authorization to log in to a particular phone. The login service is programmable so that system administrators or third parties can replace some of its components. For example, authenticating by smart card readers or automating the login process according to a desk sharing Web application are capabilities that could be added to the standard login service provided in CallManager release 3.1.

External Route Plan Wizard

CallManager Administration provides an external route plan wizard that you can use to create a basic route plan for geographically dispersed locations. The wizard uses gateway device settings in CallManager Administration and information you provide. You can learn more about this feature in Chapter 2.

FXS Support for Cisco Catalyst 6000 (WS-6624) 24 Port Gateways

CallManager provides support for Cisco Catalyst 6000 (WS-6624) 24 port FXS gateways.

Gain Attenuation for Audio Levels on Cisco Catalyst 6000 E1/T1 PRI (WS-6608-x1) 8 Port Gateways, Cisco Catalyst 6000 FXS (WS-6624) 24 Port Gateways, and Cisco Access DT-24+/DE-30+ Gateways

The Gateway Configuration screen in CallManager Administration (**Device > Gateway >** *find and click gateway > click port*) allows you to set the gain on transmit or to receive directions channel by channel for T1 or E1 spans.

Group Call Pickup/GPickUp

Group call pickup allows users who belong to one call pickup group to answer incoming calls in other groups. Users must dial the appropriate call pickup group number when using this feature. Group call pickup is available for all Cisco IP Phone models. On Cisco IP Phone models 12SP+, 30VIP, and 7910, the button is called **Group Call Pickup** and must be configured on the button template. On Cisco IP Phone models 7960 and 7940, the soft key is called **GPickUp** and is automatically available.

For the pickup feature to be operational, you must configure one or more call pickup groups in the Call Pickup Configuration screen in CallManager Administration (**Feature > Call Pickup**). Only directory numbers that belong to a call pickup group can use the call pickup feature. You must specify a call pickup group directory number for each phone that should belong to that group. See the section "Call Pickup/PickUp" for more information. For users of one call pickup group to retrieve calls destined for members of another call pickup group, they must know the group number. Once multiple call pickup groups have been established, the system administrator should advise relevant parties of the call pickup group directory numbers.

To use group call pickup, the user goes off-hook and presses the **Group Call Pickup** button/**GPickUp** soft key when he or she hears an incoming call ringing on another phone, then dials the appropriate group number for the ringing phone. This causes the ringing call to be redirected to the user's phone. Figure A-4 illustrates the group call pickup operation.

Figure A-4 *Group Call Pickup Operation*

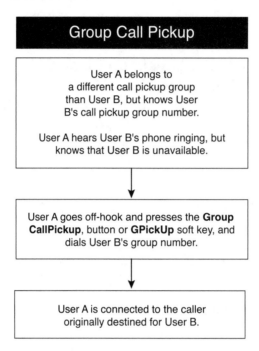

<GroupCallPickup>

User A belongs to
a different call pickup group
than User B, but knows User
B's call pickup group number.

User A hears User B's phone ringing, but
knows that User B is unavailable.

↓

User A goes off-hook and presses the **Group
CallPickup**, button or **GPickUp** soft key, and
dials User B's group number.

↓

User A is connected to the caller
originally destined for User B.

GSM-EFR/FR Support Through Use of Hardware Transcoder

NOTE   This is a new feature for CallManager release 3.1.

CallManager release 3.1 supports Groupe Speciale Mobile-Enhanced Full Rate/Full Rate
(GSM-EFR/FR). With this enhancement, cell phone users can enter a building, register to
the local picocell and call agent, and be part of the local Cisco AVVID IP Telephony
network. This feature also allows calls from a GSM phone to a G.729 or G.711 endpoint.
This feature is available in conjunction with a third-party service provider. You can learn
more about the GSM codec in Chapter 5.

H.323-Compliant Interface to H.323 Clients, Gateways, and Gatekeepers

CallManager provides configuration for H.323 clients, gateways, and gatekeepers.

Hold/Resume

Depending on the phone model in use, one or both of the following features are available:

- For Cisco IP Phone models 12SP+, 30VIP, and 7910, hold is available.
- For Cisco IP Phone models 7960 and 7940, hold and resume are available.

Hold allows a user to store a call at his or her extension. It is automatically available for Cisco IP Phone models 30VIP, 7960, 7940, and 7910. There are no configuration requirements for these models. The Cisco IP Phone 12SP+ requires a button template with the **Hold** button configured. Each line on a Cisco IP Phone actually provides two lines—a primary line and a secondary line—although only one directory number is in use per line. Therefore, a user can have two calls on hold per line.

Pressing the **Resume** soft key allows a user to retrieve a call placed on hold. It is automatically available for Cisco IP Phone models 7960 and 7940. There are no configuration requirements.

Hold on Cisco IP Phone Model 12SP+

Hold is a programmable feature button on Cisco IP Phone 12SP+. To place an active call on hold, the user presses the **Hold** button. The display indicates the held call. To retrieve the call, the user presses the **Hold** button again and is reconnected with the held call.

Hold on Cisco IP Phone Models 30VIP and 7910

Hold is a static button on Cisco IP Phone models 30VIP and 7910. To place an active call on hold, the user presses the **Hold** button. The light for the line with the call on hold remains lit. To retrieve the call, the user presses the line button and is reconnected with the held call.

Hold/Resume on Cisco IP Phone Models 7960 and 7940

Hold and **Resume** are soft keys on Cisco IP Phone models 7960 and 7940. To place an active call on hold, the user presses the **Hold** soft key. To retrieve the call on hold, the user selects the line on which the call is being held and then presses the **Resume** soft key. The caller is reconnected to the held call. The soft keys, **Hold** and **Resume,** are automatically available with no configuration required.

Table A-9 provides information about Hold service parameters.

Table A-9 *Hold Values*

Value	Default	Range	Cisco CallManager Administration Location
HoldType In the case where two different Cisco IP Phones, models 12SP+ or 30VIP, share the same directory number, this parameter determines whether the hold light flashes more rapidly for the user who placed the call on hold.	F	T (rapid flashing) or F (normal flashing)	Service Parameters Configuration screen (**Service > Service Parameters >** *select server >* **Cisco CallManager**)
AutoSelectHeldCallFlag Determines whether to automatically select the call on hold as soon as the phone goes off-hook if the held call was the last signal sent to the phone.	F	T or F	Service Parameters Configuration screen (**Service > Service Parameters >** *select server >* **Cisco CallManager**)
ToneOnHoldTime Determines the time interval between tones when a call is on hold.	10 seconds	3 to 99,999 seconds	Service Parameters Configuration screen (**Service > Service Parameters >** *select server >* **Cisco CallManager**)

HTTPD Server

NOTE   This is a new feature for CallManager release 3.1.

Cisco IP Phone models 7960 and 7940 support HTTP server functionality. Additionally, Cisco Digital Access DT-24+, DE-30+, and Cisco Catalyst 6000 gateways support HTTP server functionality. This functionality is referred to as the HTTP Daemon, or HTTPD. The daemon can run on a variety of platforms using the operating system on the Cisco IP Phone.

Integrated Call Distributor

NOTE	This is a new feature that works in conjunction with CallManager release 3.1.

The IP Integrated Contact Distribution (IP ICD) program provides simple automatic call distribution (ACD) features for CallManager release 3.1 and provides the basic infrastructure for developing more sophisticated queuing and routing features in the future.

The IP ICD provides several methods of selecting resources (agents) for incoming calls, including hunt group, distribution group, and longest-waiting agent algorithms. It provides flexible grouping of agents to service calls for a particular service by allowing the specification of multiple criteria when assigning resources to a particular call type. The IP ICD also provides a means for you to customize the logic for managing events and resources, allowing you to adapt the application to your particular needs.

JTAPI Computer Telephony Interface (CTI)

An SDK is available for third-party developers.

LDAPv3 Directory Interface

Support is provided for Microsoft ActiveDirectory and Netscape Directory Services.

Line

A line allows a user to access incoming calls or place outgoing calls. At least one line must be configured in CallManager Administration for each Cisco IP Phone on the system (**Device > Phone >** *find and click phone > click line*). Each line on a Cisco IP Phone can support two concurrent calls, one active and one on hold, although only one directory number is in use per line.

To use a Cisco IP Phone, one or more lines must be configured. Each line on a given phone must have a unique directory number assigned to it; two lines on the same phone cannot have the same directory number assigned. Configuration and use of line buttons differs depending on the phone model.

Line on Cisco IP Phone 7910

Cisco IP Phone 7910 provides one line. You must assign a directory number for that line on a Cisco IP Phone.

To use the line, the user simply presses the **Line** button. Alternatively, the user can lift the handset or press the **SPEAKER** button for hands-free dialing.

Lines on Cisco IP Phone Models 12SP+ and 30VIP

Cisco IP Phone models 12SP+ and 30VIP allow as many lines as there are programmable feature buttons. The system administrator assigns a directory number for each line on a Cisco IP Phone. The button template assigned to the phone determines the number of lines available to each phone.

To access a line, the user simply presses the line button that corresponds to the directory number they want to use. Alternatively, the user can press the **SPKR** button to access a line or lift the handset. The user is automatically connected to the first available line.

Lines on Cisco IP Phone Models 7960 and 7940

Cisco IP Phone 7960 allows up to six lines per phone, while Cisco IP Phone 7940 allows up to two lines per phone. You must assign a directory number for each line on a Cisco IP Phone.

Lines are accessed by buttons on the right side of the phone. To access a line, the user can press the line button that corresponds to the directory number he or she wants to use, or the user can press the **SPEAKER** button, lift the handset, or press the **NewCall** soft key. The user is automatically connected to the first available line if multiple lines have been configured.

Table A-10 provides information about the Line service parameter.

Table A-10   *Line Value*

Value	Default	Range	Cisco CallManager Administration Location
AlwayUsePrimeLine Determines whether, regardless of the state of the phone, the primary line (Line 1) will always be selected when the phone goes off-hook.	F	T (always select primary line) or F (select any line, depending on state)	Service Parameters Configuration screen (**Service > Service Parameters** > *select server* > **Cisco CallManager**)

Media Resource Group List Support

NOTE   This is a new feature for CallManager release 3.1.

Within a cluster, devices can be grouped together and associated with transcoder and conference bridge resources using the Media Resource Group List (MRGL). You can learn more about MRGLs in Chapter 5.

Meet-Me Conference/MeetMe

NOTE   CallManager provides two types of conferences: Ad Hoc and Meet-Me. Ad Hoc conferences require the conference controller to include attendees individually to the conference by calling them. Meet-Me conferences allow attendees to dial into the conference once the conference controller has established it. This section covers the Meet-Me Conference feature. The Ad Hoc Conference feature is covered in this appendix in the section "Conference/Confrn."

Meet-Me conference allows a user to establish a conference that attendees can direct-dial into. Meet-Me conference is available for all Cisco IP Phone models. On Cisco IP Phone models 12SP+, 30VIP, and 7910, the button is called **Meet Me Conference** and must be configured on the button template. On Cisco IP Phone models 7960 and 7940, the soft key is called **MeetMe** and is automatically available when the phone is off-hook. For the Meet-Me conference feature to be available to users, you must install a Unicast conference bridge and then establish one or more directory numbers to be used for Meet-Me conferences. This can be done in the Meet Me Number/Pattern Configuration screen in CallManager Administration on a conference bridge that has already been configured (**Service > Conference Bridge > Meet Me Number/Pattern Configuration**). You do not need a Meet-Me button to participate in a conference call, only to initiate one.

Figure A-5 illustrates the Meet-Me conference operation.

Figure A-5 *Meet-Me Conference Operation*

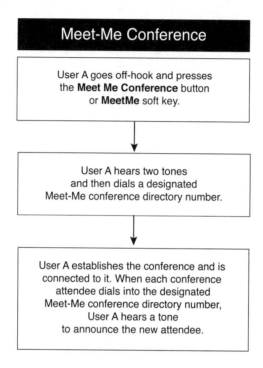

You can learn more about this feature in Chapter 5.

Message Waiting Indicator

The message waiting indicator provides visual notification that there is a message in the user's voice mailbox. The indicator is available for all Cisco IP Phones, but implementation differs depending on model. For the feature to work in conjunction with your voice mail system, the voice mail system must be configured to work with CallManager and the **message** or **Message Waiting** button must be programmed to connect directly to the voice mail system.

Message Waiting Indicator on Cisco IP Phone Models 12SP+ and 30VIP

Message Waiting is a programmable feature button on Cisco IP Phone models 12SP+ or 30VIP. For this feature to be available, the Cisco IP Phone button template must have a **Message Waiting** button assigned. The light next to the **Message Waiting** button remains lit when there is a new message in the user's voice mailbox.

Message Waiting Indicator on Cisco IP Phone Models 7960, 7940, and 7910

Message waiting indicators appear on the handset and body of Cisco IP Phone models 7960, 7940, and 7910. The indicator is lit in the color red when there is a message waiting. See the section "Messages" for information about retrieving messages from voice mail.

Messages

The **messages** button on Cisco IP Phone models 7960 and 7940 provides access to a voice mail system, if the voice mail system is integrated with CallManager.

Microsoft NetMeeting

All Cisco IP Phone models can call Microsoft NetMeeting devices that have been configured with CallManager.

Multiple Line Appearances per Phone

Cisco IP Phone models 12SP+, 30VIP, 7960, and 7940 provide multiple line appearances. See the section "Line" for more information.

Music on Hold

NOTE	This is a new feature for CallManager release 3.1.

The integrated music on hold feature provides the ability to place OnNet and OffNet users on hold with music streamed from a streaming source. OnNet devices include Cisco IP Phones and applications placed on any form of hold by an Integrated Voice Response (IVR) system or call distributor. OffNet users include those connected through MGCP or Skinny Protocol-based gateways, Cisco IOS H.323 gateways, and Cisco IOS MGCP gateways. Chapter 5 provides complete information about music on hold.

Mute

Cisco IP Phone models 12SP+, 30VIP, 7960, and 7940 allow the user to disconnect the handset or speakerphone microphone so the other party cannot hear the user. **Mute** buttons toggle on and off.

NewCall

The **NewCall** soft key on Cisco IP Phone models 7960 and 7940 allows the user to access an available line without lifting the handset. The line is opened automatically by speakerphone, unless a headset is attached. The soft key is automatically available and there are no configuration requirements.

Off-Hook Dialing

All Cisco IP Phone models provide a dial tone automatically when the phone goes off-hook (user lifts the handset or presses a line button, a speakerphone button, or the **NewCall** soft key).

Outbound Hookflash Support to Adjunct PBXs from H.323 Clients

Outbound hookflash support to adjunct Private Branch eXchanges (PBXs) from H.323 clients is available through Cisco VG200 FXO ports.

Overlap Sending

NOTE This is a new feature for CallManager release 3.1.

CallManager supports Q.931 overlap sending procedure for E1 PRI in both User and Network modes. Overlap sending procedure is a part of International Telecommunication Union (ITU) standard but not in American National Standards Institute (ANSI). For this reason, overlap sending is not supported for the T1 PRI interfaces. With this procedure, the route plan for a CallManager system can be simplified in the environments where route patterns with various lengths and patterns are required.

Paperless Phone

Cisco IP Phone models 7960 and 7940 provide LCD button labels directly on the phone's display, eliminating the need for printed button labeling. This is also true for Cisco IP Phone 7910 when the default template is used.

Performance Monitoring

You can monitor the performance of the CallManager system by way of SNMP statistics from applications to either the SNMP manager or Microsoft Performance (a Microsoft monitoring application) or the Admin. Serviceability Tool in CallManager Serviceability. You can learn more about monitoring in Chapter 6.

Privacy

In a shared-line appearance situation, the user that first goes off-hook on the shared line appearance has privacy on the line. Privacy indicates that other users with the same line appearance cannot access the line.

QoS Statistics for the Phone

All Cisco IP Phone models provide quality of service (QoS) statistics per call, per device. This information is also referred to as Call Management Records (CMRs). You can learn more about this feature in Chapter 7. Cisco IP Phone models 7960 and 7940 provide QoS statistics on the phone itself. During an active call, press the **i** button twice quickly. QoS statistics are shown on the phone's display.

Redial/REDL

Redial allows the user to automatically speed dial the last number dialed on a line. If the Cisco IP Phone has multiple lines, the user can press a specific line button and then press **Redial** to redial the last number dialed on that line. If a specific line is not selected before pressing **Redial**, the phone automatically redials the last number dialed on Line 1. Redial is automatically available for all Cisco IP Phone models except 12SP+ and 7910, where it can be configured on the button template (**Device > Phone Button Template**). No configuration is necessary for other Cisco IP Phone models.

Remote Site Survivability

NOTE	This is a new feature for CallManager release 3.1

MGCP gateway fallback support is provided on a local Cisco Catalyst 4224 IOS-based router. This allows remote offices a low-cost fallback solution when the WAN connection to CallManager fails.

The Cisco Catalyst 4224 gateway connects a Cisco AVVID IP Telephony network to traditional telephone trunks or analog devices. The trunks can be connected to the PSTN or existing PBX systems. The Cisco Catalyst 4224 communicates with CallManager using MGCP or H.323 version 2 network. This fallback support on the Cisco Catalyst 4224 allows the default H.323 protocol to be used for basic call handling for FXS, FXO, and T1-CAS interfaces during the fallback period.

Scalability Enhancements Through H.323 Gatekeeper (Beyond Ten Sites)

Support is provided for registering multiple CallManager servers in a cluster with a gatekeeper.

Select Specified Line Appearance

CallManager Administration allows you to disable one or more lines on a Cisco IP Phone. On a phone with multiple line appearances, you can disable all but one line, thereby allowing only calls received on the remaining line to ring through to the phone (**Device > Phone >** *find and click phone > click line*).

Serviceability Enhancements Through SNMP, CDP, CiscoWorks2000

Serviceability enhancements are available through SNMP, Cisco Discovery Protocol (CDP), and CiscoWorks2000. Refer to Chapter 6 for more information about serviceability.

Services on Cisco IP Phone Models 7960 and 7940

Cisco IP Phone models 7960 and 7940 provide access to customer-created XML services by way of the **services** button on the phone. Services can be integrated with CallManager through CallManager Administration (**Feature > Cisco IP Phone Services**).

Settings

The **settings** button on Cisco IP Phone models 7960, 7940, and 7910 provides access to the following features:

- Contrast/LCD Contrast
- Ring Type
- Network Configuration/Network Settings
- Status/Phone Info

Contrast/LCD Contrast

Contrast allows the user to adjust the contrast of the display panel on the phone.

Ring Type

Ring type allows the user to select the type of ring tone used by the phone.

Network Configuration/Network Settings

Network Configuration displays configuration information for the phone. Only a system administrator can unlock the phone and make changes. Use this feature to view or update the following configuration settings:

- Dynamic Host Configuration Protocol (DHCP) server address
- BOOTP server designation
- MAC address
- Host name
- Domain name
- IP address
- Subnet mask
- Trivial File Transfer Protocol (TFTP) server
- Default routers 1 through 5
- DNS servers 1 through 5
- Operational VLAN ID
- Admin. VLAN ID
- CallManager servers 1 through 5
- Information URL
- Directories URL
- Messages URL
- Services URL
- DHCP enabled designation
- DHCP address released designation
- Alternate TFTP designation
- Erase configuration option

- Forwarding delay designation
- Idle URL
- Idle URL time

Status/Phone Info

Status displays status messages, network statistics, and firmware version information (application load ID and boot load ID) for the phone.

Shared Line Appearance on Multiple Phones

The same directory number can be configured on multiple phones, providing a shared (bridged) line appearance.

Single CDR per Cluster

CallManager provides a common synchronized record of calls per cluster. You can learn more about this feature in Chapter 7.

Single Point for System/Device Configuration

CallManager Administration provides a single point for all system and device configuration. Because it operates as a collection of Web pages, you can administer systems anywhere in the world from a Web browser.

Speakerphone/SPKR

Cisco IP Phone models 12SP+, 30VIP, 7960, and 7940 provide a speakerphone for hands-free communication. Users can press a speakerphone button to place and answer calls without using the handset. Cisco IP Phone 7910 uses the **Speaker** and **Mute** button combination to provide hands-free dialing only.

Speed Dial

Speed dial allows a user to dial a designated phone number with the press of a single button. This feature is available for all Cisco IP Phone models, if configured.

Speed dial buttons can be configured on the button templates for all Cisco IP Phones. You can program as many speed dial buttons as there are feature buttons on the phone, except for Line 1, which must always be a line button. Once you designate speed dial buttons on the button template, the user can specify the speed dial numbers in the Cisco IP Phone User Options Web page.

Supplementary Services to Cisco IOS H.323 Gateways Without Media Termination Point (MTP)

Previously, a media termination point (MTP) resource was required to offer supplementary services, such as hold and transfer, to calls through an H.323 gateway. Now supplementary services are available during calls routed through Cisco IOS H.323 gateways (includes Cisco gateway models 26xx, 36xx, 53xx, 65xx, and 7xx), because of implementation of H.323 version 2 empty capabilities set.

System Event Reporting

CallManager reports system events to a common syslog or Windows Event Viewer.

T1/E1 PRI Support for Cisco Catalyst 6000 (WS-6608-x1) 8 Port Gateways

CallManager provides support for Cisco Catalyst 6000 (WS-6608-x1) 8 port E1/T1 PRI gateways.

T1-CAS Support on Cisco Digital Access DT-24+ and Cisco Catalyst 6000 T1 Interfaces

NOTE   This is a new feature for CallManager release 3.1.

The following types of T1-CAS are supported:

- E&M wink start (DID/DOD)
- E&M immediate start (DID/DOD)
- E&M delay dial (DID/DOD)

TAPI CTI

An SDK is available for third-party developers.

TAPI/JTAPI Interface and Applications Support (Cisco IP Contact Center, Cisco IP IVR, Cisco IP AA, Cisco IP SoftPhone)

An SDK is available for third-party developers. See Appendix B, "Cisco Integrated Solutions," for more information.

TAPI/JTAPI Redundancy Support

NOTE	This feature has been updated for CallManager release 3.1.

In CallManager release 3.1, Cisco JTAPI supports redundancy across CallManager clusters by way of the CTI Manager. The CTI Manager communicates with all CallManager nodes in the cluster. JTAPI applications communicate with the CTI Manager instead of a specific CallManager node. If a CallManager node fails, the devices rehome to the next CallManager node in the group, as defined by the prioritized list of CallManager nodes contained in the device pool configured for each device. JTAPI abstracts this transition to the applications.

Time Zone Configuration

Devices can be configured with the appropriate time zone using CallManager Administration (**System > Device Pool**).

Tone on Hold

When a user places a caller on hold, CallManager can provide an intermittent tone. Table A-11 provides information about the Tone on Hold service parameter.

Table A-11 *Tone on Hold Value*

Value	Default	Range	Cisco CallManager Administration Location
ToneOnHoldTime Determines the time interval between tones when a call is on hold	10 seconds	3 to 99,999 seconds	Service Parameters Configuration screen (**Service > Service Parameters** > *select server* > **Cisco CallManager**)

Transfer/XFER

Transfer allows a user to send a call to another extension. It is automatically available for any Cisco IP Phone on the system except the Cisco IP Phone 12SP+, where it must be configured on the button template. For all other models, there are no configuration requirements. On Cisco IP Phone 12SP+, transfer is a button called **Transfer**. On Cisco IP Phone 30VIP, transfer is a static button called **XFER**. On Cisco IP Phone 7910, transfer is a static button called **Transfer**. On Cisco IP Phone models 7960 and 7940, transfer is a soft key called **Trnsfer**.

There are two types of transfer:

- **Blind transfer**—The user transfers a call to another extension.
- **Consultation transfer**—The user discusses the transferred call with the intended recipient before completing the transfer.

A consultation transfer allows the person receiving the transferred call to be apprised of the situation before connecting with the caller. Figure A-6 illustrates the blind transfer operation.

Figure A-6 *Blind Transfer Operation*

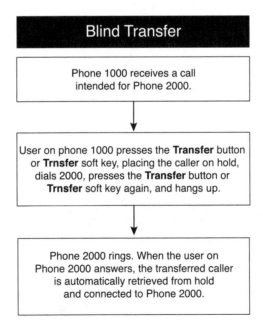

Figure A-7 illustrates the consultation transfer operation.

Figure A-7   *Consultation Transfer Operation*

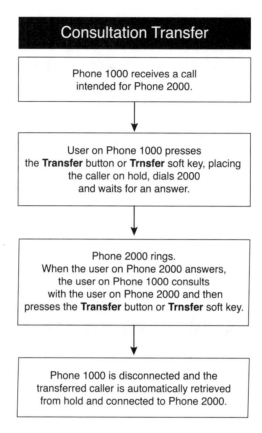

Transfer is available during an active call. To transfer a call, the user presses the transfer soft key or button and dials the directory number to which the user wants to transfer the call. To complete the transfer, the user presses the transfer soft key or button again, before or after discussing the call with the intended recipient. Refer to Figures A-4 and A-5 for more information about blind transfer and consultation transfer.

Unicast Conference

Conferences are provided in conjunction with software on CallManager. You can learn more about the Unicast conference feature in Chapter 5.

Vendor-Specific MGCP Information Configuration

NOTE	This is a new feature for CallManager release 3.1.

CallManager Administration provides a single point of configuration for MGCP and Skinny Protocol-based components on a Cisco AVVID IP Telephony network. CallManager, MGCP Cisco IOS gateways, Skinny Protocol gateways, and Cisco IP Phones can download XML-based configuration files at startup and when CallManager indicates a configuration change.

Visual Indicator of Ringing Phone

All Cisco IP Phone models provide visual notification of an incoming call. Cisco IP Phone models 12SP+ and 30VIP provide a red LED next to the line button. When a call is ringing on the line button, the LED next to it flashes. Cisco IP Phone models 7960, 7940, and 7910 provide an indicator on the handset and the phone body itself. An incoming call is signaled by the indicator, which strobes in the color red.

Volume Controls

All Cisco IP Phone models provide volume control for one or more of the following:

- Handset
- Speakerphone
- Ringer
- Headset

Wideband Stereo Codec on 79*xx*

NOTE	This is a new feature for CallManager release 3.1.

Wideband audio is an encoding method that provides 16-bit 16-kHz sampling, which is the highest precedence codec in Cisco IP Phone models 7960, 7940, and 7910.

Year 2000 Compliance

All Cisco IP Phone models, Cisco gateways, CallManager, and CallManager
Administration were certified year 2000 compliant.

Zero Cost Automated Phone Moves

Cisco IP Phone models automatically reregister with the same device information
(directory number and other settings) when moved from one Ethernet port to another, as
long as they are on the same subnet or have DHCP enabled. This results in zero cost for
countless moves.

Zero Cost Phone Adds

Cisco IP Phone models can auto-register with the system without incurring any cost for
doing so, as long as there are available directory numbers and the phones are on the same
subnet or have DHCP enabled.

Cisco Integrated Solutions

This appendix provides basic descriptions for Cisco solutions that can be integrated with Cisco CallManager. Additional information about each of the solutions can be found on Cisco Connection Online (CCO) at www.cisco.com.

The Cisco AVVID IP Telephony system is built from five main components:

- **Infrastructure**—Devices that provide media transport and manipulation. Includes telephony service-enabled switches, routers, conference bridges, and transcoders. This appendix describes the following infrastructure solution: Cisco IP Videoconferencing (Cisco IP/VC).

- **Telephony Services**—Provides the services required for call processing, management, directory, database, application, and other features. Includes CallManager (call processing), CiscoWorks2000, Lightweight Directory Access Protocol (LDAP) directory, configuration database, and computer telephony application programming interfaces (APIs). This appendix describes the following telephony services solutions: Administrative Reporting Tool (ART), Bulk Administration Tool (BAT), Tool for Auto-Registered Phone Support (TAPS), Cisco CallManager Serviceability, Admin. Serviceability Tool (AST), CiscoWorks2000, Cisco IP Phone User Options Web page, Cisco Messaging Interface, and LDAP Support.

- **Gateway**—Connects the enterprise IP Telephony networks to the Public Switched Telephone Network (PSTN) and to other private telephone systems, such as Private Branch eXchange (PBX). Includes router-based, switch-based, and standalone Voice over IP (VoIP) gateways, and video packet to time-division multiplexing (TDM) video gateways. This appendix describes the following gateway solutions: Cisco DPA, Cisco IP Videoconferencing (Cisco IP/VC).

- **Clients**—Multimedia, client-facing endpoints including Cisco IP Phones, Cisco IP SoftPhones, and video phones (coming soon). This appendix describes the following client solutions: Cisco WebAttendant and Cisco IP SoftPhone.

- **Applications**—Software-only applications and tools that provide extended multimedia services to clients and administrators. Applications include IP Interactive Voice Response (IP IVR), IP Auto Attendant (IP AA), IP Contact Centers (IPCC), Meet-Me conferencing, Cisco WebAttendant, and others. Development tools include

TAPI, JTAPI, Cisco IP Phone Productivity Services (Cisco XML SDK), and configuration database APIs, in addition to the Applications Engine, a tool for rapidly prototyping and deploying sophisticated multimedia applications. This appendix describes the following application solutions: Cisco IPCC, Cisco IP ICD, Cisco XML SDK, Cisco IP/VC, Cisco Personal Assistant, Cisco Unity, Cisco Applications SDK, Cisco IP SoftPhone, and Cisco WebAttendant.

The following solutions are described in this appendix:

- Administrative Reporting Tool (ART)
- Bulk Administration Tool (BAT)
- Tool for Auto-Registered Phone Support (TAPS)
- Cisco CallManager Serviceability
- Admin. Serviceability Tool (AST)
- Cisco DPA Voice Mail Gateways
- Cisco Customer Response
- Cisco IP Contact Center (IPCC)
- Cisco IP Integrated Contact Distribution (IP ICD)
- Cisco IP Phone Productivity Services Software Development Kit (Cisco XML SDK)
- Cisco IP Videoconferencing (Cisco IP/VC)
- Cisco Personal Assistant
- Cisco Unity
- CiscoWorks2000
- Cisco Applications Software Development Kit (SDK)
- Cisco IP Auto Attendant (Cisco IP AA)
- Cisco Interactive Voice Response (IVR)
- Cisco IP Phone User Options Web Page
- Cisco IP SoftPhone
- Cisco Messaging Interface (CMI)
- Cisco WebAttendant
- Lightweight Directory Access Protocol (LDAP) Support

Administrative Reporting Tool (ART)

The Administrative Reporting Tool (ART), a Web-based application, provides performance information on the CallManager system, including end-to-end management information for voice quality, system capacity, QoS metrics, call and billing information, inventory reporting, usage reporting, and more. The initial release of ART provided support for CallManager release 3.0(6). Subsequent ART releases target the various releases of CallManager 3.0(x) and 3.1(x).

Calls are grouped into a voice quality category based on the call information provided by Call Detail Records (CDRs), the diagnostic Call Management Records (CMRs), and quality of service (QoS) parameters you specify. Information that is not present in CDRs and CMRs, but that is required for various reports, is retrieved from the LDAP or must be supplied by the ART administrator. Once this information is retrieved, it is stored in an ART database. ART can then use this information to generate voice quality and other reports for the CallManager system.

Chapter 6, "Manageability and Monitoring Tools," provides additional information about ART. You can view the user guide for ART at the following location:

```
www.cisco.com/univercd/cc/td/doc/product/voice/sw_ap_to/admin/
index.htm
```

Bulk Administration Tool (BAT)

The Bulk Administration Tool (BAT), a Web-based application, lets you perform bulk modifications to the Cisco CallManager database. With BAT, you can create templates and comma separated value (CSV) files that can be reused for future bulk modifications. BAT can be used for database changes (including add, update, or delete, depending on the device type) for users, Cisco IP Phone models 12SP+, 30VIP, 7960, 7940, 7910, 7935, and expansion modules 7914, speed dials, lines, services, Cisco VG200 gateways, FXS ports on Cisco Catalyst 6000 gateways, and combinations such as adding phones and users all at once. With BAT, you minimize the amount of time you spend manually adding, updating, or deleting users and devices in Cisco CallManager Administration.

BAT was introduced for use with CallManager release 3.0(6). Subsequent BAT releases target the various releases of CallManager 3.0(x) and 3.1(x). You can learn more about BAT in Chapter 6 or on the Web at the following location:

```
www.cisco.com/univercd/cc/td/doc/product/voice/sw_ap_to/admin/
bulk_adm/index.htm
```

Tool for Auto-Registered Phone Support (TAPS)

The Tool for Auto-Registered Phone Support (TAPS) is an optional application for BAT that lets you or users automatically update Media Access Control (MAC) addresses in the Cisco CallManager database simply by plugging a phone into the network and dialing a directory number that has been assigned to TAPS. TAPS must be used in conjunction with BAT and the auto-registration feature in CallManager. Using BAT, you bulk-add phones using dummy MAC addresses. This saves you the labor of manually entering valid MAC addresses for each phone in the bulk operation. You can then use TAPS to update the dummy MAC address automatically in the CallManager database with the phone's actual MAC address. Once the phones with dummy MAC addresses have been added to the CallManager database using BAT, either you or the phone's end user can plug the phone into the data port, apply power, and call into the TAPS directory number to initialize the IP phone. TAPS provides voice prompts to walk the user through the short initialization process.

You can learn more about TAPS in Chapter 6 or on the Web at the following location:

```
www.cisco.com/univercd/cc/td/doc/product/voice/sw_ap_to/admin/
bulk_adm/index.htm
```

Cisco CallManager Serviceability

Cisco CallManager Serviceability is bundled with Cisco CallManager and provides alarm, trace, version, and real-time monitoring information about CallManager, Cisco IP Phones, gateways, applications, and infrastructure components within the IP telephony network. CallManager Serviceability monitors status and alarm information from these devices and can be configured to relay this service information onward to service managers through SNMP and HTTP/XML. CallManager Serviceability is automatically installed with CallManager and is accessible from the **Application** menu in Cisco CallManager Administration. CallManager Serviceability is a new feature for CallManager release 3.1(x).

CallManager Serviceability provides alarm configuration and detailed alarm definitions. It also provides simplified tracing with the option to display trace results in easy-to-read extensible markup language (XML) format. You can check version information for components installed in the CallManager system and monitor system and device status and alarms in real time using the Admin. Serviceability Tool.

Admin. Serviceability Tool (AST)

The Admin. Serviceability Tool (AST) provides real-time monitoring information for your CallManager system. AST is a part of CallManager Serviceability, which is installed automatically with CallManager. AST is accessible from the **Tools** menu in CallManager Serviceability.

Like Microsoft Performance, AST uses objects and counters to allow you to monitor and troubleshoot the enterprise IP telephony system. AST also provides alerting capability so that you can be advised with server messages or e-mails when specified conditions occur.

Cisco DPA Voice Mail Gateways

Cisco DPA 7630 and 7610 are voice mail gateways that enable legacy voice mail equipment to connect to a Cisco AVVID IP Telephony network. If you have an existing Octel 2*xx* or 3*xx* voice mail system, you can use a Cisco DPA gateway to connect to the Cisco CallManager system without any changes to the voice mail system. The Cisco DPA 7630 allows the voice mail system to be used solely by CallManager or to be shared between CallManager and the PBX. Figure B-1 shows the Cisco DPA 7630 integrated with an Avaya Definity PBX and Avaya (Octel) Messaging Server 2*xx*/3*xx*.

Figure B-1 *Using Cisco DPA 7630 with Octel and Definity*

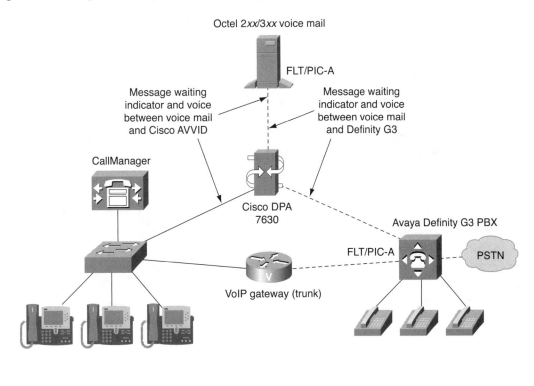

Cisco DPA gateways communicate with CallManager by emulating IP phones using an auto-sensing 10/100 Ethernet port. Cisco DPA gateways communicate with the PBX and voice mail system using 24 digital station lines, and they are easily configured using a simple menu system accessed by Telnet. On the CallManager side, configuration is performed in CallManager Administration or automatically using auto-registration. Figure B-2 shows the Cisco DPA 7610 integrated with a Nortel Meridian PBX and Avaya Messaging Server 2*xx*/3*xx*.

Figure B-2 *Using the Cisco DPA 7610 with Octel and Meridian*

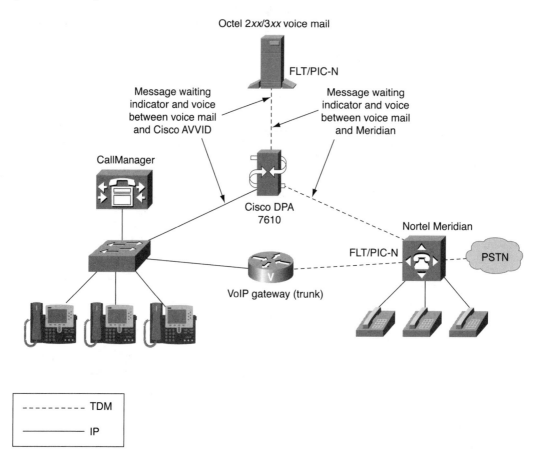

You can learn more about Cisco DPA voice mail gateways on the Web at the following location:

```
www.cisco.com/univercd/cc/td/doc/product/voice/c_access/7630adpt/
index.htm
```

Cisco Customer Response

Cisco Customer Response (formerly Cisco eServices) is a combination of the Application Editor and an Application Engine. The editor component allows application developers to develop applications rapidly that include call control services derived from Cisco CallManager, HTML services, database services, and other services. These applications are developed using a graphical editor tool by constructing customized application steps. These steps abstract the more complex TAPI and JTAPI programming calls. These applications can be developed entirely without the use of C or C++ programming tools. Alternately, more sophisticated applications can be developed by including C++/TAPI/JTAPI modules inserted into the application's steps. The Application Engine component executes Customer Response applications constructed with the editor. Effectively, the engine is a real-time interpreter of Customer Response application steps. The Application Engine uses Java Telephony Application Programming Interface (JTAPI) to request and receive services from CallManager and is implemented as a Windows service that supports multiple applications.

The server includes up to four subsystems:

- **JTAPI**—Manages the connection between CallManager and the application server.
- **Database**—Handles the connection between the application server and the enterprise database.
- **Cisco Intelligent Contact Manager (Cisco ICM)**—Manages the connection between the application server and Cisco ICM. The Cisco ICM subsystem is only used if you are using Cisco IP IVR with Cisco IP Contact Center (Cisco IPCC), which includes Cisco ICM.
- **Resource Manager**—Monitors agent phones, controls agent states, and routes and queues calls using the Cisco IP Integrated Contact Distributor (IP ICD) Resource Manager.

You can administer the Application Engine and your Customer Response applications from any computer on your network by using a Web browser to access the Cisco Customer Response Application Administration Web pages.

Examples of Customer Response applications include:

- Cisco IP IVR
- Cisco IP AA
- Cisco IPCC
- Cisco IP ICD

You can learn more about Cisco Customer Response on the Web at the following location:

www.cisco.com/univercd/cc/td/doc/product/voice/sw_ap_to/

Cisco IP Contact Center (IPCC)

Cisco IPCC is an IP-based, high-function contact center for use with Cisco CallManager. Up to 200 agents can be served by the IPCC. The IPCC is fully compatible with the Cisco IP IVR.

The IPCC uses JTAPI to control IP phones and to convey call control messages to CallManager. The IPCC can be internetworked to other vendors' call centers and PBXs through a Cisco proprietary protocol. Through internetworking, a large, distributed, feature-transparent call center network can be constructed where each node has access to telephony and data information for every call. Sophisticated agent interaction is available through a software-based agent application.

You can learn more about IPCC on the Web at the following locations:

```
www.cisco.com/warp/public/779/largeent/avvid/solutions/
call_center.html
```

```
www.cisco.com/univercd/cc/td/doc/product/voice/sw_ap_to/index.htm
```

Cisco IP Integrated Contact Distribution (IP ICD)

Cisco IP ICD is an IP-based, low-cost, entry-level, easy-to-install, and easy-to-use automatic call distribution (ACD) for use with Cisco CallManager. Up to 48 agents can be served by IP ICD. The IP ICD is fully compatible with the Cisco IP IVR.

The IP ICD uses JTAPI to control IP phones and to convey call control messages to CallManager. When the call is destined for the IP ICD, or the call needs to be transferred from ICD to an IP Phone, CallManager signals the IP ICD (and vice versa) with JTAPI. Through LDAP version 3, the IP ICD queries the LDAP directory for application-specific information, such as dial-by-name information, workflow steps, and configuration data. The IP ICD also uses the LDAP directory as a flow repository; therefore, all flows are saved in the LDAP directory and not in the Application Engine.

CallManager should be configured with a CTI Route Point as the main number for the IP ICD. The CTI ports are used for controlling voice streams. On the IP ICD side, the CTI Route Point and CTI port numbers must be configured to match CallManager. You do not need to limit an IP ICD deployment to a single CTI port. For example, you could assign one CTI port to each agent group.

You can learn more about IP ICD on the Web at the following locations:

```
www.cisco.com/warp/public/cc/pd/unco/ipicd/prodlit/ipicd_ds.htm
```

```
www.cisco.com/univercd/cc/td/doc/product/voice/sw_ap_to/
```

Cisco IP Phone Productivity Services Software Development Kit (Cisco XML SDK)

The Cisco XML SDK makes it easier for Web developers to format and deliver content to Cisco IP Phone models 7960 and 7940 by providing Web server components for LDAP directory access, Web proxy, and graphics conversion. Access to these services is provided through an XML API into the phone. An embedded XML parser within the phone is able to parse selected XML tags. The SDK also contains several sample applications that illustrate the use of the various XML tags that the phone supports. The Cisco XML SDK includes the following items:

- Utilities, such as LDAP Search, which can perform queries on any LDAP-compliant directory server and return the output in the Cisco IP Phones services XML data format; Proxy Web Server Content Retriever, which retrieves Web documents from a proxy server for processing by the application; and graphics conversion tools.

- Sample code, including a calendar application, stock quote application for displaying the stock price for a stock symbol the user enters, speed dials, graphic image converter, and more.

- Documentation, including the Cisco XML SDK Development Notes and the Programming Guides for the included ActiveX components.

See the section "Cisco IP Phone User Options Web Page" in this appendix for more information about how users subscribe or unsubscribe to services you create or install from the SDK. You can learn more about the Cisco XML SDK on the Web at the following locations:

```
www.cisco.com/univercd/cc/td/doc/product/voice/sw_ap_to/devguide/
index.htm
www.cisco.com/go/developersupport/
```

Cisco IP Videoconferencing (Cisco IP/VC)

The Cisco IP Videoconferencing (Cisco IP/VC) product family provides an IP-based network videoconferencing solution. Cisco IP/VC includes multipoint conference units that enable interactive collaboration between three or more endpoints, gateways that provide connectivity between networks of IP-based H.323 endpoints and ISDN-based H.320 videoconferencing systems, and video terminal adapters that connect single H.320 systems to IP networks. In addition, the T.120 data collaboration servers expand the capability of any videoconference to include application sharing, cooperative white boarding, and file transfer.

These products, and the solutions they enable, are developed for organizations that want a reliable, easy-to-manage, and cost-effective network infrastructure for videoconferencing applications deployment. Figure B-3 shows the Cisco IP/VC solution at work.

Figure B-3 *The Cisco IP/VC Solution at Work*

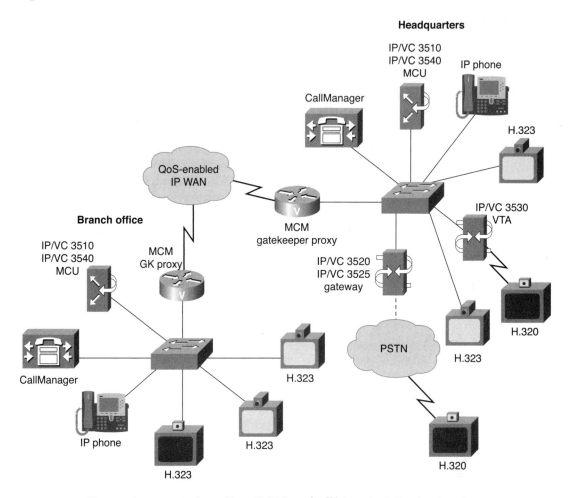

You can learn more about Cisco IP/VC on the Web at the following locations:

www.cisco.com/warp/public/cc/pd/mxsv/ipvc3500/

www.cisco.com/univercd/cc/td/doc/product/ipvc/

Interoperability with H.320 Videoconferencing Systems

If you have already made substantial investments in H.320 videoconferencing, be aware that the H.323 standard enables interoperation with H.320-based systems. Cisco IP/VC products enable an enterprise that has already experienced the benefits of videoconferencing over ISDN to leverage and protect its original investment while implementing new IP-based solutions.

Cisco Personal Assistant

Cisco Personal Assistant is an application that plays the role of a virtual personal assistant. Personal Assistant can be used by anyone in your company to redirect incoming calls based on rules that individual users devise. Incoming calls can be handled differently based on caller ID, date and time of day, and the user's meeting status based on the user's calendar. Personal Assistant can also selectively route calls to other telephone numbers so that an incoming call to a desk phone can be routed to a cell phone, home phone, or other phone based on the call routing rules created by the user. An incoming call can even generate an e-mail-based page. For example, if you are in a meeting from 2 to 3 p.m., you can configure Personal Assistant to send your calls to voice mail and page you with details of the call *except* if it is caller Y. In that case, you can direct Personal Assistant to forward the call to your cell phone.

Personal Assistant includes speech recognition as well. By simply speaking to Personal Assistant, you can access your voice mail and perform directory dialing and conferencing. Speech-enabled features are described in the following list:

- **Speech-enabled directory dialing**—This feature allows a user to pick up the phone and speak a person's name to reach that person, instead of having to dial an extension.

- **Speech-enabled voice mail browsing**—This feature provides a speech interface to Cisco Unity whereby a user can perform common voice mail operations by speaking to the Personal Assistant.

- **Simple speech-enabled Ad Hoc conferencing**—This feature allows a user to initiate a conference with several parties simply by speaking to the Personal Assistant.

You can learn more about Personal Assistant on the Web at the following location:

www.cisco.com/univercd/cc/td/doc/product/voice/assist/index.htm

Cisco Unity

Cisco Unity provides voice mail and unified messaging so you can access voice, fax, and e-mail messages using your desktop PC, a touch-tone telephone, or the Internet. With simplified message management, you can have all voice, fax, and e-mail messages delivered into your Microsoft Outlook inbox. Unity provides a self-enrollment conversation that is so easy to use, new employees can personalize their voice mailboxes and begin using Unity within minutes. Users can choose between full menu options or brief menus for faster system navigation, depending on their familiarity with the system. There is a text-to-speech capability, allowing users to listen to e-mail messages, numerous configurable personal greetings, and many more features.

Cisco Unity supports Cisco CallManager as well as leading traditional telephone systems, even simultaneously, to help you transition to IP telephony at your own pace and protect the investment you have in existing infrastructure. Unity integrates with CallManager using a software-only solution, requiring no additional hardware.

You can learn more about Unity on the Web at the following locations:

> `www.cisco.com/warp/public/180/prod_plat/avi/sys_admin_datasheet.html`
>
> `www.cisco.com/univercd/cc/td/doc/product/voice/c_unity/index.htm`

CiscoWorks2000

CiscoWorks2000 is the network management system (NMS) of choice for all Cisco devices and the Cisco CallManager system. CiscoWorks2000 is an overarching suite of network management modules that consolidate not only IP telephony system management modules, but also management modules for network data components such as switches and routers. Some Cisco IP Telephony applications routinely use CiscoWorks2000 to expedite management of the system. Currently, some remote serviceability features can be most efficiently used with CiscoWorks2000.

The CiscoWorks2000 family of Web-based products supports maintenance of Cisco enterprise networks and devices. The products include Resource Management Essentials, Voice Health Monitor, and Campus Manager. Campus Manager provides the functions Syslog Analysis, Topology Services, Path Analysis, User Tracking, and other network management services.

CiscoWorks2000 is accessible from any Web browser. Network administrators use CiscoWorks2000 to manage diagnostic and troubleshooting information collected from a Cisco IP Telephony system. The Simple Network Management Protocol (SNMP) is an industry-standard interface that can be used by any NMS to capture network monitoring information about CallManager. SNMP allows system administrators and technical support engineers to remotely monitor the status of any CallManager system. SNMP instrumentation can be used with a CiscoWorks2000 interface, and it can also be adapted for use with other NMSs that support the standard SNMP implementation.

SNMP Management Information Base (MIB) tables organize and distribute the information gathered from your company site. The information in these tables is also accessible by Cisco technical support engineers, who can remotely monitor the status of your CallManager system. However, as an on-site administrator, you have the ability to stop and start services and to gain access to and control some diagnostic information. You can use the MIB table that supports CallManager to provide all of the management interfaces for monitoring and managing your CallManager network. This MIB table is periodically updated, reflecting the current status of your CallManager network.

The CallManager MIB tables are defined in Chapter 6. You can also learn more about CiscoWorks2000 in Chapter 6.

Cisco Applications Software Development Kit (SDK)

Cisco provides an Applications SDK that includes Telephony Application Programming Interface (TAPI) and Java Telephony Application Programming Interface (JTAPI). You can use the SDK to develop applications to use in conjunction with Cisco CallManager.

TAPI

TAPI is the set of classes and principles of operation that constitute a telephony application programming interface. TAPI implementations are the interface between computer telephony applications and telephony services. CallManager includes TAPI Service Provider (Cisco TSP). Cisco TSP allows developers to create customized IP telephony applications for Cisco users, for example, voice mail with other TAPI-compliant systems, ACD, and caller ID screen pops. Cisco TSP enables the Cisco IP Telephony system to understand commands from the user-level application, such as Cisco IP SoftPhone, with the operating system.

The Cisco TAPI implementation uses the Microsoft TAPI v2.1 specification and supplies extension functions to support the Cisco IP Telephony solutions.

Cisco TAPI Service Provider (Cisco TSP)

The Cisco TSP is a TAPI-based application programming interface that allows applications to communicate with CallManager using a standard set of functions. Cisco TSP is a plug-in application to CallManager Administration (**Application > Install Plugins**). TAPI implementation consists of a Cisco TSP client that resides on all client machines running Cisco TAPI applications. Installation of the Cisco TSP is necessary before Cisco TAPI applications will function correctly. The Cisco TSP software is installed wherever the Cisco TSP will run, whether on CallManager, on a separate machine, or on both.

Cisco TSP supports up to 16 parties in a conference call. Cisco TSP also supports the TAPI Conference Call model.

Cisco TSP Processes

Cisco TSP supports a variety of features in TAPI. Initialization and security are processes that are generally invisible to the application but are important components of Cisco TSP. They are specific to the device with which Cisco TSP is communicating.

Initialization in Cisco TSP must cover connection to CallManager, authenticating the user, and device and line enumeration. It also has to handle failures at any point in the process and provide recovery options. Security has been added to provide a mechanism for administering lines to users. To configure security, the user must enter a user name and password on the TSP configuration screen. This user name and password must match the user name and password entered in CallManager Administration.

Cisco Wave Driver

The Cisco wave driver is used by third-party applications and IVR applications that use TAPI. To use first-party call control, you must install the Cisco wave driver (do this even if you are performing your own media termination).

JTAPI

JTAPI is an object-oriented application programming interface (API) for telephony applications written in Java. JTAPI is an abstract telephony model capable of uniformly representing the characteristics of a wide variety of telecommunication systems. Because it is defined without direct reference to any particular telephony hardware or software, JTAPI is well suited to the task of controlling or observing nearly any telephone system. For instance, a computer program that makes telephone calls using an implementation of JTAPI for modems might work without modification using the Cisco JTAPI implementation.

JTAPI Service Provider

JTAPI implementation consists of a Cisco JTAPI Service Provider (Cisco JTSP) client that resides on all client machines running Cisco JTAPI applications. Installation of the Cisco JTSP is necessary before Cisco JTAPI applications will function correctly. Cisco JTSP is a plug-in application to CallManager Administration (**Application > Install Plugins**). The Cisco JTSP software is installed wherever the Cisco JTSP will run, whether on CallManager, on a separate machine, or on both.

After you install the Cisco JTSP, you have access to the CallManager directory. The directory stores user profiles, application logic, and network-specific configuration information, such as the location of network resources and system administrator authentication. The Cisco JTSP uses the directory to determine which devices it has the privilege to control.

You can learn more about TAPI and JTAPI development on the Web at the following locations:

www.cisco.com/univercd/cc/td/doc/product/voice/sw_ap_to/tapi/index.htm

www.cisco.com/univercd/cc/td/doc/product/voice/sw_ap_to/jtapi/index.htm

Cisco IP Auto Attendant (Cisco IP AA)

Cisco IP Auto Attendant (Cisco IP AA) is an auto attendant flow that provides simple call answering and forwarding services. Cisco IP AA provides both dial-by-extension and telephone keypad mapping to allow callers to identify an extension by entering the first few characters of the user's name. Figure B-4 shows the IP AA structure.

Figure B-4   *Using Cisco IP AA*

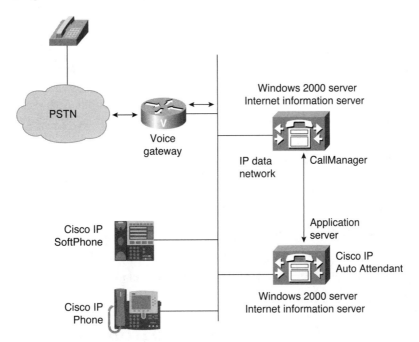

Cisco IP AA answers calls and plays a user-configurable welcome message. From the main menu, a caller can dial 0 for an operator, dial 1 to enter an extension number (such as 1234), or dial 2 to spell a name. The extension or a name is validated against the User Directory, and the caller is transferred to the desired extension. If the caller chooses the spell-by-name feature, Cisco IP AA compares the letters entered with user names and their available extensions. If a match is made, Cisco IP AA transfers the call to that user's primary extension. In the case of multiple possible matches, Cisco IP AA prompts the user to select the desired extension. In the case of too many matches, Cisco IP AA prompts the user to enter more characters. Once the desired extension has been determined, Cisco IP AA transfers the call.

System administration and monitoring are accomplished using the Application Administration on a standard Web browser. You upload the Cisco IP AA application logic to the LDAP directory using an installation utility provided with Cisco IP AA. You can then implement one or more instances of Cisco IP AA on application servers (servers designated for CallManager plug-in applications). Application Administration lets you start and stop applications, configure different system parameters, and launch the Cisco IP AA configuration wizard.

You can learn more about Cisco IP AA on the Web at the following location:

```
www.cisco.com/univercd/cc/td/doc/product/voice/sw_ap_to/ip_auto/
index.htm
```

Cisco Interactive Voice Response (IVR)

Cisco IP IVR is an IP-powered IVR solution that automates the handling of calls by autonomously interacting with users. You can use the IP IVR to build menu-driven prompts for any practical application, such as checking-account information. The menu prompts the user to enter the account number and PIN. Based on the user inputs, the Cisco IP IVR can extract and parse Web-based content so that the account information can be played over the phone for the user.

Voice prompt recording and editing is available using the Microsoft Sound Recorder, which is part of Microsoft Windows. Using this tool, voice prompts are saved as .wav files. The text-prompt creation tool can be any text editor, and the text prompts are saved as .txt files. Prerecorded voice prompts and vocabulary are also provided.

The key benefits are as follows:

- Cisco IP IVR can be located anywhere on the IP network.
- Cisco IP IVR offers Web-based activation and administration.
- Application construction can be done rapidly; it does not require users to learn a complicated high-level language.
- Flows (the IP IVR applications) are stored in an LDAP directory.
- Applications are tested and debugged easily with built-in debug tools.
- Cisco IP IVR supports Open DataBase Connectivity (ODBC) access to Microsoft SQL Server, Oracle, and Sybase databases.

The Cisco IP IVR architecture is open and extensible, allowing you to incorporate custom-developed Java classes and enabling independent developer extension of the Cisco IP IVR solution to meet your unique business needs. You can learn more about Cisco IP IVR on the Web at the following locations:

www.cisco.com/warp/public/cc/pd/unco/ipivr/index.shtml

www.cisco.com/univercd/cc/td/doc/product/voice/sw_ap_to/

Cisco IP Phone User Options Web Page

The Cisco IP Phone User Options Web page allows users to configure their own speed dial numbers, forward calls, change their password, change their PIN for extension mobility, and configure a personal address book. Additional features are provided depending on the phone model in use. Users of Cisco IP Phone models 7960 and 7940 can subscribe to or unsubscribe from Cisco IP Phone services. Users of Cisco IP Phone models 12SP+ and 30VIP can print the button template.

To have access to the Cisco IP Phone User Options Web page, users must be configured in the User area of Cisco CallManager Administration and have a phone associated with them. The Cisco IP Phone User Options Web page is available by default, but you can turn access off if desired. Also, for security reasons, you can disable external call forwarding so that users cannot set a call forwarding directive for a number that is outside of the CallManager system.

Configuring Speed Dials

The Speed Dial Configuration page allows users of Cisco IP Phone models 7960 and 7940 to enter the speed dial number and display text for each speed dial button assigned to their phone. The phone's template determines the number of speed dials available. Users of Cisco IP Phone models 12SP+, 30VIP, and 7910 can enter the speed dial number and then print a button template that displays the text for each line and feature button.

Forwarding All Calls

The Call Forwarding page allows users to enter the number to which they want all calls forwarded on a per-line basis or to cancel an existing call forwarding directive. Users can also set or cancel call forwarding using the buttons or soft keys on their phone. The number to which calls should be forwarded must be entered exactly as it would need to be dialed from the system, including any access number (such as a 9 for external calls or another number for internal calls). You can prevent users from forwarding calls to numbers outside the CallManager system for security reasons by allowing them to forward only to internal numbers.

Only system administrators can set Call Forward Busy and Call Forward No Answer directives using CallManager Administration.

Configuring IP Phone Services

The Cisco IP Phone Services page allows users of Cisco IP Phone models 7960 and 7940 to subscribe to a list of available services. Users can also see a list of services to which they have subscribed and unsubscribe from services. Services can be custom-configured by your company (see Chapter 3, "Station Devices," and the section "Cisco IP Phone Productivity Services (by XML API)" in Appendix A, "Feature List," for more information). Once the user subscribes to the services, the user can press the **services** button on his or her phone to access the subscribed services.

Changing the Password

The Update Your Password page allows users to update their passwords. Passwords must be a minimum of four and a maximum of eight alphanumeric characters.

Changing the PIN

The Update Your PIN page allows users to update their personal identification number (PIN). PINs must be a minimum of four and a maximum of eight numerals.

Configuring the Cisco Personal Address Book

The Cisco Personal Address Book allows users to create a personal address book that can be accessed from the Cisco IP Phone User Options Web page or from a Cisco IP Phone model 7960 or 7940. A Synchronization utility allows users to import contacts from Microsoft Outlook or Outlook Express directly into the Cisco Personal Address Book. Two services, PersonalAddressBook and PersonalFastDials, allow users to access the information from their phone.

Cisco IP SoftPhone

Cisco IP SoftPhone is a desktop application that turns a computer into a full-featured IP telephone with the added advantages of call tracking, desktop collaboration, and one-click dialing from online (personal) directories. Cisco IP SoftPhone is used in collaboration with a Cisco IP Phone to place, receive, and control calls from a desktop or laptop PC. The Cisco IP SoftPhone can also be used to perform audio, video, and desktop collaboration with multiple parties on a call. Figure B-5 shows the Cisco IP SoftPhone user interface.

Figure B-5 *Cisco IP SoftPhone*

Cisco IP SoftPhone uses the services of the Cisco CallManager to route calls through an IP telephony network. You must configure a line on the CallManager system before a user can send and receive calls with the Cisco IP SoftPhone.

Virtual Conference Room

With Cisco IP SoftPhone, setting up conference calls is quick and intuitive. Participants can be invited by dragging and dropping directory entries onto the Cisco IP SoftPhone's user interface to create a virtual conference room. Once a voice conference is established, you can share applications running on your desktop with all participants by selecting them from a list or by dragging associated documents onto the virtual conference room.

Voice Mail Integration

Cisco IP SoftPhone integrates with your voice mail system. It can transfer calls to a voice mailbox or place calls directly into a voice mailbox. When a user has a voice mail message, the messages icon on the Cisco IP SoftPhone turns red until the messages have been checked. Dialing the voice mailbox is as simple as clicking on the voice mail message icon.

You can learn more about Cisco IP SoftPhone on the Web at the following locations:

```
www.cisco.com/warp/public/cc/pd/unco/ipsfph/
```

```
www.cisco.com/univercd/cc/td/doc/product/voice/c_ipphon/softphon/
index.htm
```

```
www.cisco.com/warp/public/779/largeent/avvid/products/softphone/
read_me.htm
```

Cisco Messaging Interface (CMI)

Cisco Messaging Interface allows you to use an external voice mail system with Cisco CallManager. The voice mail system must meet the following requirements:

- The voice mail system must have a simplified message desk interface (SMDI) accessible with a null-modem RS-232 cable (and an available serial port).
- The voice mail system must use analog ports for connecting voice lines.
- A Cisco Access Analog Station gateway or other Cisco MGCP-based gateway must be installed and configured to interface with the analog ports on the voice mail system.

The SMDI-compliant voice mail system is connected to CallManager in two ways:

- Using a standard serial connection to CallManager.
- Using plain old telephone service (POTS) line connections to a Cisco Access Analog Station gateway or a Cisco VG200 gateway.

You can learn more about CMI on the Web at the following location:

```
www.cisco.com/univercd/cc/td/doc/product/voice/c_callmg/index.htm
```

Cisco WebAttendant

Cisco WebAttendant is an affordable and scalable Web-based solution that replaces the traditional PBX manual attendant console.

Cisco WebAttendant works in conjunction with a Cisco IP Phone to allow the attendant to quickly accept and dispatch calls to enterprise users. The application is Web-enabled and portable to multiple platforms. An integrated directory service provides traditional busy lamp field (BLF) and direct station select (DSS) functions for any line in the system. One of its primary benefits over traditional attendant console systems is its ability to monitor the state of every line in the system and to efficiently dispatch calls. The absence of a hardware-based line monitor device offers a much more affordable and easily distributed manual attendant solution than traditional consoles. Figure B-6 shows the Cisco WebAttendant interface.

Figure B-6 *Cisco WebAttendant Interface*

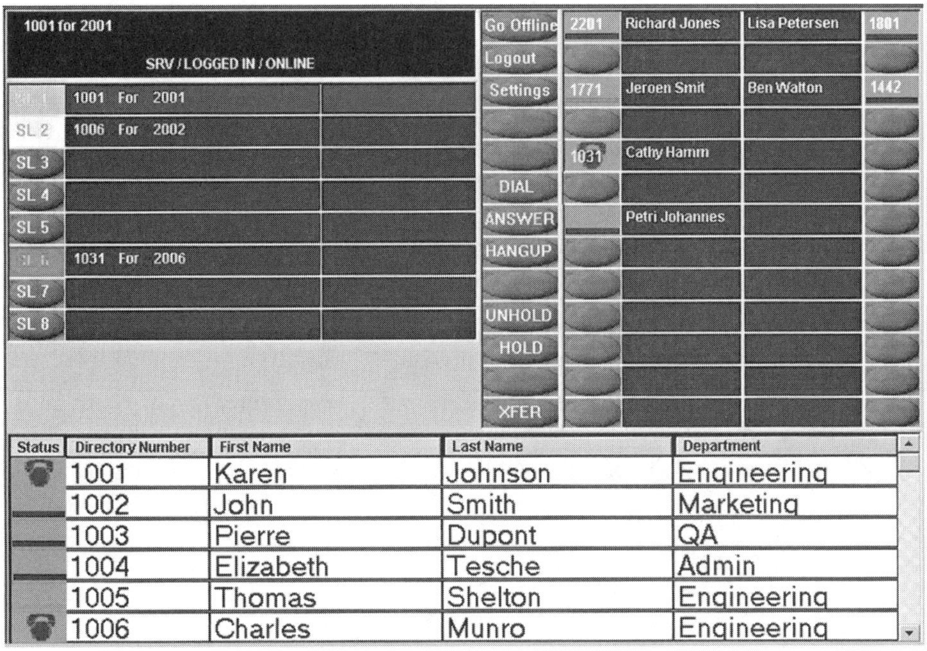

The initial release of Cisco WebAttendant provided support for Cisco CallManager 2.*x*
releases. Subsequent Cisco WebAttendant releases target the various releases of
CallManager 3.0(5) and higher and 3.1(*x*).

Note to U.K. Administrators

Cisco WebAttendant cannot be installed or used in the United Kingdom.

You can learn more about Cisco WebAttendant on the Web at the following locations:

www.cisco.com/univercd/cc/td/doc/product/voice/att_cons/index.htm

www.cisco.com/warp/public/cc/pd/unco/wbat/prodlit/watnd_ds.htm

Lightweight Directory Access Protocol (LDAP) Support

CallManager uses an LDAP directory to store authentication and authorization information about telephony application users. Authentication establishes a user's right to access the system, while authorization identifies the telephony resources that a user is permitted to use, such as a specific telephone extension.

You can upload completed workflow application files to the LDAP directory once it has been properly configured. The application server downloads these files to run workflow applications when you use CallManager Administration to start a specific application. This design allows you to start workflow applications from anywhere in the network and to run them on application servers throughout the enterprise network.

You can learn more about LDAP support in the Cisco AVVID IP Telephony system on the Web at the following locations:

    www.cisco.com/univercd/cc/td/doc/product/voice/sw_ap_to/ip_auto/
    aaadmxa.htm

    www.cisco.com/univercd/cc/td/doc/product/voice/c_callmg/index.htm

GLOSSARY

This appendix provides a list of terms and acronyms applicable to the *Cisco CallManager Fundamentals: A Cisco AVVID Solution* book. Additional information can be found at the following location:

www.cisco.com/univercd/cc/td/doc/product/voice/evbug14.htm

A

AA. Auto Attendant; an application designed to permit a switchboard attendant to efficiently distribute calls received by an enterprise.

ACD. automatic call distribution; a call routing application whose primary function is to deliver calls that arrive at an enterprise to an available user. This application is commonly used to deliver calls to call centers or groups of attendants.

ACF. Admission Confirm; an H.323 gatekeeper sends this RAS message when it permits an H.323 endpoint to make a call.

ACK. Acknowledgement.

Ad Hoc. A type of conference in which a controlling station manually adds conferees one at a time. Contrast with Meet-Me conference.

ALI. Automatic Location Identification; information about the physical location of a caller that emergency response centers use when handling E911 calls.

ANSI. American National Standards Institute; an American organization chartered with the development of standards in the United States.

API. Application programming interface; usually a set of libraries with accompanying header files that application programmers can use in their programs to interact with a third-party application.

ARJ. Admission Reject; an H.323 gatekeeper sends this RAS message when it denies an H.323 endpoint's request to place a call.

ARQ. Admission Request; H.323 endpoints that rely on a gatekeeper to route their calls send this RAS message, which requests permission from the gatekeeper for the endpoint to place a call.

ART. Administrative Reporting Tool; a Web-based application used to generate various reports about the CallManager system.

ASN1. Abstract Syntax Notation One; an ITU-T language designed for the description of data types. H.323 defines certain parts of certain messages in ASN.1.

ASP. Active Server Page; a Web page that uses ActiveX scripting to dynamically control the content of the Web page. Cisco CallManager Administration relies on Active Server Pages.

AST. Admin. Serviceability Tool; a CallManager Serviceability tool that can be used to view performance information for the CallManager cluster.

AUCX. Audit Connection; an MGCP message that the call agent sends to the gateway to audit the specified connection on an endpoint.

AUEP. Audit Endpoint; an MGCP message that the call agent sends to the gateway to audit a specified gateway.

AVVID IP Telephony. Cisco Architecture for Voice, Video, and Integrated Data; a suite of applications that is designed to handle enterprise voice networks and which processes user calls over an enterprise's IP network.

B

B-channel. Bearer Channel; one of 23 or 30 timeslots of information that can carry a user's voice or data content over an ISDN interface. See also *D-channel*.

backhaul. The practice of passing signaling information from PSTN ports transparently through a gateway to a call agent, rather than relying on the gateway to process the signaling information itself.

bandwidth. A measurement of the amount of data per unit of time that a communications interface is capable of sending or receiving.

BAT. Bulk Administration Tool; a Web-based application used to bulk-add, bulk-update, or bulk-delete large numbers of devices and users in the CallManager database.

BCF. Bandwidth Confirm; an H.323 gatekeeper sends this RAS message when it honors an H.323 endpoint's request to change the bandwidth of the media stream that the endpoint is using.

BHCC. Busy Hour Call Completion; interval between off-hook and immediate dial of four digits to a second on-net IP Phone and a ring and immediate off-hook at the target phone. Media streams are connected and an immediate on-hook and device state change to idle in CallManager occurs. BHCC is the number of these transactions that CallManager or clusters can process in one hour, with the assumption that all call transactions are evenly spaced.

blade. Cards that are the width of the chassis that they are going into and contain the DSPs for transcoding, conferencing, and media termination. See also *VICs*.

BLF. Busy Lamp Field; an indicator at a station that displays the busy or idle status of other users in the enterprise.

BRI. Basic Rate Interface; a version of ISDN designed for phones that uses two B-channels for media and one D-channel for signaling.

BRJ. Bandwidth Reject; an H.323 gatekeeper sends this RAS message when it denies an H.323 endpoint's request to change the bandwidth of the media stream that the endpoint is using.

BRQ. Bandwidth Request; a gatekeeper-enabled H.323 endpoint sends this RAS message when it wishes to change the codec (and thus the bandwidth) that it is using for a particular media session.

BSD. Berkeley Software Distribution; an open source code distribution originated at the University of California at Berkeley.

C

call appearances. A configuration of CallManager whereby the administrator makes it appear as if the same line appearance occurs multiple times on an individual phone.

call leg ID. A value appearing in Call Detail Records (CDRs), unique among all CallManager nodes in a cluster, that identifies each participant in a call.

call preservation. The process by which a Cisco AVVID IP Telephony network maintains the media exchange of a call in progress when a network error or server failure interrupts the signaling and media control for the call.

caller ID. The calling number of a station that places a call.

calling search space. Along with partitions, a call routing concept that allows CallManager to provide individualized routing to users for purposes of routing by class of calling user, geographic location, or organization.

CAMA. Centralized Automatic Message Accounting; a system in a central location capable of collecting data, usually call accounting-related, on behalf of multiple switches.

CAS. Channel Associated Signaling; a scheme for transmission of call signaling information that relies on interleaving the call signaling within the media information that the interface transmits.

CCM. Cisco CallManager; a Cisco AVVID IP Telephony service whose primary function is the control and routing of calls from voice-enabled IP devices.

CCO. Cisco Connection Online; Cisco's Web site for customer support and distribution of software, www.cisco.com.

CDP. Cisco Discovery Protocol; a device discovery protocol that runs on Cisco devices and allows devices to advertise their existence to other devices on a LAN or WAN.

CDR. Call Detail Record; a record that CallManager logs after a call completes to permit billing or auditing of system use.

CDR data. The grouping together of Call Detail Records (CDRs) and Call Management Records (CMRs).

centralized call processing. A cluster deployment model whereby a cluster in a campus provides IP telephony service across the IP WAN for phones and gateways in branch offices that lack a CallManager.

CFNA. Call Forward No Answer; a feature of CallManager that allows calls placed to a given directory number to be forwarded in the event that they are not answered.

Cgpn. Calling Party Number.

circuit switching. A process of completing calls whereby a call agent manages the transport of the media from one endpoint to another through commands to switch cards that form an actual end-to-end analog or digital circuit.

Cisco CallManager server. A Cisco-certified Windows 2000 server that is running CallManager software.

Cisco uOne. A voice mail system that integrates with CallManager. Formerly known as Amteva.

Cisco Unity. A voice mail system that integrates with CallManager. Formerly known as Active Voice.

CiscoWorks2000. A family of Web-based products used to manage Cisco enterprise networks and devices. See www.cisco.com/univercd/cc/td/doc/product/rtrmgmt/cw2000/.

Class 5 switch. A switch in a national telephone system operated by a local telephone company. Class 5 switches directly handle residential and commercial subscribers.

CLI. Command-line Interface; an interface to Cisco switches and routers running the IOS operating system in which a user types text commands to provision a device.

CLID. Calling Line ID; the calling number of a station that is placing a call.

clustering. A process by which CallManager nodes cooperatively processes an enterprise's calls with such tight integration that users cannot detect which CallManager nodes are processing their calls. Clustering relies on direct communication among CallManager nodes in a cluster.

CMF. Common Management Framework; the Cisco management foundation on which CiscoWorks2000 network management application suites run.

CMI. Cisco Messaging Interface; a Windows 2000 service that is part of Cisco AVVID IP Telephony and that coordinates SMDI communications with legacy voice mail systems.

CMR. Call Management Record; also known as a diagnostic record, a record that CallManager logs that provides information about the media session on which a device participated.

CNID. Calling Party Name Identification; if enabled, CallManager provides the user's phone number to the called party.

CO. Central Office; a switch in the PSTN, usually Class 5, that handles calls on behalf of residential and commercial subscribers.

codec. Coder-decoder; a media-encoding scheme by which an end device encodes speech or visual information into a digital representation for transmission across a media connection. It decodes the digital representation into speech or visual information for playback by the recipient.

COM. Component Object Model; A Microsoft framework used in many companies' applications that is designed to permit the interoperation of software objects running in separate tasks in a computer network.

community. In the context of SNMP, a relationship between an agent and a set of SNMP managers that defines security characteristics.

conference controller. A conference controller is the user who initiates a conference. For Ad Hoc conferences, the conference controller calls each conference participant and individually connects each participant to the conference. For Meet-Me conferences, the conference controller sets up the directory number that conference participants dial into.

conference device. A media device that mixes multiple signals from different stations or gateways and sends the combined signals to all the conference participants.

CoS. Class of Service; a method of classifying the data that a network routes to provide preferential packet routing treatment to data related to certain types of media: voice, data, and video, for example.

CPU. Central Processing Unit; the chip or chips inside a computer that execute the instructions that permit applications to function.

CRCX. Create Connection; an MGCP message the call agent sends to gateway to create a new connection on an endpoint

CSV. Comma Separated Value; a type of file in which commas are used to separate individual fields of a complex data record and new lines indicate the end of an individual record.

CTI. Computer Telephone Integration or Computer Telephony Interface; for the purposes of this book, CTI most commonly means Computer Telephony Interface. This is an interface exported by CallManager that allows application developers to create programs that work with the telephone system.

D

D-channel. Data Channel; one timeslot on an ISDN interface that is dedicated to handling the call signaling related to the bearer channels that the interface manages. See also *B-channel*.

DBL. Database Layer; a set of software components that provide a programming interface to the SQL database containing all of the CallManager configuration information.

DCF. Disengage Confirm; an H.323 gatekeeper sends this RAS message when it wishes to honor an H.323 endpoint's request to terminate a call.

DHCP. Dynamic Host Control Protocol; a network service whose primary purpose is to automatically assign IP addresses to new devices that connect or existing devices that reconnect to the network.

diagnostic record. See *CMR*.

dialing transformations. Any CallManager setting that permits CallManager to modify the calling or called number as the call is being established.

DID. Direct Inward Dial; a type of central office trunk that provides additional routing information on incoming calls. This allows trunk calls to be routed directly to a specific directory number, instead of being routed to a common attendant.

distributed call processing. A CallManager cluster deployment model whereby independent CallManager clusters, possibly gatekeeper-enabled, handle the call routing and call establishment for an enterprise and its branch offices.

DLCX. Delete Connection; an MGCP message the call agent sends to gateway to delete a connection on the endpoint.

DLL. Dynamic Link Library; a software component used by a larger program that the operating system on which the program runs includes only when the program requires the functionality provided by the software component. Dynamic link libraries allow large programs to use less RAM because they only take up memory when the larger program actually executes them.

DN. Directory number; the numerical address assigned to phones within an enterprise.

DNS. Domain Name System; a network service whose primary function is to convert fully qualified domain names (textual) into numerical IP addresses, and vice versa.

DOD. Direct Outward Dial; a service that permits a device in the enterprise to place calls directly to the public network.

DoS attacks. Denial of Service attacks; this is a form of attack that can be launched against various network systems. In general, a DoS attack is performed by launching a flood of network requests to a computer, thereby monopolizing its resources.

dotted decimal notation. A formatting convention for an IP address whereby each octet of a four-octet IP address is converted to a decimal value from 0 to 255 and delimited by periods.

DPA. Digital PBX Adapter; Cisco DPAs provide Lucent Octel voice mail integration with CallManager.

DRJ. Disengage Reject; an H.323 gatekeeper sends this RAS message when it wishes to deny an H.323 endpoint's request to terminate a call.

DRQ. Disengage Request; a gatekeeper-enabled H.323 endpoint sends this RAS message to the gatekeeper when it wishes to terminate a call.

DSP. Digital Signal Processor; a specialized type of CPU used for computationally intensive tasks. CallManager has DSP resources that are typically used to process voice streams. For example, DSPs are used to transcode voice and conference multiple streams.

DSS. Direct Station Select; a telephony feature that permits a user to dial a destination by pressing a single button.

DTD. Document Type Definition; a specific definition that describes the structure of documents that conform to the Standard Generalized Markup Language (SMGL)— for example, HTML and XML—through the insertion of tags within the documents themselves. Programs interpret the tags and use them to render the document context.

DTMF. Dual Tone Multifrequency; a common tone signaling method used by touchtone phones in which two pure frequencies are superimposed.

E

E1. A digital trunk specification that permits the transfer of 2.048 Mbps of information per second.

E164 address. A fully qualified numerical address for a device attached to a national network. The ITU-T specification E.164 defines the framework in which nations manage their national numbering plans.

EDS. Event Distribution System; the event distribution of the Cisco Management Framework (CMF).

EFR. Enhanced Full Rate; a codec optimized for speech primarily used in digital wireless networks.

E&M. Ear and Mouth; an analog trunk interface that carries signaling information over a different pair of wires (called "ear" and "mouth") than audio information.

endpoint. A device or software application that provides real-time, two-way communication for users.

ESN. Emergency Service Number; a numerical address that the North American national network uses to identify emergency response centers.

F

failover. The process whereby devices on a Cisco AVVID IP Telephony network seek out backup CallManager nodes if they lose their connection to their primary CallManager.

fallback. The process of offering a call to a less-desirable gateway after all desirable gateways have been exhausted.

fastStart. A provision of H.323, version 2, which permits an endpoint to embed media control information in the call signaling phase of a call, thus dramatically speeding up the rate at with an end-to-end media connection can be established.

firewall. A computer system placed at the junction between a private computer network and other computer networks. It is designed to protect users of a private network from users in the other networks.

first-party call control. A method of application control by which the application controls an endpoint as if it was a user at that endpoint.

flashhook. On a POTS phone, the process of temporarily interrupting the circuit to gain access to network features; on a digital phone, a brief depression of the hookswitch to gain access to network features.

forwarding. A process whereby a call agent can divert a call from the dialed destination to an alternate destination, either unconditionally or if the called user is busy or does not respond within a specified period of time.

FR. Full Rate; a codec optimized for speech primarily used in digital wireless networks.

fully meshed topology. A topology in which every node in a network maintains a communications channel with every other node in a network. CallManager clustering relies on a fully meshed topology.

FXO. Foreign Exchange Office; a VoIP gateway providing analog access to central office's line termination.

FXS. Foreign Exchange Station; a VoIP gateway providing analog access to a POTS station.

G

G.711. A simple codec used to encode voice communications that requires 64 kbps bandwidth.

G.723. A codec used to encode voice communications that requires either 5 or 6 kbps bandwidth.

G.729. A codec used to encode voice communications that requires 8 kbps bandwidth.

gatekeeper. An H.323 entity that provides address resolution, controls access to the network, and can terminate calls. In a Cisco AVVID IP Telephony network, H.323 gatekeepers provide call routing and admissions control functions only.

gateway. A device that provides real-time, two-way communications between the packet-based network and other stations on a switched network.

GCF. Gatekeeper Confirm; an H.323 gatekeeper sends this RAS message to an H.323 endpoint's search for gatekeepers on a network if it wishes to advertise its existence.

GCID. Global Call Identifier; a common identifier that identifies all calls that are related to each other in some way. Used in CDR data.

GMT. Greenwich Mean Time.

grep. General Regular Expressions Parser; a text-matching capability originally developed for the UNIX operating system. It permits a user to determine whether a particular text string conforms to a user-specified structure.

GRJ. Gatekeeper Reject; an H.323 gatekeeper sends this RAS message to an H.323 endpoint's search for gatekeepers on a network if it wishes to prevent the H.323 endpoint from registering with it.

GRQ. Gatekeeper Request; a gatekeeper-enabled H.323 endpoint sends this RAS message when it needs to find out which gatekeepers it can register with.

GSM. Groupe Speciale Mobile; a voice codec commonly used in wireless devices that requires 13 kbps bandwidth.

H

H.225. A protocol that forms the call signaling portion of the ITU-T H.323 protocol.

H.245. A protocol that forms the media control portion of the ITU-T H.323 protocol.

H.320. An ITU-T recommendation that covers videoconferencing in a circuit-switched environment.

H.323. An umbrella ITU-T specification that describes terminals, gateways, and other entities that provide communication services over packet-based networks. It references other specifications for the call signaling, media control, and coding and decoding control specifications.

H.450. A protocol that defines feature transparency for the ITU-T H.323 protocol.

hotline. A call routing feature whereby a call agent immediately places a call to a specified destination when certain phones are taken off-hook.

HP-UX. Hewlett-Packard's version of UNIX.

HTML. Hypertext Markup Language; a document type definition (DTD) used by Web pages and browsers on the World Wide Web that tells a Web browser how to render the content of a Web page.

HTTP. Hypertext Transfer Protocol; a method by which applications can exchange multimedia files on the World Wide Web.

hub. A nexus in a network where data arriving from one endpoint can select multiple routes of egress.

I

IACK. Information Request Acknowledgement; a RAS message.

ICCS. Intracluster Control Signaling; proprietary signaling that CallManager nodes in a cluster exchange to cooperatively manage calls.

ICD. Integrated Contact Distribution.

ICM. Intelligent Contact Manager; an application that manages distribution of voice, Web, and e-mail across an enterprise of automatic call distribution (ACD), Private Branch eXchange (PBX), Interactive Voice Response (IVR), database, and desktop applications.

ICMP. Internet Control Message Protocol; a message control and error reporting protocol carried over an IP network.

IE. Information Element; an individual field in an ISDN message.

IETF. Internet Engineering Task Force; a standards body that issues recommended protocols for applications that interact over the Internet.

I-frame. The link layer message that the ITU-T Q.921 standard defines for the purpose of encapsulating user data.

IIS. Internet Information Server; a Microsoft service designed to permit users to create and manage Internet services such as Web servers.

INAK. Information Request N Acknowledgement; a RAS message.

intercluster. Commonly used in the term *intercluster trunks*, this term refers to any interaction that occurs between CallManager nodes that are not members of the same cluster.

interdigit timeout. An event that causes CallManager to cease collecting a dialing user's dialed digits (and to route based on the entered digits) when CallManager detects that no digits have been entered for a specified period of time.

IOS. Internetwork Operating System; the operating system used by many Cisco routers and switches, including the gateways used by CallManager.

IP. Internet Protocol; a method by which one computer can communicate packets of information to another computer on a network.

IPCC. IP Contact Center; a software package that works with CallManager to perform call distribution and the management functions needed by call centers.

IP Centrex. A business model whereby a service provider sells IP telephony connectivity to the PSTN to different subscribers.

IP Telephony. The establishment of primarily voice, but also video and data communications over the same type of data network that makes up the Internet.

IP/VC. Internet Protocol/Videoconferencing; a family of Cisco videoconferencing devices.

IRQ. Information Request; a RAS message that H.323 gatekeepers often use to monitor the status of H.323 terminals for which they maintain registrations.

IRR. Information Request Response; a RAS message that H.323 terminals send in response to a RAS Information Request message.

ISDN. Integrated Services Digital Network; a digital circuit-switched-based telephony protocol that relies on interfaces that consist of a single D-channel for signaling and multiple B-channels for media.

ISUP. Integrated Services User Part; a component of the SS7 telephony standard that handles call signaling. SS7 is a protocol widely used in the PSTN.

ITU-T. International Telecommunication Union Telecommunication Standardization Sector; the branch of an international standards body that develops and publishes standards related to telecommunications.

IVR. Interactive Voice Response; a voice application that provides a telephone user interface and that is capable of retrieving data and redirecting calls.

IXC. Interexchange Carrier, or long-distance company; a company whose chief responsibility is the interconnection of local exchange carriers.

J

JMF. Java Media Framework; an application programming interface (API) that enables audio, video and other time-based media to be added to Java applications and applets.

JTAPI. Java Telephony Application Program Interface; an API that enables the development of Java applications that work with CallManager.

JTSP. Java TAPI Service Provider; a library that makers of telephony systems provide to permit third-parties to control the telephony system over JTAPI.

K

key system. Very small-scale telephone system designed to handle telephone communications for a small office of 1 to 25 users.

L

LAN. Local-area network; a group of independent computers and network appliances within a small geographic area that access common resources and each other over communications protocols.

LATA. Local Access and Transport Area; in North America, geographical regions within the same LATA can generally place unmetered calls.

LCD. Liquid Crystal Display.

LCF. Location Confirm; an H.323 gatekeeper sends this RAS message, which provides the network address of an H.323 endpoint, to a requesting H.323 gatekeeper when the requesting H.323 gatekeeper needs to discover the endpoint's network address.

LDAP. Lightweight Directory Access Protocol; an API that defines a programming interface that can be used to access computer-based directories. LDAP directories are a specialized format of database that is often used to hold user information in large organizations.

LEC. Local Exchange Carrier, or local telephone company; a company whose chief responsibility is providing PSTN connectivity to residential and commercial subscribers.

LED. Light Emitting Diode; a semiconductor device that emits light when an electric current passes through it.

legacy. Using established, possibly outdated, methods.

line appearance. A logical entity on a phone capable of terminating calls, often associated with a particular button on a phone. Line appearances have addresses called DNs.

logical channel. A network pathway that carries a streaming data connection between two endpoints.

LRJ. Location Reject; an H.323 gatekeeper sends this RAS message to a requesting H.323 gatekeeper when it does not know the network address of the device that the requesting H.323 gatekeeper is seeking.

LRQ. Location Request; an H.323 gatekeeper might send this RAS message to find out from other gatekeepers the network address associated with a particular E.164 or endpoint alias.

M

managed device. A device containing a network management agent implementation. The media server, MCS-7835-1000, is a managed device.

mask. A mechanism commonly used by the call routing component of CallManager to enable you to change a number substantially while retaining some of the original number's digits.

MCL. Media Control Layer; the layer within CallManager responsible for coordinating the media control phase of call establishment.

MCS. Media Convergence Server; a Cisco-certified server that comes preinstalled with the components that make up Cisco AVVID IP Telephony.

MDCX. Modify Connection; an MGCP message that the call agent sends to the gateway to modify the specified connection on an endpoint.

MGCP. Media Gateway Control Protocol; a protocol used by devices in an IP Telephony environment.

MIB. Management Information Base; a virtual information store that is used with network management protocol and network management application to provide information on a managed object.

Management Information Base; a single specification (an MIB), the union of all specifications implemented (the MIB), or the actual values of management information in a system.

MOH. Music On Hold.

MOH audio source. A file on a disk or a fixed device from which a source stream obtains the streaming data, which it provides to all connected streams.

MOH data source. A file on a disk or a fixed device from which a source obtains the streaming data that it provides to all connected streams.

MOH group. MOH audio sources having the same filename and content. Usually spans multiple MOH servers. The MOH group is implemented as MRG in CallManager release 3.1.

MOH group session. One or more streams connected to an MOH audio source on an MOH server.

MOH server. Software application that provides MOH audio sources and connects an MOH audio source to a number of streams.

MRG. Media Resource Group; a logical grouping of media servers that can be used to provide geographically specific, class of service, or class of user access to a set of media resources.

MRGL. Media Resource Group List; a list that consists of prioritized MRGs. An application can select required media resources among the available ones according to the priority order defined in the MRGL.

MRM. Media Resource Manager; software component in CallManager that locates media resources based on a provided MRGL.

MTP. Media Termination Point; a device that terminates a media stream for the purpose of allowing the stream to be redirected.

multiple tenant. Also multitenant. A type of CallManager installation in which one administrator manages a Cisco AVVID IP Telephony network on behalf of a group of different enterprise or residential customers. This type of deployment is smaller in scale than IP Centrex.

N

NAK. Negative Acknowledge; a message sent by the remote end of a Transmission Control Protocol (TCP) connection that indicates failure of the connection's establishment.

NANP. North American Numbering Plan; the set of valid dialable addresses on the North American PSTN.

Network hold. The hold action that is initialized by system as the result of a feature invocation such as transfer or conference.

NMS. Network Management Station; a server where SNMP management applications run.

NTFY. Notify; an MGCP message indicating certain requested event has occurred on the gateway.

NT Registry. A repository of configuration data maintained by the Windows NT operating system. All applications on a computer can access the registry to store and retrieve configuration information.

O

object. In the context of SNMP, a data variable that represents some resource or other aspect of a managed device.

object type. Defines a particular kind of managed object. The definition of an object type is therefore a syntactic description.

octet. An eight-bit binary number corresponding to values 0 to 255 in the decimal system.

ODBC. Open Database Connectivity; a vendor-independent standard that enables applications to interact with different databases.

off-hook. The action whereby a user initiates a call or accepts an incoming call.

OffNet. A term applied to calls between the enterprise and another telephone network (generally the PSTN).

on-hook. The action whereby a user returns a station to an idle state.

OnNet. A term applied to calls that are placed and received within the same enterprise.

operator. One of a set of three tests (EXISTS, DOES-NOT-EXIST, ==) that route filters apply when determining which route patterns in the national numbering plan should be included as part of CallManager's expansion of the @ wildcard.

orphan timeout. A CallManager setting that dictates how long a media resource device, such as Cisco IP Voice Media Streaming Application, waits until it tears down resources relating to a conversation. This happens when the Cisco IP Voice Media Streaming Application has lost its connection to CallManager and it has detected no voice activity from an endpoint in the conversation.

OS. Operating System; a set of services running on a hardware platform that provide other applications with access to the resources (such as processor, memory, network interfaces) that the hardware platform provides.

outside dial tone. A high-pitched audio indication that CallManager applies during dialing to alert a calling user that the entered address may cause the call to route to a public network.

overlapped dialing. The process whereby CallManager collects dialed digits one at a time from a user. See also *overlapped sending*.

overlapped sending. The process whereby CallManager collects dialed digits one at a time from a user.

The process whereby CallManager passes dialed digits from a calling user to switches in connected networks that actually manage the address.

P

PA. Personal Assistant; an application that works with CallManager. This application is designed to permit a user to customize call forwarding behavior based on who is calling and to track a user down given multiple possible destinations.

packet switching. A process of completing calls whereby a call agent manages call signaling and media control of two endpoints in a call but in which the media is streamed directly from one device to the other over a network of routers.

In a peer-to-peer network, a process of completing calls whereby two endpoints negotiate their call signaling, media control, and media session directly with each other over a network of routers.

partition. Along with calling search spaces, a call routing concept that allows CallManager to provide individualized routing to users for purposes of routing by class of calling user, geographic location, or organization.

PBX. Private Branch Exchange; a small phone system located at a customer premise site. The PBX is used to supplement or replace functionality that might normally be provided by a Central Office (CO).

PC. Personal Computer.

PCM. Pulse Code Modulation; the standard for voice encoding in the circuit-switched world.

PDU. Protocol Data Unit; a unit of information that peer entities in a network exchange for control purposes.

picocell. A transmission and reception area for wireless devices less than 100 meters in radius.

PIN. Personal Identification Number.

PLAR. Private Line Automatic Ringdown; see *hotline*.

POTS. Plain Old Telephone Service.

power cycle. To reset a device by interrupting and restoring power to the device.

PreDot. The section of a route pattern that corresponds to all matched digits before the . wildcard's position in the route pattern.

presentation bit. A field in an ISDN information element that specifically indicates whether a call recipient is permitted or forbidden from viewing the calling number.

PRI. Primary Rate Interface; an ISDN interface containing 24 or 32 channels for the communication of media and signaling information.

primary line. The first line appearance on a station device.

PSAP. Public Safety Answering Point; an emergency response center dedicated specifically to handling emergency calls from subscribers on the PSTN. Emergency response centers have special facilities for contacting public safety and health officers.

PSTN. Public Switched Telephone Network; the international phone system we all know and love. Typically displayed on block diagrams as a puffy, friendly looking cloud. Appearances can be deceiving.

Publisher. The master database for CallManager.

Q

Q.921. Layer 2 protocol for ISDN telephony.

Q.931. Layer 3 protocol for ISDN telephony.

QBE. Quick Buffer Encoding; commonly pronounced "cube."

QoS. Quality of Service; the traffic management mechanisms of a distributed multimedia system that permit it to guarantee the transmission of coherent information. Such mechanisms include traffic classification, traffic prioritization, bandwidth management, and admissions control.

R

RAID. Redundant Array of Independent Disks; a device containing a set of disks that appears as a single disk to an operating system. RAIDs store copies of the same piece of data in different physical locations, thus providing security against component failure and possibly improving disk performance, because information can be written simultaneously to two different disks.

RAS. Registration, Admission, and Status; part of the ITU-T H.323 protocol that defines how H.323 endpoints and gatekeepers communicate.

redundancy. The process whereby backup systems assume responsibility for providing network services if primary components fail or become unreachable.

reorder tone. A fast, cyclical tone that CallManager uses to indicate some sort of problem during call establishment.

RFC. Request For Comments; a document that proposes Internet standards and is produced for public review by the Internet Engineering Task Force (IETF). RFCs that are accepted become official Internet standards.

RIS. Real-Time Information Server; a Cisco AVVID IP Telephony service that collects serviceability information for multiple CallManager nodes in a cluster.

RME. Resource Manager Essentials; a suite of Web-based network management solutions for Cisco switches, access servers, and routers. Essential features include configuration management, change auditing, software image management, inventory, availability, and Syslog Analysis, while also allowing integration with other Cisco Web management tools and third-party applications.

route filter. A textual clause composed of tags, operators, and values that CallManager uses to restrict which route patterns it includes when performing a macro expansion of the @ wildcard.

route list. A CallManager feature that allows CallManager to search serially for and extend a call to an available gateway from among the gateways that the route list contains.

route pattern. An expression that describes a numerical address (telephone number) or range of addresses; also, this expression as assigned to a gateway or route list.

RQNT. Request Notify; a Media Gateway Control Protocol (MGCP) message that a call agent sends to a gateway to request the gateway to inform the call agent when a particular event (such as dialed digits) occurs.

RR. Receiver Ready; an ITU-T Q.921 message that a message recipient sends when it is ready to receive a transmission from its peer.

RRQ. Registration Request; a gatekeeper-enabled H.323 endpoint sends this RAS message to an H.323 gatekeeper when it wishes the gatekeeper to maintain the address information (and possibly route calls for) the endpoint.

RS-232. A recommendation published by Electronic Industries Association (EIA) that defines the physical and signaling characteristics of serial data communications.

RSIP. Restart In Progress; a Media Control Gateway Protocol (MGCP) message that a gateway sends to a call agent to indicate that an endpoint or group of endpoints is being brought into or taken out of service.

RTCP. Real-Time Control Protocol; Internet-standard protocol for the transport of control data relating to data transmitted by Real-Time Transport Protocol (RTP).

RTP. Real-Time Transport Protocol; Internet-standard protocol for the transport of real-time data, including audio and video.

RUDP. Reliable User Datagram Protocol; a simple packet-based transport protocol that is layered on the UDP/IP protocols and provides reliable in-order delivery for virtual connections.

S

SA. Syslog Analyzer; one of the CiscoWorks2000 features that provides reports and analysis of syslog messages from the Cisco devices.

SABME. Set Asynchronous Balanced Mode (Extended); a link layer control message requesting the establishment of a connection over which numbered I-frames can be sent.

SCCP. Skinny Client Control Protocol; a protocol used by devices to communicate with CallManager. Commonly referred to as Skinny Protocol.

SDI. System Diagnostic Interface; a trace interface that is used in CallManager.

SDK. Software Development Kit; a set of programming interfaces and documentation provided to programmers seeking to interface to a given operating system, application, or other product.

SDL. Signal Distribution Layer; an application framework that provides all of the components required to implement a state-machine-based application. It provides for creation of state machines and the interprocessor communication of signals between those state machines.

Specification and Description Language; an ITU-T language defined in specification Z.100 that describes a notation for state-machine-based systems.

secondary line. Any line appearance on a station other than the first.

service parameters. Settings for Cisco AVVID IP Telephony services that take effect on a service-wide basis.

SGCP. Skinny Gateway Control Protocol; a protocol used by devices to communicate with CallManager.

signed integer. 32-bit numbers that contain a 31-bit value plus a high order sign bit.

silence suppression. The process whereby, to save network bandwidth, a voice-enabled IP device ceases transmitting media when the volume level of the speaker drops below a certain threshold.

SMDI. Simplified Message Desk Interface; an RS-232 protocol that can be used to integrate a voice mail system with a PBX. CallManager provides an interface to voice mail systems with the Cisco Messaging Interface service, also known as CMI.

SMI. Structure of Management Information; specifications that define the model of management information, the allowed data types, and the rules for specifying classes (or types) of management information.

SNMP. Simple Network Management Protocol; a protocol designed to permit monitoring and management of devices on a computer network.

soft key. Context-sensitive digital display buttons on the bottom row of the display of Cisco IP Phones 7940 and 7960.

software Unicast bridge. A server-based conference mixer capable of mixing G.711 and Wideband audio streams and rebroadcasting them to conference participants.

source. A connection point on an MOH server where streams can be connected. It provides the audio-streaming data to all connected streams.

SQL. Structured Query Language; a standard language defined to permit reading from and writing to databases.

SS7. Signaling System 7; a protocol used on the Public Switched Telephone Network (PSTN) that uses a separate packet-switched network for the carriage of signaling information between switches in the PSTN.

station. Any device that provides a user with a direct interface to a voice network.

steering code. An initial sequence of digits used to direct calls to a particular set of gateways.

stream. A one-way, active media session connected through a simplex logical channel from an MOH server to a device.

Subscriber. One or more duplicate databases serving the CallManager system. Subscriber databases are updated with information from the Publisher database.

subscriber. A user of a (usually public) telephone network.

switchback. The process whereby devices unregister with one CallManager node and reregister with a higher-priority CallManager node.

switchover. A process whereby where a secondary call agent can assume control of the call signaling and media control for a call that was earlier controlled by a different call agent.

T

T1. A digital trunk interface that provides twenty-four 64-kbps timeslots for a total of 1.544 Mbps of bandwidth.

T3. A digital trunk interface that provides 44.736 Mbps of bandwidth.

TAC. Cisco Technical Assistance Center; a customer support organization.

tag. A text string that characterizes a meaningful portion of one or more route patterns in a dial plan file. Route filters rely on tags to classify numbers within a dial plan.

TAPI. Telephony Application Programming Interface; a Microsoft API that permits programmers to create telephony applications on Windows systems.

TcdSrv. Cisco Telephony Call Dispatcher Service; the server-side process from which Cisco WebAttendant clients obtain their call control services.

TCP. Transmission Control Protocol; a connection-oriented protocol that provides for the reliable end-to-end, ordered delivery of IP packets.

TDM. Time-division Multiplexing; a method of transporting information for multiple endpoints across a single interface that relies on assigning each endpoint a specific window of time when it has exclusive access to the interface.

TFTP. Trivial File Transfer Protocol; a User Datagram Protocol (UDP)-based protocol that permits the transmission of files between network devices.

third-party call control. A method of application control by which the application controls one or more endpoints and simultaneously maintains a view of all controlled endpoints.

TLA. Telealue, a geographical routing prefix in the Finnish national numbering plan.

toll restriction. A configuration whereby an enterprise routes calls between geographical regions over its own IP network instead of the PSTN, thereby avoiding any charges that the PSTN levies for placing the call.

ToS. Type of Service; a method of classifying the data that a network routes to provide preferential packet routing treatment to data related to certain types of media: voice, data, and video, for example.

traffic prioritization. The process of assigning preferential routing treatment to media streams based on the type of information they contain.

transcoder. A hardware or software device that provides a means of allowing devices that do not have a matching set of capabilities for the allowed bandwidth to communicate. Transcoders convert one media stream type into a different media stream type to allow devices to communicate.

translation pattern. A CallManager call routing feature that permits you to define aliases for route patterns.

trap. A trap is an unsolicited message sent by an agent to a management station in an asynchronous manner. The purpose is to notify the management station of some unusual event. The traps are sent to trap-receiving hosts configured in the Windows

2000 SNMP Service. With this enhancement, network management applications such as Voice Health Manager (VHM) can gather more data that can be used for fault management and analysis purpose.

trunk. A circuit between a station and the network that serves it or between two networks.

TSP. TAPI Service Provider or Telephony Service Provider; a library that makers of telephony systems provide to permit third parties to control the telephony system over Microsoft's Telephony Application Program Interface (TAPI).

TSV. Tab Separated Values; a file format in which individual data fields of a record are separated by a tab character and records are separated by new lines.

TTL. Time-to-live; a piece of information embedded in broadcast and multicast packets that dictates how many router hops a packet is permitted to traverse.

U

UDP. User Datagram Protocol.

UMS. Unified Messaging System; a system that provides a unified way of accessing voice mail, e-mail, and fax.

Unicast conference bridge. A hardware or software device that receives multiple media streams from parties on a conference, sums the information contained within, and rebroadcasts the summed information to each conference participant.

unsigned integer. 32-bit numbers that contain a 32-bit value that is assumed to be a positive number.

URJ. Unregister reject; an H.323 gatekeeper sends this RAS message to an H.323 endpoint when it denies the endpoint's request that the gatekeeper purge registration information related to the endpoint.

URL. Uniform Resource Locator; an Internet addressing format.

URQ. Unregistration request; a gatekeeper-enabled H.323 endpoint sends this RAS message to an H.323 gatekeeper to ask the gatekeeper to purge registration information related to the endpoint.

user. A person or software application that makes use of a system.

User hold. A hold action that is initialized by an end user who presses the hold button on a phone.

UUIE. User-User Information Element; a field defined by ITU-T Q.931. H.323 messages use this field to encapsulate H.323-specific values.

V

VAD. Voice Activity Detection; see *silence suppression*.

varbind. Variable Binding; in Simple Network Management Protocol (SNMP), a pairing of an object instance name and its associated value.

VHM. Voice Health Manager; a CiscoWorks2000 application that provides proactive fault management and root cause analysis for Cisco AVVID IP Telephony system. It was also previously known as Voice Health and Fault Manager (VHFM).

VICs. Voice Interface Cards; typically small trunk interface modules that are inserted into IOS gateways to allow for OffNet communication.

VoIP. Voice over IP; the process of routing voice communications over a network running Internet Protocol.

W-X-Y-Z

WAN. Wide-area Network.

wildcards. Elements within route patterns that describe a range of matching digits, cause a previous wildcard to match multiple digits, delimit portions of the route pattern, or direct CallManager to perform a macro expansion.

wink start. An analog trunk signaling method that coordinates the collection of dialed digits in which the originating device goes off-hook, awaits an off-hook and on-hook signal from the remote end (the "wink"), and outpulses dialed digits.

XML. Extensible Markup Language; a simple dialect of SGML that enables generic SGML to be served, received, and processed on the Web.

INDEX

Symbols

Numerics

A

B

background mode, 510
background noise, 321
bandwidth consumption, voice codecs, 320
bandwidth messages (H.225), fields, 305–306
BAT (Bulk Administration Tool), 407–408, 561, 617
    adding users with CSV files, 410–412
    goal of using, 408
    managing established CallManager
        systems, 409
    misconfiguration, 408–409
    setting up CallManager database, 408–409
    TAPs (Tool for Auto-Registered Phones
        Support), 412
billing, OnNet versus OffNet calls, 551
bit rates, voice codecs, 320
blades, 19
blind transfers, 609
block structure of CallManager, 316
blocking calls, 79
    900 numbers, 99–101, 179
    international calls, 96
    long distance carrier selection, 96
Bridged Telnet, 495–496
broadcast paging support, 560
bulk transactions, performing with CSV files,
    410–412
busy signals, no-circuits available call
    treatment, 276

C

call admission control messages, fields, 302–305
call appearances, 206
call attempts during switchover/switchback
    conditions, 400
Call Control, processing gateway directory
    numbers, 551
Call Control Layer, 31, 228, 269, 315–317
call control signaling, H.323 gateways, 273
call detail reports (ART), 418

call establishment
    in circuit-switched networks, 7–9
    in Cisco AVVID IP Telephony networks, 22–24
    media exchange phase, 9
    session establishment, 7
call forwarding, 562–565
    Call Forward Busy, 564
    Call Forward No Answer, 564–565
    enabling, 167
    for third-party applications, 565
    reason codes, 561
call forwarding search space, 166–167
call leg IDs, 517
call legs, 322, 517
Call Management Records (CMRs), 501.
    See also CDR data
Call Park, 566
    configuring, 566–567
Call Pickup, 567–568
call preservation, 388–390, 568–569
    algorithms, 398
    examples, 393–396
    supported devices, 397–398
call reports (ART), 417
call routing
    address translation, 59–60
    by organization, 60, 156
    by security level of user, 157
    calling search spaces, 62
    delays, troubleshootiong, 222
    dialing behavior, 66–67
    dialing transformations, 62
    endpoint determination, 58
    geographical routing, 183–196
    individualized routing, 60
    overlapped sending, 76–77
    partitions, 62
    route filters, 62–64, 87–88, 92–95
        7-digit dialing, 99
        for North American numbering plan,
            95–102
        INTERNATIONAL-ACCESS
            DOES-NOT-EXIST, 96
        length limitations, 88
        toll-free numbers, 99
    route lists, 62
    route patterns, 62–64
        . wildcard, 87

G

J-L

M

N

O

Q

R

S

T

X-Z

Hey, you've got enough worries.

Don't let IT training be one of them.

Get on the fast track to IT training at InformIT,
your total Information Technology training network.

 | **www.informit.com** |

■ Hundreds of timely articles on dozens of topics ■ Discounts on IT books from all our publishing partners, including Cisco Press ■ Free, unabridged books from the InformIT Free Library ■ "Expert Q&A"—our live, online chat with IT experts ■ Faster, easier certification and training from our Web- or classroom-based training programs ■ Current IT news ■ Software downloads ■ Career-enhancing resources